THE PROBLEMS OF PHILOSOPHY

EDITED BY MICHAEL S. RUSSO

SophiaOmni

ISBN-13:   978-1478295198
ISBN-10:   1478295198

SophiaOmni

Visit our website at:
www.sophiaomni.org

CONTENTS

HISTORICAL ARRANGEMENT OF READINGS

PREFACE

Welcome to the amazing world of philosophy. You are about to embark on an adventure that will transform your way of thinking about your own life and the world around you. And who knows: it might just make you a better person as a result!

The formal discipline of philosophy arose during the fifth century B.C. in Athens. The Athenians had just defeated the armies of Darius the Great and his son Xerxes in the Persian Wars (499-480 B.C.) and had amassed a huge treasury that enabled the average citizen to enjoy what had been virtually unheard of in the ancient world before then—something called leisure time. And what did the Athenians do with their newfound leisure, you might be wondering? They did what any truly civilized group of people would do: they began to reflect critically on their human experience, to formulate rational theories about the essential essence of the universe, to contemplate the nature of justice and beauty, and to speculate on the right way to live in human society. In short, they began to do philosophy. And they were very, very good at it, producing three of the greatest thinkers that the world has ever known in fairly short succession: Socrates, Plato, and Aristotle.

The discipline of philosophy has given us almost 2,500 years of amazing thought by men and women who understood, as Socrates did, that "the unexamined life is not worth living." Epicurus, Augustine, Aquinas, Descartes, Hobbes, Locke, Hume, Rousseau, Kant, Hegel, Marx, Mill, Kierkegaard, Nietzsche, Sartre, and De Beauvoir are some of the great intellectual heroes of our human family. Each of these men and women contributed to the great story of philosophy, producing works that have literally changed the course of history. Their writings are a living testimony to that which makes all of us most fully human: the ability to use reason to understand who we are as human beings, why we are here, and where we are ultimately heading as individuals and as a species.

So, as you embark on your journey through the discipline of philosophy, you should do so with humility and at least a small amount of trepidation. You are standing on the shoulders of the giants who came before you.

Now a few words about the text you are about to read: this anthology has been designed to give you, the newcomer to the field of philosophy, the "big picture" of the discipline of philosophy. We haven't tried to include every significant text in philosophy ever written, but have tried to give you what we think are the essential ones—those that have had the greatest impact on human thought throughout the centuries. Naturally, we had to make judgment calls about which philosophical texts to include in this work and which to leave out, or this volume would have been twice its current size. If one of your favorite philosophers or philosophical works have been omitted, we sincerely hope that you'll accept our apologies.

There are many ways that one can go about creating a text like this one; we've opted to focus on what is known as the "problems of philosophy." Since classical times there have been a handful of problems that have dominated the writing of the great philosophers. What is reality? Is there a God? Is there a correlation between perception and reality? What is the right way to live? What is a truly just society? And what makes something beautiful? Because these questions are so important in philosophy, they have been given their own subdivisions within the discipline: Metaphysics, Philosophy of Religion, Epistemology, Ethics, Political Philosophy, and Aesthetics. We think that the "big problems" approach to philosophy is the best way to get an introduction to the discipline, although we also recognize that there are those who might prefer a more historical approach. If you fit into this latter category, feel free to refer to the page entitled "Historical Arrangement of Readings," and read the selections in this text chronologically rather than topically. Both approaches to studying philosophy are equally valid and each approach has its own unique benefits.

As you work your way through this text, you probably will notice that reading great works in philosophy requires no small amount of effort. For some students, in fact, philosophy can be a maddeningly complex and bewilderingly obscure field of study. So take your time reading these texts and don't get too frustrated if you have trouble understanding them the first time around. At the same time, you should also realize that the old saying, "no pain, no gain," is applicable not only to physical fitness but to intellectual fitness as well. If you try to read through works of philosophy the way you would a popular novel, you probably won't get anything at all out of your reading. Don't give up too quickly, then, if you are having difficulty comprehending any of the selections in this text. They are not meant to be easy…just profound.

This volume would not have been possible without the support and contributions of numerous individuals. I would like to thank the members of the Molloy College Department of Philosophy for supporting the project from its inception. I would also like to acknowledge the efforts of Stephan T. Mayo, Elisa Rapaport, Eric Karahalis, Patrick J. Casey, and Marie Dollard, who provided constant feedback on the work while it was in development, and all those who generously contributed essays for this edition.

As I've already mentioned, we who are living in the 21st century have benefitted greatly from the work done in past by the giants of the discipline of philosophy. But philosophy is not a stagnant discipline, by any means. Each and every day, new philosophical giants have the potential to arise and transform human society the way the philosophical giants of the past did. This volume, therefore, is dedicated to the future heroes of the story of philosophy. And who knows: one of those heroes might very well be you!

Good luck in your pursuit of wisdom!

Michael S. Russo, Ph.D.
Editor

1

WHAT IS PHILOSOPHY?

ELISA RAPAPORT

Chances are you are reading this book because it was required for your class. And chances are you're taking this class because someone said you should. After asking yourself, "what is philosophy?" you might also have asked, "and why on earth do I have to take it?" Don't worry. Your professor probably is neither offended nor surprised. What *you* might be surprised to learn is not just that there are many legitimate answers to these questions, but that the purpose of philosophy itself is to continue to ask what you're asking.

Literally, 'philosophy' means love of wisdom, coming from the original Greek words *philos sophia.* But that only tells you so much. Philosophy means a lot more than that, and it *doesn't* mean that you have to be passionate about knowing all there is to know. The fact is the study we call Western 'philosophy' has grown a lot in the past 3,000 years. Yes, the foundations go back to the Ancient Greeks—philosophers like Socrates, Plato, and Aristotle, whose ideas are the basis for the structure of our society and education today. Even before Socrates a group of thinkers we call the Pre-Socratics were busy asking themselves all sorts of questions about the world. Who are we? Why are we here? What kind of a world is this? What is everything made of? The Ancients were fond of noting that "philosophy begins in wonder." A more contemporary philosopher, Alfred North Whitehead, continued: "at the end, when philosophic thought has done its best, the wonder remains." Philosophy isn't about having all the answers as much as asking the right questions —about anything and everything.

So, philosophy is about questions. And by now you're realizing it has something to do with asking ourselves some perhaps odd questions we don't usually think about every day. We are perfectly capable of going through our lives without seriously contemplating the stuff that everything is made of, whether or not there is a God, and what the meaning is to life. But what kind of a life would that be, if you only ever accepted everything as it was presented to you and never tried to understand the way things work? Just before he was going to be sentenced to death, Socrates famously said, "the unexamined life is not worth living." What he meant was that if he were to live a life without asking questions, without thinking and challenging and being a true philosopher, he might as well give up his life. It was asking questions all the time that got him into trouble, of course. As you'll learn in just a few pages, he challenged authority, embarrassed political leaders, questioned established religion, and inspired his students to think for themselves—challenges that were not much appreciated by those in power at the time. Can you think of anything you believe in strongly enough to be willing to give up your life for that cause? For Socrates, that cause was philosophy. He was so committed to asking questions and seeking the truth about the world that he agreed to be executed by poison rather than give up philosophical inquiry. His prosecutors actually begged him to save his own life; all he had to do was take back what he had said and give up the study of philosophy forever. But such a life, he said, would be a lie. It would not be worth the effort. What would have been the point? Not all philosophers since then would necessarily have been willing to die for their beliefs—although far too many have. But most would agree that what has propelled them through life is the very process of trying to make sense of it, similar to the Ralph Waldo Emerson (and Aerosmith) sentiment that "life is a journey, not a destination." In that sense, philosophy is the process of trying to get to the bottom of things.

What sorts of things? All things. Philosophers will proudly tell you that every single other discipline you could imagine studying today has its roots in philosophy. And this is pretty much true. Philosophers were the first to develop the formal study of politics, biology, literary criticism, and math. Philosophy asks what kind of a life is best living, what sort of behavior is expected and acceptable in any society, and what sorts of personalities are best suited for different professions. Modern psychology (particularly psycho-analysis) owes the concepts of *id, ego,* and superego to Plato's theory that the soul is influenced by appetite, emotion, and reason. The earliest mathematicians, including Thales, Democritus, Pythagoras, Euclid, Archimedes, and others, were usually philosophers as well as paradigm-shifting scientists, architects, and inventors. Hippocrates famously professionalized the practice of medicine, influencing the Hippocratic Oath still promised by doctors today. Parmenides was a philosopher, poet, and politician whose questions about truth and change pervaded the way he saw the world. Such wide-ranging interests are typical in philosophy. Even today philosophy itself is difficult to narrow down to a single topic of inquiry. But we generally categorize philosophy into a handful of different sub-disciplines.

Metaphysics, epistemology, logic, ethics, aesthetics, political philosophy, philosophy of religion, and the study of human nature are some of the areas philosophy covers. Like most subjects, philosophy has its own jargon, but the big words usually represent concepts you've already thought about. **Metaphysics** is the study of existence, asking some of the most basic questions we can ask about our environment. Who are we? What kinds of things are there in the world? What happens when we die? How am I different from everybody else? How are we the same? Why does fire burn and ice melt? Why is there something rather than nothing? Am I really here? Does anything last forever? The questions might be basic to the extent that they are essential; that is, they deal with the essence of people and objects in our world. Modern-day metaphysicians still deal with these same lingering questions, and they're also concerned with the sorts of categories everything should be placed within, a field related to metaphysics that we call 'ontology.' There are ontologists today employed by software developers to identify classes of diseases and ways of integrating medical information into usable websites and encyclopedias. Some work for government agencies classifying weapons systems and geographic data. Still others collaborate with physicists and astronomers as we learn more about how our world fits within the workings of the universe.

Epistemology is the study of knowledge, which basically asks, "what do we know?" and "how do we know it?" Some philosophers wonder whether it's possible to know anything at all. If we clearly can be wrong sometimes, how can we know with certainty that any of our beliefs are truly justified? Most of what we think we know we have to interpret from sensory perception— sight, hearing, taste, smell, and touch. Computer images and video games utilizing virtual reality are quick to show that our senses can't be completely trusted. And yet it seems wrong, somehow, to say we know nothing at all. René Descartes famously said, "I think, therefore I am" *(cogito, ergo sum)*. He recognized that he could doubt pretty much everything he thought he knew about the world, if it had come to his understanding through his senses, which he had reason to question. But if he were able to be questioning, doubting, thinking about anything at all, then at least he had to exist in some form in order to be doubting everything else. He was able to think, therefore even if he could prove and know for certain absolutely nothing else about the world, at the very least he had to know that *he* existed. This is a good example of how the sub-branches of philosophy frequently overlap with each other: metaphysics and epistemology concern Descartes' existence and how he knows it. Many of the other sub-branches work closely together, as well.

Logic, for example, affects all areas of philosophy (and science, math, and more), because logic defines the way philosophers approach all of our questions and attempted answers. Logic is the study of rational thought and argument, using strict rules of reason as a guide for sorting out what we should and shouldn't accept. You can thank the Ancient Greek philosopher Aristotle for this. He organized into a standard form and mathematical sort of language a structure for recognizing what people are really trying to say and analyzing whether or not they have made their point. "Do the premises support the conclusion?" That's a question frequently asked by philosophers in determining whether or not to accept what someone has said. If I tell you philosophy will make you smart, you ask why, and I say, "because Betrand Russell was brilliant," you're not likely to be convinced. Even if you know that Russell was a brilliant philosopher, that doesn't mean that reading one of his books will make you brilliant, as well. If I tell you, however, that passing your test is necessary to pass this class, and that reading your textbook will help you pass your test, we've probably accomplished something in terms of encouraging you to take the reading seriously. If nothing else, it's clear that you need to pass your test in the class. So if we learn Martin didn't pass his test, we wouldn't be surprised to learn he also failed the class. Do you follow this? It makes sense because when we presume the truth of our statements, there are only so many possible outcomes that also make sense. Congratulations! You're a philosopher. Or at least a logician-in-training (who will hopefully pass his test). Of course, there are many ways to accomplish that task, some more acceptable than others.

Ethics is perhaps the easiest to grasp of the various sub-branches of philosophy. Ethics is the study of right and wrong. We won't belabor the "right" vs. "wrong" ways of passing a test at this time. Most of us understand it intuitively, and if it isn't second-nature, we quickly learn what is and isn't considered appropriate, ethical behavior in our society. Not surprisingly, the philosophical study of ethics is a bit more complicated than that. Philosophers want to know not just what actions are right and wrong, but *why*. We want to know who is being harmed, who is responsible for any damage done, whether it could have been prevented — and if so, if those in control had an *obligation* to prevent harm being inflicted on someone else. There are huge implications for these questions for individual people and how we behave, as well as for governments, law makers, parents, teachers, and even clergy. As you've probably noticed, philosophers love the question, "why?" For ethicists, it's not just why someone acted a certain way that matters but why we ought to act a certain way to begin with — assuming there even is such a thing as right and wrong. Remember metaphysics, the study of existence? Ethicists have been known to debate the existence of good and evil, but especially good. Do we even know that there is some objective, undeniable answer to what the right thing to do in a given situation would be? Or do we rely on someone else's conception of morality? These are the sorts of questions that intrigue ethicists.

As you can imagine, ethics affects nearly every aspect of our lives. It would be a challenge to turn on the tv or to catch headlines in the news without finding half a dozen stories of how someone has done something wrong. There's an assessment being made in such judgments. We are determining value, assuming that some actions are better than others, much in the way we might prefer certain hairstyles, movies, or vacation destinations. Ethics would evaluate the severity and implications of possible actions when faced with a dilemma. Is it right to support a film that glamorizes intentional violence against women? That's an ethical question, but with aspects of personal preference involved if we're evaluating style, performance, or comedic success. What something is worth might be subject to personal preferences or cultural trends. Or there might be some objective reality that says relaxation is unequivocally better than the stress of gunshots and violence, for instance when debating between a spa or a war zone for summer break. Maybe the war zone is a severe example. Maybe a shopping spree would be sufficiently stressful for some but euphoric for others. Is there something wrong with either of these choices, or are they just matters of opinion? Not all decisions involve ethics. Wasting money that should be spent on college tuition could be problematic, or even throwing money away to keep up with fashion instead of donating your money to others in need. But ethics aside, our personal preferences for how we spend our time could be causing harm to no one.

Aesthetics has in common with ethics these questions about value, and both sub-branches fall under what we would call 'value theory.' But where ethics evaluates actions, motives, and decision-making, aesthetics makes judgments about what is more or less beautiful. Aesthetics studies art, literature, music, almost anything that could in some way be considered along a continuous scale of beauty. Plato tied aesthetics inseparably from metaphysics, proposing that what we experience in this world can at best only be a shadow cast by the true and ultimate form of beauty that exists in the heavens — a depiction that should sound familiar to the religions that suggest an afterlife. But even in our finite world there are ways of evaluating aspects and objects of our experience. What is good art? Is there such a thing as *bad* art? What is the purpose of art? Does it have to reveal some recognizable reality to others, or is it still art if it's an expression satisfying only the artist's aspirations? Does a work of literature remain the property of its author? Does Shakespeare gain or lose credibility when interpreted in a 21st-century setting? Even if someone doesn't care for the music of Wagner, should she still recognize the genius of his compositions? There are subjective experiences that affect people's perceptions and their conclusions that inform value, beauty, and the sublime. Aesthetics explores this phenomenon.

Political philosophy is in a way self-explanatory. It involves philosophical questioning of all things political. Like the sub-branches above, you're probably beginning to get a sense of how politics cannot exist in a vacuum. Different sorts of government, political parties, and elected representatives involve metaphysical status. What sorts of decisions are best made on behalf of an entire population have obvious ethical implications, with issues of justice — fairness and respect—informing most political theories. The leaders of society in many ways represent the people they govern, and the people's decisions and actions reflect their attitudes about the meaning of their existence.

Human nature, or the human condition, asks deeply personal sorts of questions and at the same time asks if there is a common course through which we all travel. The question, "Why are we here?" illustrates both perspectives. It also is fundamental to the study of religion, beginning with the presumption that there is, in fact, a pre-established purpose.

Philosophy of religion is one of numerous examples of how philosophical inquiry can be directed towards a somewhat related, interdisciplinary field (philosophy of language, philosophy of law, philosophy of education, etc.). Philosophy of religion is inseparable from theology to the extent that they both study God. Where theology often presumes God's existence, however, philosophy asks whether and how God could exist, then moves from that point towards an examination of religion as a human phenomenon. Many philosophers have believed in God, despite a reputation philosophy has developed for harboring atheists (those who don't believe in God) and agnostics (those who are undecided one way or another). Recall the opening comments on logic: philosophy asks for reasonable support for whatever claim anyone should make. It is possible that the existence of God is something that simply defies documentation or proof; likewise, it is possible that *belief* in God is not the sort of thing that should be subject to epistemological verification. Nevertheless, philosophers of religion have for centuries tried to convince others of their various reasons for or against the existence of an infinite, all-powerful being. Religion is also inseparable from ethics to the extent that an all-knowing and ultimately good God would be responsible for the existence of pain, suffering, and seeming evil in the world. These questions are explored within this sub-discipline.

Now that you've plowed through 3,000 years of deep thoughts in as many words, relax and ask yourself what 'philosophy' means to you. We each have philosophies — our particular approach and opinions about child raising, learning styles, even food preparation (gourmet meals vs. fast food, dine-in or take-out, etc.). The academic study of philosophy is a bit more focused than those general approaches, but each area of our lives can be accommodated within the field. Who are we? What kind of world would we like to live in? How do we get along with other countries? What kind of values are we passing on to young children? Philosophy can be intense. Many of the selections in this text will admittedly be challenging for you as you read them. But it is worth every effort. Philosophy is about you as much as it is about the famous philosophers you're about to get to know through their ideas. What is philosophy? It is questioning your own reality. Why should you take this class? Whatever your profession, you'll be a better teacher, nurse, social worker, *human being,* when you know how to ask the right questions.

APOLOGY

PLATO (424-348 BCE)

Socrates, the father of Philosophy, wasn't exactly appreciated as a prophet in his own times. In the year 399 BCE Socrates was put on trial by the people of Athens for atheism and for corrupting the youth of the city. The Apology *is Plato's account of that trial. The term apology (from the Greek "apologia") literally means "speech before." The term should not be understood in the English sense of "a statement expressing remorse or regret" (as you read the* Apology, *it will be clear that Socrates in no way regrets the way he has lived his life). An apology is a statement of defense of one way of life against accusers: in this specific case, it is Socrates' defense of his philosophical way of life against the charges raised by his accusers.*

Keep in mind that the Apology was written by Plato after Socrates' death. Although Plato undoubtedly took some creative liberties in transcribing Socrates' speech, we should probably regard the text as more or less historically accurate. For one thing, many of the readers of Plato's text would have been present at the trial, and certainly would have raised a stink if Plato had stretched the truth too far. The text, therefore, provides an interesting perspective on the historical Socrates, and, in particular, his attitudes towards his own life and philosophical mission.

1. Main Defense Speech

How you have felt, O men of Athens, at hearing the speeches of my accusers, I cannot tell; but I know that their persuasive words almost made me forget who I was—such was the effect of them; and yet they have hardly spoken a word of truth. But many as their falsehoods were, there was one of them which quite amazed me;—I mean when they told you to be upon your guard, and not to let yourselves be deceived by the force of my eloquence. They ought to have been ashamed of saying this, because they were sure to be detected as soon as I opened my lips and displayed my deficiency; they certainly did appear to be most shameless in saying this, unless by the force of eloquence they mean the force of truth; for then I do indeed admit that I am eloquent. But in how different a way from theirs!

Well, as I was saying, they have hardly uttered a word, or not more than a word, of truth; but you shall hear from me the whole truth: not, however, delivered after their manner, in a set oration duly ornamented with words and phrases. No indeed! but I shall use the words and arguments which occur to me at the moment; for I am certain that this is right, and that at my time of life I ought not to be appearing before you, O men of Athens, in the character of a juvenile orator—let no one expect this of me.

And I must beg of you to grant me one favor, which is this—If you hear me using the same words in my defense which I have been in the habit of using, and which most of you may have heard in the agora, and at the tables of the money-changers, or anywhere else, I would ask you not to be surprised at this, and not to interrupt me. For I am more than seventy years of age, and this is the first time that I have ever appeared in a court of law, and I am quite a stranger to the ways of the place; and therefore I would have you regard me as if I were really a stranger, whom you would excuse if he spoke in his native tongue, and after the fashion of his country;—that I think is not an unfair request. Never mind the manner, which may or may not be good; but think only of the justice of my cause, and give heed to that: let the judge decide justly and the speaker speak truly....

1.1. Socrates' Wisdom

I dare say, Athenians, that someone among you will reply, "Why is this, Socrates, and what is the origin of these accusations of you: for there must have been something strange which you have been doing? All this great fame and talk about you would never have arisen if you had been like other men: tell us, then, why this is, as we should be sorry to judge hastily of you." Now I regard this as a fair challenge, and I will endeavor to explain to you the origin of this name of "wise," and of this evil fame. Please to attend then. And although some of you may think I am joking, I declare that I will tell you the entire truth. Men of Athens, this reputation of mine has come of a certain sort of wisdom which I possess.

If you ask me what kind of wisdom, I reply, such wisdom as is attainable by man, for to that extent I am inclined to believe that I am wise; whereas the persons of whom I was speaking have a superhuman wisdom, which I may fail to describe, because I have it not myself; and he who says that I have, speaks falsely, and is taking away my character. And here, O men of Athens, I must beg you not to interrupt me, even if I seem to say something extravagant. For the word which I will speak is not mine. I will refer you to a witness who is worthy of credit, and will tell you about my wisdom — whether I have any, and of what sort—and that witness shall be the god of Delphi. You must have known Chaerephon; he was early a friend of mine, and also a friend of yours, for he shared in the exile of the people, and returned with you. Well, Chaerephon, as you know, was very impetuous in all his doings, and he went to Delphi and boldly asked the oracle to tell him whether—as I was saying, I must beg you not to interrupt—he asked the oracle to tell him whether there was anyone wiser than I was, and the Pythian prophetess answered that there was no man wiser. Chaerephon is dead himself, but his brother, who is in court, will

confirm the truth of this story.

Why do I mention this? Because I am going to explain to you why I have such an evil name. When I heard the answer, I said to myself, What can the god mean? and what is the interpretation of this riddle? for I know that I have no wisdom, small or great. What can he mean when he says that I am the wisest of men? And yet he is a god and cannot lie; that would be against his nature. After a long consideration, I at last thought of a method of trying the question. I reflected that if I could only find a man wiser than myself, then I might go to the god with a refutation in my hand. I should say to him, "Here is a man who is wiser than I am; but you said that I was the wisest." Accordingly I went to one who had the reputation of wisdom, and observed to him—his name I need not mention; he was a politician whom I selected for examination—and the result was as follows: When I began to talk with him, I could not help thinking that he was not really wise, although he was thought wise by many, and wiser still by himself; and I went and tried to explain to him that he thought himself wise, but was not really wise; and the consequence was that he hated me, and his enmity was shared by several who were present and heard me. So I left him, saying to myself, as I went away: Well, although I do not suppose that either of us knows anything really beautiful and good, I am better off than he is — for he knows nothing, and thinks that he knows. I neither know nor think that I know. In this latter particular, then, I seem to have slightly the advantage of him. Then I went to another, who had still higher philosophical pretensions, and my conclusion was exactly the same. I made another enemy of him, and of many others besides him.

After this I went to one man after another, being not unconscious of the enmity which I provoked, and I lamented and feared this: but necessity was laid upon me—the word of God, I thought, ought to be considered first. And I said to myself, Go I must to all who appear to know, and find out the meaning of the oracle. And I swear to you, Athenians, by the dog I swear!—for I must tell you the truth—the result of my mission was just this: I found that the men most in repute were all but the most foolish; and that some inferior men were really wiser and better. I will tell you the tale of my wanderings and of the "Herculean" labors, as I may call them, which I endured only to find at last the oracle irrefutable. When I left the politicians, I went to the poets; tragic, dithyrambic, and all sorts. And there, I said to myself, you will be detected; now you will find out that you are more ignorant than they are. Accordingly, I took them some of the most elaborate passages in their own writings, and asked what was the meaning of them—thinking that they would teach me something. Will you believe me? I am almost ashamed to speak of this, but still I must say that there is hardly a person present who would not have talked better about their poetry than they did themselves. That showed me in an instant that not by wisdom do poets write poetry, but by a sort of genius and inspiration; they are like diviners or soothsayers who also say many fine things, but do not understand the meaning of them. And the poets appeared to me to be much in the same case; and I further observed that upon the strength of their poetry they believed themselves to be the wisest of men in other things in which they were not wise. So I departed, conceiving myself to be superior to them for the same reason that I was superior to the politicians.

At last I went to the artisans, for I was conscious that I knew nothing at all, as I may say, and I was sure that they knew many fine things; and in this I was not mistaken, for they did know many things of which I was ignorant, and in this they certainly were wiser than I was. But I observed that even the good artisans fell into the same error as the poets; because they were good workmen they thought that they also knew all sorts of high matters, and this defect in them overshadowed their wisdom—therefore I asked myself on behalf of the oracle, whether I would like to be as I was, neither having their knowledge nor their ignorance, or like them in both; and I made answer to myself and the oracle that I was better off as I was.

1.2. The Results of Socrates' Investigations

This investigation has led to my having many enemies of the worst and most dangerous kind, and has given occasion also to many calumnies, and I am called wise, for my hearers always imagine that I myself possess the wisdom which I find wanting in others: but the truth is, O men of Athens, that God only is wise; and in this oracle he means to say that the wisdom of men is little or nothing; he is not speaking of Socrates, he is only using my name as an illustration, as if he said, He, O men, is the wisest, who, like Socrates, knows that his wisdom is in truth worth nothing. And so I go my way, obedient to the god, and make inquisition into the wisdom of anyone, whether citizen or stranger, who appears to be wise; and if he is not wise, then in vindication of the oracle I show him that he is not wise; and this occupation quite absorbs me, and I have no time to give either to any public matter of interest or to any concern of my own, but I am in utter poverty by reason of my devotion to the god.

There is another thing:—young men of the richer classes, who have not much to do, come about me of their own accord; they like to hear the pretenders examined, and they often imitate me, and examine others themselves; there are plenty of persons, as they soon enough discover, who think that they know something, but really know little or nothing: and then those who are examined by them instead of being angry with themselves are angry with me: This confounded Socrates, they say; this villainous misleader of youth!—and then if somebody asks them, Why, what evil does he practice or teach? they do not know, and cannot tell; but in order that they may not appear to be at a loss, they repeat the ready-made charges which are used against all philosophers about teaching things up in the clouds and under the earth, and having no gods, and making the worse appear the better cause; for they do not like to confess that their pretence of knowledge has been detected—which is the truth: and as they are numerous and ambitious and energetic, and are all in battle array and have persuasive tongues, they have filled your ears with their loud and inveterate calumnies. And this is the reason why my three accusers, Meletus and Anytus and Lycon, have set upon me; Meletus, who has a quarrel with me on behalf of the poets; Anytus, on behalf of the craftsmen; Lycon, on behalf of the rhetoricians: and as I said at the beginning, I cannot expect to get rid of this mass of calumny all in a moment. And this, O men of Athens, is the truth and the whole truth; I have concealed nothing, I have dissembled nothing. And yet I know that this plainness of speech makes them hate me, and what is their hatred but a proof that I am speaking the truth?—this is the occasion and reason of their slander of me, as you will find out either in this or in any future inquiry....

1.3. Socrates' Mission

I have said enough in answer to the charge of Meletus: any elaborate defense is unnecessary; but as I was saying before, I certainly have many enemies, and this is what will be my destruction if I am destroyed; of that I am certain; — not Meletus, nor yet Anytus, but the envy and detraction of the world, which has been the death of many good men, and will probably be the death of many more; there is no danger of my being the last of them.

Someone will say: And are you not ashamed, Socrates, of a course of life which is likely to bring you to an untimely end? To him I may fairly answer: There you are mistaken: a man who is good for anything ought not to calculate the chance of living or dying; he ought only to consider whether in doing anything he is doing right or wrong—acting the part of a good man or of a bad. Whereas, according to your view, the heroes who fell at Troy were not good for much, and the son of Thetis above all, who altogether despised danger in comparison with disgrace; and when his goddess mother said to him, in his eagerness to slay Hector, that if he avenged his companion Patroclus, and slew Hector, he would die himself — "Fate," as she said, "waits upon you next after Hector"; he, hearing this, utterly despised danger and death, and instead of fearing them, feared rather to live in dishonor, and not to avenge his friend. "Let me die next," he replies, "and be avenged of my enemy, rather than abide here by the beaked ships, a scorn and a burden of the earth." Had Achilles any thought of death and danger? For wherever a man's place is, whether the place which he has chosen or that in which he has been placed by a commander, there he ought to remain in the hour of danger; he should not think of death or of anything, but of disgrace. And this, O men of Athens, is a true saying.

Strange, indeed, would be my conduct, O men of Athens, if I who, when I was ordered by the generals whom you chose to command me at Potidaea and Amphipolis and Delium, remained where they placed me, like any other man, facing death; if, I say, now, when, as I conceive and imagine, God orders me to fulfill the philosopher's mission of searching into myself and other men, I were to desert my post through fear of death, or any other fear; that would indeed be strange, and I might justly be arraigned in court for denying the existence of the gods, if I disobeyed the oracle because I was afraid of death: then I should be fancying that I was wise when I was not wise.

For this fear of death is indeed the pretence of wisdom, and not real wisdom, being the appearance of knowing the unknown; since no one knows whether death, which they in their fear apprehend to be the greatest evil, may not be the greatest good. Is there not here conceit of knowledge, which is a disgraceful sort of ignorance? And this is the point in which, as I think, I am superior to men in general, and in which I might perhaps fancy myself wiser than other men, — that whereas I know but little of the world below, I do not suppose that I know: but I do know that injustice and disobedience to a better, whether God or man, is evil and dishonorable, and I will never fear or avoid a possible good rather than a certain evil.

And therefore if you let me go now, and reject the counsels of Anytus, who said that if I were not put to death I ought not to have been prosecuted, and that if I escape now, your sons will all be utterly ruined by listening to my words—if you say to me, Socrates, this time we will not mind Anytus, and will let you off, but upon one condition, that are to inquire and speculate in this way any more, and that if you are caught doing this again you shall die;—if this was the condition on which you let me go, I should reply: Men of Athens, I honor and love you; but I shall obey God rather than you, and while I have life and strength I shall never cease from the practice and teaching of philosophy, exhorting anyone whom I meet after my manner, and convincing him, saying: O my friend, why do you who are a citizen of the great and mighty and wise city of Athens, care so much about laying up the greatest amount of money and honor and reputation, and so little about wisdom and truth and the greatest improvement of the soul, which you never regard or heed at all? Are you not ashamed of this?

And if the person with whom I am arguing says:

Yes, but I do care; I do not depart or let him go at once; I interrogate and examine and cross-examine him, and if I think that he has no virtue, but only says that he has, I reproach him with undervaluing the greater, and overvaluing the less. And this I should say to everyone whom I meet, young and old, citizen and alien, but especially to the citizens, inasmuch as they are my brethren. For this is the command of God, as I would have you know; and I believe that to this day no greater good has ever happened in the state than my service to the God. For I do nothing but go about persuading you all, old and young alike, not to take thought for your persons and your properties, but first and chiefly to care about the greatest improvement of the soul. I tell you that virtue is not given by money, but that from virtue come money and every other good of man, public as well as private. This is my teaching, and if this is the doctrine which corrupts the youth, my influence is ruinous indeed. But if anyone says that this is not my teaching, he is speaking an untruth. Wherefore, O men of Athens, I say to you, do as Anytus bids or not as Anytus bids, and either acquit me or not; but whatever you do, know that I shall never alter my ways, not even if I have to die many times.

1.4. Socrates as Athen's Gadfly

Men of Athens, do not interrupt, but hear me; there was an agreement between us that you should hear me out. And I think that what I am going to say will do you good: for I have something more to say, at which you may be inclined to cry out; but I beg that you will not do this. I would have you know that, if you kill such a one as I am, you will injure yourselves more than you will injure me. Meletus and Anytus will not injure me: they cannot; for it is not in the nature of things that a bad man should injure a better than himself. I do not deny that he may, perhaps, kill him, or drive him into exile, or deprive him of civil rights; and he may imagine, and others may imagine, that he is doing him a great injury: but in that I do not agree with him; for the evil of doing as Anytus is doing—of unjustly taking away another man's life—is greater far. And now, Athenians, I am not going to argue for my own sake, as you may think, but for yours, that you may not sin

against the God, or lightly reject his boon by condemning me. For if you kill me you will not easily find another like me, who, if I may use such a ludicrous figure of speech, am a sort of gadfly, given to the state by the God; and the state is like a great and noble steed who is tardy in his motions owing to his very size, and requires to be stirred into life. I am that gadfly which God has given the state and all day long and in all places am always fastening upon you, arousing and persuading and reproaching you. And as you will not easily find another like me, I would advise you to spare me. I dare say that you may feel irritated at being suddenly awakened when you are caught napping; and you may think that if you were to strike me dead, as Anytus advises, which you easily might, then you would sleep on for the remainder of your lives, unless God in his care of you gives you another gadfly.

And that I am given to you by God is proved by this:—that if I had been like other men, I should not have neglected all my own concerns, or patiently seen the neglect of them during all these years, and have been doing yours, coming to you individually, like a father or elder brother, exhorting you to regard virtue; this I say, would not be like human nature. And had I gained anything, or if my exhortations had been paid, there would have been some sense in that: but now, as you will perceive, not even the impudence of my accusers dares to say that I have ever exacted or sought pay of anyone; they have no witness of that. And I have a witness of the truth of what I say; my poverty is a sufficient witness....

1.5 Concluding Comments

Well, Athenians, this and the like of this is nearly all the defense which I have to offer. Yet a word more. Perhaps there may be someone who is offended at me, when he calls to mind how he himself, on a similar or even a less serious occasion, had recourse to prayers and supplications with many tears, and how he produced his children in court, which was a moving spectacle, together with a posse of his relations and friends; whereas I, who am probably in danger of my life, will do none of these things. Perhaps this may come into his mind, and he may be set against me, and vote in anger because he is displeased at this. Now if there be such a person among you, which I am far from affirming, I may fairly reply to him: My friend, I am a man, and like other men, a creature of flesh and blood, and not of wood or stone, as Homer says; and I have a family, yes, and sons. O Athenians, three in number, one of whom is growing up, and the two others are still young; and yet I will not bring any of them hither in order to petition you for an acquittal. And why not? Not from any self-will or disregard of you. Whether I am or am not afraid of death is another question, of which I will not now speak. But my reason simply is that I feel such conduct to be discreditable to myself, and you, and the whole state. One who has reached my years, and who has a name for wisdom, whether deserved or not, ought not to debase himself. At any rate, the world has decided that Socrates is in some way superior to other men. And if those among you who are said to be superior in wisdom and courage, and any other virtue, demean themselves in this way, how shameful is their conduct! I have seen men of reputation, when they have been condemned, behaving in the strangest manner: they seemed to fancy that they were going to suffer something dreadful if they died, and that they could be immortal if you only allowed them to live; and I think that they were a dishonor to the state, and that any stranger coming in would say of them that the most eminent men of Athens, to whom the Athenians themselves give honor and command, are no better than women. And I say that these things ought not to be done by those of us who are of reputation; and if they are done, you ought not to permit them; you ought rather to show that you are more inclined to condemn, not the man who is quiet, but the man who gets up a doleful scene, and makes the city ridiculous.

But, setting aside the question of dishonor, there seems to be something wrong in petitioning a judge, and thus procuring an acquittal instead of informing and convincing him. For his duty is, not to make a present of justice, but to give judgment; and he has sworn that he will judge according to the laws, and not according to his own good pleasure; and neither he nor we should get into the habit of perjuring ourselves—there can be no piety in that. Do not then require me to do what I consider dishonorable and impious and wrong, especially now, when I am being tried for impiety on the indictment of Meletus.

For if, O men of Athens, by force of persuasion and entreaty, I could overpower your oaths, then I should be teaching you to believe that there are no gods, and convict myself, in my own defense, of not believing in them. But that is not the case; for I do believe that there are gods, and in a far higher sense than that in which any of my accusers believe in them. And to you and to God I commit my cause, to be determined by you as is best for you and me.

The jury finds Socrates guilty.

2. Proposal of the Counter Penalty

There are many reasons why I am not grieved, O men of Athens, at the vote of condemnation. I expected it, and am only surprised that the votes are so nearly equal; for I had thought that the majority against me would have been far larger; but now, had thirty votes gone over to the other side, I should have been acquitted. And I may say that I have escaped Meletus. And I may say more; for without the assistance of Anytus and Lycon, he would not have had a fifth part of the votes, as the law requires, in which case he would have incurred a fine of a thousand drachmae, as is evident.

And so he proposes death as the penalty. And what shall I propose on my part, O men of Athens? Clearly that which is my due. And what is that which I ought to pay or to receive? What shall be done to the man who has never had the wit to be idle during his whole life; but has been careless of what the many care about—wealth, and family interests, and military offices, and speaking in the assembly, and magistracies, and plots, and parties. Reflecting that I was really too honest a man to follow in this way and live, I did not go where I could do no good to you or to myself; but where I could do the greatest good privately to everyone of you, thither I went, and sought to persuade every man among you that he must look to himself, and seek virtue and wisdom before he looks to his private interests, and look to the state before he looks to the interests of the state; and that this should be the order which he observes in all his actions. What shall be done to such a one? Doubtless some good thing, O men of Athens, if he has his reward; and the good should be of a kind suitable to him. What would be a reward suitable to a poor man who is your benefactor, who desires leisure that he may instruct you? There can be no more fitting reward than [public meals for life] in the Prytaneum, O men of Athens, a reward which he deserves far more than the citizen who has won the prize at Olympia in the horse or chariot race, whether the chariots were drawn by two horses or by many. For I am in want, and he has enough; and he only gives you the appearance of happiness, and I give you the reality. And if I am to estimate the penalty justly, I say that maintenance in the Prytaneum is the just return.

Perhaps you may think that I am braving you in saying this, as in what I said before about the tears and prayers. But that is not the case. I speak rather because I am convinced that I never intentionally wronged anyone, although I cannot convince you of that—for we have had a short conversation only; but if there were a law at Athens, such as there is in other cities, that a capital cause should not be decided in one day, then I believe that I should have convinced you; but now the time is too short. I cannot in a moment refute great slanders; and, as I am convinced that I never wronged another, I will assuredly not wrong myself. I will not say of myself that I deserve any evil, or propose any penalty. Why should I? Because I am afraid of the penalty of death which Meletus proposes? When I do not know whether death is a good or an evil, why should I propose a penalty which would certainly be an evil? Shall I say imprisonment? And why should I live in prison, and be the slave of the magistrates of the year—of the Eleven? Or shall the penalty be a fine, and imprisonment until the fine is paid? There is the same objection. I should have to lie in prison, for money I have none, and I cannot pay. And if I say exile (and this may possibly be the penalty which you will affix), I must indeed be blinded by the love of life if I were to consider that when you, who are my own citizens, cannot endure my discourses and words, and have found them so grievous and odious that you would fain have done with them, others are likely to endure me. No, indeed, men of Athens, that is not very likely. And what a life should I lead, at my age, wandering from city to city, living in ever-changing exile, and always being driven out! For I am quite sure that into whatever place I go, as here so also there,

the young men will come to me; and if I drive them away, their elders will drive me out at their desire: and if I let them come, their fathers and friends will drive me out for their sakes.

Someone will say: Yes, Socrates, but cannot you hold your tongue, and then you may go into a foreign city, and no one will interfere with you? Now I have great difficulty in making you understand my answer to this. For if I tell you that this would be a disobedience to a divine command, and therefore that I cannot hold my tongue, you will not believe that I am serious; and if I say again that the greatest good of man is daily to converse about virtue, and all that concerning which you hear me examining myself and others, and the unexamined life is not worth living—that you are still less likely to believe. And yet what I say is true, although a thing of which it is hard for me to persuade you. Moreover, I am not accustomed to think that I deserve any punishment. Had I money I might have proposed to give you what I had, and have been none the worse. But you see that I have none, and can only ask you to proportion the fine to my means. However, I think that I could afford a minae, and therefore I propose that penalty; Plato, Crito, Critobulus, and Apollodorus, my friends here, bid me say thirty minae, and they will be the sureties. Well then, say thirty minae, let that be the penalty; for that they will be ample security to you.

The jury condemns Socrates to death.

3. Final Address

Not much time will be gained, O Athenians, in return for the evil name which you will get from the detractors of the city, who will say that you killed Socrates, a wise man; for they will call me wise even although I am not wise when they want to reproach you. If you had waited a little while, your desire would have been fulfilled in the course of nature. For I am far advanced in years, as you may perceive, and not far from death.

I am speaking now only to those of you who have condemned me to death. And I have another thing to say to them: You think that I was convicted through deficiency of words—I mean, that if I had thought fit to leave nothing undone, nothing un-said, I might have gained an acquittal. Not so; the deficiency which led to my conviction was not of words—certainly not. But I had not the boldness or impudence or inclination to address you as you would have liked me to address you, weeping and wailing and lamenting, and saying and doing many things which you have been accustomed to hear from others, and which, as I say, are unworthy of me. But I thought that I ought not to do anything common or mean in the hour of danger: nor do I now repent of the manner of my defence, and I would rather die having spoken after my manner, than speak in your manner and live. For neither in war nor yet at law ought any man to use every way of escaping death. For often in battle there is no doubt that if a man will throw away his arms, and fall on his knees before his pursuers, he may escape death; and in other dangers there are other ways of escaping death, if a man is willing to say and do anything. The difficulty, my friends, is not in avoiding death, but in avoid-ing unrighteousness; for that runs faster than death. I am old and move slowly, and the slower runner has overtaken me, and my accusers are keen and quick, and the faster runner, who is unrighteousness, has overtaken them. And now I depart hence condemned by you to suffer the penalty of death, and they, too, go their ways condemned by the truth to suffer the penalty of villainy and wrong; and I must abide by my award—let them abide by theirs. I suppose that these things may be regarded as fated, — and I think that they are well.

3.1. Reflections on Death

And now, O men who have condemned me, I would fain prophesy to you; for I am about to die, and that is the hour in which men are gifted with prophetic power. And I prophesy to you who are my murder-ers, that immediately after my death punishment far heavier than you have inflicted on me will surely await you. Me you have killed because you wanted to escape the accuser, and not to give an account of your lives. But that will not be as you suppose: far otherwise. For I say that there will be more accusers of you than there are now; accusers whom hitherto I have restrained: and as they are younger they will be more severe with you, and you will be more of-

fended at them. For if you think that by killing men you can avoid the accuser censuring your lives, you are mistaken; that is not a way of escape which is either possible or honorable; the easiest and noblest way is not to be crushing others, but to be improving yourselves. This is the prophecy which I utter before my departure, to the judges who have condemned me.

Friends, who would have acquitted me, I would like also to talk with you about this thing which has happened, while the magistrates are busy, and be-fore I go to the place at which I must die. Stay then awhile, for we may as well talk with one another while there is time. You are my friends, and I should like to show you the meaning of this event which has happened to me. O my judges—for you I may truly call judges—I should like to tell you of a wonder-ful circumstance. Hitherto the familiar oracle within me has constantly been in the habit of opposing me even about trifles, if I was going to make a slip or error about anything; and now as you see there has come upon me that which may be thought, and is generally believed to be, the last and worst evil. But the oracle made no sign of opposition, either as I was leaving my house and going out in the morning, or when I was going up into this court, or while I was speaking, at anything which I was going to say; and yet I have often been stopped in the middle of a speech; but now in nothing I either said or did touch-ing this matter has the oracle opposed me. What do I take to be the explanation of this? I will tell you. I regard this as a proof that what has happened to me is a good, and that those of us who think that death is an evil are in error. This is a great proof to me of what I am saying, for the customary sign would surely have opposed me had I been going to evil and not to good.

Let us reflect in another way, and we shall see that there is great reason to hope that death is a good, for one of two things:—either death is a state of noth-ingness and utter unconsciousness, or, as men say, there is a change and migration of the soul from this world to another. Now if you suppose that there is no consciousness, but a sleep like the sleep of him who is undisturbed even by the sight of dreams, death will be an unspeakable gain. For if a person were to select the night in which his sleep was undisturbed even by dreams, and were to compare with this the other days and nights of his life, and then were to tell us how many days and nights he had passed in the course of his life better and more pleasantly than this one, I think that any man, I will not say a private man, but even the great king, will not find many such days or nights, when compared with the others. Now if death is like this, I say that to die is gain; for eternity is then only a single night. But if death is the journey to another place, and there, as men say, all the dead are, what good, O my friends and judges, can be greater than this? If indeed when the pilgrim arrives in the world below, he is delivered from the professors of justice in this world, and finds the true judges who are said to give judgment there, Minos and Rhadamanthus and Aeacus and Triptolemus, and other sons of God who were righteous in their own life, that pilgrimage will be worth making. What would not a man give if he might converse with Orpheus and Musaeus and Hesiod and Homer? Nay, if this be true, let me die again and again. I, too, shall have a wonderful interest in a place where I can converse with Palamedes, and Ajax the son of Telamon, and other heroes of old, who have suffered death through an unjust judgment; and there will be no small pleasure, as I think, in comparing my own sufferings with theirs. Above all, I shall be able to continue my search into true and false knowledge; as in this world, so also in that; I shall find out who is wise, and who pretends to be wise, and is not. What would not a man give, O judges, to be able to examine the leader of the great Trojan expedition; or Odysseus or Sisyphus, or numberless others, men and women too! What infinite delight would there be in conversing with them and asking them questions!

For in that world they do not put a man to death for this; certainly not. For besides being happier in that world than in this, they will be immortal, if what is said is true.

3.2. *Concluding Comments*

Wherefore, O judges, be of good cheer about death, and know this for a fact—that no evil can happen to a good man, either in life or after death. He and his are not neglected by the gods; nor has my own approaching end happened by mere chance. But I see clearly that to die and be released was better for me; and therefore the oracle gave no sign. For which reason also, I am not angry with my accusers, or my condemners; they have done me no harm, although neither of them meant to do me any good; and for this I may gently blame them. Still I have a favor to ask of them. When my sons are grown up, I would ask you, O my friends, to punish them; and I would have you trouble them, as I have troubled you, if they seem to care about riches, or anything, more than about virtue; or if they pretend to be something when they are really nothing,—then reprove them, as I have reproved you, for not caring about that for which they ought to care, and thinking that they are something when they are really nothing. And if you do this, I and my sons will have received justice at your hands.

The hour of departure has arrived, and we go our ways—I to die, and you to live. Which is better God only knows.

Plato. "Apology." *The Dialogues of Plato.* Vol. 2. Trans. by Benjamin Jowett. Oxford: Oxford University Press, 1892.

THE VALUE OF PHILOSOPHY

BERTRAND RUSSELL (1872-1970)

One of the great philosophers of the 20th century, Bertrand Russell was also a gifted mathematician, a devout atheist, and a committed pacifist. He wrote his first work, Principles of Mathematics *in 1903. During World War 1, he was sentenced to six months for a pacifist article he produced, and, while in prison, wrote his* Introduction to Mathematical Philosophy *(1919). In the following selection from* The Problems of Philosophy *(1912), Russell provides a useful overview of the benefits of philosophical study that at the same time lays out his own vision for what the discipline is all about.*

Having now come to the end of our brief and very incomplete review of the problems of philosophy, it will be well to consider, in conclusion, what is the value of philosophy and why it ought to be studied. It is the more necessary to consider this question, in view of the fact that many men, under the influence of science or of practical affairs, are inclined to doubt whether philosophy is anything better than innocent but useless trifling, hair-splitting distinctions, and controversies on matters concerning which knowledge is impossible.

1. Mistaken Ideas About Philosophy

This view of philosophy appears to result, partly from a wrong conception of the ends of life, partly from a wrong conception of the kind of goods which philosophy strives to achieve. Physical science, through the medium of inventions, is useful to innumerable people who are wholly ignorant of it; thus the study of physical science is to be recommended, not only, or primarily, because of the effect on the student, but rather because of the effect on mankind in general. This utility does not belong to philosophy. If the study of philosophy has any value at all for others than students of philosophy, it must be only indirectly, through its effects upon the lives of those who study it. It is in these effects, therefore, if anywhere, that the value of philosophy must be primarily sought.

But further, if we are not to fail in our endeavour to determine the value of philosophy, we must first free our minds from the prejudices of what are wrongly called 'practical' men. The 'practical' man, as this word is often used, is one who recognizes only material needs, who realizes that men must have food for the body, but is oblivious of the necessity of providing food for the mind. If all men were well off, if poverty and disease had been reduced to their lowest possible point, there would still remain much to be done to produce a valuable society; and even in the existing world the goods of the mind are at least as important as the goods of the body. It is exclusively among the goods of the mind that the value of philosophy is to be found; and only those who are not indifferent to these goods can be persuaded that the study of philosophy is not a waste of time.

2. The True Aims of Philosophy

Philosophy, like all other studies, aims primarily at knowledge. The knowledge it aims at is the kind of knowledge which gives unity and system to the body of the sciences, and the kind which results from a critical examination of the grounds of our convictions, prejudices, and beliefs. But it cannot be maintained that philosophy has had any very great measure of success in its attempts to provide definite answers to its questions. If you ask a mathematician, a mineralogist, a historian, or any other man of learning, what definite body of truths has been ascertained by his science, his answer will last as long as you are willing to listen. But if you put the same question to a philosopher, he will, if he is candid, have to confess that his study has not achieved positive results such as have been achieved by other sciences. It is true that this is partly accounted for by the fact that, as soon as definite knowledge concerning any subject becomes possible, this subject ceases to be called philosophy, and becomes a separate science. The whole study of the heavens, which now belongs to astronomy, was once included in philosophy; Newton's great work was called 'the mathematical principles of natural philosophy'. Similarly, the study of the human mind, which was a part of philosophy, has now been separated from philosophy and has become the science of psychology. Thus, to a great extent, the uncertainty of philosophy is more apparent than real: those questions which are already capable of definite answers are placed in the sciences, while those only to which, at present, no definite answer can be given, remain to form the residue which is called philosophy.

This is, however, only a part of the truth concerning the uncertainty of philosophy. There are many questions—and among them those that are of the profoundest interest to our spiritual life —which, so far as we can see, must remain insoluble to the human intellect unless its powers become of quite a different order from what they are now. Has the universe any unity of plan or purpose, or is it a fortuitous concourse of atoms? Is consciousness a permanent part of the universe, giving hope of indefinite growth in wisdom, or is it a transitory accident on a small planet on which life must ultimately become impossible? Are good and evil of importance to the universe or only to man? Such questions are asked by philosophy, and variously answered by various philosophers. But it would seem that, whether answers be otherwise discoverable or not, the answers suggested by philosophy are none of them demonstrably true. Yet, however slight may be the hope of discovering an answer, it is part of the business of philosophy to continue the consideration of such questions, to make us aware of their importance, to examine all the approaches to them, and to keep alive that speculative interest in the universe which is apt to be killed by confining ourselves to definitely ascertainable knowledge.

3. The Value of Uncertainty

Many philosophers, it is true, have held that philosophy could establish the truth of certain answers to such fundamental questions. They have supposed that what is of most importance in religious beliefs could be proved by strict demonstration to be true. In order to judge of such attempts, it is necessary to take a survey of human knowledge, and to form an opinion as to its methods and its limitations. On such a subject it would be unwise to pronounce dogmatically; but if the investigations of our previous chapters have not led us astray, we shall be compelled to renounce the hope of finding philosophical proofs of religious beliefs. We cannot, therefore, include as part of the value of philosophy any definite set of answers to such questions. Hence, once more, the value of philosophy must not depend upon any supposed body of definitely ascertainable knowledge to be acquired by those who study it.

The value of philosophy is, in fact, to be sought largely in its very uncertainty. The man who has no tincture of philosophy goes through life imprisoned in the prejudices derived from common sense, from the habitual beliefs of his age or his nation, and from convictions which have grown up in his mind without the co-operation or consent of his deliberate reason. To such a man the world tends to become definite, finite, obvious; common objects rouse no questions, and unfamiliar possibilities are contemptuously rejected. As soon as we begin to philosophize, on the contrary, we find...that even the most everyday things lead to problems to which only very incomplete answers can be given. Philosophy, though unable to tell us with certainty what is the true answer to the doubts which it raises, is able to suggest many possibilities which enlarge our thoughts and free them from the tyranny of custom. Thus, while diminishing our feeling of certainty as to what things are, it greatly increases our knowledge as to what they may be; it removes the somewhat arrogant dogmatism of those who have never travelled into the region of liberating doubt, and it keeps alive our sense of wonder by showing familiar things in an unfamiliar aspect.

4. The Objects of Philosophy Contemplation and their Benefits

Apart from its utility in showing unsuspected possibilities, philosophy has a value—perhaps its chief value—through the greatness of the objects which it contemplates, and the freedom from narrow and personal aims resulting from this contemplation. The life of the instinctive man is shut up within the circle of his private interests: family and friends may be included, but the outer world is not regarded except as it may help or hinder what comes within the circle of instinctive wishes. In such a life there is something feverish and confined, in comparison with which the philosophic life is calm and free. The private world of instinctive interests is a small one, set in the midst of a great and powerful world which must, sooner or later, lay our private world in ruins. Unless we can so enlarge our interests as to include the whole outer world, we remain like a garrison in a beleaguered fortress, knowing that the enemy prevents escape and that ultimate surrender is inevitable. In such a life there is no peace, but a constant strife between the insistence of desire and the powerlessness of will. In one way or another, if our life is to be great and free, we must escape this prison and this strife.

One way of escape is by philosophic contemplation. Philosophic contemplation does not, in its widest survey, divide the universe into two hostile camps—friends and foes, helpful and hostile, good and bad—it views the whole impartially. Philosophic contemplation, when it is unalloyed, does not aim at proving that the rest of the universe is akin to man. All acquisition of knowledge is an enlargement of the Self, but this enlargement is best attained when it is not directly sought. It is obtained when the desire for knowledge is alone operative, by a study which does not wish in advance that its objects should have this or that character, but adapts the Self to the characters which it finds in its objects. This enlargement of Self is not obtained when, taking the Self as it is, we try to show that the world is so similar to this Self that knowledge of it is possible without any admission of what seems alien. The desire to prove this is a form of self-assertion and, like all self-assertion, it

is an obstacle to the growth of Self which it desires, and of which the Self knows that it is capable. Self-assertion, in philosophic speculation as elsewhere, views the world as a means to its own ends; thus it makes the world of less account than Self, and the Self sets bounds to the greatness of its goods. In contemplation, on the contrary, we start from the not-Self, and through its greatness the boundaries of Self are enlarged; through the infinity of the universe the mind which contemplates it achieves some share in infinity.

For this reason greatness of soul is not fostered by those philosophies which assimilate the universe to Man. Knowledge is a form of union of Self and not-Self; like all union, it is impaired by dominion, and therefore by any attempt to force the universe into conformity with what we find in ourselves. There is a widespread philosophical tendency towards the view which tells us that Man is the measure of all things, that truth is man-made, that space and time and the world of universals are properties of the mind, and that, if there be anything not created by the mind, it is unknowable and of no account for us. This view, if our previous discussions were correct, is untrue; but in addition to being untrue, it has the effect of robbing philosophic contemplation of all that gives it value, since it fetters contemplation to Self. What it calls knowledge is not a union with the not-Self, but a set of prejudices, habits, and desires, making an impenetrable veil between us and the world beyond. The man who finds pleasure in such a theory of knowledge is like the man who never leaves the domestic circle for fear his word might not be law.

The true philosophic contemplation, on the contrary, finds its satisfaction in every enlargement of the not-Self, in everything that magnifies the objects contemplated, and thereby the subject contemplating. Everything, in contemplation, that is personal or private, everything that depends upon habit, self-interest, or desire, distorts the object, and hence impairs the union which the intellect seeks. By thus making a barrier between subject and object, such personal and private things become a prison to the intellect. The free intellect will see as God might see, without a here and now, without hopes and fears, without the trammels of customary beliefs and traditional prejudices, calmly, dispassionately, in the sole and exclusive desire of knowledge—knowledge as impersonal, as purely contemplative, as it is possible for man to attain. Hence also the free intellect will value more the abstract and universal knowledge into which the accidents of private history do not enter, than the knowledge brought by the senses, and dependent, as such knowledge must be, upon an exclusive and personal point of view and a body whose sense-organs distort as much as they reveal.

The mind which has become accustomed to the freedom and impartiality of philosophic contemplation will preserve something of the same freedom and impartiality in the world of action and emotion. It will view its purposes and desires as parts of the whole, with the absence of insistence that results from seeing them as infinitesimal fragments in a world of which all the rest is unaffected by any one man's deeds. The impartiality which, in contemplation, is the unalloyed desire for truth, is the very same quality of mind which, in action, is justice, and in emotion is that universal love which can be given to all, and not only to those who are judged useful or admirable. Thus contemplation enlarges not only the objects of our thoughts, but also the objects of our actions and our affections: it makes us citizens of the universe, not only of one walled city at war with all the rest. In this citizenship of the universe consists man's true freedom, and his liberation from the thraldom of narrow hopes and fears.

Thus, to sum up our discussion of the value of philosophy; Philosophy is to be studied, not for the sake of any definite answers to its questions since no definite answers can, as a rule, be known to be true, but rather for the sake of the questions themselves; because these questions enlarge our conception of what is possible, enrich our intellectual imagination and diminish the dogmatic assurance which closes the mind against speculation; but above all because, through the greatness of the universe which philosophy contemplates, the mind also is rendered great, and becomes capable of that union with the universe which constitutes its highest good.

Bertrand Russell. *The Problems of Philosophy*. New York: Henry Holt, 1912.

2

READING A
PHILOSOPHICAL TEXT

You may have heard that philosophical texts are extremely difficult to read and that they often require a great deal of effort to comprehend. We are not going to try to deceive you into thinking that reading philosophy will be a "piece of cake" or that you won't have to struggle a bit to understand what's going on in a philosophical work. Certainly the kind of reading that you will be asked to do in philosophy will present a much greater intellectual challenge than you may typically be accustomed to—even in your other college classes.

Our promise to you is that if you faithfully follow the suggestions in this guide, you should be able to navigate your way through the complex arguments in the typical philosophical work. And perhaps—if you are very fortunate indeed—you may even become part of that elite group of college students who actually derive some kind of pleasure from joining the great philosophers in their pursuit of wisdom.

Reading for Understanding

Before we get down to the nitty-gritty of how to read a philosophical work, a distinction should be made between reading for information and reading for understanding. In reading for information, one reads something that requires very little effort to comprehend—an article in the *New York Post*, for example—and which therefore increases information about the world, but not understanding about yourself and the world in which you live. Growth in understanding, by comparison, comes when one reads material that is difficult to comprehend, and which forces one to rise to the more elevated level of the written material. In general, the more effort that you are forced to make in reading, the greater will be your growth in understanding. To quote the old adage, "No pain, no gain."

Try to keep in mind that the goal of reading in a liberal arts education—and this is particularly true in the discipline of philosophy—is neither pleasure nor information per se; it is rather to help expand your understanding of yourself and your universe. This is not to say that you shouldn't derive some pleasure from reading Milton's *Paradise Lost* or receive useful information from reading a work like Plato's *Republic*. But these concerns should be secondary to your ultimate aim of reading great works in order to expand your intellectual horizons and to broaden your understanding of the meaning of your existence.

Helpful Hints on Philosophical Reading

Because philosophical reading is by its very nature deep reading, in your attempt to derive some understanding of a philosophical text, you are probably going to have to put aside some of the lazy reading habits that you've developed over the years. Many students have the tendency to breeze through most of their college readings rather quickly and haphazardly in order to get through reading assignments as "painlessly" as possible. While this kind of quick-read might work if you are reading the typical college textbook that is written on a 9th grade reading level, it will not work if you are reading the works of great philosophers.

1. Savoring the Delectable. Almost all philosophers tend to write in a very dense style that demands a slow and careful reading. You should try to savor their ideas the way you would a delicious meal at a fancy restaurant. If you were dining at the Russian Tea Room you would dine slowly, attempting to appreciate every mouthful of food. Try to read philosophy in the same way: take the time to mull over every sentence that you read, and to reflect carefully upon the author's meaning. You may even have to reread a section of text several times before you get what the author is trying to say.

As an illustration of what I mean, try reading the following selection from the opening paragraphs of Kierkegaard's *Sickness Unto Death* in your normal style of reading:

A human being is spirit. But what is spirit? Spirit is the self. But what is the self? The self is a relation that relates itself to itself or is the relation's relating itself to itself in the relation; the self is not the relation but is the relation's relating itself to itself. A human being is a synthesis of the infinite and the finite, of the temporal and the eternal, of freedom and necessity, in short, a synthesis. A synthesis is a relation between two. Considered in this way, a human being is still not a self.

In the relation between the two, the relation is the third as a negative unity, and the two relate to the relation and in the relation to the relation; thus under the qualification of the psychical the relation between the psychical and the physical is a relation. If, however, the relation relates itself to itself, this relation is the positive third, and this is the self.

Søren Kierkegaard. *The Sickness Unto Death.* Trans. Howard V. Hong and Edna Hong. Princeton, NJ: Princeton Univ. Press, 1980.

Doesn't make much sense, does it? If you were asked to read this work in a philosophy class on Existentialism, you might find yourself frustrated by your inability to break through Kierkegaard's rather difficult style of writing. You might even be tempted to give up on him as soon as you got to the end of the second paragraph. So what can you do to prevent yourself from falling into despair when you encounter complicated writing of this sort in your philosophy classes? Here are just a few general suggestions:

2. Slow Down Some More. The first time I read Kierkegaard's *Sickness Unto Death* as a college student I was just as confused as you probably were reading the above selection (sometimes I still get confused when I read Kierkegaard). Confusion is perfectly natural when you are reading any kind of challenging literature. The trick is not to try to rush through your reading in the misguided hope that the author's writing will get easier later on. Instead try slowing your reading down even more, concentrating on the relations between the various terms that the author is using in each sentence and paragraph. If nothing else you should be able to figure out that Kierkegaard is defining a human being as a "self." You may not fully understand yet what a self is, but you should have a vague idea that it has something to do with being a "relation" and a "synthesis." That is more than enough for a start.

3. *Understanding Those Wacky Words.* One of the main reasons why many students have difficulty reading great works is because they get stumped by unfamiliar terms and expressions. Just try picking up Dicken's *Pickwick Papers* and you will find a large number of words that are probably completely alien to you. Sadly, the vocabulary of the average college-educated person today is much more limited than it was even 100 years ago, making it difficult for many students to read great works of literature and philosophy. One simple solution is to read these works with a dictionary beside you, and to take note of any words that are unfamiliar to you. Not only will this help you make more sense of the work that you are reading, but it may also improve your vocabulary at the same time!

Unfortunately, this problem is compounded even further in philosophy, where quite often you have a specialized vocabulary being used. Notice that in the Kierkegaard passage above none of the words that are being used are complicated in themselves. The difficulty in the passage lies in the way that Kierkegaard takes rather ordinary words and assigns them his own specific meanings ("self" and "relation" for example). If you are stuck with an author who doesn't define his terms carefully or an edition that doesn't have extensive notes on the text or a glossary, then you will just have to try to figure out the specialized meaning of these terms through their contexts or by referring to some outside source for help.

4. *Text Marking.* One way to force yourself to read more deliberately is to do what scholars for centuries have done with great works: use different devices for marking important terms, ideas, and concepts in the work. Among the most common methods of marking a text are the following:

- Underline crucial words, phrases and sentences.
- Use checks (v) and stars (*) in the margins to emphasize important sections of text.
- Make brief notes in the margins of the text to help sum up the author's main points.
- Put a question mark (?) next to passages that are problematic, ambiguous or unintelligible to you.

Text marking can help you to concentrate more intensely on a philosopher's line of argumentation, and will make life much easier when you have to go back to the text later to study for an exam or to write a paper. Consider the following suggestions for marking a text effectively:

- Use a pencil rather than a pen or highlighter to mark text.
- Mark your text lightly so that it can later be erased/changed if necessary.
- Mark a text sparingly—only in the most crucial sections.
- Never mark a book that doesn't belong to you—especially a library book.

5. *Just Keep on Trucking.* In the event that slowing yourself down and rereading a passage several times does not help you to make sense of a text, don't despair. After all, no one profits if you hurl your philosophy text against a wall, screaming obscenities about how stupid Kierkegaard is. Instead try reading further on in the work. Usually a philosophical text will get clearer as the author elaborates upon his ideas and his arguments begin to unfold. If you were

to continue to read *Sickness Unto Death*, for example, you would find that many of the terms that so confused you in the opening paragraphs are clarified by Kierkergaard later on in the first few chapters.

6. It's OK To Get Some Help. If you find it simply impossible to make any sense of a philosophical work that you have been assigned to read, then it might behoove you to get some help in understanding it. Of course, you can always ask your course instructor for assistance, but this is not going to help you to become an autonomous reader of great works. A more effective option is to find a secondary source that will help you make sense of the author's ideas. Some possibilities include:

- Don't forget to read the introduction to the work that is provided by the editor or translator. These introductions are put at the beginning of a text in order to give the reader the background information that he will need to read the text profitably.
- Read the chapter on your author from one of the many histories of philosophy that are available in every college library (Copleston's *History of Philosophy* may be a tad dull, but he does treat almost every notable figure in Western Philosophy in a fairly thorough fashion).
- Read a brief intellectual biography of your author that will help to put some of his ideas in context for you.
- Find a respectable on-line commentary on the text that can help guide you through it. Many philosophy departments around the country are developing such commentaries, and some are extremely well done.

Exercise

Instructions: Read the following selection from Kant's Groundwork of the Metaphysics of Morals *slowly, trying to get a sense of what Kant is getting at in the passage:*

Immanuel Kant
The Good Will

It is impossible to conceive anything at all in the world, or even out of it, which can be taken as good without qualification, except a good will. Intelligence, wit, judgment, and any other talents of the mind we may care to name, or courage, resolution, and constancy of the mind we may care to name, or courage, resolution, and constancy of purpose, as qualities of temperament, are without doubt good and desirable in many respects; but they can also be extremely bad and hurtful when the will is not good which has to make use of these gifts of nature, and which for this reason has the term 'character' applied to its peculiar quality. It is exactly the same with gifts of fortune. Power, wealth, honor, even health and that complete well-being and contentment with one's state which goes by the name of 'happiness,' produce boldness, and as a consequence often over-boldness as well, unless a good will is present by which their influence on the mind—and so too

---

the whole principle of action—may be corrected and adjusted to universal ends; not to mention that a rational and impartial spectator can never feel approval in contemplating the uninterrupted prosperity of a being graced by no touch of a pure and good will, and that consequently a good will seems to constitute the indispensable condition of our very worthiness to be happy.

Some qualities are even helpful to this good will itself and can make its task very much easier. They have none the less no inner unconditioned worth, but rather presuppose a good will which sets a limit to the esteem in which they are rightly held and does not permit us to regard them as absolutely good. Moderation in affections and passions, self-control, and sober reflection are not only good in many respects: they may even seem to constitute part of the inner worth of a person. Yet they are far from being properly described as good without qualification (however unconditionally they have been commended by the ancients). For without the principles of a good will they may become exceedingly bad; and the very coolness of a scoundrel makes him, not merely more dangerous, but also immediately more abominable in our eyes than we should have taken him to be without it.

Immanuel Kant, *Groundwork of the Metaphysics of Morals*. Trans. H. J. Paton. NY: Harper and Row, 1964.

1.   *List any terms in the selection that you are unfamilar with. Can you determine the meaning of these terms from their context in the passage? If not, try looking them up in the dictionary.*

2.   *Briefly summarize the point of the text in 2-3 sentences.*

Three Levels of Philosophical Reading

Our aim in the previous exercise was to help you to learn how to *make some sense* of a few rather basic philosophical passages. In fact, all you were really doing in this exercise was trying to *sum up* or *get the main point* of these passages. Believe it or not, this kind of "summing up" (what I will call explication) represents the most basic type of reading. "Summing up" is basically the same skills that you used in the seventh grade, when your teacher asked you to write a book report on *Huckleberry Finn*. The texts that we asked you to read may be a bit more difficult than those you read in the seventh grade, but the skills that you employed in summing up the text are essentially the same.

If all we did in reading a work of philosophy was to explain in the most elementary terms what the author's basic arguments are, we would not be doing anything very profound or interesting. The real task of the student of philosophy is to further investigate the text in order to discover its deeper meaning (what I refer to as the process of elucidation) and to assess whether the ideas presented in the text are right or wrong (the act of evaluation).

These three levels of philosophical reading can be broken down in the following way:

Three Levels of Philosophical Reading

SKILL	OBJECT	ACTIVITY
Explication	What does the author say?	• State the author's thesis. • Outline the author's arguments. • Sum up the author's position.
Elucidation	What does the author mean?	• Identify the implications of the author's position. • Unveil the relevance of the author's position for our own times.
Evaluation	Is the author right or wrong?	• Assess the strength of the author's arguments. • Judge the author's position as tenable/ untenable.

Reading as Explication

The term "explication" has its root in the Latin word "explicare," which means literally "to unfold." When we explicate a text what we are trying to do is to unfold or unravel the author's basic position in this text. Think of a philosophical work as a "gordian knot" that must be carefully pulled apart in order to discover the essence of the author's position. In explicating a text, all we expect you to do is to be able to explain the author's position in as simple terms as possible.

There are three steps involved in the act of explicating a text:

1. Stating the Author's Thesis. The thesis of a text is that overall point that the author is trying to make in the work. Authors typically will reveal the thesis of their work in their preface, introduction or first chapter. In other words, read the beginning of the work carefully in order to determine its overriding thesis. The first book of Aristotle's *Nicomachean Ethics*, for example, enables the careful reader to summarize the thesis of the work in the following way: "Happiness is the supreme good of human existence. It is achieved through the possession of virtue, although other worldly goods, such as health, wealth and friendship, are also necessary in order to ensure supreme happiness."

2. Outlining the Author's Arguments. Arguments are the building blocks that a philosopher will use to advance his thesis. Remember: every book has a point that it is trying to make. Every author is trying to "sell" you something. The point that the author is trying to make, the thing that he is trying to sell you, is the thesis of the text. Arguments are the tools that author uses to sell you his thesis. Unless an author backs up his thesis with strong arguments, his thesis is nothing more than mere opinion.

We will see later that arguments can either be sound or unsound. Right now it is simply important to be able to identify an author's arguments, and to understand how he uses them to support his thesis.

3. Summing Up the Author's Position (in your own words, of course). A position (literally "that which is put forth") is nothing more than the author's thesis combined with the arguments that he uses to support that thesis. It is extremely important for you to be able to sum up the author's position in your own language in order to demonstrate that you fully understand what he is arguing for or against.

To give you an example of what we mean by a position, a political candidate who is asked to give his position on the death penalty might respond in the following way: "It's my belief that the death penalty is dead wrong (thesis). In the first place, it is far more expensive than life in prison (argument 1), and in the second place it can lead to the State mistakenly taking the life of an innocent person (argument 2)." Of course, a philosophical position will probably be much longer and more complicated than the one used in this example, but it will still always involve some thesis supported by some kind of arguments

Exercise

Read the following text from Machiavelli's The Prince, making sure that you understand what you are reading. When you are finished, answer the following questions about the text:

1. State the thesis of the Machiavelli selection below in one sentence.

2. What are the arguments that Machiavelli gives to support his thesis?

Niccolò Machiavelli
In What Way Princes Must Keep Faith

How laudable it is for a prince to keep good faith and live with integrity, and not with astuteness, everyone knows. Still the experience of our times shows those princes to have done great things who have little regard for good faith, and have been able by astuteness to confuse men's brains, and who have ultimately overcome those who have made loyalty their foundation. You must know, then, that there are two methods of fighting, the one by law, the other by force: the first method is that of men, the second of beasts; but as the first method is often insufficient, one must have recourse to the second. It is therefore necessary for a prince to know well how to use both the beast and the man....

A prince being thus obligated to know well how to act as a beast must imitate the fox and the lion, for the lion cannot protect himself from traps and the fox cannot defend himself from wolves. One must therefore be a fox to recognize traps, and a lion to frighten wolves. Those who wish to be only lions do not understand this. Therefore, a prudent ruler ought not to keep faith when by doing so it would be against his interest, and when the reasons which made him bind himself no longer exist. If all men were good, this precept would not be a good one; but as they are bad, and would not observe their faith with you, so you are not bound to keep faith with them. Nor have legitimate grounds ever failed a prince who wished to show colourable excuses for the non-fulfillment of his promise. Of this one could furnish an infinite number of modern examples, and show how many times peace has been broken, and how many promises rendered worthless, by the faithlessness of princes, and those that have been best able to imitate the fox have succeeded best. But it is necessary to be able to disguise this character well, and to be a great feigner and dissembler; and men are so simple and so ready to obey present necessities, that one who deceives will always find those who allow themselves to be deceived.

Thesis

Reading as Elucidation

The second stage in reading a philosophical work is to elucidate the text. The term elucidation comes from the Latin "elucidare" meaning to shine light upon or to completely illuminate. Simply being able to sum up an author's position is not enough to fully penetrate the vast recesses of his ideas—particularly if he is a seriously profound kind of guy as most philosophers are. We need to get behind the words of the texts to "shed light" upon its deeper (less apparent) meaning.

This quest for the deeper meaning of a text will demand some kind of interpretation, and this interpretation will vary somewhat depending upon the unique perspective of the reader.

Among the tasks you will have to perform in elucidating a text are the following:

1. Identifying Implications. If we are to fully appreciate the significance of an author's position, all of the implications of that position must be fully drawn out from the text. Implications are logical outcomes of an author's position that are implied, suggested or inferred from a text, rather than being openly expressed. No author is capable of drawing out all of the implications of his ideas (he may not even be aware of all of them); it is the reader's job to do this.

When you are contemplating the implications of an author's position, always ask yourself what the consequences would be (to yourself, to human society, to our understanding of the world) if his view is accepted. If, in reading a great work of philosophy, you are unable to uncover any hidden implications in the author's position, the problem probably lies with you and not with the text. Remember: great works always have great implications!

2. Unveiling Relevance. The great philosophical works have stood the test of time and possess a depth that enables them to speak to a wide variety of people from diverse backgrounds. Plato's *Republic*, for example, has provoked readers for over 2,500 years, and continues to be cited by contemporary authors for its relevance to our own times. Such "staying power" is common to most great works, since these works typically offer an insight into the human condition that transcends the cultures in which they were written.

When you are reading a great philosophical work, then, you should always be on the lookout to see how that work may have relevance for your own life. Some of the questions that you should constantly be reflecting upon as you read are: What does this work have to say to me about the meaning of my own existence and my place in the cosmos? What can it tell me about the way to live a good life? Does it offer any positive solutions to some of the social or political problems facing the human race in the 21st century? What insights can it give me about the nature of God and my relationship to him? It is only when these questions are asked of a given text that the real work of deep reading has begun.

Exercise

1. *Read the selection from Karl Marx below.*
2. *What are the implications of Marx's position for the religious believer today?*
3. *Does Marx's view of the origins of religious belief have any relevance for your own life? Why or why not?*

Karl Marx — Stupid Man
Critique of Religious Belief

The basis of irreligious criticism is this: man makes religion; religion does not make man. Religion is indeed man's self-consciousness and self-awareness so long as he has not found himself or has lost himself again. But man is not an abstract being, squatting outside the world. Man is the human world, a state, society. This state, this society, produce religion which is an inverted world consciousness, because they are an inverted world. Religion is the general theory of this world, its encyclopedic compendium, its logic in popular form, its spiritual point d'honneur, its enthusiasm, its moral sanction, its solemn complement, its general basis of consolation and justification. It is the fantastic realization of the human being inasmuch as the human being possesses no true reality. The struggle against religion is, therefore, indirectly a struggle against that world whose spiritual aroma is religion.

Religious suffering is at the same time an expression of real suffering and a protest against real suffering. Religious is the sigh of the oppressed creature, the sentiment of a heartless world, and the soul of soulless conditions. <u>It is the opium of the people.</u>

The abolition of religion as the illusory happiness of men, is a demand for their real happiness. The call to abandon their illusions about their condition is a call to abandon a condition which requires illusions. The criticism of religion is, therefore, the embryonic criticism of this vale of tears of which religion is the halo.

Criticism has plucked the imaginary flowers from the chain, not in order that man shall bear the chain without caprice or consolation but so that he shall cast off the chain and pluck the living flower. The criticism of religion disillusions man so that he will think, act and fashion his reality as a man who has lost his illusions and regained his reason; so that he will revolve about himself as his own true sun. Religion is only the illusory sun about which man revolves so long as he does not revolve about himself.....

Karl Marx, "Critique of Hegel's Philosophy of Right." *Karl Marx: Early Writings*. Trans. T. Bottomore New York: McGraw Hill, 1963.

[Handwritten margin notes: → Metaphor. Human use their emotion to consoled themselves. To dull your sense. No religious belief and focus on yourself.]

Reading as Evaluation

Once you have figured out what the author is saying in the text (explication) and have unveiled the deeper meaning of the text (elucidation), you are then ready for the most important part of reading—entering into a critical dialogue with the author (evaluation). If we never step back from a text that we are reading and ask whether the author's perspective is right or wrong, then we are really not reading in an active way. In this case, we are just taking for granted that what the author says is true, when, in fact, this could be far from the case.

There are two steps that you will have to take as you attempt to evaluate a philosophical text:

1. Assessing the Strength of the Author's Arguments. A philosophical work will be made up of many interdependent arguments that are used by an author to advance his thesis. Some of these arguments will be stronger than others, and it is your job as a reader to assess the strengths and weaknesses of the various arguments that an author presents to you.

We'll be talking at length about what makes for a good argument. For now it suffices to say that a good argument is one in which you are almost obligated to accept the author's conclusion. If a philosopher has done he job properly the conclusions that he or she makes seem to flow by necessity from his or her premises.

2. Judging Whether the Author's Position is Tenable: An author's position is tenable if his thesis is backed up by a number of strong (sound) arguments. In other words, do the author's arguments actually offer a justification for his thesis or do they not? If they do, then you will probably feel compelled to agree with the author's position. If they don't, you are probably going to want to reject it.

Remember most philosophers will offer a number of interrelated arguments to defend their theses. Some of these arguments will be better (more sound) than others. What you need to determine is whether the author provides enough sound arguments in support of his thesis to make his position a tenable one.

Whether you agree or disagree with the author's position, it is essential to explain why you agree or disagree with it. Specify which of his arguments you find persuasive or unpersuasive and why.

Exercise

Read the following selections carefully, making sure that you understand everything that you've read. When you are finished reading, write a 1 page essay, treating the following:

- *Paragraphs 1 and 2: Summarize each author's position in 2-3 sentences and then draw out the implications of each position in 2-3 sentences.*
- *Paragraph 3: Explain which position you find the more tenable and why.*

Peter Singer
The Obligation to Assist

The path from the library at my university to the humanities lecture theatre passes a shallow ornamental pond. Suppose that on my way to give a lecture I notice that a small child has fallen in and is in danger of drowning. Would anyone deny that I ought to wade in and pull the child out? This will mean getting my clothes muddy and either canceling my lecture or delaying it until I can find something dry to change into; but compared with the avoidable death of a child this is insignificant.

A plausible principle that would support the judgment that I ought to pull the child out is this: if it is in my our power to prevent something very bad from happening, without thereby sacrificing anything of comparable moral significance, we ought to so do it. This principle seems uncontroversial....

Nevertheless the uncontroversial appearance of the principle that we ought to prevent what is bad when we can do so without sacrificing anything of comparable moral significance is deceptive. If it were taken seriously and acted upon, our lives and our world would be fundamentally changed. For the principle applies, not just to rare situations in which one can save a child from a pond, but to the everyday situation in which we can assist those living in absolute poverty. In saying this I assume that absolute poverty, with its hunger and malnutrition, lack of shelter, illiteracy, disease, high infant mortality, and low life expectancy, is a bad thing. And I assume that it is within the power of the affluent to reduce absolute poverty, without sacrificing anything of comparable moral significance. If these two assumptions and the principle we have been discussing are correct, we have an obligation to help those in absolute poverty that is no less strong than our obligation to rescue a drowning child from a pond. Not to help would be wrong, whether or not it is intrinsically equivalent to killing. Helping is not, as conventionally thought, a charitable act that is praiseworthy to do, but not wrong to omit; it is something that everyone ought to do....

I have left the notion of moral significance unexamined in order to show that the argument does not depend on any specific values or ethical principles....[The affluence of those of us living in the First World] means that we have income we can dispose of without giving up the basic necessities of life, and we can use this income to reduce absolute poverty. Just how much we think ourselves obligated to give up will depend on what we consider to be of comparable moral significance to the poverty we could prevent: stylish clothes, expensive dinners, a sophisticated stereo system, overseas holidays, a (second?) car, a large house, private schools for our children, and so on.

Peter Singer, *Practical Ethics*. Cambridge University Press, 1993.

Harry Browne
A Plea for Selfishness

It's often said that it would be a better world if everyone were unselfish. But would it be?

If it were somehow possible for everyone to give up his own happiness, what would be the result? Let's carry it to its logical conclusion and see what we find.

To visualize it, let's imagine that happiness is symbolized by a big red rubber ball. I have that ball in my hands—meaning that I hold the ability to be happy. But since I'm not going to be selfish, I quickly pass the ball to you. I've given up my happiness for you.

What will you do? Since you're not selfish either, you won't keep the ball; you'll quickly pass it on to your next-door neighbor. But he doesn't want to be selfish either, so he passes it to his wife, who likewise gives it to her children.

The children have been taught the virtue of unselfishness, so they pass it to playmates, who pass it to parents, who pass it to neighbors, and on and on and on.

I think we can stop the analogy at this point and ask what's been accomplished by all this effort. Who's better off for these demonstrations of pure unselfishness?

How would it be a better world if everyone acted that way? Whom would we be unselfish for? There would have to be a selfish person who would receive, accept, and enjoy the benefits of our unselfishness for there to be any purpose to it. But that selfish person (the object of our generosity) would be living by lower standards than we do.

For a more practical example, what is achieved by the parent who "sacrifices" himself for his children, who in turn are expected to sacrifice themselves for their children, etc.? The unselfish concept is a merry-go-round that has no ultimate purpose. No one's selfintererst is enhanced by the continual relaying of gifts from one person to another.

Perhaps most people have never carried the concept of unselfishness to this logical conclusion. If they did, they might reconsider their pleas for an unselfish world.

Harry Browne, *How I Found Freedom in an Unfree World*. New York: MacMillan, 1973.

3

Logic: The Building Blocks of Philosophy

The best way to understand what an argument is is to contrast it with what it is certainly not—namely an opinion. An opinion is simply a belief or attitude that is held about someone or something. We express our opinions all the time: we love or hate certain films, different types of food, other people. For the most part, however, people's opinions are based almost exclusively upon their feelings about certain matters and rarely if ever do they feel compelled to support their opinions with any kind of evidence.

An argument is something a bit different than this. It is an attempt to formulate reasons in support of one's claims in order to convince others that these claims are true. For example, compare the statements of the following individuals who have entered into an impromptu discussion about the Clinton presidency over a few beers at a local bar:

> Joe: I think Clinton was a lousy President. *- Stated an opinion*
> Pete: How can you say that? A good president is someone who keeps the country on the right track economically, who works with Congress to get important legislation passed, and who keeps the country out of messy wars. Clinton certainly did all that, didn't he?
> Joe: I have the right to my opinion.

What is the basic difference between the statements of Joe and Pete regarding the legacy of the Clinton presidency? As opposed to Joe, who is simply expressing his opinion, Pete is trying to give reasons in support of his views. In other words, he is attempting to argue his position by citing facts which he believes will demonstrate the truth of his claim that Clinton was a good president.

Opinions are worthless: even the most irrational person can formulate an opinion about virtually any matter under the sun. Arguments, on the other hand, are the building blocks of philosophy, and the good philosopher is one who is able to create the best—that is, the most sound and persuasive—arguments possible.

What is an Argument?

To put it simply, an argument consists of one or more premises and a conclusion. In an argument, the group of statements known as premises leads to another group of statements known as conclusions. Conclusions are nothing more than statements designed to be defended; premises are the statements designed to defend the conclusions.

There are two main kinds of arguments: inductive and deductive. The difference between these two lies primarily in the kinds of results that they produce. As we shall see, an inductive argument produces probable results, whereas a deductive argument produces certain results. This doesn't mean, however, that deductive arguments are superior to inductive ones. Both types of arguments can be extremely persuasive to different audience sand for different topics, and, should therefore be used deliberately when making speeches.

Inductive Arguments

An Inductive argument is and argument that (1) moves from particular observations to general conclusions, (2) leads to probable conclusions, not necessary ones, and (3) can be stronger or weaker depending on the degree of probability.

Most inductive arguments are based upon experience or observation, and, for this reason, they are often referred to as empirical arguments. The most common form of inductive argument occurs when we observe a particular phenomenon (e.g., noticing that people who smoke seem to get cancer) and draw general conclusions about all such phenomena from that (that lung cancer can be avoided if one avoids smoking). This is how the inductive form of this argument would appear:

Many people who smoke seem to get lung cancer.
Thus, if you want to avoid getting lung cancer, don't smoke.

Notice how in an inductive argument like this one the conclusion makes a leap beyond what is stated in the premises. We go from observing a connection between smoking and cancer among the people in a select population (family, friends, a medical study group) to making a causal link between smoking and cancer in general.

Inductive arguments, as we have seen, can be strong or weak if the conclusion follows with a high degree of probability from the premise(s). The argument cited above would be an example of strong induction, because the connection between smoking and cancer is fairly well established. But how about the following inductive argument?

All of the philosophy professors that I have had have been uptight and
    rigid.
Therefore, all philosophy professors are uptight and rigid people.

Obviously, this would be an example of a weak inductive argument, because the student speaking probably has not studied with a large enough sample of philosophy professors to draw the conclusion that "all philosophy professors are uptight and rigid people."

This example shows the inherent limitations of inductive arguments. Unless one's observations are fairly exhaustive (i.e., you have done a large scale study of the characters of thousands of philosophers all around the world), the results will be conjecture at best. The more representative the evidence one presents is, the more compelling the conclusion will be.

It should be noted again, however, that at best what we have with any inductive argument is probability. This probability can be higher or lower based upon the evidence presented, but it will never lead to absolute certainty. For this kind of result, we need to look to a different type of argument altogether—the deductive argument.

Exercise 1: Inductive Arguments

A. Indicate whether you think the following inductive arguments are strong or weak based upon the evidence provided:

- *The weather rarely gets cold enough for snow in New York in November. If we hold our conference on November 21ˢᵗ this year, we definitely won't have to worry about being snowed-out.* Week - It frequently snow in November.
- *Ruby, did you hear that old Mr Jones' house down the street was robbed last week when he was away on vacation? I'm worried that Jim had something to do with it. He's been desperate for money and was asking lots of questions about Mr. Jones lately. I happened to know that he also bought a new MP3 player this week, and where else could he have gotten the money?*
- *Polls show that 80% of all registered Republicans oppose gay marriage. Well, Sam has always been a registered Republican. So odds are he opposes gay marriage.* Week or Strong
- *It has been estimated that someone who graduates from college with a bachelor's degree can expect to earn about 66% more over the course of his or her working career than a non-graduate. According to a recent report, over the course of their adult work lives, high school graduates can expect to earn, on average, $1.2 million; those with a bachelor's degree, $2.1 million; and people with a master's degree, $2.5 million. It would seem to be the case, then, that higher education is definitely worth the price.* Strong - facts and figure
- *Santa Claus is a myth; the Easter Bunny and Tooth Fairy are myths. So wouldn't you also conclude based upon this that Jesus is a myth as well?* Week - Jesus is a Actual person

B. Write your own example of a strong inductive argument.

Deductive Arguments

A deductive argument is an argument (1) from the general to the particular, (2) that leads to certain conclusions, and (3) which can be either valid or invalid. Here is an example of a deductive argument.

P1:   All men are mortal.
P2:   Socrates was a man.
C: Therefore, Socrates was mortal.

What makes a deductive argument different from an inductive one is that the conclusion of a deductive argument should follow necessarily from the premises.

The premises in the above argument are "All men are mortal" (P1) and "Socrates was a man" (P2). Typically in a deductive argument premises are affirmed without any defense and are indicated by words such as *since, because,* and *for,* which often precede them. The conclusion in a deductive argument (C in the above example) is often indicated by words such as *therefore, thus, hence, and consequently,* which typically precede conclusions.

When we say that in a deductive argument the conclusion follows by necessity from the premises, what we mean is that if they are designed well, we are compelled to accept the conclusion that is being defended. Take the following example, for instance:

P1:   Abortion is the taking of a human life,
P2:   and the taking of a human life is murder.
 C: Therefore, it must be true that abortion is murder.

If, in fact, it is true that abortion is the taking of a human life, and if, in fact, it is also true that the taking of a human life is murder, then you are actually compelled by the force of the argument to accept the conclusion that abortion is murder. But suppose that you don't really believe that abortion is murder. Are you still obligated to accept the conclusion? The answer in short is yes, if the conclusion follows from the premises and the premises are true.

But this answer also suggests a way to challenge a deductive argument: you either must demonstrate that the conclusion doesn't follow from the premises or that at least one of the premises is false. To explain this a bit further, let's define a few more terms that are commonly used in deductive logic:

- *truth and falsity* describe the properties of statements alone (i.e., do they accord with the facts) (Note: it is possible to have valid arguments with false statements and invalid arguments with true statements).
- a *valid argument* is one in which the conclusions follow from the premises.
- an *invalid argument* is one in which the conclusions do not follow from the premises (Note: arguments can be valid or invalid).
- a *sound argument* is one with true premises and whose arguments are valid. An argument would be unsound, on the other hand, if either one of its premises was false or the argument itself was invalid.

With these terms in mind, let's reexamine that famous deductive argument about Socrates that we looked at just a little while ago:

P1:   All men are mortal.
P2:   Socrates was a man.
 C: Therefore, Socrates was mortal.

Based upon what we discussed above, it seems to be the case that the premises are true—all men are indeed mortal and Socrates was most certainly a man. The conclusion also appears to follow necessarily from the premises: if you accept that all men are mortal and that Socrates was a man, you are forced to also accept that Socrates was mortal. This argument, though hardly profound, is totally sound: the argument is valid and the premises are also true. The "All men are mortal" argument, therefore, achieves the gold standard for any deductive argument—logical soundness.

But very few arguments are so clearly sound as this one is. In the film *Love and Death*, the main character, Boris (played by Woody Allen) is contemplating whether or not to kill Napoleon, who has just invaded Russia. Here is the argument that goes through his mind as he is contemplating his decision:

"If I don't kill him he'll make war all through Europe. But murder….What would Socrates say? All those Greeks were homosexuals. Boy, they must have had some wild parties. I bet they all took a house together in Crete for the summer. A: Socrates is a man. B: All men are mortal. C: All men are Socrates. Means all men are homosexuals. Heh… I'm not a homosexual. Once, some cossacks whistled at me. I, I have the kind of body that excites both persuasions. You know, some men are heterosexual and some men are bisexual and some men don't think about sex at all, you know… they become lawyers."

It doesn't take a degree in philosophy to realize that this is a seriously problematic argument. For one thing all men are certainly not Socrates, and therefore premise C is false. For another the conclusion, "all men are homosexuals" clearly does not follow from the premises. Although this example is a joke—a pretty good one too, if you watch the movie—it shows how easy it is to distort an argument and render it completely unsound.

Let's look at a few more examples of deductive arguments to see how the questions of validity and soundness play themselves out:

The assassin of President Kennedy was either Oswald or some other party
    or parties.　　[P 1]
It wasn't Oswald.　　[P 2]
Therefore, it had to have been some other party or parties. [C]

This argument is clearly an example of a valid argument, since the conclusion follows necessarily from the premises. The only question is whether this argument is also sound. In order for it to be sound the premises also have to be true. One could argue against the truthfulness of premise 1 by maintaining that Oswald could have been involved in a conspiracy that included other parties as well. One could also argue against the truthfulness of premise 2 by maintaining that the assassin was indeed Oswald. The soundness of the argument could thus be thrown into question by challenging the truthfulness of one or more of the premises.

All pigs are cats. [P 1]
Babe is a pig.　[P 2]
Therefore babe is a cat.　[C]

You might be tempted to jump to the conclusion that this is an invalid argument because it looks strange. It is actually a valid argument, since the conclusion follows from the premises. It is not sound, however, because premise 1 is certainly false.

If I bought a ticket on the Queen Elizabeth II, I would be broke.　[P 1]
I am broke.　[P 2]
Therefore I must have bought a ticket on the Queen Elizabeth II. [C]

Let's accept that both premises are true. The argument is invalid because the conclusion does not follow from the premises. The person in question could be broke for reasons other than having bought a ticket on the QE II. The argument therefore is most assuredly unsound.

Evaluating Deductive Arguments

Now that you are armed with the basics of deductive logic, we can go back and see how you might challenge the soundness of an opponent's arguments. Remember, to do this you must attack at least one of the following:

> the argument is not valid (i.e., the conclusion does not follow necessarily from the premises).
>
> *or*
>
> at least one of the premises are not true (regardless of whether the argument is valid or not).

If you can demonstrate the either of these is the case, then your opponent's argument will be deemed unsound.

To illustrate this process, let's go back to the tricky argument about abortion that we had encountered earlier:

P1: Abortion is the taking of a human life,
P2: and the taking of a human life is murder.
C: Therefore, it must be true that abortion is murder.

Most novices to logic immediately cave in the face of this argument and accept that it automatically must be sound. To critique it we first must assess whether the argument presented is valid. Since the conclusion does indeed follow from the premises, the argument is indeed a valid one. If abortion is, in fact, the taking of a human life, and, if the taking of a human life is murder, then by necessity one would have to accept the conclusion that abortion must be murder. You really can't challenge that part of the argument.

But what you can challenge is the truthfulness of either or both of the premises. You might begin by questioning whether abortion, indeed, is actually the taking of a human life. Is an embryo really a human being? When does human life begin? At conception? At natural birth? If the embryo is not a human being, then what is it? Something else entirely (a mere conglomeration of cells)? Simply a potential human life?

Your next step would be to examine the truthfulness of premise 2: Is the taking of a human necessarily murder? Are there other situations, in fact, where a human life could be taken, when we are taking about something quite different from the "unjustifiable, illegal, intentional taking of a human life," which is the common definition of murder? How about the taking of a human life in wartime or as an act of self-defense? Are these examples of murder?

You can probably see where all this is going. There are very few deductive arguments that are impervious to any kind of challenge. Your job when assessing an argument made by an opponent—or anyone for that matter—is to find a way to poke as many holes in the argument as possible. And you do that by challenging either the validity of the argument or the truthfulness of the premises.

Exercise 2: Premises and Conclusions

A. Identify the premises and conclusions in the following arguments:

- All spiders have six legs. All six-legged creatures have wings. It follows, then, that all spiders have wings. *Premises – Premises – Conclusion*
- If Bacon wrote Hamlet, then Bacon was a great writer. Bacon was a great writer. Therefore Bacon wrote Hamlet. *All Premises no argument*
- *Premises →* Government-funded efforts to save the whooping crane from extinction are paying off. Therefore, (government funding of programs to preserve endangered species should be continued.) *Conclusion*
- One should be extremely cautious to judge another human beings, since we are all sinners. *Premises – no Conclusion. All Statements.*
- *Premises →* Almost every known carcinogen causes cancer in animals. (Therefore, it is reasonable to expect that compounds that cause cancer in animals are also potential human carcinogens.— *Conclusion*
- *Premises →* Since happiness consists in peace of mind, and since durable peace of mind depends on the confidence we have in the future, and since that confidence is based on the science we should have of the nature of God and the soul, (it follows that science is necessary for happiness.— *Conclusion*
- *Premises* All rational beings are responsible for their actions, and since all human beings are rational, it follows that (all human beings are responsible for their actions.— *Conclusion*
- Old man Brown claims that he saw a flying saucer land on his farm. But old man Brown never got beyond the fourth grade in school and can hardly read or write. He is completely ignorant of what scientists have written on the subject, so his report cannot possibly be true.— *All Premises*
- *Conclusion →* It is immoral to use rabbits in cosmetic experiments, because causing pain is immoral, and animals such as rabbits are capable of feeling pain — *Premise*
- *Conclusion →* (It seems that mercy cannot be attributed to God.) For mercy is a kind of sorrow. But — *Premises* there is no sorrow in God; (and so there can be no mercy in Him either.) – *Conclusion*

B. Fill in the blank spaces with the appropriate premises or conclusions.

Premise 1:   If President Bush had any integrity he would have resigned from office after failing to find weapons of mass destruction in Iraq.

Premise 2:   President Bush did not resign from office after failing to find weapons of mass destruction in Iraq.

Conclusion:

Premise 1:   If God were a deceiver, we could have no certain knowledge about the world around us.

Premise 2:

Conclusion: Therefore, God is not a deceiver.

Premise 1:   Anyone who kills and steals to earn a living is evil.

Premise 2:

Conclusion: Therefore, Bonnie and Clyde were evil.

Premise 1:   *We should not commit acts which break the law.*
Premise 2:   *Acts of civil disobedience break the law.*
Conclusion:

Premise 1:   *It is always wrong to treat people as a means to my own personal ends.*
Premise 2:   *Engaging in sexual activity with a prostitute is to use him or her as a means to my own ends—e.g., physical pleasure.*
Conclusion:

C. Write your own example of an argument.

Four Common Argument Forms

At times it's possible to intuitively recognize when an argument is valid or invalid. Fortunately, however, logicians have a simpler way to determine when an argument is automatically going to be true, which is a bit of a help for those of us who are not quite so innately logical.

What logicians as far back as ancient times discovered is that there are a few distinct argument forms that will always be valid. The most common of these forms go by the names modus ponens, modus tollens, the hypothetical syllogism, and the disjunctive syllogism. Naturally, we could spend pages just discussing these four basic argument forms, but we can simplify things for the sake of brevity:

Modus Ponens

If P, then Q.	When the Dow Jones shows a decline for two months, we are in a recession.
P.	The Dow Jones has showed a decline for the past three months.
Therefore, Q.	Therefore, we must be in a recession.

Modus Tollens

If P, then Q.	If I owned property in Manhattan today, I would be rich.
- Q.	I'm not rich.
Therefore, –P.	Therefore, I don't own property in Manhattan today.

Hypothetical Syllogism

If P, then Q.	If I get an A on my calculus final, I will get an A in the course.
If Q, then R.	If I get an A in the course, I will have a 3.5 average for the semester.
Therefore, if P then R	Therefore, if I get an A on the final, I will get a 3.5 average for the semester.

Disjunctive Syllogism

P or Q.   Either we should fight the Spartans or retreat until help comes.
- Q.   We cannot afford to retreat.
Therefore, P.   Therefore, we should fight the Spartans.

Remember, if an argument takes any of the above forms, it will automatically be valid. But you also have to be very careful that arguments you are making (or investigating) actually follow these forms rather strictly. For example, there are invalid forms of modus ponens and modus tollens that are always invalid:

Invalid form of Modus Ponens [Affirming the Consequent]

If P, then Q.   If you win the lottery, you will have a lot of money.
Q.   You have a lot of money.
Therefore, P.   Therefore, you won the lottery.

Invalid Form of Modus Tollens [Denying the Antecedent]

If P, then Q.   If you win the lottery, you will have a lot of money.
-P.   You didn't win the lottery.
Therefore, - Q   Therefore, you don't have a lot of money.

Why are these two arguments invalid? Quite simply, because of the invalid argument form, the conclusion must certainly does not follow from the premises. Reexamine these arguements carefully, and you'll see that this is the case. Make sure to be on guard against these invalid argument forms, and try to avoid using them by accident in your own attempts at persuasion. You may not ever be caught making an invalid argument, but if you are, it will most certainly damage the case you are trying to make with the audience.

Naturally, there are many other argument forms, both valid and invalid, but to do justice to them would require an entire course in logic. For now, it's enough to be able to recognize the four most common argument forms and to be able to spot their illegitimate counterfeits.

Exercise 2: Identifying Valid Arguments

A. Identify the underlying basic argument form of the following, and explain whether the argument is valid or invalid.

- *Either he is a damned liar or he is completely nuts. Well, he sure as hell ain't nuts, so he must be a liar.*
- *If you spend a few hours a week taking care of your equipment, it won't get rusty. If it doesn't get rusty, you'll have it for the rest of your life. So, if you take care of your equipment, you'll have it for the rest of your life.*
- *If you like working for the Boy Scouts, then you've gotta like camping out. But you know how much you hate camping out. So the Boy Scouts isn't for you.*
- *Ladies and Gentlemen of the Jury. If a person was sane, he would not go around*

killing dozens of innocent women. Theodore Bundy killed dozens of innocent women. Therefore, he can hardly be considered sane, now can he?

- *If then, it is agreed that things are either the result of coincidence or for an end, and things cannot be the result of coincidence or spontaneity, it follows that they must be for an end (Aristotle).*
- *Either wealth is an evil or a good; but wealth is not an evil; therefore wealth is a good (Sextus Empiricus).*
- *If the North Koreans are smart—and we know damn well how smart they are—they will move in the direction of reform.*
- *If each man has a definite set of rules of conduct by which he regulated his life, he would be no better than a machine. But there are no rules, so men cannot be machines.*
- *If error was something positive, God would be its cause, and by Him it would continually be procreated. But this is absurd (Spinoza).*
- *If pornography has a harmful effect on one's character, then it would certainly be best to avoid it. Many religious leaders and teachers of morality have warned us to avoid pornography. Therefore, it certainly must have a harmful effect on a person's character.*

B. Write you own examples of arguments using the four valid argument forms, modus tollens, modus ponens, hypothetical syllogism, and disjunctive syllogism.

Logical Fallacies

A fallacy is a type of argument that is psychologically persuasive but completely invalid. Very often fallacies, especially when used in the heat of debate can seem to be valid, but they are actually flawed arguments.

It is precisely because these sorts of arguments can be rhetorically persuasive that they are often used in speeches. At times the use of fallacies can actually help to demolish an opponents position or to bolster your own flimsy one—at least if the audience is not paying much attention. The problem with using fallacies like the one we will examine, is that if you get caught, your credibility will be demolished in the eyes of your audience: they'll either think that you are ignorant or duplicitous, and being accused of either of these will certainly not help you make your case.

On the positive side, an understanding of what common logical fallacies are can help you to tear down an opponent's argument. Most audiences, even those who lack a formal knowledge of logic, will be impressed if you can challenge an opponent's argument by stating that he is guilty of committing some kind of logical fallacy that you can identify with a fancy name. Your credibility at such times soars, and your opponent's plummets.

Among the commonly used types of logical fallacies are the following:

Appeal to Force occurs when one uses or threatens to use force—whether physical, psychological or legal—in an attempt to coerce another person to accept their conclusion.

> "Oh Senators, I would strongly advise you to make Claudius our next emperor. The Praetorian guard has already rallied around him, and I fear for this august body if you thwart their desires."
> "If you don't convict this murderer, one of you may be his next victim."

Ad Hominum Attack ("against the man"): An attempt to refute another's position by attacking the character, circumstance, or actions of the person making a claim rather than the argument itself.

> "I don't think we should accept the councilman's arguments in favor of Sunday shopping in our town. He's a godless communist after all."
> "You shouldn't listen to Billy-Bob's argument because he spent a year in prison."

The reason why ad hominum attacks are always fallacious is because the character, circumstances, or actions of the person being attacked have absolutely nothing to do with the validity of his arguments.

Argumentum ad Populum ("Argument to the People"): this sort of fallacy occurs when one attempts to appeal to popular sentiment by arguing that everybody is doing something and therefore it must be right. This fallacy also includes appeals to patriotism or religion. Of course, the fact that everyone is doing something or believes something to be true has absolutely no bearing on the validity of the argument being proposed:

> 85% of consumers choose PCs rather than Macs. Therefore, the PC must be a better computer.
> Real Americans eat red meat. Therefore, if you are a vegetarian, there must be something seriously wrong with you.

Argument from Ignorance: An attempt to argue that a proposition is true because it hasn't be proven false or that a certain proposition is false because it hasn't been proven true.

> "God is clearly the creator of the moral order. Try as hard as they may, ethicists have been unable to come up with any other explanation of the source of universal moral principles or why moral principles are binding on us."
> "The superb quality of her character can be demonstrated by the fact that I have never heard a word spoken against her."

Appeal to (Inappropriate) Authority involves using the testimony of someone who is an expert or authority in a field other than the one under discussion, from a source that may not be reliable, or from a biased authority.

> "My priest says that genetic engineering and in vitro fertilization are dangerous. Therefore, all experiments in this field should be stopped immediately."
> "All this talk about global warming is a lot of hooey. Why, I just heard Rush Limbaugh say today that we have absolutely nothing to worry about."

Hasty Generalization occurs when one uses unusual or atypical cases to support a general point covering all cases.

> "I know for a fact that drinking alcohol is evil. My father was an alcoholic and his drinking damned near ruined our family."
> "I have a friend who lives near Brookhaven National Laboratories who has just been

diagnosed with breast cancer. I think that we can safely conclude, then, that the research being done at Brookhaven is responsible for the high rate of breast cancer on Long Island."

Begging the Question occurs when a person assumes what the argument is trying to prove. [i.e., when the conclusion and premises are rewordings of each other]

> "To allow complete, unfettered freedom of speech is advantageous to the interests of the state. For it is clearly helpful to the community to have each individual freely express his or her own point of view."
>
> "You can't expect eighteen-year-olds to vote intelligently, because they are too young to have good judgment about the issues."

Straw Man: An attempt to substitute for your opponent's argument a simplistic caricature. By defeating the caricature (the straw man), the fallacious impression is created that you have defeated your opponent's position.

> "Of course the Equal Rights Amendment must be defeated. Do you want men and women sharing the same toilet facilities?"

Exercise 3: Logical Fallacies

Identify the logical fallacies in the following passages:

- *Women are so sentimental! My mother and sister always cry at the movies. My father and I never do.*
- *No breath of scandal has ever touched the senator. Therefore he must be incorruptibly honest.*
- *How can you take Sartre's philosophical views seriously? The man, after all, led an abysmal life and was certainly no paragon of morality.*
- *After all, my views on gun control have been endorsed by some of Hollywood's most notable actors—Sylvester Stallone, Barbra Streisand, and Alec Baldwin, among others. How could you not agree with me?*
- *Gentlemen, we cannot let Honduras be ruled by a communist government. If we do then sooner or later Mexico will become communist along with the islands in the Caribbean and no doubt Canada.*
- *The governor supports tax increases for middle-income earners. This doesn't surprise me. He has always been against unions and this is just another measure designed to undermine them. If we allow for these tax increases and the undermining of unions, democracy in this country will be threatened.*
- *It is necessary to confine criminals and to lock up dangerous lunatics. Therefore, there is nothing intrinsically wrong with depriving people of their liberties.*
- *If you hold that nothing is self-evident, I will not argue with you, for it is clear that you are a quibbler and not to be convinced.*
- *God exists because the Bible tells us so, and we know what the Bible tells us is true because it is the revealed word of God.*
- *Narcotics are habit forming. Therefore, if you allow your physician to ease your pain with an opiate you will become a hopeless drug addict.*

- *You can't park here. I don't care what the sign says. If you don't drive on, I'll give you a ticket.*
- *I also admit that there are people for whom the reality of the external world constitutes a grave problem. My answer is that I do not address them, but that I presuppose a minimum of reason in my readers.*
- *She says that she loves me and she must be telling the truth, because she certainly wouldn't lie to someone that she loves.*
- *It is totally idiotic to try to prevent teens from having sexual relations. Everybody's "doing it" anyway, so what can possibly be wrong with sex before marriage?*
- *There is no proof that the secretary "leaked" the news to the papers, so it couldn't have been the secretary who did it.*
- *Gentlemen, I am sure that if you think it over you will see that my suggestion has real merit. It is only a suggestion of course, and not an order. As I mentioned at our last conference, I am planning to reorganize the whole business. I still hope, however, that it will not be necessary to curtail the operations of your department.*
- *The Rolls-Royce is a foreign made automobile and gets very few miles per gallon. Therefore all foreign made automobiles get very few miles per gallon.*
- *Two students were having a disagreement about cars. Student A said, "I can prove to you that Toyota Carolla's are faster than Honda Civic's. John owns a Carolla and he told me he beats every Civic he has ever raced." Student B asked, "How do you know John is telling the truth?" Student A replied by saying, "Someone who drives the fastest car wouldn't have to lie."*

4

THE HUMAN CONDITION:
WHY ARE WE HERE?

What does it mean to be a human being? Is there any real (i.e., higher) purpose to a human life? And, if so, what might this purpose be?

These are among the most fundamental and profound questions that anyone can ask. They are also the questions that ultimately drive the discipline of philosophy, since philosophical speculation usually begins with an attitude of wonder concerning our human condition. Primitive man, struggling each day for basic survival, probably didn't have much time to ponder these sorts of questions. It was difficult enough for him just to ensure that there was enough food to eat and adequate clothing and shelter to keep warm. Abstract reflection on the human condition would have been a luxury that our early ancestors simply couldn't afford.

Once human civilization began to develop—in ancient Mesopotamia and Egypt around 3,500 B.C.—increases in leisure time generated by the division of labor enabled the big questions to be asked in a much more systematic way than would have been possible. It was in response to questions like "who am I?", "why am I here?" and "where am I ultimately going?" that the early religions of man sprung up. In India, Egypt, and the Middle East, humans created myths, rituals, and complex systems of belief to explain how the universe came into being and to provide some kind of consolation in a world that, despite the increases in material comfort, was still filled with terrible violence and insecurity.

In classical Greece, however, something rather unique happened during the 5th century B.C. The Greeks struggled over the same perplexing questions as their counterparts in the ancient world, but the approach that they took to answering these questions was dramatically different from that of the Sumerians, Egyptians and Jews. The Greeks began to rely less on appeals to ancient myths and authority figures and more on the use of reason, logic, and argumentation to solve some of the questions they had concerning the nature of the cosmos and man's place within it. With philosophers like Socrates, Plato, and Aristotle, then, we have the first serious philosophical attempt to answer the question, "Who am I?" The world would never be the same after that.

Reflection on the Human Condition

Philosophical reflection on the human condition, if it is to be anything other than fanciful, must begin by examining the way things actually are. If we look objectively at a human life, there are certain basic facts about existence that seem to apply to everyone. As a starting point for our discussion on the human condition, therefore, we might begin by reflecting on what these "basic facts" of life are and how we might respond to them. Let's call this "your story" to make this exercise really personal, although, in point of fact, it really should be called "everyone's story":

(Your Name)'s Story

1. You were born into this life with no control over where you were born, to whom you were born, or in what social and economic conditions you were born. You couldn't decide to stay in the womb rather than being thrust out into the world naked and screaming, and once you were born, you pretty much were handed a dealt deck in terms of your genetic make-up and your environment. If you were very lucky, you weren't born in a war zone or to abusive parents or with a life-threatening disability or mentally incapacitated.
2. For approximately 18-25 years of your life, you grew physically and developed, to a greater or lesser degree, the intellectual, psychological, and social skills needed to navigate your way through life and find your place within human society.
3. For much of the rest of your life, you put the skills you learned to use working in some kind of job—in all likelihood, one that you didn't enjoy very much or that didn't pay you the kind of salary that you thought you deserved. The money that you earned from working, however, enabled you eventually to leave your parent's home and pay for those items necessary for survival (food, clothing, housing) and those that contribute to human felicity (cars, Iphones, designer handbags, etc.).
4. Like all animals, you have a built-in desire to procreate and to spread your gene pool as widely as possible to ensure the survival of the species. If conditions were right, you may have found a suitable partner with whom to produce offspring. You would then spend the most productive years of your mid-life providing for those offspring, attempting to ensure their survival into adulthood, and training them—with greater or lesser success—to become autonomous individuals in their own right.
5. If you were lucky, you didn't die accidentally, perish from a disease, or get killed, and made it into old age. At that point your body began to break down, you got sick, you suffered physically (and perhaps emotionally as well) and eventually died. Within moments after your death, your body began to decompose, and within a few years, almost nothing was left of you at all.
6. Within one or two generations of your death, you were forgotten by every other human being on the planet (unless you were one of the ridiculously small percentage of human beings who were skillful or lucky enough to make an impact on human history, in which case, you might be remembered a bit longer). Your grandchildren will probably only have fleeting memories of you and their children will only know who you were through dusty, old photographs that have been left behind (if they haven't already been tossed away by a careless descendant, that is).
7. Within a relatively short amount of time—planetarily speaking—humanity itself will be destroyed through some kind of global cataclysm or pandemic and nothing will remain of our species. At some point in time a new species may evolve from the bugs that have managed to survive, but this species will probably have little or nothing in common with our own. Eventually, the planet, and even the universe itself, will sim-

ply cease to exist, and all that will remain will be the infinite void.

These are the basic facts about the human condition. These are not the facts about the existence of some people; they would seem to be facts that apply to everyone equally, no matter how privileged or fortunate a person's life may appear on the surface. The question that philosophers have raised throughout the centuries in response to these basic facts is how are we to make rational sense of them. In other words, how do we interpret these facts and fit them into some kind of coherent narrative that can help us live our lives in a more meaningful way?

Indeed, there are several different ways that people throughout history have chosen to respond to the brute facts about human existence—and in particular the objective truth that we will eventually die and be completely forgotten and that eventually everything that exists now as we know it will also disappear into cosmic oblivion. As we'll see, some of these approaches are more profound than others, but most people tend to fit into one or more types, depending upon how they relate to the reality of their human condition:

Option 1: The Hedonist

The most common approach to dealing with the stark facts of reality goes by the name of "hedonism." The hedonist's ultimate meaning in life is derived almost exclusively from the pleasure that he experiences. Food, drink, sex, and the acquisition of material possessions and creature comforts are the ultimate goal of his life. Even his most intimate relationships with family, friends, and sexual partners are to be weighed based upon how much pleasure the hedonist derives from these relationships.

Hedonists can be extremely bright, refined people: you'll often find them in extremely high positions in government and business. The problem is that the hedonist often goes through his life completely unreflectively. Living for the moment, he rarely thinks about unpleasant subjects like the inevitability of personal annihilation. Distressing topics like this would mar the pleasure he experiences in life and therefore he does all he can to avoid them at all costs.

In a certain respect, the hedonist, therefore, seems to have an advantage here over his more introspective counterpart. He can block out all unpleasant thoughts as he swills his beer and focuses on life's immediate pleasure (what the ancient Romans would call "bread and circuses"). But even the most unreflective person eventually will be confronted by the stark fact of his own finitude in the form of the physical pain, suffering, and death that is inevitable in life. In some ways, his completely unconscious mode of existing will leave the hedonist totally unprepared to face the end of his existence and, as a result, he will likely experience far more fear and depression than a more introspective person might.

Option 2: The Existentialist

On the opposite end of the spectrum from the hedonist is the existential-type of person, who thinks about the brute facts of life all the time and whose whole existence is filled with anxiety and despair. If you've ever watched a Woody Allen film, you know exactly what this type of person is like. He tends to be fairly intellectual, given to obsessing over the minutest aspects of the human condition and finding human existence lacking. Unlike the hedonist, the existentialist can't ever enjoy even the most innocent of human pleasures, because he knows that they are fleeting at best. Likewise, he often keeps others at arm's length and avoids truly intimate relationships, because he knows that they will all end in death.

For the existentialist, human existence is characterized by absurdity—the idea that there is no ultimate meaning or purpose to the world or to our lives. Really horrible and tragic things happen to really good people (shit happens) and basically there is not much we can do about it. The act of having to live in a world without any real meaning fills the heart of the existentialist with anxiety, despair, and dread (otherwise referred to as existential angst). All this leads Albert Camus, a notable 20th century existentialist, to claim that there really is only one true philosophical problem—that of suicide. Keep living, in other words, in the face of the absurdity and pointlessness of life, or end your life totally and be done with it. Those are really the only two viable options an existentialist has.

What the unreflective person and the existentialist have in common is recognition of the fundamental banality of the human condition. We're born, we live, we suffer, we die, and ultimately we are forgotten. The unreflective individual tries to run from this truth by drowning himself in distracting pleasures (To quote a famous Peggy Lee song from the 1960s: "Is that all there is, my friends? Break out the booze and have a ball, if that's all there is."). The existentialist doesn't take this easy way out, but his life is no less bleak. In the end all he has is his despair and the troubling thoughts of whether human life is at all worth it in the end.

Option 3: The Superman

Another type typical in philosophical literature is what has come to be known as the "superman" (*Übermensch* in German). The hedonist blocks out all unpleasant thoughts about the human condition; the existentialist is more self-reflective, but despairs over the brute facts of life. In contrast to these two, the superman is self-reflective enough to recognize life is unpleasant, harsh, and filled with suffering and death, but, unlike the existentialist, he doesn't use this as an excuse to wallow in anxiety and despair. For the superman, both the hedonists and the existentialist are living inauthentic existences, because they refuse to take ultimate responsibility for their lives.

Like the existentialist, the superman also recognizes that human life has no intrinsic meaning. But while the existentialist is forced simply to accept this fact, the superman feels compelled to create his own meaning in life. There is no God, so he becomes the creator of his own identity and the ultimate master of his own destiny. Because he rejects the idea of a transcendent law-giver, he is also forced to create his own values in life, which often stand in marked contrast the values of the "herd" (i.e., those human beings who compliantly accept whatever values and beliefs are transmitted to them by religious authorities).

Like the existentialist, the superman stands alone, but his isolation is completely self-imposed. He cannot be one of the herd, because his superior self-awareness necessarily leads him to be contemptuous of those who live unreflective lives. His "master morality" also marks him as other in the eyes of those who are content to practice the "slave morality" preached by organized religion.

Option 4: The Mystic

A final option for dealing with the unpleasant facts of the human condition is to do what the practitioners of most of the world's great religions have done for centuries—simply change the narrative so that what initially appears to be tragic actually becomes the greatest of all triumphs.

All of the world's great religions have their mystic types. These are men and women who, either through heroic self-effort, or God's grace, or through some combination of the two, have a glimpse of an eternal bliss that the rest of us could barely even imagine. This mystical glimpse is called the beatific vision. Although it is fleeting, it offers the mystic a taste of what eternal life with God would be like and provides the consolation that the mystic needs to endure this "veil of tears" we call human existence.

The narrative of the human condition for the mystic thus becomes changed in several crucial ways. In contrast to the "brute facts" of life that I outlined above, the mystic is convinced, as a result of his vision of the divine, that things simply aren't as they appear to be. Here, then, would be the mystic's spin on your life story:

(Your Name)'s Story

1. The universe and everything in it was created by an all-perfect, all-knowing, and all-loving Supreme Being (SB). From before time began, this Being knew that you would come into existence and had a very special plan just for you. You are precious to Him, because you are, in fact, one with Him, and his love for you is constant and all-enduring.

2. Your life has ultimate meaning because it is part of the SB's ultimate plan for mankind. This plan, furthermore, has been revealed through the SB's word as it exists in the sacred texts of your particular faith tradition. All you have to do is follow the blueprint for your life as it has been revealed through this sacred text and interpreted by the SB's anointed ministers and teachers and you will experience happiness in this life and salvation in the next.

3. During your life, you may experience suffering and pain, but these are merely tests to see if you are worthy enough to receive eternal life. Assuming you endure your suffering with equanimity, follow SB's blueprint for your life, and remain faithful, you can be assured that, despite any adversities you experience, you will receive an eternal reward in the next life. The heavenly bliss that you will experience in the next life, in fact, will make even the most exquisite pleasures of this life pale by comparison.

4. Of course, you have also been created with the gift of free will and can use the freedom you have to transgress the SB's law, reject his love, or engage in despair about your condition. If you do this, you will experience misery in this life and unspeakable torment in the next (i.e., eternal separation from the SB, the source of all love and goodness).

5. The world will come to an end, but the faithful who are part of the SB's chosen people (i.e., the elect) will continue to enjoy supreme bliss with the SB in heaven for all eternity.

Naturally, there are some variations on this narrative depending upon which of the world's great religious traditions you are examining. Some branches of Judaism, for example, reject the idea of an afterlife altogether, and Christian denominations have argued for centuries over the question of whether faith, works, or grace is the key to salvation. The narrative would also be somewhat different in Hinduism (with its numerous gods and emphasis on karma and reincarnation) and probably doesn't apply at all to Buddhism, which some have called a philosophy of life, rather than a religion *per se*. In general, however, all of the great theistic religious traditions of the world would ascribe to something like the above narrative.

The mystic, who represents the culmination of the spiritual life of a given faith tradition, is one who has been blessed with the vision of God that allows him to have a keen sense of certainty that the narrative outlined above is true, despite the lack of evidence to support the most important features of this narrative (the existence of a Supreme Being and the reality of life after death). This enables him to act like a traveler to a distant marvelous land (heaven), who passes through different countries offering a variety of seductions and pleasures (earthly life), but never regards any of them as his true home. This life and everything in it for the mystic is to be used in the service of God and for the sake of attaining eternal life with him after death. Everything else for him pales in comparison to the ultimate goal.

Assessing the Four Types

The four philosophical types described above, of course, are generalized ways of looking at our human condition. There are undoubtedly other possible philosophical types, but most people can probably fit themselves quite comfortably into one of these four types. Whether one type is any better or worse than any other is undoubtedly the subject of a lifetime's worth of philosophical reflection and debate.

Which type you yourself embody is something that only you can determine. If you're still unclear about which type you fit into, you might try answering the following question.

If I knew that I was going to die in a year, I would...

(a) *enjoy myself completely for the time I had left.*
(b) *get seriously depressed and probably lose all hope.*
(c) *take it upon myself to try to beat the odds and live as long as possible.*
(d) *begin praying to God and ask for his help enduring this crisis.*

Death is the termination and culmination of our human project. The way one thinks about death, therefore, is often indicative of the attitudes and beliefs one has about life and the human condition. If you answered "a" to this question, odds are you are probably a hedonist at heart, if you answered "b," an existentialist, "c," a superman, and "d," a mystic-type.

Depending upon what philosophical type you are, there are radically different implications and challenges for the way you live your life. The hedonist, for example, is dependent upon objects of pleasure to keep him happy and motivated. When these objects of pleasure become difficult to enjoy—because of reversal of fortune, sickness, and old age—so too ends any motivation that the hedonist has for life. The existentialist has to either learn to endure a life devoid of meaning or have the courage to end his own life (neither a very palatable option for most people). On the surface, the superman would seem to be in a far better position than these other two, but he is forced to live as the ultimate outcast. In scorning the common morality of those around him, he must become an island unto himself—a state that requires a degree of self-autonomy that very few people possess. Finally, by focusing on the blessings of the next life, the mystic, for all practical purposes, is forced to scorn all of the pleasures that this life provides. The adoption of this life-denying sensibility leads him to treat all objects of earthly love as means, rather than as proper ends in themselves.

As I've pointed out, no particular philosophical type is better or worse necessarily than any other. But it probably is helpful to know your type and to understand the implications that particular way of looking at the human condition has for your life. As the Siddartha Gautama (otherwise known as the Buddha) understood, we have to take our human lives seriously and this requires constant introspection and a high degree of self-awareness. As you think about the meaning of your own life, try to keep the insight of the Buddha in your mind as much as possible:

"Let me respectfully remind you,
Life and death are of supreme importance.
Time swiftly passes by and opportunity is lost.
Each of us should strive to awaken.
Awaken! Take heed!
This night your days are diminished by one.
Do not squander your lives...."

Letter to Menoeceus

Epicurus (341-270 BCE)

Founder of the philosophical school of late antiquity that bears his name, Epicurus wrote numerous works, but none of them survive in their original form. It is believed that his works were destroyed by Christian authorities, who found his ideas incompatible with their own more ascetic world view. The principle source of his doctrines is found in Diogenes Laertius' Lives of the Eminent Philosophers, which was written in the third century A.D. Among the works of Epicurus that was preserved is the "Letter to Menoeceus," a summary of his teachings on ethics that was believed to have been written by Epicurus for the benefit of his students. Epicurus is definitely in the hedonistic school of ethics, since he clearly believed that pleasure is the highest good in life. What separates him from less sophisticated hedonists is his belief that the pursuit of pleasure must be guided by reason and that pleasures of the body (food, drink, sex) are less important than higher pleasures such as those derived from friendship, freedom, and philosophical contemplation.

Epicurus to Menoeceus, greetings:

Let no one be slow to seek wisdom when he is young nor weary in the search of it when he has grown old. For no age is too early or too late for the health of the soul. And to say that the season for studying philosophy has not yet come, or that it is past and gone, is like saying that the season for happiness is not yet or that it is now no more. Therefore, both old and young alike ought to seek wisdom, the former in order that, as age comes over him, he may be young in good things because of the grace of what has been, and the latter in order that, while he is young, he may at the same time be old, because he has no fear of the things which are to come. So we must exercise ourselves in the things which bring happiness, since, if that be present, we have everything, and, if that be absent, all our actions are directed towards attaining it.

1. The Gods

Those things which without ceasing I have declared unto you, do them, and exercise yourself in them, holding them to be the elements of right life. First believe that God is a living being immortal and blessed, according to the notion of a god indicated by the common sense of mankind; and so believing, you shall not affirm of him anything that is foreign to his immortality or that is repugnant to his blessedness. Believe about him whatever may uphold both his blessedness and his immortality. For there are gods, and the knowledge of them is manifest; but they are not such as the multitude believe, seeing that men do not steadfastly maintain the notions they form respecting them. Not the man who denies the gods worshipped by the multitude, but he who affirms of the gods what the multitude believes about them is truly impious. For the utterances of the multitude about the gods are not true preconceptions but false assumptions; hence it is that the greatest evils happen to the wicked and the greatest blessings happen to the good from the hand of the gods, seeing that they are always favorable to their own good qualities and take pleasure in men like themselves, but reject as alien whatever is not of their kind.

2. Death

Accustom yourself to believing that death is nothing to us, for good and evil imply the capacity for sensation, and death is the privation of all sentience;

therefore a correct understanding that death is nothing to us makes the mortality of life enjoyable, not by adding to life a limitless time, but by taking away the yearning after immortality. For life has no terrors for him who has thoroughly understood that there are no terrors for him in ceasing to live. Foolish, therefore, is the man who says that he fears death, not because it will pain when it comes, but because it pains in the prospect. Whatever causes no annoyance when it is present, causes only a groundless pain in the expectation. Death, therefore, the most awful of evils, is nothing to us, seeing that, when we are, death is not come, and, when death is come, we are not. It is nothing, then, either to the living or to the dead, for with the living it is not and the dead exist no longer.

But in the world, at one time men shun death as the greatest of all evils, and at another time choose it as a respite from the evils in life. The wise man does not deprecate life nor does he fear the cessation of life. The thought of life is no offense to him, nor is the cessation of life regarded as an evil. And even as men choose of food not merely and simply the larger portion, but the more pleasant, so the wise seek to enjoy the time which is most pleasant and not merely that which is longest. And he who admonishes the young to live well and the old to make a good end speaks foolishly, not merely because of the desirability of life, but because the same exercise at once teaches to live well and to die well. Much worse is he who says that it were good not to be born, but when once one is born to pass quickly through the gates of Hades. For if he truly believes this, why does he not depart from life? It would be easy for him to do so once he were firmly convinced. If he speaks only in jest, his words are foolishness as those who hear him do not believe.

We must remember that the future is neither wholly ours nor wholly not ours, so that neither must we count upon it as quite certain to come nor despair of it as quite certain not to come.

3. The Ultimate Goal of Life

We must also reflect that of desires some are natural, others are groundless; and that of the natural some are necessary as well as natural, and some natural

only. And of the necessary desires some are necessary if we are to be happy, some if the body is to be rid of uneasiness, some if we are even to live. He who has a clear and certain understanding of these things will direct every preference and aversion toward securing health of body and tranquillity of mind, seeing that this is the sum and end of a blessed life. For the end of all our actions is to be free from pain and fear, and, when once we have attained all this, the tempest of the soul is laid; seeing that the living creature has no need to go in search of something that is lacking, nor to look for anything else by which the good of the soul and of the body will be fulfilled. When we are pained because of the absence of pleasure, then, and then only, do we feel the need of pleasure. Wherefore we call pleasure the alpha and omega of a blessed life. Pleasure is our first and kindred good. It is the starting-point of every choice and of every aversion, and to it we come back, inasmuch as we make feeling the rule by which to judge of every good thing.

4. Guidlines Concering the Pursuit of Pleasure

And since pleasure is our first and native good, for that reason we do not choose every pleasure whatsoever, but will often pass over many pleasures when a greater annoyance ensues from them. And often we consider pains superior to pleasures when submission to the pains for a long time brings us as a consequence a greater pleasure. While therefore all pleasure because it is naturally akin to us is good, not all pleasure is should be chosen, just as all pain is an evil and yet not all pain is to be shunned. It is, however, by measuring one against another, and by looking at the conveniences and inconveniences, that all these matters must be judged. Sometimes we treat the good as an evil, and the evil, on the contrary, as a good.

Again, we regard independence of outward things as a great good, not so as in all cases to use little, but so as to be contented with little if we have not much, being honestly persuaded that they have the sweetest enjoyment of luxury who stand least in need of it, and that whatever is natural is easily procured and only the vain and worthless hard to win.

Plain fare gives as much pleasure as a costly diet, when once the pain of want has been removed, while bread and water confer the highest possible pleasure when they are brought to hungry lips. To habituate one's self, therefore, to simple and inexpensive diet supplies all that is needful for health, and enables a man to meet the necessary requirements of life without shrinking, and it places us in a better condition when we approach at intervals a costly fare and renders us fearless of fortune.

When we say, then, that pleasure is the end and aim, we do not mean the pleasures of the prodigal or the pleasures of sensuality, as we are understood to do by some through ignorance, prejudice, or willful misrepresentation. By pleasure we mean the absence of pain in the body and of trouble in the soul. It is not an unbroken succession of drinking-bouts and of revelry, not sexual lust, not the enjoyment of the fish and other delicacies of a luxurious table, which produce a pleasant life; it is sober reasoning, searching out the grounds of every choice and avoidance, and banishing those beliefs through which the greatest tumults take possession of the soul. Of all this the beginning and the greatest good is wisdom. Therefore wisdom is a more precious thing even than philosophy ; from it spring all the other virtues, for it teaches that we cannot live pleasantly without living wisely, honorably, and justly; nor live wisely, honorably, and justly without living pleasantly. For the virtues have grown into one with a pleasant life, and a pleasant life is inseparable from them.

Who, then, is superior in your judgment to such a man? He holds a holy belief concerning the gods, and is altogether free from the fear of death. He has diligently considered the end fixed by nature, and understands how easily the limit of good things can be reached and attained, and how either the duration or the intensity of evils is but slight. Fate, which some introduce as sovereign over all things, he scorns, affirming rather that some things happen of necessity, others by chance, others through our own agency. For he sees that necessity destroys responsibility and that chance is inconstant; whereas our own actions are autonomous, and it is to them that praise and blame naturally attach. It were better, indeed, to accept the legends of the gods than to bow beneath that yoke of destiny which the natural philosophers have imposed. The one holds out some faint hope that we may escape if we honor the gods, while the necessity of the naturalists is deaf to all entreaties. Nor does he hold chance to be a god, as the world in general does, for in the acts of a god there is no disorder; nor to be a cause, though an uncertain one, for he believes that no good or evil is dispensed by chance to men so as to make life blessed, though it supplies the starting-point of great good and great evil. He believes that the misfortune of the wise is better than the prosperity of the fool. It is better, in short, that what is well judged in action should not owe its successful issue to the aid of chance.

Exercise yourself in these and related precepts day and night, both by yourself and with one who is like-minded; then never, either in waking or in dream, will you be disturbed, but will live as a god among men. For man loses all semblance of mortality by living in the midst of immortal blessings.

Diogenes Laertius. *Lives of the Eminent Philosophers*. Trans. R.D. Hicks. Cambridge University Press, 1926.

NOTES FROM THE UNDERGROUND

FYODOR DOSTOYEVSKY (1821-1881)

Fedyor Dostoyevski is often considered one of the greatest existential authors of all time. In works such as The Brothers Karamazov *and* Crime and Punishment *he offers a keen insight into the soul of characters suffering from alienation, despair, and anxiety. Published in 1864,* Notes From the Underground *is a portrait of human alienation. The work takes the form of a confession in which the "underground man, a retired civil servant living in St. Petersburg, produces a stream-of-consciousness narrative that reveals his deep despair about his own existential condition. In the end, the underground man is impotent to do anything more than lament his fate—the curse of both his "unhappy consciousness" and his inability to take any action that would alleviate his suffering.*

PART ONE

1

I am a sick man....I am a spiteful man. I am an unattractive man. I believe my liver is diseased. However, I know nothing at all about my disease, and do not know for certain what ails me. I don't consult a doctor for it, and never have, though I have a respect for medicine and doctors. Besides, I am extremely superstitious, sufficiently so to respect medicine, anyway (I am well-educated enough not to be superstitious, but I am superstitious). No, I refuse to consult a doctor from spite. That you probably will not understand. Well, I understand it, though. Of course, I can't explain who it is precisely that I am mortifying in this case by my spite: I am perfectly well aware that I cannot "pay out" the doctors by not consulting them; I know better than anyone that by all this I am only injuring myself and no one else. But still, if I don't consult a doctor it is from spite. My liver is bad, well—let it get worse!

I have been going on like that for a long time —twenty years. Now I am forty. I used to be in the government service, but am no longer. I was a spiteful official. I was rude and took pleasure in being so. I did not take bribes, you see, so I was bound to find a recompense in that, at least. (A poor jest, but I will not scratch it out. I wrote it thinking it would sound very witty; but now that I have seen myself that I only wanted to show off in a despicable way, I will not scratch it out on purpose!)

When petitioners used to come for information to the table at which I sat, I used to grind my teeth at them, and felt intense enjoyment when I succeeded in making anybody unhappy. I almost did succeed. For the most part they were all timid people—of course, they were petitioners. But of the uppish ones there was one officer in particular I could not endure. He simply would not be humble, and clanked his sword in a disgusting way. I carried on a feud with him for eighteen months over that sword. At last I got the better of him. He left off clanking it. That happened in my youth, though.

But do you know, gentlemen, what was the chief point about my spite? Why, the whole point, the real sting of it lay in the fact that continually, even in the moment of the acutest spleen, I was inwardly conscious with shame that I was not only not a spiteful but not even an embittered man, that I was simply scaring sparrows at random and amusing myself by it. I might foam at the mouth, but bring me a doll to play with, give me a cup of tea with sugar in it, and maybe I should be appeased. I might even be genuinely touched, though probably I should grind my teeth at myself afterwards and lie awake at night with shame for months after. That was my way.

I was lying when I said just now that I was a spiteful official. I was lying from spite. I was simply amusing myself with the petitioners and with the officer, and in reality I never could become spiteful. I was conscious every moment in myself of many, very many elements absolutely opposite to that. I felt them positively swarming in me, these opposite elements. I knew that they had been swarming in me all my life and craving some outlet from me, but I would not let them, would not let them, purposely would not let them come out. They tormented me till I was ashamed: they drove me to convulsions and--sickened me, at last, how they sickened me! Now, are not you fancying, gentlemen, that I am expressing remorse for something now, that I am asking your forgiveness for something? I am sure you are fancying that...However, I assure you I do not care if you are....

It was not only that I could not become spiteful, I did not know how to become anything; neither spiteful nor kind, neither a rascal nor an honest man, neither a hero nor an insect. Now, I am living out my life in my corner, taunting myself with the spiteful and useless consolation that an intelligent man cannot become anything seriously, and it is only the fool who becomes anything. Yes, a man in the nineteenth century must and morally ought to be pre-eminently a characterless creature; a man of character, an active man is pre-eminently a limited creature. That is my conviction of forty years. I am forty years old now, and you know forty years is a whole lifetime; you know it is extreme old age. To live longer than forty years is bad manners, is vulgar, immoral. Who does live beyond forty? Answer that, sincerely and honestly I will tell you who do: fools and worthless fellows. I tell all old men that to their face, all these venerable old men, all these silver-haired and reverend seniors! I tell the whole world that to its face! I have a right to say so, for I shall go on living to sixty myself. To seventy! To eighty!...Stay, let me take breath...

You imagine no doubt, gentlemen, that I want to amuse you. You are mistaken in that, too. I am by no means such a mirthful person as you imagine, or as you may imagine; however, irritated by all this babble (and I feel that you are irritated) you think fit to ask me who I am—then my answer is, I am a collegiate assessor. I was in the service that I might have something to eat (and solely for that reason), and when last year a distant relation left me six thousand roubles in his will I immediately retired from the service and settled down in my corner. I used to live in this corner before, but now I have settled down in it. My room is a wretched, horrid one in the outskirts of the town. My servant is an old countrywoman, ill-natured from stupidity, and, moreover, there is always a nasty smell about her. I am told that the Petersburg climate is bad for me, and that with my small means it is very expensive to live in Petersburg. I know all that better than all these sage and experienced counsellors and monitors.... But I am remaining in Petersburg; I am not going away from Petersburg! I am not going away because ...ech! Why, it is absolutely no matter whether I am going away or not going away.

But what can a decent man speak of with most pleasure?

Answer: Of himself.

Well, so I will talk about myself.

2

I want now to tell you, gentlemen, whether you care to hear it or not, why I could not even become an insect. I tell you solemnly, that I have many times tried to become an insect. But I was not equal even to that. I swear, gentlemen, that to be too conscious is an illness—a real thorough-going illness. For man's everyday needs, it would have been quite enough to have the ordinary human consciousness, that is, half or a quarter of the amount which falls to the lot of a cultivated man of our unhappy nineteenth century, especially one who has the fatal ill-luck to inhabit Petersburg, the most theoretical and intentional town on the whole terrestrial globe. (There are intentional and unintentional towns.) It would have been quite enough, for instance, to have the consciousness by which all so-called direct persons and men of action live. I bet you think I am writing all this from affectation, to be witty at the expense of men of action; and what is more, that from ill-bred affectation, I am clanking a sword like my officer. But, gentlemen, whoever can pride himself on his diseases and even swagger over them?

Though, after all, everyone does do that; people

do pride themselves on their diseases, and I do, may be, more than anyone. We will not dispute it; my contention was absurd. But yet I am firmly persuaded that a great deal of consciousness, every sort of consciousness, in fact, is a disease. I stick to that. Let us leave that, too, for a minute. Tell me this: why does it happen that at the very, yes, at the very moments when I am most capable of feeling every refinement of all that is "sublime and beautiful," as they used to say at one time, it would, as though of design, happen to me not only to feel but to do such ugly things, such that ... Well, in short, actions that all, perhaps, commit; but which, as though purposely, occurred to me at the very time when I was most conscious that they ought not to be committed. The more conscious I was of goodness and of all that was "sublime and beautiful," the more deeply I sank into my mire and the more ready I was to sink in it altogether. But the chief point was that all this was, as it were, not accidental in me, but as though it were bound to be so. It was as though it were my most normal condition, and not in the least disease or depravity, so that at last all desire in me to struggle against this depravity passed. It ended by my almost believing (perhaps actually believing) that this was perhaps my normal condition. But at first, in the beginning, what agonies I endured in that struggle! I did not believe it was the same with other people, and all my life I hid this fact about myself as a secret. I was ashamed (even now, perhaps, I am ashamed): I got to the point of feeling a sort of secret abnormal, despicable enjoyment in returning home to my corner on some disgusting Petersburg night, acutely conscious that that day I had committed a loathsome action again, that what was done could never be undone, and secretly, inwardly gnawing, gnawing at myself for it, tearing and consuming myself till at last the bitterness turned into a sort of shameful accursed sweetness, and at last—into positive real enjoyment! Yes, into enjoyment, into enjoyment! I insist upon that. I have spoken of this because I keep wanting to know for a fact whether other people feel such enjoyment? I will explain; the enjoyment was just from the too intense consciousness of one's own degradation; it was from feeling oneself that one had reached the last barrier, that it was horrible, but that it could not be otherwise; that there was no escape for you; that you never could become a different man; that

even if time and faith were still left you to change into something different you would most likely not wish to change; or if you did wish to, even then you would do nothing; because perhaps in reality there was nothing for you to change into.

And the worst of it was, and the root of it all, that it was all in accord with the normal fundamental laws of over-acute consciousness, and with the inertia that was the direct result of those laws, and that consequently one was not only unable to change but could do absolutely nothing. Thus it would follow, as the result of acute consciousness, that one is not to blame in being a scoundrel; as though that were any consolation to the scoundrel once he has come to realise that he actually is a scoundrel. But enough....Ech, I have talked a lot of nonsense, but what have I explained? How is enjoyment in this to be explained? But I will explain it. I will get to the bottom of it! That is why I have taken up my pen....

I, for instance, have a great deal of *amour propre* (self-love). I am as suspicious and prone to take offence as a humpback or a dwarf. But upon my word I sometimes have had moments when if I had happened to be slapped in the face I should, perhaps, have been positively glad of it. I say, in earnest, that I should probably have been able to discover even in that a peculiar sort of enjoyment—the enjoyment, of course, of despair; but in despair there are the most intense enjoyments, especially when one is very acutely conscious of the hopelessness of one's position. And when one is slapped in the face—why then the consciousness of being rubbed into a pulp would positively overwhelm one. The worst of it is, look at it which way one will, it still turns out that I was always the most to blame in everything. And what is most humiliating of all, to blame for no fault of my own but, so to say, through the laws of nature. In the first place, to blame because I am cleverer than any of the people surrounding me. (I have always considered myself cleverer than any of the people surrounding me, and sometimes, would you believe it, have been positively ashamed of it. At any rate, I have all my life, as it were, turned my eyes away and never could look people straight in the face.) To blame, finally, because even if I had had magnanimity, I should only have had more suffering from the sense of its uselessness. I should certainly have never been able to do anything from being magnanimous-

-neither to forgive, for my assailant would perhaps have slapped me from the laws of nature, and one cannot forgive the laws of nature; nor to forget, for even if it were owing to the laws of nature, it is insulting all the same. Finally, even if I had wanted to be anything but magnanimous, had desired on the contrary to revenge myself on my assailant, I could not have revenged myself on any one for anything because I should certainly never have made up my mind to do anything, even if I had been able to. Why should I not have made up my mind? About that in particular I want to say a few words.

3

With people who know how to revenge themselves and to stand up for themselves in general, how is it done? Why, when they are possessed, let us suppose, by the feeling of revenge, then for the time there is nothing else but that feeling left in their whole being. Such a gentleman simply dashes straight for his object like an infuriated bull with its horns down, and nothing but a wall will stop him. (By the way: facing the wall, such gentlemen—that is, the "direct" persons and men of action—are genuinely nonplussed. For them a wall is not an evasion, as for us people who think and consequently do nothing; it is not an excuse for turning aside, an excuse for which we are always very glad, though we scarcely believe in it ourselves, as a rule. No, they are nonplussed in all sincerity. The wall has for them something tranquillising, morally soothing, final—maybe even something mysterious...but of the wall later.)

Well, such a direct person I regard as the real normal man, as his tender mother nature wished to see him when she graciously brought him into being on the earth. I envy such a man till I am green in the face. He is stupid. I am not disputing that, but perhaps the normal man should be stupid, how do you know? Perhaps it is very beautiful, in fact. And I am the more persuaded of that suspicion, if one can call it so, by the fact that if you take, for instance, the antithesis of the normal man, that is, the man of acute consciousness, who has come, of course, not out of the lap of nature but out of a retort (this is almost mysticism, gentlemen, but I suspect this, too), this retort-made man is sometimes so nonplussed in the

presence of his antithesis that with all his exaggerated consciousness he genuinely thinks of himself as a mouse and not a man. It may be an acutely conscious mouse, yet it is a mouse, while the other is a man, and therefore, et caetera, et caetera. And the worst of it is, he himself, his very own self, looks on himself as a mouse; no one asks him to do so; and that is an important point. Now let us look at this mouse in action. Let us suppose, for instance, that it feels insulted, too (and it almost always does feel insulted), and wants to revenge itself, too. There may even be a greater accumulation of spite in it than in *l'homme de la nature et de la vérité* (the man of nature and truth). The base and nasty desire to vent that spite on its assailant rankles perhaps even more nastily in it than in *l'homme de la nature et de la vérité*. For through his innate stupidity the latter looks upon his revenge as justice pure and simple; while in consequence of his acute consciousness the mouse does not believe in the justice of it. To come at last to the deed itself, to the very act of revenge. Apart from the one fundamental nastiness the luckless mouse succeeds in creating around it so many other nastinesses in the form of doubts and questions, adds to the one question so many unsettled questions that there inevitably works up around it a sort of fatal brew, a stinking mess, made up of its doubts, emotions, and of the contempt spat upon it by the direct men of action who stand solemnly about it as judges and arbitrators, laughing at it till their healthy sides ache. Of course the only thing left for it is to dismiss all that with a wave of its paw, and, with a smile of assumed contempt in which it does not even itself believe, creep ignominiously into its mouse-hole. There in its nasty, stinking, underground home our insulted, crushed and ridiculed mouse promptly becomes absorbed in cold, malignant and, above all, everlasting spite. For forty years together it will remember its injury down to the smallest, most ignominious details, and every time will add, of itself, details still more ignominious, spitefully teasing and tormenting itself with its own imagination. It will itself be ashamed of its imaginings, but yet it will recall it all, it will go over and over every detail, it will invent unheard of things against itself, pretending that those things might happen, and will forgive nothing. Maybe it will begin to revenge itself, too, but, as it were, piecemeal, in trivial ways, from behind the stove, incognito, without believing either in its own right to vengeance, or in the success of its revenge, knowing that from all its efforts at revenge it will suffer a hundred times more than he on whom it revenges itself, while he, I daresay, will not even scratch himself. On its deathbed it will recall it all over again, with interest accumulated over all the years and...

But it is just in that cold, abominable half despair, half belief, in that conscious burying oneself alive for grief in the underworld for forty years, in that acutely recognised and yet partly doubtful hopelessness of one's position, in that hell of unsatisfied desires turned inward, in that fever of oscillations, of resolutions determined for ever and repented of again a minute later—that the savour of that strange enjoyment of which I have spoken lies. It is so subtle, so difficult of analysis, that persons who are a little limited, or even simply persons of strong nerves, will not understand a single atom of it. "Possibly," you will add on your own account with a grin, "people will not understand it either who have never received a slap in the face," and in that way you will politely hint to me that I, too, perhaps, have had the experience of a slap in the face in my life, and so I speak as one who knows. I bet that you are thinking that. But set your minds at rest, gentlemen, I have not received a slap in the face, though it is absolutely a matter of indifference to me what you may think about it. Possibly, I even regret, myself, that I have given so few slaps in the face during my life. But enough...not another word on that subject of such extreme interest to you.

I will continue calmly concerning persons with strong nerves who do not understand a certain refinement of enjoyment. Though in certain circumstances these gentlemen bellow their loudest like bulls, though this, let us suppose, does them the greatest credit, yet, as I have said already, confronted with the impossible they subside at once. The impossible means the stone wall! What stone wall? Why, of course, the laws of nature, the deductions of natural science, mathematics. As soon as they prove to you, for instance, that you are descended from a monkey, then it is no use scowling, accept it for a fact. When they prove to you that in reality one drop of your own fat must be dearer to you than a hundred thousand of your fellow-creatures, and that this conclu-

sion is the final solution of all so-called virtues and duties and all such prejudices and fancies, then you have just to accept it, there is no help for it, for twice two is a law of mathematics. Just try refuting it.

"Upon my word, they will shout at you, it is no use protesting: it is a case of twice two makes four! Nature does not ask your permission, she has nothing to do with your wishes, and whether you like her laws or dislike them, you are bound to accept her as she is, and consequently all her conclusions. A wall, you see, is a wall...and so on, and so on."

Merciful Heavens! but what do I care for the laws of nature and arithmetic, when, for some reason I dislike those laws and the fact that twice two makes four? Of course I cannot break through the wall by battering my head against it if I really have not the strength to knock it down, but I am not going to be reconciled to it simply because it is a stone wall and I have not the strength.

As though such a stone wall really were a consolation, and really did contain some word of conciliation, simply because it is as true as twice two makes four. Oh, absurdity of absurdities! How much better it is to understand it all, to recognise it all, all the impossibilities and the stone wall; not to be reconciled to one of those impossibilities and stone walls if it disgusts you to be reconciled to it; by the way of the most inevitable, logical combinations to reach the most revolting conclusions on the everlasting theme, that even for the stone wall you are yourself somehow to blame, though again it is as clear as day you are not to blame in the least, and therefore grinding your teeth in silent impotence to sink into luxurious inertia, brooding on the fact that there is no one even for you to feel vindictive against, that you have not, and perhaps never will have, an object for your spite, that it is a sleight of hand, a bit of juggling, a cardsharper's trick, that it is simply a mess, no knowing what and no knowing who, but in spite of all these uncertainties and jugglings, still there is an ache in you, and the more you do not know, the worse the ache.

4

"Ha, ha, ha! You will be finding enjoyment in toothache next," you cry, with a laugh.

"Well, even in toothache there is enjoyment," I answer. I had toothache for a whole month and I know there is. In that case, of course, people are not spiteful in silence, but moan; but they are not candid moans, they are malignant moans, and the malignancy is the whole point. The enjoyment of the sufferer finds expression in those moans; if he did not feel enjoyment in them he would not moan. It is a good example, gentlemen, and I will develop it. Those moans express in the first place all the aimlessness of your pain, which is so humiliating to your consciousness; the whole legal system of nature on which you spit disdainfully, of course, but from which you suffer all the same while she does not. They express the consciousness that you have no enemy to punish, but that you have pain; the consciousness that in spite of all possible Wagenheims you are in complete slavery to your teeth; that if someone wishes it, your teeth will leave off aching, and if he does not, they will go on aching another three months; and that finally if you are still contumacious and still protest, all that is left you for your own gratification is to thrash yourself or beat your wall with your fist as hard as you can, and absolutely nothing more. Well, these mortal insults, these jeers on the part of someone unknown, end at last in an enjoyment which sometimes reaches the highest degree of voluptuousness. I ask you, gentlemen, listen sometimes to the moans of an educated man of the nineteenth century suffering from toothache, on the second or third day of the attack, when he is beginning to moan, not as he moaned on the first day, that is, not simply because he has toothache, not just as any coarse peasant, but as a man affected by progress and European civilisation, a man who is "divorced from the soil and the national elements," as they express it now-a-days. His moans become nasty, disgustingly malignant, and go on for whole days and nights. And of course he knows himself that he is doing himself no sort of good with his moans; he knows better than anyone that he is only lacerating and harassing himself and others for nothing; he knows that even the audience before whom he is making his efforts, and his whole family, listen to him with loathing, do not put a ha'porth of faith in him, and inwardly understand that he might moan differently, more simply, without trills and flourishes, and that he is only amusing himself like that from ill-humour, from malignancy.

Well, in all these recognitions and disgraces it is that there lies a voluptuous pleasure. As though he would say: "I am worrying you, I am lacerating your hearts, I am keeping everyone in the house awake. Well, stay awake then, you, too, feel every minute that I have toothache. I am not a hero to you now, as I tried to seem before, but simply a nasty person, an impostor. Well, so be it, then! I am very glad that you see through me. It is nasty for you to hear my despicable moans: well, let it be nasty; here I will let you have a nastier flourish in a minute...." You do not understand even now, gentlemen? No, it seems our development and our consciousness must go further to understand all the intricacies of this pleasure. You laugh? Delighted. My jests, gentlemen, are of course in bad taste, jerky, involved, lacking self-confidence. But of course that is because I do not respect myself. Can a man of perception respect himself at all?

5

Come, can a man who attempts to find enjoyment in the very feeling of his own degradation possibly have a spark of respect for himself? I am not saying this now from any mawkish kind of remorse. And, indeed, I could never endure saying, "Forgive me, Papa, I won't do it again," not because I am incapable of saying that—on the contrary, perhaps just because I have been too capable of it, and in what a way, too. As though of design I used to get into trouble in cases when I was not to blame in any way. That was the nastiest part of it. At the same time I was genuinely touched and penitent, I used to shed tears and, of course, deceived myself, though I was not acting in the least and there was a sick feeling in my heart at the time....For that one could not blame even the laws of nature, though the laws of nature have continually all my life offended me more than anything. It is loathsome to remember it all, but it was loathsome even then. Of course, a minute or so later I would realise wrathfully that it was all a lie, a revolting lie, an affected lie, that is, all this penitence, this emotion, these vows of reform. You will ask why did I worry myself with such antics: answer, because it was very dull to sit with one's hands folded, and so one began cutting capers. That is really it. Observe yourselves more carefully, gentlemen, then you will understand that it is so. I invented adventures for myself and made up a life, so as at least to live in some way. How many times it has happened to me—well, for instance, to take offence simply on purpose, for nothing; and one knows oneself, of course, that one is offended at nothing; that one is putting it on, but yet one brings oneself at last to the point of being really offended. All my life I have had an impulse to play such pranks, so that in the end I could not control it in myself. Another time, twice, in fact, I tried hard to be in love. I suffered, too, gentlemen, I assure you. In the depth of my heart there was no faith in my suffering, only a faint stir of mockery, but yet I did suffer, and in the real, orthodox way; I was jealous, beside myself ... and it was all from *ennui*, gentlemen, all from *ennui*; inertia overcame me. You know the direct, legitimate fruit of consciousness is inertia, that is, conscious sitting-with-the-hands-folded. I have referred to this already. I repeat, I repeat with emphasis: all "direct" persons and men of action are active just because they are stupid and limited. How explain that? I will tell you: in consequence of their limitation they take immediate and secondary causes for primary ones, and in that way persuade themselves more quickly and easily than other people do that they have found an infallible foundation for their activity, and their minds are at ease and you know that is the chief thing. To begin to act, you know, you must first have your mind completely at ease and no trace of doubt left in it. Why, how am I, for example, to set my mind at rest? Where are the primary causes on which I am to build? Where are my foundations? Where am I to get them from? I exercise myself in reflection, and consequently with me every primary cause at once draws after itself another still more primary, and so on to infinity. That is just the essence of every sort of consciousness and reflection. It must be a case of the laws of nature again. What is the result of it in the end? Why, just the same. Remember I spoke just now of vengeance. (I am sure you did not take it in.) I said that a man revenges himself because he sees justice in it. Therefore he has found a primary cause, that is, justice. And so he is at rest on all sides, and consequently he carries out his revenge calmly and successfully, being persuaded that he is doing a just and honest thing. But I see no justice in it, I find no sort of virtue in it either, and consequently if I attempt to revenge myself, it is only out of spite. Spite, of course, might overcome everything, all my doubts, and so might serve quite successfully in place of a primary cause, precisely because it is not a cause. But what is to be done if I have not even spite (I began with that just now, you know). In consequence again of those accursed laws of consciousness, anger in me is subject to chemical disintegration. You look into it, the object flies off into air, your reasons evaporate, the criminal is not to be found, the wrong becomes not a wrong but a phantom, something like the toothache, for which no one is to blame, and consequently there is only the same outlet left again—that is, to beat the wall as hard as you can. So you give it up with a wave of the hand because you have not found a fundamental cause. And try letting yourself be carried away by your feelings, blindly, without reflection, without a primary cause, repelling consciousness at least for a time; hate or love, if only not to sit with your hands folded. The day after tomorrow, at the latest, you will begin despising yourself for having knowingly deceived yourself. Result: a soap-bubble and inertia. Oh, gentlemen, do you know, perhaps I consider myself an intelligent man, only because all my life I have been able neither to begin nor to finish anything. Granted I am a babbler, a harmless vexatious babbler, like all of us. But what is to be done if the direct and sole vocation of every intelligent man is babble, that is, the intentional pouring of water through a sieve?

6

Oh, if I had done nothing simply from laziness! Heavens, how I should have respected myself, then. I should have respected myself because I should at least have been capable of being lazy; there would at least have been one quality, as it were, positive in me, in which I could have believed myself. Question: What is he? Answer: A sluggard; how very pleasant it would have been to hear that of oneself! It would mean that I was positively defined, it would mean that there was something to say about me. "Sluggard"—why, it is a calling and vocation, it is a career. Do not jest, it is so. I should then be a member of the best club by right, and should find my occupation in continually respecting myself. I knew a gentleman who prided himself all his life on being a connoisseur of Lafitte. He considered this as his positive virtue, and never doubted himself. He died, not simply with a tranquil, but with a triumphant conscience, and he was quite right, too. Then I should have chosen a career for myself, I should have been a sluggard and a glutton, not a simple one, but, for instance, one with sympathies for everything sublime and beautiful. How do you like that? I have long had visions of it. That "sublime and beautiful" weighs heavily on my mind at forty But that is at forty; then—oh, then it would have been different! I should have found for myself a form of activity in keeping with it, to be precise, drinking to the health of everything "sublime and beautiful." I should have snatched at every opportunity to drop a tear into my glass and then to drain it to all that is "sublime and beautiful." I should then have turned everything into the sublime and the beautiful; in the nastiest, unquestionable trash, I should have sought out the sublime and the beautiful. I should have exuded tears like a wet sponge. An artist, for instance, paints a picture worthy of Gay. At once I drink to the health of the artist who painted the picture worthy of Gay, because I love all that is "sublime and beautiful." An author has written AS YOU WILL: at once I drink to the health of "anyone you will" because I love all that is "sublime and beautiful."

I should claim respect for doing so. I should persecute anyone who would not show me respect. I should live at ease, I should die with dignity, why, it is charming, perfectly charming! And what a good round belly I should have grown, what a treble chin I should have established, what a ruby nose I should have coloured for myself, so that everyone would have said, looking at me: "Here is an asset! Here is something real and solid!" And, say what you like, it is very agreeable to hear such remarks about oneself in this negative age.

7

But these are all golden dreams. Oh, tell me, who was it first announced, who was it first proclaimed, that man only does nasty things because he does not know his own interests; and that if he were enlight-

ened, if his eyes were opened to his real normal interests, man would at once cease to do nasty things, would at once become good and noble because, being enlightened and understanding his real advantage, he would see his own advantage in the good and nothing else, and we all know that not one man can, consciously, act against his own interests, consequently, so to say, through necessity, he would begin doing good? Oh, the babe! Oh, the pure, innocent child! Why, in the first place, when in all these thousands of years has there been a time when man has acted only from his own interest? What is to be done with the millions of facts that bear witness that men, CONSCIOUSLY, that is fully understanding their real interests, have left them in the background and have rushed headlong on another path, to meet peril and danger, compelled to this course by nobody and by nothing, but, as it were, simply disliking the beaten track, and have obstinately, wilfully, struck out another difficult, absurd way, seeking it almost in the darkness. So, I suppose, this obstinacy and perversity were pleasanter to them than any advantage.... Advantage! What is advantage? And will you take it upon yourself to define with perfect accuracy in what the advantage of man consists? And what if it so happens that a man's advantage, SOMETIMES, not only may, but even must, consist in his desiring in certain cases what is harmful to himself and not advantageous. And if so, if there can be such a case, the whole principle falls into dust. What do you think—are there such cases? You laugh; laugh away, gentlemen, but only answer me: have man's advantages been reckoned up with perfect certainty? Are there not some which not only have not been included but cannot possibly be included under any classification? You see, you gentlemen have, to the best of my knowledge, taken your whole register of human advantages from the averages of statistical figures and politico-economical formulas. Your advantages are prosperity, wealth, freedom, peace—and so on, and so on. So that the man who should, for instance, go openly and knowingly in opposition to all that list would to your thinking, and indeed mine, too, of course, be an obscurantist or an absolute madman: would not he? But, you know, this is what is surprising: why does it so happen that all these statisticians, sages and lovers of humanity, when they reckon up human advantages invariably leave out one? They don't even take it into their reckoning in the form in which it should be taken, and the whole reckoning depends upon that. It would be no greater matter, they would simply have to take it, this advantage, and add it to the list. But the trouble is, that this strange advantage does not fall under any classification and is not in place in any list. I have a friend for instance....Ech! gentlemen, but of course he is your friend, too; and indeed there is no one, no one to whom he is not a friend! When he prepares for any undertaking this gentleman immediately explains to you, elegantly and clearly, exactly how he must act in accordance with the laws of reason and truth. What is more, he will talk to you with excitement and passion of the true normal interests of man; with irony he will upbraid the short-sighted fools who do not understand their own interests, nor the true significance of virtue; and, within a quarter of an hour, without any sudden outside provocation, but simply through something inside him which is stronger than all his interests, he will go off on quite a different tack—that is, act in direct opposition to what he has just been saying about himself, in opposition to the laws of reason, in opposition to his own advantage, in fact in opposition to everything ... I warn you that my friend is a compound personality and therefore it is difficult to blame him as an individual. The fact is, gentlemen, it seems there must really exist something that is dearer to almost every man than his greatest advantages, or (not to be illogical) there is a most advantageous advantage (the very one omitted of which we spoke just now) which is more important and more advantageous than all other advantages, for the sake of which a man if necessary is ready to act in opposition to all laws; that is, in opposition to reason, honour, peace, prosperity—in fact, in opposition to all those excellent and useful things if only he can attain that fundamental, most advantageous advantage which is dearer to him than all. "Yes, but it's advantage all the same," you will retort. But excuse me, I'll make the point clear, and it is not a case of playing upon words. What matters is, that this advantage is remarkable from the very fact that it breaks down all our classifications, and continually shatters every system constructed by lovers of mankind for the benefit of mankind. In fact, it upsets everything. But before I mention this advantage to you, I want to compromise myself personally, and therefore I boldly declare that all these fine systems, all these theories for explaining to mankind their real normal interests, in order that inevitably striving to pursue these interests they may at once become good and noble—are, in my opinion, so far, mere logical exercises! Yes, logical exercises. Why, to maintain this theory of the regeneration of mankind by means of the pursuit of his own advantage is to my mind almost the same thing...as to affirm, for instance, following Buckle, that through civilisation mankind becomes softer, and consequently less bloodthirsty and less fitted for warfare. Logically it does seem to follow from his arguments. But man has such a predilection for systems and abstract deductions that he is ready to distort the truth intentionally, he is ready to deny the evidence of his senses only to justify his logic. I take this example because it is the most glaring instance of it. Only look about you: blood is being spilt in streams, and in the merriest way, as though it were champagne. Take the whole of the nineteenth century in which Buckle lived. Take Napoleon—the Great and also the present one. Take North America—the eternal union. Take the farce of Schleswig-Holstein....And what is it that civilisation softens in us? The only gain of civilisation for mankind is the greater capacity for variety of sensations—and absolutely nothing more. And through the development of this many-sidedness man may come to finding enjoyment in bloodshed. In fact, this has already happened to him. Have you noticed that it is the most civilised gentlemen who have been the subtlest slaughterers, to whom the Attilas and Stenka Razins could not hold a candle, and if they are not so conspicuous as the Attilas and Stenka Razins it is simply because they are so often met with, are so ordinary and have become so familiar to us. In any case civilisation has made mankind if not more bloodthirsty, at least more vilely, more loathsomely bloodthirsty. In old days he saw justice in bloodshed and with his conscience at peace exterminated those he thought proper. Now we do think bloodshed abominable and yet we engage in this abomination, and with more energy than ever. Which is worse? Decide that for yourselves. They say that Cleopatra (excuse an instance from Roman history) was fond of sticking gold pins into her slave-girls' breasts and derived gratification from their screams and writhings. You will say that that was in the comparatively barbarous times; that these are barbarous times too, because also, comparatively speaking, pins are stuck in even now; that though man has now learned to see more clearly than in barbarous ages, he is still far from having learnt to act as reason and science would dictate. But yet you are fully convinced that he will be sure to learn when he gets rid of certain old bad habits, and when common sense and science have completely re-educated human nature and turned it in a normal direction. You are confident that then man will cease from INTENTIONAL error and will, so to say, be compelled not to want to set his will against his normal interests. That is not all; then, you say, science itself will teach man (though to my mind it's a superfluous luxury) that he never has really had any caprice or will of his own, and that he himself is something of the nature of a piano-key or the stop of an organ, and that there are, besides, things called the laws of nature; so that everything he does is not done by his willing it, but is done of itself, by the laws of nature. Consequently we have only to discover these laws of nature, and man will no longer have to answer for his actions and life will become exceedingly easy for him. All human actions will then, of course, be tabulated according to these laws, mathematically, like tables of logarithms up to 108,000, and entered in an index; or, better still, there would be published certain edifying works of the nature of encyclopaedic lexicons, in which everything will be so clearly calculated and explained that there will be no more incidents or adventures in the world.

Then—this is all what you say—new economic relations will be established, all ready-made and worked out with mathematical exactitude, so that every possible question will vanish in the twinkling of an eye, simply because every possible answer to it will be provided. Then the "Palace of Crystal" will be built. Then...In fact, those will be halcyon days. Of course there is no guaranteeing (this is my comment) that it will not be, for instance, frightfully dull then (for what will one have to do when everything will be calculated and tabulated), but on the other hand everything will be extraordinarily rational. Of course boredom may lead you to anything. It is boredom sets one sticking golden pins into people, but all that would not matter. What is bad (this is my comment again) is that I dare say people will be thankful for the gold pins then. Man is stupid, you know, phenomenally stupid; or rather he is not at all stupid, but he is so ungrateful that you could not find another like him in all creation. I, for instance, would not be in the least surprised if all of a sudden, A PROPOS of nothing, in the midst of general prosperity a gentleman with an ignoble, or rather with a reactionary and ironical, countenance were to arise and, putting his arms akimbo, say to us all: "I say, gentleman, hadn't we better kick over the whole show and scatter rationalism to the winds, simply to send these logarithms to the devil, and to enable us to live once more at our own sweet foolish will!" That again would not matter, but what is annoying is that he would be sure to find followers—such is the nature of man. And all that for the most foolish reason, which, one would think, was hardly worth mentioning: that is, that man everywhere and at all times, whoever he may be, has preferred to act as he chose and not in the least as his reason and advantage dictated. And one may choose what is contrary to one's own interests, and sometimes one POSITIVELY OUGHT (that is my idea). One's own free unfettered choice, one's own caprice, however wild it may be, one's own fancy worked up at times to frenzy—is that very "most advantageous advantage" which we have overlooked, which comes under no classification and against which all systems and theories are continually being shattered to atoms. And how do these wiseacres know that man wants a normal, a virtuous choice? What has made them conceive that man must want a rationally advantageous choice? What man wants is simply INDEPENDENT choice, whatever that independence may cost and wherever it may lead. And choice, of course, the devil only knows what choice.

8

"Ha! ha! ha! But you know there is no such thing as choice in reality, say what you like," you will interpose with a chuckle. "Science has succeeded in so far analysing man that we know already that choice and what is called freedom of will is nothing else than—"

Stay, gentlemen, I meant to begin with that myself I confess, I was rather frightened. I was just going to say that the devil only knows what choice depends on, and that perhaps that was a very good thing, but I remembered the teaching of science... and pulled myself up. And here you have begun upon it. Indeed, if there really is some day discovered a formula for all our desires and caprices—that is, an explanation of what they depend upon, by what laws they arise, how they develop, what they are aiming at in one case and in another and so on, that is a real mathematical formula—then, most likely, man will at once cease to feel desire, indeed, he will be certain to. For who would want to choose by rule? Besides, he will at once be transformed from a human being into an organ-stop or something of the sort; for what is a man without desires, without free will and without choice, if not a stop in an organ? What do you think? Let us reckon the chances—can such a thing happen or not?

"H'm!" you decide. "Our choice is usually mistaken from a false view of our advantage. We sometimes choose absolute nonsense because in our foolishness we see in that nonsense the easiest means for attaining a supposed advantage. But when all that is explained and worked out on paper (which is perfectly possible, for it is contemptible and senseless to suppose that some laws of nature man will never understand), then certainly so-called desires will no longer exist. For if a desire should come into conflict with reason we shall then reason and not desire, because it will be impossible retaining our reason to be SENSELESS in our desires, and in that way knowingly act against reason and desire to injure ourselves. And as all choice and reasoning can be really calculated—because there will some day be discovered the laws of our so-called free will—so, joking apart, there may one day be something like a table constructed of them, so that we really shall choose in accordance with it. If, for instance, some day they calculate and prove to me that I made a long nose at someone because I could not help making a long nose at him and that I had to do it in that particular way, what FREEDOM is left me, especially if I am a learned man and have taken my degree somewhere? Then I should be able to calculate my whole life for thirty years beforehand. In short, if this could be arranged there would be nothing left for us to do; anyway, we should have to understand that. And, in fact,

we ought unwearyingly to repeat to ourselves that at such and such a time and in such and such circumstances nature does not ask our leave; that we have got to take her as she is and not fashion her to suit our fancy, and if we really aspire to formulas and tables of rules, and well, even...to the chemical retort, there's no help for it, we must accept the retort too, or else it will be accepted without our consent...."

Yes, but here I come to a stop! Gentlemen, you must excuse me for being over-philosophical; it's the result of forty years underground! Allow me to indulge my fancy. You see, gentlemen, reason is an excellent thing, there's no disputing that, but reason is nothing but reason and satisfies only the rational side of man's nature, while will is a manifestation of the whole life, that is, of the whole human life including reason and all the impulses. And although our life, in this manifestation of it, is often worthless, yet it is life and not simply extracting square roots. Here I, for instance, quite naturally want to live, in order to satisfy all my capacities for life, and not simply my capacity for reasoning, that is, not simply one twentieth of my capacity for life. What does reason know? Reason only knows what it has succeeded in learning (some things, perhaps, it will never learn; this is a poor comfort, but why not say so frankly?) and human nature acts as a whole, with everything that is in it, consciously or unconsciously, and, even if it goes wrong, it lives. I suspect, gentlemen, that you are looking at me with compassion; you tell me again that an enlightened and developed man, such, in short, as the future man will be, cannot consciously desire anything disadvantageous to himself, that that can be proved mathematically. I thoroughly agree, it can—by mathematics. But I repeat for the hundredth time, there is one case, one only, when man may consciously, purposely, desire what is injurious to himself, what is stupid, very stupid—simply in order to have the right to desire for himself even what is very stupid and not to be bound by an obligation to desire only what is sensible. Of course, this very stupid thing, this caprice of ours, may be in reality, gentlemen, more advantageous for us than anything else on earth, especially in certain cases. And in particular it may be more advantageous than any advantage even when it does us obvious harm, and contradicts the soundest conclusions of our reason concerning our advantage—for in any circumstances it preserves for us what is most precious and most important—that is, our personality, our individuality. Some, you see, maintain that this really is the most precious thing for mankind; choice can, of course, if it chooses, be in agreement with reason; and especially if this be not abused but kept within bounds. It is profitable and sometimes even praiseworthy. But very often, and even most often, choice is utterly and stubbornly opposed to reason ... and ... and ... do you know that that, too, is profitable, sometimes even praiseworthy? Gentlemen, let us suppose that man is not stupid. (Indeed one cannot refuse to suppose that, if only from the one consideration, that, if man is stupid, then who is wise?) But if he is not stupid, he is monstrously ungrateful! Phenomenally ungrateful. In fact, I believe that the best definition of man is the ungrateful biped. But that is not all, that is not his worst defect; his worst defect is his perpetual moral obliquity, perpetual—from the days of the Flood to the Schleswig-Holstein period. Moral obliquity and consequently lack of good sense; for it has long been accepted that lack of good sense is due to no other cause than moral obliquity. Put it to the test and cast your eyes upon the history of mankind. What will you see? Is it a grand spectacle? Grand, if you like. Take the Colossus of Rhodes, for instance, that's worth something. With good reason Mr. Anaevsky testifies of it that some say that it is the work of man's hands, while others maintain that it has been created by nature herself. Is it many-coloured? May be it is many-coloured, too: if one takes the dress uniforms, military and civilian, of all peoples in all ages—that alone is worth something, and if you take the undress uniforms you will never get to the end of it; no historian would be equal to the job. Is it monotonous? May be it's monotonous too: it's fighting and fighting; they are fighting now, they fought first and they fought last— you will admit, that it is almost too monotonous. In short, one may say anything about the history of the world—anything that might enter the most disordered imagination. The only thing one can't say is that it's rational. The very word sticks in one's throat. And, indeed, this is the odd thing that is continually happening: there are continually turning up in life moral and rational persons, sages and lovers of humanity who make it their object to live all their lives as morally and rationally as possible, to be, so

to speak, a light to their neighbours simply in order to show them that it is possible to live morally and rationally in this world. And yet we all know that those very people sooner or later have been false to themselves, playing some queer trick, often a most unseemly one. Now I ask you: what can be expected of man since he is a being endowed with strange qualities? Shower upon him every earthly blessing, drown him in a sea of happiness, so that nothing but bubbles of bliss can be seen on the surface; give him economic prosperity, such that he should have nothing else to do but sleep, eat cakes and busy himself with the continuation of his species, and even then out of sheer ingratitude, sheer spite, man would play you some nasty trick. He would even risk his cakes and would deliberately desire the most fatal rubbish, the most uneconomical absurdity, simply to introduce into all this positive good sense his fatal fantastic element. It is just his fantastic dreams, his vulgar folly that he will desire to retain, simply in order to prove to himself--as though that were so necessary—that men still are men and not the keys of a piano, which the laws of nature threaten to control so completely that soon one will be able to desire nothing but by the calendar. And that is not all: even if man really were nothing but a piano-key, even if this were proved to him by natural science and mathematics, even then he would not become reasonable, but would purposely do something perverse out of simple ingratitude, simply to gain his point. And if he does not find means he will contrive destruction and chaos, will contrive sufferings of all sorts, only to gain his point! He will launch a curse upon the world, and as only man can curse (it is his privilege, the primary distinction between him and other animals), may be by his curse alone he will attain his object—that is, convince himself that he is a man and not a piano-key! If you say that all this, too, can be calculated and tabulated—chaos and darkness and curses, so that the mere possibility of calculating it all beforehand would stop it all, and reason would reassert itself, then man would purposely go mad in order to be rid of reason and gain his point! I believe in it, I answer for it, for the whole work of man really seems to consist in nothing but proving to himself every minute that he is a man and not a piano-key! It may be at the cost of his skin, it may be by cannibalism! And this being so, can one help being tempted to rejoice that it has not yet come off, and that desire still depends on something we don't know?

You will scream at me (that is, if you condescend to do so) that no one is touching my free will, that all they are concerned with is that my will should of itself, of its own free will, coincide with my own normal interests, with the laws of nature and arithmetic.

Good heavens, gentlemen, what sort of free will is left when we come to tabulation and arithmetic, when it will all be a case of twice two make four? Twice two makes four without my will. As if free will meant that!

9

Gentlemen, I am joking, and I know myself that my jokes are not brilliant, but you know one can take everything as a joke. I am, perhaps, jesting against the grain. Gentlemen, I am tormented by questions; answer them for me. You, for instance, want to cure men of their old habits and reform their will in accordance with science and good sense. But how do you know, not only that it is possible, but also that it is DESIRABLE to reform man in that way? And what leads you to the conclusion that man's inclinations NEED reforming? In short, how do you know that such a reformation will be a benefit to man? And to go to the root of the matter, why are you so positively convinced that not to act against his real normal interests guaranteed by the conclusions of reason and arithmetic is certainly always advantageous for man and must always be a law for mankind? So far, you know, this is only your supposition. It may be the law of logic, but not the law of humanity. You think, gentlemen, perhaps that I am mad? Allow me to defend myself. I agree that man is pre-eminently a creative animal, predestined to strive consciously for an object and to engage in engineering--that is, incessantly and eternally to make new roads, WHEREVER THEY MAY LEAD. But the reason why he wants sometimes to go off at a tangent may just be that he is PREDESTINED to make the road, and perhaps, too, that however stupid the "direct" practical man may be, the thought sometimes will occur to him that the road almost always does lead

SOMEWHERE, and that the destination it leads to is less important than the process of making it, and that the chief thing is to save the well-conducted child from despising engineering, and so giving way to the fatal idleness, which, as we all know, is the mother of all the vices. Man likes to make roads and to create, that is a fact beyond dispute. But why has he such a passionate love for destruction and chaos also? Tell me that! But on that point I want to say a couple of words myself. May it not be that he loves chaos and destruction (there can be no disputing that he does sometimes love it) because he is instinctively afraid of attaining his object and completing the edifice he is constructing? Who knows, perhaps he only loves that edifice from a distance, and is by no means in love with it at close quarters; perhaps he only loves building it and does not want to live in it, but will leave it, when completed, for the use of domestic animals—such as the ants, the sheep, and so on. Now the ants have quite a different taste. They have a marvellous edifice of that pattern which endures for ever—the ant-heap.

With the ant-heap the respectable race of ants began and with the ant-heap they will probably end, which does the greatest credit to their perseverance and good sense. But man is a frivolous and incongruous creature, and perhaps, like a chess player, loves the process of the game, not the end of it. And who knows (there is no saying with certainty), perhaps the only goal on earth to which mankind is striving lies in this incessant process of attaining, in other words, in life itself, and not in the thing to be attained, which must always be expressed as a formula, as positive as twice two makes four, and such positiveness is not life, gentlemen, but is the beginning of death. Anyway, man has always been afraid of this mathematical certainty, and I am afraid of it now. Granted that man does nothing but seek that mathematical certainty, he traverses oceans, sacrifices his life in the quest, but to succeed, really to find it, dreads, I assure you. He feels that when he has found it there will be nothing for him to look for. When workmen have finished their work they do at least receive their pay, they go to the tavern, then they are taken to the police-station--and there is occupation for a week. But where can man go? Anyway, one can observe a certain awkwardness about him when he has attained such objects. He loves the process of attaining, but does not quite like to have attained, and that, of course, is very absurd. In fact, man is a comical creature; there seems to be a kind of jest in it all. But yet mathematical certainty is after all, something insufferable. Twice two makes four seems to me simply a piece of insolence. Twice two makes four is a pert coxcomb who stands with arms akimbo barring your path and spitting. I admit that twice two makes four is an excellent thing, but if we are to give everything its due, twice two makes five is sometimes a very charming thing too.

And why are you so firmly, so triumphantly, convinced that only the normal and the positive—in other words, only what is conducive to welfare—is for the advantage of man? Is not reason in error as regards advantage? Does not man, perhaps, love something besides well-being? Perhaps he is just as fond of suffering? Perhaps suffering is just as great a benefit to him as well-being? Man is sometimes extraordinarily, passionately, in love with suffering, and that is a fact. There is no need to appeal to universal history to prove that; only ask yourself, if you are a man and have lived at all. As far as my personal opinion is concerned, to care only for well-being seems to me positively ill-bred. Whether it's good or bad, it is sometimes very pleasant, too, to smash things. I hold no brief for suffering nor for well-being either. I am standing for ... my caprice, and for its being guaranteed to me when necessary. Suffering would be out of place in vaudevilles, for instance; I know that. In the "Palace of Crystal" it is unthinkable; suffering means doubt, negation, and what would be the good of a "palace of crystal" if there could be any doubt about it? And yet I think man will never renounce real suffering, that is, destruction and chaos. Why, suffering is the sole origin of consciousness. Though I did lay it down at the beginning that consciousness is the greatest misfortune for man, yet I know man prizes it and would not give it up for any satisfaction. Consciousness, for instance, is infinitely superior to twice two makes four. Once you have mathematical certainty there is nothing left to do or to understand. There will be nothing left but to bottle up your five senses and plunge into contemplation. While if you stick to consciousness, even though the same result is attained, you can at least flog yourself at times, and that will, at any rate, liven you up. Reactionary as it is, corporal punishment is better than nothing.

10

You believe in a palace of crystal that can never be destroyed—a palace at which one will not be able to put out one's tongue or make a long nose on the sly. And perhaps that is just why I am afraid of this edifice, that it is of crystal and can never be destroyed and that one cannot put one's tongue out at it even on the sly.

You see, if it were not a palace, but a hen-house, I might creep into it to avoid getting wet, and yet I would not call the hen-house a palace out of gratitude to it for keeping me dry. You laugh and say that in such circumstances a hen-house is as good as a mansion. Yes, I answer, if one had to live simply to keep out of the rain.

But what is to be done if I have taken it into my head that that is not the only object in life, and that if one must live one had better live in a mansion? That is my choice, my desire. You will only eradicate it when you have changed my preference. Well, do change it, allure me with something else, give me another ideal. But meanwhile I will not take a hen-house for a mansion. The palace of crystal may be an idle dream, it may be that it is inconsistent with the laws of nature and that I have invented it only through my own stupidity, through the old-fashioned irrational habits of my generation. But what does it matter to me that it is inconsistent? That makes no difference since it exists in my desires, or rather exists as long as my desires exist. Perhaps you are laughing again? Laugh away; I will put up with any mockery rather than pretend that I am satisfied when I am hungry. I know, anyway, that I will not be put off with a compromise, with a recurring zero, simply because it is consistent with the laws of nature and actually exists. I will not accept as the crown of my desires a block of buildings with tenements for the poor on a lease of a thousand years, and perhaps with a sign-board of a dentist hanging out. Destroy my desires, eradicate my ideals, show me something better, and I will follow you. You will say, perhaps, that it is not worth your trouble; but in that case I can give you the same answer. We are discussing things seriously; but if you won't deign to give me your attention, I will drop your acquaintance. I can retreat into my underground hole.

But while I am alive and have desires I would rather my hand were withered off than bring one brick to such a building! Don't remind me that I have just rejected the palace of crystal for the sole reason that one cannot put out one's tongue at it. I did not say because I am so fond of putting my tongue out. Perhaps the thing I resented was, that of all your edifices there has not been one at which one could not put out one's tongue. On the contrary, I would let my tongue be cut off out of gratitude if things could be so arranged that I should lose all desire to put it out. It is not my fault that things cannot be so arranged, and that one must be satisfied with model flats. Then why am I made with such desires? Can I have been constructed simply in order to come to the conclusion that all my construction is a cheat? Can this be my whole purpose? I do not believe it.

But do you know what: I am convinced that we underground folk ought to be kept on a curb. Though we may sit forty years underground without speaking, when we do come out into the light of day and break out we talk and talk and talk....

11

The long and the short of it is, gentlemen, that it is better to do nothing! Better conscious inertia! And so hurrah for underground! Though I have said that I envy the normal man to the last drop of my bile, yet I should not care to be in his place such as he is now (though I shall not cease envying him). No, no; anyway the underground life is more advantageous. There, at any rate, one can ... Oh, but even now I am lying! I am lying because I know myself that it is not underground that is better, but something different, quite different, for which I am thirsting, but which I cannot find! Damn underground!

I will tell you another thing that would be better, and that is, if I myself believed in anything of what I have just written. I swear to you, gentlemen, there is not one thing, not one word of what I have written that I really believe. That is, I believe it, perhaps, but

at the same time I feel and suspect that I am lying like a cobbler.

"Then why have you written all this?" you will say to me. "I ought to put you underground for forty years without anything to do and then come to you in your cellar, to find out what stage you have reached! How can a man be left with nothing to do for forty years?"

"Isn't that shameful, isn't that humiliating?" you will say, perhaps, wagging your heads contemptuously. "You thirst for life and try to settle the problems of life by a logical tangle. And how persistent, how insolent are your sallies, and at the same time what a scare you are in! You talk nonsense and are pleased with it; you say impudent things and are in continual alarm and apologising for them. You declare that you are afraid of nothing and at the same time try to ingratiate yourself in our good opinion. You declare that you are gnashing your teeth and at the same time you try to be witty so as to amuse us. You know that your witticisms are not witty, but you are evidently well satisfied with their literary value. You may, perhaps, have really suffered, but you have no respect for your own suffering. You may have sincerity, but you have no modesty; out of the pettiest vanity you expose your sincerity to publicity and ignominy. You doubtlessly mean to say something, but hide your last word through fear, because you have not the resolution to utter it, and only have a cowardly impudence. You boast of consciousness, but you are not sure of your ground, for though your mind works, yet your heart is darkened and corrupt, and you cannot have a full, genuine consciousness without a pure heart. And how intrusive you are, how you insist and grimace! Lies, lies, lies!"

Of course I have myself made up all the things you say. That, too, is from underground. I have been for forty years listening to you through a crack under the floor. I have invented them myself, there was nothing else I could invent. It is no wonder that I have learned it by heart and it has taken a literary form....

But can you really be so credulous as to think that I will print all this and give it to you to read too? And another problem: why do I call you "gentlemen," why do I address you as though you really were my readers? Such confessions as I intend to make are never printed nor given to other people to read. Anyway, I am not strong-minded enough for that, and I don't see why I should be. But you see a fancy has occurred to me and I want to realise it at all costs. Let me explain.

Every man has reminiscences which he would not tell to everyone, but only to his friends. He has other matters in his mind which he would not reveal even to his friends, but only to himself, and that in secret. But there are other things which a man is afraid to tell even to himself, and every decent man has a number of such things stored away in his mind. The more decent he is, the greater the number of such things in his mind. Anyway, I have only lately determined to remember some of my early adventures. Till now I have always avoided them, even with a certain uneasiness. Now, when I am not only recalling them, but have actually decided to write an account of them, I want to try the experiment whether one can, even with oneself, be perfectly open and not take fright at the whole truth. I will observe, in parenthesis, that Heine says that a true autobiography is almost an impossibility, and that man is bound to lie about himself. He considers that Rousseau certainly told lies about himself in his confessions, and even intentionally lied, out of vanity. I am convinced that Heine is right; I quite understand how sometimes one may, out of sheer vanity, attribute regular crimes to oneself, and indeed I can very well conceive that kind of vanity. But Heine judged of people who made their confessions to the public. I write only for myself, and I wish to declare once and for all that if I write as though I were addressing readers, that is simply because it is easier for me to write in that form. It is a form, an empty form—I shall never have readers. I have made this plain already....

I don't wish to be hampered by any restrictions in the compilation of my notes. I shall not attempt any system or method. I will jot things down as I remember them.

But here, perhaps, someone will catch at the word and ask me: if you really don't reckon on readers, why do you make such compacts with yourself—and on paper too—that is, that you won't attempt any system or method, that you jot things down as you remember them, and so on, and so on? Why are you explaining? Why do you apologise?

Well, there it is, I answer.

There is a whole psychology in all this, though. Perhaps it is simply that I am a coward. And perhaps that I purposely imagine an audience before me in order that I may be more dignified while I write. There are perhaps thousands of reasons. Again, what is my object precisely in writing? If it is not for the benefit of the public why should I not simply recall these incidents in my own mind without putting them on paper?

Quite so; but yet it is more imposing on paper. There is something more impressive in it; I shall be better able to criticise myself and improve my style. Besides, I shall perhaps obtain actual relief from writing. Today, for instance, I am particularly oppressed by one memory of a distant past. It came back vividly to my mind a few days ago, and has remained haunting me like an annoying tune that one cannot get rid of. And yet I must get rid of it somehow. I have hundreds of such reminiscences; but at times some one stands out from the hundred and oppresses me. For some reason I believe that if I write it down I should get rid of it. Why not try?

Besides, I am bored, and I never have anything to do. Writing will be a sort of work. They say work makes man kind-hearted and honest. Well, here is a chance for me, anyway.

Snow is falling today, yellow and dingy. It fell yesterday, too, and a few days ago. I fancy it is the wet snow that has reminded me of that incident which I cannot shake off now. And so let it be a story *a propos* of the falling snow.

Fyodor Dostovesky. *Notes from the Underground*. Trans. Constance Garnett. New York: McMillan, 1918.

THE DEATH OF IVAN ILYCH

LEO TOLSTOY (1828-1910)

One of the great novelists of the 19ᵗʰ century, Leo Tolstoy produced such literary masterpieces as War and Peace *and* Anna Karenina *before he fell into a suicidal despair about the meaninglessness of his life. As a result of his personal crisis, he underwent a deep spiritual conversion in the 1870s to a radical form of Christianity that espoused a lifestyle of poverty, chastity, pacifism, and a renunciation of worldly glory. After his conversion, Tolstoy stopped writing novels and began writing short stories and essays that explicated his unique Christian vision.* The Death of Ivan Ilych, *written during this period, is the story of a high court judge who has lived a life of hedonist self-indulgence. At the age of 45 he suddenly discovers that he is dying and experiences a profound existential crisis that forces him to completely reevaluate his life.*

1

During an interval in the Melvinski trial in the large building of the Law Courts the members and public prosecutor met in Ivan Egorovich Shebek's private room, where the conversation turned on the celebrated Krasovski case. Fedor Vasilievich warmly maintained that it was not subject to their jurisdiction, Ivan Egorovich maintained the contrary, while Peter Ivanovich, not having entered into the discussion at the start, took no part in it but looked through the Gazette which had just been handed in.

"Gentlemen," he said, "Ivan Ilych has died!"

"You don't say so!"

"Here, read it yourself," replied Peter Ivanovich, handing Fedor Vasilievich the paper still damp from the press. Surrounded by a black border were the words: "Praskovya Fedorovna Golovina, with profound sorrow, informs relatives and friends of the demise of her beloved husband Ivan Ilych Golovin, Member of the Court of Justice, which occurred on February the 4th of this year 1882. The funeral will take place on Friday at one o'clock in the afternoon."

Ivan Ilych had been a colleague of the gentlemen present and was liked by them all. He had been ill for some weeks with an illness said to be incurable. His post had been kept open for him, but there had been conjectures that in case of his death Alexeev might receive his appointment, and that either Vinnikov or Shtabel would succeed Alexeev. So on receiving the news of Ivan Ilych's death the first thought of each of the gentlemen in that private room was of the changes and promotions it might occasion among themselves or their acquaintances.

"I shall be sure to get Shtabel's place or Vinnikov's," thought Fedor Vasilievich. "I was promised that long ago, and the promotion means an extra eight hundred rubles a year for me besides the allowance."

"Now I must apply for my brother-in-law's transfer from Kaluga," thought Peter Ivanovich. "My wife will be very glad, and then she won't be able to say that I never do anything for her relations."

"I thought he would never leave his bed again," said Peter Ivanovich aloud. "It's very sad."

"But what really was the matter with him?"

"The doctors couldn't say—at least they could, but each of them said something different. When last I saw him I thought he was getting better."

"And I haven't been to see him since the holidays. I always meant to

go."

"Had he any property?"

"I think his wife had a little—but something quiet trifling."

"We shall have to go to see her, but they live so terribly far away."

"Far away from you, you mean. Everything's far away from your place."

"You see, he never can forgive my living on the other side of the river," said Peter Ivanovich, smiling at Shebek. Then, still talking of the distances between different parts of the city, they returned to the Court.

Besides considerations as to the possible transfers and promotions likely to result from Ivan Ilych's death, the mere fact of the death of a near acquaintance aroused, as usual, in all who heard of it the complacent feeling that, "it is he who is dead and not I."

Each one thought or felt, "Well, he's dead but I'm alive!" But the more intimate of Ivan Ilych's acquaintances, his so-called friends, could not help thinking also that they would now have to fulfil the very tiresome demands of propriety by attending the funeral service and paying a visit of condolence to the widow.

Fedor Vasilievich and Peter Ivanovich had been his nearest acquaintances. Peter Ivanovich had studied law with Ivan Ilych and had considered himself to be under obligations to him.

Having told his wife at dinner-time of Ivan Ilych's death, and of his conjecture that it might be possible to get her brother transferred to their circuit, Peter Ivanovich sacrificed his usual nap, put on his evening clothes and drove to Ivan Ilych's house.

At the entrance stood a carriage and two cabs. Leaning against the wall in the hall downstairs near the cloakstand was a coffin-lid covered with cloth of gold, ornamented with gold cord and tassels, that had been polished up with metal powder. Two ladies in black were taking off their fur cloaks. Peter Ivanovich recognized one of them as Ivan Ilych's sister, but the other was a stranger to him. His colleague Schwartz was just coming downstairs, but on seeing Peter Ivanovich enter he stopped and winked at him, as if to say: "Ivan Ilych has made a mess of things—not like you and me."

Schwartz's face with his Piccadilly whiskers, and his slim figure in evening dress, had as usual an air of elegant solemnity which contrasted with the playfulness of his character and had a special piquancy here, or so it seemed to Peter Ivanovich.

Peter Ivanovich allowed the ladies to precede him and slowly followed them upstairs. Schwartz did not come down but remained where he was, and Peter Ivanovich understood that he wanted to arrange where they should play bridge that evening. The ladies went upstairs to the widow's room, and Schwartz with seriously compressed lips but a playful look in his eyes, indicated by a twist of his eyebrows the room to the right where the body lay.

Peter Ivanovich, like everyone else on such occasions, entered feeling uncertain what he would have to do. All he knew was that at such times it is always safe to cross oneself. But he was not quite sure whether one should make obeisances while doing so. He therefore adopted a middle course. On entering the room he began crossing himself and made a slight movement resembling a bow. At the same time, as far as the motion of his head and arm allowed, he surveyed the room. Two young men—apparently nephews, one of whom was a high-school pupil—were leaving the room, crossing themselves as they did so. An old woman was standing motionless, and a lady with strangely arched eyebrows was saying something to her in a whisper. A vigorous, resolute Church Reader, in a frock-coat, was reading something in a loud voice with an expression that precluded any contradiction. The butler's assistant, Gerasim, stepping lightly in front of Peter Ivanovich, was strewing something on the floor. Noticing this, Peter Ivanovich was immediately aware of a faint odour of a decomposing body.

The last time he had called on Ivan Ilych, Peter Ivanovich had seen Gerasim in the study. Ivan Ilych had been particularly fond of him and he was performing the duty of a sick nurse.

Peter Ivanovich continued to make the sign of the cross slightly inclining his head in an intermediate direction between the coffin, the Reader, and the icons on the table in a corner of the room. Afterwards, when it seemed to him that this movement of his arm in crossing himself had gone on too long, he stopped and began to look at the corpse.

The dead man lay, as dead men always lie, in a specially heavy way, his rigid limbs sunk in the soft cushions of the coffin, with the head forever bowed on the pillow. His yellow waxen brow with bald patches over his sunken temples was thrust up in the way peculiar to the dead, the protruding nose seeming to press on the upper lip. He was much changed and grown even thinner since Peter Ivanovich had last seen him, but, as is always the case with the dead, his face was handsomer and above all more dignified than when he was alive. The expression on the face said that what was necessary had been accomplished, and accomplished rightly. Besides this there was in that expression a reproach and a warning to the living. This warning seemed to Peter Ivanovich out of place, or at least not applicable to him. He felt a certain discomfort and so he hurriedly crossed himself once more and turned and went out of the door—too hurriedly and too regardless of propriety, as he himself was aware.

Schwartz was waiting for him in the adjoining room with legs spread wide apart and both hands toying with his top-hat behind his back. The mere sight of that playful, well-groomed, and elegant figure refreshed Peter Ivanovich. He felt that Schwartz was above all these happenings and would not surrender to any depressing influences. His very look said that this incident of a church service for Ivan Ilych could not be a sufficient reason for infringing the order of the session—in other words, that it would certainly not prevent his unwrapping a new pack of cards and shuffling them that evening while a footman placed fresh candles on the table: in fact, that there was no reason for supposing that this incident would hinder their spending the evening agreeably. Indeed he said this in a whisper as Peter Ivanovich passed him, proposing that they should meet for a game at Fedor Vasilievich's. But apparently Peter Ivanovich was not destined to play bridge that evening. Praskovya Fedorovna (a short, fat woman who despite all efforts to the contrary had continued to broaden steadily from her shoulders downwards and who had the same extraordinarily arched eyebrows as the lady who had been standing by the coffin), dressed all in black, her head covered with lace, came out of her own room with some other ladies, conducted them to the room where the dead body lay, and said: "The service will begin immediately. Please go in."

Schwartz, making an indefinite bow, stood still, evidently neither accepting nor declining this invitation. Praskovya Fedorovna recognizing Peter Ivanovich, sighed, went close up to him, took his hand, and said: "I know you were a true friend to Ivan Ilych . . ." and looked at him awaiting some suitable response. And Peter Ivanovich knew that, just as it had been the right thing to cross himself in

that room, so what he had to do here was to press her hand, sigh, and say, "Believe me . . ." So he did all this and as he did it felt that the desired result had been achieved: that both he and she were touched.

"Come with me. I want to speak to you before it begins," said the widow. "Give me your arm."

Peter Ivanovich gave her his arm and they went to the inner rooms, passing Schwartz who winked at Peter Ivanovich compassionately.

"That does for our bridge! Don't object if we find another player. Perhaps you can cut in when you do escape," said his playful look.

Peter Ivanovich sighed still more deeply and despondently, and Praskovya Fedorovna pressed his arm gratefully. When they reached the drawing-room, upholstered in pink cretonne and lighted by a dim lamp, they sat down at the table—she on a sofa and Peter Ivanovich on a low pouffe, the springs of which yielded spasmodically under his weight. Praskovya Fedorovna had been on the point of warning him to take another seat, but felt that such a warning was out of keeping with her present condition and so changed her mind. As he sat down on the pouffe Peter Ivanovich recalled how Ivan Ilych had arranged this room and had consulted him regarding this pink cretonne with green leaves. The whole room was full of furniture and knick-knacks, and on her way to the sofa the lace of the widow's black shawl caught on the edge of the table. Peter Ivanovich rose to detach it, and the springs of the pouffe, relieved of his weight, rose also and gave him a push. The widow began detaching her shawl herself, and Peter Ivanovich again sat down, suppressing the rebellious springs of the pouffe under him. But the widow had not quite freed herself and Peter Ivanovich got up again, and again the pouffe rebelled and even creaked. When this was all over she took out a clean cambric handkerchief and began to weep. The episode with the shawl and the struggle with the pouffe had cooled Peter Ivanovich's emotions and he sat there with a sullen look on his face. This awkward situation was interrupted by Sokolov, Ivan Ilych's butler, who came to report that the plot in the cemetery that Praskovya Fedorovna had chosen would cost two hundred rubles. She stopped weeping and, looking at Peter Ivanovich with the air of a victim, remarked in French that it was very hard for her. Peter Ivanovich made a silent gesture signifying his full conviction that it must indeed be so.

"Please smoke," she said in a magnanimous yet crushed voice, and turned to discuss with Sokolov the price of the plot for the grave.

Peter Ivanovich while lighting his cigarette heard her inquiring very circumstantially into the prices of different plots in the cemetery and finally decide which she would take. When that was done she gave instructions about engaging the choir. Sokolov then left the room.

"I look after everything myself," she told Peter Ivanovich, shifting the albums that lay on the table; and noticing that the table was endangered by his cigarette-ash, she immediately passed him an ash-tray, saying as she did so: "I consider it an affectation to say that my grief prevents my attending to practical affairs. On the contrary, if anything can—I won't say console me, but—distract me, it is seeing to everything concerning him." She again took out her handkerchief as if preparing to cry, but suddenly, as if mastering her feeling, she shook herself and began to speak calmly. "But there is something I want to talk to you about."

Peter Ivanovich bowed, keeping control of the springs of the pouffe, which immediately began quivering under him.

"He suffered terribly the last few days."

"Did he?" said Peter Ivanovich.

"Oh, terribly! He screamed unceasingly, not for minutes but for hours. For the last three days he screamed incessantly. It was unendurable. I cannot understand how I bore it; you could hear him three rooms off. Oh, what I have suffered!"

"Is it possible that he was conscious all that time?" asked Peter Ivanovich.

"Yes," she whispered. "To the last moment. He took leave of us a quarter of an hour before he died, and asked us to take Volodya away."

The thought of the suffering of this man he had known so intimately, first as a merry little boy, then as a schoolmate, and later as a grown-up colleague, suddenly struck Peter Ivanovich with horror, despite an unpleasant consciousness of his own and this woman's dissimulation. He again saw that brow, and that nose pressing down on the lip, and felt afraid for himself.

"Three days of frightful suffering and the death! Why, that might suddenly, at any time, happen to me," he thought, and for a moment felt terrified. But—he did not himself know how—the customary reflection at once occurred to him that this had happened to Ivan Ilych and not to him, and that it should not and could not happen to him, and that to think that it could would be yielding to depressing which he ought not to do, as Schwartz's expression plainly showed. After which reflection Peter Ivanovich felt reassured, and began to ask with interest about the details of Ivan Ilych's death, as though death was an accident natural to Ivan Ilych but certainly not to himself.

After many details of the really dreadful physical sufferings Ivan Ilych had endured (which details he learnt only from the effect those sufferings had produced on Praskovya Fedorovna's nerves) the widow apparently found it necessary to get to business.

"Oh, Peter Ivanovich, how hard it is! How terribly, terribly hard!" and she again began to weep.

Peter Ivanovich sighed and waited for her to finish blowing her nose. When she had done so he said, "Believe me . . ." and she again began talking and brought out what was evidently her chief concern with him—namely, to question him as to how she could obtain a grant of money from the government on the occasion of her husband's death. She made it appear that she was asking Peter Ivanovich's advice about her pension, but he soon saw that she already knew about that to the minutest detail, more even than he did himself. She knew how much could be got out of the government in consequence of her husband's death, but wanted to find out whether she could not possibly extract something more. Peter Ivanovich tried to think of some means of doing so, but after reflecting for a while and, out of propriety, condemning the government for its niggardliness, he said he thought that nothing more could be got. Then she sighed and evidently began to devise means of getting rid of her visitor. Noticing this, he put out his cigarette, rose, pressed her hand, and went out into the anteroom.

In the dining-room where the clock stood that Ivan Ilych had liked so much and had bought at an antique shop, Peter Ivanovich met a priest and a few acquaintances who had come to attend the service, and he recognized Ivan Ilych's daughter, a handsome young woman. She was in black and her slim figure appeared slimmer than ever. She had a gloomy, determined, almost angry expression, and bowed to Peter Ivanovich as though he were in some way to blame. Behind her, with the same offended look, stood a wealthy young man, an examining magistrate, whom Peter Ivanovich also knew and who was her fiance, as he had heard. He bowed mournfully to them and was about to pass into the death-chamber, when from under the stairs appeared the figure of Ivan Ilych's schoolboy son, who was extremely like his father. He seemed a little Ivan Ilych, such as Peter Ivanovich remembered when they studied law together. His tear-stained eyes had in them the look that is seen in the eyes of boys of thirteen or fourteen who are not pure-minded. When he saw Peter Ivanovich he scowled morosely and shamefacedly. Peter Ivanovich nodded to him and entered the death-chamber. The service began: candles, groans, incense, tears, and sobs. Peter Ivanovich stood looking gloomily down at his feet. He did not look once at the dead man, did not yield to any depressing influence, and was one of the first to leave the room. There was no one in the anteroom, but Gerasim darted out of the dead man's room, rummaged with his strong hands among the fur coats to find Peter Ivanovich's and helped him on with it.

"Well, friend Gerasim," said Peter Ivanovich, so as to say something. "It's a sad affair, isn't it?"

"It's God's will. We shall all come to it some day," said Gerasim, displaying his teeth—the even white teeth of a healthy peasant—and, like a man in the thick of urgent work, he briskly opened the front door, called the coachman, helped Peter Ivanovich into the sledge, and sprang back to the porch as if in readiness for what he had to do next.

Peter Ivanovich found the fresh air particularly pleasant after the smell of incense, the dead body, and carbolic acid.

"Where to sir?" asked the coachman.

"It's not too late even now....I'll call round on Fedor Vasilievich."

He accordingly drove there and found them just finishing the first rubber, so that it was quite convenient for him to cut in.

2

Ivan Ilych's life had been most simple and most ordinary and therefore most terrible.

He had been a member of the Court of Justice, and died at the age of forty-five. His father had been an official who after serving in various ministries and departments in Petersburg had made the sort of career which brings men to positions from which by reason of their long service they cannot be dismissed, though they are obviously unfit to hold any responsible position, and for whom therefore posts are specially created, which though fictitious carry salaries of from six to ten thousand rubles that are not fictitious, and in receipt of which they live on to a great age.

Such was the Privy Councillor and superfluous member of various superfluous institutions, Ilya Epimovich Golovin.

He had three sons, of whom Ivan Ilych was the second. The eldest son was following in his father's footsteps only in another department, and was already approaching that stage in the service at which a similar sinecure would be reached. The third son was a failure. He had ruined his prospects in a number of positions and was not serving in the railway department. His father and brothers, and still more their wives, not merely disliked meeting him, but avoided remembering his existence unless compelled to do so. His sister had married Baron Greff, a Petersburg official of her father's type. Ivan Ilych was *le phenix de la famille* as people said. He was neither as cold and formal as his elder brother nor as wild as the younger, but was a happy mean between them—an intelligent polished, lively and agreeable man. He had studied with his younger brother at the School of Law, but the latter had failed to complete the course and was expelled when he was in the fifth class. Ivan Ilych finished the course well. Even when he was at the School of Law he was just what he remained for the rest of his life: a capable, cheerful, good-natured, and sociable man, though strict in the fulfillment of what he considered to be his duty: and he considered his duty to be what was so considered by those in authority. Neither as a boy nor as a man was he a toady, but from early youth was by nature attracted to people of high station as a fly is drawn to the light, assimilating their ways and views of life and establishing friendly relations with them. All the enthusiasms of childhood and youth passed without leaving much trace on him; he succumbed to sensuality, to vanity, and latterly among the highest classes to liberalism, but always within limits which his instinct unfailingly indicated to him as correct.

At school he had done things which had formerly seemed to him very horrid and made him feel disgusted with himself when he did them; but when later on he saw that such actions were done by people of good position and that they did not regard them as wrong, he was able not exactly to regard them as right, but to forget about them entirely or not be at all troubled at remembering them.

Having graduated from the School of Law and qualified for the tenth rank of the civil service, and having received money from his father for his equipment, Ivan Ilych ordered himself clothes at Scharmer's, the fashionable tailor, hung a medallion inscribed respice finem on his watch-chain, took leave of his professor and the prince who was patron of the school, had a farewell dinner with his comrades at Donon's first-class restaurant, and with his new and fashionable portmanteau, linen, clothes, shaving and other toilet appliances, and a travelling rug, all purchased at the best shops, he set off for one of the provinces where through his father's influence, he had been attached to the governor as an official for special service.

In the province Ivan Ilych soon arranged as easy and agreeable a position for himself as he had had at the School of Law. He performed his official task, made his career, and at the same time amused himself pleasantly and decorously. Occasionally he paid official visits to country districts where he behaved with dignity both to his superiors and inferiors, and performed the duties entrusted to him, which related chiefly to the sectarians, with an exactness and incorruptible honesty of which he could not but feel proud.

In official matters, despite his youth and taste for frivolous gaiety, he was exceedingly reserved, punctilious, and even severe; but in society he was often amusing and witty, and always good-natured, correct in his manner, and bon enfant, as the governor and his wife—with whom he was like one of the family—used to say of him.

In the province he had an affair with a lady who made advances to the elegant young lawyer, and there was also a milliner; and there were carousals with aides-de-camp who visited the district, and after-supper visits to a certain outlying street of doubtful reputation; and there was too some obsequiousness to his chief and even to his chief's wife, but all this was done with such a tone of good breeding that no hard names could be applied to it. It all came under the heading of the French saying: "Il faut que jeunesse se passe." It was all done with clean hands, in clean linen, with French phrases, and above all among people of the best society and consequently with the approval of people of rank.

So Ivan Ilych served for five years and then came a change in his official life. The new and reformed judicial institutions were introduced, and new men were needed. Ivan Ilych became such a new man. He was offered the post of examining magistrate, and he accepted it though the post was in another province and obliged him to give up the connexions he had formed and to make new ones. His friends met to give him a send-off; they had a group photograph taken and presented him with a silver cigarette-case, and he set off to his new post.

As examining magistrate Ivan Ilych was just as comme il faut and decorous a man, inspiring general respect and capable of separating his official duties from his private life, as he had been when acting as an official on special service. His duties now as examining magistrate were fare more interesting and attractive than before. In his former position it had been pleasant to wear an undress uniform made by Scharmer, and to pass through the crowd of petitioners and officials who were timorously awaiting an audience with the governor, and who envied him as with free and easy gait he went straight into his chief's private room to have a cup of tea and a cigarette with him. But not many people had then been directly dependent on him—only police officials and the sectarians when he went on special missions—and he liked to treat them politely, almost as comrades, as if he were letting them feel that he who had the power to crush them was treating them in this simple, friendly way. There were then but few such people. But now, as an examining magistrate, Ivan Ilych felt that everyone without exception, even the most important and self-satisfied, was in his power, and that he need only write a few words on a sheet of paper with a certain heading, and this or that important, self-satisfied person would be brought before him in the role of an accused person or a witness, and if he did not choose to allow him to sit down, would have to stand before him and answer his questions. Ivan Ilych never abused his power; he tried on the contrary to soften its expression, but the consciousness of it and the possibility of softening its effect, supplied the chief interest and attraction of his office. In his work itself, especially in his examinations, he very soon acquired a method of eliminating all considerations irrelevant to the legal aspect of the case, and reducing even the most complicated case to a form in which it would be presented on paper only in its externals, completely excluding his personal opinion of the matter, while above all observing every prescribed formality. The work was new and Ivan Ilych was one of the first men to apply the new Code of 1864.

On taking up the post of examining magistrate in a new town, he made new acquaintances and connexions, placed himself on a new footing and assumed a somewhat different tone. He took up an attitude of rather dignified aloofness towards the provincial authorities, but picked out the best circle of legal gentlemen and wealthy gentry living in the town and assumed a tone of slight dissatisfaction with the government, of moderate liberalism, and of enlightened citizenship. At the same time, without at all altering the elegance of his toilet, he ceased shaving his chin and allowed his beard to grow as it pleased.

Ivan Ilych settled down very pleasantly in this new town. The society there, which inclined towards opposition to the governor was friendly, his salary was larger, and he began to play vint [a form of bridge], which he found added not a little to the pleasure of life, for he had a capacity for cards, played good-humouredly, and calculated rapidly and astutely, so that he usually won.

After living there for two years he met his future wife, Praskovya Fedorovna Mikhel, who was the most attractive, clever, and brilliant girl of the set in which he moved, and among other amusements and relaxations from his labours as examining magistrate, Ivan Ilych established light and playful relations with her.

While he had been an official on special service he had been accustomed to dance, but now as an examining magistrate it was exceptional for him to do so. If he danced now, he did it as if to show

that though he served under the reformed order of things, and had reached the fifth official rank, yet when it came to dancing he could do it better than most people. So at the end of an evening he sometimes danced with Praskovya Fedorovna, and it was chiefly during these dances that he captivated her. She fell in love with him. Ivan Ilych had at first no definite intention of marrying, but when the girl fell in love with him he said to himself: "Really, why shouldn't I marry?"

Praskovya Fedorovna came of a good family, was not bad looking, and had some little property. Ivan Ilych might have aspired to a more brilliant match, but even this was good. He had his salary, and she, he hoped, would have an equal income. She was well connected, and was a sweet, pretty, and thoroughly correct young woman. to say that Ivan Ilych married because he fell in love with Praskovya Fedorovna and found that she sympathized with his views of life would be as incorrect as to say that he married because his social circle approved of the match. He was swayed by both these considerations: the marriage gave him personal satisfaction, and at the same time it was considered the right thing by the most highly placed of his associates.

So Ivan Ilych got married.

The preparations for marriage and the beginning of married life, with its conjugal caresses, the new furniture, new crockery, and new linen, were very pleasant until his wife became pregnant—so that Ivan Ilych had begun to think that marriage would not impair the easy, agreeable, gay and always decorous character of his life, approved of by society and regarded by himself as natural, but would even improve it. But from the first months of his wife's pregnancy, something new, unpleasant, depressing, and unseemly, and from which there was no way of escape, unexpectedly showed itself.

His wife, without any reason—de gaiete de coeur as Ivan Ilych expressed it to himself—began to disturb the pleasure and propriety of their life. She began to be jealous without any cause, expected him to devote his whole attention to her, found fault with everything, and made coarse and ill-mannered scenes.

At first Ivan Ilych hoped to escape from the unpleasantness of this state of affairs by the same easy and decorous relation to life that had served him heretofore: he tried to ignore his wife's disagreeable moods, continued to live in his usual easy and pleasant way, invited friends to his house for a game of cards, and also tried going out to his club or spending his evenings with friends. But one day his wife began upbraiding him so vigorously, using such coarse words, and continued to abuse him every time he did not fulfil her demands, so resolutely and with such evident determination not to give way till he submitted—that is, till he stayed at home and was bored just as she was—that he became alarmed. He now realized that matrimony—at any rate with Praskovya Fedorovna—was not always conducive to the pleasures and amenities of life, but on the contrary often infringed both comfort and propriety, and that he must therefore entrench himself against such infringement. And Ivan Ilych began to seek for means of doing so. His official duties were the one thing that imposed upon Praskovya Fedorovna, and by means of his official work and the duties attached to it he began struggling with his wife to secure his own independence.

With the birth of their child, the attempts to feed it and the various failures in doing so, and with the real and imaginary illnesses of mother and child, in which Ivan Ilych's sympathy was demanded but about which he understood nothing, the need of securing for himself an existence outside his family life became still more imperative.

As his wife grew more irritable and exacting and Ivan Ilych transferred the center of gravity of his life more and more to his official work, so did he grow to like his work better and became more ambitious than before.

Very soon, within a year of his wedding, Ivan Ilych had realized that marriage, though it may add some comforts to life, is in fact a very intricate and difficult affair towards which in order to perform one's duty, that is, to lead a decorous life approved of by society, one must adopt a definite attitude just as towards one's official duties.

And Ivan Ilych evolved such an attitude towards married life. He only required of it those conveniences—dinner at home, housewife, and bed—which it could give him, and above all that propriety of external forms required by public opinion. For the rest he looked for lighthearted pleasure and propriety, and was very thankful when he found them, but if he met with antagonism and querulousness he at once retired into his separate fenced-off world of official duties, where he found satisfaction.

Ivan Ilych was esteemed a good official, and after three years was made Assistant Public Prosecutor. His new duties, their importance, the possibility of indicting and imprisoning anyone he chose, the publicity his speeches received, and the success he had in all these things, made his work still more attractive.

More children came. His wife became more and more querulous and ill-tempered, but the attitude Ivan Ilych had adopted towards his home life rendered him almost impervious to her grumbling.

After seven years' service in that town he was transferred to another province as Public Prosecutor. They moved, but were short of money and his wife did not like the place they moved to. Though the salary was higher the cost of living was greater, besides which two of their children died and family life became still more unpleasant for him.

Praskovya Fedorovna blamed her husband for every inconvenience they encountered in their new home. Most of the conversations between husband and wife, especially as to the children's education, led to topics which recalled former disputes, and these disputes were apt to flare up again at any moment. There remained only those rare periods of amorousness which still came to them at times but did not last long. These were islets at which they anchored for a while and then again set out upon that ocean of veiled hostility which showed itself in their aloofness from one another. This aloofness might have grieved Ivan Ilych had he considered that it ought not to exist, but he now regarded the position as normal, and even made it the goal at which he aimed in family life. His aim was to free himself more and more from those unpleasantness and to give them a semblance of harmlessness and propriety. He attained this by spending less and less time with his family, and when obliged to be at home he tried to safeguard his position by the presence of outsiders. The chief thing however was that he had his official duties. The whole interest of his life now centered in the official world and that interest absorbed him. The consciousness of his power, being able to ruin anybody he wished to ruin, the importance, even the external dignity of his entry into court, or meetings with his subordinates, his success with superiors and inferiors, and above all his masterly handling of cases, of which he was conscious—all this gave him pleasure and filled his life, together with chats with his colleagues, dinners, and bridge. So that on the whole Ivan Ilych's life continued to flow as he considered it should do—pleasantly and properly.

So things continued for another seven years. His eldest daughter was already sixteen, another child had died, and only one son was left, a schoolboy and a subject of dissension. Ivan Ilych wanted to put him in the School of Law, but to spite him Praskovya Fedorovna entered him at the High School. The daughter had been educated at home and had turned out well: the boy did not learn badly either.

3

So Ivan Ilych lived for seventeen years after his marriage. He was already a Public Prosecutor of long standing, and had declined several proposed transfers while awaiting a more desirable post, when an unanticipated and unpleasant occurrence quite upset the peaceful course of his life. He was expecting to be offered the post of presiding judge in a University town, but Happe somehow came to the front and obtained the appointment instead. Ivan Ilych became irritable, reproached Happe, and quarrelled both him and with his immediate superiors—who became colder to him and again passed him over when other appointments were made.

This was in 1880, the hardest year of Ivan Ilych's life. It was then that it became evident on the one hand that his salary was insufficient for them to live on, and on the other that he had been forgotten, and not only this, but that what was for him the greatest and most cruel injustice appeared to others a quite ordinary occurrence. Even his father did not consider it his duty to help him. Ivan Ilych felt himself abandoned by everyone, and that they regarded his position with a salary of 3,500 rubles as quite normal and even fortunate. He alone knew that with the consciousness of the injustices done him, with his wife's incessant nagging, and with the debts he had contracted by living beyond his means, his position was far from normal.

In order to save money that summer he obtained leave of absence and went with his wife to live in the country at her brother's place.

In the country, without his work, he experienced ennui for the first time in his life, and not only ennui but intolerable depression, and he decided that it was impossible to go on living like that, and that it was necessary to take energetic measures.

Having passed a sleepless night pacing up and down the veranda, he decided to go to Petersburg and bestir himself, in order to punish those who had failed to appreciate him and to get transferred to another ministry.

Next day, despite many protests from his wife and her brother, he started for Petersburg with the sole object of obtaining a post with a salary of five thousand rubles a year. He was no longer bent on any particular department, or tendency, or kind of activity. All he now wanted was an appointment to another post with a salary of five thousand rubles, either in the administration, in the banks, with the railways in one of the Empress Marya's Institutions, or even in the customs—but it had to carry with it a salary of five thousand rubles and be in a ministry other than that in which they had failed to appreciate him.

And this quest of Ivan Ilych's was crowned with remarkable and unexpected success. At Kursk an acquaintance of his, F. I. Ilyin, got into the first-class carriage, sat down beside Ivan Ilych, and told him of a telegram just received by the governor of Kursk announcing that a change was about to take place in the ministry: Peter Ivanovich was to be superseded by Ivan Semonovich.

The proposed change, apart from its significance for Russia, had a special significance for Ivan Ilych, because by bringing forward a new man, Peter Petrovich, and consequently his friend Zachar Ivanovich, it was highly favourable for Ivan Ilych, since Sachar Ivanovich was a friend and colleague of his.

In Moscow this news was confirmed, and on reaching Petersburg Ivan Ilych found Zachar Ivanovich and received a definite promise of an appointment in his former Department of Justice.

A week later he telegraphed to his wife: "Zachar in Miller's place. I shall receive appointment on presentation of report."

Thanks to this change of personnel, Ivan Ilych had unexpectedly obtained an appointment in his former ministry which placed him two states above his former colleagues besides giving him five thousand rubles salary and three thousand five hundred rubles for expenses connected with his removal. All his ill humour towards his former enemies and the whole department vanished, and Ivan Ilych was completely happy.

He returned to the country more cheerful and contented than he had been for a long time. Praskovya Fedorovna also cheered up and a truce was arranged between them. Ivan Ilych told of how he had been feted by everybody in Petersburg, how all those who had been his enemies were put to shame and now fawned on him, how envious they were of his appointment, and how much everybody in Petersburg had liked him.

Praskovya Fedorovna listened to all this and appeared to believe it. She did not contradict anything, but only made plans for their life in the town to which they were going. Ivan Ilych saw with delight that these plans were his plans, that he and his wife agreed, and that, after a stumble, his life was regaining its due and natural character of pleasant lightheartedness and decorum.

Ivan Ilych had come back for a short time only, for he had to take up his new duties on the 10th of September. Moreover, he needed time to settle into the new place, to move all his belongings from the province, and to buy and order many additional things: in a word, to make such arrangements as he had resolved on, which were almost exactly what Praskovya Fedorovna too had decided on.

Now that everything had happened so fortunately, and that he and his wife were at one in their aims and moreover saw so little of one another, they got on together better than they had done since the first years of marriage. Ivan Ilych had thought of taking his family away with him at once, but the insistence of his wife's brother and her sister-in-law, who had suddenly become particularly amiable and friendly to him and his family, induced him to depart alone.

So he departed, and the cheerful state of mind induced by his success and by the harmony between his wife and himself, the one intensifying the other, did not leave him. He found a delightful house, just the thing both he and his wife had dreamt of. Spacious, lofty reception rooms in the old style, a convenient and dignified study, rooms for his wife and daughter, a study for his son—it might have been specially built for them. Ivan Ilych himself superintended the arrangements, chose the wallpapers, supplemented the furniture (preferably with antiques which he considered particularly comme il faut), and supervised the upholstering. Everything progressed and progressed and approached the ideal he had set himself: even when things were only half completed they exceeded his expectations. He saw what a refined and elegant character, free from vulgarity, it would all have when it was ready. On falling asleep he pictured to himself how the reception room would look. Looking at the yet unfinished drawing room he could see the fireplace, the screen, the what-not, the little chairs dotted here and there, the dishes and plates on the walls, and the bronzes, as they would be when everything was in place. He was pleased by the thought of how his wife and daughter, who shared his taste n this matter, would be impressed by it. They were certainly not expecting as much. He had been particularly successful in finding, and buying cheaply, antiques which gave a particularly aristocratic character to the whole place. But in his letters he intentionally understated everything in order to be able to surprise them. All this so absorbed him that his new duties—though he liked his official work—interested him less than he had expected. Sometimes he even had moments of absent-mindedness during the court sessions and would consider whether he should have straight or curved cornices for his curtains. He was so interested in it all that he often did things himself, rearranging the furniture, or rehanging the curtains. Once when mounting a step-ladder to show the upholsterer, who did not understand, how he wanted the hangings draped, he mad a false step and slipped, but being a strong and agile man he clung on and only knocked his side against the knob of the window frame. The bruised place was painful but the pain soon passed, and he felt particularly bright and well just then. He wrote: "I feel fifteen years younger." He thought he would have everything ready by September, but it dragged on till mid-October. But the result was charming not only in his eyes but to everyone who saw it.

In reality it was just what is usually seen in the houses of people of moderate means who want to appear rich, and therefore succeed only in resembling others like themselves: there are damasks, dark wood, plants, rugs, and dull and polished bronzes—all the things people of a certain class have in order to resemble other people of that class. His house was so like the others that it would never have been noticed, but to him it all seemed to be quite exceptional. He was very happy when he met his family at the station and brought them to the newly furnished house all lit up, where a footman in a white tie opened the door into the hall decorated with plants, and when they went on into the drawing-room and the study uttering exclamations of delight. He conducted them everywhere, drank in their praises eagerly, and beamed with pleasure. At tea that evening, when Praskovya Fedorovna among others things asked him about his fall, he laughed, and showed them how he had gone flying and had frightened the upholsterer.

"It's a good thing I'm a bit of an athlete. Another man might have been killed, but I merely knocked myself, just here; it hurts when it's touched, but it's passing off already—it's only a bruise."

So they began living in their new home—in which, as always happens, when they got thoroughly settled in they found they were just one room short—and with the increased income, which as always was just a little (some five hundred rubles) too little, but it was all very nice.

Things went particularly well at first, before everything was finally arranged and while something had still to be done: this thing bought, that thing ordered, another thing moved, and something else adjusted. Though there were some disputes between husband and wife, they were both so well satisfied and had so much to do that it all passed off without any serious quarrels. When nothing was left to arrange it became rather dull and something seemed to be lacking, but they were then making acquaintances, forming habits, and life was growing fuller.

Ivan Ilych spent his mornings at the law court and came home to dinner, and at first he was generally in a good humour, though he occasionally became irritable just on account of his house. (Every spot on the tablecloth or the upholstery, and every broken window-blind string, irritated him. He had devoted so much trouble to arranging it all that every disturbance of it distressed him.) But on the whole his life ran its course as he believed life should do: easily, pleasantly, and decorously.

He got up at nine, drank his coffee, read the paper, and then put on his undress uniform and went to the law courts. there the harness in which he worked had already been stretched to fit him and he donned it without a hitch: petitioners, inquiries at the chancery, the chancery itself, and the sittings public and administrative. In all this the thing was to exclude everything fresh and vital, which always disturbs the regular course of official business, and to admit only official relations with people, and then only on official grounds. A man would come, for instance, wanting some information. Ivan Ilych, as one in whose sphere the matter did not lie, would have nothing to do with him: but if the man had some business with him in his official capacity, something that could be expressed on officially stamped paper, he would do everything, positively everything he could within the limits of such relations, and in doing so would maintain the semblance of friendly human relations, that is, would observe the courtesies of life. As soon as the official relations ended, so did everything else. Ivan Ilych possessed this capacity to separate his real life from the official side of affairs and not mix the two, in the highest degree, and by long practice and natural aptitude had brought it to such a pitch that sometimes, in the manner of a virtuoso, he would even allow himself to let the human and official relations mingle. He let himself do this just because he felt that he could at any time he chose resume the strictly official attitude again and drop the human relation. and he did it all easily, pleasantly, correctly, and even artistically. In the intervals between the sessions he smoked, drank tea, chatted a little about politics, a little about general topics, a little about cards, but most of all about official appointments. Tired, but with the feelings of a virtuoso—one of the first violins who has played his part in an orchestra with precision—he would return home to find that his wife and daughter had been out paying calls, or had a visitor, and that his son had been to school, had done his homework with his tutor, and was surely learning what is taught at High Schools. Everything was as it should be. After dinner, if they had no visitors, Ivan Ilych sometimes read a book that was being much discussed at the time, and in the evening settled down to work, that is, read official papers, compared the depositions of witnesses, and noted paragraphs of the Code applying to them. This was neither dull nor amusing. It was dull when he might have been playing bridge, but if no bridge was available it was at any rate better than doing nothing or sitting with his wife. Ivan Ilych's chief pleasure was giving little dinners to which he invited men and women of good social position, and just as his drawing-room resembled all other drawing-rooms so did his enjoyable little parties resemble all other such parties.

Once they even gave a dance. Ivan Ilych enjoyed it and everything went off well, except that it led to a violent quarrel with his wife about the cakes and sweets. Praskovya Fedorovna had made her own plans, but Ivan Ilych insisted on getting everything from an expensive confectioner and ordered too many cakes, and the quarrel occurred because some of those cakes were left over and the confectioner's bill came to forty-five rubles. It was a great and disagreeable quarrel. Praskovya Fedorovna called him "a fool and an imbecile," and he clutched at his head and made angry allusions to divorce.

But the dance itself had been enjoyable. The best people were there, and Ivan Ilych had danced with Princess Trufonova, a sister of the distinguished founder of the Society "Bear My Burden".

The pleasures connected with his work were pleasures of ambition; his social pleasures were those of vanity; but Ivan Ilych's greatest pleasure was playing bridge. He acknowledged that whatever disagreeable incident happened in his life, the pleasure that beamed like a ray of light above everything else was to sit down to bridge with goo players, not noisy partners, and of course to four-handed bridge (with five players it was annoying to have to stand out, though one pretended not to mind), to play a clever and serious game (when the cards allowed it) and then to have supper and drink a glass of wine. after a game of bridge, especially if he had won a little (to win a large sum was unpleasant), Ivan Ilych went to bed in a specially good humour.

So they lived. They formed a circle of acquaintances among the best people and were visited by people of importance and by young folk. In their views as to their acquaintances, husband, wife and daughter were entirely agreed, and tacitly and unanimously kept at arm's length and shook off the various shabby friends and relations who, with much show of affection, gushed into the drawing-room with its Japanese plates on the walls. Soon these shabby friends ceased to obtrude themselves and only the best people remained in the Golovins' set.

Young men made up to Lisa, and Petrishchev, an examining magistrate and Dmitri Ivanovich Petrishchev's son and sole heir, began to be so attentive to her that Ivan Ilych had already spoken to Praskovya Fedorovna about it, and considered whether they should not arrange a party for them, or get up some private theatricals.

So they lived, and all went well, without change, and life flowed pleasantly.

4

They were all in good health. It could not be called ill health if Ivan Ilych sometimes said that he had a queer taste in his mouth and felt some discomfort in his left side.

But this discomfort increased and, though not exactly painful, grew into a sense of pressure in his side accompanied by ill humour. And his irritability became worse and worse and began to mar the agreeable, easy, and correct life that had established itself in the Golovin family. Quarrels between husband and wife became more and more frequent, and soon the ease and amenity disappeared and even the decorum was barely maintained. Scenes again became frequent, and very few of those islets remained on which husband and wife could meet without an explosion. Praskovya Fedorovna now had good reason to say that her husband's temper was trying. With characteristic exaggeration she said he had always had a dreadful temper, and that it had needed all her good nature to put up with it for twenty years. It was true that now the quarrels were started by him. His bursts of temper always came just before dinner, often just as he began to eat his soup. Sometimes he noticed that a plate or dish was chipped, or the food was not right, or his son put his elbow on the table, or his daughter's hair was not done as he liked it, and for all this he blamed Praskovya Fedorovna. At first she retorted and said disagreeable things to him, but once or twice he fell into such a rage at the beginning of dinner that she realized it was due to some physical derangement brought on by taking food, and so she restrained herself and did not answer, but only hurried to get the dinner over. She regarded this self-restraint as highly praiseworthy. Having come to the conclusion that her husband had a dreadful temper and made her life miserable, she began to feel sorry for herself, and the more she pitied herself the more she hated her husband. She began to wish he would die; yet she did not want him to die because then his salary would cease. And this irritated her against him still more. She considered herself dreadfully unhappy just because not even his death could save her, and though she concealed her exasperation, that hidden exasperation of hers increased his irritation also.

After one scene in which Ivan Ilych had been particularly unfair and after which he had said in explanation that he certainly was irritable but that it was due to his not being well, she said that if he was ill it should be attended to, and insisted on his going to see a celebrated doctor.

He went. Everything took place as he had expected and as it always does. There was the usual waiting and the important air assumed by the doctor, with which he was so familiar (resembling that which he himself assumed in court), and the sounding and listening, and the questions which called for answers that were foregone conclusions and were evidently unnecessary, and the look of importance which implied that "if only you put yourself in our hands we will arrange everything–we know indubitably how it has to be done, always in the same way for everybody alike." It was all just as it was in the law courts. The doctor put on just the same air towards him as he himself put on towards an accused person.

The doctor said that so-and-so indicated that there was so-and-so inside the patient, but if the investigation of so-and-so did not confirm this, then he must assume that and that. If he assumed that and that, then . . . and so on. To Ivan Ilych only one question was important: was his case serious or not? But the doctor ignored that inappropriate question. From his point of view it was not the one under consideration, the real question was to decide between a floating kidney, chronic catarrh, or appendicitis. It was not a question the doctor solved brilliantly, as it seemed to Ivan Ilych, in favour of the appendix, with the reservation that should an examination of the urine give fresh indications the matter would be reconsidered. All this was just what Ivan Ilych had himself brilliantly accomplished a thousand times in

dealing with men on trial. The doctor summed up just as brilliantly, looking over his spectacles triumphantly and even gaily at the accused. From the doctor's summing up Ivan Ilych concluded that things were bad, but that for the doctor, and perhaps for everybody else, it was a matter of indifference, though for him it was bad. And this conclusion struck him painfully, arousing in him a great feeling of pity for himself and of bitterness towards the doctor's indifference to a matter of such importance.

He said nothing of this, but rose, placed the doctor's fee on the table, and remarked with a sigh: "We sick people probably often put inappropriate questions. But tell me, in general, is this complaint dangerous, or not?..."

The doctor looked at him sternly over his spectacles with one eye, as if to say: "Prisoner, if you will not keep to the questions put to you, I shall be obliged to have you removed from the court."

"I have already told you what I consider necessary and proper. The analysis may show something more." And the doctor bowed.

Ivan Ilych went out slowly, seated himself disconsolately in his sledge, and drove home. All the way home he was going over what the doctor had said, trying to translate those complicated, obscure, scientific phrases into plain language and find in them an answer to the question: "Is my condition bad? Is it very bad? Or is there as yet nothing much wrong?" And it seemed to him that the meaning of what the doctor had said was that it was very bad. Everything in the streets seemed depressing. The cabmen, the houses, the passers-by, and the shops, were dismal. His ache, this dull gnawing ache that never ceased for a moment, seemed to have acquired a new and more serious significance from the doctor's dubious remarks. Ivan Ilych now watched it with a new and oppressive feeling.

He reached home and began to tell his wife about it. She listened, but in the middle of his account his daughter came in with her hat on, ready to go out with her mother. She sat down reluctantly to listen to this tedious story, but could not stand it long, and her mother too did not hear him to the end.

"Well, I am very glad," she said. "Mind now to take your medicine regularly. Give me the prescription and I'll send Gerasim to the chemist's." And she went to get ready to go out.

While she was in the room Ivan Ilych had hardly taken time to breathe, but he sighed deeply when she left it.

"Well," he thought, "perhaps it isn't so bad after all."

He began taking his medicine and following the doctor's directions, which had been altered after the examination of the urine. but then it happened that there was a contradiction between the indications drawn from the examination of the urine and the symptoms that showed themselves. It turned out that what was happening differed from what the doctor had told him, and that he had either forgotten or blundered, or hidden something from him. He could not, however, be blamed for that, and Ivan Ilych still obeyed his orders implicitly and at first derived some comfort from doing so.

From the time of his visit to the doctor, Ivan Ilych's chief occupation was the exact fulfillment of the doctor's instructions regarding hygiene and the taking of medicine, and the observation of his pain and his excretions. His chief interest came to be people's ailments and people's health. When sickness, deaths, or recoveries were mentioned in his presence, especially when the illness resembled his own, he listened with agitation which he tried to hide, asked questions, and applied what he heard to his own case.

The pain did not grow less, but Ivan Ilych made efforts to force himself to think that he was better. And he could do this so long as nothing agitated him. But as soon as he had any unpleasantness with his wife, any lack of success in his official work, or held bad cards at bridge, he was at once acutely sensible of his disease. He had formerly borne such mischances, hoping soon to adjust what was wrong, to master it and attain success, or make a grand slam. But now every mischance upset him and plunged him into despair. He would say to himself: "there now, just as I was beginning to get better and the medicine had begun to take effect, comes this accursed misfortune, or unpleasantness...." And he was furious with the mishap, or with the people who were causing the unpleasantness and killing him, for he felt that this fury was killing him but he could not restrain it. One would have thought that it should have been clear to him that this exasperation with circumstances and people aggravated his illness, and

that he ought therefore to ignore unpleasant occurrences. But he drew the very opposite conclusion: he said that he needed peace, and he watched for everything that might disturb it and became irritable at the slightest infringement of it. His condition was rendered worse by the fact that he read medical books and consulted doctors. The progress of his disease was so gradual that he could deceive himself when comparing one day with another—the difference was so slight. But when he consulted the doctors it seemed to him that he was getting worse, and even very rapidly. Yet despite this he was continually consulting them.

That month he went to see another celebrity, who told him almost the same as the first had done but put his questions rather differently, and the interview with this celebrity only increased Ivan Ilych's doubts and fears. A friend of a friend of his, a very good doctor, diagnosed his illness again quite differently from the others, and though he predicted recovery, his questions and suppositions bewildered Ivan Ilych still more and increased his doubts. A homeopathist diagnosed the disease in yet another way, and prescribed medicine which Ivan Ilych took secretly for a week. But after a week, not feeling any improvement and having lost confidence both in the former doctor's treatment and in this one's, he became still more despondent. One day a lady acquaintance mentioned a cure effected by a wonder-working icon. Ivan Ilych caught himself listening attentively and beginning to believe that it had occurred. This incident alarmed him. "Has my mind really weakened to such an extent?" he asked himself. "Nonsense! It's all rubbish. I mustn't give way to nervous fears but having chosen a doctor must keep strictly to his treatment. That is what I will do. Now it's all settled. I won't think about it, but will follow the treatment seriously till summer, and then we shall see. From now there must be no more of this wavering!" this was easy to say but impossible to carry out. The pain in his side oppressed him and seemed to grow worse and more incessant, while the taste in his mouth grew stranger and stranger. It seemed to him that his breath had a disgusting smell, and he was conscious of a loss of appetite and strength. There was no deceiving himself: something terrible, new, and more important than anything before in his life, was taking place within him of which he alone was aware.

Those about him did not understand or would not understand it, but thought everything in the world was going on as usual. That tormented Ivan Ilych more than anything. He saw that his household, especially his wife and daughter who were in a perfect whirl of visiting, did not understand anything of it and were annoyed that he was so depressed and so exacting, as if he were to blame for it. Though they tried to disguise it he saw that he was an obstacle in their path, and that his wife had adopted a definite line in regard to his illness and kept to it regardless of anything he said or did. Her attitude was this: "You know," she would say to her friends, "Ivan Ilych can't do as other people do, and keep to the treatment prescribed for him. One day he'll take his drops and keep strictly to his diet and go to bed in good time, but the next day unless I watch him he'll suddenly forget his medicine, eat sturgeon—which is forbidden—and sit up playing cards till one o'clock in the morning."

"Oh, come, when was that?" Ivan Ilych would ask in vexation. "Only once at Peter Ivanovich's."

"And yesterday with shebek."

"Well, even if I hadn't stayed up, this pain would have kept me awake."

"Be that as it may you'll never get well like that, but will always make us wretched."

Praskovya Fedorovna's attitude to Ivan Ilych's illness, as she expressed it both to others and to him, was that it was his own fault and was another of the annoyances he caused her. Ivan ilych felt that this opinion escaped her involuntarily—but that did not make it easier for him.

At the law courts too, Ivan Ilych noticed, or thought he noticed, a strange attitude towards himself. It sometimes seemed to him that people were watching him inquisitively as a man whose place might soon be vacant. Then again, his friends would suddenly begin to chaff him in a friendly way about his low spirits, as if the awful, horrible, and unheard-of thing that was going on within him, incessantly gnawing at him and irresistibly drawing him away, was a very agreeable subject for jests. Schwartz in particular irritated him by his jocularity, vivacity, and savoir-faire, which reminded him of what he himself had been ten years ago.

Friends came to make up a set and they sat down to cards. They dealt, bending the new cards to soften them, and he sorted the diamonds in his hand and found he had seven. His partner said "No trumps" and supported him with two diamonds. What more could be wished for? It ought to be jolly and lively. They would make a grand slam. But suddenly Ivan Ilych was conscious of that gnawing pain, that taste in his mouth, and it seemed ridiculous that in such circumstances he should be pleased to make a grand slam.

He looked at his partner Mikhail Mikhaylovich, who rapped the table with his strong hand and instead of snatching up the tricks pushed the cards courteously and indulgently towards Ivan Ilych that he might have the pleasure of gathering them up without the trouble of stretching out his hand for them. "Does he think I am too weak to stretch out my arm?" thought Ivan Ilych, and forgetting what he was doing he over-trumped his partner, missing the grand slam by three tricks. And what was most awful of all was that he saw how upset Mikhail Mikhaylovich was about it but did not himself care. And it was dreadful to realize why he did not care.

They all saw that he was suffering, and said: "We can stop if you are tired. Take a rest." Lie down? No, he was not at all tired, and he finished the rubber. All were gloomy and silent. Ivan Ilych felt that he had diffused this gloom over them and could not dispel it. They had supper and went away, and Ivan Ilych was left alone with the consciousness that his life was poisoned and was poisoning the lives of others, and that this poison did not weaken but penetrated more and more deeply into his whole being.

With this consciousness, and with physical pain besides the terror, he must go to bed, often to lie awake the greater part of the night. Next morning he had to get up again, dress, go to the law courts, speak, and write; or if he did not go out, spend at home those twenty-four hours a day each of which was a torture. And he had to live thus all alone on the brink of an abyss, with no one who understood or pitied him.

5

So one month passed and then another. Just before the New Year his brother-in-law came to town and stayed at their house. Ivan Ilych was at the law courts and Praskovya Fedorovna had gone shopping. When Ivan Ilych came home and entered his study he found his brother-in-law there—a healthy, florid man—unpacking his portmanteau himself. He raised his head on hearing Ivan Ilych's footsteps and looked up at him for a moment without a word. That stare told Ivan Ilych everything. His brother-in-law opened his mouth to utter an exclamation of surprise but checked himself, and that action confirmed it all.

"I have changed, eh?"

"Yes, there is a change."

And after that, try as he would to get his brother-in-law to return to the subject of his looks, the latter would say nothing about it. Praskovya Fedorovna came home and her brother went out to her. Ivan Ilych locked to door and began to examine himself in the glass, first full face, then in profile. He took up a portrait of himself taken with his wife, and compared it with what he saw in the glass. The change in him was immense. Then he bared his arms to the elbow, looked at them, drew the sleeves down again, sat down on an ottoman, and grew blacker than night.

"No, no, this won't do!" he said to himself, and jumped up, went to the table, took up some law papers and began to read them, but could not continue. He unlocked the door and went into the reception-room. The door leading to the drawing-room was shut. He approached it on tiptoe and listened.

"No, you are exaggerating!" Praskovya Fedorovna was saying.

"Exaggerating! Don't you see it? Why, he's a dead man! Look at his eyes—there's no life in them. But what is it that is wrong with him?"

"No one knows. Nikolaevich [that was another doctor] said something, but I don't know what. And Seshchetitsky [this was the celebrated specialist] said quite the contrary . . ."

Ivan Ilych walked away, went to his own room, lay down, and began musing; "The kidney, a floating kidney." He recalled all the doctors had told him of how it detached itself and swayed about. And by an effort of imagination he tried to catch that kidney and arrest it and support it. So little was needed for this, it seemed to him. "No, I'll go to see Peter Ivanovich again." [That was the friend whose friend was a doctor.] He rang, ordered the carriage, and got ready to go.

"Where are you going, Jean?" asked his wife with a specially sad and exceptionally kind look.

This exceptionally kind look irritated him. He looked morosely at her.

"I must go to see Peter Ivanovich."

He went to see Peter Ivanovich, and together they went to see his friend, the doctor. He was in, and Ivan Ilych had a long talk with him.

Reviewing the anatomical and physiological details of what in the doctor's opinion was going on inside him, he understood it all.

There was something, a small thing, in the vermiform appendix. It might all come right. Only stimulate the energy of one organ and check the activity of another, then absorption would take place and everything would come right. He got home rather late for dinner, ate his dinner, and conversed cheerfully, but could not for a long time bring himself to go back to work in his room. At last, however, he went to his study and did what was necessary, but the consciousness that he had put something aside—an important, intimate matter which he would revert to when his work was done—never left him. When he had finished his work he remembered that this intimate matter was the thought of his vermiform appendix. But he did not give himself up to it, and went to the drawing-room for tea. There were callers there, including the examining magistrate who was a desirable match for his daughter, and they were conversing, playing the piano, and singing. Ivan Ilych, as Praskovya Fedorovna remarked, spent that evening more cheerfully than usual, but he never for a moment forgot that he had postponed the important matter of the appendix. At eleven o'clock he said goodnight and went to his bedroom. Since his illness he had slept alone in a small room next to his study. He undressed and took up a novel by Zola, but instead of reading it he fell into thought, and in his imagination that desired improvement in the vermiform appendix occurred. There was the absorption and evacuation and the re-establishment of normal activity. "Yes, that's it!" he said to himself. "One need only assist nature, that's all." He remembered his medicine, rose, took it, and lay down on his back watching for the beneficent action of the medicine and for it to lessen the pain. "I need only take it regularly and avoid all injurious influences. I am already feeling better, much better." He began touching his side: it was not painful to the touch. "There, I really don't feel it. It's much better already." He put out the light and turned on his side . . . "The appendix is getting better, absorption is occurring." Suddenly he felt the old, familiar, dull, gnawing pain, stubborn and serious. There was the same familiar loathsome taste in his mouth. His heart sank and he felt dazed. "My God! My God!" he muttered. "Again, again! And it will never cease." And suddenly the matter presented itself in a quite different aspect. "Vermiform appendix! Kidney!" he said to himself. "It's not a question of appendix or kidney, but of life and . . . death. Yes, life was there and now it is going, going and I cannot stop it. Yes. Why deceive myself? Isn't it obvious to everyone but me that I'm dying, and that it's only a question of weeks, days . . . it may happen this moment. There was light and now there is darkness. I was here and now I'm going there! Where?" A chill came over him, his breathing ceased, and he felt only the throbbing of his heart.

"When I am not, what will there be? There will be nothing. Then where shall I be when I am no more? Can this be dying? No, I don't want to!" He jumped up and tried to light the candle, felt for it with trembling hands, dropped candle and candlestick on the floor, and fell back on his pillow.

"What's the use? It makes no difference," he said to himself, staring with wide-open eyes into the darkness. "Death. Yes, death. And none of them knows or wishes to know it, and they have no pity for me. Now they are playing." (He heard through the door the distant sound of a song and its accompaniment.) "It's all the same to them, but they will die too! Fools! I first, and they later, but it will be the same for them. And now they are merry . . . the beasts!"

Anger choked him and he was agonizingly, unbearably miserable. "It is impossible that all men have been doomed to suffer this awful horror!" He raised himself.

"Something must be wrong. I must calm myself—must think it all over from the beginning." And he again began thinking. "Yes, the beginning of my illness: I knocked my side, but I was still quite well that day and the next. It hurt a little, then rather more. I saw the doctors, then followed despondency and anguish, more doctors, and I drew nearer to the abyss. My strength grew less and I kept coming near-er and nearer, and now I have wasted away and there is no light in my eyes. I think of the appendix—but this is death! I think of mending the appendix, and all the while here is death! Can it really be death?" Again terror seized him and he gasped for breath. He leant down and began feeling for the matches, pressing with his elbow on the stand beside the bed. It was in his way and hurt him, he grew furious with it, pressed on it still harder, and upset it. Breathless and in despair he fell on his back, expecting death to come immediately.

Meanwhile the visitors were leaving. Praskovya Fedorovna was seeing them off. She heard something fall and came in.

"What has happened?"

"Nothing. I knocked it over accidentally."

She went out and returned with a candle. He lay there panting heavily, like a man who has run a thousand yards, and stared upwards at her with a fixed look.

"What is it, Jean?"

"No . . . o . . . thing. I upset it." ("Why speak of it? She won't understand," he thought.)

And in truth she did not understand. She picked up the stand, lit his candle, and hurried away to see another visitor off. When she came back he still lay on his back, looking upwards.

"What is it? Do you feel worse?"

"Yes."

She shook her head and sat down.

"Do you know, Jean, I think we must ask Leshchetitsky to come and see you here."

This meant calling in the famous specialist, regardless of expense. He smiled malignantly and said "No." She remained a little longer and then went up to him and kissed his forehead.

While she was kissing him he hated her from the bottom of his soul and with difficulty refrained from pushing her away.

"Good night. Please God you'll sleep."

"Yes."

6

Ivan Ilych saw that he was dying, and he was in continual despair.

In the depth of his heart he knew he was dying, but not only was he not accustomed to the thought, he simply did not and could not grasp it.

The syllogism he had learnt from Kiesewetter's Logic: "Caius is a man, men are mortal, therefore Caius is mortal," had always seemed to him correct as applied to Caius, but certainly not as applied to himself. That Caius—man in the abstract—was mortal, was perfectly correct, but he was not Caius, not an abstract man, but a creature quite, quite separate from all others. He had been little Vanya, with a mamma and a papa, with Mitya and Volodya, with the toys, a coachman and a nurse, afterwards with Katenka and will all the joys, griefs, and delights of childhood, boyhood, and youth. What did Caius know of the smell of that striped leather ball Vanya had been so fond of? Had Caius kissed his mother's hand like that, and did the silk of her dress rustle so for Caius? Had he rioted like that at school when the pastry was bad? Had Caius been in love like that? Could Caius preside at a session as he did? "Caius really was mortal, and it was right for him to die; but for me, little Vanya, Ivan Ilych, with all my thoughts and emotions, it's altogether a different matter. It cannot be that I ought to die. That would be too terrible."

Such was his feeling.

"If I had to die like Caius I would have known it was so. An inner voice would have told me so, but there was nothing of the sort in me and I and all my friends felt that our case was quite different from that of Caius. and now here it is!" he said to himself. "It can't be. It's impossible! But here it is. How is this? How is one to understand it?"

He could not understand it, and tried to drive this false, incorrect, morbid thought away and to replace it by other proper and healthy thoughts. But that thought, and not the thought only but the reality itself, seemed to come and confront him.

And to replace that thought he called up a succession of others, hoping to find in them some support. He tried to get back into the former current of thoughts that had once screened the thought of death from him. But strange to say, all that had formerly shut off, hidden, and destroyed his consciousness of death, no longer had that effect. Ivan Ilych now spent most of his time in attempting to re-establish that old current. He would say to himself: "I will take up my duties again—after all I used to live by them." And banishing all doubts he would go to the law courts, enter into conversation with his colleagues, and sit carelessly as was his wont, scanning the crowd with a thoughtful look and leaning both his emaciated arms on the arms of his oak chair; bending over as usual to a colleague and drawing his papers nearer he would interchange whispers with him, and then suddenly raising his eyes and sitting erect would pronounce certain words and open the proceedings. But suddenly in the midst of those proceedings the pain in his side, regardless of the stage the proceedings had reached, would begin its own gnawing work. Ivan Ilych would turn his attention to it and try to drive the thought of it away, but without success. It would come and stand before him and look at him, and he would be petrified and the light would die out of his eyes, and he would again begin asking himself whether It alone was true. And his colleagues and subordinates would see with surprise and distress that he, the brilliant and subtle judge, was becoming confused and making mistakes. He would shake himself, try to pull himself together, manage somehow to bring the sitting to a close, and return home with the sorrowful consciousness that his judicial labours could not as formerly hide from him what he wanted them to hide, and could not deliver him from It. And what was worst of all was that It drew his attention to itself not in order to make him take some action but only that he should look at It, look it straight in the face: look at it and without doing anything, suffer inexpressibly.

And to save himself from this condition Ivan Ilych looked for consolations—new screens—and new screens were found and for a while seemed to save him, but then they immediately fell to pieces or rather became transparent, as if It penetrated them and nothing could veil It.

In these latter days he would go into the drawing-room he had arranged—that drawing-room where he had fallen and for the sake of which (how bitterly ridiculous it seemed) he had sacrificed his life—for he knew that his illness originated with that knock. He would enter and see that something had scratched the polished table. He would look for the cause of this and find that it was the bronze ornamentation of an album, that had got bent. He would take up the expensive album which he had lovingly arranged, and feel vexed with his daughter and her friends for their untidiness—for the album was torn here and there and some of the photographs turned upside down. He would put it carefully in order and bend the ornamentation back into position. Then it would occur to him to place all those things in another corner of the room, near the plants. He would call the footman, but his daughter or wife would come to help him. They would not agree, and his wife would contradict him, and he would dispute and grow angry. But that was all right, for then he did not think about It. It was invisible.

But then, when he was moving something himself, his wife would say: "Let the servants do it. You will hurt yourself again." And suddenly It would flash through the screen and he would see it. It was just a flash, and he hoped it would disappear, but he would involuntarily pay attention to his side. "It sits there as before, gnawing just the same!" And he could no longer forget It, but could distinctly see it looking at him from behind the flowers. "What is it all for?"

"It really is so! I lost my life over that curtain as I might have done when storming a fort. Is that possible? How terrible and how stupid. It can't be true! It can't, but it is."

He would go to his study, lie down, and again be alone with It: face to face with It. And nothing could be done with It except to look at it and shudder.

7

How it happened it is impossible to say because it came about step by step, unnoticed, but in the third month of Ivan Ilych's illness, his wife, his daughter, his son, his acquaintances, the doctors, the servants, and above all he himself, were aware that the whole interest he had for other people was whether he would soon vacate his place, and at last release the living from the discomfort caused by his presence and be himself released from his sufferings.

He slept less and less. He was given opium and hypodermic injections of morphine, but this did not relieve him. The dull depression he experienced in a somnolent condition at first gave him a little relief, but only as something new, afterwards it became as distressing as the pain itself or even more so.

Special foods were prepared for him by the doctors' orders, but all those foods became increasingly distasteful and disgusting to him.

For his excretions also special arrangements had to be made, and this was a torment to him every time—a torment from the uncleanliness, the unseemliness, and the smell, and from knowing that another had to take part in it.

But just through his most unpleasant matter, Ivan Ilych obtained comfort. Gerasim, the butler's young assistant, always came in to carry the things out. Gerasim was a clean, fresh peasant lad, grown stout on town food and always cheerful and bright. At first the sight of him, in his clean Russian peasant costume, engaged on that disgusting task embarrassed Ivan Ilych.

Once when he got up from the commode too weak to draw up his trousers, he dropped into a soft armchair and looked with horror at his bare, enfeebled thighs with the muscles so sharply marked on them.

Gerasim with a firm light tread, his heavy boots emitting a pleasant smell of tar and fresh winter air, came in wearing a clean Hessian apron, the sleeves of his print shirt tucked up over his strong bare young arms; and refraining from looking at his sick master out of consideration for his feelings, and restraining the joy of life that beamed from his face, he went up to the commode.

"Gerasim!" said Ivan Ilych in a weak voice.

"Gerasim started, evidently afraid he might have committed some blunder, and with a rapid movement turned his fresh, kind, simple young face which just showed the first downy signs of a beard."

"Yes, sir?"

"That must be very unpleasant for you. You must forgive me. I am helpless."

"Oh, why, sir," and Gerasim's eyes beamed and he showed his glistening white teeth, "what's a little trouble? It's a case of illness with you, sir."

And his deft strong hands did their accustomed task, and he went out of the room stepping lightly. Five minutes later he as lightly returned.

Ivan Ilych was still sitting in the same position in the armchair.

"Gerasim," he said when the latter had replaced the freshly-washed utensil. "Please come here and help me." Gerasim went up to him. "Lift me up. It is hard for me to get up, and I have sent Dmitri away."

Gerasim went up to him, grasped his master with

his strong arms deftly but gently, in the same way that he stepped—lifted him, supported him with one hand, and with the other drew up his trousers and would have set him down again, but Ivan Ilych asked to be led to the sofa. Gerasim, without an effort and without apparent pressure, led him, almost lifting him, to the sofa and placed him on it.

"Thank you. How easily and well you do it all!"

Gerasim smiled again and turned to leave the room. But Ivan Ilych felt his presence such a comfort that he did not want to let him go.

"One thing more, please move up that chair. No, the other one—under my feet. It is easier for me when my feet are raised."

Gerasim brought the chair, set it down gently in place, and raised Ivan Ilych's legs on it. It seemed to Ivan Ilych that he felt better while Gerasim was holding up his legs.

"It's better when my legs are higher," he said. "Place that cushion under them."

Gerasim did so. He again lifted the legs and placed them, and again Ivan Ilych felt better while Gerasim held his legs. When he set them down Ivan Ilych fancied he felt worse.

"Gerasim," he said. "Are you busy now?"

"Not at all, sir," said Gerasim, who had learnt from the townsfolk how to speak to gentlefolk.

"What have you still to do?"

"What have I to do? I've done everything except chopping the logs for tomorrow."

Then hold my legs up a bit higher, can you?"

"Of course I can. Why not?" and Gerasim raised his master's legs higher and Ivan Ilych thought that in that position he did not feel any pain at all.

"And how about the logs?"

"Don't trouble about that, sir. There's plenty of time."

Ivan Ilych told Gerasim to sit down and hold his legs, and began to talk to him. And strange to say it seemed to him that he felt better while Gerasim held his legs up.

After that Ivan Ilych would sometimes call Gerasim and get him to hold his legs on his shoulders, and he liked talking to him. Gerasim did it all easily, willingly, simply, and with a good nature that touched Ivan Ilych. Health, strength, and vitality in other people were offensive to him, but Gerasim's strength and vitality did not mortify but soothed him.

What tormented Ivan Ilych most was the deception, the lie, which for some reason they all accepted, that he was not dying but was simply ill, and the only need keep quiet and undergo a treatment and then something very good would result. He however knew that do what they would nothing would come of it, only still more agonizing suffering and death. This deception tortured him—their not wishing to admit what they all knew and what he knew, but wanting to lie to him concerning his terrible condition, and wishing and forcing him to participate in that lie. Those lies—lies enacted over him on the eve of his death and destined to degrade this awful, solemn act to the level of their visitings, their curtains, their sturgeon for dinner—were a terrible agony for Ivan Ilych. And strangely enough, many times when they were going through their antics over him he had been within a hairbreadth of calling out to them: "Stop lying! You know and I know that I am dying. Then at least stop lying about it!" But he had never had the spirit to do it. The awful, terrible act of his dying was, he could see, reduced by those about him to the level of a casual, unpleasant, and almost indecorous incident (as if someone entered a drawing room defusing an unpleasant odour) and this was done by that very decorum which he had served all his life long. He saw that no one felt for him, because no one even wished to grasp his position. Only Gerasim recognized it and pitied him. And so Ivan Ilych felt at ease only with him. He felt comforted when Gerasim supported his legs (sometimes all night long) and refused to go to bed, saying: "Don't you worry, Ivan Ilych. I'll get sleep enough later on," or when he suddenly became familiar and exclaimed: "If you weren't sick it would be another matter, but as it is, why should I grudge a little trouble?" Gerasim alone did not lie; everything showed that he alone understood the facts of the case and did not consider it necessary to disguise them, but simply felt sorry for his emaciated and enfeebled master. Once when Ivan Ilych was sending him away he even said straight out: "We shall all of us die, so why should I grudge a little trouble?"—expressing the fact that he did not think his work burdensome, because he was doing it for a dying man and hoped someone would do the same for him when his time came.

Apart from this lying, or because of it, what most tormented Ivan Ilych was that no one pitied him as he wished to be pitied. At certain moments after prolonged suffering he wished most of all (though he would have been ashamed to confess it) for someone to pity him as a sick child is pitied. He longed to be petted and comforted. he knew he was an important functionary, that he had a beard turning grey, and that therefore what he long for was impossible, but still he longed for it. and in Gerasim's attitude towards him there was something akin to what he wished for, and so that attitude comforted him. Ivan Ilych wanted to weep, wanted to be petted and cried over, and then his colleague Shebek would come, and instead of weeping and being petted, Ivan Ilych would assume a serious, severe, and profound air, and by force of habit would express his opinion on a decision of the Court of Cassation and would stubbornly insist on that view. This falsity around him and within him did more than anything else to poison his last days.

8

It was morning. He knew it was morning because Gerasim had gone, and Peter the footman had come and put out the candles, drawn back one of the curtains, and begun quietly to tidy up. Whether it was morning or evening, Friday or Sunday, made no difference, it was all just the same: the gnawing, unmitigated, agonizing pain, never ceasing for an instant, the consciousness of life inexorably waning but not yet extinguished, the approach of that ever dreaded and hateful Death which was the only reality, and always the same falsity. What were days, weeks, hours, in such a case?

"Will you have some tea, sir?"

"He wants things to be regular, and wishes the gentlefolk to drink tea in the morning," thought Ivan Ilych, and only said "No."

"Wouldn't you like to move onto the sofa, sir?"

"He wants to tidy up the room, and I'm in the way. I am uncleanliness and disorder," he thought, and said only:

"No, leave me alone."

The man went on bustling about. Ivan Ilych stretched out his hand. Peter came up, ready to help.

"What is it, sir?"

"My watch."

Peter took the watch which was close at hand and gave it to his master.

"Half-past eight. Are they up?"

"No sir, except Vladimir Ivanovich" (the son) "who has gone to school. Praskovya Fedorovna ordered me to wake her if you asked for her. Shall I do so?"

"No, there's no need to." "Perhaps I's better have some tea," he thought, and added aloud: "Yes, bring me some tea."

Peter went to the door, but Ivan Ilych dreaded being left alone. "How can I keep him here? Oh yes, my medicine." "Peter, give me my medicine." "Why not? Perhaps it may still do some good." He took a spoonful and swallowed it. "No, it won't help. It's all tomfoolery, all deception," he decided as soon as he became aware of the familiar, sickly, hopeless taste. "No, I can't believe in it any longer. But the pain, why this pain? If it would only cease just for a moment!" And he moaned. Peter turned towards him. "It's all right. Go and fetch me some tea."

Peter went out. Left alone Ivan Ilych groaned not so much with pain, terrible though that was, as from mental anguish. Always and for ever the same, always these endless days and nights. If only it would come quicker! If only what would come quicker? Death, darkness? . . . No, no! anything rather than death!

When Peter returned with the tea on a tray, Ivan Ilych stared at him for a time in perplexity, not realizing who and what he was. Peter was disconcerted by that look and his embarrassment brought Ivan Ilych to himself.

"Oh, tea! All right, put it down. Only help me to wash and put on a clean shirt."

And Ivan Ilych began to wash. With pauses for rest, he washed his hands and then his face, cleaned his teeth, brushed his hair, looked in the glass. He was terrified by what he saw, especially by the limp way in which his hair clung to his pallid forehead.

While his shirt was being changed he knew that he would be still more frightened at the sight of his body, so he avoided looking at it. Finally he was ready. He drew on a dressing-gown, wrapped himself in a plaid, and sat down in the armchair to take his tea. For a moment he felt refreshed, but as soon as he began to drink the tea he was again aware of the same taste, and the pain also returned. He finished it with an effort, and then lay down stretching out his legs, and dismissed Peter.

Always the same. Now a spark of hope flashes up, then a sea of despair rages, and always pain; always pain, always despair, and always the same. When alone he had a dreadful and distressing desire to call someone, but he knew beforehand that with others present it would be still worse. "Another dose of morphine—to lose consciousness. I will tell him, the doctor, that he must think of something else. It's impossible, impossible, to go on like this."

An hour and another pass like that. But now there is a ring at the door bell. Perhaps it's the doctor? It is. He comes in fresh, hearty, plump, and cheerful, with that look on his face that seems to say: "There now, you're in a panic about something, but we'll arrange it all for you directly!" The doctor knows this expression is out of place here, but he has put it on once for all and can't take it off—like a man who has put on a frock-coat in the morning to pay a round of calls.

The doctor rubs his hands vigorously and reassuringly.

"Brr! How cold it is! There's such a sharp frost; just let me warm myself!" he says, as if it were only a matter of waiting till he was warm, and then he would put everything right.

"Well now, how are you?"

Ivan Ilych feels that the doctor would like to say: "Well, how are our affairs?" but that even he feels that this would not do, and says instead: "What sort of a night have you had?"

Ivan Ilych looks at him as much as to say: "Are you really never ashamed of lying?" But the doctor does not wish to understand this question, and Ivan Ilych says: "Just as terrible as ever. The pain never leaves me and never subsides. If only something...."

"Yes, you sick people are always like that.... There, now I think I am warm enough. Even Praskovya Fedorovna, who is so particular, could find no fault with my temperature. Well, now I can say good-morning," and the doctor presses his patient's hand.Then dropping his former playfulness, he begins with a most serious face to examine the patient, feeling his pulse and taking his temperature, and then begins the sounding and auscultation.

Ivan Ilych knows quite well and definitely that all this is nonsense and pure deception, but when the doctor, getting down on his knee, leans over him, putting his ear first higher then lower, and performs various gymnastic movements over him with a significant expression on his face, Ivan Ilych submits to it all as he used to submit to the speeches of the lawyers, though he knew very well that they were all lying and why they were lying.

The doctor, kneeling on the sofa, is still sounding him when Praskovya Fedorovna's silk dress rustles at the door and she is heard scolding Peter for not having let her know of the doctor's arrival.

She comes in, kisses her husband, and at once proceeds to prove that she has been up a long time already, and only owing to a misunderstanding failed to be there when the doctor arrived.

Ivan Ilych looks at her, scans her all over, sets against her the whiteness and plumpness and cleanness of her hands and neck, the gloss of her hair, and the sparkle of her vivacious eyes. He hates her with his whole soul. And the thrill of hatred he feels for her makes him suffer from her touch.

Her attitude towards him and his diseases is still the same. Just as the doctor had adopted a certain relation to his patient which he could not abandon, so had she formed one towards him—that he was not doing something he ought to do and was himself to blame, and that she reproached him lovingly for this—and she could not now change that attitude.

"You see he doesn't listen to me and doesn't take his medicine at the proper time. And above all he lies in a position that is no doubt bad for him—with his legs up."

She described how he made Gerasim hold his legs up.

The doctor smiled with a contemptuous affability that said: "What's to be done? These sick people do have foolish fancies of that kind, but we must forgive them."

When the examination was over the doctor looked at his watch, and then Praskovya Fedorovna announced to Ivan Ilych that it was of course as he pleased, but she had sent today for a celebrated specialist who would examine him and have a consultation with Michael Danilovich (their regular doctor).

"Please don't raise any objections. I am doing

this for my own sake," she said ironically, letting it be felt that she was doing it all for his sake and only said this to leave him no right to refuse. He remained silent, knitting his brows. He felt that he was surrounded and involved in a mesh of falsity that it was hard to unravel anything.

Everything she did for him was entirely for her own sake, and she told him she was doing for herself what she actually was doing for herself, as if that was so incredible that he must understand the opposite.

At half-past eleven the celebrated specialist arrived. Again the sounding began and the significant conversations in his presence and in another room, about the kidneys and the appendix, and the questions and answers, with such an air of importance that again, instead of the real question of life and death which now alone confronted him, the question arose of the kidney and appendix which were not behaving as they ought to and would now be attached by Michael Danilovich and the specialist and forced to amend their ways.

The celebrated specialist took leave of him with a serious though not hopeless look, and in reply to the timid question Ivan Ilych, with eyes glistening with fear and hope, put to him as to whether there was a chance of recovery, said that he could not vouch for it but there was a possibility. The look of hope with which Ivan Ilych watched the doctor out was so pathetic that Praskovya Fedorovna, seeing it, even wept as she left the room to hand the doctor his fee.

The gleam of hope kindled by the doctor's encouragement did not last long. The same room, the same pictures, curtains, wall-paper, medicine bottles, were all there, and the same aching suffering body, and Ivan Ilych began to moan. They gave him a subcutaneous injection and he sank into oblivion.

It was twilight when he came to. They brought him his dinner and he swallowed some beef tea with difficulty, and then everything was the same again and night was coming on.

After dinner, at seven o'clock, Praskovya Fedorovna came into the room in evening dress, her full bosom pushed up by her corset, and with traces of powder on her face. She had reminded him in the morning that they were going to the theatre. Sarah Bernhardt was visiting the town and they had a box, which he had insisted on their taking. Now he had forgotten about it and her toilet offended him, but he concealed his vexation when he remembered that he had himself insisted on their securing a box and going because it would be an instructive and aesthetic pleasure for the children.

Praskovya Fedorovna came in, self-satisfied but yet with a rather guilty air. She sat down and asked how he was, but, as he saw, only for the sake of asking and not in order to learn about it, knowing that there was nothing to learn—and then went on to what she really wanted to say: that she would not on any account have gone but that the box had been taken and Helen and their daughter were going, as well as Petrishchev (the examining magistrate, their daughter's fiance) and that it was out of the question to let them go alone; but that she would have much preferred to sit with him for a while; and he must be sure to follow the doctor's orders while she was away.

"Oh, and Fedor Petrovich" (the fiance) "would like to come in. May he? And Lisa?"

"All right."

Their daughter came in in full evening dress, her fresh young flesh exposed (making a show of that very flesh which in his own case caused so much suffering), strong, healthy, evidently in love, and impatient with illness, suffering, and death, because they interfered with her happiness.

Fedor Petrovich came in too, in evening dress, his hair curled a la Capoul, a tight stiff collar round his long sinewy neck, an enormous white shirt-front and narrow black trousers tightly stretched over his strong thighs. He had one white glove tightly drawn on, and was holding his opera hat in his hand.

Following him the schoolboy crept in unnoticed, in a new uniform, poor little fellow, and wearing gloves. Terribly dark shadows showed under his eyes, the meaning of which Ivan Ilych knew well.

His son had always seemed pathetic to him, and now it was dreadful to see the boy's frightened look of pity. It seemed to Ivan Ilych that Vasya was the only one besides Gerasim who understood and pitied him.

They all sat down and again asked how he was. A silence followed. Lisa asked her mother about the opera glasses, and there was an altercation between mother and daughter as to who had taken them and where they had been put. This occasioned some unpleasantness.

Fedor Petrovich inquired of Ivan Ilych whether he had ever seen Sarah Bernhardt. Ivan Ilych did not at first catch the question, but then replied: "No, have you seen her before?"

"Yes, in Adrienne Lecouvreur."

Praskovya Fedorovna mentioned some roles in which Sarah Bernhardt was particularly good. Her daughter disagreed. Conversation sprang up as to the elegance and realism of her acting—the sort of conversation that is always repeated and is always the same.

In the midst of the conversation Fedor Petrovich glanced at Ivan Ilych and became silent. The others also looked at him and grew silent. Ivan Ilych was staring with glittering eyes straight before him, evidently indignant with them. This had to be rectified, but it was impossible to do so. The silence had to be broken, but for a time no one dared to break it and they all became afraid that the conventional deception would suddenly become obvious and the truth become plain to all. Lisa was the first to pluck up courage and break that silence, but by trying to hide what everybody was feeling, she betrayed it.

"Well, if we are going it's time to start," she said, looking at her watch, a present from her father, and with a faint and significant smile at Fedor Petrovich relating to something known only to them. She got up with a rustle of her dress.

They all rose, said good-night, and went away.

When they had gone it seemed to Ivan Ilych that he felt better; the falsity had gone with them. But the pain remained—that same pain and that same fear that made everything monotonously alike, nothing harder and nothing easier. Everything was worse.

Again minute followed minute and hour followed hour. Everything remained the same and there was no cessation. And the inevitable end of it all became more and more terrible.

"Yes, send Gerasim here," he replied to a question Peter asked.

9

His wife returned late at night. She came in on tiptoe, but he heard her, opened his eyes, and made haste to close them again. She wished to send Gerasim away and to sit with him herself, but he opened his eyes and said: "No, go away."

"Are you in great pain?"

"Always the same."

"Take some opium."

He agreed and took some. She went away.

Till about three in the morning he was in a state of stupefied misery. It seemed to him that he and his pain were being thrust into a narrow, deep black sack, but though they were pushed further and further in they could not be pushed to the bottom. And this, terrible enough in itself, was accompanied by suffering. He was frightened yet wanted to fall through the sack, he struggled but yet co-operated. And suddenly he broke through, fell, and regained consciousness. Gerasim was sitting at the foot of the bed dozing quietly and patiently, while he himself lay with his emaciated stockinged legs resting on Gerasim's shoulders; the same shaded candle was there and the same unceasing pain.

"Go away, Gerasim," he whispered.

"It's all right, sir. I'll stay a while."

"No. Go away."

He removed his legs from Gerasim's shoulders, turned sideways onto his arm, and felt sorry for himself. He only waited till Gerasim had gone into the next room and then restrained himself no longer but wept like a child. He wept on account of his helplessness, his terrible loneliness, the cruelty of man, the cruelty of God, and the absence of God.

"Why hast Thou done all this? Why hast Thou brought me here? Why, why dost Thou torment me so terribly?"

He did not expect an answer and yet wept because there was no answer and could be none. The pain again grew more acute, but he did not stir and did not call. He said to himself: "Go on! Strike me! But what is it for? What have I done to Thee? What is it for?"

Then he grew quiet and not only ceased weeping but even held his breath and became all attention. It was as though he were listening not to an audible voice but to the voice of his soul, to the current of thoughts arising within him.

"What is it you want?" was the first clear conception capable of expression in words, that he heard.

"What do you want? What do you want?" he repeated to himself.

"What do I want? To live and not to suffer," he answered.

And again he listened with such concentrated attention that even his pain did not distract him.

"To live? How?" asked his inner voice.

"Why, to live as I used to—well and pleasantly."

"As you lived before, well and pleasantly?" the voice repeated.

And in imagination he began to recall the best moments of his pleasant life. But strange to say none of those best moments of his pleasant life now seemed at all what they had then seemed—none of them except the first recollections of childhood. There, in childhood, there had been something really pleasant with which it would be possible to live if it could return. But the child who had experienced that happiness existed no longer, it was like a reminiscence of somebody else.

As soon as the period began which had produced the present Ivan Ilych, all that had then seemed joys now melted before his sight and turned into something trivial and often nasty.

And the further he departed from childhood and the nearer he came to the present the more worthless and doubtful were the joys. This began with the School of Law. A little that was really good was still found there—there was light-heartedness, friendship, and hope. But in the upper classes there had already been fewer of such good moments. Then during the first years of his official career, when he was in the service of the governor, some pleasant moments again occurred: they were the memories of love for a woman. Then all became confused and there was still less of what was good; later on again there was still less that was good, and the further he went the less there was. His marriage, a mere accident, then the disenchantment that followed it, his wife's bad breath and the sensuality and hypocrisy: then that deadly official life and those preoccupations about money, a year of it, and two, and ten, and twenty, and always the same thing. And the longer it lasted the more deadly it became. "It is as if I had been going downhill while I imagined I was going up. And that is really what it was. I was going up in public opinion, but to the same extent life was ebbing away from me. And now it is all done and there is only death."

Then what does it mean? Why? It can't be that life is so senseless and horrible. But if it really has been so horrible and senseless, why must I die and die in agony? There is something wrong!

"Maybe I did not live as I ought to have done," it suddenly occurred to him. "But how could that be, when I did everything properly?" he replied, and immediately dismissed from his mind this, the sole solution of all the riddles of life and death, as something quite impossible.

"Then what do you want now? To live? Live how? Live as you lived in the law courts when the usher proclaimed, 'The judge is coming! The judge is coming, the judge!'" he repeated to himself. "Here he is, the judge. But I am not guilty!" he exclaimed angrily. "What is it for?" And he ceased crying, but turning his face to the wall continued to ponder on the same question: Why, and for what purpose, is there all this horror? But however much he pondered he found no answer. And whenever the thought occurred to him, as it often did, that it all resulted from his not having lived as he ought to have done, he at once recalled the correctness of his whole life and dismissed so strange an idea.

10

Another fortnight passed. Ivan Ilych now no longer left his sofa. He would not lie in bed but lay on the sofa, facing the wall nearly all the time. He suffered ever the same unceasing agonies and in his loneliness pondered always on the same insoluble question: "What is this? Can it be that it is Death?" And the inner voice answered: "Yes, it is Death."

"Why these sufferings?" And the voice answered, "For no reason—they just are so." Beyond and besides this there was nothing.

From the very beginning of his illness, ever since he had first been to see the doctor, Ivan Ilych's life had been divided between two contrary and alternating moods: now it was despair and the expectation of this uncomprehended and terrible death, and now hope and an intently interested observation of the functioning of his organs. Now before his eyes there was only a kidney or an intestine that temporarily evaded its duty, and now only that incomprehensible and dreadful death from which it was impossible to escape.

These two states of mind had alternated from the very beginning of his illness, but the further it progressed the more doubtful and fantastic became the conception of the kidney, and the more real the sense of impending death.

He had but to call to mind what he had been three months before and what he was now, to call to mind with what regularity he had been going downhill, for every possibility of hope to be shattered.

Latterly during the loneliness in which he found himself as he lay facing the back of the sofa, a loneliness in the midst of a populous town and surrounded by numerous acquaintances and relations but that yet could not have been more complete anywhere—either at the bottom of the sea or under the earth—during that terrible loneliness Ivan ilych had lived only in memories of the past. Pictures of his past rose before him one after another. They always began with what was nearest in time and then went back to what was most remote—to his childhood—and rested there. If he thought of the stewed prunes that had been offered him that day, his mind went back to the raw shrivelled French plums of his childhood, their peculiar flavour and the flow of saliva when he sucked their stones, and along with the memory of that taste came a whole series of memories of those days: his nurse, his brother, and their toys. "No, I mustn't think of that. . . . It is too painful," Ivan Ilych said to himself, and brought himself back to the present—to the button on the back of the sofa and the creases in its morocco. "Morocco is expensive, but it does not wear well: there had been a quarrel about it. It was a different kind of quarrel and a different kind of morocco that time when we tore father's portfolio and were punished, and mamma brought us some tarts. . . ." And again his thoughts dwelt on his childhood, and again it was painful and he tried to banish them and fix his mind on something else.

Then again together with that chain of memories another series passed through his mind—of how his illness had progressed and grown worse. There also the further back he looked the more life there had been. There had been more of what was good in life and more of life itself. The two merged together. "Just as the pain went on getting worse and worse, so my life grew worse and worse," he thought. "There is one bright spot there at the back, at the be-ginning of life, and afterwards all becomes blacker and blacker and proceeds more and more rapidly—in inverse ration to the square of the distance from death," thought Ivan Ilych. And the example of a stone falling downwards with increasing velocity entered his mind. Life, a series of increasing sufferings, flies further and further towards its end—the most terrible suffering. "I am flying. . . ." He shuddered, shifted himself, and tried to resist, but was already aware that resistance was impossible, and again with eyes weary of gazing but unable to cease seeing what was before them, he stared at the back of the sofa and waited—awaiting that dreadful fall and shock and destruction.

"Resistance is impossible!" he said to himself. "If I could only understand what it is all for! But that too is impossible. An explanation would be possible if it could be said that I have not lived as I ought to. But it is impossible to say that," and he remembered all the legality, correctitude, and propriety of his life. "That at any rate can certainly not be admitted," he thought, and his lips smiled ironically as if someone could see that smile and be taken in by it. "There is no explanation! Agony, death....What for?"

11

Another two weeks went by in this way and during that fortnight an even occurred that Ivan Ilych and his wife had desired. Petrishchev formally proposed. It happened in the evening. The next day Praskovya Fedorovna came into her husband's room considering how best to inform him of it, but that very night there had been a fresh change for the worse in his condition. She found him still lying on the sofa but in a different position. He lay on his back, groaning and staring fixedly straight in front of him.

She began to remind him of his medicines, but he turned his eyes towards her with such a look that she did not finish what she was saying; so great an animosity, to her in particular, did that look express.

"For Christ's sake let me die in peace!" he said.

She would have gone away, but just then their daughter came in and went up to say good morning. He looked at her as he had done at his wife, and in reply to her inquiry about his health said dryly that he would soon free them all of himself. They were both silent and after sitting with him for a while went away.

"Is it our fault?" Lisa said to her mother. "It's as if we were to blame! I am sorry for papa, but why should we be tortured?"

The doctor came at his usual time. Ivan Ilych answered "Yes" and "No," never taking his angry eyes from him, and at last said: "You know you can do nothing for me, so leave me alone."

"We can ease your sufferings."

"You can't even do that. Let me be."

The doctor went into the drawing room and told Praskovya Fedorovna that the case was very serious and that the only resource left was opium to allay her husband's sufferings, which must be terrible.

It was true, as the doctor said, that Ivan Ilych's physical sufferings were terrible, but worse than the physical sufferings were his mental sufferings which were his chief torture.

His mental sufferings were due to the fact that that night, as he looked at Gerasim's sleepy, good-natured face with it prominent cheek-bones, the question suddenly occurred to him: "What if my whole life has been wrong?"

It occurred to him that what had appeared perfectly impossible before, namely that he had not spent his life as he should have done, might after all be true. It occurred to him that his scarcely perceptible attempts to struggle against what was considered good by the most highly placed people, those scarcely noticeable impulses which he had immediately suppressed, might have been the real thing, and all the rest false. And his professional duties and the whole arrangement of his life and of his family, and all his social and official interests, might all have been false. He tried to defend all those things to himself and suddenly felt the weakness of what he was defending. There was nothing to defend.

"But if that is so," he said to himself, "and I am leaving this life with the consciousness that I have lost all that was given me and it is impossible to rectify it—what then?"

He lay on his back and began to pass his life in review in quite a new way. In the morning when he saw first his footman, then his wife, then his daughter, and then the doctor, their every word and movement confirmed to him the awful truth that had been revealed to him during the night. In them he saw himself—all that for which he had lived—and saw clearly that it was not real at all, but a terrible and huge deception which had hidden both life and death. This consciousness intensified his physical suffering tenfold. He groaned and tossed about, and pulled at his clothing which choked and stifled him. And he hated them on that account.

He was given a large dose of opium and became unconscious, but at noon his sufferings began again. He drove everybody away and tossed from side to side.

His wife came to him and said:

"Jean, my dear, do this for me. It can't do any harm and often helps. Healthy people often do it."

He opened his eyes wide.

"What? Take communion? Why? It's unnecessary! However..."

She began to cry.

"Yes, do, my dear. I'll send for our priest. He is such a nice man."

"All right. Very well," he muttered.

When the priest came and heard his confession, Ivan Ilych was softened and seemed to feel a relief from his doubts and consequently from his sufferings, and for a moment there came a ray of hope. He again began to think of the vermiform appendix and the possibility of correcting it. He received the sacrament with tears in his eyes.

When they laid him down again afterwards he felt a moment's ease, and the hope that he might live awoke in him again. He began to think of the operation that had been suggested to him. "To live! I want to live!" he said to himself.

His wife came in to congratulate him after his communion, and when uttering the usual conventional words she added:

"You feel better, don't you?"

Without looking at her he said "Yes."

Her dress, her figure, the expression of her face, the tone of her voice, all revealed the same thing. "This is wrong, it is not as it should be. All you have lived for and still live for is falsehood and deception, hiding life and death from you." And as soon as he admitted that thought, his hatred and his agonizing physical suffering again sprang up, and with that suffering a consciousness of the unavoidable, approaching end. And to this was added a new sensation of grinding shooting pain and a feeling of suffocation.

The expression of his face when he uttered that "Yes" was dreadful. Having uttered it, he looked her straight in the eyes, turned on his face with a rapidity extraordinary in his weak state and shouted:

"Go away! Go away and leave me alone!"

12

From that moment the screaming began that continued for three days, and was so terrible that one could not hear it through two closed doors without horror. At the moment he answered his wife realized that he was lost, that there was no return, that the end had come, the very end, and his doubts were still unsolved and remained doubts.

"Oh! Oh! Oh!" he cried in various intonations. he had begun by screaming "I won't!" and continued screaming on the letter "O".

For three whole days, during which time did not exist for him, he struggled in that black sack into which he was being thrust by an invisible, resistless force. He struggled as a man condemned to death struggles in the hands of the executioner, knowing that he cannot save himself. And every moment he felt that despite all his efforts he was drawing nearer and nearer to what terrified him. He felt that his agony was due to his being thrust into that black hole and still more to his not being able to get right into it. He was hindered from getting into it by his conviction that his life had been a good one. That very justification of his life held him fast and prevented his moving forward, and it caused him most torment of all.

Suddenly some force struck him in the chest and side, making it still harder to breathe, and he fell through the hole and there at the bottom was a light. What had happened to him was like the sensation one sometimes experiences in a railway carriage when one thinks one is going backwards while one is really going forwards and suddenly becomes aware of the real direction.

"Yes, it was not the right thing," he said to himself, "but that's no matter. It can be done. But what is the right thing?" he asked himself, and suddenly grew quiet.

This occurred at the end of the third day, two hours before his death. Just then his schoolboy son had crept softly in and gone up to the bedside. The dying man was still screaming desperately and waving his arms. His hand fell on the boy's head, and the boy caught it, pressed it to his lips, and began to cry.

At that very moment Ivan Ilych fell through and caught sight of the light, and it was revealed to him that though his life had not been what it should have been, this could still be rectified. He asked himself, "What is the right thing?" and grew still, listening. Then he felt that someone was kissing his hand. He opened his eyes, looked at his son, and felt sorry for him. His wife came up to him and he glanced at her. She was gazing at him open-mouthed, with undried tears on her nose and cheek and a despairing look on her face. He felt sorry for her too.

"Yes, I am making them wretched," he thought. "They are sorry, but it will be better for them when I die." He wished to say this but had not the strength to utter it. "Besides, why speak? I must act," he thought. with a look at his wife he indicated his son and said: "Take him away. . . sorry for him . . . sorry for you too. . . ." He tried to add, "Forgive me," but said "Forego" and waved his hand, knowing that He whose understanding mattered would understand.

And suddenly it grew clear to him that what had been oppressing him and would not leave him was all dropping away at once from two sides, from ten sides, and from all sides. He was sorry for them, he must act so as not to hurt them: release them and free himself from these sufferings. "How good and how simple!" he thought. "And the pain?" he asked himself. "What has become of it? Where are you, pain?"

He turned his attention to it.

"Yes, here it is. Well, what of it? Let the pain be."

"And death...where is it?"

He sought his former accustomed fear of death and did not find it. "Where is it? What death?" There was no fear because there was no death.

In place of death there was light.

"So that's what it is!" he suddenly exclaimed aloud. "What joy!"

To him all this happened in a single instant, and the meaning of that instant did not change. For those present his agony continued for another two hours. Something rattled in his throat, his emaciated body twitched, then the gasping and rattle became less and less frequent.

"It is finished!" said someone near him.

He heard these words and repeated them in his soul.

"Death is finished," he said to himself. "It is no more!"

He drew in a breath, stopped in the midst of a sigh, stretched out, and died.

Leo Tolstoy. *The Death of Ivan Ilych*. Trans. Louise and Aylmer Maude, 1886.

THUS SPOKE ZARATHUSTRA

FRIEDRICH NIETZSCHE (1844-1900)

*Friedrich Nietzsche is often considered the "bad boy" of modern philosophy for his rejection of organized religion, popular morality, and his radical ideas concerning the "superman" (*Übermensch*) and the "will to power." Because his philosophy was twisted by the Nazis to justify their expansionistic wars and extermination of the Jews, Nietzsche's reputation suffered in the years following the Second World War. In more recent years, however, Nietzsche has begun to be recognized as a groundbreaking and visionary philosopher—one of the first existentialist and post-modern thinkers in philosophy. In* Thus Spoke Zarathustra, *from which a selection has been included below, Nietzsche invents the character of Zarathustra, a prophet, who announces the death of God and the coming of the superman—a being who represents the final evolution of mankind.*

ZARATHUSTRA'S PROLOGUE

1

When Zarathustra was thirty years old, he left his home and the lake of his home, and went into the mountains. There he enjoyed his spirit and solitude, and for ten years did not weary of it. But at last his heart changed,—and rising one morning with the rosy dawn, he went before the sun, and spoke thus to it:

You great star! What would be your happiness if you had not those for whom thou shine?

For ten years you have climbed into my cave: you would have wearied of your light and of the journey, had it not been for me, my eagle, and my serpent.

But we awaited you every morning, took from you your overflow and blessed you for it.

Behold! I am weary of my wisdom, like the bee that has gathered too much honey; I need hands out-stretched to take it.

I would bestow and distribute, until the wise have once more become joyous in their folly, and the poor happy in their riches.

Therefore must I descend into the deep: as you do in the evening, when you go behind the sea, and

give light also to the underworld, you exuberant star!

Like you I must *go down*, as men say, to whom I shall descend.

Bless me, then, you tranquil eye, that can behold even the greatest happiness without envy!

Bless the cup that is about to overflow, that the water may flow golden out of it, and carry every-where the reflection of your bliss!

Behold! This cup is again going to empty itself, and Zarathustra is again going to be a man. "

Thus began Zarathustra's down-going.

2

Zarathustra went down the mountain alone, no one meeting him. When he entered the forest, however, there suddenly stood before him an old man, who had left his holy cot to seek roots. And thus spoke the old man to Zarathustra:

"No stranger to me is this wanderer: many years ago passed he by. Zarathustra he was called; but he has altered.

Then you carried your ashes into the mountains: will you now carry your fire into the valleys? Don't you fear the incendiary's doom?

Yes, I recognise Zarathustra. Pure is his eye, and no loathing lurks about his mouth. Does he not walk along like a dancer?

Zarathustra is changed; a child has Zarathustra become; an awakened one is Zarathustra: what will you do in the land of the sleepers?

As in the sea have you lived in solitude, and it has carried you up. Alas, will you now go ashore? Alas, will you again drag your own body"

Zarathustra answered: "I love mankind."

"Why," said the saint, "did I go into the forest and the desert? Was it not because I loved men far too well?

Now I love God: men, I do not love. Man is a thing too imperfect for me. Love to man would be fatal to me."

Zarathustra answered: "Did I speak of love! I am bringing gifts to men."

"Give them nothing," said the saint. "Take rather part of their load, and carry it along with them—that will be most agreeable unto them: if only it be agreeable to you!

If, however, you will give anything to them, give them no more than alms, and let them also beg for it!"

"No," replied Zarathustra, "I give no alms. I am not poor enough for that."

The saint laughed at Zarathustra, and spoke thus: "Then see to it that they accept your treasures! They are distrustful of hermits, and do not believe that we come with gifts.

The fall of our footsteps rings too hollow through their streets. And just as at night, when they are in bed and hear a man abroad long before sunrise, so they ask themselves concerning us: Where does the thief go?

Go not to men, but stay in the forest! Go rather to the animals! Why not be like me—a bear amongst bears, a bird amongst birds?"

"And what does the saint do in the forest?" asked Zarathustra.

The saint answered: "I make hymns and sing them; and in making hymns I laugh and weep and mumble: thus do I praise God.

With singing, weeping, laughing, and mumbling do I praise the God who is my God. But what do you bring us as a gift?"

When Zarathustra had heard these words, he bowed to the saint and said: "What should I have to give you! Let me rather hurry away lest I take something away from you!"—And thus they parted from one another, the old man and Zarathustra, laughing like schoolboys.

When Zarathustra was alone, however, he said to his heart: "Could it be possible! This old saint in the forest has not yet heard of it, that *God is dead*!"

3

When Zarathustra arrived at the nearest town which adjoineth the forest, he found many people assembled in the market-place; for it had been announced that a rope-dancer would give a performance. And Zarathustra spoke thus unto the people:

I teach you the Superman. Man is something that is to be surpassed. What have you done to surpass man?

All beings so far have created something beyond themselves: and you want to be the ebb of that great tide, and would rather go back to the beast than surpass man?

What is the ape to man? A laughing-stock, a thing of shame. And just the same shall man be to the Superman: a laughing-stock, a thing of shame.

You have made your way from the worm to man, and much within you is still worm. Once were you apes, and even yet man is more of an ape than any of the apes.

Even the wisest among you is only a disharmony and hybrid of plant and phantom. But do I bid you become phantoms or plants?

Behold, I teach you the Superman!

The Superman is the meaning of the earth. Let your will say: The Superman *shall be* the meaning of the earth!

I conjure you, my brethren, *remain true to the earth*, and believe not those who speak to you of superearthly hopes! Poisoners are they, whether they know it or not.

Despisers of life are they, decaying ones and poisoned ones themselves, of whom the earth is weary: so away with them!

Once blasphemy against God was the greatest blasphemy; but God died, and with him also died those blasphemers. To blaspheme the earth is now the most dreadful sin, and to rate the heart of the unknowable higher than the meaning of the earth!

Once the soul looked contemptuously on the body, and then that contempt was the supreme thing:—the soul wished the body meagre, ghastly, and famished. Thus it thought to escape from the body and the earth.

Oh, that soul was itself meagre, ghastly, and famished; and cruelty was the delight of that soul!

But you, also, my brothers, tell me: What does your body say about your soul? Is your soul not poverty and pollution and wretched self-complacency?

Truly, a polluted stream is man. One must be a sea, to receive a polluted stream without becoming impure.

Behold, I teach you the Superman: he is that sea; in him can your great contempt be submerged.

What is the greatest thing you can experience? It is the hour of great contempt. The hour in which even your happiness becomes loathsome unto you, and so also your reason and virtue.

The hour when you say: "What good is my happiness! It is poverty and pollution and wretched self-complacency. But my happiness should justify existence itself!"

The hour when you say: "What good is my reason! Does it long for knowledge as the lion for his food? It is poverty and pollution and wretched self-complacency!"

The hour when you say: "What good is my virtue! As yet it hath not made me passionate. How weary I am of my good and my bad! It is all poverty and pollution and wretched self-complacency!"

The hour when you say: "What good is my justice! I do not see that I am fervour and fuel. The just, however, are fervour and fuel!"

The hour when you say: "What good is my pity! Is not pity the cross on which he is nailed who loveth man? But my pity is not a crucifixion."

Have ye ever spoken thus? Have you ever cried thus? Ah! would that I had heard you crying thus!

It is not your sin—it is your self-satisfaction that cries to heaven; your very sparingness in sin cries to heaven!

Where is the lightning to lick you with its tongue? Where is the frenzy with which you should be inoculated?

Behold, I teach you the Superman: he is that lightning, he is that frenzy!—

When Zarathustra had thus spoken, one of the people called out: "We have now heard enough of the rope-dancer; it is time now for us to see him!" And all the people laughed at Zarathustra. But the rope-dancer, who thought the words applied to him, began his performance.

4

Zarathustra, however, looked at the people and wondered. Then he spoke thus:

Man is a rope stretched between the animal and the Superman—a rope over an abyss.

A dangerous crossing, a dangerous wayfaring, a dangerous looking-back, a dangerous trembling and halting.

What is great in man is that he is a bridge and not a goal: what is lovable in man is that he is an *over-going* and a *down-going*.

I love those that know not how to live except as down-goers, for they are the over-goers.

I love the great despisers, because they are the great adorers, and arrows of longing for the other shore.

I love those who do not first seek a reason beyond the stars for going down and being sacrifices, but sacrifice themselves to the earth, that the earth of the Superman may hereafter arrive.

I love him who lives in order to know, and seeks to know in order that the Superman may hereafter live. Thus he seeks his own down-going.

I love him who labours and invents, that he may build the house for the Superman, and prepare for him earth, animal, and plant: for thus he seeks his own down-going.

I love him who loves his virtue: for virtue is the will to down-going, and an arrow of longing.

I love him who reserves no share of spirit for himself, but wants to be wholly the spirit of his virtue: thus he walks as spirit over the bridge.

I love him who makes his virtue his inclination and destiny: thus, for the sake of his virtue, he is willing to live on, or live no more.

I love him who desires not too many virtues. One virtue is more of a virtue than two, because it is more of a knot for one's destiny to cling to.

I love him whose soul is lavish, who wants no thanks and doth not give back: for he always bestowes, and desires not to keep for himself.

I love him who is ashamed when the dice fall in his favour, and who then asks: "Am I a dishonest player?"—for he is willing to succumb.

I love him who scatters golden words in advance of his deeds, and always does more than he promiseth: for he seeks his own down-going.

I love him who justifies the future ones, and redeemeth the past ones: for he is willing to succumb through the present ones.

I love him who chastens his God, because he loves his God: for he must succumb through the wrath of his God.

I love him whose soul is deep even in the wounding, and may succumb through a small matter: thus he goes willingly over the bridge.

I love him whose soul is so overfull that he forgets himself, and all things are in him: thus all things become his down-going.

I love him who is of a free spirit and a free heart: thus is his head only the bowels of his heart; his heart, however, causes his down-going.

I love all who are like heavy drops falling one by one out of the dark cloud that lowers over man: they herald the coming of the lightning, and succumb as heralds.

Behold, I am a herald of the lightning, and a heavy drop out of the cloud: the lightning, however, is the *Superman*.—

5

When Zarathustra had spoken these words, he again looked at the people, and was silent. "There they stand," said he to his heart; "there they laugh: they understand me not; I am not the mouth for these ears.

Must one first batter their ears, that they may learn to hear with their eyes? Must one clatter like kettledrums and penitential preachers? Or do they only believe the stammerer?

They have something of which they are proud. What do they call it, that which makes them proud? Culture, they call it; it distinguishes them from the goatherds.

They dislike, therefore, to hear of 'contempt' of themselves. So I will appeal to their pride.

I will speak to them of the most contemptible thing: that, however, is the *last man*!"

And thus spoke Zarathustra to the people:

It is time for man to fix his goal. It is time for man to plant the germ of his highest hope.

Still is his soil rich enough for it. But that soil will one day be poor and exhausted, and no lofty tree will any longer be able to grow in it.

Alas! there will come the time when man will no longer launch the arrow of his longing beyond man—and the string of his bow will have unlearned to whizz!

I tell you: one must still have chaos in one, to give birth to a dancing star. I tell you: you have still chaos in you.

Alas! There will come the time when man will no longer give birth to any star. Alas! There will come the time of the most despicable man, who can no longer despise himself.

Behold! I show you *the last man*.

"What is love? What is creation? What is longing? What is a star?"—so asks the last man and he blinks.

The earth has then become small, and on it there hops the last man who makes everything small. His species is ineradicable like that of the ground-flea; the last man lives longest.

"We have discovered happiness"—say the last men, and they blink.

They have left the regions where it is hard to live; for they need warmth. One still love one's neighbour and rub against him; for one needs warmth.

Turning ill and being distrustful, they consider sinful: they walk warily. He is a fool who still stumbles over stones or men!

A little poison now and then: that makes for pleasant dreams. And much poison in the end for a pleasant death.

One still works, for work is a pastime. But one is careful lest the pastime should hurt one.

One no longer becomes poor or rich; both are too burdensome. Who still wants to rule? Who still wants to obey? Both are too burdensome.

No shepherd, and one herd! Every one wants the same; every one is equal: he who has other sentiments goes voluntarily into the madhouse.

"Formerly all the world was insane,"—say the subtlest of them, and they blink.

They are clever and know all that has happened: so there is no end to their mockery. People still fall out, but are soon reconciled—otherwise it spoils their stomachs.

They have their little pleasures for the day, and their little pleasures for the night, but they have a regard for health.

"We have discovered happiness,"—say the last men, and they blink.—

And here ended the first discourse of Zarathustra, which is also called "The Prologue": for at this point the shouting and mirth of the multitude interrupted him. "Give us this last man, O Zarathustra,"—they called out—"make us into these last men! Then will we make you a present of the Superman!" And all the people exulted and smacked their lips. Zarathustra, however, turned sad, and said to his heart:

"They do not understand me: I am not the mouth for these ears.

Too long, perhaps, have I lived too long in the mountains; I have listened to long to the brooks and trees: now I speak to them as to the goatherds.

Calm is my soul, and clear, like the mountains in the morning. But they think me cold, and a mocker with terrible jests.

And now do they look at me and laugh: and while they laugh they hate me too. There is ice in their laughter."

6

Then, however, something happened which made every mouth mute and every eye fixed. In the meantime, of course, the rope-dancer had commenced his performance: he had come out at a little door, and was going along the rope which was stretched between two towers, so that it hung above the market-place and the people. When he was just midway across,

the little door opened once more, and a gaudily-dressed fellow like a buffoon sprang out, and went rapidly after the first one. "Go on, halt-foot,""cried his frightful voice, "go on, lazy-bones, interloper, sallow-face!—lest I tickle you with my heel! What are you doing here between the towers? In the tower is the place for you, thou should be locked up; to one better than yourself you block the way!"—And with every word he came nearer and nearer the first one. When, however, he was but a step behind, there happened the frightful thing which made every mouth mute and every eye fixed—he uttered a yell like a devil, and jumped over the other who was in his way. The latter, however, when he thus saw his rival triumph, lost at the same time his head and his footing on the rope; he threw his pole away, and shot downwards faster than it, like an eddy of arms and legs, into the depth. The market-place and the people were like the sea when the storm comes on: they all flew apart and in disorder, especially where the body was about to fall.

Zarathustra, however, remained standing, and just beside him fell the body, badly injured and disfigured, but not yet dead. After a while consciousness returned to the shattered man, and he saw Zarathustra kneeling beside him. "What are you doing there?" said he at last, "I knew long ago that the devil would trip me up. Now he will drag me to hell: will you prevent him?"

"On my honor, my friend," answered Zarathustra, "there is nothing at all to what you say: there is no devil and no hell. Your soul will be dead even sooner than your body: fear, therefore, nothing any more!"

The man looked up distrustfully. "If you speak the truth," said he, "I lose nothing when I lose my life. I am not much more than an animal which has been taught to dance by blows and scanty fare."

"Not at all," said Zarathustra, "you have made danger your calling; in that there is nothing contemptible. Now you perish by your calling: therefore will I bury you with mine own hands."

When Zarathustra had said this the dying one did not reply further; but he moved his hand as if he sought the hand of Zarathustra in gratitude.

7

Meanwhile the evening came on, and the market-place veiled itself in gloom. Then the people dispersed, for even curiosity and terror become fatigued. Zarathustra, however, still sat beside the dead man on the ground, absorbed in thought: so he forgot the time. But at last it became night, and a cold wind blew upon the lonely one. Then arose Zarathustra and said to his heart:

Truly, a fine catch of fish hath Zarathustra made today! It is not a man he hath caught, but a corpse.

Sombre is human life, and as yet without meaning: a buffoon may be fateful to it.

I want to teach men the sense of their existence, which is the Superman, the lightning out of the dark cloud of man.

But still am I far from them, and my sense speaks not to their sense. To men I am still something between a fool and a corpse.

Gloomy is the night, gloomy are the ways of Zarathustra. Come, you cold and stiff companion! I will carry you to the place where I shall bury you with my own hands....

THE THREE METAMORPHOSES

Three metamorphoses of the spirit do I designate to you: how the spirit becomes a camel, the camel a lion, and the lion at last a child.

Many heavy things are there for the spirit, the strong load-bearing spirit in which reverence dwells: for strength demands the heavy and the heaviest burdens.

What is heavy? so asks the load-bearing spirit; then it kneels down like the camel, and wants to be well laden.

What is the heaviest thing, you heroes? asks the load-bearing spirit, that I may take it upon me and rejoice in my strength.

Is it not this: To humiliate oneself in order to mortify one's pride? To exhibit one's folly in order to mock at one's wisdom?

Or is it this: To desert our cause when it celebrates its triumph? To ascend high mountains to tempt the tempter?

Or is it this: To feed on the acorns and grass of knowledge, and for the sake of truth to suffer hunger of soul?

Or is it this: To be sick and dismiss comforters, and make friends of the deaf, who never hear your requests?

Or is it this: To go into foul water when it is the water of truth, and not disclaim cold frogs and hot toads?

Or is it this: To love those who despise us, and give one's hand to the phantom when it is going to frighten us?

All these heaviest things the load-bearing spirit takes upon itself: and like the camel, which, when laden, hastens into the wilderness, so hastens the spirit into its wilderness.

But in the loneliest wilderness there happens the second metamorphosis: here the spirit becomes a lion; freedom will it capture, and lordship in its own wilderness.

Its last Lord it here seeks: hostile will it be to him, and to its last God; for victory will it struggle with the great dragon.

What is the great dragon which the spirit is no longer inclined to call Lord and God? "Thou-shalt," is the great dragon called. But the spirit of the lion saith, "I will."

"Thou-shalt," lies in its path, sparkling with gold—a scale-covered beast; and on every scale glitters golden, "Thou shalt!"

The values of a thousand years glitter on those scales, and thus speaks the mightiest of all dragons: "All the values of things—glitter on me.

All values have already been created, and all created values—do I represent. Truly, there shall be no 'I will' any more. Thus speaks the dragon.

My brothers, why is there no need of the lion in the spirit? Why is the beast of burden, which renounces and is reverent, not sufficient?

To create new values—that, even the lion cannot yet accomplish: but to create itself freedom for new creating—that can the might of the lion do.

To create itself freedom, and give a holy "No" even to duty: for that, my brothers, there is need of the lion.

To assume the right to new values—that is the

most formidable assumption for a load-bearing and reverent spirit. Truly, to such a spirit it is preying, and the work of a beast of prey.

As its holiest, it once loved "Thou-shalt": now is it forced to find illusion and arbitrariness even in the holiest things, that it may capture freedom from its love: the lion is needed for this capture.

But tell me, my brethren, what the child can do, which even the lion could not do? Why has the preying lion still to become a child?

Innocence is the child, and forgetfulness, a new beginning, a game, a self-rolling wheel, a first movement, a holy Yea.

Yes, for the game of creating, my brothers, there is needed a holy "Yes" unto life: *its own* will, wills now the spirit; *his own* world wins the world's outcast.

Three metamorphoses of the spirit have I designated to you: how the spirit became a camel, the camel a lion, and the lion at last a child.—

Thus spoke Zarathustra.

Friedrich Nietzsche. *Thus Spake Zarathustra*. Trans. Thomas Common. Edinbugh: 1909.

CONFESSIONS

AUGUSTINE (354-430)

The Confessions *is St. Augustine's autobiographical account of his life from birth until his conversion to the Christian faith. Born of a Christian mother and pagan father in 4ᵗʰ century Northern Africa, Augustine's youth was filled with pride, ambition, and sexual desire. Throughout his life, Augustine toyed with many different types of philosophical and religious systems—Stoicism, Skepticism, Manichaeanisn, NeoPlatonism—in his never-ending quest to find happiness in life. None of these approaches, however, could provide him with the consolation he sought. While he was in Milan, however, Augustine was exposed to the Christian thought of St. Ambrose, which led him to reconsider the Christian faith of his childhood. Soon Augustine came to recognize the truth of Christianity, although he found that a lifetime of sinful habits had left him incapable of doing the good that he willed to do. The following selection from Book VIII of the* Confessions *represents the climax of Augustine's tale. He is at a crossroads, incapable of embracing Christianity whole-heartedly but knowing that there are no other options left for him. Just at the moment when he is about to give up all hope, God mysteriously intervenes in his life, dispelling all his doubt and despair.*

From the moment the Confessions *was promulgated in 396 BC, Augustine's autobiography became the classic spiritual text in Christian literature and remains so till this day. The work also offers something of a blueprint of the Christian mystic's journey to attain union with God, and in this sense is vitally important for understanding the entire Christian mystical tradition.*

1. In a spirit of gratitude, O my God, let me remember and confess to you the mercies that you bestowed upon me. Let my bones be penetrated with your love, and let them cry out to you, "Who is like you, O Lord?" You have completely broken my bonds; let me offer you a sacrifice of praise. I will tell how you have severed these shackles, so that all who worship you, when they hear my tale will say, "Blessed be the Lord, in heaven and in earth, for great and wonderful is his name."

Your words had now firmly fixed themselves in my heart, and I was besieged on all sides by you. Of your eternal life, I was now quite certain, though I saw it obscurely, as through a looking glass. But I no longer doubted that there was an incorruptible substance from which all other substances were derived. And I no longer desired to be more certain of you, but only to stand more firmly in you. As for my temporal life, everything was in a state of flux, and my heart needed to be purged of its old ways. The Way—the Savior Himself—pleased me, but I still

hesitated to enter the narrowness of that path….

The Two Wills

5. The enemy held my will, and made a chain out of it, and bound me with it. From from a perverse will came lust, and lust given into became habit, and habit not resisted became necessity. These links, as it were, joined together—for this reason I called it a chain—and held me fast in harsh slavery. But that new will, which had begun to develop in me, freely to serve you and to enjoy you, O God, was not yet able to overcome the old will, which had become strengthened by long custom. And so, my two wills—one new and the other old, one carnal and the other spiritual—struggled within me; and they laid waste to my soul by their discord.

Thus, I understood by my own experience what I had read—that the flesh lusts against the spirit and the spirit against the flesh. I certainly was on both sides, but more when I was on that side which I approved in myself than on that side which I disapproved. For the latter was not really "me," because, for the most part, I suffered things against my will rather than doing them willingly. And yet it was my own fault that custom became more powerful against me, since I had come willingly where I now wished not to be. And who has any right to complain when just punishment overtakes the sinner?

Nor had I any longer my former excuse that the reason I continued to hesitate to turn my back to the world and serve you was because I could not see the truth clearly. For now I could see it with perfect clarity. But I was still bound to the earth and refused to be your soldier. I was as much afraid of being freed of my encumbrances as I was of being encumbered by them.

So I was held down by the pleasant burdens of this world, like one who is asleep, and the thoughts in which I attempted to meditate on you were like the efforts of one who tries to wake up but who sinks back again into sleep. No one, of course, wants to sleep forever, and sensible people all agree that it is better to be awake; yet a man, feeling the sleepiness of his limbs, generally puts off waking up and, even after it is time to arise, often defers to shake off sleep, though he knows he should not be doing so. In the same way, I was quite sure that it was much better to give myself up to your charity than to give myself over to my own desires; but though the former course satisfied me and was beginning to gain mastery over me, the latter pleased me and ensnared me. Nor had I any answer to give to you as you called out to me, "Awake, you who sleep, and arise from the dead, and Christ shall give you light." And when you showed me in every possible way that what you said was true, I had no answer, except the dull and drowsy words, "A minute. Just a minute. Let me have just a little while longer." But these minutes never ended, and my little while went on for a very long while.

In vain, I tried to delight in your law according to the inner man, while another law in my members rebelled against the law of my mind and led me captive under the law of sin which was in my members. For the law of sin is the strong force of habit, whereby the mind is drawn and held, even against its will—but deservedly, for the mind fell into the habit willingly. Who then shall deliver me, wretched man

that I am, from the body of this death, but only your grace, through Jesus Christ our Lord?...

[Augustine goes to visit the priest Simplicianus, who recounts the tales of several men and women who had converted to the Christian faith, thus inflaming Augustine with the strong desire to do likewise.]

The Struggle in the Garden

8. In the midst, then, of this great quarrel of my inner dwelling,…disturbed both in mind and appearance, I rushed to Alypius and cried: "What is wrong with us? What is this that you have just heard? The unlearned are rising up and taking heaven, while we, with all our learning, are wallowing in the world of flesh and blood! Are we ashamed to follow because they have gone ahead of us? And aren't we ashamed of not having the courage to follow at all?" I spoke words like these, and the disturbance of my mind tore me away from him, while he gazed on in silent bewilderment. For I spoke in strange tones, and my forehead, cheeks, eyes, color, and tone of voice all expressed my emotions more fully than the words I had uttered.

There was a small garden attached to the house where we were staying. We were free to make use of it as well as the house, since the owner of the house, our host, was not living there. The turmoil in my heart had driven me to this garden, and no one would interfere with the debate I had started within myself until it could be resolved—the outcome of which you knew, though I did not. I only knew that I was going mad so that I might be whole, and dying that I might have life, knowing what an evil thing I was, but not knowing what a good thing I was soon to become.

So I retired into the garden, and Alypius followed behind me. My privacy was not lessened by his presence, and, in any event, how could he have abandoned me in the state that I was in? We sat down as far from the house as possible. I was troubled in spirit for not entering into your will and covenant, my God, which all my bones cried out to me to enter, and praised it to the heavens. And the way to go there is not by ships, or chariots, or feet; nor did it even demand going so far as the short distance I had come from the house to the place where we were sitting. For to go there, all I had had to do was to will to go, but to will it resolutely and sincerely; not to toss and turn, this way and that of a will half-maimed by the struggle, with one part falling as another rose.

While still consumed by the fever of my irresoluteness, I made many bodily movements—the kind that people often want to perform, but cannot, either because they lack limbs, or because they are bound, or weakened by sickness, or in some other way prevented from acting. If I tore out my hair, beat my forehead, locked my fingers together around my knee, I did so because I willed it. But I might have willed to do so and not have done it, if the power of motion in my limbs had not obeyed. So I did many things where "willing" was not the same as "being able." And yet I was not able to do the thing that I longed to do so much more, and which very shortly, when I willed it, would be able to do, because when I willed, I should will thoroughly. For in this particular instance the ability was one with the will, and to will was to do. And yet it was not done. It was much easier for my body to obey the weakest willing of my soul to move my limbs than it was for the soul to carry out its own major act of willing, which could be accomplished in the will alone.

9. What is the cause of this absurd situation? Let your mercy illuminate my inquiry, so that an answer can be found in the mysterious punishment of humanity and the darkest pains of the children of Adam. What is the cause, then, of this absurd situation? The mind commands the body, and the body obeys immediately; the mind commands itself, and is resisted. The mind commands the hand to move, and so complete is the compliance that the command is hardly to be distinguished from its execution. Yet the mind is mind and the hand is body. The mind commands the mind—its own self—to will, and yet it does not. Again, what is the cause of this absurd situation? The mind, I say, commands itself to will something, and it would not command, unless it willed, and yet what it commands is not done. But it does not will the thing entirely, and therefore it does not command entirely. Insofar as it commands the thing, it does will it, but insofar as the thing is not done, it does not will it. For the will commands that there be a will—not a different will, but itself.

But it does not command entirely, and therefore the command is not obeyed. For if the will was entire, it would not command itself to act, since the will would already be there. This partial willing and partial non-willing is not quite so absurd, but is rather a sickness of the soul, which was so weighed down by habit that it cannot be raised up by the truth. There are two wills, then, and neither is entire, because one has what the other lacks.

Rejection of the Manichaean Solution

10. There are those who, having perceived two deliberating wills, conclude that there are two natures within us—one good and one evil. Let them perish from your presence, O God, as do all those idle talkers who lead our minds astray. They themselves are truly evil when they assert such things, and yet these same people could become good if they would just assent to the truth, so that your Apostle may say to them, "You were in darkness once, but now light in the Lord." Unfortunately, they want to be light, not in the Lord, but in themselves, and, imagining the nature of the soul to be that what God is, are made more gross darkness still through their dreadful arrogance; for they have moved further away from you, the true light that enlightens everyone who comes into the world. I say to these men, be wary of what you say and blush for shame; but draw near to him and be enlightened, and you shall no longer be ashamed.

When I was deliberating about whether to serve the Lord my God now, as I had long intended, I was the one who wanted to do it and I was also the one who wanted not to do it. I was the only one involved. But I neither willed this course entirely nor rejected it entirely. I was at war with myself and was torn apart by myself. This tearing apart took place against my will, but what it indicated was not the presence of an alien mind, but a punishment that I was suffering in my own mind. Therefore, it was not I who caused it, but the sin that dwelled within me—the penalty for a sin more freely committed, for I was a son of Adam.

For, if there are as many conflicting natures as there are conflicting wills, there would not be two such natures only, but many. Suppose a man is wondering whether he should go to the Manichaean conventicler or to the theater. These Manichaeans will say, "You see, here are two natures, one good, pulling him in one direction, the other evil, pulling him in another. For what else could this indecision be except a conflict between wills?" But I say that both are equally bad—that which pulls towards them and that which pulls towards the theater. But they believe that a will which pulls towards them must be good.

But suppose one of us should deliberate, and through a conflict of his two wills, should be in confusion as to whether he should go to the theater or to our Church. Wouldn't these same Manichaeans be perplexed as to what to say on this point? For they must either confess that the will which leads to our Church is good as well as theirs (something they would not be willing to do)…; or they must assume that in the same man there are two evil natures and two evil souls, and that it is not true, as they say, that there is one good and another bad; or they must be converted to the truth, and no longer deny that when a person is deliberating there is a soul fluctuating between two conflicting wills.

Let them stop saying, therefore, when they perceive two conflicting wills in the same man, that the conflict is between two opposing souls, of two opposing substances, from two opposing principles, one good and the other bad. For you, O God of truth, have disproved, checked, and overthrown them. Such is the case when both wills being bad, one debates whether he should kill a man by poison or by the sword; whether he should seize this or that part of a man's property, when he cannot have both; whether he should squander his money for pleasure or hoard his money like a miser; whether he should go to the circus or the theater, if both are opened on the same day (a third option being to rob another's house if he has the opportunity and a fourth being to commit adultery)—assuming he has the means to do all these things at the time, and all are equally desired, although impossible to enact at the same time. The mind is then torn apart by four or even more…conflicting wills. But the Manichaeans do not hold that there are a similar number of conflicting substances.

The same holds true in wills which are good. Let me ask: Is it a good thing to take pleasure in reading the apostle? Or a good thing to take pleasure in a sober psalm? Or a good thing to discuss the Gospel? For each of these, they will answer, "It is good." But what if all of these give equal pleasure at the same time? Doesn't this mean that different wills distract the mind, while he deliberates which to select? Yet they are all good, but they compete among themselves until one is chosen….It is likewise the case when eternity delights us from above and the pleasure of temporal goods holds us down from below: our one soul is not ready to embrace either with its entire will. And so the soul is torn apart with great distress, with truth pulling in one direction and habit pulling in the other.

Inner Debate

11. So I was soul-sick and tormented. And I accused myself far more severely than I usually did, tossing and turning in my chain, as I strove to break free from it completely. I was held by it only slightly, but I was still held. And you, O Lord, pressed upon me in my innermost being by a severe mercy, redoubling the lashes of fear and shame, so that I would not give way once more, and that small piece of chain that still bound me would not get stronger and bind me even more. I said to myself, "Let it be done now, let it be done now." And as I spoke these words, I was all but moving in that direction. I nearly did it, but yet did not do it. But I didn't slip back into my own ways, but took a breath and kept my stand. And I tried again…and all but touched and grasped it; and yet still I did not come to it, or touch it, or grasp it; for I hesitated to die to death and to live to life….At that very moment in which I was to become something other than I was, the nearer it approached me, the greater was my horror, but it did not strike me back, nor turn me away, but held me in suspense.

The very toys of toys and vanities of vanities, my ancient mistresses, were still holding me back, as they plucked the garment of my flesh and whispered softly, "Do you think you can be done with us? From this moment shall we no longer be with you forever? And from this moment shall this-and-that no longer be lawful for you forever?" And what did they suggest to me by "this" and "that"? What did they suggest, O my God? Let your mercy turn it away from the soul of your servant. What foul deed were they suggesting? What shameful acts? But now their voices were half as loud, and they did not openly show themselves to contradict me, but muttered, as it were, behind my back, and slyly grasping at me as I walked away to make me look back at them. And yet they did delay me as I hesitated to tear free and shake them off and move in the direction in which I was being called. They had an aggressive habit of taunting me by saying, "Do you really think that you can live without them?"

But now it spoke very faintly. For on that side where I had turned my face and where I hesitated to go, there appeared to me the chaste, dignified figure of Continence. She was serene and calm, honestly beckoning me to come and doubt no longer. As she stretched forth to receive and embrace me, her holy hands filled with multitudes of good examples of all ages, there were some young men and women here and grave widows and aged virgins. And in them all was Continence herself, not barren, but a fruitful mother of children, her joys given by you, her husband, O Lord. She smiled on me with encouraging prodding, as though to say, "Can't you do what these youths and maidens have done? Or do you think that they did it all by themselves and without the help of the Lord their God? The Lord their God gave me to them. Why do you insist upon standing by yourself, and so not really stand firm at all? Cast yourself upon him and fear not. He will not draw away and let you fall. Lean fearlessly upon him and he will receive you and heal you." And I was blushing with shame, for I could still hear the whisperings of those vanities of mine, and hung back in suspense. And yet again she seemed to say, "Close your ears to those unclean parts of you that belong to the earth, so that they might be mortified. They might tell you of delights, but nothing like the delights that are told by the law of the Lord your God."

And so continued the debate in my heart, waged between myself and myself. But Alypius, sitting by my side, silently waited to see how this extreme agitation within me would end.

Augustine's Conversion

12. But this deep reflection, from the secret depths of my soul, drew together and heaped up all my misery…, and there arose a great storm within me, bringing with it a mighty shower of tears. So that I might be free to give vent to these feelings without self-consciousness, I left Alypius, since solitude was more appropriate for the act of weeping. So I went far enough away that even his presence would not be a burden to me. This was how I was feeling, and he understood it; for I suppose that I had said something, and the tones of my voice must have appeared choked with tears. And so I arose to leave and he remained where we were sitting, filled with extreme astonishment. I threw myself down—I don't really know how—under a certain fig tree, and gave full reign to my tears. They poured out from my eyes like a flood, an acceptable sacrifice to you. And, I said to you, not in these exact words, but in this sense, "And you, O Lord, how long? How long, Lord? Will you be angry forever? O do not remember our former sins." For I felt it was these that were holding me back. I uttered these cries of despair to you: "How long, how long this "tomorrow and tomorrow? Why not now? Why can't my depravity be put to an end at this every hour?"

So I was saying words of this sort and crying in the bitter contrition of my heart, when suddenly a voice reached my ears from a nearby house. It was the voice of a boy or girl—I don't know which—and it kept repeating, "Take it and read. Take it and read." Immediately, my expression changed. I began to reflect upon whether words like these were ever used in the kinds of games that children play, but couldn't remember ever before hearing words of that kind. So I stemmed the flood of my tears and arose, interpreting it to be nothing other than a command from God to open the book and read the first chapter I came upon. For I had once heard that Anthony, coming in during the reading of the Gospels, believed the words to be directed to him, when he heard, "Go and sell all you have, and give the money to the poor, and you will have treasure in heaven, and come follow me." By such a divine message was he converted to you. Eagerly, I then returned to the place where Alypius was sitting, since it was in that spot that I had left the book of the Apostle when I had gotten up. Snatching it up and opening it, in silence I read that section upon which my eyes first fell: "Not in rioting and drunkenness, not in debauchery and wantonness, not in strife and envying; but put on the Lord Jesus Christ, and make not provision for the flesh, in concupiscence." I didn't need to read any further, for immediately at the end of this sentence, the light of certainty flooded my heart, and the darkness of doubt vanished away.

I closed the book, and either using my fingers or some other means to mark the page, and with complete calmness told Alypius what had happened. And he told me in his turn what had been going on with him, which I didn't know anything about. He asked to see what I had read and I showed him. And he looked beyond even what I had read. I didn't know the words that followed, which were, "He that is weak in faith, receive"—which he applied to himself and interpreted for me. He became strengthened by the admonition; and he joined me with the kind of strong resolution and commitment that was totally in keeping with his character (for in this respect he was quite superior to me).

We then went inside to my mother and told her what had transpired, and she rejoiced. We described to her what took place and she leapt with joyful triumph, and blessed you, who have the power to do much more than we ask for or understand. For she understood that you had given her much more in my regard than she had even asked for in her pitiful and sorrowful pleadings. For you had converted me to yourself, so that I no longer sought a wife or any worldly ambitions. I was now standing in that rule of faith that many years earlier you had shown to her in a vision of me. And, in doing so, you converted her sorrow into joy—a joy far more plentiful than she could have hoped for, and much more precious and purer than she desired by having grandchildren from my flesh.

Augustine. *Confessions*. Trans. by Michael S. Russo, 2012.

5

PHILOSOPHY OF RELIGION: DOES GOD EXIST?

ERIC KARAHALIS

As if the word "philosophy" is not daunting enough to the average college student, adding the word "religion" at the end makes it even more fearsome. What is philosophy of religion? To a modern reader the phrase 'Philosophy of Religion' might seem strange or even an apparent contradiction of terms. But let us try to simplify and classify to better understand the subject.

The word philosophy can be divided into two Greek terms: *philia,* which means love, and *sophia* which translates into wisdom. So at its core philosophy is a love of wisdom and truth. The Oxford dictionary defines philosophy as, "the use of reason and argument in seeking the truth and knowledge of reality, especially of the causes and nature of things and of the principles governing existence, the material universe, perception of physical phenomena, and human behavior." Philosophy of religion is an attempt to use reason and analysis to understand the root and foundation of religion, holding it up to the light of truth to see through its many layers and seek to reveal its core. One of the central questions in the philosophy of religion is the relationship between religion and reason. Is religion blind and irrational? Is religion a sophisticated form of superstition? Is religion a human construct for social control? Is religion a psychological or emotional need? Is religion a projection of humanity's highest ideals? Or is religion rooted in reality? Does religion lead us to truth–indeed, the deepest truths? Can reason lead to faith? All of these questions and more become the focal point and subject matter of philosophy of religion.

Religion is more difficult to simply define. The word "Religion" is rooted in the Latin words *re*— "again" and *ligare*— "to bind back," as well as the Latin *religio* "respect for what is sacred, reverence for the gods." In other words religion is being bound and committed in reverence and devotion to something, and in most cases that something is God or gods. Religion is not a simple word to pin down but rather a term that can be divided into several categories.

Modes of Religious-Mindedness

As a crystal exposes the color spectrum contained in white light as light passes through it - so too the lens of philosophy can help us to differentiate between the many shades or modes of religious mindedness when we hold the light of reason to religion. We will focus primarily on the western Christian tradition, although much of the following can be applied to all of the great theistic religious traditions of the world.

Fundamentalism

The first mode of religious-mindedness is religious fundamentalism. In its purest form fundamentalism is understood to entail an absolute, unquestioning loyalty to certain basics or "fundamentals" of a given faith tradition. Religious fundamentalism today is understood as relying on pure faith and a literal reading of sacred scriptures. Simply, religious fundamentalism is grounded on faith, feeling, and irrationality and is often categorized as rejecting many modern scientific findings. This form of religion is extremely skeptical of philosophy and science and relies solely on devotion to God and scripture. This understanding was best vocalized by the ancient church father Tertullian of Carthage. Tertullian lived at a time when many early Christians sought to use and reconcile ancient philosophy to the Christian worldview. He felt that philosophy would only pull the mind further away from God into heresies and that the truest way to understand God was pure faith. Tertullian states, "Worldly wisdom culminates in philosophy with its rash interpretations of God's nature and purpose…it is philosophy that supplies heresies with their equipment."[1]

Fundamentalism is more than just a rejection of reason and an extremely literal reading of scripture; it is also a psychological condition that desires to possess an ungrounded and unreasonable certainty. Fundamentalists are absolutely certain that their subjective position is the only objective reality. Every other belief, position, or understanding is misguided and false. When fundamentalists focus solely on the basic principles of their faith, often a form of legalistic religion emerges, where any lack of strict adherence to the practice condemns the violator as a sinner and someone in need of God's punishment rather than love and forgiveness. This form of religion is very unaccepting of those who do not share their viewpoint. It is this form of extreme fundamentalism that is the cause of violence perpetrated in the name of God. From the standpoint of philosophy it is hard not to recognize that when people possess an extreme, polarizing position on any given subject they are likely to be vehemently dismissive of any contrary vantage point.

This explains the zealous rejection of science by many fundamental religious extremists and the rejection of religion by many scientific fundamentalist extremists. Scientific fundamentalist extremism is a viewpoint held by many modern scientists, like Richard Dawkins, who maintains that all religions and religious mindedness is inherently bad and the root of most of the world's troubles and evils. This is a fundamentalism that states if something cannot be observed, examined, and studied through the senses and reason it cannot have any reality or claim to exist. Therefore any belief in God is inherently irrational and dangerous. This position is as intolerant of religion as extreme religious fundamentalism is of the sciences. The religious variances that comprise the rest of the spectrum of religious modes fall somewhere in the middle of these two extreme, opposite poles.

Mysticism

The Mystic tradition is another form of religious-mindedness. Mysticism is a submission of reason and the will to pure faith. The mystic recognizes that reason cannot understand God and so only faith can bridge the infinite gap between God and humanity. Unlike the fundamentalist who rejects reason as uncertain and attributes an irrational certainty to faith, the mystic recognizes the limits of reason and certainty and embraces faith as an indeterminate openness to God. The mystic often practices a detachment from earthly desires and concerns freeing oneself in action and meditative passivity to receive communion with the divine. The mystic experience transcends the world and reason in an ecstatic (outside oneself) experience of God.

Among those who follow this mode of the religious traditions is where we find many saints and religious heroes who submitted their lives to God and lived abundant lives of charity, love, and wisdom, transforming the world by their actions and words. There is something inspiring in dedicating one's life to God through great acts of love and kindness. Mother Theresa is one such example: She lived her life caring for those sick and dying in Calcutta, India. She did not possess a deep rational understanding of God yet she was a living example of unwavering faith, absolute commitment and submission, and deep unconditional love. Considering examples like Mother Theresa it is plain to see that faith without a rational understanding is not inherently bad.

Apologetics

Apologetics, another mode of religion, is an attempt to defend and ground the belief in God through the use of reason and philosophy. Apologetics is derived from the Greek word *apologetikos* which means "defensible" This form of religious mindedness marries the tradition of philosophy to the tradition of religion in an attempt to explain rationally the doctrines, practices, and issues of the faith community.

This way of conceiving philosophy as a useful tool is apparent in the writings of the early church father Clement of Alexandria. He states, "Philosophy came into existence for the advantages reaped by us from knowledge...Accordingly before the advent of the Lord, philosophy was necessary to the Greeks for righteousness…Philosophy therefore was a preparation, paving the way for him who is perfected in Christ." Clement tells us that philosophy is a kindred and useful tool of religion and not to be considered detrimental or dangerous to the faithful.

St. Augustine, Bishop of Hippo, is one of the most prolific writers of late antiquity in the Christian apologetic tradition. He uses philosophy to examine the human condition, the nature of God, time, evil, love, the Trinity, government, and scripture. Augustine declares, "I believe in order that I may understand" (*Credo ut intelligam*). This statement demonstrates that faith is not the absence of reason but rather the prerequisite and root of reason. In his text on Christian Teaching Augustine states, "Any statements by those who are called philosophers, especially the Platonists, which happen to be true and consistent with our faith should not cause alarm, but be claimed for our own use." Augustine views philosophy as a great assistant and useful discipline in bringing humanity to truth and suggests that faith adds a new depth to the understanding. It is Augustine's seamless synthesis of Greek Neo-Platonic philosophy to Christianity that has drawn people into his teachings and religious understandings to this day. Augustine's influence can be traced through later mathematicians and scientists like René Descartes and Sigmund Freud.

Arguments for the Existence of God

A major topic in apologetics is the existence of God. Remember that the apologetic thinkers accept God on faith and they recognize that God is known primarily in the heart, soul, and spirit of mankind. There is no real need to prove God's existence for these believers for in their view there can be no doubt as to whether God exists. However, the apologetic thinkers were aware that many people held a contrary position and possessed a great skepticism towards God's existence. In an attempt to dispel disbelief and convert this opposing viewpoint, apologetic thinkers like Anselm and Aquinas set out to rationally prove that God does exist.

In philosophy there are two schools of thought regarding how humans come to knowledge and understanding: rationalism and empiricism. Rationalism is the philosophical position that all knowledge comes to humans through reason alone (*a priori* —Latin meaning knowledge is prior to experience). This understanding holds that all knowledge is hidden in the recesses of our minds waiting to be explored and discovered. Rationalism and its pure logic is the basis for the science of mathematics.

Empiricism, on the other hand, is the position that all knowledge comes to humans through the senses and experience (*a posteriori*—Latin meaning knowledge comes from the posterior, outside world). Empiricists hold that if you wish to understand the world you must observe and look to nature and experience to enlighten our minds with knowledge. It is this position that grounds all of the natural sciences, for how else can we come to understand our natural world without taking in data through the five senses and then trying to understand the underlying similarities and patterns. The best arguments and proofs for truth, particularly with respect for God's existence tend to be empirically-based or at least an amalgamation of both rationalism and empiricism.

The Ontological Argument

St. Anselm, Archbishop of Canterbury, also follows the Christian apologetic tradition. Like Augustine, he eloquently explains that the use of philosophy in religion is not to prove rationally that God exists as a pretext for faith but rather to believe in order to understand. Faith proceeds understanding. In Anselm's own Latin: "*Fides quaerens intellectum*" which translates to, faith seeking understanding.[2] In other words, Anselm is full of faith and seeks to reason an indisputable argument for the existence of God. Anselm is best known for his ontological proof for the existence of God, so named because "ontos" in Greek means "being" and it is an argument on God's being or existence. Anselm's proof is an attempt to demonstrate that God must exist necessarily and rationally. Anselm tries to formulate a purely rational and impenetrable argument in support of God's existence. Anselm's argument is often criticized for not going deep enough. It is merely a logical rational syllogism (mathematical like rational arguments) based on pure reason rather than an argument from experience and observation.

The Cosmological Argument

St. Thomas Aquinas is another church father who is responsible for the promulgation of Christian apologetics. Aquinas, like Augustine, was extremely prolific and married Greek philosophy to the Christian tradition. Aquinas integrates the teaching and writings of the ancient Greek philosopher Aristotle to Christianity. Aristotle is often credited as a founding father to the scientific community and method. The scientific method is the use of reason and observation to dissect, divide, classify, and understand the essential characteristics and causes of all natural phenomena, i.e. humans, animals, plants, elements, soul, God, etc. Thomas, like Aristotle, is an empiricist who looks to nature and reason to discover the truth. He borrows some of Aristotle's own arguments and baptizes them to present a very natural and rational argument in support of God's existence. Known as the "five ways," Aquinas' proofs attempt to demonstrate rationally from experience and nature that God must necessarily exist. Unlike Anselm who uses a purely rational argument to prove God's existence, Aquinas makes use of natural observation and grounded experience to rationally show that God logically must exist.

Aquinas' five ways can be divided into two main types of arguments: the cosmological argument and the teleological argument. Aquinas borrows the cosmological argument from Aristotle This argument draws on the existence of the world and universe to conclude that God must necessarily exist as the first cause of everything. From nothing, nothing comes, or in Latin, *ex nihilo nihil fit*. Therefore, if there is a world—the word "cosmological" comes from the Greek word cosmos meaning "world" or "universe"—something must be responsible for its existence and that something is God

The *Teleological Argument*

The teleological argument is one of the strongest experience-based arguments that seek to conclude the absolute reality of God's existence. Teleology is a word derived from the Greek word *telos*, "purpose" or "end." This proof is grounded on the observation that everything in nature possesses an inner purpose and is aimed at some objective end. All one needs to do is contemplate the miracle of human reproduction: how from a fertilized egg, to human infant, to an adult human being—nature possesses an ingrained order and rationale. Everything in the universe and nature follows an inherent, knowable, predictable, and rational path and where there is order and rationality there is an intelligent being. The seasons, the tides, day and night, the weather, astrological events, life cycles, food cycles, mathematics, genetics and chemistry are only a short list of the apparent examples of the world's apparent order. A world of observable intelligible order cannot be the product of chaos or chance, but rather a divine intelligent being/creator God. This argument—also known as the argument from design—is one of Thomas' greatest contributions to both philosophy and religion. The happy union of reason and religion bears witness to the coherence and compatibility of philosophy and religion. This tradition allows for an acceptance of empirical science rather than a rejection due to scripture or doctrine.

Arguments Against the Existence of God

In a world drunk with labels and polarizations religion is often classified by atheists ("atheism"— from Greek *a* "without" and *theos* "God"—is the philosophical position that God does not exist) as belonging to the realm of pure speculation and illusion. They claim it is an irrational otherworldly childish belief in imaginary beings that makes humanity feel better about the hardships of life, as well as an abandonment of reason and submission to religious authority. It is such authorities, the atheists might continue, that have terrorized the world with bitter hatred, pious rivalries, holy wars, inquisitions, and, in the present age jihads. Many people might point to the reality of global terrorism fueled by radical Islamic fundamentalism, as well as Christian fundamentalists who say that Jesus hates gays and a good Christian should bomb abortion clinics. The events of September 11, 2001 can testify to the atrocities humans have unleashed on each other in the name of God and religion. Under the impartial light of philosophy it is apparent that doubt and disbelief in God is a justified position and can be argued rationally.

So, we must ask ourselves: Is religion inherently bad? Does it tend toward violence and hatred? Has it only darkened the world we live in, or is there a great light of truth to religion illuminating the world? Is it purely irrational? Does God exist or is this merely a human hope and projection?

Religion as Projection

Throughout time humans have stood in awe and amazement of the world and universe. Awe is a state of mental bafflement—things that are beyond our ability to comprehend cause awe within us. An awe experience can be positive or negative (a beautiful sunset, child birth, or death) and leaves the observer in a state of confusion, anxiety, and insecurity. Without an understanding of the world and things around them, humans become overwhelmed with fear and anxiety. This state of fear and anxiety is not sustainable for the human psyche and demands an acceptable explanation and rationale for the things we encounter in existence. A deep anxiety of the mystery, the unknown and mortality fosters the innate human desire to understanding the world, our place in it, as well as our meaning and purpose. If the answer to our quest for meaning takes a leap of faith towards God, be it a rational or irrational faith we are on the path of religion. If, however, we examine this inner anxiety or trepid malaise from the vantage point of rationality, philosophically we discover our final mode of religious mindedness: religion as psychological projection.

The mode of religious mindedness known as a psychological projection is not a religious mindset at all. It is this mode of philosophy of religion that denies the existence of God as an objective, rational, existing being. This branch of philosophy of religion looks to the emotional roots: anxiety, fear, the desire for certainty and order, and the need for meaning as the rational cause of theism and religious traditions. In other words, God and religion are merely human constructions invented to help mankind overcome the anxieties and fears inherent in the world. Ludwig Feuerbach and Karl Marx are two such modern thinkers who understand religion as being rooted in the human psyche. Feuerbach explains that God is truly an outward projection of the inner ideals and truest desires of mankind. In this analysis God is not a supernatural being, not the source of existence, not to be worshipped, but rather humanity's greatest hopes and ideals elevated into the heavens, as an ever-present deity, reminding of us of our noblest and greatest possibilities.

Karl Marx accuses religion of being a fabrication to comfort mankind's pain and anxiety in the face of a meaningless, unfeeling, and heartless world. It is Marx's position that humanity creates illusions like God and heaven to assuage the hardships and heartaches of both life and death. Freud takes a similar approach to Marx in developing his psychological understanding of the origins of religion. He argues that fear of the harshness of the world that we inhabit and the inevitability of death leads human beings to create the illusion of a divine father figure who will ultimately make everything turn out alright in our lives. It is in lines of argument like these that many modern radical fundamental atheists such as Christopher Hitchens and Richard Dawkins find their rational justifications.

Religion and the Problem of Evil

The problem of evil—also known as theodicy—is one of the major stumbling blocks of for the belief in God. The problem of evil is centered on the question: If God is a good, all-powerful, and all-loving God, why is there evil in the world? Evil's existence implicitly demonstrates that God may not be good, loving, omnipotent, or real at all—for how can absolute love and goodness allow evil to flourish. Augustine understands evil as the privation of good—evil is merely the corruption of goodness—much like a cancer cell exists as a mutation or corruption of a healthy cell, so too evil cannot exist without the presence of healthy cells. According to Augustine, God did in fact create everything good; however, through free will mankind has corrupted its goodness and that is what has become evil. Despite Augustine's insightful explanation, the problem of evil is still a central issue for Christian apologetics and belief in God, highlighted in the writings of the Russian novelist Fyodor Dostoyevski.

Reflecting on philosophy of religion yields a rich human tradition of applying reason to help clarify, understand, and uncover the core of religion. Examining the spectrum of religion has revealed the polar extremes from fundamentalism and radical atheism; the skeptic's and atheist's rejection of belief to the mystic's leap beyond reason; and the middle hue of apologetics skillfully synthesizing religion and reason. It is the judgment of philosophy that religion is not inherently evil (bad), (though it may be used to this end), but rather a belief that has assisted humanity in edifying the individual, the community, and the world. Standing always as the highest human ideal to love, to forgive, to seek to reconcile, and to understand others, religion has much truth to offer us in our insatiable quest for wisdom. Therefore, in the true spirit of philosophy (a love of wisdom) we should be excited and encouraged to examine for ourselves the rich writings on the history of the philosophy of religion to see what truth it may offer and uncover.

In a modern world that is being shaped and affected by the radical beliefs of religious fundamentalists it is a moral imperative to rationally examine the core of religion to enlighten and judge for oneself its merits and faults. From American Christian fundamentalists trying to effect government policy, to radical Islamic extremists killing civilians in the name of God – there is a pressing need to understand the religious minded to resolve the modern conflicts that have arisen from such misguided positions. As conscientious ambassadors of truth and reason it is our duty to engage in a study of religion from the vantage point of philosophy.

THE ONTOLOGICAL ARGUMENT

ANSELM OF CANTERBURY (1034-1109)

Anslem's ontological argument is the classic a priori argument for the existence of God. The starting point for this famous—and controversial—"proof" for the existence of God is the definition of a God as "a being greater than which none can be conceived." From that definition, Anselm argues that, if this being exists in the understanding, then it must exist in reality as well, or a greater being could be conceived—namely one that exists in the understanding as well as in reality. For some, the argument is the ultimate logical proof for the existence of God, but, Anselm's detractors throughout the centuries have maintained that the argument is logically suspect.

Gaunilo of Marmoutiers was a contemporary of Anselm and one of the first—though certainly not the last—to offer a challenge to Anselm's argument. Gaunilo maintains that arguments similar in structure can be used to prove the existence of many things that clearly do not exist—the greatest possible island, for example. In his reply to Gaunilo, Anselm states that Gaunilo's analogy is fallacious because there can be no island greater than which none can be conceived. The argument, therefore, applies to one being and one being only—God.

Anselm's Original Argument

Chapter 1: Encouraging the Mind to Contemplate God

Come on now little man, get away from your worldly occupations for a while, escape from your tumultuous thoughts. Lay aside your burdensome cares and put off your laborious exertions. Give yourself over to God for a little while, and rest for a while in Him. Enter into the cell of your mind, shut out everything except God and whatever helps you to seek Him once the door is shut. Speak now, my heart, and say to God, "I seek your face; your face, Lord, I seek."

Come on then, my Lord God, teach my heart where and how to seek you, where and how to find you. Lord, if you are not here, where shall I find you? If, however, you are everywhere, why do I not see you here? But certainly you dwell in inaccessible light. And where is that inaccessible light? Or how do I reach it? Or who will lead me to it and into it, so that I can see you in it? And then by what signs, under what face shall I seek you? I have never seen you, my Lord God, or known your face. What shall I

do, Highest Lord, what shall this exile do, banished far from you as he is? What should your servant do, desperate as he is for your love yet cast away from your face? He longs to see you, and yet your face is too far away from him. He wants to come to you, and yet your dwelling place is unreachable. He yearns to discover you, and he does not know where you are. He craves to seek you, and does not know how to recognize you. Lord, you are my Lord and my God, and I have never seen you. You have made me and nurtured me, given me every good thing I have ever received, and I still do not know you. I was created for the purpose of seeing you, and I still have not done the thing I was made to do.

Oh, how miserable man's lot is when he has lost what he was made for! Oh how hard and dire was that downfall! Alas, what did he lose and what did he find? What was taken away and what remains? He has lost beatitude for which he was made, and he has found misery for which he was not made. That without which he cannot be happy has been taken away, and that remains which in itself can only make him miserable. Back then man ate the bread of angels for which he now hungers, and now he eats the bread of griefs which he did not even know back then. Alas for the common grief of man, the universal lamentation of Adam's sons! He belched in his satiety, while we sigh in our want. He was rich, we are beggars. He happily possessed and miserably abandoned, we unhappily lack and miserably desire, yet alas, we remain empty. Why, since it would have been easy for him, did he not keep what we so disastrously lack? Why did he deprive us of light, and cover us with darkness instead? Why did he take life away from us and inflict death instead? From what have we poor wretches been expelled, and toward what are we being driven? From what have we been cast down, in what buried? From our fatherland into exile, from the vision of God into blindness. From the happiness of immortality into the bitterness and horror of death. What a miserable transformation! From so much good into so much evil! A heavy injury, a heavy, heavy grief.

I have come to you as a poor man to a rich one, as a poor rich to a merciful giver. May I not return empty and rejected! And if "I sigh before I eat" (Job 3:4), once I have sighed give me something to eat. Lord, turned in (incurvatus) as I am I can only look down, so raise me up so that I can look up. "My iniquities heaped on my head" cover me over and weigh me down "like a heavy load" (Ps. 37:5). Dig me out and set me free before "the pit" created by them "shuts its jaws over me" (Ps. 67:16).Let me see your light, even if I see it from afar or from the depths. Teach me to seek you, and reveal yourself to this seeker. For I cannot seek you unless you teach me how, nor can I find you unless you show yourself to me. Let me seek you in desiring you, and desire you in seeking you. Let me find you in loving you and love you in finding you.

I acknowledge, Lord, and I give thanks that you have created in me this your image, so that I can remember you, think about you and love you. But it is so worn away by sins, so smudged over by the smoke of sins, that it cannot do what it was created to do unless you renew and reform it. I do not even try, Lord, to rise up to your heights, because my intellect does not measure up to that task; but I do want to understand in some small measure your truth, which my heart believes in and loved. Nor do I seek to un-

derstand so that I can believe, but rather I believe so that I can understand. For I believe this too, that "unless I believe I shall not understand" (Isa. 7:9).

Chapter 2: That God Really Exists

Therefore, Lord, you who give knowledge of the faith, give me as much knowledge as you know to be fitting for me, because you are as we believe and that which we believe. And indeed we believe you are something greater than which cannot be thought. Or is there no such kind of thing, for "the fool said in his heart, '"there is no God'"" (Ps. 13:1, 52:1)? But certainly that same fool, having heard what I just said, "something greater than which cannot be thought," understands what he heard, and what he understands is in his thought, even if he does not think it exists. For it is one thing for something to exist in a person's thought and quite another for the person to think that thing exists. For when a painter thinks ahead to what he will paint, he has that picture in his thought, but he does not yet think it exists, because he has not done it yet. Once he has painted it he has it in his thought and thinks it exists because he has done it. Thus even the fool is compelled to grant that something greater than which cannot be thought exists in thought, because he understands what he hears, and whatever is understood exists in thought. And certainly that greater than which cannot be understood cannot exist only in thought, for if it exists only in thought it could also be thought of as existing in reality as well, which is greater. If, therefore, that than which greater cannot be thought exists in thought alone, then that than which greater cannot be thought turns out to be that than which something greater actually can be thought, but that is obviously impossible. Therefore something than which greater cannot be thought undoubtedly exists both in thought and in reality.

Chapter 3: That God Cannot be Thought Not to Exist

In fact, it so undoubtedly exists that it cannot be thought of as not existing. For one can think there exists something that cannot be thought of as not existing, and that would be greater than something which can be thought of as not existing. For if that greater than which cannot be thought can be thought of as not existing, then that greater than which cannot be thought is not that greater than which cannot be thought, which does not make sense. Thus that than which nothing can be thought so undoubtedly exists that it cannot even be thought of as not existing.

And you, Lord God, are this being. You exist so undoubtedly, my Lord God, that you cannot even be thought of as not existing. And deservedly, for if some mind could think of something greater than you, that creature would rise above the creator and could pass judgment on the creator, which is absurd. And indeed whatever exists except you alone can be thought of as not existing. You alone of all things most truly exists and thus enjoy existence to the fullest degree of all things, because nothing else exists so undoubtedly, and thus everything else enjoys being in a lesser degree. Why therefore did the fool say in his heart "there is no God," since it is so evident to any rational mind that you above all things exist? Why indeed, except precisely because he is stupid and foolish

Chapter 4: How the Fool Managed to Say in His Heart That Which Cannot be Thought

How in the world could he have said in his heart what he could not think? Or how indeed could he not have thought what he said in his heart, since saying it in his heart is the same as thinking it? But if he really thought it because he said it in his heart, and did not say it in his heart because he could not possibly have thought it — and that seems to be precisely what happened — then there must be more than one way in which something can be said in one's heart or thought. For a thing is thought in one way when the words signifying it are thought, and it is thought in quite another way when the thing signified is understood. God can be thought not to exist in the first way but not in the second. For no one who understands what God is can think that he does not exist. Even though he may say those words in his heart he will give them some other meaning or no meaning at all. For God is that greater than which cannot be thought. Whoever understands this also understands that God exists in such a way that one cannot even think of him as not existing.

Gaunilo's "On Behalf of the Fool"

To one who questions whether (or simply denies that) there exists something of such a nature that nothing greater can be imagined, it is said that its existence is proved in the first place by the fact that anyone denying it already has it in his thought, since upon hearing it said he understands what is said; and in the second place by the fact that what he understands necessarily exists not only in the mind but in reality as well. Thus its existence is proved, because it is a greater thing to exist in reality as well than to exist in the mind alone, and if it exists only in the mind, then what exists in reality as well will be greater, and thus that which is greater than all else will be less than something else and not greater than all else, which is nonsense. Thus what is greater than all else must necessarily exist, not only in the mind (which has already been acknowledge to be the case), in reality as well, or else it could not be greater than all else.

But perhaps the fool could reply that this thing is said to exist in my mind only in the sense that I understand what is said. For could I not say that all sorts of false and completely nonexistent things exist in my mind since when someone speaks of them I understand what is said? Unless perhaps what is being said here is that one entertains this particular thing in the mind in a completely different way than one thinks of false or doubtful things, and thus what is being said is that having heard this particular thing I do not merely think it but understand it, for I cannot think of this thing in any other way except by understanding it, and that means understanding with certainty that it actually exists. But if this is true, then in the first place there will be no difference between first entertaining that thing in the mind and then understanding that it exists. Imagine the case of that picture which is first in the painter's mind, then exists in reality. It seems unthinkable that, once such an object was spoken of the words heard, the object could not be thought not to exist in the same way God can be thought not to exist. For if God cannot be thought not to exist, then what is the point of launching this whole argument against someone who might deny that something of such a nature actually exists? And in the second place, this basic notion—that God is such that, as soon as he is thought of, he must be perceived by the mind as unquestionably existing—this notion, I say, must be proved to me by some unquestionable argument, but not by the one offered here, namely that this must be in my understanding because I understand what I'm hearing. For as far as I am concerned one might say the same thing about other things that are certain or even false, things about which I might be deceived (as I believe I often am).

Thus the example of the painter who already has in his mind the picture he is about to produce cannot be made to support this argument. For that picture, before it comes into being, exists in the art of the painter, and such a thing existing in the art of some painter is nothing other than a certain part of his understanding; for as Saint Augustine says, "If a craftsman is going to make a box, he first has it in his art. The box he actually produces is not life, but that in his art is life, because the artisan's soul, in which all such things exist before they are brought forth, is alive. And how are these things alive in the living soul of the artisan unless because are nothing other than the knowledge or understanding of the soul itself? But leaving aside those things which are known to belong to the nature of the mind itself, in the case of those things which are perceived as true by the mind through hearing or thought, in this case there is a difference between the thing itself and the mind which grasps it. Thus even if it should be true that there is something greater than which cannot be thought, this thing, whether heard or understood, would not be like the as-yet-unmade picture in the painter's mind.

Moreover, there is the point already suggested earlier, namely that when hear of something greater than all other things which can be thought of—and that something can be nothing other than God himself—I can no more entertain a thought of this being in terms of species or genera familiar to me than I can entertain such a thought of God himself, and for this reason I am able to think he does not exist. For I have not known the thing itself and I cannot form a similitude of it from other things. For if I hear about some man completely unknown to me, whom I do not even know exists, I could at least think about him through that specific and generic knowledge by which I know what a man is or what men are like Yet it could be true that, because the speaker was lying, the man I thought about actually did not exist at all, even though I had thought of him as an existing thing, my idea of him being based, not on knowledge of this particular man, but on knowledge of man in general. But when I hear someone say "God" or "something greater than everything else" I cannot think of it as I thought of that nonexistent man, for I was able to think of the latter in terms of some truly existing thing known to me, while in the former case I can think only of the bare words, and on this basis alone one can seldom or never gain any true knowledge. For when one thinks in this way, one thinks not so much of the word itself - which, insofar as it is the sound of letters or syllables is itself a real thing, but of what is signified by the sound heard. But a phrase like "that which is greater than everything else" is not thought of as one thinks about words when one knows what they mean. It is not thought of, that is, as one thinks about something he knows is true either in reality or in thought alone. It is thought of, instead, as one does when he does not really know what the words mean, but thinks of it only in terms of an affection produced by the words within his soul, yet tries to imagine what the words mean. On this basis, though, it would be amazing if he was ever able to penetrate to the truth of the thing. It is in this way and only in this way that this being is in my mind when I hear and understand someone saying there is something greater than everything else that can be thought of. So much for the claim that the supreme nature already exists in my mind.

Nevertheless, that this being must exist not only in my mind but in reality as well is proved to me by the following argument: If it did not, then whatever did exist in reality would be greater, and thus the thing which has already been proved to exist in my mind will not be greater than everything else. If it is said that this being, which cannot be conceived of in terms of any existing thing, exists in the mind, I do not deny that it exists in mine. But through this alone it can hardly be said to attain existence in reality. I will not concede that much to it unless convinced by some indubitable argument. For whoever says that it must exist because otherwise that which is greater than all other beings will not be greater than all other beings, that person isn't paying careful enough attention to what he says. For I do not yet grant, in fact I deny it or at least question it, that the thing existing in my mind is greater than any real thing. Nor do I concede that it exists in any way except this: the sort of existence (if you can call it such) a thing has when the mind attempts to form some image of a thing unknown to it on the basis of nothing more than some words the person has heard. How then is it demonstrated to me that the thing exists in reality merely because it is said to be greater than everything else? For I continue to deny and doubt that this is established, since I continue to question whether this greater thing is in my mind or thought even in the way that many doubtful or unreal things are. It would first have to be proved to me that this greater thing really exists somewhere. Only then will we be able to infer from the fact that is greater than everything else that it also subsists in itself.

For example, they say there is in the ocean somewhere an island which, due to the difficulty (or rather the impossibility) of finding what does not actually exist, is called "the lost island." And they say that this island has all manner of riches and delights, even more of them than the Isles of the Blest, and having no owner or inhabitant it is superior in the abundance of its riches to all other lands which are inhabited by men. If someone should tell me that such is the case, I will find it easy to understand what he says, since there is nothing difficult about it. But suppose he then adds, as if he were stating a logical consequence, "Well then, you can no longer doubt that this island more excellent than all other lands really exists somewhere, since you do not doubt that it is in your mind; and since it is more excellent to exist not only in the mind but in reality as well, this island must necessarily exist, because if it didn't, any other island really existing would be more excellent than it, and thus that island now thought of by you as more excellent will not be such." If, I say, someone tries to convince me though this argument that the island really exists and there should be no more

doubt about it, I will either think he is joking or I will have a hard time deciding who is the bigger fool, me if I believe him or him if he thinks he has proved its existence without having first convinced me that this excellence is something undoubtedly existing in reality and not just something false or uncertain existing in my mind.

In the meantime, this is how the fool answers. If it is asserted in the first place that this being is so great that its nonbeing is logically inconceivable (this in turn being proved by nothing except that otherwise it would not be greater than all other beings), then the fool can answer, "When did I say that such a being, namely one greater than all others, actually exists, thus allowing you to proceed from there to argue that it so really exists that its very nonexistence is inconceivable?" It should first be proved conclusively that some being superior to (that is, greater and better than) all others exists, so that on this basis we can go on to prove the attributes such a greater and better being must possess. When, however, it is said that this highest being cannot be thought of as not existing, perhaps it would have been better to say that its nonbeing or the possibility of its nonbeing is unintelligible. For strictly speaking false things are unintelligible even though they can be thought of in the same way the fool thought God did not exist. I am absolutely certain that I exist, although I nevertheless know that my nonexistence is possible. And I understand without doubting it that the highest thing there is, namely God, exists and cannot not exist. I do not know, however, whether I can think of myself as nonexistant when I know for certain that I exist. If it turns out that I can do so in this case, why should I not be able to do the same concerning other things I know with equal certainty? If I cannot, though, the impossibility of doing so will not be something peculiar to thinking about God.

The other parts of that book are argued with such veracity, brilliance and splendor, and filled with such value, such an intimate fragrance of devout and holy feeling, that they should in no way be condemned because of those things which, at the beginning"it also prove that he exists are rightly intuited but less firmly argued. Rather those things should be argued more robustly and the entire work thus received with great respect and praise.

Anselm's Reply

Since whoever wrote this reply to me is not the fool against whom I wrote in my treatise but instead one who, though speaking on behalf of the fool, is a Catholic Christian and no fool himself, I can speak to him as a Catholic Christian.

You say—whoever you are who claim that the fool can say these things—that something greater than which cannot be thought of is in the mind only as something that cannot be thought of in terms of some [existent thing known to us]. And you say that one can no more argue, "since a being greater than which cannot be thought of exists in my mind it must also exist in reality," than one can argue, "the lost island certainly exists in reality because when it is described in words the hearer has no doubt that it exists in his mind." I say in reply that if "a being greater than which cannot be thought of" is neither understood nor thought of, nor is it in our understanding or our thought, then God either is not that greater than which cannot be thought of or he is not understood or thought of, nor is he in the understanding or mind. In proving that this is false I appeal to your faith and conscience. Therefore "a being greater than which cannot be thought of" is really understood and thought of and it really is in our understanding and thought. And that is why the arguments by which you attempt to prove the contrary either are not true or what you think follows from them does not follow from them at all.

Moreover, you imagine that although "a being greater than which cannot be thought of" is understood, it does not follow that it exists in our understanding nor does it follow that, since it is in our understanding, it must exist in reality. I myself say with certainty that if such a being can even be thought of as existing, it must necessarily exist. For "a being greater than which cannot be thought of" cannot be thought of except as having no beginning; but whatever can be thought of as existing yet does not actually exist can be thought of as having a beginning. Therefore "a being greater than which cannot be thought of" cannot be thought of yet not actually exist. Therefore, if it can be thought of, it necessarily exists.

Furthermore, if it can be thought of at all, it must necessarily exist. For no one who denies or doubts the existence of "a being greater than which cannot be thought of" denies or doubts that, if it did exist, it would be impossible for it not to exist either in reality or in the mind. Otherwise it would not be "a being greater than which cannot be thought of." But whatever can be thought of yet does not actually exist, could, if it did come to exist, not existence again in reality and in the mind. That is why, if it can even be thought of, "a being greater than which cannot be thought of" cannot be nonexistent.

But let us suppose that it does not exist (if it is even possible to suppose as much). Whatever can be thought of yet does not exist, even if it should come into existence, would not be 'a being greater than which cannot be thought of.' Thus "a being greater than which cannot be thought of" would not be "a being greater than which cannot be thought of," which is absurd. Thus if "a being greater than which cannot be thought of" can even be thought of, it is false to say that it does not exist; and it is even more false if such can be understood and exist in the understanding.

I will go even farther. Without doubt whatever does not exist somewhere or at some time, even if it does exist somewhere or at some time, can be thought of as capable of as existing never and nowhere, just as it does not exist somewhere or at some time. For what did not exist yesterday and exists today can be thought of as never existing, just as it is thought of as not having existed yesterday. And what does not exist here but does exist somewhere else can be thought of as not existing anywhere. And it is the same with something some parts of which are absent at times. If that is the case, then all of its parts and thus the thing in its entirety can be thought of as existing never and nowhere. For if it is said that time always exists and the world is everywhere, it is nevertheless true that time as a whole does not exist forever, nor does the entire world exist everywhere. And if individual parts of time exist when other parts do not, they can be thought of as never existing at all. And just as particular parts of the world do not exist where other parts do, so they can be thought of as never existing at all, anywhere. And what is composed of parts can be broken up in the mind and be nonexistent. Thus whatever does not exist as a whole sometime or somewhere can be thought of as not existing, even if it actually exists at the moment. But "a being greater than which cannot be thought of," if it exists, cannot be thought of as not existing. Otherwise it is not "a being greater than which cannot be thought of," which is absurd. Thus it cannot fail to exist in its totality always and everywhere.

Do you not believe that the being of which these things are understood can be thought about or understood or be in the thought or understanding to some extent? For if he is not, then we cannot understand these things about him. If you say that he is not understood or in the understanding because he is not fully understood, say as well that one who cannot look directly at the sun does not see the light of day, which is nothing other than the light of the sun. Certainly "a being greater than which cannot be thought of" is understood and exists in the understanding at least to the extent that these statements about it are understood.

Anselm continues as some length, but much of what he says seems repetitive. He does eventually note one important difference in the way he and Gaunilo have been phrasing the matter..

You often picture me as offering this argument: Because what is greater than all other things exists in the understanding, it must also exist in reality or else the being which is greater than all others would not be such. Never in my entire treatise do I say this. For there is a big difference between saying "greater than all other things" and "a being greater than which cannot be thought of." If someone says "a being greater than which cannot be thought of" is not something actually existing or is something which could possibly not exist or something which cannot even be understood, such assertions are easily refuted. For what does not exist is capable of not existing, and what is capable of not existing can be thought of as not existing. But whatever can be thought of as not existing, if it does actually exist, is not "a being greater than which cannot be thought of."

Anselm goes on to present his standard argument that the nonexistence of such a being is inconceivable. Then he adds a key observation.

It is not, it seems, so easy to prove the same thing of "that which is greater than all other things," for it is not all that obvious that something which can be thought of as not existing is not nevertheless greater than all things which actually exist.

Anselm of Canterbury. *Proslogion.* Trans. David Burr. 1996. Used with permission.

THE COSMOLOGICAL ARGUMENT

THOMAS AQUINAS (1225-1274)

After the maddening logical complexity of Anselm's ontological argument, the cosmological proofs for the existence of God offered by the 13th century theological Thomas Aquinas will probably seem much more straightforward. These arguments are a posteriori because they begin from observations about the way things are in the material universe in attempt to demonstrate a first cause—namely God—that is responsible for that reality which we experience.

Question 2: On the Existence of God

First Article: Whether the Existence of God is Self-Evident?

Objection 1: It seems that the existence of God is self-evident. Now those things are said to be self-evident to us the knowledge of which is naturally implanted in us, as we can see in regard to first principles. But as Damascene says (De Fide Orth. 1.1.3), "the knowledge of God is naturally implanted in all." Therefore the existence of God is self-evident.

Objection 2: Further, those things are said to be self-evident which are known as soon as the terms are known, which the Philosopher (1 Poster. 3) says is true of the first principles of demonstration. Thus, when the nature of a whole and of a part is known, it is at once recognized that every whole is greater than its part. But as soon as the signification of the word "God" is understood, it is at once seen that God exists. For by this word is signified that thing than which nothing greater can be conceived. But that which exists actually and mentally is greater than that which exists only mentally. Therefore, since as soon as the word "God" is understood it exists mentally, it also follows that it exists actually. Therefore the proposition "God exists" is self-evident.

Objection 3: Further, the existence of truth is self-evident. For whoever denies the existence of truth grants that truth does not exist: and, if truth does not exist, then the proposition "Truth does not exist" is true: and if there is anything true, there must be truth. But God is truth itself: "I am the way, the truth, and the life" (Jn. 14:6) Therefore "God exists" is self-evident.

On the contrary, No one can mentally admit the opposite of what is self-evident; as the Philosopher (Metaph. 4.6) states concerning the first principles of demonstration. But the opposite of the proposition "God is" can be mentally admitted: "The fool said in his heart, There is no God" (Ps. 52:1). Therefore, that God exists is not self-evident.

I answer that, A thing can be self-evident in either of two ways: on the one hand, self-evident in itself, though not to us; on the other, self-evident in itself, and to us. A proposition is self-evident because the predicate is included in the essence of the subject, as "Man is an animal," for animal is contained in the essence of man. If, therefore the essence of the predicate and subject be known to all, the proposition will be self-evident to all; as is clear with regard to the first principles of demonstration, the terms of which are common things that no one is ignorant of, such as being and non-being, whole and part, and such like. If, however, there are some to whom the essence of the predicate and subject is unknown, the proposition will be self-evident in itself, but not to those who do not know the meaning of the predicate and subject of the proposition. Therefore, it happens, as Boethius says..., "that there are some mental concepts self-evident only to the learned, as that incorporeal substances are not in space."

Therefore I say that this proposition, "God exists," of itself is self-evident, for the predicate is the same as the subject, because God is His own existence as will be hereafter shown....Now because we do not know the essence of God, the proposition is not self-evident to us; but needs to be demonstrated by things that are more known to us, though less known in their nature—namely, by effects.

Reply to Objection 1: To know that God exists in a general and confused way is implanted in us by nature, inasmuch as God is man's beatitude. For man naturally desires happiness, and what is naturally desired by man must be naturally known to him. This, however, is not to know absolutely that God exists; just as to know that someone is approaching is not the same as to know that Peter is approaching, even though it is Peter who is approaching; for many there are who imagine that man's perfect good which is happiness, consists in riches, and others in pleasures, and others in something else.

Reply to Objection 2: Perhaps not everyone who hears this word "God" understands it to signify something than which nothing greater can be thought, seeing that some have believed God to be a body. Yet, granted that everyone understands that by this word "God" is signified something than which nothing greater can be thought, nevertheless, it does not therefore follow that he understands that what the word signifies exists actually, but only that it exists mentally. Nor can it be argued that it actually exists, unless it be admitted that there actually exists something than which nothing greater can be thought; and this precisely is not admitted by those who hold that God does not exist.

Reply to Objection 3: The existence of truth in general is self-evident but the existence of a Primal Truth is not self-evident to us.

Second Article: Whether it can be Demonstrated that God Exists?

Objection 1: It seems that the existence of God cannot be demonstrated. For it is an article of faith that God exists. But what is of faith cannot be demonstrated, because a demonstration produces scientific knowledge; whereas faith is of the unseen (Heb. 11:1). Therefore it cannot be demonstrated that God

exists.

Objection 2: Further, the essence is the middle term of demonstration. But we cannot know in what God's essence consists, but solely in what it does not consist; as Damascene says (De Fide Orth. i, 4). Therefore we cannot demonstrate that God exists.

Objection 3: Further, if the existence of God were demonstrated, this could only be from His effects. But His effects are not proportionate to Him, since He is infinite and His effects are finite; and between the finite and infinite there is no proportion. Therefore, since a cause cannot be demonstrated by an effect not proportionate to it, it seems that the existence of God cannot be demonstrated.

On the contrary, The Apostle says: "The invisible things of Him are clearly seen, being understood by the things that are made" (Rom. 1:20). But this would not be unless the existence of God could be demonstrated through the things that are made; for the first thing we must know of anything is whether it exists.

I answer that, Demonstration can be made in two ways: One is through the cause, and is called "a priori," and this is to argue from what is prior absolutely. The other is through the effect, and is called a demonstration "a posteriori"; this is to argue from what is prior relatively only to us. When an effect is better known to us than its cause, from the effect we proceed to the knowledge of the cause. And from every effect the existence of its proper cause can be demonstrated, so long as its effects are better known to us; because since every effect depends upon its cause, if the effect exists, the cause must pre-exist. Hence the existence of God, in so far as it is not self-evident to us, can be demonstrated from those of His effects which are known to us.

Reply to Objection 1: The existence of God and other like truths about God, which can be known by natural reason, are not articles of faith, but are preambles to the articles; for faith presupposes natural knowledge, even as grace presupposes nature, and perfection supposes something that can be perfected. Nevertheless, there is nothing to prevent a man, who cannot grasp a proof, accepting, as a matter of faith, something which in itself is capable of being scientifically known and demonstrated.

Reply to Objection 2: When the existence of a cause is demonstrated from an effect, this effect takes the place of the definition of the cause in proof of the cause's existence. This is especially the case in regard to God, because, in order to prove the existence of anything, it is necessary to accept as a middle term the meaning of the word, and not its essence, for the question of its essence follows on the question of its existence. Now the names given to God are derived from His effects; consequently, in demonstrating the existence of God from His effects, we may take for the middle term the meaning of the word "God".

Reply to Objection 3: From effects not proportionate to the cause no perfect knowledge of that cause can be obtained. Yet from every effect the existence of the cause can be clearly demonstrated, and so we can demonstrate the existence of God from His effects; though from them we cannot perfectly know God as He is in His essence.

Third Article: Whether God exists?

Objection 1: It seems that God does not exist; because if one of two contraries be infinite, the other would be altogether destroyed. But the word "God" means that He is infinite goodness. If, therefore, God existed, there would be no evil discoverable; but there is evil in the world. Therefore God does not exist.

Objection 2: Further, it is superfluous to suppose that what can be accounted for by a few principles has been produced by many. But it seems that everything we see in the world can be accounted for by other principles, supposing God did not exist. For all natural things can be reduced to one principle which is nature; and all voluntary things can be reduced to one principle which is human reason, or will. Therefore there is no need to suppose God's existence.

On the contrary, It is said in the person of God: "I am Who am." (Ex. 3:14)

I answer that, The existence of God can be proved in five ways.

The first and more manifest way is the argument from motion. It is certain, and evident to our senses, that in the world some things are in motion. Now whatever is in motion is put in motion by another, for nothing can be in motion except it is in potentiality to that towards which it is in motion; whereas a thing moves inasmuch as it is in act. For motion is nothing else than the reduction of something from potentiality to actuality. But nothing can be reduced from potentiality to actuality, except by something in a state of actuality. Thus that which is actually hot, as fire, makes wood, which is potentially hot, to be actually hot, and thereby moves and changes it. Now it is not possible that the same thing should be at once in actuality and potentiality in the same respect, but only in different respects. For what is actually hot cannot simultaneously be potentially hot; but it is simultaneously potentially cold. It is therefore impossible that in the same respect and in the same way a thing should be both mover and moved, i.e. that it should move itself. Therefore, whatever is in motion must be put in motion by another. If that by which it is put in motion be itself put in motion, then this also must needs be put in motion by another, and that by another again. But this cannot go on to infinity, because then there would be no first mover, and, consequently, no other mover; seeing that subsequent movers move only inasmuch as they are put in motion by the first mover; as the staff moves only because it is put in motion by the hand. Therefore it is necessary to arrive at a first mover, put in motion by no other; and this everyone understands to be God.

The second way is from the nature of the efficient cause. In the world of sense we find there is an order of efficient causes. There is no case known (neither is it, indeed, possible) in which a thing is found to be the efficient cause of itself; for so it would be prior to itself, which is impossible. Now in efficient causes it is not possible to go on to infinity, because in all efficient causes following in order, the first is the cause of the intermediate cause, and the intermediate is the cause of the ultimate cause, whether the intermediate cause be several, or only one. Now to take away the cause is to take away the effect. Therefore, if there be no first cause among efficient causes, there will be no ultimate, nor any intermediate cause. But if in efficient causes it is possible to go on to infinity, there will be no first efficient cause, neither will there be an ultimate effect, nor any intermediate efficient causes; all of which is plainly false. Therefore it is necessary to admit a first efficient cause, to which everyone gives the name of God.

The third way is taken from possibility and necessity, and runs thus. We find in nature things that are possible to be and not to be, since they are found to be generated, and to corrupt, and consequently, they are possible to be and not to be. But it is impossible for these always to exist, for that which is possible not to be at some time is not. Therefore, if everything is possible not to be, then at one time there could have been nothing in existence. Now if this were true, even now there would be nothing in existence, because that which does not exist only begins to exist by something already existing. Therefore, if at one time nothing was in existence, it would have been impossible for anything to have begun to exist; and thus even now nothing would be in existence—which is absurd. Therefore, not all beings are merely possible, but there must exist something the existence of which is necessary. But every necessary thing either has its necessity caused by another, or not. Now it is impossible to go on to infinity in necessary things which have their necessity caused by another, as has been already proved in regard to efficient causes. Therefore we cannot but postulate the existence of some being having of itself its own necessity, and not receiving it from another, but rather causing in others their necessity. This all men speak of as God.

The fourth way is taken from the gradation to be found in things. Among beings there are some more and some less good, true, noble and the like. But "more" and "less" are predicated of different things, according as they resemble in their different ways something which is the maximum, as a thing is said to be hotter according as it more nearly resembles that which is hottest; so that there is something which is truest, something best, something noblest and, consequently, something which is uttermost being; for those things that are greatest in truth are greatest in being, as it is written in Metaph. ii. Now the maximum in any genus is the cause of all in that genus; as fire, which is the maximum heat, is the cause of all hot things. Therefore there must also be something which is to all beings the cause of their being, goodness, and every other perfection; and this we call God.

The fifth way is taken from the governance of the world. We see that things which lack intelligence, such as natural bodies, act for an end, and this is evident from their acting always, or nearly always, in the same way, so as to obtain the best result. Hence it is plain that not fortuitously, but designedly, do they achieve their end. Now whatever lacks intelligence cannot move towards an end, unless it be directed by some being endowed with knowledge and intelligence; as the arrow is shot to its mark by the archer. Therefore some intelligent being exists by whom all natural things are directed to their end; and this being we call God.

Reply to Objection 1: As Augustine says (Enchiridion xi): "Since God is the highest good, He would not allow any evil to exist in His works, unless His omnipotence and goodness were such as to bring good even out of evil." This is part of the infinite goodness of God, that He should allow evil to exist, and out of it produce good.

Reply to Objection 2: Since nature works for a determinate end under the direction of a higher agent, whatever is done by nature must needs be traced back to God, as to its first cause. So also whatever is done voluntarily must also be traced back to some higher cause other than human reason or will, since these can change or fail; for all things that are changeable and capable of defect must be traced back to an immovable and self-necessary first principle....

Thomas Aquinas. *Summa Theologica* I, Q.2. Trans. Fathers of the English Dominican Province. London: Washbourne, 1912.

THE WAGER

BLAISE PASCAL (1623-1662)

Blaise Pascal, a 17ᵗʰ century philosopher, scientist, and mathematician underwent a religious conversion in 1654, and as a result became personally convinced of the existence of God. As a member of the Jansenists, a radical Catholic movement, he spent the rest of his life working to promote the "true faith." In his most famous work of philosophy, Pensées (Thoughts), Pascal rejects the idea that God's existence can be proven rationally. Using an early form of probability theory, Pascal instead argues that, based upon the odds, belief in God gives one the greatest possible amount of benefit with the least possible cost.

We know that there is an infinite, and are ignorant of its nature. As we know it to be false that numbers are finite, it is therefore true that there is an infinity in number. But we do not know what it is. It is false that it is even, it is false that it is odd; for the addition of a unit can make no change in its nature. Yet it is a number, and every number is odd or even (this is certainly true of every finite number. So we may well know that there is a God without knowing what He is. Is there not one substantial truth, seeing that there are so many things which are not the truth itself?

We know the existence and nature of the finite, because we also are finite and have extension. We know the existence of the infinite, and are ignorant of its nature, because it has extension like us, but not limits like us. But we know neither the existence nor the nature of God, because He has neither extension nor limits.

But by faith we know His existence; in glory we shall know His nature. Now, I have already shown that we may well know the existence of a thing, without knowing its nature.

Let us now speak according to natural lights. If there is a God, He is infinitely incomprehensible, since, having neither parts nor limits, He has no affinity to us. We are then incapable of knowing either what He is or if He is. This being so, who will dare to undertake the decision of the question? Not we, who have no affinity to Him.

Who then will blame Christians for not being able to give a reason for their belief since they profess a religion for which they cannot give a reason? They declare, in expounding it to the world, that it is a foolishness; and then you complain that they do not prove it! If they proved it, they would not keep their words; it is in lacking proofs, that they are not lacking in sense. "Yes, but although this excuses those who offer it as such, and take away from them the blame of putting it forward without reason, it does not excuse those who receive it." Let us then examine this point, and say, "God is, or He is not." But to which side shall we incline? Reason can decide nothing here. There is an infinite chaos which separates us. A game is being played at the extremity of this infinite distance where heads or tails will turn up. What will you wager? According to reason, you can do neither the one thing nor the other; according to reason, you can defend neither of the propositions.

Do not then reprove for error those who have made a choice; for you know nothing about it. "No, but I blame them for having made, not this choice, but a choice; for again both he who chooses heads and he who chooses tails are equally at fault, they are both in the wrong. The true course is not to wager at all."

Yes; but you must wager. It is not optional. You are embarked. Which will you choose then; Let us see.

Since you must choose, let us see which interests you least. You have two things to lose, the true and the good; and two things to stake, your reason and your will, your knowledge and your happiness; and your nature has two things to shun, error and misery. Your reason is no more shocked in choosing one rather than the other, since you must of necessity choose. This is one point settled. But your happiness? Let us weigh the gain and the loss in wagering that God is. Let us estimate these two chances. If you gain, you gain all; if you lose, you lose nothing. Wager them without hesitation that He is. "That is very fine. Yes, I must wager; but I may perhaps wager too much."—Let us see. Since there is an equal risk of gain and of loss, if you had only to gain two lives, instead of one, you might still wager. But if there were three lives to gain, you would have to play (since you are under the necessity of playing), and you would be imprudent, when you are forced to play, not to chance your life to gain three at a game where there is an equal risk of loss and gain. But there is an eternity of life and happiness. And this being so, if there were an infinity of chances, of which one only would be for you, you would still be right in wagering one to win two, and you would act stupidly, being obliged to play, by refusing to stake one life against three at a game in which out of an infinity of chances there is one for you, if there were an infinity of an infinitely happy life to gain. But there is here an infinity of an infinitely happy life to gain, a chance of gain against a finite number of chances of loss, and what you stake is finite. It is all divided; wherever the infinite is and there is not an infinity of chances of loss against that of gain, there is no time to hesitate, you must give all. And thus, when one is forced to play, he must renounce reason to preserve his life, rather than risk it for infinite gain, as likely to happen as the loss of nothingness.

For it is no use to say it is uncertain if we will gain, and it is certain that we risk, and that the infinite distance between the certainty of what is staked and the uncertainty of what will be gained, equals the finite good which is certainly staked against the uncertain infinite. It is not so, as every player stakes a certainty to gain an uncertainty, and yet he stakes a finite certainty to gain a finite uncertainty, without transgressing against reason. There is not an infinite distance between the certainty staked and the uncertainty of the gain; that is untrue. In truth, there is an infinity between the certainty of gain and the certainty of loss. But the uncertainty of the gain is proportioned to the certainty of the stake according to the proportion of the chances of gain and loss.

Hence it comes that, if there are as many risks on one side as on the other, the course is to play even; and then the certainty of the stake is equal to the uncertainty of the gain, so far is it from the fact that there is an infinite distance between them. And so our proposition is of infinite force, when there is the finite to stake in a game where there are equal risks of gain and of loss, and the infinite to gain. This is demonstrable; and if men are capable of any truths, this is one. "I confess it, I admit it. But still is there no means of seeing the faces of the cards?"—Yes, Scripture and the rest, &c.—"Yes, but I have my hands tied and my mouth closed; I am forced to wager, and am not free. I am not released, and am so made that I cannot believe. What then would you have me do?"

Blaise Pascal. *Thoughts*. Trans. W. F. Trotter. New York: Collier & Son, 1910.

THE ARGUMENT FROM DESIGN

WILLIAM PALEY (1743-1805)

William Paley's argument from design (also known as the watchmaker analogy) is a teleological argument for the existence of God. The argument has been resurrected in recent years as "intelligent design" theory, which is often posed as an alternative to Darwin's theory of evolution. Paley's argument is extremely seductive in its simplicity. A watch, he argues, is a complex device which presupposes the existence of an intelligent designer who fashioned it. Likewise, the universe is filled with even more complex organisms and therefore presupposes the existence of a supreme being who serves as a kind of cosmic designer.

1. State of the Argument

In crossing a beach, suppose I hit my foot against a stone. Suppose I were asked how the stone came to be there. I might possibly answer that, for anything I knew to the contrary, it had lain there forever. It would be difficult to show that this answer is absurd.

But suppose I had found a watch upon the ground, and it should be asked how the watch happened to be in that place. I should hardly think of the answer which I had before given—that for anything I knew the watch might have always been there—would be an acceptable answer.

Yet why should not this answer serve for the watch as well as for the stone? Why is it not as admissible in the second case as in the first? For this reason, and for no other: namely, that when we come to inspect the watch, we perceive—what we could not discover in the stone—that its several parts are framed and put together for a purpose. The parts are so formed and adjusted as to produce motion, and that motion so regulated as to point out the hour of the day. If the different parts had been differently shaped from what they are, of a different size from what they are, or placed after any other manner or in any other order than that in which they are placed, either no motion at all would have been carried on in the machine, or none which would have answered the use that is now served by it.

To reckon up a few of the plainest of these parts and of their offices, all tending to one result; we see a cylindrical box containing a coiled elastic spring, which, by its endeavor to relax itself, turns round the box. We next observe a flexible chain—artificially wrought for the sake of flexure—communicating the action of the spring from the box to the fusee. We then find a series of wheels, the teeth of which catch in and apply to each other, conducting the motion from the fusee to the balance and from the balance to the pointer, and at the same time, by the size and shape of those wheels, so regulating that motion as to terminate in causing an index, by an equable and measured progression, to pass over a given space in a given time. We take notice that the wheels are made of brass, in order to keep them from rust; the springs of steel, no other metal being so elastic; that over the face of the watch there is placed a glass, a material employed in no other part of the work, but in the room of which, if there had been any other than a transparent substance, the hour could not be seen without opening the case. This mechanism being observed—it requires indeed an examination of the instrument, and perhaps some previous knowledge of the subject, to perceive and understand it; but being once, as we have said, observed and understood —the inference we think is inevitable, that the watch must have had a maker-that there must have existed, at some time and at some place or other, an artificer or artificers who formed it for the purpose which we find it actually to answer, who comprehended its construction and designed its use.

I. It wouldn't, I think, weaken the conclusion that the watch had a maker if we had never seen a watch made, if we had never known an artist capable of making one, if we were altogether incapable of executing such a piece of workmanship ourselves, or if we did not understanding the details of how watches are made (suppose watchmaking was a lost ancient art, or that it was, to most of humanity, one of the more curious productions of modern manufacture). Does one man in a million know how oval frames are turned? Ignorance of this kind exalts our opinion of the unseen and unknown artist's skiff, if he be unseen and unknown, but raises no doubt in our minds of the existence and agency of such an artist, at some former time and in some place or other. Nor can I perceive that it varies at all the inference that the watch has a maker, whether the question arise concerning a human agent or concerning an agent of a different species, or an agent possessing in some respects a different nature.

II. Neither, secondly, would it invalidate our conclusion, that the watch sometimes went wrong or that it seldom went exactly right. The purpose of the machinery, the design, and the designer might be evident, and in the case supposed, would be evident, in whatever way we accounted for the irregularity of the movement, or whether we could account for it or not. It is not necessary that a machine be perfect in order to show with what design it was made: still less necessary, where the only question is whether it were made with any design at all.

III. Nor, thirdly, would it bring any uncertainty into the argument, if there were a few parts of the watch which we could not discover or had not yet discovered what their purpose was for the general working of the watch; or even some parts which we could not ascertain whether they contributed to that general functioning of the watch in any manner whatever. For, as to the first branch of the case, if by the loss, or disorder, or decay of the parts in question, the movement of the watch were found in fact to be stopped, or disturbed, or retarded, no doubt would remain in our minds as to the utility or intention of these parts. Howeverly, we should be unable to investigate the manner according to which, or the connection by which, the ultimate effect depended upon their action or assistance. The more complex the machine, the more likely is this obscurity to arise. Then, as to the second thing supposed, namely, that there were parts which might be spared without causing problems to the movement of the watch, and that we had proved this by experiment, these superfluous parts, even if we were completely assured that they were such, would not vacate the reasoning which we had instituted concerning other parts. The reasons to think there's a designer remained, with respect to them, nearly as it was before.

IV. Nor, fourthly, would any man in his senses think the existence of the watch with its various machinery accounted for, by being told that it was one out of possible combinations of material forms; that whatever he had found in the place where he found the watch, must have contained some internal configuration or other; and that this configuration might be the structure now exhibited, namely, of the works of a watch, as well as a different structure.

V. Nor, fifthly, would it yield his inquiry more satisfaction, to be answered that there existed in things a principle of order, which had disposed the parts of the watch into their present form and situation. He never knew a watch made by the principle of order; nor can he even form to himself an idea of what is meant by a principle of order distinct from the intelligence of the watchmaker.

VI. Sixthly, he would be surprised to hear that the mechanism of the watch was no proof of contrivance, only a motive to induce the mind to think so:

VII. And not less surprised to be informed that the watch in his hand was nothing more than the result of the laws of metallic nature. It is a perversion of language to assign any law as the efficient, operative cause of any thing. A law presupposes an agent, for it is only the mode according to which an agent proceeds: it implies a power, for it is the order according to which that power acts. Without this agent, without this power, which are both distinct from itself, the law does nothing, is nothing. The expression, "the law of metallic nature," may sound strange and harsh to a philosophic ear; but it seems quite as justifiable as some others which are more familiar to him, such as "the law of vegetable nature," "the law of animal nature," or, indeed, as "the law of nature" in general, when assigned as the cause of phenomena, in exclusion of agency and power, or when it is substituted into the place of these.

VIII. Neither, lastly, would our observer be driven out of his conclusion or from his confidence in its truth by being told that he knew nothing at all about the matter. He knows enough for his argument; he knows the utility of the end; he knows the subserviency and adaptation of the means to the end. These points being known, his ignorance of other points, his doubts concerning other points affect not the certainty of his reasoning. The consciousness of knowing little need not beget a distrust of that which he does know.

2. State of the Argument Continued

Suppose, in the next place, that the person who found the watch should after some time discover that, in addition to all the properties which he had hitherto observed in it, it possessed the unexpected property of producing in the course of its movement another watch like itself—the thing is conceivable; that it contained within it a mechanism, a system of parts—a mold, for instance, or a complex adjustment of lathes, baffles, and other tools—evidently and separately calculated for this purpose; let us inquire what effect ought such a discovery to have upon his former conclusion.

I. The first effect would be to increase his admiration of the contrivance, and his conviction of the consummate skill of the contriver. Whether he regarded the object of the contrivance, the distinct apparatus, the intricate, yet in many parts intelligible mechanism by which it was carried on, he would perceive in this new observation nothing but an additional reason for doing what he had already done—for referring the construction of the watch to design and to supreme art. If that construction without this property, or, which is the same thing, before this property had been noticed, proved intention and art to have been employed about it, still more strong would the proof appear when he came to the knowledge of this further property, the crown and perfection of all the rest.

II. He would reflect, that though the watch before him were, in some sense, the maker of the watch, which, was fabricated in the course of its movements, yet it was in a very different sense from that in which a carpenter, for instance, is the maker of a chair—the author of its contrivance, the cause of the relation of its parts to their use. With respect to these, the first watch was no cause at all to the second; in no such sense as this was it the author of the constitution and order, either of the arts which the new watch contained, or of the parts by the aid and instrumentality of which it was produced. We might possibly say, but with great latitude of expression, that a stream of water ground corn; but no latitude of expression would allow us to say, no stretch of conjecture could lead us to think that the stream of water built the mill, though it were too ancient for us to know who the builder was. What the stream of water does in the affair is neither more nor less than this: by the application of an unintelligent impulse to a mechanism previously arranged, arranged independently of it and arranged by intelligence, an effect is produced, namely, the corn is ground. But the effect results from the arrangement. The force of the stream cannot be said to be the cause or author of the effect, still less of the arrangement. Understanding and plan in the formation of the mill were not the less necessary for any share which the water has in grinding the corn; yet is this share the same as that which the watch would have contributed to the production of the new watch, upon the supposition assumed in the last section. Therefore,

III. Though it be now no longer probable that the individual watch which our observer had found was made immediately by the hand of an artificer, yet does not this alteration in anyway affect the inference that an artificer had been originally employed and concerned in the production. The argument from design remains as it was. Marks of design and contrivance are no more accounted for now than they were before. In the same thing, we may ask for the cause of different properties. We may ask for the cause of the color of a body, of its hardness, of its heat; and these causes may be all different. We are now asking for the cause of that subserviency to a use, that relation to an end, which we have remarked in the watch before us. No answer is given to this question by telling us that a preceding watch produced it. There cannot be design without a designer; contrivance without a contriver; order without choice; arrangement without anything capable of arranging; subserviency and relation to a purpose without that which could intend a purpose; means suitable to an end, and executing their office in accomplishing that end, without the end ever having been contemplated or the means accommodated to it. Arrangement, disposition of parts, subserviency of means to an end, relation of instruments to a use imply the presence of intelligence and mind. No one, therefore, can rationally believe that the insensible, inanimate watch, from which the watch before us issued, was the proper cause of the mechanism we so much admire in it—could be truly said to have constructed the instrument, disposed its parts, assigned their office, determined their order, action, and mutual dependency, combined their several motions into one result, and that also a result connected with the utilities of other beings. All these properties, therefore, are as much unaccounted for as they were before.

IV. Nor is anything gained by running the difficulty farther back, that is, by supposing the watch before us to have been produced from another watch, that from a former, and so on indefinitely. Our going back ever so far brings us no nearer to the least degree of satisfaction upon the subject. Contrivance is still unaccounted for. We still want a contriver. A designing mind is neither supplied by this supposition nor dispensed with. If the difficulty were diminished the farther we went back, by going back indefinitely we might exhaust it. And this is the only case to which this sort of reasoning applies. Where there is a tendency, or, as we increase the number of terms, a continual approach toward a limit, there, by supposing the number of terms to be what is called infinite, we may conceive the limit to be attained; but where there is no such tendency or approach, nothing is effected by lengthening the series. There is no difference as to the point in question, whatever there may be as to many points, between one series and another—between a series which is finite and a series which is infinite. A chain composed of an infinite number of links, can no more support itself, than a chain composed of a finite number of links. And of this we are assured, though we never can have tried the experiment; because, by increasing the number of links, from ten, for instance, to a hundred, from a hundred to a thousand, etc., we make not the smallest approach, we observe not the smallest tendency toward self support. There is no difference in this respect—yet there may be a great difference in sev-

eral respects—between a chain of a greater or less length, between one chain and another, between one that is finite and one that is infinite. This very much resembles the case before us. The machine which we are inspecting demonstrates, by its construction, contrivance and design. Contrivance must have had a contriver, design a designer, whether the machine immediately proceeded from another machine or not. That circumstance alters not the case. That other machine may, in like manner, have proceeded from a former machine: nor does that alter the case; contrivance must have had a contriver. That former one from one preceding it: no alteration still; a contriver is still necessary. No tendency is perceived, no approach toward a diminution of this necessity. It is the same with any and every succession of these machines—a succession of ten, of a hundred, of a thousand; with one series, as with another -- a series which is finite, as with a series which is infinite. In whatever other respects they may differ, in this they do not. In all equally, contrivance and design are unaccounted for.

The question is not simply, How came the first watch into existence? which question, it may be pretended, is done away by supposing the series of watches thus produced from one another to have been infinite, and consequently to have had no such first for which it was necessary to provide a cause. This, perhaps, would have been nearly the state of the question, if nothing had been before us but an unorganized, unmechanized substance, without mark or indication of contrivance. It might be difficult to show that such substance could not have existed from eternity, either in succession—if it were possible, which I think it is not, for unorganized bodies to spring from one another—or by individual perpetuity. But that is not the question now. To suppose it to be so is to suppose that it made no difference whether he had found a watch or a stone. As it is, the metaphysics of that question have no place; for, in the watch which we are examining are seen contrivance, design, an end, a purpose, means for the end, adaptation to the purpose. And the question which irresistibly presses upon our thoughts is, whence this contrivance and design? The thing required is the intending mind, the adapting hand, the intelligence by which that hand was directed. This question, this demand is not shaken off by increasing a number or succession of substances destitute of these properties; nor the more, by increasing that number to infinity. If it be said that, upon the supposition of one watch being produced from another in the course of that other's movements and by means of the mechanism within it, we have a cause for the watch in my hand, namely, the watch from which it proceeded; I deny that for the design, the contrivance, the suitableness of means to an end, the adaptation of instruments to a use, all of which we discover in the watch, we have any cause whatever. It is in vain, therefore, to assign a series of such causes or to allege that a series may be carried back to infinity; for I do not admit that we have yet any cause at all for the phenomena, still less any series of causes either finite or infinite. Here is contrivance but no contriver; proofs of de- sign, but no designer.

V. Our observer would further also reflect that the maker of the watch before him was in truth and reality the maker of every watch produced from it: there being no difference, except that the latter manifests a more exquisite skill, between the making of another watch with his own hands, by the mediation of ffles, lathes, chisels, etc., and the disposing, fixing, and inserting of these instruments, or of others equivalent to them, in the body of the watch already made, in such a manner as io form a new watch in the course of the movements which he had given to the old one. It is only working by one set of tools instead of another.

The conclusion which the first examination of the watch, of its works, construction, and movement, suggested, was that it must have had, for cause and author of that construction, an artificer who understood its mechanism and designed its use. This conclusion is invincible. A second examination presents us with a new discovery. The watch is found, in the course of its movement, to produce another watch similar to itself; and not only so, but we perceive in it a system of organization separately calculated for that purpose. What effect would this discovery have or ought it to have upon our former inference? What, as has already been said, but to increase beyond measure our admiration of the skill which had been employed in the formation of such a machine? Or shall it, instead of this, all at once turn us round to an opposite conclusion, namely, that no art or skill whatever has been concerned in the business,

although all other evidences of art and skill remain as they were, and this last and supreme piece of art be now added to the rest? Can this be maintained without absurdity? Yet this is atheism....

5. Application of the Argument Continued

Every observation which was made in our first chapter concerning the watch may be repeated with strict propriety concerning the eye, concerning animals, concerning plants, concerning, indeed, all the organized parts of the works of nature. As,

I. When we are inquiring simply after the existence of an intelligent Creator, imperfection, inaccuracy, liability to disorder, occasional irregularities may subsist in a considerable degree without inducing any doubt into the question; just as a watch may frequently go wrong, seldom perhaps exactly right, may be faulty in some parts, defective in some, without the smallest ground of suspicion from thence arising that it was not a watch, not made, or not made for the purpose ascribed to it. When faults are pointed out, and when a question is started concerning the skill of the artist or dexterity with which the work is executed, then, indeed, in order to defend these qualities from accusation, we must be able either to expose some intractableness and imperfection in the materials or point out some invincible difficulty in the execution, into which imperfection and difficulty the matter of complaint may be resolved; or, if we cannot do this, we must ad- duce such specimens of consummate art and contrivance proceeding from the same hand as may convince the inquirer of the existence, in the case before him, of impediments like those which we have mentioned, although, what from the nature of the case is very likely to happen, they be unknown and unperceived by him. This we must do in order to vindicate the artist's skill, or at least the perfection of it; as we must also judge of his intention and of the provisions employed in fulfilling that intention, not from an instance in which they fail but from the great plurality of instances in which they succeed. But, after all, these are different questions from the question of the artist's existence; or, which is the same, whether the thing before us be a work of art or not; and the questions ought always to be kept separate in the mind. So likewise it is in the works of nature. Irregularities and imperfections are of little or no weight in the consideration when that consideration relates simply to the existence of a Creator. When the argument respects His attributes, they are of weight; but are then to be taken in conjunction-the attention is not to rest upon them, but they are to be taken in conjunction with the unexceptionable evidence which we possess of skill, power, and benevolence displayed in other instances; which evidences may, in strength, number, and variety, be such and may so overpower apparent blemishes as to induce us, upon the most reasonable ground, to believe that these last ought to be referred to some cause, though we be ignorant of it, other than defect of knowledge or of benevolence in the author. . . .

William Paley. *Natural Theology* (1800).

RELIGION AS THE OPIATE OF THE PEOPLE

KARL MARX (1818-1883)

Rejecting Feuerbach's anthropological arguments against the existence of God, Karl Marx instead focuses on the social and economic conditions that give rise to the belief in a supreme being and a heavenly afterlife. For Marx, religion is the ultimate drug, an illusion that human beings create as a psychic balm for what is essentially a harsh and unjust existence in this world. The rejection of God, then, becomes the means whereby human beings can begin to materially improve the world in which they actually live.

For Germany, the criticism of religion has been essentially completed, and the criticism of religion is the prerequisite of all criticism.

The profane existence of error is compromised as soon as its heavenly *oratio pro aris et focis* ("speech for the altars and hearths") has been refuted. Man, who has found only the reflection of himself in the fantastic reality of heaven, where he sought a superman, will no longer feel disposed to find the mere appearance of himself, the non-man ("*Unmensch*"), where he seeks and must seek his true reality.

The foundation of irreligious criticism is: Man makes religion, religion does not make man.

Religion is, indeed, the self-consciousness and self-esteem of man who has either not yet won through to himself, or has already lost himself again. But, man is no abstract being squatting outside the world. Man is the world of man—state, society. This state and this society produce religion, which is an inverted consciousness of the world, because they are an inverted world. Religion is the general theory of this world, its encyclopaedic compendium, its logic in popular form, its spiritual *point d'honneur*, it enthusiasm, its moral sanction, its solemn complement, and its universal basis of consolation and justification. It is the fantastic realization of the human essence since the human essence has not acquired any true reality. The struggle against religion is,

therefore, indirectly the struggle against that world whose spiritual aroma is religion.

Religious suffering is, at one and the same time, the expression of real suffering and a protest against real suffering. Religion is the sigh of the oppressed creature, the heart of a heartless world, and the soul of soulless conditions. It is the opium of the people.

The abolition of religion as the illusory happiness of the people is the demand for their real happiness. To call on them to give up their illusions about their condition is to call on them to give up a condition that requires illusions.

The criticism of religion is, therefore, in embryo, the criticism of that vale of tears of which religion is the halo.

Criticism has plucked the imaginary flowers on the chain not in order that man shall continue to bear that chain without fantasy or consolation, but so that he shall throw off the chain and pluck the living flower. The criticism of religion disillusions man, so that he will think, act, and fashion his reality like a man who has discarded his illusions and regained his senses, so that he will move around himself as his own true Sun. Religion is only the illusory Sun which revolves around man as long as he does not revolve around himself.

It is, therefore, the task of history, once the other-world of truth has vanished, to establish the truth of this world. It is the immediate task of philosophy, which is in the service of history, to unmask self-estrangement in its unholy forms once the holy form of human self-estrangement has been unmasked.

Thus, the criticism of Heaven turns into the criticism of Earth, the criticism of religion into the criticism of law, and the criticism of theology into the criticism of politics.

Karl Marx. *Introduction to a Contribution to the Critique of Hegel's Philosophy of Right.* Deutsch-Französische Jahrbucher (February, 1844).

RELIGION AS ILLUSION

SIGMUND FREUD (1856-1939)

The 19th century was the age of the great "masters of suspicion"— Marx, Nietzsche, and Freud. Each of these thinkers in his own way sought to challenge the theistic foundations of Western society by formulating innovative theories about the "true" origins of religious ideas and beliefs. For Freud, religious beliefs are entirely human constructs and, therefore, nothing more than illusions we create to help us endure the harsh realities of our human condition and the inevitability of death. The rejection of religion, which Freud regarded as a kind of infantile neurosis, is the first step in attaining psychological maturity.

In what does the peculiar value of religious ideas lie?

We have spoken of the hostility to civilization which is produced by the pressure that civilization exercises, the renunciations of instinct which it demands. If one imagines its prohibitions lifted if, then, one may take any woman one pleases as a sexual object, if one may without hesitation kill one's rival for her love or anyone else who stands in one's way, if, too, one can carry off any of the other man's belongings without asking leave how splendid, what a string of satisfactions one's life would be! True, one soon comes across the first difficulty: everyone else has exactly the same wishes as I have and will treat me with no more consideration than I treat him. And so in reality only one person could be made unrestrictedly happy by such a removal of the restrictions of civilization, and he would be a tyrant, a dictator, who had seized all the means to power. And even he would have every reason to wish that the others would observe at least one cultural commandment: 'thou shalt not kill'.

1. Civilization as Defense Against Nature

But how ungrateful, how short-sighted after all, to strive for the abolition of civilization! What would then remain would be a state of nature, and that would be far harder to bear. It is true that nature would not demand any restrictions of instinct from us, she would let us do as we liked; but she has her own particularly effective method of restricting us. She destroys us coldly, cruelly, relentlessly, as it seems to us, and possibly through the very things that occasioned our satisfaction. It was precisely because of these dangers with which nature threatens us that we came together and created civilization, which is also, among other things, intended to make our communal life possible. For the principal task of civilization, its actual raison d'être, is to defend us against nature.

We all know that in many ways civilization does this fairly well already, and clearly as time goes on it will do it much better. But no one is under the illusion that nature has already been vanquished; and few dare hope that she will ever be entirely subjected to man. There are the elements, which seem to mock at all human control: the earth, which quakes and is torn apart and buries all human life and its works; water, which deluges and drowns everything in a turmoil; storms, which blow everything before them; there are diseases, which we have only recently recognized as attacks by other organisms; and finally there is the painful riddle of death, against which no medicine has yet been found, nor probably will be. With these forces nature rises up against us, majestic, cruel and inexorable; she brings to our mind once more our weakness and helplessness, which we thought to escape through the work of civilization. One of the few gratifying and exalting impressions which mankind can offer is when, in the face of an elemental catastrophe, it forgets the discordancies of its civilization and all its internal difficulties and animosities, and recalls the great common task of preserving itself against the superior power of nature.

For the individual, too, life is hard to bear, just as it is for mankind in general. The civilization in which he participates imposes some amount of privation on him, and other men bring him a measure of suffering, either in spite of the precepts of his civilization or because of its imperfections. To this are added the injuries which untamed nature he calls it Fate inflicts on him. One might suppose that this condition of things would result in a permanent state of anxious expectation in him and a severe injury to his natural narcissism. We know already how the individual reacts to the injuries which civilization and other men inflict on him: he develops a corresponding degree of resistance to the regulations of civilization and of hostility to it. But how does he defend himself against the superior powers of nature, of Fate, which threaten him as they threaten all the rest?

2. Humanizing the Forces of Nature

Civilization relieves him of this task; it performs it in the same way for all alike; and it is noteworthy that in this almost all civilizations act alike. Civilization does not call a halt in the task of defending man against nature, it merely pursues it by other means. The task is a manifold one. Man's self-regard, seriously menaced, calls for consolation; life and the universe must be robbed of their terrors; moreover his curiosity, moved, it is true, by the strongest practical interest, demands an answer.

A great deal is already gained with the first step: the humanization of nature. Impersonal forces and destinies cannot be approached; they remain eternally remote. But if the elements have passions that rage as they do in our own souls, if death itself is not something spontaneous but the violent act of an evil Will, if everywhere in nature there are Beings around us of a kind that we know in our own society, then we can breathe freely, can feel at home in the uncanny and can deal by psychical means with our senseless anxiety. We are still defenceless, perhaps, but we are no longer helplessly paralysed; we can at least react. Perhaps, indeed, we are not even defenceless. We can apply the same methods against these violent supermen outside that we employ in our own society; we can try to adjure them, to appease them, to bribe them, and, by so influencing them, we may rob them of a part of their power. A replacement like this of natural science by psychology not only provides immediate relief, but also points the way to a further mastering of the situation.

For this situation is nothing new. It has an infantile prototype, of which it is in fact only the continuation. For once before one has found oneself in a similar state of helplessness: as a small child, in relation to one's parents. One had reason to fear them, and especially one's father; and yet one was sure of his protection against the dangers one knew. Thus it was natural to assimilate the two situations. Here, too, wishing played its part, as it does in dream-life. The sleeper may be seized with a presentiment of death, which threatens to place him in the grave. But the dream-work knows how to select a condition that will turn even that dreaded event into a wish-fulfilment: the dreamer sees himself in an ancient Etruscan grave which he has climbed down into, happy to find his archaeological interests satisfied. In the same way, a man makes the forces of nature not simply into persons with whom he can associate as he would with his equals—that would not do justice to the overpowering impression which those forces make on him—but he gives them the character of a father. He turns them into gods, following in this, as I have tried to show, not only an infantile prototype but a phylogenetic one.

In the course of time the first observations were made of regularity and conformity to law in natural phenomena, and with this the forces of nature lost their human traits. But man's helplessness remains and along with it his longing for his father, and the gods. The gods retain their threefold task: they must exorcize the terrors of nature, they must reconcile men to the cruelty of Fate, particularly as it is shown in death, and they must compensate them for the sufferings and privations which a civilized life in common has imposed on them.

But within these functions there is a gradual displacement of accent. It was observed that the phenomena of nature developed automatically according to internal necessities. Without doubt the gods were the lords of nature; they had arranged it to be as it was and now they could leave it to itself. Only occasionally, in what are known as miracles, did they intervene in its course, as though to make it plain that they had relinquished nothing of their original sphere of power. As regards the apportioning of destinies, an unpleasant suspicion persisted that the perplexity and helplessness of the human race could not be remedied. It was here that the gods were most apt to fail. If they themselves created Fate, then their counsels must be deemed inscrutable. The notion dawned on the most gifted people of antiquity that Moira [Fate] stood above the gods and that the gods themselves had their own destinies. And the more autonomous nature became and the more the gods withdrew from it, the more earnestly were all expectations directed to the third function of the gods—the more did morality become their true domain. It now became the task of the gods to even out the defects and evils of civilization, to attend to the sufferings which men inflict on one another in their life together and to watch over the fulfilment of the precepts of civilization, which men obey so imperfectly. Those precepts themselves were credited with a divine origin; they were elevated beyond human society and were extended to nature and the universe.

3. Creating a Religious Mythology

And thus a store of ideas is created, born from man's need to make his helplessness tolerable and built up from the material of memories of the helplessness of his own childhood and the childhood of the human race. It can clearly be seen that the possession of these ideas protects him in two directions against the dangers of nature and Fate, and against the injuries that threaten him from human society itself. Here is the gist of the matter. Life in this world serves a higher purpose; no doubt it is not easy to guess what that purpose is, but it certainly signifies a perfecting of man's nature. It is probably the spiritual part of man, the soul, which in the course of time has so slowly and unwillingly detached itself from the body, that is the object of this elevation and exaltation. Everything that happens in this world is an expression of the intentions of an intelligence superior to us, which in the end, though its ways and byways are difficult to follow, orders everything for the best— that is, to make it enjoyable for us. Over each one of us there watches a benevolent Providence which is only seemingly stern and which will not suffer us to become a plaything of the overmighty and pitiless forces of nature. Death itself is not extinction, is not a return to inorganic lifelessness, but the beginning of a new kind of existence which lies on the path of development to something higher. And, looking in the other direction, this view announces that the same moral laws which our civilizations have set up govern the whole universe as well, except that they are maintained by a supreme court of justice with incomparably more power and consistency. In the end all good is rewarded and all evil punished, if not actually in this form of life then in the later existences that begin after death. In this way all the terrors, the sufferings and the hardships of life are destined to be obliterated. Life after death, which continues life on earth just as the invisible part of the spectrum joins on to the visible part, brings us all the perfection that we may perhaps have missed here. And the superior wisdom which directs this course of things, the infinite goodness that expresses itself in it, the justice that achieves its aim in it these are the attributes of the divine beings who also created us and the world as a whole, or rather, of the one divine being into which, in our civilization, all the gods of antiquity have been condensed. The people which first succeeded in thus concentrating the divine attributes was not a little proud of the advance. It had laid open to view the father who had all along been hidden behind every divine figure as its nucleus. Fundamentally this was a return to the historical beginnings of the idea of God....

4. Religion as Wish Fulfillment

Let us now take up the thread of our enquiry. What, then, is the psychological significance of religious ideas and under what heading are we to classify them? The question is not at all easy to answer immediately. After rejecting a number of formulations, we will take our stand on the following one. Religious ideas are teachings and assertions about facts and conditions of external (or internal) reality which tell one something one has not discovered for oneself and which lay claim to one's belief. Since they give us information about what is most important and interesting to us in life, they are particularly highly prized. Anyone who knows nothing of them is very ignorant; and anyone who has added them to his knowledge may consider himself much the richer....

We must ask where the inner force of those doctrines lies and to what it is that they owe their efficacy, independent as it is of recognition by reason.

I think we have prepared the way sufficiently for an answer to both these questions. It will be found if we turn our attention to the psychical origin of religious ideas. These, which are given out as teachings, are not precipitates of experience or end-results of thinking: they are illusions, fulfilments of the oldest, strongest and most urgent wishes of mankind. The secret of their strength lies in the strength of those wishes. As we already know, the terrifying impression of helplessness in childhood aroused the need for protection for protection through love which was provided by the father; and the recognition that this helplessness lasts throughout life made it necessary to cling to the existence of a father, but this time a more powerful one. Thus the benevolent rule of a divine Providence allays our fear of the dangers of life; the establishment of a moral world-order ensures the fulfilment of the demands of justice, which have so often remained unfulfilled in human civilization; and the prolongation of earthly existence in a future life provides the local and temporal framework in which these wish-fulfilments shall take place. Answers to the riddles that tempt the curiosity of man, such as how the universe began or what the relation is between body and mind, are developed in conformity with the underlying assumptions of this system. It is an enormous relief to the individual psyche if the conflicts of its childhood arising from the father-complex—conflicts which it has never wholly overcome—are removed from it and brought to a solution which is universally accepted.

5. Religious Beliefs as Illusions

When I say that these things are all illusions, I must define the meaning of the word. An illusion is not the same thing as an error; nor is it necessarily an error. Aristotle's belief that vermin are developed out of dung (a belief to which ignorant people still cling) was an error; so was the belief of a former generation of doctors that *tabes dorsalis* is the result of sexual excess. It would be incorrect to call these errors illusions. On the other hand, it was an illusion of Columbus's that he had discovered a new sea-route to the Indies. The part played by his wish in this error is very clear. One may describe as an illusion the assertion made by certain nationalists that the Indo-Germanic race is the only one capable of civilization; or the belief, which was only destroyed by psycho-analysis, that children are creatures without sexuality. What is characteristic of illusions is that they are derived from human wishes. In this respect they come near to psychiatric delusions. But they differ from them, too, apart from the more complicated structure of delusions. In the case of delusions, we emphasize as essential their being in contradiction with reality. Illusions need not necessarily be false that is to say, unrealizable or in contradiction to reality. For instance, a middle-class girl may have the illusion that a prince will come and marry her. This is possible; and a few such cases have occurred. That the Messiah will come and found a golden age is much less likely.

Whether one classifies this belief as an illusion or as something analogous to a delusion will depend on one's personal attitude. Examples of illusions which have proved true are not easy to find, but the illusion of the alchemists that all metals can be turned into gold might be one of them. The wish to have a great deal of gold, as much gold as possible, has, it is true, been a good deal damped by our present-day knowledge of the determinants of wealth, but chemistry no longer regards the transmutation of metals into gold as impossible. Thus we call a belief an illusion when a wish-fulfilment is a prominent factor in its motivation, and in doing so we disregard its relations to reality, just as the illusion itself sets no store by verification.

Having thus taken our bearings, let us return once more to the question of religious doctrines. We can now repeat that all of them are illusions and insusceptible of proof. No one can be compelled to think them true, to believe in them. Some of them are so improbable, so incompatible with everything we have laboriously discovered about the reality of the world, that we may compare them—if we pay proper regard to the psychological differences—to delusions. Of the reality value of most of them we cannot judge; just as they cannot be proved, so they cannot be refuted. We still know too little to make a critical approach to them. The riddles of the universe reveal themselves only slowly to our investigation; there are many questions to which science to-day can give no answer. But scientific work is the only road which can lead us to a knowledge of reality outside ourselves. It is once again merely an illusion to expect anything from intuition and introspection; they can give us nothing but particulars about our own mental life, which are hard to interpret, never any information about the questions which religious doctrine finds it so easy to answer....

6. Religion as Universal Obsessive Neurosis

We now observe that the store of religious ideas includes not only wish-fulfilments but important historical recollections. This concurrent influence of past and present must give religion a truly incomparable wealth of power. But perhaps with the help of an analogy yet another discovery may begin to dawn on us. Though it is not a good plan to transplant ideas far from the soil in which they grew up, yet here is a conformity which we cannot avoid pointing out. We know that a human child cannot successfully complete its development to the civilized stage without passing through a phase of neurosis sometimes of greater and sometimes of less distinctness. This is because so many instinctual demands which will later be unserviceable cannot be suppressed by the rational operation of the child's intellect but have to be tamed by acts of repression, behind which, as a rule, lies the motive of anxiety. Most of these infantile neuroses are overcome spontaneously in the course of growing up, and this is especially true of the obsessional neuroses of childhood. The remainder can be cleared up later still by psycho-analytic treatment. In just the same way, one might assume, humanity as a whole, in its development through the ages, fell into states analogous to the neuroses, and for the same reasons—namely because in the times of its ignorance and intellectual weakness the instinctual renunciations indispensable for man's communal existence had only been achieved by it by means of purely affective forces. The precipitates of these processes resembling repression which took place in prehistoric times still remained attached to civilization for long periods. Religion would thus be the universal obsessional neurosis of humanity; like the obsessional neurosis of children, it arose out of the Oedipus complex, out of the relation to the father. If this view is right, it is to be supposed that a turning-away from religion is bound to occur with the fatal inevitability of a process of growth, and that we find ourselves at this very juncture in the middle of that phase of development....

Thus I must contradict you when you go on to argue that men are completely unable to do without the consolation of the religious illusion, that without it they could not bear the troubles of life and the cruelties of reality. That is true, certainly, of the men into whom you have instilled the sweet—or bitter-sweet poison—from childhood onwards. But what of the other men, who have been sensibly brought up? Perhaps those who do not suffer from the neurosis will need no intoxicant to deaden it. They

will, it is true, find themselves in a difficult situation. They will have to admit to themselves the full extent of their helplessness and their insignificance in the machinery of the universe; they can no longer be the centre of creation, no longer the object of tender care on the part of a beneficent Providence. They will be in the same position as a child who has left the parental house where he was so warm and comfortable. But surely infantilism is destined to be surmounted. Men cannot remain children for ever; they must in the end go out into 'hostile life'. We may call this 'education to reality'. Need I confess to you that the sole purpose of my book is to point out the necessity for this forward step?

You are afraid, probably, that they will not stand up to the hard test? Well, let us at least hope they will. It is something, at any rate, to know that one is thrown upon one's own resources. One learns then to make a proper use of them. And men are not entirely without assistance. Their scientific knowledge has taught them much since the days of the Deluge, and it will increase their power still further. And, as for the great necessities of Fate, against which there is no help, they will learn to endure them with resignation. Of what use to them is the mirage of wide acres in the moon, whose harvest no one has ever yet seen? As honest smallholders on this earth they will know how to cultivate their plot in such a way that it supports them. By withdrawing their expectations from the other world and concentrating all their liberated energies into their life on earth, they will probably succeed in achieving a state of things in which life will become tolerable for everyone and civilization no longer oppressive to anyone. Then, with one of our fellow-unbelievers, they will be able to say without regret:

Den Himmel überlassen wir
Den Engeln und den Spatzen.

[We leave Heaven
to the angels and the sparrows.]

Sigmund Freud. *The Future of an Illusion. Complete Psychological Works of Sigmund Freud. Volume 21.* Trans. James Strachey. London: Hogarth Press, 1927.

EVIL AND THE EXISTENCE OF GOD

FYODOR DOSTOYEVSKY (1821-1881)

One of the great stumbling blocks for a belief in God throughout the centuries has been the existence of evil in the world. The problem of evil argument goes as follows: God is good, but evil seems to thrive in the world and innocents suffer unjustly (Think about the six million Jews who were killed in the Holocaust or children who are regularly tormented at the hands of sadistic parents.). The implication is that either God doesn't really care about such suffering (or why wouldn't he stop it?) or he doesn't really exist at all. In the following selection from The Brothers Karamazov, *this essentially is the argument that Ivan Karamazov makes to his pious brother, Alyosha. In the end, Alyosha is simply unable to accept Ivan's argument, calling it "rebellion." But Ivan is given the last word and the devout Alyosha finds himself unable to meet Ivan's challenge to his faith.*

"Well, tell me where to begin, give your orders. The existence of God, eh?" [Ivan said]

"Begin where you like. You declared yesterday at father's that there was no God." Alyosha looked searchingly at his brother.

"I said that yesterday at dinner on purpose to tease you and I saw your eyes glow. But now I've no objection to discussing with you, and I say so very seriously. I want to be friends with you, Alyosha, for I have no friends and want to try it. Well, only fancy, perhaps I too accept God," laughed Ivan; "that's a surprise for you, isn't it?"

"Yes of course, if you are not joking now."

"Joking? I was told at the elder's yesterday that I was joking. You know, dear boy, there was an old sinner in the eighteenth century who declared that, if there were no God, he would have to be invented. S'il n'existait pas Dieu, il faudrait l'inventer.* And man has actually invented God. And what's strange, what would be marvellous, is not that God should really exist; the marvel is that such an idea, the idea of the necessity of God, could enter the head of such a savage, vicious beast as man. So holy it is, so touching, so wise and so great a credit it does to man. As for me, I've long resolved not to think whether man created God or God man. And I won't go through all the axioms laid down by Russian boys on that subject, all derived from European hy-

potheses; for what's a hypothesis there is an axiom with the Russian boy, and not only with the boys but with their teachers too, for our Russian professors are often just the same boys themselves. And so I omit all the hypotheses. For what are we aiming at now? I am trying to explain as quickly as possible my essential nature, that is what manner of man I am, what I believe in, and for what I hope, that's it, isn't it? And therefore I tell you that I accept God simply. But you must note this: if God exists and if He really did create the world, then, as we all know, He created it according to the geometry of Euclid and the human mind with the conception of only three dimensions in space. Yet there have been and still are geometricians and philosophers, and even some of the most distinguished, who doubt whether the whole universe, or to speak more widely, the whole of being, was only created in Euclid's geometry; they even dare to dream that two parallel lines, which according to Euclid can never meet on earth, may meet somewhere in infinity. I have come to the conclusion that, since I can't understand even that, I can't expect to understand about God. I acknowledge humbly that I have no faculty for settling such questions, I have a Euclidian earthly mind, and how could I solve problems that are not of this world? And I advise you never to think about it either, my dear Alyosha, especially about God, whether He exists or not. All such questions are utterly inappropriate for a mind created with an idea of only three dimensions. And so I accept God and am glad to, and what's more, I accept His wisdom, His purpose which are utterly beyond our ken; I believe in the underlying order and the meaning of life; I believe in the eternal harmony in which they say we shall one day be blended. I believe in the Word to Which the universe is striving, and Which Itself was 'with God,' and Which Itself is God and so on, and so on, to infinity. There are all sorts of phrases for it. I seem to be on the right path, don't I'? Yet would you believe it, in the final result I don't accept this world of God's, and, although I know it exists, I don't accept it at all. It's not that I don't accept God, you must understand, it's the world created by Him I don't and cannot accept. Let me make it plain. I believe like a child that suffering will be healed and made up for, that all the humiliating absurdity of human contradictions will vanish like a pitiful mirage, like the despicable fabrication of the impotent and infinitely small Euclidian mind of man, that in the world's finale, at the moment of eternal harmony, something so precious will come to pass that it will suffice for all hearts, for the comforting of all resentments, for the atonement of all the crimes of humanity, of all the blood they've shed; that it will make it not only possible to forgive but to justify all that has happened with men- but thought all that may come to pass, I don't accept it. I won't accept it. Even if parallel lines do meet and I see it myself, I shall see it and say that they've met, but still I won't accept it. That's what's at the root of me, Alyosha; that's my creed. I am in earnest in what I say. I began our talk as stupidly as I could on purpose, but I've led up to my confession, for that's all you want. You didn't want to hear about God, but only to know what the brother you love lives by. And so I've told you."

Ivan concluded his long tirade with marked and unexpected feeling.

"And why did you begin 'as stupidly as you could?'" asked Alyosha, looking dreamily at him.

"To begin with, for the sake of being Russian. Russian conversations on such subjects are always carried on inconceivably stupidly. And secondly, the stupider one is, the closer one is to reality. The stupider one is, the clearer one is. Stupidity is brief and artless, while intelligence wriggles and hides itself.

Intelligence is a knave, but stupidity is honest and straight forward. I've led the conversation to my despair, and the more stupidly I have presented it, the better for me."

"You will explain why you don't accept the world?" said Alyosha.

"To be sure I will, it's not a secret, that's what I've been leading up to. Dear little brother, I don't want to corrupt you or to turn you from your stronghold, perhaps I want to be healed by you." Ivan smiled suddenly quite like a little gentle child. Alyosha had never seen such a smile on his face before.

Rebellion

"I must make one confession" Ivan began. "I could never understand how one can love one's neighbours. It's just one's neighbours, to my mind, that one can't love, though one might love those at a distance. I once read somewhere of John the Merciful, a saint, that when a hungry, frozen beggar came to him, he took him into his bed, held him in his arms, and began breathing into his mouth, which was putrid and loathsome from some awful disease. I am convinced that he did that from 'self-laceration,' from the self-laceration of falsity, for the sake of the charity imposed by duty, as a penance laid on him. For anyone to love a man, he must be hidden, for as soon as he shows his face, love is gone."

"Father Zossima has talked of that more than once," observed Alyosha; "he, too, said that the face of a man often hinders many people not practised in love, from loving him. But yet there's a great deal of love in mankind, and almost Christ-like love. I know that myself, Ivan."

"Well, I know nothing of it so far, and can't understand it, and the innumerable mass of mankind are with me there. The question is, whether that's due to men's bad qualities or whether it's inherent in their nature. To my thinking, Christ-like love for men is a miracle impossible on earth. He was God. But we are not gods. Suppose I, for instance, suffer intensely. Another can never know how much I suffer, because he is another and not I. And what's more, a man is rarely ready to admit another's suffering (as though it were a distinction). Why won't he admit it, do you think? Because I smell unpleasant, because

I have a stupid face, because I once trod on his foot. Besides, there is suffering and suffering; degrading, humiliating suffering such as humbles me--hunger, for instance—my benefactor will perhaps allow me; but when you come to higher suffering--for an idea, for instance—he will very rarely admit that, perhaps because my face strikes him as not at all what he fancies a man should have who suffers for an idea. And so he deprives me instantly of his favour, and not at all from badness of heart. Beggars, especially genteel beggars, ought never to show themselves, but to ask for charity through the newspapers. One can love one's neighbours in the abstract, or even at a distance, but at close quarters it's almost impossible. If it were as on the stage, in the ballet, where if beggars come in, they wear silken rags and tattered lace and beg for alms dancing gracefully, then one might like looking at them. But even then we should not love them. But enough of that. I simply wanted to show you my point of view. I meant to speak of the suffering of mankind generally, but we had better confine ourselves to the sufferings of the children. That reduces the scope of my argument to a tenth of what it would be. Still we'd better keep to the children, though it does weaken my case. But, in the first place, children can be loved even at close quarters, even when they are dirty, even when they are ugly (I fancy, though, children never are ugly). The second reason why I won't speak of grown-up people is that, besides being disgusting and unworthy of love, they have a compensation—they've eaten the apple and know good and evil, and they have become 'like gods.' They go on eating it still. But the children haven't eaten anything, and are so far innocent. Are you fond of children, Alyosha? I know you are, and you will understand why I prefer to speak of them. If they, too, suffer horribly on earth, they must suffer for their fathers' sins, they must be punished for their fathers, who have eaten the apple; but that reasoning is of the other world and is incomprehensible for the heart of man here on earth. The innocent must not suffer for another's sins, and especially such innocents! You may be surprised at me, Alyosha, but I am awfully fond of children, too. And observe, cruel people, the violent, the rapacious, the Karamazovs are sometimes very fond of children. Children while they are quite little—up to seven, for instance—are so remote from grown-up people they are different

creatures, as it were, of a different species. I knew a criminal in prison who had, in the course of his career as a burglar, murdered whole families, including several children. But when he was in prison, he had a strange affection for them. He spent all his time at his window, watching the children playing in the prison yard. He trained one little boy to come up to his window and made great friends with him... You don't know why I am telling you all this, Alyosha? My head aches and I am sad."

"You speak with a strange air," observed Alyosha uneasily, "as though you were not quite yourself."

"By the way, a Bulgarian I met lately in Moscow," Ivan went on, seeming not to hear his brother's words, "told me about the crimes committed by Turks and Circassians in all parts of Bulgaria through fear of a general rising of the Slavs. They burn villages, murder, outrage women and children, they nail their prisoners by the ears to the fences, leave them so till morning, and in the morning they hang them—all sorts of things you can't imagine. People talk sometimes of bestial cruelty, but that's a great injustice and insult to the beasts; a beast can never be so cruel as a man, so artistically cruel. The tiger only tears and gnaws, that's all he can do. He would never think of nailing people by the ears, even if he were able to do it. These Turks took a pleasure in torturing children, too; cutting the unborn child from the mothers womb, and tossing babies up in the air and catching them on the points of their bayonets before their mothers' eyes. Doing it before the mothers' eyes was what gave zest to the amusement. Here is another scene that I thought very interesting. Imagine a trembling mother with her baby in her arms, a circle of invading Turks around her. They've planned a diversion: they pet the baby, laugh to make it laugh. They succeed, the baby laughs. At that moment a Turk points a pistol four inches from the baby's face. The baby laughs with glee, holds out its little hands to the pistol, and he pulls the trigger in the baby's face and blows out its brains. Artistic, wasn't it? By the way, Turks are particularly fond of sweet things, they say."

"Brother, what are you driving at?" asked Alyosha.

"I think if the devil doesn't exist, but man has created him, he has created him in his own image and likeness."

"Just as he did God, then?" observed Alyosha.

"'It's wonderful how you can turn words,' as Polonius says in Hamlet," laughed Ivan. "You turn my words against me. Well, I am glad. Yours must be a fine God, if man created Him in his image and likeness. You asked just now what I was driving at. You see, I am fond of collecting certain facts, and, would you believe, I even copy anecdotes of a certain sort from newspapers and books, and I've already got a fine collection. The Turks, of course, have gone into it, but they are foreigners. I have specimens from home that are even better than the Turks. You know we prefer beating—rods and scourges—that's our national institution. Nailing ears is unthinkable for us, for we are, after all, Europeans. But the rod and the scourge we have always with us and they cannot be taken from us. Abroad now they scarcely do any beating. Manners are more humane, or laws have been passed, so that they don't dare to flog men now. But they make up for it in another way just as national as ours. And so national that it would be practically impossible among us, though I believe we are being inoculated with it, since the religious movement began in our aristocracy. I have a charming pamphlet, translated from the French, describing how, quite recently, five years ago, a murderer, Richard, was executed—a young man, I believe, of three and twenty, who repented and was converted to the Christian faith at the very scaffold. This Richard was an illegitimate child who was given as a child of six by his parents to some shepherds on the Swiss mountains. They brought him up to work for them. He grew up like a little wild beast among them. The shepherds taught him nothing, and scarcely fed or clothed him, but sent him out at seven to herd the flock in cold and wet, and no one hesitated or scrupled to treat him so. Quite the contrary, they thought they had every right, for Richard had been given to them as a chattel, and they did not even see the necessity of feeding him. Richard himself describes how in those years, like the Prodigal Son in the Gospel, he longed to eat of the mash given to the pigs, which were fattened for sale. But they wouldn't even give that, and beat him when he stole from the pigs. And that was how he spent all his childhood and his youth, till he grew up and was strong enough to go away and be a thief. The savage began to earn his living as a day labourer in Geneva. He drank what he earned, he lived like a brute, and finished by killing and robbing an old man. He was caught, tried, and condemned to death. They are not sentimentalists there. And in prison he was immediately surrounded by pastors, members of Christian brotherhoods, philanthropic ladies, and the like. They taught him to read and write in prison, and expounded the Gospel to him. They exhorted him, worked upon him, drummed at him incessantly, till at last he solemnly confessed his crime. He was converted. He wrote to the court himself that he was a monster, but that in the end God had vouchsafed him light and shown grace. All Geneva was in excitement about him--all philanthropic and religious Geneva. All the aristocratic and well-bred society of the town rushed to the prison, kissed Richard and embraced him; 'You are our brother, you have found grace.' And Richard does nothing but weep with emotion, 'Yes, I've found grace! All my youth and childhood I was glad of pigs' food, but now even I have found grace. I am dying in the Lord.' 'Yes, Richard, die in the Lord; you have shed blood and must die. Though it's not your fault that you knew not the Lord, when you coveted the pigs' food and were beaten for stealing it (which was very wrong of you, for stealing is forbidden); but you've shed blood and you must die.' And on the last day, Richard, perfectly limp, did nothing but cry and repeat every minute: 'This is my happiest day. I am going to the Lord.' 'Yes,' cry the pastors and the judges and philanthropic ladies. 'This is the happiest day of your life, for you are going to the Lord!' They all walk or drive to the scaffold in procession behind the prison van. At the scaffold they call to Richard: 'Die, brother, die in the Lord, for even thou hast found grace!' And so, covered with his brothers' kisses, Richard is dragged on to the scaffold, and led to the guillotine. And they chopped off his head in brotherly fashion, because he had found grace. Yes, that's characteristic. That pamphlet is translated into Russian by some Russian philanthropists of aristocratic rank and evangelical aspirations, and has been distributed gratis for the enlightenment of the people. The case of Richard is interesting because it's national. Though to us it's absurd to cut off a man's head, because he has become our brother and has found grace, yet we have our own speciality, which is all but worse. Our historical pastime is the direct satisfaction of inflicting pain. There are lines in

Nekrassov describing how a peasant lashes a horse on the eyes, 'on its meek eyes,' everyone must have seen it. It's peculiarly Russian. He describes how a feeble little nag has foundered under too heavy a load and cannot move. The peasant beats it, beats it savagely, beats it at last not knowing what he is doing in the intoxication of cruelty, thrashes it mercilessly over and over again. 'However weak you are, you must pull, if you die for it.' The nag strains, and then he begins lashing the poor defenceless creature on its weeping, on its 'meek eyes.' The frantic beast tugs and draws the load, trembling all over, gasping for breath, moving sideways, with a sort of unnatural spasmodic action—it's awful in Nekrassov. But that only a horse, and God has made horses to be beaten. So the Tatars have taught us, and they left us the knout as a remembrance of it. But men, too, can be beaten. A well-educated, cultured gentleman and his wife beat their own child with a birch-rod, a girl of seven. I have an exact account of it. The papa was glad that the birch was covered with twigs. 'It stings more,' said he, and so be began stinging his daughter. I know for a fact there are people who at every blow are worked up to sensuality, to literal sensuality, which increases progressively at every blow they inflict. They beat for a minute, for five minutes, for ten minutes, more often and more savagely. The child screams. At last the child cannot scream, it gasps, 'Daddy daddy!' By some diabolical unseemly chance the case was brought into court. A counsel is engaged. The Russian people have long called a barrister 'a conscience for hire.' The counsel protests in his client's defence. 'It's such a simple thing,' he says, 'an everyday domestic event. A father corrects his child. To our shame be it said, it is brought into court.' The jury, convinced by him, give a favourable verdict. The public roars with delight that the torturer is acquitted. Ah, pity I wasn't there! I would have proposed to raise a subscription in his honour! Charming pictures.

"But I've still better things about children. I've collected a great, great deal about Russian children, Alyosha. There was a little girl of five who was hated by her father and mother, 'most worthy and respectable people, of good education and breeding.' You see, I must repeat again, it is a peculiar characteristic of many people, this love of torturing children, and children only. To all other types of humanity these torturers behave mildly and benevolently, like cultivated and humane Europeans; but they are very fond of tormenting children, even fond of children themselves in that sense. it's just their defencelessness that tempts the tormentor, just the angelic confidence of the child who has no refuge and no appeal, that sets his vile blood on fire. In every man, of course, a demon lies hidden—the demon of rage, the demon of lustful heat at the screams of the tortured victim, the demon of lawlessness let off the chain, the demon of diseases that follow on vice, gout, kidney disease, and so on.

"This poor child of five was subjected to every possible torture by those cultivated parents. They beat her, thrashed her, kicked her for no reason till her body was one bruise. Then, they went to greater refinements of cruelty—shut her up all night in the cold and frost in a privy, and because she didn't ask to be taken up at night (as though a child of five sleeping its angelic, sound sleep could be trained to wake and ask), they smeared her face and filled her mouth with excrement, and it was her mother, her mother did this. And that mother could sleep, hearing the poor child's groans! Can you understand why a little creature, who can't even understand what's done to her, should beat her little aching heart with her tiny fist in the dark and the cold, and weep her meek unresentful tears to dear, kind God to protect her? Do you understand that, friend and brother, you pious and humble novice? Do you understand why this infamy must be and is permitted? Without it, I am told, man could not have existed on earth, for he could not have known good and evil. Why should he know that diabolical good and evil when it costs so much? Why, the whole world of knowledge is not worth that child's prayer to dear, kind God'! I say nothing of the sufferings of grown-up people, they have eaten the apple, damn them, and the devil take them all! But these little ones! I am making you suffer, Alyosha, you are not yourself. I'll leave off if you like."

"Nevermind. I want to suffer too," muttered Alyosha.

"One picture, only one more, because it's so curious, so characteristic, and I have only just read it in some collection of Russian antiquities. I've forgotten the name. I must look it up. It was in the darkest days of serfdom at the beginning of the century, and long live the Liberator of the People! There was in those days a general of aristocratic connections, the owner of great estates, one of those men--somewhat exceptional, I believe, even then—who, retiring from the service into a life of leisure, are convinced that they've earned absolute power over the lives of their subjects. There were such men then. So our general, settled on his property of two thousand souls, lives in pomp, and domineers over his poor neighbours as though they were dependents and buffoons. He has kennels of hundreds of hounds and nearly a hundred dog-boys—all mounted, and in uniform. One day a serf-boy, a little child of eight, threw a stone in play and hurt the paw of the general's favourite hound. 'Why is my favourite dog lame?' He is told that the boy threw a stone that hurt the dog's paw. 'So you did it.' The general looked the child up and down. 'Take him.' He was taken—taken from his mother and kept shut up all night. Early that morning the general comes out on horseback, with the hounds, his dependents, dog-boys, and huntsmen, all mounted around him in full hunting parade. The servants are summoned for their edification, and in front of them all stands the mother of the child. The child is brought from the lock-up. It's a gloomy, cold, foggy, autumn day, a capital day for hunting. The general orders the child to be undressed; the child is stripped naked. He shivers, numb with terror, not daring to cry... 'Make him run,' commands the general. 'Run! run!' shout the dog-boys. The boy runs... 'At him!' yells the general, and he sets the whole pack of hounds on the child. The hounds catch him, and tear him to pieces before his mother's eyes!... I believe the general was afterwards declared incapable of administering his estates. Well—what did he deserve? To be shot? To be shot for the satisfaction of our moral feelings? Speak, Alyosha!

"To be shot," murmured Alyosha, lifting his eyes to Ivan with a pale, twisted smile.

"Bravo!" cried Ivan delighted. "If even you say so... You're a pretty monk! So there is a little devil sitting in your heart, Alyosha Karamazov!"

"What I said was absurd, but —"

"That's just the point, that 'but'!" cried Ivan. "Let me tell you, novice, that the absurd is only too necessary on earth. The world stands on absurdities, and perhaps nothing would have come to pass in it without them. We know what we know!"

"What do you know?"

"I understand nothing," Ivan went on, as though in delirium. "I don't want to understand anything now. I want to stick to the fact. I made up my mind long ago not to understand. If I try to understand anything, I shall be false to the fact, and I have determined to stick to the fact."

"Why are you trying me?" Alyosha cried, with sudden distress. "Will you say what you mean at last?"

"Of course, I will; that's what I've been leading up to. You are dear to me, I don't want to let you go, and I won't give you up to your Zossima."

Ivan for a minute was silent, his face became all at once very sad.

"Listen! I took the case of children only to make my case clearer. Of the other tears of humanity with which the earth is soaked from its crust to its centre, I will say nothing. I have narrowed my subject on purpose. I am a bug, and I recognise in all humility that I cannot understand why the world is arranged as it is. Men are themselves to blame, I suppose; they were given paradise, they wanted freedom, and stole fire from heaven, though they knew they would become unhappy, so there is no need to pity them. With my pitiful, earthly, Euclidian understanding, all I know is that there is suffering and that there are none guilty; that cause follows effect, simply and directly; that everything flows and finds its level— but that's only Euclidian nonsense, I know that, and I can't consent to live by it! What comfort is it to me that there are none guilty and that cause follows effect simply and directly, and that I know it?—I must have justice, or I will destroy myself. And not justice in some remote infinite time and space, but here on earth, and that I could see myself. I have believed in it. I want to see it, and if I am dead by then, let me rise again, for if it all happens without me, it will be too unfair. Surely I haven't suffered simply that I, my crimes and my sufferings, may manure the soil of the future harmony for somebody else. I want to see with my own eyes the hind lie down with the lion and the victim rise up and embrace his murderer. I want to be there when everyone suddenly understands what it has all been for. All the religions of the world are built on this longing, and I am a believer. But then there are the children, and what am I to do about them? That's a question I can't answer. For the hundredth time I repeat, there are numbers of questions, but I've only taken the children, because in their case what I mean is so unanswerably clear. Listen! If all must suffer to pay for the eternal harmony, what have children to do with it, tell me, please? It's beyond all comprehension why they should suffer, and why they should pay for the harmony. Why should they, too, furnish material to enrich the soil for the harmony of the future? I understand solidarity in sin among men. I understand solidarity in retribution, too; but there can be no such solidarity with children. And if it is really true that they must share responsibility for all their fathers' crimes, such a truth is not of this world and is beyond my comprehension. Some jester will say, perhaps, that the child would have grown up and have sinned, but you see he didn't grow up, he was torn to pieces by the dogs, at eight years old. Oh, Alyosha, I am not blaspheming! I understand, of course, what an upheaval of the universe it will be when everything in heaven and earth blends in one hymn of praise and everything that lives and has lived cries aloud: 'Thou art just, O Lord, for Thy ways are revealed.' When the mother embraces the fiend who threw her child to the dogs, and all three cry aloud with tears, 'Thou art just, O Lord!' then, of course, the crown of knowledge will be reached and all will be made clear. But what pulls me up here is that I can't accept that harmony. And while I am on earth, I make haste to take my own measures. You see, Alyosha, perhaps it really may happen that if I live to that moment, or rise again to see it, I, too, perhaps, may cry aloud with the rest, looking at the mother embracing the child's torturer, 'Thou art just, O Lord!' but I don't want to cry aloud then. While there is still time, I hasten to protect myself, and so I renounce the higher harmony altogether. It's not worth the tears of that one tortured child who beat itself on the breast with its little fist and prayed in its stinking outhouse, with its unexpiated tears to 'dear, kind God!' It's not worth it, because those tears are unatoned for. They must be atoned for, or there can be no harmony. But how? How are you going to atone for them? Is it possible? By their being avenged? But what do I care for aveng-

ing them? What do I care for a hell for oppressors? What good can hell do, since those children have already been tortured? And what becomes of harmony, if there is hell? I want to forgive. I want to embrace. I don't want more suffering. And if the sufferings of children go to swell the sum of sufferings which was necessary to pay for truth, then I protest that the truth is not worth such a price. I don't want the mother to embrace the oppressor who threw her son to the dogs! She dare not forgive him! Let her forgive him for herself, if she will, let her forgive the torturer for the immeasurable suffering of her mother's heart. But the sufferings of her tortured child she has no right to forgive; she dare not forgive the torturer, even if the child were to forgive him! And if that is so, if they dare not forgive, what becomes of harmony? Is there in the whole world a being who would have the right to forgive and could forgive? I don't want harmony. From love for humanity I don't want it. I would rather be left with the unavenged suffering. I would rather remain with my unavenged suffering and unsatisfied indignation, even if I were wrong. Besides, too high a price is asked for harmony; it's beyond our means to pay so much to enter on it. And so I hasten to give back my entrance ticket, and if I am an honest man I am bound to give it back as soon as possible. And that I am doing. It's not God that I don't accept, Alyosha, only I most respectfully return him the ticket."

"That's rebellion," murmered Alyosha, looking down.

"Rebellion? I am sorry you call it that," said Ivan earnestly. "One can hardly live in rebellion, and I want to live. Tell me yourself, I challenge your answer. Imagine that you are creating a fabric of human destiny with the object of making men happy in the end, giving them peace and rest at last, but that it was essential and inevitable to torture to death only one tiny creature—that baby beating its breast with its fist, for instance—and to found that edifice on its unavenged tears, would you consent to be the architect on those conditions? Tell me, and tell the truth."

"No, I wouldn't consent," said Alyosha softly.

Fyodor Dostoyevsky. *The Brothers Karamazov*. Trans. Constance Garnett. London: Heinemann, 1912.

6

EPISTEMOLOGY: WHAT CAN WE KNOW?

PATRICK J. CASEY

Epistemology (from the Greek *epistēmē*, meaning 'knowledge' and *logos*, meaning 'an account' or 'study of') is the branch of philosophy that attempts to give an account, or theory of, knowledge. It studies, in particular, the sources, scope and quality of human knowledge. Epistemology is about getting the right beliefs—about how we acquire them, how to know that they're the right ones, and how to tell when you have them. It is of enormous importance to be able to sift through our beliefs and to do our best to tell which of them actually merit the designation 'knowledge' and which do not.

Perhaps the biggest obstacle to understanding and benefiting from epistemology is the climate of opinion nowadays which suggests that it does not matter *what* you believe, so long as you believe what you do sincerely or that you have good intentions. Sometimes people will express this idea in a relativistic manner and will say things like, "each person has his or her own beliefs and those beliefs are true for them" or "each person's beliefs are true in their own way." Again, the idea is that it does not matter what you believe, so long as you mean well. Oddly enough, people tend to think this way especially about beliefs which are most important to us as humans—like religious and ethical beliefs—and less about beliefs which are of comparatively little importance, like who the starting point guard for the Knicks is. But a little reflection shows that this way of thinking—that it does not matter what you believe, provided that you believe it sincerely—cannot be right. For example, if you think that drinking lots of alcohol before pitching in a baseball game will make you a better player, or that carrying an onion in your pocket will make you invisible, how will that work out for you? Whether you're trying to earn a spot in the starting rotation or trying to rob a bank, it's not going to end well. It doesn't matter how sincerely you hold these beliefs, they are false; consequently, the actions which you based on these beliefs won't achieve your intended goals. More seriously, and in order to grasp the gravity of the matter, imagine you are backpacking through the woods with some friends and you come upon a person who is obviously starving to death. Without a medical background you might think that the best thing to do would be to give them a good, solid meal. As a result, and with the best intentions in the world, you would end up killing the person you were trying to help. Even when you have the best intentions in the world, if you're acting on beliefs which you *think* are true but aren't, then you can do a great deal of harm to yourself and to others.

So we see that sincerity, or good intentions, is not enough. *What* you believe matters—it matters a great deal. Beliefs are important to human life because they inform the way that we behave and the choices that we make. If you believe that the best way to stimulate the economy is for the government to borrow money and invest it in public works, then this will affect how you vote. If you don't believe that God exists, chances are you're not going to go pray or go to church (unless your girlfriend makes you). If you believe that taking the Verrazano Bridge is the best way to get to Manhattan, this will affect how what route you take when you want to see a Broadway show. Whether it's stimulating the economy, caring for your soul, or simply trying to find the best way to Manhattan, whether you have knowledge or simply think that you do, matters. You don't want to make a mistake and end up with a struggling economy, in hell, or even worse, Staten Island. We now begin to see why epistemology is of such great importance. Because our beliefs are so important, and because whether the beliefs we act upon are true or false determine whether or not our actions have the consequences we desire, it is essential to be able to tell when we actually have knowledge and when we only *think* we have knowledge. That is, we need a reliable way of picking out knowledge from the whole body of our beliefs. This is what epistemology is about.

Distinction Between Knowledge and Opinion

In order to be able to pick out knowledge from the whole set of our beliefs or opinions, we need to know what we are looking for. So, what is knowledge? A reasonable place to start is with the observation that everything we know is believed. It would be very odd to say something like, "I know that God exists, but I don't believe it." If you know something, you have to believe it. This tells us that belief is a necessary condition for knowledge. In the context of philosophy, 'belief' is used in a broad way to mean anything that a person thinks is *true*. In fact, though it may seem strange at first, it is not actually possible to believe something that you think is false. After all, if you thought the belief was false, you would not believe it! This creates an interesting situation because everything you believe, you think is true. But yet it should be obvious from your own experience that not everything you believe *is* true.

In casual conversation people will sometimes say things like, "You only *believe* that, you don't *know* it" implying that belief is not enough, that it's not sufficient for one to claim that one has knowledge. What this way of talking calls attention to is the fact that not everything that we believe do we know. Why is this? Well, for starters, it is possible to believe things that are not true. Indeed, anytime you believe something that you don't know, the belief may turn out to be false. But conversely, when you really know something, that belief could not turn out to be false. A person can believe what is false, but not *know* something that is false. This tells us that not only must we have a belief in order to have knowledge, but that it is necessary that the belief be *true* if we are to have knowledge.

So, our definition of knowledge so far is that it is true belief. Is this enough to pick our knowledge as opposed to other beliefs? Is having a true belief sufficient to say that it's knowledge? Epistemologists have agreed that it is not. Imagine that you're trying to decide whether the element Zinc has a higher atomic weight than Iron (if you actually do know, pretend that you don't). You could decide what to believe based on the result of a coin flip – if the coin comes up "heads", you'll believe that Iron has a higher atomic weight than Zinc, but if it comes up "tails", you'll believe that Zinc has a higher atomic weight than Iron. You flip the coin and lo and behold, it comes up "tails", so you believe that Zinc has a higher atomic weight than Iron. Now, it turns out in this case that your belief is true. So you have a true belief, but would you say that you *know* that Zinc has a higher atomic weight than Iron? Intuitively, the thought is that *even though your belief turned out to be true*, we wouldn't want to call it knowledge. You came up with a true belief by sheer luck! The idea here is that true beliefs have to be formed in the right kind of way—broadly speaking, a reliable way—for them to count as knowledge. Otherwise, the person is not entitled to call their belief knowledge. In other words, there needs to be a good reason to think that their belief is *true*; there needs to be what philosophers call a *justification* for the belief. The results of a coin flip doesn't count as a solid basis for thinking that a belief about atomic weight is true. Rather, you need something like an argument, or empirical evidence as a justification for your beliefs. And although there is considerable disagreement among philosophers about what exactly justification is and how it works, all philosophers agree that there needs to be at least a third element to knowledge which captures this intuition that beliefs that are true by accident or sheer luck aren't knowledge. There is a sense in which justification is the most practical aspect of epistemology. It's the part of the philosopher's toolkit which enables us to evaluate the beliefs that we hold and attempts to provide methods for distinguishing true beliefs from false beliefs.

Now that we have a working definition of knowledge, we can begin to evaluate our beliefs and pick out which beliefs merit the status of *knowledge* and which do not. In this context of evaluating beliefs and determining what counts as knowledge, it is easier to see the distinction between psychology and epistemology. Psychology seeks to describe the human mind and how beliefs are formed etc., while epistemology seeks to give a *normative* theory of knowledge. This is just a technical way of saying that while psychology describes *how* the mind operates, epistemology tells us how we *ought* to think or govern our beliefs if we want to procure knowledge about the world. Epistemology gives rules or *norms* for evaluating beliefs and determining which beliefs deserve to be called *knowledge*. There is a sense in which epistemology underwrites, not just psychology, but all forms of science insofar as they are disciplines for acquiring knowledge themselves (indeed, the Latin root of our modern word 'science' (*scientia*) is derived from the Greek *epistēmē* —both words mean "knowledge"). Indeed, part of what epistemologists concern themselves with is the status of scientific knowledge itself. Do, for example, biologists' or anthropologists' claims have the same status as mathematical claims to knowledge? And if not, why not?

A potentially helpful way of making distinctions in different kinds of claims to knowledge is by degree of justification. An important thing to keep in mind when thinking about knowledge is that philosophers disagree among themselves about how strong exactly the criterion of justification needs to be to merit being called knowledge. This is a very old debate in philosophy and goes all the way back to Plato and Aristotle. Some philosophers maintain that in order for a belief to count as real knowledge, it must not be possible to be wrong about our belief. René Descartes was the quintessential representative of this position. His idea was that if you can possibly doubt a belief, then it's not knowledge. He thought that knowledge entailed *certainty*, that is, it entails that you can't possibly be wrong about it. He thought that the best way to avoid error and the terrible consequences that can follow, is to not believe anything which you don't know with certainty. Only those beliefs which you can't be wrong about properly merit being called knowledge. This is a very stringent criterion of justification indeed. A weaker standard is that knowledge is a belief which you have a good reason to hold, or which makes the truth of the belief probable but not certain. Philosophers who advocate this more modest theory of knowledge point out that human beings are fallible, we often get things wrong. They argue that the criterion of certainty for knowledge limits the term knowledge to such an extent that it's not very helpful at all. And if the point of epistemology is to evaluate our actions in a way that is helpful to human life, we should employ a weaker standard for knowledge.

On the far end of the spectrum is the claim that humans aren't justified in believing much, if anything, at all. This position, called *skepticism*, implies that humans can't have knowledge (since justification is a necessary requirement for knowledge). It is important to keep this position separate from that of *fallibilism*, which makes the more moderate claim that human beings simply sometimes make errors in their beliefs. Skeptics argue that we should give up our claims to know things all together. Hence, skepticism t is a much stronger claim than fallibilism, and one should not infer that we can't know anything simply because we sometimes make mistakes. Moreover, a truly consistent skeptic can't even say that they *know* that humans can't have knowledge as this would *itself* be a claim to know at least one thing—that humans can't know anything! As most philosophers throughout history have believed that it is possible to have knowledge, there is very real sense in which the whole history of epistemology is essentially a variety of responses to skepticism. On the whole, skepticism in any kind of robust form is not a desirable position because it prohibits people from making positive claims about the world altogether.

Sources of Knowledge: How is Knowledge Acquired?

Another way of evaluating our beliefs is to examine the *sources* of knowledge. Philosophers have broken knowledge into two types: knowledge acquired through reason and knowledge derived from experience. The former kind of knowledge, which is acquired independent of experience, is called *a priori* knowledge. Examples of this kind of knowledge are propositions such as $2 + 3 = 5$, that the interior angles of a triangle add up to 180 degrees and that all bachelors are unmarried males. One can see the truth of these propositions simply through reason and by paying attention to the terms which make up the sentences. The latter kind of knowledge, which is derived from, or dependent upon experience, is called *a posteriori* knowledge. Anything which you actually need experience to know would fall under this kind of knowledge. For example, that grass is green, that penguins can't fly, that the average temperature in Anchorage, Alaska is colder than New York City. None of these things could you come to know by just sitting in your room and thinking very hard—you'd have to get out and use your senses. It is not clear whether human knowledge is fundamentally *a priori* or *a posteriori*, and philosophers have lined up on each side of the issue. Philosophers who believe that the most important truths about the world can be discovered through reason are called *rationalists*. Philosophers who think that the most important truths about the world can be discovered through experience or by inference from what we know through experience are called *empiricists*.

Interestingly, information which is gained empirically, that is, through experience, tells us a great deal about the world we live in. But it is also subject to error and correction by further experience. For example, in the ancient world it was thought that the Sun revolved around the Earth. And indeed, from the perspective of observers on the Earth, the Sun does appear to move while the Earth stays fixed. However, subsequent experience (like the observation of the phases of the planet Venus, among other things) caused natural philosophers to change their minds about the model of the solar system, moving the Earth from the physical center of the universe into the heavens. The point here is that while experience gives us a great deal of information about the world, the information it provides is never certain. What we thought we knew, we turned out to be wrong about. Importantly, it is usually thought that there is no parallel with knowledge which is gained *a priori*—no new information could cause us to revise *a priori* knowledge. For example, it is not possible that new information would show us that $2 + 3 = 5$ is wrong, nor is it possible that an anthropologist would somewhere find a married bachelor, if only they would look hard enough. On the other hand, *a priori* reflection doesn't produce new knowledge about the world; it is gained by an analysis of terms, like 'bachelor' or 'triangle' or various numbers. So *a priori* knowledge is certain, but it doesn't tell us anything new. Conversely, experience can tell us many new things, but it is never certain.

The eventual realization of philosophers was that if you demand certainty, you can't say much, if anything, about the world we find ourselves in. On the other hand, if you want to say things about the world, you have to give up demanding certainty. The development of philosophy through the modern period (from which most of our readings are drawn) is in some ways a progressive acceptance of this point. Philosophers began to doubt the powers of reason to access truths about the world around us and became more and more comfortable with mere probability in our knowledge. This retreat from the high criterion of certainty for knowledge —of which Descartes was in many ways the last and greatest exponent—was coincident with the rise of the empirical and experimental sciences. But again, knowledge based on the senses (though it works out for us well enough in practice) is never certain—it could always turn out to be wrong and is subject to revision. If you now find yourself thinking, "Wait a minute, if we can be wrong about knowledge based on the senses, then it can't be *true* knowledge", then congratulations, you're officially a philosopher. Basically what you are asking is, "Wasn't Descartes right to say that true knowledge entailed certainty? Doesn't having real knowledge mean that you can't turn out to be wrong about it?" Consequently, you may find yourself back where we started—"What, *really*, is knowledge?" If this is where you find yourself, you're in an excellent position to read the following selections. Be warned that there are no easy answers to be found here. But this is what philosophy is really about: learning to think about some of life's most challenging and important questions and trying to figure out what you should believe yourself.

THE ARGUMENT FOR SKEPTICISM

SEXTUS EMPIRICUS (C 200 BCE)

The Skeptics were a group of philosophers living in ancient Greece who questioned whether it was possible at all to have justified belief, and therefore knowledge. There were two main groups of skeptics in the ancient world, though there was a considerable diversity among thinkers within each group. The first were called the Academics, and the second, Pyrrhonists. The Academics were a group of skeptics living around the time of Plato (3rd century BC) who took as their starting point an extension of Socrates' claim in the Apology that his wisdom consisted only in his recognition of the limits of his own knowledge, making the further claim that we couldn't really know anything at all. They argued that since there is no fool-proof way to distinguish between true perceptions and illusions, the best human beings were capable of was probable true belief. The only thing, they claimed, that human beings could have certainty about was that they couldn't be certain of anything. Thus, they reasoned, the best policy is to remain skeptical, or to suspend judgment about the truth or falsity of how the world appears to us. The other school of Skepticism was known as Pyrrhonian Skepticism (named after the founder of this school, Pyrrho of Elis, who lived in Alexandria during the 1st century BC). The Pyrrhonians were even more extreme than their earlier counterparts, denying that human beings could have any certainty at all…even to the point of remaining skeptical about whether they could be certain that they couldn't know anything. Thus, their proposal was that, since the question of whether we can have knowledge or not is ultimately not settled, we ought to keep investigating. However, the goal of the Pyrrhonists was not simply a suspension of judgment about whether we could have knowledge, but rather to attain the mental tranquility or peace of mind which results from giving up the hopeless task of settling which perceptions are true and which are illusions.

The following selection comes from Outlines of Pyrrhonism, *written by the Greek physician Sextus Empiricus, who lived around the second century in Greece. The text represents one of the few first-hand accounts of the system of Pyrrhonian skepticism that we possess and provides an interesting perspective on how the skeptic's way of life alone offers the possibility of attaining happiness.*

BOOK I

1. The Main Differences between Philosophical Systems

For those that investigate about any matter the reasonable result is that they discover the object they pursue or they deny it is discoverable and concede it is inapprehensible (*akatalêpsias*) or they continue searching for it. In like manner, regarding the objects investigated by the philosophies some have said they discovered the truth, others deny the apprehensibility of it to be possible while still others continue to seek it. The philosophers who seem to have discovered the truth are called Dogmatic, like for instance Aristotle, Epicurus, the Stoics, and some others, while Academics, like Clitomachus and Carneades deny the apprehensibility of the truth, whereas the Skeptics continue their search for it. Thus it is well said that there are three foremost types of philosophy: Dogmatic, Academic and Skeptic. Concerning the former two kinds of philosophy it is suitable for others to discourse. Presently we will enquire about the main outlines of Skepticism. By way of preface, none of the matters to be discussed do we strongly maintain that things certainly are just as we say they are: rather we inquisitively report about each of them, according to the way they appear to us at the time....

4. What is Scepticism?

Skepticism is the ability to oppose appearances to objects of thought "in anyway whatsoever," from which, because of the equipollence of the opposing facts and accounts, we will go first into suspension of judgment (*epoche*) and subsequently into a state of tranquility (*ataraxia*). We call it an ability not in any elaborate sense but simply in the sense of "to be able to". Presently we take appearances to be percepts, which we distinguish from objects of thought. "In anyway whatsoever" can be taken with ability in which case it simply means ability or else, as we have said, we take it with the opposition of appearances and objects of thought. When we oppose these in a number of ways, either appearances to appearances or objects of thought to objects of thought or crosswise, appearances to objects of thought in order that all of the opposites are encompassed. We say in anyway at all in order that we don't just investigate how appearances appear or how objects of thought are thought but so that we take them in the simple sense. We do not take up contrasting accounts entirely by negation and affirmation but simply by opposing conflicting accounts. We say equipollence then in regard to being equally plausible or implausible, as none of the conflicting accounts is set out beforehand as being the most credible. Suspension of judgment is an intellectual state by which we neither posit nor negate anything. But tranquility is calmness and undisturbedness of the soul. How tranquility enters along with suspension of judgment we will be reminded in the chapters about the objectives of skepticism....

6. The Principles of Scepticism

We say the causal principle of skepticism is the hope of attaining tranquility. The disorders of talented men are on account of an anomaly in things and being puzzled as to which of them they should assent to. They came to investigate what is true and what is false in things, believing that being tranquil results from the determination of them. The system of skepticism is most of all the principle, which to every account opposes an equal account. As a result of this we seem not to dogmatize.

7. Does the Sceptic Dogmatize?

We assert the Skeptic does not dogmatize, not according to this meaning of the word dogma which they say is most common—as to approve of something. (The Skeptic assents to the affections and the imagination. For instance, he does not say, when becoming hot or cold, that I seem not to be heated or chilled). But we say he does not dogmatize according to what they say dogma is: they assent to some unclear object of investigation in the sciences. For Pyrrhonists assent to none of the unclear objects. He does not even dogmatize in uttering the Skeptical phrases pertaining to the aforementioned unclear objects of scientific investigation, for example "no more" or "I determine nothing" or any of the others about which we will speak later. For the one who dogmatizes posits as existing this thing about which he is said to dogmatize. But the Skeptic posits these phrases not entirely as existing. For the Skeptic conceives the phrase "everything is false" itself as false along with all the other things and likewise for the phrase "nothing is true". So also the phrase "no more" says that it itself is no more this than that and thus cancels itself along with the others. It's the same for the other Skeptical phrases we utter. What's more, if the dogmatizer posits as existing that which he dogmatizes about, the Skeptic utters his own phrase as potentially cancelling itself. Thus, in the utterance of them he should not be said to dogmatize. Most important, in the utterance of these phrases he says what is apparent to himself and he reports the impression forming no opinion about it, making no commitment regarding external substances.

8. Does the Skeptic Belong to a School?

We take the same approach to the question, does the Skeptic belong to a school? If someone says a school is an adherence to many dogmas that agree with one another and with appearances and if someone says dogma is assent to something unclear, then we shall say the Skeptic does not belong to a school. But if you deem a school to be training which follows a certain line of reasoning in accordance with appearances, which indicates how it is to seem to live correctly (the word correctly being taken not only in regard to virtue but in a looser sense) and which tends to enable one to suspend judgment then we say we belong to a school. For we follow a line of reasoning which, in accordance with appearances points us to a life in accordance with the customs of our fatherland and its laws and persuasions and our own affections.....

10. Do the Sceptics Abolish Appearances?

Those who say that the Skeptics annul appearances seem to me to be unacquainted with our arguments. For we do not take issue with the fact that we are involuntarily led into assent according to affective images, as we said before. These affective images are indeed the appearances. When we investigate if the substance is such as it appears, we concede that it appears, but we investigate not regarding the appearance but what is said about the appearance—and that is a different matter than investigating the appearance itself. For example, honey appears to us to be sweet. This we agree for we taste sweetness perceptually. But whether it actually has the quality of sweetness in reference to reason, we investigate. This is not an appearance but something that is said about an appearance. And even if we do propound arguments against appearances, we do not set them out intending to annul the appearances, but to point out the rashness—the rush to judgment of the dogmatists. For if reason is so deceptive that it even snatches appearances from under our very eyes it is necessary to view it with suspicion in the case of unclear things so that in following it we are not led into a rush to judgment.

11. Regarding the Criterion of Scepticism

That we adhere to appearances is clear from our assertion about the criterion of the Skeptical School. Criterion is said in two ways: first as being apprehended in belief as existent or non-existent, of which we will discuss in our refutation. Second there is the criterion of action adhering to which

in the course of life we either act or do not act. Of this we will now speak. We say the appearance is the criterion of the Skeptical school, implicitly being called the faculty of imagination. For lying in involuntary affection and in persuasion it is not an object of investigation. Consequently no one disputes whether the substance has this or that appearance but about the appearance, if it is such a kind as it appears is investigable.

And so adhering to appearances we live according to everyday observes without holding opinions, since we are unable to be completely inactive. Thus it seems these everyday observances are tetramerous: one part lies in the guidance of nature, another in the necessity of the affections, another in the transmission of laws and customs and another in the teachings of the arts. By nature's guidance we are naturally capable of perceiving and thinking. The necessity of the affections is that by which there is hunger for food and thirst for drink. The transmission of customs and laws is that by which we invite piety as a way of life as good and impiety as bad. The instruction of the arts, that whereby we are not inactive in such arts as we adopt. We say all of this without holding opinions.

12. What Is the Final Objective of Scepticism?

The next task is to go through the aim of the Skeptical school. Now, an objective is that for the sake of which everything is done or contemplated, while it is for the sake of nothing. Or alternatively an objective is the ultimate object of appetency. We still assert that the Skeptic's objective is tranquility in respect of matters of opinion and moderation of the passions in matters forced upon us. For Skeptics begin to philosophize in order to make a determination on sense-impressions and to apprehend which are true and which are false so as to become tranquil. They came upon equipollent disputes, of which being unable to make a determination they suspend judgment. When they stopped judgment a state of tranquility in matters of opinion happened to follow.

One who holds opinions about what is by nature good or bad will be disturbed by anything. When the things which seem to be good are not present to him he believes himself to be tormented by things naturally evil and he pursues what he thinks to be good. When he acquires these things he encounters even more disturbances for he is elated going against reason and without measure. In fear of change he will do anything in order that he does not lose the things, which to him seem good. The one who makes no determination about the things that are good or bad by nature neither flees nor pursues them with intensity; and, consequently, he is tranquil.

And so a story told about Apelles the Painter also pertains to the Skeptic. They say that when he was painting a horse he wished to represent in the painting the foam on the horses mouth, he was so unsuccessful as he gave up he flung the sponge, which he used to wipe the paints of his brush and the mark of the sponge made the likeness of horse's foam.

Similarly the Skeptics hope to acquire tranquility on account of a determination about the anomalies in appearances and in thoughts and being unable to produce this state they suspended judgment. When they suspended judgment tranquility followed by accident just as a shadow follows a body. Thus we do not hold that the Skeptic is not disturbed by anything but we assert he is disturbed by things, which are forced on him. For we agree the Skeptic shivers when cold and thirsts and suffers certain affections of this sort. In these cases ordinary people are afflicted by two sets of circumstances, by the affections themselves, and no less by the belief that these circumstances are evil by nature. The Skeptic strips away the additional opinion that each of them is bad by nature and he comes off in these cases as more moderate. This then is why we say that the objective of Skepticism is tranquility in matters of opinion and moderation of passions in matters forced upon us. Certain esteemed Skeptics have added to these, suspension of judgment in investigations.

13. Of the General Modes of Suspending Judgment

Since we have said that tranquility follows suspension of judgment it will be our next task to say how suspension of judgment happens for us. It happens generally speaking through the opposition of things. We oppose appearances to appearances and thoughts to thoughts and crosswise. For instance we oppose appearances to appearances when we say "the same tower from far away appears circular and from nearby square." Likewise we oppose thoughts to thoughts, when against he who contrives that there is providence from the order of the firmament, we counter argue that many good people are ill fated and many bad people have good fortune. We conclude from this that providence does not exist. We oppose thoughts to appearances as Anaxagoras does when to the appearance that snow is white he opposes the thought that snow is frozen water and water is black and therefore snow is black.

In another sense we oppose present things to present things, as in the previous examples and sometimes to things past or in the future. For instance when someone propounds to us an argument, which we are unable to refute we say to him that "just as before the founder of the school to which you adhere was born, the sound argument held by it was not yet apparent, although it really existed in nature. In the same way it is possible that the opposite of the argument just now propounded by you exists in nature, although not yet apparent to us so that we should not yet assent to the now seemingly strong argument.

In order to have a more precise understanding of these antitheses I shall lay down as a principle the various modes by which suspension of judgment is brought about but without making any positive assertion either about their number or their powers. For it is possible that they are unsound and that there are more than will be discussed.

14a. On the Ten Modes

The usual tradition amongst the older Sceptics is that the "modes" by which "suspension" is supposed to be brought about are ten in number; and they also give them the synonymous names of "arguments" and "positions." They are these: the first, based on the variety in animals; the second, on the differences in human beings; the third, on the different structures of the organs of sense; the fourth, on the circumstantial conditions; the fifth, on positions and intervals and locations; the sixth, on intermixtures; the seventh, on the quantities and formations of the underlying objects; the eighth, on the fact of relativity; the ninth, on the frequency or rarity of occurrence; the tenth, on the disciplines and customs and laws, the legendary beliefs and the dogmatic convictions. This order, however, we adopt without prejudice....

14b. The Fourth Mode

In order to reach suspension of judgment, either basing the argument on each sense individually or keeping far from the senses, we also take up the fourth mode of skepticism. This is the one dependent on so called circumstances, which we call dispositions. It is observed in natural or unnatural states, in waking or sleeping, depending on age, in motion or at rest, in hatred or love, either being in a state of need or satiety, either drunk or sober, on predispositions, on being courageous or cowardly, on being in distress or in a state of delight.

For instance, things produce dissimilar impressions depending on whether the state is natural or unnatural, since those who are frantic and those who are divinely possessed seem to hear demons, while we do not. Similarly they often claim to receive an offering of storax or frankincense or something of this kind and many other things, though they are not perceptible by us. The same water seems to be boiling when poured on inflamed spots, but to us is tepid. And again the same garment, which appears bright yellow to those with jaundiced eyes, does not seem so to me. And the same honey appears sweet to me but bitter to men with jaundice. Now if someone says that the intermixture of certain humors produces inappropriate sense impressions from the underlying object in those who are in an unnatural state, we reply that since those with healthy humors also have mixed humors, it is possible that these humors make the external existing objects appear differently to those who are healthy, for these realities appear naturally to those who are said to be in an unnatural state. To grant the power of the underlying object to this exchange by the humors is fanciful and since the healthy ones are in a state that is natural for the healthy but against nature for the sick and the sick ones are in a state natural for sick people but against nature for the healthy, so that they too are in a state, which is, relatively speaking, natural, and thus should be given credence.

Due to either sleep or being awake the images that come to be are different. When asleep we perceive things that we do not perceive when awake; nor conversely do we perceive awake as we perceive when asleep, so that the being or non-being of these impressions comes to be not absolutely but relatively, either to sleep or wakefulness. And so in all likelihood we see things in our sleep, which in wakefulness are non-existent, although not absolutely unreal; for they exist in sleep just as waking realities exist, but they do not exist in our sleep.

As a result of age too there are differences. For the same air seems to be chilly to the elderly while to those in their prime it seems temperate. Also the same color to those who are older appears dim while to those in their prime it appears bright. It is similar with sound. The same sound to the elderly seems dim while to the young it is clearly audible. Furthermore those who differ in age are put in motion dissimilarly in respect of choices and avoidances. For children have a great zeal for balls and wheels. Those in their prime choose other things, and old men others still. From this we conclude that different perceptions come to be from the same underlying objects, which is due to differences in age.

Objects appear dissimilar depending on being in motion or at rest. As when standing still we see them motionless, but we believe them to be moving when sailing past them. Depending on loving or hatred as some have an excessive aversion to pork while others greatly enjoy eating it. As Menander said:

> How he appears to be, even in his looks
> Since he has become like this: Beastlike!
> Committing no misdeed makes us beautiful.

Many men having ugly girlfriends believe them to be the ripest of fruits. Depending on hunger or satiety: since the same meat seems to be the tastiest to the hungry and to be unpleasant to the sated. Depending on being drunk or sober: As when sober we believe things to be shameful, when we are drunk the same things do not appear shameful. Predispositions are a factor: For the same wine appears like vinegar to those who have previously eaten dates or figs, seems sweet to those who have just consumed nuts or chickpeas. As the vestibule of a bathhouse warms those who come in from the outside, one is chilled coming out of it if one lingers too long. Depending on being afraid or courageous: since the same thing seems more frightening and terrible to the coward and never seems that way to the more courageous person. Depending on grief or joy: since the same matters are grievous to the distressed but are pleasant to the joyful.

Since, then, there are so many anomalies depending on the dispositions and that at different times people come to be in different dispositions, it is easy to say what each underlying object appears like to each man, but we can go no further and say what it *is*. For surely the one who judges is in one of the previously discussed dispositions or he is in absolutely no disposition whatsoever. But to assert that one is in no disposition at all is like saying one is neither healthy nor sick, neither moving nor at rest, nor of a certain age and also devoid of the other dispositions is a completely un-manifested phenomenon. But if one judges the sensory impressions in some disposition one will be part of the disagreement and one will not be an impartial judge of the external underlying object since one will be tainted by the dispositions which one is in. Nor will the waking person be able to compare the sense impressions of sleepers with those of waking people, nor again a healthy person compare the sense impressions of sick people with those who are well. For we assent to what is present and affects us in the present rather than to what is not present.

In another way too the anomaly of these kinds of sense-impressions is undetermined. For he who prefers one sense impression to another or one circumstance to another surely made the judgment uncritically and without adequate proof or critically and with proof. He cannot do so without these, since he will not be believed, nor yet with them. For if he judges the sense-impressions he certainly judges by a criterion. And so surely he will say the criterion is either true or false. But if false he will not be credible. If he says it is true he will assert the criterion is true either without proof or with proof. And if without proof he will not be credible. But if with proof it will be altogether necessary for the proof to be true since otherwise it will lack credibility. Then when he says the proof which he takes to make the criterion convincing is true, will he do so after judging it or without judging it? If he has not judged it then it

will not be credible. If he has judged it clearly he will say he has judged it by means of a criterion and from that criterion we shall ask for proof and for that proof again a criterion. For a proof always needs a criterion, in order to be established and the criterion needs a proof in order to be shown to be true. As such neither is a proof able to be sound absent a preexistent true criterion. Nor can a criterion be true absent previous confirmation of the proof. Thus the criterion and the proof fall into the 'reciprocal mode' in which both will be found to be unconvincing. For each one awaits the credibility of the other and so each is as lacking in credibility as the other. If then one can choose between sense-impressions neither without criteria and proof nor with them, the different sense-impressions, which come to be dependent upon the different dispositions, will be undeterminable. Therefore one is led into suspension of judgment about the nature of the underlying external objects as a result of this mode.

14c. The Tenth Mode

There is a tenth mode, which is mostly concerned with ethics. It depends on the precepts, the customs, the laws, the mythic beliefs and the dogmatic conceptions. A precept is a choice of a way of life or some way of acting engaged in by one person or many, for instance by Diogenes or the Spartans. The law is a written contract amongst citizens, the transgressor of which is punished. A custom or habit (for there is no difference) is a common acceptance by a number of people of a certain way of acting, the transgressor of which is not necessarily punished. For instance the law prohibits adultery and our custom forbids intercourse with a woman in public. Mythic belief is the acceptance of events, which did not occur and are fictitious, for example the story being told about Kronos, for these stories, led many people into belief. But the Dogmatic tradition is a firm apprehension of fact through reasoning or something seeming to be strengthened by proof, for example that atoms are the elements of existing things, or homoeomeries or irreducible parts or some other thing.

And we oppose each of these sometimes to itself and sometimes to each of the others. For example, in this we oppose custom to custom. Some of the

Ethiopians tattoo their newborn babies, which we do not. While Persians deem it becoming to wear brightly colored full-length dresses extending to their feet, while it is unbecoming to us. The Indians copulate with women in public but most of the other races hold this to be shameful. We oppose law to law in this way: Amongst the Romans the man who renounces the inheritance of his father's property does not have to pay his father's debts. But amongst the Rhodesians he must pay them entirely. Amongst the Tauri in Scythia the law was that foreigners are to be sacrificed to Artemis. Among us it is forbidden to kill a human at a religious rite.

We oppose custom to others, as for example the law—when we say amongst the Persians male homosexual acts are customary, while amongst the Romans this practice is forbidden by law.

One could have taken many more examples pertaining to each of the antitheses discussed above, but in a concise account these will suffice. We are not able to say what the underlying object is in its nature since so much anomaly has been shown in the objects on account of this mode. Rather we can say how it appears relative to the precepts, to the law, to the custom or each of the others. And so on account of this mode it is necessary for us to suspend judgment about the nature of the external underlying object. And thus, by means of the ten modes we finally end in the suspension of judgment.....

22. Of the Expression "I Suspend Judgment"

We adopt the expression "I suspend judgment" in place of "I cannot say which of the matters that lie before us you ought to believe and which you ought not to believe," showing that matters pertaining to belief and disbelief appear equal to us. As to whether they are equal we make no positive assertion. We say what appears to us about them, when it makes an impression on us. The expression "suspension of judgment" derives from the fact the intellect is "suspended" so that it neither affirms nor annuls anything, due to the equipollence of the matters being investigated.

Sextus Empiricus. *Outlines of Pyrrhonism*. Trans. Luke Amentas, 2012. Used with permission.

THE REPUBLIC

PLATO (424–348 BCE)

Besides being one of the most important works written by Plato, The Republic *is also one of the most influential works in the history of philosophy. So broad is the scope of the work that it treats virtually every important topic in philosophy—political theory, aesthetics, ethics, metaphysics, and epistemology. After laying out his vision for the ideal political community, Plato, in Book V of* The Republic, *goes on to make the surprising claim that in order for a state to be truly just, it has to be governed by philosopher-kings. The reason for this is obvious to Plato: only philosophers have the training necessary to grasp the "forms"—those abstract concepts that make justice and morality possible. In particular, it is their ability to grasp the Form of the Good, the source of all things, that makes philosophers the ideal rulers for a political community.*

All this leads to what is certainly the most complex part of The Republic, *in which Plato develops his "two world" theory, dividing reality into sensible and intellectual realms. In the following selection, we are treated to three metaphors that Plato uses to describe how we grasp reality—the analogy of the sun, the divided line, and his most famous analogy of all, the myth of the cave. What each of these analogies make clear is that, for Plato, the intellectual constructions he calls the forms actually have a much higher level of reality than those things which we perceive through the senses.*

1. The Analogy of the Sun

The many, as we say, are seen but not known, and the ideas are known but not seen.

Exactly.

And what is the organ with which we see the visible things?

The sight, he said.

And with the hearing, I said, we hear, and with the other senses perceive the other objects of sense?

True.

But have you remarked that sight is by far the most costly and complex piece of workmanship which the artificer of the senses ever contrived?

No, I never have, he said.

Then reflect: has the ear or voice need of any third or additional nature in order that the one may be able to hear and the other to be heard?

Nothing of the sort.

No, indeed, I replied; and the same is true of most, if not all, the other senses—you would not say

that any of them requires such an addition?

Certainly not.

But you see that without the addition of some other nature there is no seeing or being seen?

How do you mean?

Sight being, as I conceive, in the eyes, and he who has eyes wanting to see; color being also present in them, still unless there be a third nature specially adapted to the purpose, the owner of the eyes will see nothing and the colors will be invisible.

Of what nature are you speaking?

Of that which you term light, I replied.

True, he said.

Noble, then, is the bond which links together sight and visibility, and great beyond other bonds by no small difference of nature; for light is their bond, and light is no ignoble thing?

Nay, he said, the reverse of ignoble.

And which, I said, of the gods in heaven would you say was the lord of this element? Whose is that light which makes the eye to see perfectly and the visible to appear?

You mean the sun, as you and all mankind say.

May not the relation of sight to this deity be described as follows?

How?

Neither sight nor the eye in which sight resides is the sun?

No.

Yet of all the organs of sense the eye is the most like the sun?

By far the most like.

And the power which the eye possesses is a sort of effluence which is dispensed from the sun?

Exactly.

Then the sun is not sight, but the author of sight who is recognized by sight?

True, he said.

And this is he whom I call the child of the good, whom the good begat in his own likeness, to be in the visible world, in relation to sight and the things of sight, what the good is in the intellectual world in relation to mind and the things of mind:

Will you be a little more explicit? he said.

Why, you know, I said, that the eyes, when a person directs them toward objects on which the light of day is no longer shining, but the moon and stars only, see dimly, and are nearly blind; they seem to have no clearness of vision in them?

Very true.

But when they are directed toward objects on which the sun shines, they see clearly and there is sight in them?

Certainly.

And the soul is like the eye: when resting upon that on which truth and being shine, the soul perceives and understands, and is radiant with intelligence; but when turned toward the twilight of becoming and perishing, then she has opinion only, and goes blinking about, and is first of one opinion and then of another, and seems to have no intelligence?

Just so.

Now, that which imparts truth to the known and the power of knowing to the knower is what I would have you term the idea of good, and this you will deem to be the cause of science, and of truth in so far as the latter becomes the subject of knowledge; beautiful too, as are both truth and knowledge, you will be right in esteeming this other nature as more beautiful than either; and, as in the previous instance, light and sight may be truly said to be like the sun, and yet not to be the sun, so in this other sphere, science and truth may be deemed to be like the good, but not the good; the good has a place of honor yet higher.

What a wonder of beauty that must be, he said, which is the author of science and truth, and yet surpasses them in beauty; for you surely cannot mean to say that pleasure is the good?

God forbid, I replied; but may I ask you to consider the image in another point of view?

In what point of view?

You would say, would you not? that the sun is not only the author of visibility in all visible things, but of generation and nourishment and growth, though he himself is not generation?

Certainly.

In like manner the good may be said to be not only the author of knowledge to all things known, but of their being and essence, and yet the good is not essence, but far exceeds essence in dignity and power.

Glaucon said, with a ludicrous earnestness: By the light of heaven, how amazing!

Yes, I said, and the exaggeration may be set down to you; for you made me utter my fancies.

And pray continue to utter them; at any rate let us hear if there is anything more to be said about the similitude of the sun.

Yes, I said, there is a great deal more.

Then omit nothing, however slight.

I will do my best, I said; but I should think that a great deal will have to be omitted.

I hope not, he said.

2. The Divided Line

You have to Imagine, then, that there are two ruling powers, and that one of them is set over the intellectual world, the other over the visible. I do not say heaven, lest you should fancy that I am playing upon the name (ovpavos, opatos). May I suppose that you have this distinction of the visible and intelligible fixed in your mind?

I have.

Now take a line which has been cut into two

unequal parts, and divide each of them again in the same proportion, and suppose the two main divisions to answer, one to the visible and the other to the intelligible, and then compare the subdivisions in respect of their clearness and want of clearness, and you will find that the first section in the sphere of the visible consists of images. And by images I mean, in the first place, shadows, and in the second place, reflections in water and in solid, smooth and polished bodies and the like: Do you understand?

Yes, I understand.

Imagine, now, the other section, of which this is only the resemblance, to include the animals which we see, and everything that grows or is made.

Very good.

Would you not admit that both the sections of this division have different degrees of truth, and that the copy is to the original as the sphere of opinion is to the sphere of knowledge?

Most undoubtedly.

Next proceed to consider the manner in which the sphere of the intellectual is to be divided.

In what manner?

Thus: There are two subdivisions, in the lower of which the soul uses the figures given by the former division as images; the inquiry can only be hypothetical, and instead of going upward to a principle descends to the other end; in the higher of the two, the soul passes out of hypotheses, and goes up to a principle which is above hypotheses, making no use of images as in the former case, but proceeding only in and through the ideas themselves.

I do not quite understand your meaning, he said.

Then I will try again; you will understand me better when I have made some preliminary remarks. You are aware that students of geometry, arithmetic, and the kindred sciences assume the odd, and the even, and the figures, and three kinds of angles, and the like, in their several branches of science; these are their hypotheses, which they and everybody are supposed to know, and therefore they do not deign to give any account of them either to themselves or others; but they begin with them, and go on until they arrive at last, and in a consistent manner, at

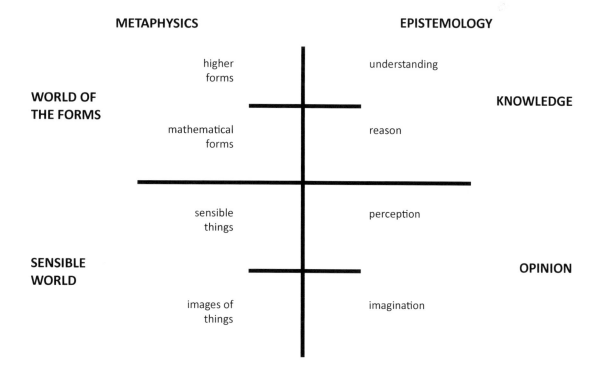

their conclusion?

Yes, he said, I know.

And do you not know also that although they make use of the visible forms and reason about them, they are thinking not of these, but of the ideals which they resemble; not of the figures which they draw, but of the absolute square and the absolute diameter, and so on—the forms which they draw or make, and which have shadows and reflections in water of their own, are converted by them into images, but they are really seeking to behold the things themselves, which can only be seen with the eye of the mind?

That is true.

And of this kind I spoke as the intelligible, although in the search after it the soul is compelled to use hypotheses; not ascending to a first principle, because she is unable to rise above the region of hypothesis, but employing the objects of which the shadows below are resemblances in their turn as images, they having in relation to the shadows and reflections of them a greater distinctness, and therefore a higher value.

I understand, he said, that you are speaking of the province of geometry and the sister arts.

And when I speak of the other division of the intelligible, you will understand me to speak of that other sort of knowledge which reason herself attains by the power of dialectic, using the hypotheses not as first principles, but only as hypotheses—that is to say, as steps and points of departure into a world which is above hypotheses, in order that she may soar beyond them to the first principle of the whole; and clinging to this and then to that which depends on this, by successive steps she descends again without the aid of any sensible object, from ideas, through ideas, and in ideas she ends.

I understand you, he replied; not perfectly, for you seem to me to be describing a task which is really tremendous; but, at any rate, I understand you to say that knowledge and being, which the science of dialectic contemplates, are clearer than the notions of the arts, as they are termed, which proceed from hypotheses only: these are also contemplated by the understanding, and not by the senses: yet, because they start from hypotheses and do not ascend to a principle, those who contemplate them appear to you not to exercise the higher reason upon them, although when a first principle is added to them they are cognizable by the higher reason. And the habit which is concerned with geometry and the cognate sciences I suppose that you would term understanding, and not reason, as being intermediate between opinion and reason.

You have quite conceived my meaning, I said; and now, corresponding to these four divisions, let there be four faculties in the soul—reason answering to the highest, understanding to the second, faith (or conviction) to the third, and perception of shadows to the last—and let there be a scale of them, and let us suppose that the several faculties have clearness in the same degree that their objects have truth.

I understand, he replied, and give my assent, and accept your arrangement....

3. The Myth of the Cave

AND now, I said, let me show in a figure how far our nature is enlightened or unenlightened: Behold! human beings living in an underground den, which has a mouth open toward the light and reaching all along the den; here they have been from their childhood, and have their legs and necks chained so that they cannot move, and can only see before them, being prevented by the chains from turning round their heads. Above and behind them a fire is blazing at a distance, and between the fire and the prisoners there is a raised way; and you will see, if you look, a low wall built along the way, like the screen which marionette players have in front of them, over which they show the puppets.

I see.

And do you see, I said, men passing along the wall carrying all sorts of vessels, and statues and figures of animals made of wood and stone and various materials, which appear over the wall? Some of them are talking, others silent.

You have shown me a strange image, and they are strange prisoners.

Like ourselves, I replied; and they see only their own shadows, or the shadows of one another, which the fire throws on the opposite wall of the cave?

True, he said; how could they see anything but the shadows if they were never allowed to move their heads?

And of the objects which are being carried in like manner they would only see the shadows?

Yes, he said.

And if they were able to converse with one another, would they not suppose that they were naming what was actually before them?

Very true.

And suppose further that the prison had an echo which came from the other side, would they not be sure to fancy when one of the passersby spoke that the voice which they heard came from the passing shadow?

No question, he replied.

To them, I said, the truth would be literally nothing but the shadows of the images.

That is certain.

And now look again, and see what will naturally follow if the prisoners are released and disabused of their error. At first, when any of them is liberated and compelled suddenly to stand up and turn his neck round and walk and look toward the light, he will suffer sharp pains; the glare will distress him, and he will be unable to see the realities of which in his former state he had seen the shadows; and then conceive someone saying to him, that what he saw before was an illusion, but that now, when he is approaching nearer to being and his eye is turned toward more real existence, he has a clearer vision— what will be his reply? And you may further imagine that his instructor is pointing to the objects as they pass and requiring him to name them—will he not be perplexed? Will he not fancy that the shadows which he formerly saw are truer than the objects which are now shown to him?

Far truer.

And if he is compelled to look straight at the light, will he not have a pain in his eyes which will make him turn away to take refuge in the objects of vision which he can see, and which he will conceive to be in reality clearer than the things which are now being shown to him?

True, he said.

And suppose once more, that he is reluctantly dragged up a steep and rugged ascent, and held fast until he is forced into the presence of the sun himself, is he not likely to be pained and irritated? When he approaches the light his eyes will be dazzled, and he will not be able to see anything at all of what are now called realities.

Not all in a moment, he said.

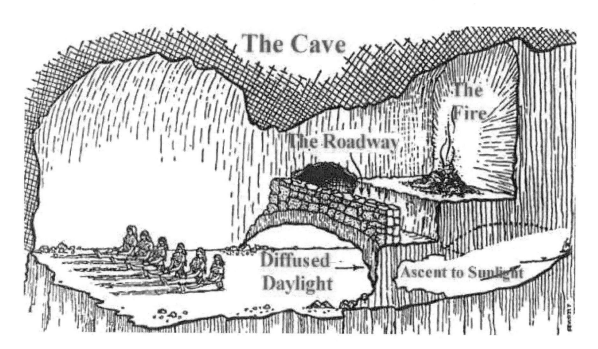

He will require to grow accustomed to the sight of the upper world. And first he will see the shadows best, next the reflections of men and other objects in the water, and then the objects themselves; then he will gaze upon the light of the moon and the stars and the spangled heaven; and he will see the sky and the stars by night better than the sun or the light of the sun by day?

Certainly.

Last of all he will be able to see the sun, and not mere reflections of him in the water, but he will see him in his own proper place, and not in another; and he will contemplate him as he is.

Certainly.

He will then proceed to argue that this is he who gives the season and the years, and is the guardian of all that is in the visible world, and in a certain way the cause of all things which he and his fellows have been accustomed to behold?

Clearly, he said, he would first see the sun and then reason about him.

And when he remembered his old habitation, and the wisdom of the den and his fellow prisoners, do you not suppose that he would felicitate himself on the change, and pity him?

Certainly, he would.

And if they were in the habit of conferring honors among themselves on those who were quickest to observe the passing shadows and to remark which of them went before, and which followed after, and which were together; and who were therefore best able to draw conclusions as to the future, do you think that he would care for such honors and glories, or envy the possessors of them? Would he not say with Homer,

"Better to be the poor servant of a poor master," and to endure anything, rather than think as they do and live after their manner?

Yes, he said, I think that he would rather suffer anything than entertain these false notions and live in this miserable manner.

Imagine once more, I said, such a one coming suddenly out of the sun to be replaced in his old situation; would he not be certain to have his eyes full of darkness?

To be sure, he said.

And if there were a contest, and he had to compete in measuring the shadows with the prisoners who had never moved out of the den, while his sight was still weak, and before his eyes had become steady (and the time which would be needed to acquire this new habit of sight might be very considerable), would he not be ridiculous? Men would say of him that up he went and down he came without his eyes; and that it was better not even to think of ascending; and if anyone tried to loose another and lead him up to the light, let them only catch the offender, and they would put him to death.

No question, he said.

This entire allegory, I said, you may now append, dear Glaucon, to the previous argument; the prisonhouse is the world of sight, the light of the fire is the sun, and you will not misapprehend me if you interpret the journey upward to be the ascent of the soul into the intellectual world according to my poor belief, which, at your desire, I have expressed—whether rightly or wrongly, God knows. But, whether true or false, my opinion is that in the world of knowledge the idea of good appears last of all, and is seen only with an effort; and, when seen, is also inferred to be the universal author of all things beautiful and right, parent of light and of the lord of light in this visible world, and the immediate source of reason and truth in the intellectual; and that this is the power upon which he who would act rationally either in public or private life must have his eye fixed.

I agree, he said, as far as I am able to understand you.

Moreover, I said, you must not wonder that those who attain to this beatific vision are unwilling to descend to human affairs; for their souls are ever hastening into the upper world where they desire to dwell; which desire of theirs is very natural, if our allegory may be trusted.

Yes, very natural.

Plato. "Republic." *The Dialogues of Plato.* Vol. 2. Translated by Benjamin Jowett. Oxford: Oxford University Press, 1892.

MEDITATIONS ON FIRST PHILOSOPHY

RENÉ DESCARTES (1596-1650)

A French philosopher and mathematician, René Descartes is often considered the "father of modern philosophy" because he begins his philosophical method by focusing on questions about how we know (epistemology), rather than about how things are (metaphysics). However, in many respects Descartes was also the last of the great line of Medieval philosophers who were concerned that we only label scientia *("knowledge") those beliefs that we knew with absolute certainty. His emphasis on rigorous method, along with an attitude of healthy skepticism, makes Descartes in those respects a forerunner of many of the modern sciences. In his* Meditations on First Philosophy, *he lays out a bold new method for philosophical inquiry—one that begins by doubting almost everything that human beings believe to be true (whether learned from the scholarly tradition, society or the senses), and accepting nothing as certain that can't be conclusively demonstrated. In the following selections he argues that there are two beliefs which have this pedigree: the belief that he himself must exist, and that God exists. By sticking to his rigorous method, Descartes believes that he has constructed a system of true and certain knowledge, founded upon pure reason.*

Meditation 1
Of the Things Which we May Doubt

1. Several years have now elapsed since I first became aware that I had accepted, even from my youth, many false opinions for true, and that consequently what I afterward based on such principles was highly doubtful; and from that time I was convinced of the necessity of undertaking once in my life to rid myself of all the opinions I had adopted, and of commencing anew the work of building from the foundation, if I desired to establish a firm and abiding superstructure in the sciences. But as this enterprise appeared to me to be one of great magnitude, I waited until I had attained an age so mature as to leave me no hope that at any stage of life more advanced I should be better able to execute my design. On this account, I have delayed so long that I should henceforth consider I was doing wrong were I still to consume in deliberation any of the time that now remains for action. To-day, then, since I have oppor-tunely freed my mind from all cares [and am happily disturbed by no passions], and since I am in the secure possession of leisure in a peaceable retirement, I will at length apply myself earnestly and freely to the general overthrow of all my former opinions.

2. But, to this end, it will not be necessary for me to show that the whole of these are false--a point, perhaps, which I shall never reach; but as even now my reason convinces me that I ought not the less carefully to withhold belief from what is not entirely certain and indubitable, than from what is manifestly false, it will be sufficient to justify the rejection of the whole if I shall find in each some ground for doubt. Nor for this purpose will it be necessary even to deal with each belief individually, which would be truly an endless labor; but, as the removal from below of the foundation necessarily involves the downfall of the whole edifice, I will at once approach the criticism of the principles on which all my former beliefs rested.

3. All that I have, up to this moment, accepted

as possessed of the highest truth and certainty, I received either from or through the senses. I observed, however, that these sometimes misled us; and it is the part of prudence not to place absolute confidence in that by which we have even once been deceived.

4. But it may be said, perhaps, that, although the senses occasionally mislead us respecting minute objects, and such as are so far removed from us as to be beyond the reach of close observation, there are yet many other of their informations (presentations), of the truth of which it is manifestly impossible to doubt; as for example, that I am in this place, seated by the fire, clothed in a winter dressing gown, that I hold in my hands this piece of paper, with other intimations of the same nature. But how could I deny that I possess these hands and this body, and withal escape being classed with persons in a state of insanity, whose brains are so disordered and clouded by dark bilious vapors as to cause them pertinaciously to assert that they are monarchs when they are in the greatest poverty; or clothed [in gold] and purple when destitute of any covering; or that their head is made of clay, their body of glass, or that they are gourds? I should certainly be not less insane than they, were I to regulate my procedure according to examples so extravagant.

5. Though this be true, I must nevertheless here consider that I am a man, and that, consequently, I am in the habit of sleeping, and representing to myself in dreams those same things, or even sometimes others less probable, which the insane think are presented to them in their waking moments. How often have I dreamt that I was in these familiar circumstances, that I was dressed, and occupied this place by the fire, when I was lying undressed in bed? At the present moment, however, I certainly look upon this paper with eyes wide awake; the head which I now move is not asleep; I extend this hand consciously and with express purpose, and I perceive it; the occurrences in sleep are not so distinct as all this. But I cannot forget that, at other times I have been deceived in sleep by similar illusions; and, attentively considering those cases, I perceive so clearly that there exist no certain marks by which the state of waking can ever be distinguished from sleep, that I feel greatly astonished; and in amazement I almost persuade myself that I am now dreaming.

6. Let us suppose, then, that we are dreaming, and that all these particulars—namely, the opening of the eyes, the motion of the head, the forth- putting of the hands--are merely illusions; and even that we really possess neither an entire body nor hands such as we see. Nevertheless it must be admitted at least that the objects which appear to us in sleep are, as it were, painted representations which could not have been formed unless in the likeness of realities; and, therefore, that those general objects, at all events, namely, eyes, a head, hands, and an entire body, are not simply imaginary, but really existent. For, in truth, painters themselves, even when they study to represent sirens and satyrs by forms the most fantastic and extraordinary, cannot bestow upon them natures absolutely new, but can only make a certain medley of the members of different animals; or if they chance to imagine something so novel that nothing at all similar has ever been seen before, and such as is, therefore, purely fictitious and absolutely false, it is at least certain that the colors of which this is composed are real. And on the same principle, although these general objects, viz. [a body], eyes, a head, hands, and the like, be imaginary, we are nevertheless absolutely necessitated to admit the reality at least of some other objects still more simple and universal than these, of which, just as of certain real colors, all those images of things, whether true and real, or false and fantastic, that are found in our consciousness (cogitatio),are formed.

7. To this class of objects seem to belong corporeal nature in general and its extension; the figure of extended things, their quantity or magnitude, and their number, as also the place in, and the time during, which they exist, and other things of the same sort.

8. We will not, therefore, perhaps reason illegitimately if we conclude from this that Physics, Astronomy, Medicine, and all the other sciences that have for their end the consideration of composite objects, are indeed of a doubtful character; but that Arithmetic, Geometry, and the other sciences of the same class, which regard merely the simplest and most general objects, and scarcely inquire whether or not these are really existent, contain somewhat that is certain and indubitable: for whether I am awake or dreaming, it remains true that two and three make five, and that a square has but four sides; nor does it seem possible that truths so apparent can

ever fall under a suspicion of falsity [or incertitude].

9. Nevertheless, the belief that there is a God who is all powerful, and who created me, such as I am, has, for a long time, obtained steady possession of my mind. How, then, do I know that he has not arranged that there should be neither earth, nor sky, nor any extended thing, nor figure, nor magnitude, nor place, providing at the same time, however, for [the rise in me of the perceptions of all these objects, and] the persuasion that these do not exist otherwise than as I perceive them ? And further, as I sometimes think that others are in error respecting matters of which they believe themselves to possess a perfect knowledge, how do I know that I am not also deceived each time I add together two and three, or number the sides of a square, or form some judgment still more simple, if more simple indeed can be imagined? But perhaps Deity has not been willing that I should be thus deceived, for he is said to be supremely good. If, however, it were repugnant to the goodness of Deity to have created me subject to constant deception, it would seem likewise to be contrary to his goodness to allow me to be occasionally deceived; and yet it is clear that this is permitted.

10. Some, indeed, might perhaps be found who would be disposed rather to deny the existence of a Being so powerful than to believe that there is nothing certain. But let us for the present refrain from opposing this opinion, and grant that all which is here said of a Deity is fabulous: nevertheless, in whatever way it be supposed that I reach the state in which I exist, whether by fate, or chance, or by an endless series of antecedents and consequents, or by any other means, it is clear (since to be deceived and to err is a certain defect) that the probability of my being so imperfect as to be the constant victim of deception, will be increased exactly in proportion as the power possessed by the cause, to which they assign my origin, is lessened. To these reasonings I have assuredly nothing to reply, but am constrained at last to avow that there is nothing of all that I formerly believed to be true of which it is impossible to doubt, and that not through thoughtlessness or levity, but from cogent and maturely considered reasons; so that henceforward, if I desire to discover anything certain, I ought not the less carefully to refrain from assenting to those same opinions than to what might be shown to be manifestly false.

11. But it is not sufficient to have made these observations; care must be taken likewise to keep them in remembrance. For those old and customary opinions perpetually recur—long and familiar usage giving them the right of occupying my mind, even almost against my will, and subduing my belief; nor will I lose the habit of deferring to them and confiding in them so long as I shall consider them to be what in truth they are, viz, opinions to some extent doubtful, as I have already shown, but still highly probable, and such as it is much more reasonable to believe than deny. It is for this reason I am persuaded that I shall not be doing wrong, if, taking an opposite judgment of deliberate design, I become my own deceiver, by supposing, for a time, that all those opinions are entirely false and imaginary, until at length, having thus balanced my old by my new prejudices, my judgment shall no longer be turned aside by perverted usage from the path that may conduct to the perception of truth. For I am assured that, meanwhile, there will arise neither peril nor error from this course, and that I cannot for the present yield too much to distrust, since the end I now seek is not action but knowledge.

12. I will suppose, then, not that Deity, who is sovereignly good and the fountain of truth, but that some malignant demon, who is at once exceedingly potent and deceitful, has employed all his artifice to deceive me; I will suppose that the sky, the air, the earth, colors, figures, sounds, and all external things, are nothing better than the illusions of dreams, by means of which this being has laid snares for my credulity; I will consider myself as without hands, eyes, flesh, blood, or any of the senses, and as falsely believing that I am possessed of these; I will continue resolutely fixed in this belief, and if indeed by this means it be not in my power to arrive at the knowledge of truth, I shall at least do what is in my power, viz, [suspend my judgment], and guard with settled purpose against giving my assent to what is false, and being imposed upon by this deceiver, whatever be his power and artifice. But this undertaking is arduous, and a certain indolence insensibly leads me back to my ordinary course of life; and just as the captive, who, perchance, was enjoying in his dreams an imaginary liberty, when he begins to suspect that it is but a vision, dreads awakening, and conspires

with the agreeable illusions that the deception may be prolonged; so I, of my own accord, fall back into the train of my former beliefs, and fear to arouse myself from my slumber, lest the time of laborious wakefulness that would succeed this quiet rest, in place of bringing any light of day, should prove inadequate to dispel the darkness that will arise from the difficulties that have now been raised.

Meditation 2
Of the Nature of the Human Mind and That It is More Easily Known Than the Body

1. The Meditation of yesterday has filled my mind with so many doubts, that it is no longer in my power to forget them. Nor do I see, meanwhile, any principle on which they can be resolved; and, just as if I had fallen all of a sudden into very deep water, I am so greatly disconcerted as to be unable either to plant my feet firmly on the bottom or sustain myself by swimming on the surface. I will, nevertheless, make an effort, and try anew the same path on which I had entered yesterday, that is, proceed by casting aside all that admits of the slightest doubt, not less than if I had discovered it to be absolutely false; and I will continue always in this track until I shall find something that is certain, or at least, if I can do nothing more, until I shall know with certainty that there is nothing certain. Archimedes, that he might transport the entire globe from the place it occupied to another, demanded only a point that was firm and immovable; so, also, I shall be entitled to entertain the highest expectations, if I am fortunate enough to discover only one thing that is certain and indubitable.

2. I suppose, accordingly, that all the things which I see are false (fictitious); I believe that none of those objects which my fallacious memory represents ever existed; I suppose that I possess no senses; I believe that body, figure, extension, motion, and place are merely fictions of my mind. What is there, then, that can be esteemed true ? Perhaps this only, that there is absolutely nothing certain.

3. But how do I know that there is not something different altogether from the objects I have now enumerated, of which it is impossible to entertain the slightest doubt? Is there not a God, or some being, by whatever name I may designate him, who causes these thoughts to arise in my mind ? But why suppose such a being, for it may be I myself am capable of producing them? Am I, then, at least not something? But I before denied that I possessed senses or a body; I hesitate, however, for what follows from that? Am I so dependent on the body and the senses that without these I cannot exist? But I had the persuasion that there was absolutely nothing in the world, that there was no sky and no earth, neither minds nor bodies; was I not, therefore, at the same time, persuaded that I did not exist? Far from it; I assuredly existed, since I was persuaded. But there is I know not what being, who is possessed at once of the highest power and the deepest cunning, who is constantly employing all his ingenuity in deceiving me. Doubtless, then, I exist, since I am deceived; and, let him deceive me as he may, he can never bring it about that I am nothing, so long as I shall be conscious that I am something. So that it must, in fine, be maintained, all things being maturely and carefully considered, that this proposition (pronunciatum) I am, I exist, is necessarily true each time it is expressed by me, or conceived in my mind.

4. But I do not yet know with sufficient clearness what I am, though assured that I am; and hence, in the next place, I must take care, lest perchance I inconsiderately substitute some other object in room of what is properly myself, and thus wander from truth, even in that knowledge (cognition) which I hold to be of all others the most certain and evident. For this reason, I will now consider anew what I formerly believed myself to be, before I entered on the present train of thought; and of my previous opinion I will retrench all that can in the least be invalidated by the grounds of doubt I have adduced, in order that there may at length remain nothing but what is certain and indubitable.

5. What then did I formerly think I was? Undoubtedly I judged that I was a man. But what is a man ? Shall I say a rational animal ? Assuredly not; for it would be necessary forthwith to inquire into what is meant by animal, and what by rational, and thus, from a single question, I should insensibly glide into others, and these more difficult than the first; nor do I now possess enough of leisure to warrant me in wasting my time amid subtleties of

this sort. I prefer here to attend to the thoughts that sprung up of themselves in my mind, and were inspired by my own nature alone, when I applied myself to the consideration of what I was. In the first place, then, I thought that I possessed a countenance, hands, arms, and all the fabric of members that appears in a corpse, and which I called by the name of body. It further occurred to me that I was nourished, that I walked, perceived, and thought, and all those actions I referred to the soul; but what the soul itself was I either did not stay to consider, or, if I did, I imagined that it was something extremely rare and subtile, like wind, or flame, or ether, spread through my grosser parts. As regarded the body, I did not even doubt of its nature, but thought I distinctly knew it, and if I had wished to describe it according to the notions I then entertained, I should have explained myself in this manner: By body I understand all that can be terminated by a certain figure; that can be comprised in a certain place, and so fill a certain space as therefrom to exclude every other body; that can be perceived either by touch, sight, hearing, taste, or smell; that can be moved in different ways, not indeed of itself, but by something foreign to it by which it is touched [and from which it receives the impression]; for the power of self-motion, as likewise that of perceiving and thinking, I held as by no means pertaining to the nature of body; on the contrary, I was somewhat astonished to find such faculties existing in some bodies.

6. But [as to myself, what can I now say that I am], since I suppose there exists an extremely powerful, and, if I may so speak, malignant being, whose whole endeavors are directed toward deceiving me? Can I affirm that I possess any one of all those attributes of which I have lately spoken as belonging to the nature of body? After attentively considering them in my own mind, I find none of them that can properly be said to belong to myself. To recount them were idle and tedious. Let us pass, then, to the attributes of the soul. The first mentioned were the powers of nutrition and walking; but, if it be true that I have no body, it is true likewise that I am capable neither of walking nor of being nourished. Perception is another attribute of the soul; but perception too is impossible without the body; besides, I have frequently, during sleep, believed that I perceived objects which I afterward observed I did not in reali-

ty perceive. Thinking is another attribute of the soul; and here I discover what properly belongs to myself. This alone is inseparable from me. I am--I exist: this is certain; but how often? As often as I think; for perhaps it would even happen, if I should wholly cease to think, that I should at the same time altogether cease to be. I now admit nothing that is not necessarily true. I am therefore, precisely speaking, only a thinking thing, that is, a mind (mens sive animus), understanding, or reason, terms whose signification was before unknown to me. I am, however, a real thing, and really existent; but what thing? The answer was, a thinking thing.

7. The question now arises: what else am I? I will stimulate my imagination with a view to discover whether I am not still something more than a thinking being. Now it is plain I am not the assemblage of members called the human body; I am not a thin and penetrating air diffused through all these members, or wind, or flame, or vapor, or breath, or any of all the things I can imagine; for I supposed that all these were not, and, without changing the supposition, I find that I still feel assured of my existence. But it is true, perhaps, that those very things which I suppose to be non-existent, because they are unknown to me, are not in truth different from myself whom I know. This is a point I cannot determine, and do not now enter into any dispute regarding it. I can only judge of things that are known to me: I am conscious that I exist, and I who know that I exist inquire into what I am. It is, however, perfectly certain that the knowledge of my existence, thus precisely taken, is not dependent on things, the existence of which is as yet unknown to me: and consequently it is not dependent on any of the things I can feign in imagination. Moreover, the phrase itself, I frame an image (efffingo), reminds me of my error; for I should in truth frame one if I were to imagine myself to be anything, since to imagine is nothing more than to contemplate the figure or image of a corporeal thing; but I already know that I exist, and that it is possible at the same time that all those images, and in general all that relates to the nature of body, are merely dreams [or chimeras]. From this I discover that it is not more reasonable to say, I will excite my imagination that I may know more distinctly what I am, than to express myself as follows: I am now awake, and perceive something real; but because my

perception is not sufficiently clear, I will of express purpose go to sleep that my dreams may represent to me the object of my perception with more truth and clearness. And, therefore, I know that nothing of all that I can embrace in imagination belongs to the knowledge which I have of myself, and that there is need to recall with the utmost care the mind from this mode of thinking, that it may be able to know its own nature with perfect distinctness.

8. But what, then, am I? A thinking thing, it has been said. But what is a thinking thing? It is a thing that doubts, understands, [conceives], affirms, denies, wills, refuses; that imagines also, and perceives....

11. Let us now accordingly consider the objects that are commonly thought to be [the most easily, and likewise] the most distinctly known, viz, the bodies we touch and see; not, indeed, bodies in general, for these general notions are usually somewhat more confused, but one body in particular. Take, for example, this piece of wax; it is quite fresh, having been but recently taken from the beehive; it has not yet lost the sweetness of the honey it contained; it still retains somewhat of the odor of the flowers from which it was gathered; its color, figure, size, are apparent (to the sight); it is hard, cold, easily handled; and sounds when struck upon with the finger. In fine, all that contributes to make a body as distinctly known as possible, is found in the one before us. But, while I am speaking, let it be placed near the fire—what remained of the taste exhales, the smell evaporates, the color changes, its figure is destroyed, its size increases, it becomes liquid, it grows hot, it can hardly be handled, and, although struck upon, it emits no sound. Does the same wax still remain after this change ? It must be admitted that it does remain; no one doubts it, or judges otherwise. What, then, was it I knew with so much distinctness in the piece of wax? Assuredly, it could be nothing of all that I observed by means of the senses, since all the things that fell under taste, smell, sight, touch, and hearing are changed, and yet the same wax remains.

12. It was perhaps what I now think, viz, that this wax was neither the sweetness of honey, the pleasant odor of flowers, the whiteness, the figure, nor the sound, but only a body that a little before appeared to me conspicuous under these forms, and which is now perceived under others. But, to speak precisely, what is it that I imagine when I think of it in this way? Let it be attentively considered, and, retrenching all that does not belong to the wax, let us see what remains. There certainly remains nothing, except something extended, flexible, and movable. But what is meant by flexible and movable? Is it not that I imagine that the piece of wax, being round, is capable of becoming square, or of passing from a square into a triangular figure? Assuredly such is not the case, because I conceive that it admits of an infinity of similar changes; and I am, moreover, unable to compass this infinity by imagination, and consequently this conception which I have of the wax is not the product of the faculty of imagination. But what now is this extension? Is it not also unknown ? for it becomes greater when the wax is melted, greater when it is boiled, and greater still when the heat increases; and I should not conceive [clearly and] according to truth, the wax as it is, if I did not suppose that the piece we are considering admitted even of a wider variety of extension than I ever imagined, I must, therefore, admit that I cannot even comprehend by imagination what the piece of wax is, and that it is the mind alone (mens, Lat., entendement, F.) which perceives it. I speak of one piece in particular; for as to wax in general, this is still more evident. But what is the piece of wax that can be perceived only by the [understanding or] mind? It is certainly the same which I see, touch, imagine; and, in fine, it is the same which, from the beginning, I believed it to be. But (and this it is of moment to observe) the perception of it is neither an act of sight, of touch, nor of imagination, and never was either of these, though it might formerly seem so, but is simply an intuition (inspectio) of the mind, which may be imperfect and confused, as it formerly was, or very clear and distinct, as it is at present, according as the attention is more or less directed to the elements which it contains, and of which it is composed.

13. But, meanwhile, I feel greatly astonished when I observe [the weakness of my mind, and] its proneness to error. For although, without at all giving expression to what I think, I consider all this in my own mind, words yet occasionally impede my progress, and I am almost led into error by the terms of ordinary language. We say, for example, that we see the same wax when it is before us, and not

that we judge it to be the same from its retaining the same color and figure: whence I should forthwith be disposed to conclude that the wax is known by the act of sight, and not by the intuition of the mind alone, were it not for the analogous instance of human beings passing on in the street below, as observed from a window. In this case I do not fail to say that I see the men themselves, just as I say that I see the wax; and yet what do I see from the window beyond hats and cloaks that might cover artificial machines, whose motions might be determined by springs ? But I judge that there are human beings from these appearances, and thus I comprehend, by the faculty of judgment alone which is in the mind, what I believed I saw with my eyes….

Meditation 3
On God's Existence

1. I will now close my eyes, I will stop my ears, I will turn away my senses from their objects, I will even efface from my consciousness all the images of corporeal things; or at least, because this can hardly be accomplished, I will consider them as empty and false; and thus, holding converse only with myself, and closely examining my nature, I will endeavor to obtain by degrees a more intimate and familiar knowledge of myself. I am a thinking (conscious) thing, that is, a being who doubts, affirms, denies, knows a few objects, and is ignorant of many,-- [who loves, hates], wills, refuses, who imagines likewise, and perceives; for, as I before remarked, although the things which I perceive or imagine are perhaps nothing at all apart from me [and in themselves], I am nevertheless assured that those modes of consciousness which I call perceptions and imaginations, in as far only as they are modes of consciousness, exist in me.

2. And in the little I have said I think I have summed up all that I really know, or at least all that up to this time I was aware I knew. Now, as I am endeavoring to extend my knowledge more widely, I will use circumspection, and consider with care whether I can still discover in myself anything further which I have not yet hitherto observed. I am certain that I am a thinking thing; but do I not therefore likewise know what is required to render me

certain of a truth ? In this first knowledge, doubtless, there is nothing that gives me assurance of its truth except the clear and distinct perception of what I affirm, which would not indeed be sufficient to give me the assurance that what I say is true, if it could ever happen that anything I thus clearly and distinctly perceived should prove false; and accordingly it seems to me that I may now take as a general rule, that all that is very clearly and distinctly apprehended (conceived) is true….

7. But among these ideas, some appear to me to be innate, others adventitious, and others to be made by myself (factitious); for, as I have the power of conceiving what is called a thing, or a truth, or a thought, it seems to me that I hold this power from no other source than my own nature; but if I now hear a noise, if I see the sun, or if I feel heat, I have all along judged that these sensations proceeded from certain objects existing out of myself; and, in fine, it appears to me that sirens, hippogryphs, and the like, are inventions of my own mind. But I may even perhaps come to be of opinion that all my ideas are of the class which I call adventitious, or that they are all innate, or that they are all factitious; for I have not yet clearly discovered their true origin.

8. What I have here principally to do is to consider, with reference to those that appear to come from certain objects without me, what grounds there are for thinking them like these objects. The first of these grounds is that it seems to me I am so taught by nature; and the second that I am conscious that those ideas are not dependent on my will, and therefore not on myself, for they are frequently presented to me against my will, as at present, whether I will or not, I feel heat; and I am thus persuaded that this sensation or idea (sensum vel ideam) of heat is produced in me by something different from myself, viz., by the heat of the fire by which I sit. And it is very reasonable to suppose that this object impresses me with its own likeness rather than any other thing.

9. But I must consider whether these reasons are sufficiently strong and convincing. When I speak of being taught by nature in this matter, I understand by the word nature only a certain spontaneous impetus that impels me to believe in a resemblance between ideas and their objects, and not a natural light that affords a knowledge of its truth. But these two things are widely different; for what the natural light shows

to be true can be in no degree doubtful, as, for example, that I am because I doubt, and other truths of the like kind; inasmuch as I possess no other faculty whereby to distinguish truth from error, which can teach me the falsity of what the natural light declares to be true, and which is equally trustworthy; but with respect to [seemingly] natural impulses, I have observed, when the question related to the choice of right or wrong in action, that they frequently led me to take the worse part; nor do I see that I have any better ground for following them in what relates to truth and error.

10. Then, with respect to the other reason, which is that because these ideas do not depend on my will, they must arise from objects existing without me, I do not find it more convincing than the former, for just as those natural impulses, of which I have lately spoken, are found in me, notwithstanding that they are not always in harmony with my will, so likewise it may be that I possess some power not sufficiently known to myself capable of producing ideas without the aid of external objects, and, indeed, it has always hitherto appeared to me that they are formed during sleep, by some power of this nature, without the aid of aught external.

11. And, in fine, although I should grant that they proceeded from those objects, it is not a necessary consequence that they must be like them. On the contrary, I have observed, in a number of instances, that there was a great difference between the object and its idea. Thus, for example, I find in my mind two wholly diverse ideas of the sun; the one, by which it appears to me extremely small draws its origin from the senses, and should be placed in the class of adventitious ideas; the other, by which it seems to be many times larger than the whole earth, is taken up on astronomical grounds, that is, elicited from certain notions born with me, or is framed by myself in some other manner. These two ideas cannot certainly both resemble the same sun; and reason teaches me that the one which seems to have immediately emanated from it is the most unlike.

12. And these things sufficiently prove that hitherto it has not been from a certain and deliberate judgment, but only from a sort of blind impulse, that I believed existence of certain things different from myself, which, by the organs of sense, or by whatever other means it might be, conveyed their ideas or images into my mind [and impressed it with their likenesses]....

17. But, among these my ideas, besides that which represents myself, respecting which there can be here no difficulty, there is one that represents a God; others that represent corporeal and inanimate things; others angels; others animals; and, finally, there are some that represent men like myself.

18. But with respect to the ideas that represent other men, or animals, or angels, I can easily suppose that they were formed by the mingling and composition of the other ideas which I have of myself, of corporeal things, and of God, although they were, apart from myself, neither men, animals, nor angels.

19. And with regard to the ideas of corporeal objects, I never discovered in them anything so great or excellent which I myself did not appear capable of originating....

22. There only remains, therefore, the idea of God, in which I must consider whether there is anything that cannot be supposed to originate with myself. By the name God, I understand a substance infinite, [eternal, immutable], independent, all-knowing, all-powerful, and by which I myself, and every other thing that exists, if any such there be, were created. But these properties are so great and excellent, that the more attentively I consider them the less I feel persuaded that the idea I have of them owes its origin to myself alone. And thus it is absolutely necessary to conclude, from all that I have before said, that God exists.

23. For though the idea of substance be in my mind owing to this, that I myself am a substance, I should not, however, have the idea of an infinite substance, seeing I am a finite being, unless it were given me by some substance in reality infinite.

24. And I must not imagine that I do not apprehend the infinite by a true idea, but only by the negation of the finite, in the same way that I comprehend repose and darkness by the negation of motion and light: since, on the contrary, I clearly perceive that there is more reality in the infinite substance than in the finite, and therefore that in some way I possess the perception (notion) of the infinite before that of the finite, that is, the perception of God before that of myself, for how could I know that I doubt, desire, or that something is wanting to me, and that I am

not wholly perfect, if I possessed no idea of a being more perfect than myself, by comparison of which I knew the deficiencies of my nature?....

39. But before I examine this with more attention, and pass on to the consideration of other truths that may be evolved out of it, I think it proper to remain here for some time in the contemplation of God himself--that I may ponder at leisure his marvelous attributes--and behold, admire, and adore the beauty of this light so unspeakably great, as far, at least, as the strength of my mind, which is to some degree dazzled by the sight, will permit. For just as we learn by faith that the supreme felicity of another life consists in the contemplation of the Divine majesty alone, so even now we learn from experience that a like meditation, though incomparably less perfect, is the source of the highest satisfaction of which we are susceptible in this life.

Meditation 4
Of Truth and Error

1. I have been habituated these bygone days to detach my mind from the senses, and I have accurately observed that there is exceedingly little which is known with certainty respecting corporeal objects, that we know much more of the human mind, and still more of God himself. I am thus able now without difficulty to abstract my mind from the contemplation of [sensible or] imaginable objects, and apply it to those which, as disengaged from all matter, are purely intelligible. And certainly the idea I have of the human mind in so far as it is a thinking thing, and not extended in length, breadth, and depth, and participating in none of the properties of body, is incomparably more distinct than the idea of any corporeal object; and when I consider that I doubt, in other words, that I am an incomplete and dependent being, the idea of a complete and independent being, that is to say of God, occurs to my mind with so much clearness and distinctness, and from the fact alone that this idea is found in me, or that I who possess it exist, the conclusions that God exists, and that my own existence, each moment of its continuance, is absolutely dependent upon him, are so manifest, as to lead me to believe it impossible that the human mind can know anything with more clearness

and certitude. And now I seem to discover a path that will conduct us from the contemplation of the true God, in whom are contained all the treasures of science and wisdom, to the knowledge of the other things in the universe.

2. For, in the first place, I discover that it is impossible for him ever to deceive me, for in all fraud and deceit there is a certain imperfection: and although it may seem that the ability to deceive is a mark of subtlety or power, yet the will testifies without doubt of malice and weakness; and such, accordingly, cannot be found in God.

3. In the next place, I am conscious that I possess a certain faculty of judging [or discerning truth from error], which I doubtless received from God, along with whatever else is mine; and since it is impossible that he should will to deceive me, it is likewise certain that he has not given me a faculty that will ever lead me into error, provided I use it aright.

4. And there would remain no doubt on this head, did it not seem to follow from this, that I can never therefore be deceived; for if all I possess be from God, and if he planted in me no faculty that is deceitful, it seems to follow that I can never fall into error. Accordingly, it is true that when I think only of God and turn wholly to him, I discover [in myself] no cause of error or falsity: but immediately thereafter, recurring to myself, experience assures me that I am nevertheless subject to innumerable errors. When I come to inquire into the cause of these, I observe that there is not only present to my consciousness a real and positive idea of God, or of a being supremely perfect, but also, so to speak, a certain negative idea of nothing, in other words, of that which is at an infinite distance from every sort of perfection, and that I am, as it were, a mean between God and nothing, or placed in such a way between absolute existence and non-existence, that there is in truth nothing in me to lead me into error, in so far as an absolute being is my creator; but that, on the other hand, as I thus likewise participate in some degree of nothing or of nonbeing, in other words, as I am not myself the supreme Being, and as I am wanting in many perfections, it is not surprising I should fall into error. And I hence discern that error, so far as error is not something real, which depends for its existence on God, but is simply defect; and therefore that, in order to fall into it, it is not necessary God

should have given me a faculty expressly for this end, but that my being deceived arises from the circumstance that the power which God has given me of discerning truth from error is not infinite.

5. Nevertheless this is not yet quite satisfactory; for error is not a pure negation, [in other words, it is not the simple deficiency or want of some knowledge which is not due], but the privation or want of some knowledge which it would seem I ought to possess. But, on considering the nature of God, it seems impossible that he should have planted in his creature any faculty not perfect in its kind, that is, wanting in some perfection due to it: for if it be true, that in proportion to the skill of the maker the perfection of his work is greater, what thing can have been produced by the supreme Creator of the universe that is not absolutely perfect in all its parts? And assuredly there is no doubt that God could have created me such as that I should never be deceived; it is certain, likewise, that he always wills what is best: is it better, then, that I should be capable of being deceived than that I should not?

6. Considering this more attentively the first thing that occurs to me is the reflection that I must not be surprised if I am not always capable of comprehending the reasons why God acts as he does; nor must I doubt of his existence because I find, perhaps, that there are several other things besides the present respecting which I understand neither why nor how they were created by him; for, knowing already that my nature is extremely weak and limited, and that the nature of God, on the other hand, is immense, incomprehensible, and infinite, I have no longer any difficulty in discerning that there is an infinity of things in his power whose causes transcend the grasp of my mind: and this consideration alone is sufficient to convince me, that the whole class of final causes is of no avail in physical [or natural] things; for it appears to me that I cannot, without exposing myself to the charge of temerity, seek to discover the (impenetrable) ends of Deity.

7. It further occurs to me that we must not consider only one creature apart from the others, if we wish to determine the perfection of the works of Deity, but generally all his creatures together; for the same object that might perhaps, with some show of reason, be deemed highly imperfect if it were alone in the world, may for all that be the most perfect pos-

sible, considered as forming part of the whole universe: and although, as it was my purpose to doubt of everything, I only as yet know with certainty my own existence and that of God, nevertheless, after having remarked the infinite power of Deity, I cannot deny that we may have produced many other objects, or at least that he is able to produce them, so that I may occupy a place in the relation of a part to the great whole of his creatures.

8. Whereupon, regarding myself more closely, and considering what my errors are (which alone testify to the existence of imperfection in me), I observe that these depend on the concurrence of two causes, viz, the faculty of cognition, which I possess, and that of election or the power of free choice,--in other words, the understanding and the will. For by the understanding alone, I [neither affirm nor deny anything but] merely apprehend (percipio) the ideas regarding which I may form a judgment; nor is any error, properly so called, found in it thus accurately taken. And although there are perhaps innumerable objects in the world of which I have no idea in my understanding, it cannot, on that account be said that I am deprived of those ideas [as of something that is due to my nature], but simply that I do not possess them, because, in truth, there is no ground to prove that Deity ought to have endowed me with a larger faculty of cognition than he has actually bestowed upon me; and however skillful a workman I suppose him to be, I have no reason, on that account, to think that it was obligatory on him to give to each of his works all the perfections he is able to bestow upon some. Nor, moreover, can I complain that God has not given me freedom of choice, or a will sufficiently ample and perfect, since, in truth, I am conscious of will so ample and extended as to be superior to all limits. And what appears to me here to be highly remarkable is that, of all the other properties I possess, there is none so great and perfect as that I do not clearly discern it could be still greater and more perfect. For, to take an example, if I consider the faculty of understanding which I possess, I find that it is of very small extent, and greatly limited, and at the same time I form the idea of another faculty of the same nature, much more ample and even infinite, and seeing that I can frame the idea of it, I discover, from this circumstance alone, that it pertains to the nature of God. In the same way, if I examine

the faculty of memory or imagination, or any other faculty I possess, I find none that is not small and circumscribed, and in God immense [and infinite]. It is the faculty of will only, or freedom of choice, which I experience to be so great that I am unable to conceive the idea of another that shall be more ample and extended; so that it is chiefly my will which leads me to discern that I bear a certain image and similitude of Deity. For although the faculty of will is incomparably greater in God than in myself, as well in respect of the knowledge and power that are conjoined with it, and that render it stronger and more efficacious, as in respect of the object, since in him it extends to a greater number of things, it does not, nevertheless, appear to me greater, considered in itself formally and precisely: for the power of will consists only in this, that we are able to do or not to do the same thing (that is, to affirm or deny, to pursue or shun it), or rather in this alone, that in affirming or denying, pursuing or shunning, what is proposed to us by the understanding, we so act that we are not conscious of being determined to a particular action by any external force. For, to the possession of freedom, it is not necessary that I be alike indifferent toward each of two contraries; but, on the contrary, the more I am inclined toward the one, whether because I clearly know that in it there is the reason of truth and goodness, or because God thus internally disposes my thought, the more freely do I choose and embrace it; and assuredly divine grace and natural knowledge, very far from diminishing liberty, rather augment and fortify it. But the indifference of which I am conscious when I am not impelled to one side rather than to another for want of a reason, is the lowest grade of liberty, and manifests defect or negation of knowledge rather than perfection of will; for if I always clearly knew what was true and good, I should never have any difficulty in determining what judgment I ought to come to, and what choice I ought to make, and I should thus be entirely free without ever being indifferent.

9. From all this I discover, however, that neither the power of willing, which I have received from God, is of itself the source of my errors, for it is exceedingly ample and perfect in its kind; nor even the power of understanding, for as I conceive no object unless by means of the faculty that God bestowed upon me, all that I conceive is doubtless rightly conceived by me, and it is impossible for me to be deceived in it. Whence, then, spring my errors ? They arise from this cause alone, that I do not restrain the will, which is of much wider range than the understanding, within the same limits, but extend it even to things I do not understand, and as the will is of itself indifferent to such, it readily falls into error and sin by choosing the false in room of the true, and evil instead of good.

10. For example, when I lately considered whether aught really existed in the world, and found that because I considered this question, it very manifestly followed that I myself existed, I could not but judge that what I so clearly conceived was true, not that I was forced to this judgment by any external cause, but simply because great clearness of the understanding was succeeded by strong inclination in the will; and I believed this the more freely and spontaneously in proportion as I was less indifferent with respect to it. But now I not only know that I exist, in so far as I am a thinking being, but there is likewise presented to my mind a certain idea of corporeal nature; hence I am in doubt as to whether the thinking nature which is in me, or rather which I myself am, is different from that corporeal nature, or whether both are merely one and the same thing, and I here suppose that I am as yet ignorant of any reason that would determine me to adopt the one belief in preference to the other; whence it happens that it is a matter of perfect indifference to me which of the two suppositions I affirm or deny, or whether I form any judgment at all in the matter.

11. This indifference, moreover, extends not only to things of which the understanding has no knowledge at all, but in general also to all those which it does not discover with perfect clearness at the moment the will is deliberating upon them; for, however probable the conjectures may be that dispose me to form a judgment in a particular matter, the simple knowledge that these are merely conjectures, and not certain and indubitable reasons, is sufficient to lead me to form one that is directly the opposite. Of this I lately had abundant experience, when I laid aside as false all that I had before held for true, on the single ground that I could in some degree doubt of it.

12. But if I abstain from judging of a thing when I do not conceive it with sufficient clearness and

distinctness, it is plain that I act rightly, and am not deceived; but if I resolve to deny or affirm, I then do not make a right use of my free will; and if I affirm what is false, it is evident that I am deceived; moreover, even although I judge according to truth, I stumble upon it by chance, and do not therefore escape the imputation of a wrong use of my freedom; for it is a dictate of the natural light, that the knowledge of the understanding ought always to precede the determination of the will. And it is this wrong use of the freedom of the will in which is found the privation that constitutes the form of error. Privation, I say, is found in the act, in so far as it proceeds from myself, but it does not exist in the faculty which I received from God, nor even in the act, in so far as it depends on him.

13. For I have assuredly no reason to complain that God has not given me a greater power of intelligence or more perfect natural light than he has actually bestowed, since it is of the nature of a finite understanding not to comprehend many things, and of the nature of a created understanding to be finite; on the contrary, I have every reason to render thanks to God, who owed me nothing, for having given me all the perfections I possess, and I should be far from thinking that he has unjustly deprived me of, or kept back, the other perfections which he has not bestowed upon me.

14. I have no reason, moreover, to complain because he has given me a will more ample than my understanding, since, as the will consists only of a single element, and that indivisible, it would appear that this faculty is of such a nature that nothing could be taken from it [without destroying it]; and certainly, the more extensive it is, the more cause I have to thank the goodness of him who bestowed it upon me.

15. And, finally, I ought not also to complain that God concurs with me in forming the acts of this will, or the judgments in which I am deceived, because those acts are wholly true and good, in so far as they depend on God; and the ability to form them is a higher degree of perfection in my nature than the want of it would be. With regard to privation, in which alone consists the formal reason of error and sin, this does not require the concurrence of Deity, because it is not a thing [or existence], and if it be referred to God as to its cause, it ought not to be called privation, but negation [according to the signification of these words in the schools]. For in truth it is no imperfection in Deity that he has accorded to me the power of giving or withholding my assent from certain things of which he has not put a clear and distinct knowledge in my understanding; but it is doubtless an imperfection in me that I do not use my freedom aright, and readily give my judgment on matters which I only obscurely and confusedly conceive. I perceive, nevertheless, that it was easy for Deity so to have constituted me as that I should never be deceived, although I still remained free and possessed of a limited knowledge, viz., by implanting in my understanding a clear and distinct knowledge of all the objects respecting which I should ever have to deliberate; or simply by so deeply engraving on my memory the resolution to judge of nothing without previously possessing a clear and distinct conception of it, that I should never forget it. And I easily understand that, in so far as I consider myself as a single whole, without reference to any other being in the universe, I should have been much more perfect than I now am, had Deity created me superior to error; but I cannot therefore deny that it is not somehow a greater perfection in the universe, that certain of its parts are not exempt from defect, as others are, than if they were all perfectly alike. And I have no right to complain because God, who placed me in the world, was not willing that I should sustain that character which of all others is the chief and most perfect.

16. I have even good reason to remain satisfied on the ground that, if he has not given me the perfection of being superior to error by the first means I have pointed out above, which depends on a clear and evident knowledge of all the matters regarding which I can deliberate, he has at least left in my power the other means, which is, firmly to retain the resolution never to judge where the truth is not clearly known to me: for, although I am conscious of the weakness of not being able to keep my mind continually fixed on the same thought, I can nevertheless, by attentive and oft-repeated meditation, impress it so strongly on my memory that I shall never fail to recollect it as often as I require it, and I can acquire in this way the habitude of not erring.

17. And since it is in being superior to error that the highest and chief perfection of man consists, I

deem that I have not gained little by this day's meditation, in having discovered the source of error and falsity. And certainly this can be no other than what I have now explained: for as often as I so restrain my will within the limits of my knowledge, that it forms no judgment except regarding objects which are clearly and distinctly represented to it by the understanding, I can never be deceived; because every clear and distinct conception is doubtless something, and as such cannot owe its origin to nothing, but must of necessity have God for its author-- God, I say, who, as supremely perfect, cannot, without a contradiction, be the cause of any error; and consequently it is necessary to conclude that every such conception [or judgment] is true. Nor have I merely learned to-day what I must avoid to escape error, but also what I must do to arrive at the knowledge of truth; for I will assuredly reach truth if I only fix my attention sufficiently on all the things I conceive perfectly, and separate these from others which I conceive more confusedly and obscurely; to which for the future I shall give diligent heed.

Meditation 5
Of the Essence of Material Things and, Again, of God; That He Exists

1. Several other questions remain for consideration respecting the attributes of God and my own nature or mind. I will, however, on some other occasion perhaps resume the investigation of these. Meanwhile, as I have discovered what must be done and what avoided to arrive at the knowledge of truth, what I have chiefly to do is to essay to emerge from the state of doubt in which I have for some time been, and to discover whether anything can be known with certainty regarding material objects.

2. But before considering whether such objects as I conceive exist without me, I must examine their ideas in so far as these are to be found in my consciousness, and discover which of them are distinct and which confused.

3. In the first place, I distinctly imagine that quantity which the philosophers commonly call continuous, or the extension in length, breadth, and depth that is in this quantity, or rather in the object to which it is attributed. Further, I can enumerate in it many diverse parts, and attribute to each of these all sorts of sizes, figures, situations, and local motions; and, in fine, I can assign to each of these motions all degrees of duration.

4. And I not only distinctly know these things when I thus consider them in general; but besides, by a little attention, I discover innumerable particulars respecting figures, numbers, motion, and the like, which are so evidently true, and so accordant with my nature, that when I now discover them I do not so much appear to learn anything new, as to call to remembrance what I before knew, or for the first time to remark what was before in my mind, but to which I had not hitherto directed my attention.

5. And what I here find of most importance is, that I discover in my mind innumerable ideas of certain objects, which cannot be esteemed pure negations, although perhaps they possess no reality beyond my thought, and which are not framed by me though it may be in my power to think, or not to think them, but possess true and immutable natures of their own. As, for example, when I imagine a triangle, although there is not perhaps and never was in any place in the universe apart from my thought one such figure, it remains true nevertheless that this figure possesses a certain determinate nature, form, or essence, which is immutable and eternal, and not framed by me, nor in any degree dependent on my thought; as appears from the circumstance, that diverse properties of the triangle may be demonstrated, viz., that its three angles are equal to two right, that its greatest side is subtended by its greatest angle, and the like, which, whether I will or not, I now clearly discern to belong to it, although before I did not at all think of them, when, for the first time, I imagined a triangle, and which accordingly cannot be said to have been invented by me.

6. Nor is it a valid objection to allege, that perhaps this idea of a triangle came into my mind by the medium of the senses, through my having. seen bodies of a triangular figure; for I am able to form in thought an innumerable variety of figures with regard to which it cannot be supposed that they were ever objects of sense, and I can nevertheless demonstrate diverse properties of their nature no less than of the triangle, all of which are assuredly true since I clearly conceive them: and they are therefore something, and not mere negations; for it

is highly evident that all that is true is something, [truth being identical with existence]; and I have already fully shown the truth of the principle, that whatever is clearly and distinctly known is true. And although this had not been demonstrated, yet the nature of my mind is such as to compel me to assert to what I clearly conceive while I so conceive it; and I recollect that even when I still strongly adhered to the objects of sense, I reckoned among the number of the most certain truths those I clearly conceived relating to figures, numbers, and other matters that pertain to arithmetic and geometry, and in general to the pure mathematics.

7. But now if because I can draw from my thought the idea of an object, it follows that all I clearly and distinctly apprehend to pertain to this object, does in truth belong to it, may I not from this derive an argument for the existence of God? It is certain that I no less find the idea of a God in my consciousness, that is the idea of a being supremely perfect, than that of any figure or number whatever: and I know with not less clearness and distinctness that an [actual and] eternal existence pertains to his nature than that all which is demonstrable of any figure or number really belongs to the nature of that figure or number; and, therefore, although all the conclusions of the preceding Meditations were false, the existence of God would pass with me for a truth at least as certain as I ever judged any truth of mathematics to be.

8. Indeed such a doctrine may at first sight appear to contain more sophistry than truth. For, as I have been accustomed in every other matter to distinguish between existence and essence, I easily believe that the existence can be separated from the essence of God, and that thus God may be conceived as not actually existing. But, nevertheless, when I think of it more attentively, it appears that the existence can no more be separated from the essence of God, than the idea of a mountain from that of a valley, or the equality of its three angles to two right angles, from the essence of a triangle; so that it is not less impossible to conceive a God, that is, a being supremely perfect, lacking existence, or who is devoid of a certain perfection, than to conceive a mountain without a valley.

9. But though, in truth, I cannot conceive a God unless as existing, any more than I can a mountain without a valley, yet, just as it does not follow that there is any mountain in the world merely because I conceive a mountain with a valley, so likewise, though I conceive God as existing, it does not seem to follow on that account that God exists; for my thought imposes no necessity on things; and as I may imagine a winged horse, though there be none such, so I could perhaps attribute existence to God, though no God existed.

10. But the cases are not analogous, and a fallacy lurks under the semblance of this objection: for because I cannot conceive a mountain without a valley, it does not follow that there is any mountain or valley in existence, but simply that the mountain or valley, whether they do or do not exist, are inseparable from each other; whereas, on the other hand, because I cannot conceive God unless as existing, it follows that existence is inseparable from him, and therefore that he really exists: not that this is brought about by my thought, or that it imposes any necessity on things, but, on the contrary, the necessity which lies in the thing itself, that is, the necessity of the existence of God, determines me to think in this way: for it is not in my power to conceive a God without existence, that is, a being supremely perfect, and yet devoid of an absolute perfection, as I am free to imagine a horse with or without wings.

11. Nor must it be alleged here as an objection, that it is in truth necessary to admit that God exists, after having supposed him to possess all perfections, since existence is one of them, but that my original supposition was not necessary; just as it is not necessary to think that all quadrilateral figures can be inscribed in the circle, since, if I supposed this, I should be constrained to admit that the rhombus, being a figure of four sides, can be therein inscribed, which, however, is manifestly false. This objection is, I say, incompetent; for although it may not be necessary that I shall at any time entertain the notion of Deity, yet each time I happen to think of a first and sovereign being, and to draw, so to speak, the idea of him from the storehouse of the mind, I am necessitated to attribute to him all kinds of perfections, though I may not then enumerate them all, nor think of each of them in particular. And this necessity is sufficient, as soon as I discover that existence is a perfection, to cause me to infer the

existence of this first and sovereign being; just as it is not necessary that I should ever imagine any triangle, but whenever I am desirous of considering a rectilinear figure composed of only three angles, it is absolutely necessary to attribute those properties to it from which it is correctly inferred that its three angles are not greater than two right angles, although perhaps I may not then advert to this relation in particular. But when I consider what figures are capable of being inscribed in the circle, it is by no means necessary to hold that all quadrilateral figures are of this number; on the contrary, I cannot even imagine such to be the case, so long as I shall be unwilling to accept in thought aught that I do not clearly and distinctly conceive; and consequently there is a vast difference between false suppositions, as is the one in question, and the true ideas that were born with me, the first and chief of which is the idea of God. For indeed I discern on many grounds that this idea is not factitious depending simply on my thought, but that it is the representation of a true and immutable nature: in the first place because I can conceive no other being, except God, to whose essence existence pertains; in the second, because it is impossible to conceive two or more gods of this kind; and it being supposed that one such God exists, I clearly see that he must have existed from all eternity, and will exist to all eternity; and finally, because I apprehend many other properties in God, none of which I can either diminish or change.

12. But, indeed, whatever mode of proof I in the end adopt, it always returns to this, that it is only the things I clearly and distinctly conceive which have the power of completely persuading me. And although, of the objects I conceive in this manner, some, indeed, are obvious to everyone, while others are only discovered after close and careful investigation; nevertheless after they are once discovered, the latter are not esteemed less certain than the former. Thus, for example, to take the case of a right-angled triangle, although it is not so manifest at first that the square of the base is equal to the squares of the other two sides, as that the base is opposite to the greatest angle; nevertheless, after it is once apprehended. We are as firmly persuaded of the truth of the former as of the latter. And, with respect to God if I were not pre-occupied by prejudices, and my thought beset on all sides by the continual

presence of the images of sensible objects, I should know nothing sooner or more easily then the fact of his being. For is there any truth more clear than the existence of a Supreme Being, or of God, seeing it is to his essence alone that existence pertains?

13. And although the right conception of this truth has cost me much close thinking, nevertheless at present I feel not only as assured of it as of what I deem most certain, but I remark further that the certitude of all other truths is so absolutely dependent on it that without this knowledge it is impossible ever to know anything perfectly.

14. For although I am of such a nature as to be unable, while I possess a very clear and distinct apprehension of a matter, to resist the conviction of its truth, yet because my constitution is also such as to incapacitate me from keeping my mind continually fixed on the same object and as I frequently recollect a past judgment without at the same time being able to recall the grounds of it, it may happen meanwhile that other reasons are presented to me which would readily cause me to change my opinion, if I did not know that God existed; and thus I should possess no true and certain knowledge, but merely vague and vacillating opinions. Thus, for example, when you consider the nature of the [rectilinear] triangle, it most clearly appears to me, who have been instructed in the principles of geometry, that its three angles are equal to two right angles, and I find it impossible to believe otherwise, while I apply my mind to the demonstration; but as soon as I cease from attending to the process of proof, although I still remember that I had a clear comprehension of it, yet I may readily come to doubt of the truth demonstrated, if I do not know that there is a God: for I may persuade myself that I have been so constituted by nature as to be sometimes deceived, even in matters which I think I apprehend with the greatest evidence and certitude, especially when I recollect that I frequently considered many things to be true and certain which other reasons afterward constrained me to reckon as wholly false.

15. But after I have discovered that God exists, seeing I also at the same time observed that all things depend on him, and that he is no deceiver, and thence inferred that all which I clearly and distinctly perceive is of necessity true: although I no longer attend to the grounds of a judgment, no

opposite reason can be alleged sufficient to lead me to doubt of its truth, provided only I remember that I once possessed a clear and distinct comprehension of it. My knowledge of it thus becomes true and certain. And this same knowledge extends likewise to whatever I remember to have formerly demonstrated, as the truths of geometry and the like: for what can be alleged against them to lead me to doubt of them? Will it be that my nature is such that I may be frequently deceived? But I already know that I cannot be deceived in judgments of the grounds of which I possess a clear knowledge. Will it be that I formerly deemed things to be true and certain which I afterward discovered to be false? But I had no clear and distinct knowledge of any of those things, and, being as yet ignorant of the rule by which I am assured of the truth of a judgment, I was led to give my assent to them on grounds which I afterward discovered were less strong than at the time I imagined them to be. What further objection, then, is there? Will it be said that perhaps I am dreaming (an objection I lately myself raised), or that all the thoughts of which I am now conscious have no more truth than the reveries of my dreams? But although, in truth, I should be dreaming, the rule still holds that all which is clearly presented to my intellect is indisputably true.

16. And thus I very clearly see that the certitude and truth of all science depends on the knowledge alone of the true God, insomuch that, before I knew him, I could have no perfect knowledge of any other thing. And now that I know him, I possess the means of acquiring a perfect knowledge respecting innumerable matters, as well relative to God himself and other intellectual objects as to corporeal nature, in so far as it is the object of pure mathematics.

Meditation 6

Continued in Section 7.3

René Descartes. *Meditations on First Philosophy.* Trans. John Veitch, 1901

An Essay Concerning Human Understanding

John Locke (1632-1704)

The founder of the philosophical system known as British Empiricism, John Locke was one of the most influential thinkers of the 17th century. While Descartes is known as the "father of modern philosophy", Locke was the great herald of modern conceptions of the natural sciences and the experimental method. While Descartes demanded certainty as a criterion of knowledge, a number of philosophers who came after him—especially Locke—began to argue that we must be content with imperfection in our knowledge of the world. Locke himself was deeply suspicious of the Cartesian program of basing knowledge on reason alone. Consequently, he maintained that we should focus on empirical evidence rather than pure reason to properly govern our beliefs. His pessimism about the powers of human reason to attain knowledge of the world in the strict Cartesian sense opened the path to the modern understanding of the natural sciences as less about certainty and more about probable and revisable knowledge gained through empirical investigation.

In his major philosophical work, An Essay Concerning Human Understanding, *Locke focuses on the epistemology of ideas—objects of consciousness, representing things in the outside world. In opposition to Cartesian rationalism, he argues forcefully against the existence of innate ideas; that is, the doctrine that some of the most important truths about the world are native to the mind and only need to be "dug out" or explicated by reason. Mathematical knowledge is taken as a paradigmatic example of* innate *ideas—we do not (and indeed, could not) learn mathematics from experience, but instead the mind looks within itself to realize mathematical truths as 2 + 2 = 4. Locke, however, treats innate ideas as any other hypothesis, and argues that there is not sufficient evidence for this doctrine (children, for example, don't seem to possess them). For Locke, the human mind is a* tabula rasa—*a blank slate—empty of all content until it receives sense perception. There is nothing in the mind which was not first known through the senses.*

BOOK I

Chapter 2
No Innate Speculative Principles

1. It is an established opinion amongst some men, that there are in the understanding certain innate principles; some primary notions…stamped upon the mind of man; which the soul receives in its very first being, and brings into the world with it. It would be sufficient to convince unprejudiced readers of the falseness of this supposition, if I should only show (as I hope I shall in the following parts of this Discourse) how men, barely by the use of their natural faculties, may attain to all the knowledge they have, without the help of any innate impressions; and may arrive at certainty, without any such original notions or principles. For I imagine anyone will easily grant that it would be impertinent to suppose the ideas of colours innate in a creature to whom God hath given sight, and a power to receive them by the eyes from external objects: and no less unreasonable would it be to attribute several truths to the impressions of nature, and innate characters, when we may observe in ourselves faculties fit to

attain as easy and certain knowledge of them as if they were originally imprinted on the mind.

But because a man is not permitted without censure to follow his own thoughts in the search of truth, when they lead him ever so little out of the common road, I shall set down the reasons that made me doubt of the truth of that opinion, as an excuse for my mistake, if I be in one; which I leave to be considered by those who, with me, dispose themselves to embrace truth wherever they find it.

2. There is nothing more commonly taken for granted than that there are certain principles, both speculative and practical, (for they speak of both), universally agreed upon by all mankind: which therefore, they argue, must needs be the constant impressions which the souls of men receive in their first beings, and which they bring into the world with them, as necessarily and really as they do any of their inherent faculties.

3. This argument, drawn from universal consent, has this misfortune in it, that if it were true in matter of fact, that there were certain truths wherein all mankind agreed, it would not prove them innate, if there can be any other way shown how men may come to that universal agreement, in the things they do consent in, which I presume may be done.

4. But, which is worse, this argument of universal consent, which is made use of to prove innate principles, seems to me a demonstration that there are none such: because there are none to which all mankind give a universal assent. I shall begin with the speculative, and instance in those magnified principles of demonstration, "Whatsoever is, is," and "It is impossible for the same thing to be and not to be"; which, of all others, I think have the most allowed title to innate. These have so settled a reputation of maxims universally received, that it will no doubt be thought strange if anyone should seem to question it. But yet I take liberty to say, that these propositions are so far from having an universal assent, that there are a great part of mankind to whom they are not so much as known.

5. For, first, it is evident, that all children and idiots have not the least apprehension or thought of them. And the want of that is enough to destroy that universal assent which must needs be the necessary concomitant of all innate truths: it seeming to me near a contradiction to say, that there are truths imprinted on the soul, which it perceives or understands not: imprinting, if it signify anything, being nothing else but the making certain truths to be perceived. For to imprint anything on the mind without the mind's perceiving it, seems to me hardly intelligible. If therefore children and idiots have souls, have minds, with those impressions upon them, they must unavoidably perceive them, and necessarily know and assent to these truths; which since they do not, it is evident that there are no such impressions. For if they are not notions naturally imprinted, how can they be innate? And if they are notions imprinted, how can they be unknown? To say a notion is imprinted on the mind, and yet at the same time to say, that the mind is ignorant of it, and never yet took notice of it, is to make this impression nothing.

No proposition can be said to be in the mind which it never yet knew, which it was never yet conscious of. For if any one may, then, by the same reason, all propositions that are true, and the mind is capable ever of assenting to, may be said to be in the mind, and to be imprinted: since, if any one can be said to be in the mind, which it never yet knew, it must be only because it is capable of knowing it; and so the mind is of all truths it ever shall know. Nay, thus truths may be imprinted on the mind which it never did, nor ever shall know; for a man may live long, and die at last in ignorance of many truths which his mind was capable of knowing, and that with certainty. So that if the capacity of knowing be the natural impression contended for, all the truths a man ever comes to know will, by this account, be every one of them innate; and this great point will amount to no more, but only to a very improper way of speaking; which, whilst it pretends to assert the contrary, says nothing different from those who deny innate principles. For nobody, I think, ever denied that the mind was capable of knowing several truths. The capacity, they say, is innate; the knowledge acquired. But then to what end such contest for certain innate maxims? If truths can be imprinted on the understanding without being perceived, I can see no difference there can be between any truths the mind is capable of knowing in respect of their original: they must all be innate or all adventitious: in vain shall a man go about to distinguish them. He therefore that talks of innate notions in the understanding, cannot (if he intend thereby any distinct sort of truths) mean such truths to be in the understanding as it never perceived, and is yet wholly ignorant of. For if these words "to be in the understanding" have any propriety, they signify to be understood. So that to be in the understanding, and not to be understood; to be in the mind and never to be perceived, is all one as to say anything is and is not in the mind or understanding. If therefore these two propositions, "Whatsoever is, is," and "It is impossible for the same thing to be and not to be," are by nature imprinted, children cannot be ignorant of them: infants, and all that have souls, must necessarily have them in their understandings, know the truth of them, and assent to it....

BOOK II

Chapter 1
Of Ideas in General and Their Origins

1. Every man being conscious to himself that he thinks; and that which his mind is applied about whilst thinking being the ideas that are there, it is past doubt that men have in their minds several ideas,—such as are those expressed by the words whiteness, hardness, sweetness, thinking, motion, man, elephant, army, drunkenness, and others: it is in the first place then to be inquired, How he comes by them?

I know it is a received doctrine, that men have native ideas, and original characters, stamped upon their minds in their very first being. This opinion I have at large examined already; and, I suppose what I have said in the foregoing Book will be much more easily admitted, when I have shown whence the understanding may get all the ideas it has; and by what ways and degrees they may come into the mind;- for which I shall appeal to every one's own observation and experience.

2. Let us then suppose the mind to be, as we say, white paper, void of all characters, without any ideas: How comes it to be furnished? Whence comes it by that vast store which the busy and boundless fancy of man has painted on it with an almost endless variety? Whence has it all the materials of reason and knowledge? To this I answer, in one word, from *experience*. In that all our knowledge is founded; and from that it ultimately derives itself. Our observation employed either, about external sensible objects, or about the internal operations of our minds perceived and reflected on by ourselves, is that which supplies our understandings with all the materials of thinking. These two are the fountains of knowledge, from whence all the ideas we have, or can naturally have, do spring.

3. First, our Senses, conversant about particular sensible objects, do convey into the mind several distinct perceptions of things, according to those various ways wherein those objects do affect them. And thus we come by those ideas we have of yellow, white, heat, cold, soft, hard, bitter, sweet, and all those which we call sensible qualities; which when I say the senses convey into the mind, I mean, they from external objects convey into the mind what produces there those perceptions. This great source of most of the ideas we have, depending wholly upon our senses, and derived by them to the understanding, I call *sensation*.

4. Secondly, the other fountain from which experience furnisheth the understanding with ideas is,—the perception of the operations of our own mind within us, as it is employed about the ideas it has got;—which operations, when the soul comes to reflect on and consider, do furnish the understanding with another set of ideas, which could not be had from things without. And such are perception, thinking, doubting, believing, reasoning, knowing, willing, and all the different actings of our own minds;—which we being conscious of, and observing in ourselves, do from these receive into our understandings as distinct ideas as we do from bodies affecting our senses. This source of ideas every man has wholly in himself; and though it be not sense, as having nothing to do with external objects, yet it is very like it, and might properly enough be called internal sense. But as I call the other SENSATION, so I Call this REFLECTION, the ideas it affords being such only as the mind gets by reflecting on its own operations within itself. By reflection then, in the following part of this discourse, I would be understood to mean, that notice which the mind takes of its own operations, and the manner of them, by reason whereof there come to be ideas of these operations in the understanding. These two, I say, viz. external

material things, as the objects of *sensation*, and the operations of our own minds within, as the objects of *reflection*, are to me the only originals from whence all our ideas take their beginnings. The term operations here I use in a large sense, as comprehending not barely the actions of the mind about its ideas, but some sort of passions arising sometimes from them, such as is the satisfaction or uneasiness arising from any thought.

5. The understanding seems to me not to have the least glimmering of any ideas which it doth not receive from one of these two. External objects furnish the mind with the ideas of sensible qualities, which are all those different perceptions they produce in us; and the mind furnishes the understanding with ideas of its own operations.

These, when we have taken a full survey of them, and their several modes, combinations, and relations, we shall find to contain all our whole stock of ideas; and that we have nothing in our minds which did not come in one of these two ways. Let any one examine his own thoughts, and thoroughly search into his understanding; and then let him tell me, whether all the original ideas he has there, are any other than of the objects of his senses, or of the operations of his mind, considered as objects of his reflection. And how great a mass of knowledge soever he imagines to be lodged there, he will, upon taking a strict view, see that he has not any idea in his mind but what one of these two have imprinted—though perhaps, with infinite variety compounded and enlarged by the understanding, as we shall see hereafter.

6. He that attentively considers the state of a child, at his first coming into the world, will have little reason to think him stored with plenty of ideas, that are to be the matter of his future knowledge. It is by degrees he comes to be furnished with them. And though the ideas of obvious and familiar qualities imprint themselves before the memory begins to keep a register of time or order, yet it is often so late before some unusual qualities come in the way, that there are few men that cannot recollect the beginning of their acquaintance with them. And if it were worth while, no doubt a child might be so ordered as to have but a very few, even of the ordinary ideas, till he were grown up to a man. But all that are born into the world, being surrounded with bodies that perpetually and diversely affect them, variety of ideas,

whether care be taken of it or not, are imprinted on the minds of children. Light and colours are busy at hand everywhere, when the eye is but open; sounds and some tangible qualities fail not to solicit their proper senses, and force an entrance to the mind;- but yet, I think, it will be granted easily, that if a child were kept in a place where he never saw any other but black and white till he were a man, he would have no more ideas of scarlet or green, than he that from his childhood never tasted an oyster, or a pine-apple, has of those particular relishes.

7. Men then come to be furnished with fewer or more simple ideas from without, according as the objects they converse with afford greater or less variety; and from the operations of their minds within, according as they more or less reflect on them. For, though he that contemplates the operations of his mind, cannot but have plain and clear ideas of them; yet, unless he turn his thoughts that way, and considers them attentively, he will no more have clear and distinct ideas of all the operations of his mind, and all that may be observed therein, than he will have all the particular ideas of any landscape, or of the parts and motions of a clock, who will not turn his eyes to it, and with attention heed all the parts of it. The picture, or clock may be so placed, that they may come in his way every day; but yet he will have but a confused idea of all the parts they are made up of, till he applies himself with attention, to consider them each in particular.

8. And hence we see the reason why it is pretty late before most children get ideas of the operations of their own minds; and some have not any very clear or perfect ideas of the greatest part of them all their lives. Because, though they pass there continually, yet, like floating visions, they make not deep impressions enough to leave in their mind clear, distinct, lasting ideas, till the understanding turns inward upon itself, reflects on its own operations, and makes them the objects of its own contemplation. Children when they come first into it, are surrounded with a world of new things, which, by a constant solicitation of their senses, draw the mind constantly to them; forward to take notice of new, and apt to be delighted with the variety of changing objects. Thus the first years are usually employed and diverted in looking abroad. Men's business in them is to acquaint themselves with what is to be found without;

and so growing up in a constant attention to outward sensations, seldom make any considerable reflection on what passes within them, till they come to be of riper years; and some scarce ever at all.

9. To ask, at what time a man has first any ideas, is to ask, when he begins to perceive;- having ideas, and perception, being the same thing. I know it is an opinion, that the soul always thinks, and that it has the actual perception of ideas in itself constantly, as long as it exists; and that actual thinking is as insepa-rable from the soul as actual extension is from the body; which if true, to inquire after the beginning of a man's ideas is the same as to inquire after the be-ginning of his soul. For, by this account, soul and its ideas, as body and its extension, will begin to exist both at the same time.

Chapter 2
Of Simple Ideas

1. The better to understand the nature, manner, and extent of our knowledge, one thing is carefully to be observed concerning the ideas we have; and that is, that some of them are simple and some complex.

Though the qualities that affect our senses are, in the things themselves, so united and blended, that there is no separation, no distance between them; yet it is plain, the ideas they produce in the mind enter by the senses simple and unmixed. For, though the sight and touch often take in from the same object, at the same time, different ideas—as a man sees at once motion and colour; the hand feels softness and warmth in the same piece of wax: yet the simple ideas thus united in the same subject, are as perfectly distinct as those that come in by different senses. The coldness and hardness which a man feels in a piece of ice being as distinct ideas in the mind as the smell and whiteness of a lily; or as the taste of sugar, and smell of a rose. And there is nothing can be plainer to a man than the clear and distinct perception he has of those simple ideas; which, being each in itself un-compounded, contains in it nothing but one uniform appearance, or conception in the mind, and is not distinguishable into different ideas.

2. The mind can neither make nor destroy them. These simple ideas, the materials of all our knowl-edge, are suggested and furnished to the mind only by those two ways above mentioned, viz. sensa-tion and reflection. When the understanding is once stored with these simple ideas, it has the power to repeat, compare, and unite them, even to an al-most infinite variety, and so can make at pleasure new complex ideas. But it is not in the power of the most exalted wit, or enlarged understanding, by any quickness or variety of thought, to invent or frame one new simple idea in the mind, not taken in by the ways before mentioned: nor can any force of the understanding destroy those that are there....

Chapter 8
Some Further Considerations Concerning Our Simple Ideas of Sensation

1. Concerning the simple ideas of Sensation, it is to be considered,—that whatsoever is so constituted in nature as to be able, by affecting our senses, to cause any perception in the mind, doth thereby produce in the understanding a simple idea; which, whatever be the external cause of it, when it comes to be taken notice of by our discerning faculty, it is by the mind looked on and considered there to be a real posi-tive idea in the understanding, as much as any other whatsoever; though, perhaps, the cause of it be but a privation of the subject.

2. Thus the ideas of heat and cold, light and darkness, white and black, motion and rest, are equally clear and positive ideas in the mind; though, perhaps, some of the causes which produce them are barely privations, in those subjects from whence our senses derive those ideas. These the understanding, in its view of them, considers all as distinct positive ideas, without taking notice of the causes that pro-duce them: which is an inquiry not belonging to the idea, as it is in the understanding, but to the nature of the things existing without us. These are two very different things, and carefully to be distinguished; it being one thing to perceive and know the idea of white or black, and quite another to examine what kind of particles they must be, and how ranged in the superficies, to make any object appear white or black.

3. A painter or dyer who never inquired into their causes hath the ideas of white and black, and other colours, as clearly, perfectly, and distinctly in his

understanding, and perhaps more distinctly, than the philosopher who hath busied himself in considering their natures, and thinks he knows how far either of them is, in its cause, positive or privative; and the idea of black is no less positive in his mind than that of white, however the cause of that colour in the external object may be only a privation.

4. If it were the design of my present undertaking to inquire into the natural causes and manner of perception, I should offer this as a reason why a privative cause might, in some cases at least, produce a positive idea; viz. that all sensation being produced in us only by different degrees and modes of motion in our animal spirits, variously agitated by external objects, the abatement of any former motion must as necessarily produce a new sensation as the variation or increase of it; and so introduce a new idea, which depends only on a different motion of the animal spirits in that organ.

5. But whether this be so or not I will not here determine, but appeal to every one's own experience, whether the shadow of a man, though it consists of nothing but the absence of light (and the more the absence of light is, the more discernible is the shadow) does not, when a man looks on it, cause as clear and positive idea in his mind as a man himself, though covered over with clear sunshine? And the picture of a shadow is a positive thing. Indeed, we have negative names, which stand not directly for positive ideas, but for their absence, such as insipid, silence, nihil, &c.; which words denote positive ideas, v.g. taste, sound, being, with a signification of their absence.

6. And thus one may truly be said to see darkness. For, supposing a hole perfectly dark, from whence no light is reflected, it is certain one may see the figure of it, or it may be painted; or whether the ink I write with makes any other idea, is a question. The privative causes I have here assigned of positive ideas are according to the common opinion; but, in truth, it will be hard to determine whether there be really any ideas from a privative cause, till it be determined, whether rest be any more a privation than motion.

7. To discover the nature of our ideas the better, and to discourse of them intelligibly, it will be convenient to distinguish them as they are ideas or perceptions in our minds; and as they are modifi-

cations of matter in the bodies that cause such perceptions in us: that so we may not think (as perhaps usually is done) that they are exactly the images and resemblances of something inherent in the subject; most of those of sensation being in the mind no more the likeness of something existing without us, than the names that stand for them are the likeness of our ideas, which yet upon hearing they are apt to excite in us.

8. Whatsoever the mind perceives in itself, or is the immediate object of perception, thought, or understanding, that I call idea; and the power to produce any idea in our mind, I call quality of the subject wherein that power is. Thus a snowball having the power to produce in us the ideas of white, cold, and round,—the power to produce those ideas in us, as they are in the snowball, I call qualities; and as they are sensations or perceptions in our understandings, I call them ideas; which ideas, if I speak of sometimes as in the things themselves, I would be understood to mean those qualities in the objects which produce them in us.

9. Qualities thus considered in bodies are,—First, such as are utterly inseparable from the body, in what state soever it be; and such as in all the alterations and changes it suffers, all the force can be used upon it, it constantly keeps; and such as sense constantly finds in every particle of matter which has bulk enough to be perceived; and the mind finds inseparable from every particle of matter, though less than to make itself singly be perceived by our senses: v.g. Take a grain of wheat, divide it into two parts; each part has still solidity, extension, figure, and mobility: divide it again, and it retains still the same qualities; and so divide it on, till the parts become insensible; they must retain still each of them all those qualities. For division (which is all that a mill, or pestle, or any other body, does upon another, in reducing it to insensible parts) can never take away either solidity, extension, figure, or mobility from any body, but only makes two or more distinct separate masses of matter, of that which was but one before; all which distinct masses, reckoned as so many distinct bodies, after division, make a certain number. These I call original or primary qualities of body, which I think we may observe to produce simple ideas in us, viz. solidity, extension, figure, motion or rest, and number.

10. Secondly, such qualities which in truth are nothing in the objects themselves but power to produce various sensations in us by their primary qualities, i.e. by the bulk, figure, texture, and motion of their insensible parts, as colours, sounds, tastes, &c. These I call secondary qualities. To these might be added a third sort, which are allowed to be barely powers; though they are as much real qualities in the subject as those which I, to comply with the common way of speaking, call qualities, but for distinction, secondary qualities. For the power in fire to produce a new colour, or consistency, in wax or clay,—by its primary qualities, is as much a quality in fire, as the power it has to produce in me a new idea or sensation of warmth or burning, which I felt not before—by the same primary qualities, viz. the bulk, texture, and motion of its insensible parts.

11. The next thing to be considered is, how bodies produce ideas in us; and that is manifestly by impulse, the only way which we can conceive bodies to operate in.

12. If then external objects be not united to our minds when they produce ideas therein; and yet we perceive these original qualities in such of them as singly fall under our senses, it is evident that some motion must be thence continued by our nerves, or animal spirits, by some parts of our bodies, to the brains or the seat of sensation, there to produce in our minds the particular ideas we have of them. And since the extension, figure, number, and motion of bodies of an observable bigness, may be perceived at a distance by the sight, it is evident some singly imperceptible bodies must come from them to the eyes, and thereby convey to the brain some motion; which produces these ideas which we have of them in us.

13. After the same manner, that the ideas of these original qualities are produced in us, we may conceive that the ideas of secondary qualities are also produced, viz. by the operation of insensible particles on our senses. For, it being manifest that there are bodies and good store of bodies, each whereof are so small, that we cannot by any of our senses discover either their bulk, figure, or motion,—as is evident in the particles of the air and water, and others extremely smaller than those; perhaps as much smaller than the particles of air and water, as the particles of air and water are smaller than peas or hail-stones;—let us suppose at present that the different motions and figures, bulk and number, of such particles, affecting the several organs of our senses, produce in us those different sensations which we have from the colours and smells of bodies; v.g. that a violet, by the impulse of such insensible particles of matter, of peculiar figures and bulks, and in different degrees and modifications of their motions, causes the ideas of the blue colour, and sweet scent of that flower to be produced in our minds. It being no more impossible to conceive that God should annex such ideas to such motions, with which they have no similitude, than that he should annex the idea of pain to the motion of a piece of steel dividing our flesh, with which that idea hath no resemblance.

14. What I have said concerning colours and smells may be understood also of tastes and sounds, and other the like sensible qualities; which, whatever reality we by mistake attribute to them, are in truth nothing in the objects themselves, but powers to produce various sensations in us; and depend on those primary qualities, viz. bulk, figure, texture, and motion of parts as I have said.

15. From whence I think it easy to draw this observation—that the ideas of primary qualities of bodies are resemblances of them, and their patterns do really exist in the bodies themselves, but the ideas produced in us by these secondary qualities have no resemblance of them at all. There is nothing like our ideas, existing in the bodies themselves. They are, in the bodies we denominate from them, only a power to produce those sensations in us: and what is sweet, blue, or warm in idea, is but the certain bulk, figure, and motion of the insensible parts, in the bodies themselves, which we call so.

16. Flame is denominated hot and light; snow, white and cold; and manna, white and sweet, from the ideas they produce in us. Which qualities are commonly thought to be the same in those bodies that those ideas are in us, the one the perfect resemblance of the other, as they are in a mirror, and it would by most men be judged very extravagant if one should say otherwise. And yet he that will consider that the same fire that, at one distance produces in us the sensation of warmth, does, at a nearer approach, produce in us the far different sensation of pain, ought to bethink himself what reason he has to say- that this idea of warmth, which was produced

in him by the fire, is actually in the fire; and his idea of pain, which the same fire produced in him the same way, is not in the fire. Why are whiteness and coldness in snow, and pain not, when it produces the one and the other idea in us; and can do neither, but by the bulk, figure, number, and motion of its solid parts?

17. The particular bulk, number, figure, and motion of the parts of fire or snow are really in them,—whether any one's senses perceive them or no: and therefore they may be called real qualities, because they really exist in those bodies. But light, heat, whiteness, or coldness, are no more really in them than sickness or pain is in manna. Take away the sensation of them; let not the eyes see light or colours, nor the ears hear sounds; let the palate not taste, nor the nose smell, and all colours, tastes, odours, and sounds, as they are such particular ideas, vanish and cease, and are reduced to their causes, i.e. bulk, figure, and motion of parts....

21. Ideas being thus distinguished and understood, we may be able to give an account how the same water, at the same time, may produce the idea of cold by one hand and of heat by the other: whereas it is impossible that the same water, if those ideas were really in it, should at the same time be both hot and cold. For, if we imagine warmth, as it is in our hands, to be nothing but a certain sort and degree of motion in the minute particles of our nerves or animal spirits, we may understand how it is possible that the same water may, at the same time, produce the sensations of heat in one hand and cold in the other; which yet figure never does, that never producing-the idea of a square by one hand which has produced the idea of a globe by another. But if the sensation of heat and cold be nothing but the increase or diminution of the motion of the minute parts of our bodies, caused by the corpuscles of any other body, it is easy to be understood, that if that motion be greater in one hand than in the other; if a body be applied to the two hands, which has in its minute particles a greater motion than in those of one of the hands, and a less than in those of the other, it will increase the motion of the one hand and lessen it in the other; and so cause the different sensations of heat and cold that depend thereon.

22. I have in what just goes before been engaged in physical inquiries a little further than perhaps I intended. But, it being necessary to make the nature of sensation a little understood; and to make the difference between the qualities in bodies, and the ideas produced by them in the mind, to be distinctly conceived, without which it were impossible to discourse intelligibly of them;—I hope I shall be pardoned this little excursion into natural philosophy; it being necessary in our present inquiry to distinguish the primary and real qualities of bodies, which are always in them (viz. solidity, extension, figure, number, and motion, or rest, and are sometimes perceived by us, viz. when the bodies they are in are big enough singly to be discerned), from those secondary and imputed qualities, which are but the powers of several combinations of those primary ones, when they operate without being distinctly discerned—whereby we may also come to know what ideas are, and what are not, resemblances of something really existing in the bodies we denominate from them.

23. The qualities, then, that are in bodies, rightly considered, are of three sorts:—First, The bulk, figure, number, situation, and motion or rest of their solid parts. Those are in them, whether we perceive them or not; and when they are of that size that we can discover them, we have by these an idea of the thing as it is in itself; as is plain in artificial things. These I call primary qualities.

Secondly, The power that is in any body, by reason of its insensible primary qualities, to operate after a peculiar manner on any of our senses, and thereby produce in us the different ideas of several colours, sounds, smells, tastes, &c. These are usually called sensible qualities.

Thirdly, The power that is in any body, by reason of the particular constitution of its primary qualities, to make such a change in the bulk, figure, texture, and motion of another body, as to make it operate on our senses differently from what it did before. Thus the sun has a power to make wax white, and fire to make lead fluid. These are usually called powers.

The first of these, as has been said, I think may be properly called real, original, or primary qualities; because they are in the things themselves, whether they are perceived or not: and upon their different modifications it is that the secondary qualities depend.

The other two are only powers to act differently upon other things: which powers result from the different modifications of those primary qualities.

24. But, though the two latter sorts of qualities are powers barely, and nothing but powers, relating to several other bodies, and resulting from the different modifications of the original qualities, yet they are generally otherwise thought of. For the second sort, viz, the powers to produce several ideas in us, by our senses, are looked upon as real qualities in the things thus affecting us: but the third sort are called and esteemed barely powers. v.g. The idea of heat or light, which we receive by our eyes, or touch, from the sun, are commonly thought real qualities existing in the sun, and something more than mere powers in it. But when we consider the sun in reference to wax, which it melts or blanches, we look on the whiteness and softness produced in the wax, not as qualities in the sun, but effects produced by powers in it. Whereas, if rightly considered, these qualities of light and warmth, which are perceptions in me when I am warmed or enlightened by the sun, are no otherwise in the sun, than the changes made in the wax, when it is blanched or melted, are in the sun. They are all of them equally powers in the sun, depending on its primary qualities; whereby it is able, in the one case, so to alter the bulk, figure, texture, or motion of some of the insensible parts of my eyes or hands, as thereby to produce in me the idea of light or heat; and in the other, it is able so to alter the bulk, figure, texture, or motion of the insensible parts of the wax, as to make them fit to produce in me the distinct ideas of white and fluid.

25. Why the secondary are ordinarily taken for real qualities, and not for bare powers. The reason why the one are ordinarily taken for real qualities, and the other only for bare powers, seems to be, because the ideas we have of distinct colours, sounds, &c., containing nothing at all in them of bulk, figure, or motion, we are not apt to think them the effects of these primary qualities; which appear not, to our senses, to operate in their production, and with which they have not any apparent congruity or conceivable connexion. Hence it is that we are so forward to imagine, that those ideas are the resemblances of something really existing in the objects themselves: since sensation discovers nothing of bulk, figure, or motion of parts in their production; nor can reason show how bodies, by their bulk,

figure, and motion, should produce in the mind the ideas of blue or yellow, &c. But, in the other case, in the operations of bodies changing the qualities one of another, we plainly discover that the quality produced hath commonly no resemblance with anything in the thing producing it; wherefore we look on it as a bare effect of power. For, through receiving the idea of heat or light from the sun, we are apt to think it is a perception and resemblance of such a quality in the sun; yet when we see wax, or a fair face, receive change of colour from the sun, we cannot imagine that to be the reception or resemblance of anything in the sun, because we find not those different colours in the sun itself. For, our senses being able to observe a likeness or unlikeness of sensible qualities in two different external objects, we forwardly enough conclude the production of any sensible quality in any subject to be an effect of bare power, and not the communication of any quality which was really in the efficient, when we find no such sensible quality in the thing that produced it. But our senses, not being able to discover any unlikeness between the idea produced in us, and the quality of the object producing it, we are apt to imagine that our ideas are resemblances of something in the objects, and not the effects of certain powers placed in the modification of their primary qualities, with which primary qualities the ideas produced in us have no resemblance.

26. Secondary qualities twofold; first, immediately perceivable; secondly, mediately perceivable. To conclude. Besides those before-mentioned primary qualities in bodies, viz. bulk, figure, extension, number, and motion of their solid parts; all the rest, whereby we take notice of bodies, and distinguish them one from another, are nothing else but several powers in them, depending on those primary qualities; whereby they are fitted, either by immediately operating on our bodies to produce several different ideas in us; or else, by operating on other bodies, so to change their primary qualities as to render them capable of producing ideas in us different from what before they did. The former of these, I think, may be called secondary qualities immediately perceivable: the latter, secondary qualities, mediately perceivable.

John Locke. *An Essay Concerning Human Understanding*. Vol. 1. Ed. Alexander Campbell Fraser. Oxford: Clarendon Press, 1894.

7

PHILOSOPHY OF MIND: WHAT IS MIND AND WHAT IS THE SELF?

A.J. GRUNTHALER

What exactly does it mean to be a human person?

Are you merely a physical being, whose thoughts and feelings arise from the firing of neurons in your brain? Or is the "real you" something more than the sum total of your physical properties? Do your thoughts and feelings, for example, presuppose the existence of a mind or soul that is the real you? And, if this real you is immaterial, does that mean that in some way your human identity is capable of living on beyond the death of your body?

These are the sorts of problems that Philosophy of Mind addresses. Philosophy of Mind is the branch of philosophy deals with questions about the nature and properties of the mind, the mind's relationship to the body, and problems pertaining to human identity.

Before we proceed any further, it might be helpful to define what exactly we mean by the word "mind" and what its connection is to the older term that is often used in philosophy—"soul." For this we need to do a bit of etymological investigation. In ancient Greek the term used for soul or mind was *psyche* (from which we get the word "psychology"); in Latin, the term used was *animus* (from which we get the word "animate"). For practical purposes, we can use these terms interchangeably. Both essentially refer to what the ancient Greeks and Romans understood to be the true source of human identity—that aspect of who we are that enable us to think, reason, contemplate, judge, imagine, and so on. In this sense, the mind in antiquity was always viewed in relation to the body, the two combined in some strange way to comprise who we are as human individuals.

Mind and body: the two distinct but interconnected elements that make us who we are as unique human beings. Or do they? While this composite understanding of human identity has had a long history in philosophical and religious thought, in more recent times many philosophers have come to question whether this model in fact makes sense. To understand the significance of this debate, we'll examine two very important problems in the field of

Philosophy of Mind—the mind-body problem, and the problem of personal identity. The fact that these two problems have been discussed and debated since the beginning of the modern era seems to indicate that the answer to the question, "what does it mean to be a human person?" is, in fact, much more complex an issue that we might assume.

The Mind-Body Problem

One of the great issues explored by philosophy throughout history is what precisely is the relationship of mind to body? On a very basic level, most people tend to make a distinction between mental and physical phenomenon. The mind makes a judgment or a decision about something (that there is danger, for example) and the body moves in accordance with the mind's wishes (it runs away). The question is whether there actually is a real division between mind and body, or whether we are just using this as a convenient way to talk about ourselves.

There are two basic approaches that philosophers have taken to resolve this problem—dualism and physicalism.

Dualism

Dualists argue that mind and body are distinct substances, which interact with one another but which remain separate. There is a difference, they argue, between mental acts such as thinking, deciding, or imagining and physical processes, such as those that occur in the brain. Mental acts, therefore, cannot be reduced to activities of the brain.

In the *Phaedo*, for example, mind-body dualism provided Plato with the rationale for arguing for the continued existence of a spiritual mind after the death of the material body. The body decays, he argued, but the mind freed from the "prison of the body" is able to live on beyond death. This metaphysical separation between mind and body that Plato described in the *Phaedo* would be accepted universally throughout the Middle Ages because it supported the Christian belief in the immortality of the soul.

The most prominent formulation of the dualistic position is found in the writing of René Descartes. As you may recall from the previous section of this text on Epistemology, Descartes wanted to develop a truly scientific understanding of the world—one that was founded upon the principles of pure reason rather than upon belief or appeals to authority (as was the case during the Middle Ages). Beginning from a position of skeptical doubt about everything, Descartes was looking for some unassailable truth which could provide a foundation for knowledge about the rest of the world. That certain truth became, "*cogito ergo sum*"—I think therefore I am. Descartes deduced that although he could doubt the existence of almost everything else—including his own physical body—he couldn't doubt his existence as a thinking being.

What Descartes began to realize from his investigation is that thought is essential to human existence in a way that bodily attributes are not. Mind, not body, he believed, was what made us truly human. As he himself put it, "this 'I'—that is, the soul by which I am what I am—is entirely distinct from the body, and indeed is easier to know than the body, and would not fail to be whatever it is, even if the body did not exist." (*Discourse on Method*, Part IV). For Descartes, then, human beings are comprised of two distinct substances—body and mind—both of which are capable of existing independently of one another. Bodies, he held, are spatially extended substances, incapable of feeling or thought ("*res extensa*"); minds, on the other hand, are non-extended, non-physical substances and are characterized by thought ("*res cognitans*").

If mind and body are two different types of realities, as Descartes maintains, then the question becomes, how is it possible for these two entities to interact? The mind experiences fear and causes the legs to run—an example of the mind affecting the body. Conversely, the hand moves close to a hot flame and the mind experiences pain—a case of body affecting mind. So there must be some kind of interaction between the two. But how is this possible if they are completely different realities? Descartes' solution is that mind-body interaction takes place in the pineal gland—a theory which even in his own time must have seemed implausible. Certainly, there is absolutely no reason to believe that a physical organ like the pineal gland has anything at all to do with consciousness.

Other dualistic attempts to provide an answer to how the mind and body interact have proven equally unsatisfactory. The French philosopher, Nicholas Malbranche, for instance, developed a theory known as Occasionalism. While agreeing with Descartes that mind and body were separate, Malbranche rejected Descartes's explanation of how these two interacted. Instead he argued God interceded when there was need for mind and body to interact. When human beings have a thought (the desire to get a drink of water), it is God who actually moves the person's body to act (in this case, moving the hand to turn on the faucet). Though it may seem as though mind and body are interacting, in fact, this is not the cause, because it is God who is actually intervening.

Although body-mind dualism has a long tradition in Western Philosophy, the position has been subject to a great deal of criticism in modern thought. In a 1643 letter that she wrote to Descartes, Princess Elizabeth of Bohemia wondered,

> how the human soul can determine the movement of the animal spirits in the body so as to perform voluntary acts—being as it is merely a conscious substance. For the determination of movement seems always to come about from the moving body's being propelled—to depend on the kind of impulse it gets from what is set in motion, or again, on the nature and shape of this latter thing's surface. Now the first two conditions involve contact, and the third involves that the impelling thing has extension; but you utterly exclude extension from your notion of the soul, and contact seems to me incompatible with a thing's being immaterial.

To use the example from above, the mind has a thought that danger is present and gives a command to the legs to run. The question becomes how this mental thought can lead to the physical act of running if mind and body are distinct substances as Plato and Descartes maintain.

Physicalism

One of the main problems with dualism is that it seems to violate the philosophical principle that has come to be known as Ockham's Razor. William Ockham was a 14th century English philosopher who famously argued that "entities must not be multiplied beyond necessity." According to this principle, if we are attempting to explain a given phenomenon, we shouldn't posit the existence of any object or force beyond the minimum necessary to produce an adequate explanation. In other words, all things being equal, the simplest explanation of any phenomenon is the best. Therefore, if we can devise a theory that uses only physical properties to explain how thought occurs, this theory will be preferable, according to Ockham's Razor, to one that adds another unnecessary level of mental activity to explain the same reality.

This alternative approach to the mind-body problem has come to be known as physicalism, a theory that maintains that all mental phenomenon can ultimately be reduced to physical ones. The physicalist argues that there is no need to posit a separate non-material substance for mind, because mental processes can ultimate be traced back to activity in the brain. All thoughts, feelings, judgments, etc., are nothing more than particular brain states.

Although physicalism does solve some of the difficulties associated with dualism, the theory is not without some difficulties of its own. There are those who argue, for example, that denying the reality of mental states contradicts our normal human experience. Most of us perceive our mental states as having a unique quality or feeling (*qualia*) to them. Certainly, we know what it's like to "feel" pain, desire, or joy, and we perceive these states to be different from purely physical experiences. Likewise, it is evident that mental states cause behavior. For example, we experience a state of desire for a certain object and this leads us to go to the mall to shop for it. In reducing all mental activity to physical properties, therefore, the physicalist seems to diminish the richness and complexity of our human experience.

The Problem of Personal Identity

The second important question that the field of Philosophy of Mind addresses is the question of how a person can be understood to be the same individual over a lengthy period of time. This question has come to be known as the problem of personal identity.

You've undoubtedly had the experience of flipping through old family photo albums and seeing pictures of yourself when you were a child. Is the child in the image the same "you" that exists in the present time? As your body has aged and grown, you have shed almost all the cells you had as a child. Physically, there is very little remaining of you that has anything in common with the child you once were at the age of four or five. How, then can you claim to be the same person over this period of time?

A solution to this problem was posed by the English philosopher, John Locke, who grounded personal identity on consciousness rather than on the substance of the body. In *An Essay Concerning Human Understanding*, Locke argued that continuity of personal identity was based upon the continuity of our past and future thoughts. Returning to the example of the photo album, it's clear that physically, intellectually, emotionally, and temperamentally, you undoubtedly have undergone tremendous changes since the time when you were a child. But the memories that you retain from this time are still *your* memories. You are also able to stop and reflect upon how much *you* have changed throughout the years. For Locke this means that there is a consistent and abiding you that endures through all the changes that you have gone through during the course of your lifetime.

Locke asks us to imagine that a prince's mind has entered the body of a cobbler. To anyone looking at him, the cobbler would remain a cobbler. But the prince would be aware that, despite the external change that has occurred, he is still himself, because he retains the consciousness of his own thoughts and actions over time.

Locke's theory of personal identity would be challenged by subsequent philosophers. Thomas Reid, the founder of what has come to be known as the "Common Sense" School of Philosophy, objected to Locke's theory because of the transitivity of memories. Reid asks us to imagine a soldier who at the age of 25 is a hero in battle. This officer also remembers getting beaten as a child. Later, when he is 65 years old, he recalls his heroism in battle, but not the beatings he took when he was younger. Since he can't remember these beatings, Reid argues that, based upon Locke's definition of personhood, the soldier is not the same person at 65 that he was when he was 25.

David Hume went even further than Reid by completely rejecting the idea that there was an enduring self that underlies the changes that occur to us on a physical level. He argued that self-examination leads us to the conclusion that all we have are particular acts of perception, and that what we call a person is actually nothing more than a "bundle or collection of different perceptions which succeed one another with inconceivable rapidity and are in perpetual flux and movement." Our imagination makes links between ideas that resemble one another, but in no way do they constitute the foundation of personal identity.

Mind, Body, and Immortality

After reading about the mind-body problem and the problem of personal identity, you might be tempted to think that these are merely academic issues of interest only to philosophers. Nothing can be further from the truth. Both of these problems, in fact, are intimately connected to a still greater problem that is of intrinsic interest to all human beings—the problem of whether we continue to live on in some form after death. The inevitability of death is one of the greatest existential challenges for human beings. Death potentially means the end of all of our hopes, desires, and prospects for the future. It is no wonder, then, that throughout the history of mankind, human beings endlessly speculated on whether "something more" awaited us after the death of the body.

If we are merely material beings—as the physicalist maintains—then there is absolutely no hope that anything at all exists beyond what we experience in this life. Our individual identities would come to an end when the body ceases to live any longer. On the other hand, if Plato and Descartes are correct, and the body is actually something unessential to who we are as human beings, then the possibility of our continued existence after death becomes much more conceivable. In this latter view, death even becomes something positive because it means liberation from the trials and tribulations of corporeal existence. It means an end to suffering, disease, and pain, and the unleashing of our true potentials as purely spiritual beings.

It's unlikely however, that we'll ever definitively be able to answer the question of whether our human identity continues in some form after death. Philosophy can provide a starting point for speculation about this issue, but the philosophical method itself can lead to no certain conclusions on this topic. Whether or not you and I will continue to exist after death is a subject that, for better or worse, we'll have to leave in the hands of mystics and theologians.

PHAEDO

PLATO (424-348 BCE)

One of the earliest philosophical texts dealing with the question of the relation of body to mind (or soul), and whether the mind lives on after death is Plato's Phaedo. *The text describes the last hours of Socrates before his death from hemlock poisoning. The prologue of the dialogue is set at Phlius a few months after Socrates' death. Phaedo has been asked by Ecrates and others to describe the manner of Socrates' death. Phaedo transports us back to Socrates' prison cell on the evening before he is to die. Socrates' execution has been put off for 30 days until the sacred ship from Delos arrives in Athens. During this interval, Socrates has used the time to continue his practice of engaging in philosophical discourse with his disciples. Now the period of waiting is over, and Socrates will be put to death in the morning. At this crucial time, Socrates is tended to by some of his favorite disciples, including Simmias, Cebes, and Crito (Plato, however, is notably absent). All of them know that this will be the last conversation that they have with their friend and mentor. Xantippe, Socrates' wife, and their children are also present, but they are promptly dismissed so that the men can get down to some serious philosophizing. After this we get into the meat of the discussion on why the philosopher need not fear death and the reason we'll see is that the real Socrates is actually other than the physical being who is about to be put to death.*

1. Prologue to the Dialogue

Echecrates. Were you yourself, Phaedo, in the prison with Socrates on the day when he drank the poison?

Phaedo. Yes, Echecrates, I was.

Ech. I wish that you would tell me about his death. What did he say in his last hours? We were informed that he died by taking poison, but no one knew anything more; for no Phliasian ever goes to Athens now, and a long time has elapsed since any Athenian found his way to Phlius, and therefore we had no clear account.

Phaed. Did you not hear of the proceedings at the trial?

Ech. Yes; someone told us about the trial, and we could not understand why, having been condemned, he was put to death, as appeared, not at the time, but long afterwards. What was the reason of this?

Phaed. An accident, Echecrates. The reason was that the stern of the ship which the Athenians send to Delos happened to have been crowned on the day before he was tried.

Ech. What is this ship?

Phaed. This is the ship in which, as the Athenians say, Theseus went to Crete when he took with him the fourteen youths, and was the saviour of them and of himself. And they were said to have vowed to Apollo at the time, that if they were saved they would make an annual pilgrimage to Delos. Now this custom still continues, and the whole period of the voyage to and from Delos, beginning when the priest of Apollo crowns the stern of the ship, is a holy season, during which the city is not allowed to be polluted by public executions; and often, when the vessel is detained by adverse winds, there may be a very considerable delay. As I was saying, the ship was crowned on the day before the trial, and this was the reason why Socrates lay in prison and was not put to death until long after he was condemned.

Ech. What was the manner of his death, Phaedo? What was said or done? And which of his friends had he with him? Or were they not allowed by the authorities to be present? And did he die alone?

Phaed. No; there were several of his friends with him.

Ech. If you have nothing to do, I wish that you would tell me what passed, as exactly as you can.

Phaed. I have nothing to do, and will try to gratify your wish. For to me, too, there is no greater pleasure than to have Socrates brought to my recollection, whether I speak myself or hear another speak of him.

Ech. You will have listeners who are of the same mind with you, and I hope that you will be as exact as you can.

Phaed. I remember the strange feeling which came over me at being with him. For I could hardly believe that I was present at the death of a friend, and therefore I did not pity him, Echecrates; his manner and his language were so noble and fearless in the hour of death that to me he appeared blessed. I thought that in going to the other world he could not be without a divine call, and that he would be happy, if any man ever was, when he arrived there, and therefore I did not pity him as might seem natural at such a time. But neither could I feel the pleasure which I usually felt in philosophical discourse (for philosophy was the theme of which we spoke). I was pleased, and I was also pained, because I knew that he was soon to die, and this strange mixture of feeling was shared by us all; we were laughing and weeping by turns, especially the excitable Apollodorus—you know the sort of man?

Ech. Yes.

Phaed. He was quite overcome; and I myself and all of us were greatly moved.

Ech. Who were present?

Phaed. Of native Athenians there were, besides Apollodorus, Critobulus and his father Crito, Hermogenes, Epigenes, Aeschines, and Antisthenes; likewise Ctesippus of the deme of Paeania, Menexenus, and some others; but Plato, if I am not mistaken, was ill.

Ech. Were there any strangers?

Phaed. Yes, there were; Simmias the Theban, and Cebes, and Phaedondes; Euclid and Terpison, who came from Megara.

Ech. And was Aristippus there, and Cleombrotus?

Phaed. No, they were said to be in Aegina.

Ech. Anyone else?

Phaed. I think that these were about all.

Ech. And what was the discourse of which you spoke?

2. Flashback: Socrates in Prison

I will begin at the beginning and try to repeat the entire conversation. You must understand that we had been previously in the habit of assembling early in the morning at the court in which the trial was held, and which is not far from the prison. There we remained talking with one another until the opening of the prison doors (for they were not opened very early), and then went in and generally passed the day with Socrates. On the last morning the meeting was earlier than usual; this was owing to our having heard on the previous evening that the sacred ship had arrived from Delos, and therefore we agreed to meet very early at the accustomed place. On our going to the prison, the jailer who answered the door, instead of admitting us, came out and bade us wait and he would call us. "For the Eleven," he said, "are now with Socrates; they are taking off his chains, and giving orders that he is to die to-day." He soon returned and said that we might come in.

On entering we found Socrates just released from chains, and Xanthippe, whom you know, sitting by him, and holding his child in her arms. When she saw us she uttered a cry and said, as women will: "O Socrates, this is the last time that either you will converse with your friends, or they with you." Socrates turned to Crito and said: "Crito, let someone take her home." Some of Crito's people accordingly led her away, crying out and beating herself. And when she was gone, Socrates, sitting up on the couch, began to bend and rub his leg, saying, as he rubbed: "How singular is the thing called pleasure, and how curiously related to pain, which might be thought to be the opposite of it; for they never come to a man together, and yet he who pursues either of them is generally compelled to take the other. They are two, and yet they grow together out of one head or stem; and I cannot help thinking that if Aesop had noticed them, he would have made a fable about God trying to reconcile their strife, and when he could not, he fastened their heads together; and this is the reason why when one comes the other follows, as I find in my own case pleasure comes following after the pain in my leg, which was caused by the chain."

Upon this Cebes said: I am very glad indeed, Socrates, that you mentioned the name of Aesop. For that reminds me of a question which has been asked by others, and was asked of me only the day before yesterday by Evenus the poet, and as he will be sure to ask again, you may as well tell me what I should say to him, if you would like him to have an answer. He wanted to know why you who never before wrote a line of poetry, now that you are in prison are putting Aesop into verse, and also composing that hymn in honor of Apollo.

Tell him, Cebes, he replied, that I had no idea of rivaling him or his poems; which is the truth, for I knew that I could not do that. But I wanted to see whether I could purge away a scruple which I felt about certain dreams. In the course of my life I have often had intimations in dreams "that I should make music." The same dream came to me sometimes in one form, and sometimes in another, but always saying the same or nearly the same words: Make and cultivate music, said the dream. And thus far I had imagined that this was only intended to exhort and encourage me in the study of philosophy, which has always been the pursuit of my life, and is the noblest and best of music. The dream was bidding me to do what I was already doing, in the same way that the competitor in a race is bidden by the spectators to run when he is already running. But I was not certain of this, as the dream might have meant music in the popular sense of the word, and being under sentence of death, and the festival giving me a respite, I thought that I should be safer if I satisfied the scruple, and, in obedience to the dream, composed a few verses before I departed. And first I made a hymn in honor of the god of the festival, and then considering that a poet, if he is really to be a poet or maker, should not only put words together but make stories, and as I have no invention, I took some fables of Esop, which I had ready at hand and knew, and turned them into verse.

Tell Evenus this, and bid him be of good cheer; that I would have him come after me if he be a wise man, and not tarry; and that to-day I am likely to be going, for the Athenians say that I must.

3. Death as a Good and The Prohibition against Suicide

Simmias said: What a message for such a man! having been a frequent companion of his, I should say that, as far as I know him, he will never take your advice unless he is obliged.

Why, said Socrates,—is not Evenus a philosopher?

I think that he is, said Simmias.

Then he, or any man who has the spirit of philosophy, will be willing to die, though he will not take his own life, for that is held not to be right.

Here he changed his position, and put his legs off the couch on to the ground, and during the rest of the conversation he remained sitting.

Why do you say, inquired Cebes, that a man ought not to take his own life, but that the philosopher will be ready to follow the dying?

Socrates replied: And have you, Cebes and Simmias, who are acquainted with Philolaus, never heard him speak of this?

I never understood him, Socrates.

My words, too, are only an echo; but I am very willing to say what I have heard: and indeed, as I am going to another place, I ought to be thinking and talking of the nature of the pilgrimage which I am about to make. What can I do better in the interval between this and the setting of the sun?

Then tell me, Socrates, why is suicide held not to be right? as I have certainly heard Philolaus affirm when he was staying with us at Thebes: and there are others who say the same, although none of them has ever made me understand him.

But do your best, replied Socrates, and the day may come when you will understand. I suppose that you wonder why, as most things which are evil may be accidentally good, this is to be the only exception (for may not death, too, be better than life in some cases?), and why, when a man is better dead, he is not permitted to be his own benefactor, but must wait for the hand of another.

By Jupiter! yes, indeed, said Cebes, laughing, and speaking in his native Doric.

I admit the appearance of inconsistency, replied Socrates, but there may not be any real inconsistency after all in this.

There is a doctrine uttered in secret that man is a prisoner who has no right to open the door of his prison and run away; this is a great mystery which I do not quite understand. Yet I, too, believe that the gods are our guardians, and that we are a possession of theirs. Do you not agree?

Yes, I agree to that, said Cebes.

And if one of your own possessions, an ox or an ass, for example took the liberty of putting himself out of the way when you had given no intimation of your wish that he should die, would you not be angry with him, and would you not punish him if you could?

Certainly, replied Cebes.

Then there may be reason in saying that a man should wait, and not take his own life until God summons him, as he is now summoning me.

Yes, Socrates, said Cebes, there is surely reason in that. And yet how can you reconcile this seemingly true belief that God is our guardian and we his possessions, with that willingness to die which we were attributing to the philosopher? That the wisest of men should be willing to leave this service in which they are ruled by the gods who are the best of rulers is not reasonable, for surely no wise man thinks that when set at liberty he can take better care of himself than the gods take of him. A fool may perhaps think this—he may argue that he had better run away from his master, not considering that his duty is to remain to the end, and not to run away from the good, and that there is no sense in his running away. But the wise man will want to be ever with him who is better than himself. Now this, Socrates, is the reverse of what was just now said; for upon this view the wise man should sorrow and the fool rejoice at passing out of life.

The earnestness of Cebes seemed to please Socrates. Here, said he, turning to us, is a man who is always inquiring, and is not to be convinced all in a moment, nor by every argument.

4. Socrates Attitude Towards His Own Death

And in this case, added Simmias, his objection does appear to me to have some force. For what can be the meaning of a truly wise man wanting to fly away and lightly leave a master who is better than himself? And I rather imagine that Cebes is referring to you; he thinks that you are too ready to leave us, and too ready to leave the gods who, as you acknowledge, are our good rulers.

Yes, replied Socrates; there is reason in that. And this indictment you think that I ought to answer as if I were in court?

That is what we should like, said Simmias.

Then I must try to make a better impression upon you than I did when defending myself before the judges. For I am quite ready to acknowledge, Simmias and Cebes, that I ought to be grieved at death, if I were not persuaded that I am going to other gods who are wise and good (of this I am as certain as I can be of anything of the sort) and to men departed (though I am not so certain of this), who are better than those whom I leave behind; and therefore I do not grieve as I might have done, for I have good hope that there is yet something remaining for the dead, and, as has been said of old, some far better thing for the good than for the evil.

But do you mean to take away your thoughts with you, Socrates? said Simmias. Will you not communicate them to us?—the benefit is one in which we too may hope to share. Moreover, if you succeed in convincing us, that will be an answer to the charge against yourself.

I will do my best, replied Socrates. But you must first let me hear what Crito wants; he was going to say something to me.

Only this, Socrates, replied Crito: the attendant who is to give you the poison has been telling me that you are not to talk much, and he wants me to let you know this; for that by talking heat is increased, and this interferes with the action of the poison; those who excite themselves are sometimes obliged to drink the poison two or three times.

Then, said Socrates, let him mind his business and be prepared to give the poison two or three times, if necessary; that is all.

I was almost certain that you would say that, replied Crito; but I was obliged to satisfy him.

Never mind him, he said.

5. The Philosopher Embraces Death

And now I will make answer to you, O my judges, and show that he who has lived as a true philosopher has reason to be of good cheer when he is about to die, and that after death he may hope to receive the greatest good in the other world. And how this may be, Simmias and Cebes, I will endeavor to explain. For I deem that the true disciple of philosophy is likely to be misunderstood by other men; they do not perceive that he is ever pursuing death and dying; and if this is true, why, having had the desire of death all his life long, should he repine at the arrival of that which he has been always pursuing and desiring?

Simmias laughed and said: Though not in a laughing humor, I swear that I cannot help laughing when I think what the wicked world will say when they hear this. They will say that this is very true, and our people at home will agree with them in saying that the life which philosophers desire is truly death, and that they have found them out to be deserving of the death which they desire.

And they are right, Simmias, in saying this, with the exception of the words "They have found them out"; for they have not found out what is the nature of this death which the true philosopher desires, or how he deserves or desires death. But let us leave them and have a word with ourselves: Do we believe that there is such a thing as death?

To be sure, replied Simmias.

And is this anything but the separation of soul and body? And being dead is the attainment of this separation; when the soul exists in herself, and is parted from the body and the body is parted from the soul—that is death?

Exactly: that and nothing else, he replied.

And what do you say of another question, my friend, about which I should like to have your opinion, and the answer to which will probably throw light on our present inquiry: Do you think that the philosopher ought to care about the pleasures—if they are to be called pleasures—of eating and drinking?

Certainly not, answered Simmias.

And what do you say of the pleasures of love—should he care about them?

By no means.

And will he think much of the other ways of indulging the body—for example, the acquisition of costly raiment, or sandals, or other adornments of the body? Instead of caring about them, does he not rather despise anything more than nature needs? What do you say?

I should say the true philosopher would despise them.

Would you not say that he is entirely concerned with the soul and not with the body? He would like, as far as he can, to be quit of the body and turn to the soul.

That is true.

In matters of this sort philosophers, above all other men, may be observed in every sort of way to dissever the soul from the body.

That is true.

Whereas, Simmias, the rest of the world are of opinion that a life which has no bodily pleasures and no part in them is not worth having; but that he who thinks nothing of bodily pleasures is almost as though he were dead.

That is quite true.

6. Death and Knowledge

What again shall we say of the actual acquirement of knowledge?—is the body, if invited to share in the inquiry, a hinderer or a helper? I mean to say, have sight and hearing any truth in them? Are they not, as the poets are always telling us, inaccurate witnesses? and yet, if even they are inaccurate and indistinct, what is to be said of the other senses?—for you will allow that they are the best of them?

Certainly, he replied.

Then when does the soul attain truth?—for in attempting to consider anything in company with the body she is obviously deceived.

Yes, that is true.

Then must not existence be revealed to her in thought, if at all?

Yes.

And thought is best when the mind is gathered into herself and none of these things trouble her—neither sounds nor sights nor pain nor any pleasure—when she has as little as possible to do with the body, and has no bodily sense or feeling, but is aspiring after being?

That is true.

And in this the philosopher dishonors the body; his soul runs away from the body and desires to be alone and by herself?

That is true.

Well, but there is another thing, Simmias: Is there or is there not an absolute justice?

Assuredly there is.

And an absolute beauty and absolute good?

Of course.

But did you ever behold any of them with your eyes?

Certainly not.

Or did you ever reach them with any other bodily sense? (and I speak not of these alone, but of absolute greatness, and health, and strength, and of the essence or true nature of everything). Has the reality of them ever been perceived by you through the bodily organs? or rather, is not the nearest approach to the knowledge of their several natures made by him who so orders his intellectual vision as to have the most exact conception of the essence of that which he considers?

Certainly.

And he attains to the knowledge of them in their highest purity who goes to each of them with the mind alone, not allowing when in the act of thought the intrusion or introduction of sight or any other sense in the company of reason, but with the very light of the mind in her clearness penetrates into the very fight of truth in each; he has got rid, as far as he can, of eyes and ears and of the whole body, which he conceives of only as a disturbing element, hindering the soul from the acquisition of knowledge when in company with her—is not this the sort of man who, if ever man did, is likely to attain the knowledge of existence?

There is admirable truth in that, Socrates, replied Simmias.

And when they consider all this, must not true philosophers make a reflection, of which they will speak to one another in such words as these: We have found, they will say, a path of speculation which seems to bring us and the argument to the conclusion that while we are in the body, and while the soul is mingled with this mass of evil, our desire will not be satisfied, and our desire is of the truth.

For the body is a source of endless trouble to us by reason of the mere requirement of food; and also is liable to diseases which overtake and impede us in the search after truth: and by filling us so full of loves, and lusts, and fears, and fancies, and idols, and every sort of folly, prevents our ever having, as people say, so much as a thought. For whence come wars, and fightings, and factions? whence but from the body and the lusts of the body? For wars are occasioned by the love of money, and money has to be acquired for the sake and in the service of the body; and in consequence of all these things the time which ought to be given to philosophy is lost.

Moreover, if there is time and an inclination toward philosophy, yet the body introduces a turmoil and confusion and fear into the course of speculation, and hinders us from seeing the truth: and all experience shows that if we would have pure knowledge of anything we must be quit of the body, and the soul in herself must behold all things in themselves: then I suppose that we shall attain that which we desire, and of which we say that we are lovers, and that is wisdom, not while we live, but after death, as the argument shows; for if while in company with the body the soul cannot have pure knowledge, one of two things seems to follow—either knowledge is not to be attained at all, or, if at all, after death. For then, and not till then, the soul will be in herself alone and without the body. In this present life, I reckon that we make the nearest approach to knowledge when we have the least possible concern or interest in the body, and are not saturated with the bodily nature, but remain pure until the hour when God himself is pleased to release us. And then the foolishness of the body will be cleared away and we shall be pure and hold converse with other pure souls, and know of ourselves the clear light everywhere; and this is surely the light of truth. For no impure thing is allowed to approach the pure. These are the sort of words, Simmias, which the true lovers of wisdom cannot help saying to one another, and thinking. You will agree with me in that?

Certainly, Socrates.

7. Death As Purification

But if this is true, O my friend, then there is great

hope that, going whither I go, I shall there be satisfied with that which has been the chief concern of you and me in our past lives. And now that the hour of departure is appointed to me, this is the hope with which I depart, and not I only, but every man who believes that he has his mind purified.

Certainly, replied Simmias.

And what is purification but the separation of the soul from the body, as I was saying before; the habit of the soul gathering and collecting herself into herself, out of all the courses of the body; the dwelling in her own place alone, as in another life, so also in this, as far as she can; the release of the soul from the chains of the body?

Very true, he said.

And what is that which is termed death, but this very separation and release of the soul from the body?

To be sure, he said.

And the true philosophers, and they only, study and are eager to release the soul. Is not the separation and release of the soul from the body their especial study?

That is true.

And as I was saying at first, there would be a ridiculous contradiction in men studying to live as nearly as they can in a state of death, and yet repining when death comes.

Certainly.

Then, Simmias, as the true philosophers are ever studying death, to them, of all men, death is the least terrible. Look at the matter in this way: how inconsistent of them to have been always enemies of the body, and wanting to have the soul alone, and when this is granted to them, to be trembling and repining; instead of rejoicing at their departing to that place where, when they arrive, they hope to gain that which in life they loved (and this was wisdom), and at the same time to be rid of the company of their enemy. Many a man has been willing to go to the world below in the hope of seeing there an earthly love, or wife, or son, and conversing with them. And will he who is a true lover of wisdom, and is persuaded in like manner that only in the world below he can worthily enjoy her, still repine at death? Will he not depart with joy? Surely he will, my friend, if he be a true philosopher. For he will have a firm conviction that there only, and nowhere else, he can find

wisdom in her purity. And if this be true, he would be very absurd, as I was saying, if he were to fear death.

He would, indeed, replied Simmias....

8. Cebes' Objection

Cebes answered: I agree, Socrates, in the greater part of what you say. But in what relates to the soul, men are apt to be incredulous; they fear that when she leaves the body her place may be nowhere, and that on the very day of death she may be destroyed and perish—immediately on her release from the body, issuing forth like smoke or air and vanishing away into nothingness. For if she could only hold together and be herself after she was released from the evils of the body, there would be good reason to hope, Socrates, that what you say is true. But much persuasion and many arguments are required in order to prove that when the man is dead the soul yet exists, and has any force of intelligence.

True, Cebes, said Socrates; and shall I suggest that we talk a little of the probabilities of these things?

I am sure, said Cebes, that I should gready like to know your opinion about them.

I reckon, said Socrates, that no one who heard me now, not even if he were one of my old enemies, the comic poets, could accuse me of idle talking about matters in which I have no concern. Let us, then, if you please, proceed with the inquiry....

9. The Cycle of Opposites Argument

Whether the souls of men after death are or are not in the world below, is a question which may be argued in this manner: The ancient doctrine of which I have been speaking affirms that they go from this into the other world, and return hither, and are born from the dead. Now if this be true, and the living come from the dead, then our souls must be in the other world, for if not, how could they be born again? And this would be conclusive, if there were any real evidence that the living are only born from the dead; but if there is no evidence of this, then other arguments will have to be adduced.

That is very true, replied Cebes.

Then let us consider this question, not in relation

to man only, but in relation to animals generally, and to plants, and to everything of which there is generation, and the proof will be easier. Are not all things which have opposites generated out of their opposites? I mean such things as good and evil, just and unjust—and there are innumerable other opposites which are generated out of opposites. And I want to show that this holds universally of all opposites; I mean to say, for example, that anything which becomes greater must become greater after being less.

True.

And that which becomes less must have been once greater and then become less.

Yes.

And the weaker is generated from the stronger, and the swifter from the slower.

Very true.

And the worse is from the better, and the more just is from the more unjust.

Of course.

And is this true of all opposites? and are we convinced that all of them are generated out of opposites?

Yes.

And in this universal opposition of all things, are there not also two intermediate processes which are ever going on, from one to the other, and back again; where there is a greater and a less there is also an intermediate process of increase and diminution, and that which grows is said to wax, and that which decays to wane?

Yes, he said.

And there are many other processes, such as division and composition, cooling and heating, which equally involve a passage into and out of one another. And this holds of all opposites, even though not always expressed in words—they are generated out of one another, and there is a passing or process from one to the other of them?

Very true, he replied.

Well, and is there not an opposite of life, as sleep is the opposite of waking?

True, he said.

And what is that?

Death, he answered.

And these, then, are generated, if they are opposites, the one from the other, and have there

their two intermediate processes also?

Of course.

Now, said Socrates, I will analyze one of the two pairs of opposites which I have mentioned to you, and also its intermediate processes, and you shall analyze the other to me. The state of sleep is opposed to the state of waking, and out of sleeping waking is generated, and out of waking, sleeping, and the process of generation is in the one case falling asleep, and in the other waking up. Are you agreed about that?

Quite agreed.

Then suppose that you analyze life and death to me in the same manner. Is not death opposed to life?

Yes.

And they are generated one from the other?

Yes.

What is generated from life?

Death.

And what from death?

I can only say in answer—life.

Then the living, whether things or persons, Cebes, are generated from the dead?

That is clear, he replied.

Then the inference is, that our souls are in the world below?

That is true.

And one of the two processes or generations is visible—for surely the act of dying is visible?

Surely, he said.

And may not the other be inferred as the complement of nature, who is not to be supposed to go on one leg only? And if not, a corresponding process of generation in death must also be assigned to her?

Certainly, he replied.

And what is that process?

Revival.

And revival, if there be such a thing, is the birth of the dead into the world of the living?

Quite true.

Then there is a new way in which we arrive at the inference that the living come from the dead, just as the dead come from the living; and if this is true, then the souls of the dead must be in some place out of which they come again. And this, as I think, has been satisfactorily proved.

Yes, Socrates, he said; all this seems to flow

necessarily out of our previous admissions.

And that these admissions are not unfair, Cebes, he said, may be shown, as I think, in this way: If generation were in a straight line only, and there were no compensation or circle in nature, no turn or return into one another, then you know that all things would at last have the same form and pass into the same state, and there would be no more generation of them.

What do you mean? he said.

A simple thing enough, which I will illustrate by the case of sleep, he replied. You know that if there were no compensation of sleeping and waking, the story of the sleeping Endymion would in the end have no meaning, because all other things would be asleep, too, and he would not be thought of. Or if there were composition only, and no division of substances, then the chaos of Anaxagoras would come again. And in like manner, my dear Cebes, if all things which partook of life were to die, and after they were dead remained in the form of death, and did not come to life again, all would at last die, and nothing would be alive—how could this be otherwise? For if the living spring from any others who are not the dead, and they die, must not all things at last be swallowed up in death?

There is no escape from that, Socrates, said Cebes; and I think that what you say is entirely true.

Yes, he said, Cebes, I entirely think so, too; and we are not walking in a vain imagination; but I am confident in the belief that there truly is such a thing as living again, and that the living spring from the dead, and that the souls of the dead are in existence, and that the good souls have a better portion than the evil.

10. The Affinity Argument

Must we not, said Socrates, ask ourselves some question of this sort? What is that which, as we imagine, is liable to be scattered away, and about which we fear? and what again is that about which we have no fear? And then we may proceed to inquire whether that which suffers dispersion is or is not of the nature of soul—our hopes and fears as to our own souls will turn upon that.

That is true, he said.

Now the compound or composite may be supposed to be naturally capable of being dissolved in like manner as of being compounded; but that which is uncompounded, and that only, must be, if anything is, indissoluble.

Yes; that is what I should imagine, said Cebes.

And the uncompounded may be assumed to be the same and unchanging, where the compound is always changing and never the same?

That I also think, he said.

Then now let us return to the previous discussion. Is that idea or essence, which in the dialectical process we define as essence of true existence -- whether essence of equality, beauty, or anything else: are these essences, I say, liable at times to some degree of change? or are they each of them always what they are, having the same simple, self-existent and unchanging forms, and not admitting of variation at all, or in any way, or at any time?

They must be always the same, Socrates, replied Cebes.

And what would you say of the many beautiful—whether men or horses or garments or any other things which may be called equal or beautiful—are they all unchanging and the same always, or quite the reverse? May they not rather be described as almost always changing and hardly ever the same either with themselves or with one another?

The latter, replied Cebes; they are always in a state of change.

And these you can touch and see and perceive with the senses, but the unchanging things you can only perceive with the mind—they are invisible and are not seen?

That is very true, he said.

Well, then, he added, let us suppose that there are two sorts of existences, one seen, the other unseen.

Let us suppose them.

The seen is the changing, and the unseen is the unchanging.

That may be also supposed.

And, further, is not one part of us body, and the rest of us soul?

To be sure.

And to which class may we say that the body is more alike and akin?

Clearly to the seen: no one can doubt that.

And is the soul seen or not seen?

Not by man, Socrates.

And by "seen" and "not seen" is meant by us that which is or is not visible to the eye of man?

Yes, to the eye of man.

And what do we say of the soul? is that seen or not seen?

Not seen.

Unseen then?

Yes.

Then the soul is more like to the unseen, and the body to the seen?

That is most certain, Socrates.

And were we not saying long ago that the soul when using the body as an instrument of perception, that is to say, when using the sense of sight or hearing or some other sense (for the meaning of perceiving through the body is perceiving through the senses)—were we not saying that the soul too is then dragged by the body into the region of the changeable, and wanders and is confused; the world spins round her, and she is like a drunkard when under their influence?

Very true.

But when returning into herself she reflects; then she passes into the realm of purity, and eternity, and immortality, and unchangeableness, which are her kindred, and with them she ever lives, when she is by herself and is not let or hindered; then she ceases from her erring ways, and being in communion with the unchanging is unchanging. And this state of the soul is called wisdom?

That is well and truly said, Socrates, he replied.

And to which class is the soul more nearly alike and akin, as far as may be inferred from this argument, as well as from the preceding one?

I think, Socrates, that, in the opinion of everyone who follows the argument, the soul will be infinitely more like the unchangeable even the most stupid person will not deny that.

And the body is more like the changing?

Yes.

Yet once more consider the matter in this light: When the soul and the body are united, then nature orders the soul to rule and govern, and the body to obey and serve.

Now which of these two functions is akin to the divine? and which to the mortal? Does not the divine appear to you to be that which naturally orders and rules, and the mortal that which is subject and servant?

True.

And which does the soul resemble?

The soul resembles the divine and the body the mortal—there can be no doubt of that, Socrates.

Then reflect, Cebes: is not the conclusion of the whole matter this?—that the soul is in the very likeness of the divine, and immortal, and intelligible, and uniform, and indissoluble, and unchangeable; and the body is in the very likeness of the human, and mortal, and unintelligible, and multiform, and dissoluble, and changeable. Can this, my dear Cebes, be denied?

No, indeed.

But if this is true, then is not the body liable to speedy dissolution? And is not the soul almost or altogether indissoluble?

Certainly.

11. Doctrines Concerning Body and Soul

And do you not observe, that after a man is dead, the body, which is the visible part of man, and has a visible framework, which is called a corpse, and which would naturally be dissolved and decomposed and dissipated, is not dissolved or decomposed at once, but may remain for a good while, if the constitution be sound at the time of death, and the season of the year favorable? For the body when shrunk and embalmed, as is the custom in Egypt, may remain almost entire through infinite ages; and even in decay, still there are some portions, such as the bones and ligaments, which are practically indestructible. You allow that?

Yes.

And are we to suppose that the soul, which is invisible, in passing to the true Hades, which like her is invisible, and pure, and noble, and on her way to the good and wise God, whither, if God will, my soul is also soon to go—that the soul, I repeat, if this be her nature and origin, is blown away and perishes immediately on quitting the body as the many say? That can never be, dear Simmias and Cebes. The truth rather is that the soul which is pure at departing draws after her no bodily taint, having never voluntarily had connection with the body, which she is ever avoiding, herself gathered into herself (for such abstraction has been the study of her life). And what does this mean but that she has been a true disciple of philosophy and has practised how to die easily? And is not philosophy the practice of death?

Certainly.

That soul, I say, herself invisible, departs to the invisible world to the divine and immortal and rational: thither arriving, she lives in bliss and is released from the error and folly of men, their fears and wild passions and all other human ills, and forever dwells, as they say of the initiated, in company with the gods. Is not this true, Cebes?

Yes, said Cebes, beyond a doubt.

12. The "Pollution" of Souls

But the soul which has been polluted, and is impure at the time of her departure, and is the companion and servant of the body always, and is in love with and fascinated by the body and by the desires and pleasures of the body, until she is led to believe that the truth only exists in a bodily form, which a man may touch and see and taste and use for the purposes of his lusts—the soul, I mean, accustomed to hate and fear and avoid the intellectual principle, which to the bodily eye is dark and invisible, and can be attained only by philosophy—do you suppose that such a soul as this will depart pure and unalloyed?

That is impossible, he replied.

She is engrossed by the corporeal, which the continual association and constant care of the body have made natural to her.

Very true.

And this, my friend, may be conceived to be that heavy, weighty, earthy element of sight by which such a soul is depressed and dragged down again into the visible world, because she is afraid of the invisible and of the world below—prowling about tombs and sepulchres, in the neighborhood of which, as they tell us, are seen certain ghostly apparitions of souls which have not departed pure, but are cloyed with sight and therefore visible.

That is very likely, Socrates.

Yes, that is very likely, Cebes; and these must be the souls, not of the good, but of the evil, who are compelled to wander about such places in payment of the penalty of their former evil way of life; and they continue to wander until the desire which haunts them is satisfied and they are imprisoned in another body. And they may be supposed to be fixed in the same natures which they had in their former life.

What natures do you mean, Socrates?

I mean to say that men who have followed after gluttony, and wantonness, and drunkenness, and have had no thought of avoiding them, would pass into asses and animals of that sort. What do you think?

I think that exceedingly probable.

And those who have chosen the portion of injustice, and tyranny, and violence, will pass into wolves, or into hawks and kites; whither else can we suppose them to go?

Yes, said Cebes; that is doubtless the place of natures such as theirs. And there is no difficulty, he said, in assigning to all of them places answering to their several natures and propensities?

There is not, he said.

Even among them some are happier than others; and the happiest both in themselves and their place of abode are those who have practised the civil and social virtues which are called temperance and justice, and are acquired by habit and attention without philosophy and mind.

Why are they the happiest?

Because they may be expected to pass into some gentle, social nature which is like their own, such as that of bees or ants, or even back again into the form of man, and just and moderate men spring from them.

That is not impossible.

13. Philosophy as Purification of the Soul

But he who is a philosopher or lover of learning, and is entirely pure at departing, is alone permitted to reach the gods. And this is the reason, Simmias and Cebes, why the true votaries of philosophy abstain from all fleshly lusts, and endure and refuse to give themselves up to them -- not because they fear poverty or the ruin of their families, like the lovers of money, and the world in general; nor like the lovers of power and honor, because they dread the dishonor or disgrace of evil deeds.

No, Socrates, that would not become them, said Cebes.

No, indeed, he replied; and therefore they who have a care of their souls, and do not merely live in the fashions of the body, say farewell to all this; they will not walk in the ways of the blind: and when philosophy offers them purification and release from evil, they feel that they ought not to resist her influence, and to her they incline, and whither she leads they follow her.

What do you mean, Socrates?

14. The Body as Prison of the Soul

I will tell you, he said. The lovers of knowledge are conscious that their souls, when philosophy receives them, are simply fastened and glued to their bodies: the soul is only able to view existence through the bars of a prison, and not in her own nature; she is wallowing in the mire of all ignorance; and philosophy, seeing the terrible nature of her confinement, and that the captive through desire is led to conspire in her own captivity (for the lovers of knowledge are aware that this was the original state of the soul, and that when she was in this state philosophy received and gently counseled her, and wanted to release her, pointing out to her that the eye is full of deceit, and also the ear and other senses, and persuading her to retire from them in all but the necessary use of them and to be gathered up and collected into herself, and to trust only to herself and her own intuitions of absolute existence, and mistrust that which comes to her through others and is subject to vicissitude)— philosophy shows her that this is visible and tangible, but that what she sees in her own nature is intellectual and invisible. And the soul of the true philosopher thinks that she ought not to resist this deliverance, and therefore abstains from pleasures and desires and pains and fears, as far as she is able; reflecting that when a man has great joys or sorrows or fears or desires he suffers from them, not the sort of evil which might be anticipated —as, for example, the loss of his health or property, which he has sacrificed to his lusts—but he has suffered an evil greater far, which is the greatest and worst of all

evils, and one of which he never thinks.

And what is that, Socrates? said Cebes.

Why, this: When the feeling of pleasure or pain in the soul is most intense, all of us naturally suppose that the object of this intense feeling is then plainest and truest: but this is not the case.

Very true.

And this is the state in which the soul is most enthralled by the body.

How is that?

Why, because each pleasure and pain is a sort of nail which nails and rivets the soul to the body, and engrosses her and makes her believe that to be true which the body affirms to be true; and from agreeing with the body and having the same delights she is obliged to have the same habits and ways, and is not likely ever to be pure at her departure to the world below, but is always saturated with the body; so that she soon sinks into another body and there germinates and grows, and has therefore no part in the communion of the divine and pure and simple.

That is most true, Socrates, answered Cebes.

And this, Cebes, is the reason why the true lovers of knowledge are temperate and brave; and not for the reason which the world gives.

Certainly not.

Certainly not! For not in that way does the soul of a philosopher reason; she will not ask philosophy to release her in order that when released she may deliver herself up again to the thraldom of pleasures and pains, doing a work only to be undone again, weaving instead of unweaving her Penelope's web. But she will make herself a calm of passion and follow Reason, and dwell in her, beholding the true and divine (which is not matter of opinion), and thence derive nourishment. Thus she seeks to live while she lives, and after death she hopes to go to her own kindred and to be freed from human ills. Never fear, Simmias and Cebes, that a soul which has been thus nurtured and has had these pursuits, will at her departure from the body be scattered and blown away by the winds and be nowhere and nothing....

15. The Death of Socrates

When he had done speaking, Crito said: And have you any commands for us, Socrates—anything to say about your children, or any other matter in which we can serve you?

Nothing particular, he said: only, as I have always told you, I would have you look to yourselves; that is a service which you may always be doing to me and mine as well as to yourselves. And you need not make professions; for if you take no thought for yourselves, and walk not according to the precepts which I have given you, not now for the first time, the warmth of your professions will be of no avail.

We will do our best, said Crito. But in what way would you have us bury you?

In any way that you like; only you must get hold of me, and take care that I do not walk away from you. Then he turned to us, and added with a smile: I cannot make Crito believe that I am the same Socrates who have been talking and conducting the argument; he fancies that I am the other Socrates whom he will soon see, a dead body—and he asks, How shall he bury me? And though I have spoken many words in the endeavor to show that when I have drunk the poison I shall leave you and go to the joys of the blessed—these words of mine, with which I comforted you and myself, have had, I perceive, no effect upon Crito. And therefore I want you to be surety for me now, as he was surety for me at the trial: but let the promise be of another sort; for he was my surety to the judges that I would remain, but you must be my surety to him that I shall not remain, but go away and depart; and then he will suffer less at my death, and not be grieved when he sees my body being burned or buried. I would not have him sorrow at my hard lot, or say at the burial, Thus we lay out Socrates, or, Thus we follow him to the grave or bury him; for false words are not only evil in themselves, but they infect the soul with evil. Be of good cheer, then, my dear Crito, and say that you are burying my body only, and do with that as is usual, and as you think best.

When he had spoken these words, he arose and went into the bath chamber with Crito, who bade us wait; and we waited, talking and thinking of the subject of discourse, and also of the greatness of our sorrow; he was like a father of whom we were being bereaved, and we were about to pass the rest of our lives as orphans. When he had taken the bath his children were brought to him—(he had two young sons and an elder one); and the women of his family

also came, and he talked to them and gave them a few directions in the presence of Crito; and he then dismissed them and returned to us.

Now the hour of sunset was near, for a good deal of time had passed while he was within. When he came out, he sat down with us again after his bath, but not much was said. Soon the jailer, who was the servant of the Eleven, entered and stood by him, saying: To you, Socrates, whom I know to be the noblest and gentlest and best of all who ever came to this place, I will not impute the angry feelings of other men, who rage and swear at me when, in obedience to the authorities, I bid them drink the poison—indeed, I am sure that you will not be angry with me; for others, as you are aware, and not I, are the guilty cause. And so fare you well, and try to bear lightly what must needs be; you know my errand. Then bursting into tears he turned away and went out.

Socrates looked at him and said: I return your good wishes, and will do as you bid. Then, turning to us, he said, How charming the man is: since I have been in prison he has always been coming to see me, and at times he would talk to me, and was as good as could be to me, and now see how generously he sorrows for me. But we must do as he says, Crito; let the cup be brought, if the poison is prepared: if not, let the attendant prepare some.

Yet, said Crito, the sun is still upon the hilltops, and many a one has taken the draught late, and after the announcement has been made to him, he has eaten and drunk, and indulged in sensual delights; do not hasten then, there is still time.

Socrates said: Yes, Crito, and they of whom you speak are right in doing thus, for they think that they will gain by the delay; but I am right in not doing thus, for I do not think that I should gain anything by drinking the poison a little later; I should be sparing and saving a life which is already gone: I could only laugh at myself for this. Please then to do as I say, and not to refuse me.

Crito, when he heard this, made a sign to the servant, and the servant went in, and remained for some time, and then returned with the jailer carrying a cup of poison. Socrates said: You, my good friend, who are experienced in these matters, shall give me directions how I am to proceed. The man answered: You have only to walk about until your legs are heavy, and then to lie down, and the poison will act. At the same time he handed the cup to Socrates, who in the easiest and gentlest manner, without the least fear or change of color or feature, looking at the man with all his eyes, Echecrates, as his manner was, took the cup and said: What do you say about making a libation out of this cup to any god? May I, or not? The man answered: We only prepare, Socrates, just so much as we deem enough. I understand, he said: yet I may and must pray to the gods to prosper my journey from this to that other world—may this, then, which is my prayer, be granted to me. Then holding the cup to his lips, quite readily and cheerfully he drank off the poison. And hitherto most of us had been able to control our sorrow; but now when we saw him drinking, and saw too that he had finished the draught, we could no longer forbear, and in spite of myself my own tears were flowing fast; so that I covered my face and wept over myself, for certainly I was not weeping over him, but at the thought of my own calamity in having lost such a companion. Nor was I the first, for Crito, when he found himself unable to restrain his tears, had got up and moved away, and I followed; and at that moment. Apollodorus, who had been weeping all the time, broke out in a loud cry which made cowards of us all. Socrates alone retained his calmness: What is this strange outcry? he said. I sent away the women mainly in order that they might not offend in this way, for I have heard that a man should die in peace. Be quiet, then, and have patience.

When we heard that, we were ashamed, and refrained our tears; and he walked about until, as he said, his legs began to fail, and then he lay on his back, according to the directions, and the man who gave him the poison now and then looked at his feet and legs; and after a while he pressed his foot hard and asked him if he could feel; and he said, no; and then his leg, and so upwards and upwards, and showed us that he was cold and stiff. And he felt them himself, and said: When the poison reaches the heart, that will be the end. He was beginning to grow cold about the groin, when he uncovered his face, for he had covered himself up, and said (they were his last words)—he said: Crito, I owe a cock to Asclepius; will you remember to pay the debt? The debt shall be paid, said Crito; is there anything else? There was no answer to this question; but in a minute or two a movement was heard, and the attendants uncovered him; his eyes were set, and Crito closed his eyes and mouth.

Such was the end, Echecrates, of our friend, whom I may truly call the wisest, and justest, and best of all the men whom I have ever known.

Plato. "Phaedo." *The Dialogues of Plato*. Vol. 2. Trans. Benjamin Jowett. Oxford: Oxford University Press, 1892.

ON THE HUMAN SOUL

THOMAS AQUINAS (1225-1274)

The goal of the 13ᵗʰ century medieval philosopher, Thomas Aquinas, was to reconcile the thought of Aristotle with the teaching of the Catholic Church to which he belonged. This reconciliation of Greek and Christian thought was, of course, fraught with difficulties, and nowhere were the challenges that Aquinas faced in "Christianizing" Aristotle's philosophy more evident than in his treatment of the soul. Aristotle defined the soul as "the act of the body," but Aquinas goes beyond Aristotle's thought when he argues that the soul is independent of the body and therefore capable of existing without it after death. Although his approach to philosophy in general may be Aristotelian, in this text from his Summa Theologica, *Aquinas also shows how indebted he is to Platonic dualism when it comes to his understanding of the relationship of soul to body.*

Article 1: Whether the soul is a body?

Objection 1: It would seem that the soul is a body. For the soul is the moving principle of the body. Nor does it move unless moved. First, because seemingly nothing can move unless it is itself moved, since nothing gives what it has not; for instance, what is not hot does not give heat. Secondly, because if there be anything that moves and is not moved, it must be the cause of eternal, unchanging movement, as we find proved Phys. viii, 6; and this does not appear to be the case in the movement of an animal, which is caused by the soul. Therefore the soul is a mover moved. But every mover moved is a body. Therefore the soul is a body.

Objection 2: Further, all knowledge is caused by means of a likeness. But there can be no likeness of a body to an incorporeal thing. If, therefore, the soul were not a body, it could not have knowledge of corporeal things.

Objection 3: Further, between the mover and the moved there must be contact. But contact is only between bodies. Since, therefore, the soul moves the body, it seems that the soul must be a body.

On the contrary, Augustine says (De Trin. vi, 6) that the soul "is simple in comparison with the body, inasmuch as it does not occupy space by its bulk."

I answer that, To seek the nature of the soul, we must premise that the soul is defined as the first principle of life of those things which live: for we call living things "animate," [*i.e. having a soul], and those things which have no life, "inanimate." Now life is shown principally by two actions, knowledge and movement. The philosophers of old, not being able to rise above their imagination, supposed that the principle of these actions was something corporeal: for they asserted that only bodies were real things; and that what is not corporeal is nothing: hence they maintained that the soul is something corporeal. This opinion can be proved to be false in many ways; but we shall make use of only one proof, based on universal and certain principles, which shows clearly that the soul is not a body.

It is manifest that not every principle of vital action is a soul, for then the eye would be a soul, as it is a principle of vision; and the same might be applied to the other instruments of the soul: but it is the "first" principle of life, which we call the soul. Now, though a body may be a principle of life, or to be a living thing, as the heart is a principle of life in an animal, yet nothing corporeal can be the first principle of life. For it is clear that to be a principle of life, or to be a living thing, does not belong to a body as such; since, if that were the case, every body would be a living thing, or a principle of life. Therefore a body is competent to be a living thing or even a principle of life, as "such" a body. Now that it is actually such a body, it owes to some principle which is called its act. Therefore the soul, which is the first principle of life, is not a body, but the act of a body; thus heat, which is the principle of calefaction, is not a body, but an act of a body.

Reply to Objection 1: As everything which is in motion must be moved by something else, a process which cannot be prolonged indefinitely, we must allow that not every mover is moved. For, since to be moved is to pass from potentiality to actuality, the mover gives what it has to the thing moved, inasmuch as it causes it to be in act. But, as is shown in Phys. viii, 6, there is a mover which is altogether immovable, and not moved either essentially, or accidentally; and such a mover can cause an invariable movement. There is, however, another kind of mover, which, though not moved essentially, is moved accidentally; and for this reason it does not cause an invariable movement; such a mover, is the soul. There is, again, another mover, which is moved essentially---namely, the body. And because the philosophers of old believed that nothing existed but bodies, they maintained that every mover is moved; and that the soul is moved directly, and is a body.

Reply to Objection 2: The likeness of a thing known is not of necessity actually in the nature of the knower; but given a thing which knows potentially, and afterwards knows actually, the likeness of the thing known must be in the nature of the knower, not actually, but only potentially; thus color is not actually in the pupil of the eye, but only potentially. Hence it is necessary, not that the likeness of corporeal things should be actually in the nature of the soul, but that there be a potentiality in the soul for such a likeness. But the ancient philosophers omitted to distinguish between actuality and potentiality; and so they held that the soul must be a body in order to have knowledge of a body; and that it must be composed of the principles of which all bodies are formed in order to know all bodies.

Reply to Objection 3: There are two kinds of contact; of "quantity," and of "power." By the former a body can be touched only by a body; by the latter a body can be touched by an incorporeal thing, which moves that body.

Article 2: Whether the human soul is something subsistent?

Objection 1: It would seem that the human soul is not something subsistent. For that which subsists is said to be "this particular thing." Now "this particular thing" is said not of the soul, but of that which is composed of soul and body. Therefore the soul is not something subsistent.

Objection 2: Further, everything subsistent operates. But the soul does not operate; for, as the Philosopher says (De Anima i, 4), "to say that the soul feels or understands is like saying that the soul weaves or builds." Therefore the soul is not subsistent.

Objection 3: Further, if the soul were subsistent, it would have some operation apart from the body. But it has no operation apart from the body, not even that of understanding: for the act of understanding does not take place without a phantasm, which cannot exist apart from the body. Therefore the human soul is not something subsistent.

On the contrary, Augustine says (De Trin. x, 7): "Who understands that the nature of the soul is that of a substance and not that of a body, will see that those who maintain the corporeal nature of the soul, are led astray through associating with the soul those things without which they are unable to think of any nature---i.e. imaginary pictures of corporeal things." Therefore the nature of the human intellect is not only incorporeal, but it is also a substance, that is, something subsistent.

I answer that, It must necessarily be allowed that the principle of intellectual operation which we call the soul, is a principle both incorporeal and subsistent. For it is clear that by means of the intellect man can have knowledge of all corporeal things. Now whatever knows certain things cannot have any of them in its own nature; because that which is in it naturally would impede the knowledge of anything else. Thus we observe that a sick man's tongue being vitiated by a feverish and bitter humor, is insensible to anything sweet, and everything seems bitter to it. Therefore, if the intellectual principle contained the nature of a body it would be unable to know all bodies. Now every body has its own determinate nature. Therefore it is impossible for the intellectual principle to be a body. It is likewise impossible for it to understand by means of a bodily organ; since the determinate nature of that organ would impede knowledge of all bodies; as when a certain determinate color is not only in the pupil of the eye, but also in a glass vase, the liquid in the vase seems to be of that same color.

Therefore the intellectual principle which we call the mind or the intellect has an operation "per se" apart from the body. Now only that which subsists can have an operation "per se." For nothing can operate but what is actual: for which reason we do not say that heat imparts heat, but that what is hot gives heat. We must conclude, therefore, that the human soul, which is called the intellect or the mind, is something incorporeal and subsistent.

Reply to Objection 1: "This particular thing" can be taken in two senses. Firstly, for anything subsistent; secondly, for that which subsists, and is complete in a specific nature. The former sense excludes the inherence of an accident or of a material form; the latter excludes also the imperfection of the part, so that a hand can be called "this particular thing" in the first sense, but not in the second. Therefore, as the human soul is a part of human nature, it can indeed be called "this particular thing," in the first sense, as being something subsistent; but not in the second, for in this sense, what is composed of body and soul is said to be "this particular thing."

Reply to Objection 2: Aristotle wrote those words as expressing not his own opinion, but the opinion of those who said that to understand is to be moved, as is clear from the context. Or we may reply that to operate "per se" belongs to what exists "per se." But for a thing to exist "per se," it suffices sometimes that it be not inherent, as an accident or a material form; even though it be part of something. Nevertheless, that is rightly said to subsist "per se," which is neither inherent in the above sense, nor part of anything else. In this sense, the eye or the hand cannot be said to subsist "per se"; nor can it for that reason be said to operate "per se". Hence the operation of the parts is through each part attributed to the whole. For we say that man sees with the eye, and feels with the hand, and not in the same sense

as when we say that what is hot gives heat by its heat; for heat, strictly speaking, does not give heat. We may therefore say that the soul understands, as the eye sees; but it is more correct to say that man understands through the soul.

Reply to Objection 3: The body is necessary for the action of the intellect, not as its origin of action, but on the part of the object; for the phantasm is to the intellect what color is to the sight. Neither does such a dependence on the body prove the intellect to be non-subsistent; otherwise it would follow that an animal is non-subsistent, since it requires external objects of the senses in order to perform its act of perception....

Article 4: Whether the soul is man?

Objection 1: It would seem that the soul is man. For it is written: "Though our outward man is corrupted, yet the inward man is renewed day by day." But that which is within man is the soul. Therefore the soul is the inward man.

Objection 2: Further, the human soul is a substance. But it is not a universal substance. Therefore it is a particular substance. Therefore it is a "hypostasis" or a person; and it can only be a human person. Therefore the soul is man; for a human person is a man.

On the contrary, Augustine (De Civ. Dei xix, 3) commends Varro as holding "that man is not a mere soul, nor a mere body; but both soul and body."

I answer that, The assertion "the soul is man," can be taken in two senses. First, that man is a soul; though this particular man, Socrates, for instance, is not a soul, but composed of soul and body. I say this, forasmuch as some held that the form alone belongs to the species; while matter is part of the individual, and not the species. This cannot be true; for to the nature of the species belongs what the definition signifies; and in natural things the definition does not signify the form only, but the form and the matter. Hence in natural things the matter is part of the species; not, indeed, signate matter, which is the principle of individuality; but the common matter. For as it belongs to the notion of this particular man to be composed of this soul, of this flesh, and of these bones; so it belongs to the notion of man to be composed of soul, flesh, and bones; for whatever belongs in common to the substance of all the individuals contained under a given species, must belong to the substance of the species.

It may also be understood in this sense, that this soul is this man; and this could be held if it were supposed that the operation of the sensitive soul were proper to it, apart from the body; because in that case all the operations which are attributed to man would belong to the soul only; and whatever performs the operations proper to a thing, is that thing; wherefore that which performs the operations of a man is man. But it has been shown above that sensation is not the operation of the soul only. Since, then, sensation is an operation of man, but not proper to him, it is clear that man is not a soul only, but something composed of soul and body. Plato, through supposing that sensation was proper to the soul, could maintain man to be a soul making use of the body.

Reply to Objection 1: According to the Philosopher (Ethic. ix, 8), a thing seems to be chiefly what is principle in it; thus what the governor of a state does, the state is said to do. In this way sometimes what is principle in man is said to be man; sometimes, indeed, the intellectual part which, in accordance with truth, is called the "inward" man; and sometimes the sensitive part with the body is called man in the opinion of those whose observation does not go beyond the senses. And this is called the "outward" man.

Reply to Objection 2: Not every particular substance is a hypostasis or a person, but that which has the complete nature of its species. Hence a hand, or a foot, is not called a hypostasis, or a person; nor, likewise, is the soul alone so called, since it is a part of the human species.

Article 5: Whether the soul is composed of matter and form?

Objection 1: It would seem that the soul is composed of matter and form. For potentiality is opposed to actuality. Now, whatsoever things are in actuality participate of the First Act, which is God; by participation of Whom, all things are good, are beings, and are living things, as is clear from the teaching of Dionysius (Div. Nom. v). Therefore whatsoever things are in potentiality participate of the first potentiality. But the first potentiality is primary matter. Therefore, since the human soul is, after a manner, in potentiality; which appears from the fact that sometimes a man is potentially understanding; it seems that the human soul must participate of primary matter, as part of itself.

Objection 2: Further, wherever the properties of matter are found, there matter is. But the properties of matter are found in the soul---namely, to be a subject, and to be changed, for it is a subject to science, and virtue; and it changes from ignorance to knowledge and from vice to virtue. Therefore matter is in the soul.

Objection 3: Further, things which have no matter, have no cause of their existence, as the Philosopher says Metaph. viii (Did. vii, 6). But the soul has a cause of its existence, since it is created by God. Therefore the soul has matter.

Objection 4: Further, what has no matter, and is a form only, is a pure act, and is infinite. But this belongs to God alone. Therefore the soul has matter.

On the contrary, Augustine (Gen. ad lit. vii, 7,8,9) proves that the soul was made neither of corporeal matter, nor of spiritual matter.

I answer that, The soul has no matter. We may consider this question in two ways. First, from the notion of a soul in general; for it belongs to the notion of a soul to be the form of a body. Now, either it is a form by virtue of itself, in its entirety, or by virtue of some part of itself. If by virtue of itself in its entirety, then it is impossible that any part of it should be matter, if by matter we understand something purely potential: for a form, as such, is an act; and that which is purely potentiality cannot be part of an act, since potentiality is repugnant to actuality as being opposite thereto. If, however, it be a form by virtue of a part of itself, then we call that part the soul: and that matter, which it actualizes first, we call the "primary animate."

Secondly, we may proceed from the specific notion of the human soul inasmuch as it is intellectual. For it is clear that whatever is received into something is received according to the condition of the recipient. Now a thing is known in as far as its form is in the knower. But the intellectual soul knows a thing in its nature absolutely: for instance, it knows a stone absolutely as a stone; and therefore the form of a stone absolutely, as to its proper formal idea, is in the intellectual soul. Therefore the intellectual soul itself is an absolute form, and not something composed of matter and form. For if the intellectual soul were composed of matter and form, the forms of things would be received into it as individuals, and so it would only know the individual: just as it happens with the sensitive powers which receive forms in a corporeal organ; since matter is the principle by which forms are individualized. It follows, therefore, that the intellectual soul, and every intellectual substance which has knowledge of forms absolutely, is exempt from composition of matter and form.

Reply to Objection 1: The First Act is the universal principle of all acts; because It is infinite, virtually "precontaining all things," as Dionysius says (Div. Nom. v). Wherefore things participate of It not as a part of themselves, but by diffusion of Its processions. Now as potentiality is receptive of act, it must be proportionate to act. But the acts received which proceed from the First Infinite Act, and are participations thereof, are diverse, so that there cannot be one potentiality which receives all acts, as there is one act, from which all participated acts are derived; for then the receptive potentiality would equal the active potentiality of the First Act. Now the receptive potentiality in the intellectual soul is other than the receptive potentiality of first matter, as appears from the diversity of the things received by each. For primary matter receives individual forms; whereas the intelligence receives absolute forms. Hence the existence of such a potentiality in the intellectual soul does not prove that the soul is composed of matter and form.

Reply to Objection 2: To be a subject and to be changed belong to matter by reason of its being in potentiality. As, therefore, the potentiality of the intelligence is one thing and the potentiality of primary matter another, so in each is there a different reason of subjection and change. For the intelligence is subject to knowledge, and is changed from ignorance to knowledge, by reason of its being in potentiality with regard to the intelligible species.

Reply to Objection 3: The form causes matter to be, and so does the agent; wherefore the agent causes matter to be, so far as it actualizes it by transmuting it to the act of a form. A subsistent form, however, does not owe its existence to some formal principle, nor has it a cause transmuting it from potentiality to act. So after the words quoted above, the Philosopher concludes, that in things composed of matter and form "there is no other cause but that which moves from potentiality to act; while whatsoever things have no matter are simply beings at once."

Reply to Objection 4: Everything participated is compared to the participator as its act. But whatever created form be supposed to subsist "per se," must have existence by participation; for "even life," or anything of that sort, "is a participator of existence," as Dionysius says (Div. Nom. v). Now participated existence is limited by the capacity of the participator; so that God alone, Who is His own existence, is pure act and infinite. But in intellectual substances there is composition of actuality and potentiality, not, indeed, of matter and form, but of form and participated existence. Wherefore some say that they are composed of that "whereby they are" and that "which they are"; for existence itself is that by which a thing is.

Article 6: Whether the human soul is incorruptible?

Objection 1: It would seem that the human soul is corruptible. For those things that have a like beginning and process seemingly have a like end. But the beginning, by generation, of men is like that of animals, for they are made from the earth. And the process of life is alike in both; because "all things breathe alike, and man hath nothing more than the beast," as it is written. Therefore, as the same text concludes, "the death of man and beast is one, and the condition of both is equal." But the souls of brute animals are corruptible. Therefore, also, the human soul is corruptible.

Objection 2: Further, whatever is out of nothing can return to nothingness; because the end should correspond to the beginning. But as it is written, "We are born of nothing"; which is true, not only of the body, but also of the soul. Therefore, as is concluded in the same passage, "After this we shall be as if we had not been," even as to our soul.

Objection 3: Further, nothing is without its own proper operation. But the operation proper to the soul, which is to understand through a phantasm, cannot be without the body. For the soul understands nothing without a phantasm; and there is no phantasm without the body as the Philosopher says (De Anima i, 1). Therefore the soul cannot survive the dissolution of the body.

On the contrary, Dionysius says (Div. Nom. iv) that human souls owe to Divine goodness that they are "intellectual," and that they have "an incorruptible substantial life."

I answer that, We must assert that the intellectual principle which we call the human soul is incorruptible. For a thing may be corrupted in two ways---"per se," and accidentally. Now it is impossible for any substance to be generated or corrupted accidentally, that is, by the generation or corruption of something else. For generation and corruption belong to a thing, just as existence belongs to it, which is acquired by generation and lost by corruption. Therefore, whatever has existence "per se" cannot be generated or corrupted except 'per se'; while things which do not subsist, such as accidents and material forms, acquire existence or lost it through the generation or corruption of composite things. Now it was shown above that the souls of brutes are not self-subsistent, whereas the human soul is; so that the souls of brutes are corrupted, when their bodies are corrupted; while the human soul could not be corrupted unless it were corrupted "per se." This, indeed, is impossible, not only as regards the human soul, but also as regards anything subsistent that is a form alone. For it is clear that what belongs to a thing by virtue of itself is inseparable from it; but existence belongs to a form, which is an act, by virtue of itself. Wherefore matter acquires actual existence as it acquires the form; while it is corrupted so far as the form is separated from it. But it is impossible for a form to be separated from itself; and therefore it is impossible for a subsistent form to cease to exist.

Granted even that the soul is composed of matter and form, as some pretend, we should nevertheless have to maintain that it is incorruptible. For corruption is found only where there is contrariety; since generation and corruption are from contraries and into contraries. Wherefore the heavenly bodies, since they have no matter subject to contrariety, are incorruptible. Now there can be no contrariety in the intellectual soul; for it receives according to the manner of its existence, and those things which it receives are without contrariety; for the notions even of contraries are not themselves contrary, since contraries belong to the same knowledge. Therefore it is impossible for the intellectual soul to be corruptible. Moreover we may take a sign of this from the fact that everything naturally aspires to existence after its own manner. Now, in things that have knowledge, desire ensues upon knowledge. The senses indeed do not know existence, except under the conditions of "here" and "now," whereas the intellect apprehends existence absolutely, and for all time; so that everything that has an intellect naturally desires always to exist. But a natural desire cannot be in vain. Therefore every intellectual substance is incorruptible.

Reply to Objection 1: Solomon reasons thus in the person of the foolish, as expressed in the words of Wisdom 2. Therefore the saying that man and animals have a like beginning in generation is true of the body; for all animals alike are made of earth. But it is not true of the soul. For the souls of brutes are produced by some power of the body; whereas the human soul is produced by God. To signify this it is written as to other animals: "Let the earth bring forth the living soul": while of man it is written that "He breathed into his face the breath of life." And so in the last chapter of Ecclesiastes (12:7) it is concluded: "(Before) the dust return into its earth from whence it was; and the spirit return to God Who gave it." Again the process of life is alike as to the body, concerning which it is written: "All things breathe alike," and, "The breath in our nostrils is smoke." But the process is not alike of the soul; for man is intelligent, whereas animals are not. Hence it is false to say: "Man has nothing more than beasts." Thus death comes to both alike as to the body, by not as to the soul.

Reply to Objection 2: As a thing can be created by reason, not of a passive potentiality, but only of the active potentiality of the Creator, Who can produce something out of nothing, so when we say that a thing can be reduced to nothing, we do not imply in the creature a potentiality to non-existence, but in the Creator the power of ceasing to sustain existence. But a thing is said to be corruptible because there is in it a potentiality to non-existence.

Reply to Objection 3: To understand through a phantasm is the proper operation of the soul by virtue of its union with the body. After separation from the body it will have another mode of understanding, similar to other substances separated from bodies...

Thomas Aquinas. *Summa Theologica* I, Q.75. Trans. Fathers of the English Dominican Province. London: Washbourne, 1912.

MIND-BODY DUALISM

RENÉ DESCARTES (1596-1650)

Although mind-body dualism has a long tradition in philosophy (as is evident in the previous selections from Plato and Aquinas), the dualistic approach of René Descartes was so influential during the modern period that most subsequent thought on this topic can be read as a reaction to his understanding of the relationship between body and mind. In the second of his Meditations on First Philosophy, *we saw that the application of systematic doubt led Descartes to the conclusion that who he was was identical to his rational soul. In the following selection from the Sixth Meditation, Descartes goes on to argue that, not only is the soul distinct from the body, it is of an entirely different nature. The question that is more difficult for Descartes to answer is how substances so different as mind and body are capable of interacting with one another at all.*

Meditation VI

5....I will recall to my mind the things I have hitherto held as true, because perceived by the senses, and the foundations upon which my belief in their truth rested; I will, in the second place, examine the reasons that afterward constrained me to doubt of them; and, finally, I will consider what of them I ought now to believe.

6. Firstly, then, I perceived that I had a head, hands, feet and other members composing that body which I considered as part, or perhaps even as the whole, of myself. I perceived further, that that body was placed among many others, by which it was capable of being affected in diverse ways, both beneficial and hurtful; and what was beneficial I remarked by a certain sensation of pleasure, and what was hurtful by a sensation of pain. And besides this pleasure and pain, I was likewise conscious of hunger, thirst, and other appetites, as well as certain corporeal inclinations toward joy, sadness, anger, and similar passions. And, out of myself, besides the extension, figure, and motions of bodies, I likewise perceived in them hardness, heat, and the other tactile qualities, and, in addition, light, colors, odors, tastes, and sounds, the variety of which gave me the means of distinguishing the sky, the earth, the sea, and generally all the other bodies, from one another.

And certainly, considering the ideas of all these qualities, which were presented to my mind, and which alone I properly and immediately perceived, it was not without reason that I thought I perceived certain objects wholly different from my thought, namely, bodies from which those ideas proceeded; for I was conscious that the ideas were presented to me without my consent being required, so that I could not perceive any object, however desirous I might be, unless it were present to the organ of sense; and it was wholly out of my power not to perceive it when it was thus present. And because the ideas I perceived by the senses were much more lively and clear, and even, in their own way, more distinct than any of those I could of myself frame by meditation, or which I found impressed on my memory, it seemed that they could not have proceeded from myself, and must therefore have been caused in me by some other objects; and as of those objects I had no knowledge beyond what the ideas themselves gave me, nothing was so likely to occur to my mind as the supposition that the objects were similar to the ideas which they caused. And because I recollected also that I had formerly trusted to the senses, rather than to reason, and that the ideas which I myself formed were not so clear as those I perceived by sense, and that they were even for the most part composed of parts of the latter, I was readily persuaded that I had no idea in my intellect which had not formerly passed through the senses. Nor was I altogether wrong in likewise believing that that body which, by a special right, I called my own, pertained to me more properly and strictly than any of the others; for in truth, I could never be separated from it as from other bodies; I felt in it and on account of it all my appetites and affections, and in fine I was affected in its parts by pain and the titillation of pleasure, and not in the parts of the other bodies that were separated from it. But when I inquired into the reason why, from this I know not what sensation of pain, sadness of mind should follow, and why from the sensation of pleasure, joy should arise, or why this indescribable twitching of the stomach, which I call hunger, should put me in mind of taking food, and the parchedness of the throat of drink, and so in other cases, I was unable to give any explanation, unless that I was so taught by nature; for there is assuredly no affinity, at least none that I am able to comprehend, between this irritation of the stomach and the desire of food, any more than between the perception of an object that causes pain and the consciousness of sadness which springs from the perception. And in the same way it seemed to me that all the other judgments I had formed regarding the objects of sense, were dictates of nature; because I remarked that those judgments were formed in me, before I had leisure to weigh and consider the reasons that might constrain me to form them.

7. But, afterward, a wide experience by degrees sapped the faith I had reposed in my senses; for I frequently observed that towers, which at a distance seemed round, appeared square, when more closely viewed, and that colossal figures, raised on the summits of these towers, looked like small statues, when viewed from the bottom of them; and, in other instances without number, I also discovered error in judgments founded on the external senses; and not only in those founded on the external, but even in those that rested on the internal senses; for is there aught more internal than pain? And yet I have sometimes been informed by parties whose arm or leg had been amputated, that they still occasionally seemed to feel pain in that part of the body which they had lost, —a circumstance that led me to think that I could not be quite certain even that any one of

my members was affected when I felt pain in it. And to these grounds of doubt I shortly afterward also added two others of very wide generality: the first of them was that I believed I never perceived anything when awake which I could not occasionally think I also perceived when asleep, and as I do not believe that the ideas I seem to perceive in my sleep proceed from objects external to me, I did not any more observe any ground for believing this of such as I seem to perceive when awake; the second was that since I was as yet ignorant of the author of my being or at least supposed myself to be so, I saw nothing to prevent my having been so constituted by nature as that I should be deceived even in matters that appeared to me to possess the greatest truth. And, with respect to the grounds on which I had before been persuaded of the existence of sensible objects, I had no great difficulty in finding suitable answers to them; for as nature seemed to incline me to many things from which reason made me averse, I thought that I ought not to confide much in its teachings. And although the perceptions of the senses were not dependent on my will, I did not think that I ought on that ground to conclude that they proceeded from things different from myself, since perhaps there might be found in me some faculty, though hitherto unknown to me, which produced them.

8. But now that I begin to know myself better, and to discover more clearly the author of my being, I do not, indeed, think that I ought rashly to admit all which the senses seem to teach, nor, on the other hand, is it my conviction that I ought to doubt in general of their teachings.

9. And, firstly, because I know that all which I clearly and distinctly conceive can be produced by God exactly as I conceive it, it is sufficient that I am able clearly and distinctly to conceive one thing apart from another, in order to be certain that the one is different from the other, seeing they may at least be made to exist separately, by the omnipotence of God; and it matters not by what power this separation is made, in order to be compelled to judge them different; and, therefore, merely because I know with certitude that I exist, and because, in the meantime, I do not observe that aught necessarily belongs to my nature or essence beyond my being a thinking thing, I rightly conclude that my essence consists only in my being a thinking

thing or a substance whose whole essence or nature is merely thinking. And although I may, or rather, as I will shortly say, although I certainly do possess a body with which I am very closely conjoined; nevertheless, because, on the one hand, I have a clear and distinct idea of myself, in as far as I am only a thinking and unextended thing, and as, on the other hand, I possess a distinct idea of body, in as far as it is only an extended and unthinking thing, it is certain that I, that is, my mind, by which I am what I am, is entirely and truly distinct from my body, and may exist without it.

10. Moreover, I find in myself diverse faculties of thinking that have each their special mode: for example, I find I possess the faculties of imagining and perceiving, without which I can indeed clearly and distinctly conceive myself as entire, but I cannot reciprocally conceive them without conceiving myself, that is to say, without an intelligent substance in which they reside, for in the notion we have of them, or to use the terms of the schools in their formal concept, they comprise some sort of intellection; whence I perceive that they are distinct from myself as modes are from things. I remark likewise certain other faculties, as the power of changing place, of assuming diverse figures, and the like, that cannot be conceived and cannot therefore exist, any more than the preceding, apart from a substance in which they inhere. It is very evident, however, that these faculties, if they really exist, must belong to some corporeal or extended substance, since in their clear and distinct concept there is contained some sort of extension, but no intellection at all. Further, I cannot doubt but that there is in me a certain passive faculty of perception, that is, of receiving and taking knowledge of the ideas of sensible things; but this would be useless to me, if there did not also exist in me, or in some other thing, another active faculty capable of forming and producing those ideas. But this active faculty cannot be in me in as far as I am but a thinking thing, seeing that it does not presuppose thought, and also that those ideas are frequently produced in my mind without my contributing to it in any way, and even frequently contrary to my will. This faculty must therefore exist in some substance different from me, in which all the objective reality of the ideas that are produced by this faculty is contained formally or eminently, as I

before remarked; and this substance is either a body, that is to say, a corporeal nature in which is contained formally and in effect all that is objectively and by representation in those ideas; or it is God himself, or some other creature, of a rank superior to body, in which the same is contained eminently. But as God is no deceiver, it is manifest that he does not of himself and immediately communicate those ideas to me, nor even by the intervention of any creature in which their objective reality is not formally, but only eminently, contained. For as he has given me no faculty whereby I can discover this to be the case, but, on the contrary, a very strong inclination to believe that those ideas arise from corporeal objects, I do not see how he could be vindicated from the charge of deceit, if in truth they proceeded from any other source, or were produced by other causes than corporeal things: and accordingly it must be concluded, that corporeal objects exist. Nevertheless, they are not perhaps exactly such as we perceive by the senses, for their comprehension by the senses is, in many instances, very obscure and confused; but it is at least necessary to admit that all which I clearly and distinctly conceive as in them, that is, generally speaking all that is comprehended in the object of speculative geometry, really exists external to me.

11. But with respect to other things which are either only particular, as, for example, that the sun is of such a size and figure, etc., or are conceived with less clearness and distinctness, as light, sound, pain, and the like, although they are highly dubious and uncertain, nevertheless on the ground alone that God is no deceiver, and that consequently he has permitted no falsity in my opinions which he has not likewise given me a faculty of correcting, I think I may with safety conclude that I possess in myself the means of arriving at the truth. And, in the first place, it cannot be doubted that in each of the dictates of nature there is some truth: for by nature, considered in general, I now understand nothing more than God himself, or the order and disposition established by God in created things; and by my nature in particular I understand the assemblage of all that God has given me.

12. But there is nothing which that nature teaches me more expressly or more sensibly than that I have a body which is ill affected when I feel

pain, and stands in need of food and drink when I experience the sensations of hunger and thirst, etc. And therefore I ought not to doubt but that there is some truth in these informations.

13. Nature likewise teaches me by these sensations of pain, hunger, thirst, etc., that I am not only lodged in my body as a pilot in a vessel, but that I am besides so intimately conjoined, and as it were intermixed with it, that my mind and body compose a certain unity. For if this were not the case, I should not feel pain when my body is hurt, seeing I am merely a thinking thing, but should perceive the wound by the understanding alone, just as a pilot perceives by sight when any part of his vessel is damaged; and when my body has need of food or drink, I should have a clear knowledge of this, and not be made aware of it by the confused sensations of hunger and thirst: for, in truth, all these sensations of hunger, thirst, pain, etc., are nothing more than certain confused modes of thinking, arising from the union and apparent fusion of mind and body.

14. Besides this, nature teaches me that my own body is surrounded by many other bodies, some of which I have to seek after, and others to shun. And indeed, as I perceive different sorts of colors, sounds, odors, tastes, heat, hardness, etc., I safely conclude that there are in the bodies from which the diverse perceptions of the senses proceed, certain varieties corresponding to them, although, perhaps, not in reality like them; and since, among these diverse perceptions of the senses, some are agreeable, and others disagreeable, there can be no doubt that my body, or rather my entire self, in as far as I am composed of body and mind, may be variously affected, both beneficially and hurtfully, by surrounding bodies....

19. ...[T]here is a vast difference between mind and body, in respect that body, from its nature, is always divisible, and that mind is entirely indivisible. For in truth, when I consider the mind, that is, when I consider myself in so far only as I am a thinking thing, I can distinguish in myself no parts, but I very clearly discern that I am somewhat absolutely one and entire; and although the whole mind seems to be united to the whole body, yet, when a foot, an arm, or any other part is cut off, I am conscious that nothing has been taken from my mind; nor can the faculties of willing, perceiving, conceiving, etc., properly be called its parts, for it is the same mind that is exercised all entire in willing, in perceiving, and in conceiving, etc. But quite the opposite holds in corporeal or extended things; for I cannot imagine any one of them how small soever it may be, which I cannot easily sunder in thought, and which, therefore, I do not know to be divisible. This would be sufficient to teach me that the mind or soul of man is entirely different from the body, if I had not already been apprised of it on other grounds....

René Descartes. *Meditations on First Philosophy*. Trans. John Veitch 1901.

THE MYTH OF THE GHOST IN THE MACHINE

GILBERT RYLE (1900-1976)

Gilbert Ryle was a Professor of Philosophy at Oxford, the editor of the highly influential journal Mind, *and the author of* The Concept of Mind, *from which the following selection is taken. Ryle rejects Descartes' idea that mind is distinct from body and that mental states are separable from physical ones. He argues that Cartesian dualism involves a "category mistake." Mental events, he argues, are not separate events existing alongside bodily events any more than a university is separate from and existing alongside its libraries, laboratories, administration and students. When we talk about mental states, Ryle says, we are talking less about some private and inaccessible events going on in the mind than we are about how a person is disposed to act in certain circumstances.*

1. The "Official" Doctrine of Mind

There is a doctrine about the nature and place of minds which is so prevalent among theorists and even among laymen that it deserves to be described as the official theory. Most philosophers, psychologists and religious teachers subscribe, with minor reservations, to its main articles and, although they admit certain theoretical difficulties in it, they tend to assume that these can be overcome without serious modifications being made to the architecture of the theory. It will be argued here that the central principles of the doctrine are unsound and conflict with the whole body of what we know about minds when we are not speculating about them.

The official doctrine, which hails chiefly from Descartes, is something like this. With the doubtful exceptions of idiots and infants in arms every human being has both a body and a mind. Some would prefer to say that every human being is both a body and a mind. His body and his mind are ordinarily harnessed together, but after the death of the body his mind may continue to exist and function.

Human bodies are in space and are subject to the mechanical laws whicfh govern all other bodies in space. Bodily processes and states can be inspected by external observers. So a man's bodily life is as mtich a publicTaffair as are the lives of animals and reptiles and even as the careers of trees, crystals and planets.

But minds are not in space, nor are their operations subject to mechanical laws. The workings of one mind are not witnessable by other observers; its career is private. Only I can take direct cognisance of the states and processes of my own mind. A person therefore lives through two collateral histories, one consisting of what happens in and to his body, the other consisting of what happens in and to his mind. The first is public, the second private. The events in the first history are events in the physical world, those in the second are events in the mental world.

It has been disputed whether a person does or can directly monitor all or only some of the episodes of his own private history; but, according to the official doctrine, of at least some of these episodes he has direct and unchallengeable cognisance. In consciousness, self-consciousness and introspection he is directly and authentically apprised of the present states and operations of his mind. He may have great or small uncertainties about concurrent and adjacent episodes in the physical world, but he can have none about at least part of what is momentarily occupying his mind.

It is customary to express this bifurcation of his two lives and of his two worlds by saying that the things and events which belong to the physical world, including his own body, are external, while the workings of his own mind are internal. This antithesis of outer and inner is of course meant to be construed as a metaphor, since minds, not being in space, could not be described as being spatially inside anything else, or as having things going on spatially inside themselves. But relapses from this good intention are common and theorists are found speculating how stimuli, the physical sources of which are yards or miles outside a person's skin, can generate mental responses inside his skull, or how decisions framed inside his cranium can set going movements of his extremities.

Even when 'inner' and 'outer are construed as metaphors, the problem how a person's mind and body influence one another is notoriously charged with theoretical difficulties. What the mind wills, die legs, arms and the tongue execute] what affects the ear and the eye has something to do with what the mind perceives; grimaces and smiles betray the mind's moods and bodily castigations lead, it is hoped, to moral improvement. But the actual transactions between the episodes of the private history and those of the public history remain mysterious, since by definition they can belong to neither series. They could not be reported among the happenings described in a person's autobiography of his inner life, but nor could they be reported among those described in some one else's biography of that person's overt career. They can be inspected neither by introspection nor by laboratory experiment. They are theoretical shuttlecocks which are forever being bandied from the physiologist back to the psychologist and from the psychologist back to the physiologist.

Underlying this partly metaphorical representation of the bifurcation of a person's two lives there is a seemingly more profound and philosophical assumption. It is assumed that there are two different kinds of existence or status. What exists or happens may have the status of physical existence, or it may have the status of mental existence. Somewhat as the faces of coins are either heads or tails, or somewhat as living creatures are either male or female, so, it is supposed, some existing is physical existing, other existing is mental existing. It is a necessary feature of what has physical existence that it is in space and time; it is a necessary feature of what has mental existence that it is in time but not in space. What has physical existence is composed of matter, or else is a function of matter; what has mental existence consists of consciousness, or else is a function of consciousness.

There is thus a polar opposition between mind and matter, an opposition which is often brought out as follows. Material objects are situated in a common field, known as 'space', and what happens to one body in one part of space is mechanically connected with what happens to other bodies in other parts of space. But mental happenings occur in insulated fields, known as 'minds', and there is, apart maybe from telepathy, no direct causal connection between what happens in one mind and what happens in another. Only through the medium of the public physical world can the mind of one person make a difference to the mind of another. The mind is its own place and in his inner life each of us lives the life of a ghostly Robinson Crusoe. People can see, hear, and jolt one another's bodies, but they are irremediably blind and deaf to the workings of one another's minds and inoperative upon them….

2. The Absurdity of the Official Doctrine

Such in outline is the official theory. I shall often speak of it, with deliberate abusiveness as 'the dogma of the Ghost in the Machine.' I hope to prove that it is entirely false, and false not in detail but in principle. It is not merely an assemblage of particular mistakes. It is one big mistake and a mistake of a special kind. It is, namely, a category-mistake. It represents the facts of mental life as if they belonged to one logical type or category (or range of types or categories), when they actually belong to another. The dogma is therefore a philosopher's myth. In attempting to explode the myth I shall probably be taken to be denying well-known facts about the mental life of human beings, and my plea that I aim at doing nothing more than rectify the logic of mental-conduct concepts will probably be disallowed as mere subterfuge.

I must first indicate what is meant by the

phrase 'category-mistake'. This I do in a series of illustrations.

A foreigner visiting Oxford or Cambridge for the first time is shown a number of colleges, libraries, playing fields, museums, scientific departments and administrative offices. He then asks 'But where is the University? I have seen where the members of the Colleges live, where the Registrar works, where the scientists experiment and the rest. But I have not yet seen the University in which reside and work the members of your University.' It has then to be explained to him that the University is not another collateral institution, some ulterior counterpart to the colleges, laboratories and offices which he has seen. The University is just the way in which all that he has already seen is organized. When they are seen and when their co-ordination is understood, the University has been seen. His mistake lay in his innocent assumption that it was correct to speak of Christ Church, the Bodleian Library, the Ashmolean Museum *and* the University, to speak, that is, as if 'the University' stood for an extra member of the class of which these other units are members, (tie was mistakenly allocating the University to the same category as that to which 4 the other institutions belong.

The same mistake would be made by a child witnessing the march-past of a division, who, having had pointed out to him such and such battalions, batteries, squadrons, etc., asked when the division was going to appear. He would be supposing that a division was a counterpart to the units alrea4y seen, partly similar to them and partly unlike them. He would be shown his mistake by being told that in watching the battalions, batteries and squadrons marching past he had been watching the division marching past. The march-past was not a parade of battalions, batteries, squadrons and a division; it was a parade of the battalions, batteries and squadrons o/a division....

One more illustration. A foreigner watching his first game of cricket learns what are the functions of the bowlers, the batsmen, the fielders, the umpires and the scorers. He then says 'But there is no one left on the field to contribute the famous element of team-spirit. I see who does the bowling, the batting and the wicket-keeping; but I do not see whose role it is to exercise *esprit de corps*.' Once more,

it would have to be explained that he was looking for the wrong type of thing. Team-spirit is not another cricketing-operation supplementary to all of the other special tasks. It is, roughly, the keenness with which each of the special tasks is performed, and performing a task keenly is not performing two tasks. Certainly exhibiting team-spirit is not the same thing as bowling or catching, but nor is it a third thing such that we can say that the bowler first bowls and then exhibits team-spirit or that a fielder is at a given moment either catching or displaying *esprit de corps*.

These illustrations of category-mistakes have a common feature which must be noticed. The mistakes were made by people who did not know how to wield the concepts *University*, *division* and *team-spirit*. Their puzzles arose from inability to use certain items in the English vocabulary.

The theoretically interesting category-mistakes are those made by people who are perfectly competent to apply concepts, at least in the situations with which they are familiar, but are still liable in their abstract thinking to allocate those concepts to logical types to which they do not belong) An instance of a mistake of this sort would be the following story. A student of politics has learned the main differences between the British, the French and the American Constitutions, and has learned also the differences and connections between the Cabinet, Parliament, the various Ministries, the Judicature and the Church of England. But he still becomes embarrassed when asked questions about the connections between the Church of England, the Home Office and the British Constitution. For while the Church and the Home

Office are institutions, the British Constitution is not another institution in the same sense of that noun. So inter-institutional relations which can be asserted or denied to hold between the Church and the Home Office cannot be asserted or denied to hold between either of them and the British Constitution. 'The British Constitution' is not a term of the same logical type as 'the Home Office and 'the Church of England'. In a partially similar way, John Doe may be a relative, a friend, an enemy or a stranger to Richard Roe; but he cannot be any of these things to the Average taxpayer. He knows how to talk sense in certain sorts of discussions about the Average

Taxpayer, but he is baffled to say why he could not come across him in the street as he can come across Richard Roe.

It is pertinent to our main subject to notice that, so long as the student of politics continues to think of the British Constitution as a counterpart to the other institutions, he will tend to describe it as a mysteriously occult institution; and (so long as John Doe continues to think of the Average Taxpayer as a fellow-citizen, he will tend to think of him as an elusive insubstantial man, a ghost who is everywhere yet nowhere.

My destructive purpose is to show that a family of radical category-mistakes is the source of the double-life theory. The representation of a person as a ghost mysteriously ensconced in a machine derives from this argument. Because, as is true, a person's thinking, feeling and purposive doing cannot be described solely in the idioms of physics, chemistry and physiology, therefore they must be described in counterpart idioms. As the human body is a complex organised unit, so the human mind must be another complex organised unit, though one made of a different sort of stuff and with a different sort of structure. Or, again, as the human body, like any other parcel of matter, is a field of causes and effects, so the mind must be another field of causes and effects, though not (Heaven be praised) mechanical causes and effects.

3. The Origin of the Category-mistake

One of the chief intellectual origins of what I have yet to prove to be the Cartesian category-mistake seems to be this. When Galileo showed that his methods of scientific discovery were competent to provide a mechanical theory which should cover every occupant of space, Descartes found in himself two conflicting motives. As a man of scientific genius he could not but endorse the claims of mechanics, yet as a religious and moral man he could not accept, as Hobbes accepted, the discouraging rider to those claims, namely that human nature differs only in degree of complexity from clockwork. The mental could not be just a variety of the mechanical.

He and subsequent philosophers naturally but erroneously availed themselves of the following escape-route. Since mental-conduct words are not to be construed as signifying the occurrence of mechanical processes, they must be construed as signifying the occurrence of non-mechanical processes; since mechanical laws explain movements in space as the effects of other movements in space, other laws must explain some of the non-spatial workings of minds as the effects of other non-spatial workings of minds. The difference between the human behaviours which we describe as intelligent and those which we describe as unintelligent must be a difference in their causation; so, while some movements of human tongues and limbs are the effects of mechanical causes, others must be the effects of non-mechanical causes, i.e. some issue from movements of particles of matter, others from workings of the mind.

The differences between the physical and the mental were thus represented as differences inside the common framework of the categories of 'thing', 'stuff', 'attribute', 'state', 'process', 'change', 'cause' and 'effect'. Minds are things, but different sorts of things from bodies; mental processes are causes and effects, but different sorts of causes and effects from bodily movements. And so on. Somewhat as the foreigner expected the University to be an extra edifice, rather like a college but also considerably different, so the repudiators of mechanism represented minds as extra centres of causal processes, rather like machines but also considerably different from them. Their theory was a para-mechanical hypothesis.

That this assumption was at the heart of the doctrine is shown by the fact that there was from the beginning felt to be a major theoretical difficulty in explaining how minds can influence and be influenced by bodies. How can a mental process, such as willing, cause spatial movements likejhejnovenients of the tongue? How can a physical change in the optic nerve have among its effects a mind's perception of a flash of light?...

When two terms belong to the same category, it is proper to construct conjunctive propositions embodying them. Thus a purchaser may say that he bought a left-hand glove and a right-hand glove, but not that he bought a left-hand glove, a right-hand glove and a pair of gloves. 'She came home in a flood of tears and a sedan-chair' is a well-known joke based on the absurdity of conjoining terms of different types. It would have been equally ridiculous to construct the disjunction 'She came home either in a flood of tears or else in a sedan-chair. Now the dogma of the Ghost in the Machine does just this. It maintains that there exist both bodies and minds; that there occur physical processes and mental processes; that there are mechanical causes of corporeal movements and mental causes of corporeal movement. I shall argue that these and other analogous conjunctions are absurd; but, it must be noticed, the argument will not show that either of the illegitimately conjoined propositions is absurd in itself. I am not, for example, denying that there occur mental processes. Doing long division is a mental process and so is making a joke. But I am saying that the phrase 'there occur mental processes' does not mean the same sort of thing as 'there occur physical processes', and, therefore, that it makes no sense to conjoin or disjoin the two.

If my argument is successful, there will follow some interesting consequences. First, the hallowed contrast between Mind and Matter will be dissipated, but dissipated not by either of the equally hallowed absorptions of Mind by Matter or of Matter by Mind, but in quite a different way. For the seeming contrast of the two will be shown to be as illegitimate as would be the contrast of 'she came home in a flood of tears' and 'she came home in a sedan-chair'. The belief that there is a polar opposition between Mind and Matter is the belief that they are terms of the same logical type.

It will also follow that both Idealism and Materialism are answers to an improper question. The 'reduction' of the material world to mental states and processes, as well as the 'reduction' of mental states and processes to physical states and processes, presuppose the legitimacy of the disjunction. 'Either there exist minds or there exist bodies (but not both)'. It would be like saying, 'Either she bought a left-hand and a right-hand glove or she bought a pair of gloves (but not both)'.

It is perfectly proper to say, in one logical tone of voice, that there exist minds and to say, in another logical tone of voice, that there exist bodies. But these expressions do not indicate two different species of existence, for 'existence' is not a generic word like 'coloured' or 'sexed'. They indicate two different senses of 'exist', somewhat as 'rising' has different senses in 'the tide is rising', 'hopes are rising', and 'the average age of death is rising'. A man would be thought to be making a poor joke who said that three things are now rising, namely the tide, hopes and the average age of death. It would be just as good or bad a joke to say that there exist prime numbers and Wednesdays and public opinions and navies; or that there exist both minds and bodies....

One of the central motives of this book is to show that 'mental' does not denote a status, such that a person can sensibly ask of a given thing or event whether it is mental or physical, 'in the mind' or 'in the outside world'. To talk of a person's mind is not to talk of a repository which is permitted to house objects that something called 'the physical world' is forbidden to house; it is to talk of the person's abilities, liabilities and inclinations to do and undergo certain sorts of things, and of the doing and undergoing of these things in the ordinary world....

Gilbert Ryle. *The Concept of Mind*. London: Hutchinson, 1949.

ON PERSONAL IDENTITY

JOHN LOCKE (1632-1704)

Like Descartes, the English philosopher John Locke, was a dualist, holding that human beings were composites of material bodies and immaterial souls. When addressing the issue of personal identity in his Essay Concerning Human Understanding, *it would have been very easy for Locke to argue that personal identity consists of the identity of either the body or the mind. Instead, he develops a theory of personal identity founded upon consciousness of oneself as a being enduring through time. As evidenced by his example of the prince and the cobbler, Locke was determined to show that personal identity is independent of any changes that may or may not occur to one's body or mind.*

6…The identity of the same man consists in nothing but a participation of the same continued life, by constantly fleeting particles of matter, in succession vitally united to the same organized body. He that shall place the identity of man in anything else, but, like that of other animals, in one fitly organized body, taken in any one instant, and from thence continued, under one organization of life, in several successively fleeting particles of matter united to it, will find it hard to make an embryo, one of years, mad and sober, the same man, by any supposition, that will not make it possible for Seth, Ismael, Socrates, Pilate, St. Austin, and Caesar Borgia, to be the same man. For if the identity of soul alone makes the same man; and there be nothing in the nature of matter why the same individual spirit may not be united to different bodies, it will be possible that those men, living in distant ages, and of different tempers, may have been the same man: which way of speaking must be from a very strange use of the word man, applied to an idea out of which body and shape are excluded. And that way of speaking would agree yet worse with the notions of those philosophers who allow of transmigration, and are of opinion that the souls of men may, for their miscarriages, be detruded into the bodies of beasts, as fit habitations, with organs suited to the satisfaction of their brutal inclinations. But yet I think nobody, could he be sure that the soul of Heliogabalus were in one of his hogs, would yet say that hog were a man or Heliogabalus.

7. It is not therefore unity of substance that comprehends all sorts of identity, or will determine it in every case; but to conceive and judge of it aright, we must consider what idea the word it is applied to stands for: it being one thing to be the same substance, another the same man, and a third the same person, if person, man, and substance, are three names standing for three different ideas; for such as is the idea belonging to that name, such must be the identity; which, if it had been a little more carefully attended to, would possibly have prevented a great deal of that confusion which often occurs about this matter, with no small seeming difficulties, especially concerning personal identity, which therefore we shall in the next place a little consider.

8. An animal is a living organized body; and consequently the same animal…is the same continued life communicated to different particles of matter, as they happen successively to be united to that organized living body. And whatever is talked of other definitions, ingenious observation puts it past doubt, that the idea in our minds, of which the sound man in our mouths is the sign, is nothing else but of an animal of such a certain form. Since I think I may be confident, that, whoever should see a

creature of his own shape or make, though it had no more reason all its life than a cat or a parrot, would call him still a man; or whoever should hear a cat or a parrot discourse, reason, and philosophize, would call or think it nothing but a cat or a parrot; and say, the one was a dull irrational man, and the other a very intelligent rational parrot....

9. This being premised, to find wherein personal identity consists, we must consider what person stands for; —which, I think, is a thinking intelligent being, that has reason and reflection, and can consider itself as itself, the same thinking thing, in different times and places; which it does only by that consciousness which is inseparable from thinking, and, as it seems to me, essential to it: it being impossible for any one to perceive without perceiving that he does perceive. When we see, hear, smell, taste, feel, meditate, or will anything, we know that we do so. Thus it is always as to our present sensations and perceptions: and by this every one is to himself that which he calls self: it not being considered, in this case, whether the same self be continued in the same or divers substances. For, since consciousness always accompanies thinking, and it is that which makes every one to be what he calls self, and thereby distinguishes himself from all other thinking things, in this alone consists personal identity, i.e. the sameness of a rational being: and as far as this consciousness can be extended backwards to any past action or thought, so far reaches the identity of that person; it is the same self now it was then; and it is by the same self with this present one that now reflects on it, that that action was done.

10. But it is further inquired, whether it be the same identical substance. This few would think they had reason to doubt of, if these perceptions, with their consciousness, always remained present in the mind, whereby the same thinking thing would be always consciously present, and, as would be thought, evidently the same to itself. But that which seems to make the difficulty is this, that this consciousness being interrupted always by forgetfulness, there being no moment of our lives wherein we have the whole train of all our past actions before our eyes in one view, but even the best memories losing the sight of one part whilst they are viewing another; and we sometimes, and that the greatest part of our lives, not reflecting on our past selves, being

intent on our present thoughts, and in sound sleep having no thoughts at all, or at least none with that consciousness which remarks our waking thoughts, —I say, in all these cases, our consciousness being interrupted, and we losing the sight of our past selves, doubts are raised whether we are the same thinking thing, i.e. the same substance or no. Which, however reasonable or unreasonable, concerns not personal identity at all. The question being what makes the same person; and not whether it be the same identical substance, which always thinks in the same person, which, in this case, matters not at all: different substances, by the same consciousness (where they do partake in it) being united into one person, as well as different bodies by the same life are united into one animal, whose identity is preserved in that change of substances by the unity of one continued life. For, it being the same consciousness that makes a man be himself to himself, personal identity depends on that only, whether it be annexed solely to one individual substance, or can be continued in a succession of several substances. For as far as any intelligent being can repeat the idea of any past action with the same consciousness it had of it at first, and with the same consciousness it has of any present action; so far it is the same personal self For it is by the consciousness it has of its present thoughts and actions, that it is self to itself now, and so will be the same self, as far as the same consciousness can extend to actions past or to come. and would be by distance of time, or change of substance, no more two persons, than a man be two men by wearing other clothes to-day than he did yesterday, with a long or a short sleep between: the same consciousness uniting those distant actions into the same person, whatever substances contributed to their production.

11. That this is so, we have some kind of evidence in our very bodies, all whose particles, whilst vitally united to this same thinking conscious self, so that we feel when they are touched, and are affected by, and conscious of good or harm that happens to them, as a part of ourselves; i.e. of our thinking conscious self. Thus, the limbs of his body are to every one a part of Himself; he sympathizes and is concerned for them. Cut off a hand, and thereby separate it from that consciousness he had of its heat, cold, and other affections, and it is then no longer a part of that

which is himself, any more than the remotest part of matter. Thus, we see the substance whereof personal self consisted at one time may be varied at another, without the change of personal identity; there being no question about the same person, though the limbs which but now were a part of it, be cut off.

12. But the question is, [w]hether if the same substance which thinks be changed, it can be the same person; or, remaining the same, it can be different persons?

And to this I answer: ...This can be no question at all to those who place thought in a purely material animal constitution, void of an immaterial substance. For, whether their supposition be true or no, it is plain they conceive personal identity preserved in something else than identity of substance; as animal identity is preserved in identity of life, and not of substance. And therefore those who place thinking in an immaterial substance only, before they can come to deal with these men, must show why personal identity cannot be preserved in the change of immaterial substances, or variety of particular immaterial substances, as well as animal identity is preserved in the change of material substances, or variety of particular bodies: unless they will say, it is one immaterial spirit that makes the same life in brutes, as it is one immaterial spirit that makes the same person in men; which the Cartesians at least will not admit, for fear of making brutes thinking things too....

15. And thus may we be able, without any difficulty, to conceive the same person at the resurrection, though in a body not exactly in make or parts the same which he had here, —the same consciousness going along with the soul that inhabits it. But yet the soul alone, in the change of bodies, would scarce to any one but to him that makes the soul the man, be enough to make the same man. For should the soul of a prince, carrying with it the consciousness of the prince's past life, enter and inform the body of a cobbler, as soon as deserted by his own soul, every one sees he would be the same person with the prince, accountable only for the prince's actions: but who would say it was the same man? The body too goes to the making the man, and would, I guess, to everybody determine the man in this case, wherein the soul, with all its princely thoughts about it, would not make another

man: but he would be the same cobbler to every one besides himself. I know that, in the ordinary way of speaking, the same person, and the same man, stand for one and the same thing. And indeed every one will always have a liberty to speak as he pleases, and to apply what articulate sounds to what ideas he thinks fit, and change them as often as he pleases. But yet, when we will inquire what makes the same spirit, man, or person, we must fix the ideas of spirit, man, or person in our minds; and having resolved with ourselves what we mean by them, it will not be hard to determine, in either of them, or the like, when it is the same, and when not.

16. But though the same immaterial substance or soul does not alone, wherever it be, and in whatsoever state, make the same man; yet it is plain, consciousness, as far as ever it can be extended- should it be to ages past- unites existences and actions very remote in time into the same person, as well as it does the existences and actions of the immediately preceding moment: so that whatever has the consciousness of present and past actions, is the same person to whom they both belong. Had I the same consciousness that I saw the ark and Noah's flood, as that I saw an overflowing of the Thames last winter, or as that I write now, I could no more doubt that I who write this now, that saw' the Thames overflowed last winter, and that viewed the flood at the general deluge, was the same self,- place that self in what substance you please- than that I who write this am the same myself now whilst I write (whether I consist of all the same substance, material or immaterial, or no) that I was yesterday. For as to this point of being the same self, it matters not whether this present self be made up of the same or other substances—I being as much concerned, and as justly accountable for any action that was done a thousand years since, appropriated to me now by this self-consciousness, as I am for what I did the last moment.

17. Self is that conscious thinking thing, —whatever substance made up of, (whether spiritual or material, simple or compounded, it matters not)- which is sensible or conscious of pleasure and pain, capable of happiness or misery, and so is concerned for itself, as far as that consciousness extends. Thus every one finds that, whilst comprehended under that consciousness, the little finger is as much a

part of himself as what is most so. Upon separation of this little finger, should this consciousness go along with the little finger, and leave the rest of the body, it is evident the little finger would be the person, the same person; and self then would have nothing to do with the rest of the body. As in this case it is the consciousness that goes along with the substance, when one part is separate from another, which makes the same person, and constitutes this inseparable self: so it is in reference to substances remote in time. That with which the consciousness of this present thinking thing can join itself, makes the same person, and is one self with it, and with nothing else; and so attributes to itself, and owns all the actions of that thing, as its own, as far as that consciousness reaches, and no further; as every one who reflects will perceive.

18. In this personal identity is founded all the right and justice of reward and punishment; happiness and misery being that for which every one is concerned for himself, and not mattering what becomes of any substance, not joined to, or affected with that consciousness. For, as it is evident in the instance I gave but now, if the consciousness went along with the little finger when it was cut off, that would be the same self which was concerned for the whole body yesterday, as making part of itself, whose actions then it cannot but admit as its own now. Though, if the same body should still live, and immediately from the separation of the little finger have its own peculiar consciousness, whereof the little finger knew nothing, it would not at all be concerned for it, as a part of itself, or could own any of its actions, or have any of them imputed to him.

19. This may show us wherein personal identity consists: not in the identity of substance, but, as I have said, in the identity of consciousness, wherein if Socrates and the present mayor of Queinborough agree, they are the same person: if the same Socrates waking and sleeping do not partake of the same consciousness, Socrates waking and sleeping is not the same person. And to punish Socrates waking for what sleeping Socrates thought, and waking Socrates was never conscious of, would be no more of right,

than to punish one twin for what his brother-twin did, whereof he knew nothing, because their outsides were so like, that they could not be distinguished; for such twins have been seen.

20. But yet possibly it will still be objected,— Suppose I wholly lose the memory of some parts of my life, beyond a possibility of retrieving them, so that perhaps I shall never be conscious of them again; yet am I not the same person that did those actions, had those thoughts that I once was conscious of, though I have now forgot them? To which I answer, that we must here take notice what the word I is applied to; which, in this case, is the man only. And the same man being presumed to be the same person, I is easily here supposed to stand also for the same person. But if it be possible for the same man to have distinct incommunicable consciousness at different times, it is past doubt the same man would at different times make different persons; which, we see, is the sense of mankind in the solemnest declaration of their opinions, human laws not punishing the mad man for the sober man's actions, nor the sober man for what the mad man did, — thereby making them two persons: which is somewhat explained by our way of speaking in English when we say such an one is "not himself," or is "beside himself"; in which phrases it is insinuated, as if those who now, or at least first used them, thought that self was changed; the selfsame person was no longer in that man.

21. But yet it is hard to conceive that Socrates, the same individual man, should be two persons. To help us a little in this, we must consider what is meant by Socrates, or the same individual man.

First, it must be either the same individual, immaterial, thinking substance; in short, the same numerical soul, and nothing else.

Secondly, or the same animal, without any regard to an immaterial soul.

Thirdly, or the same immaterial spirit united to the same animal.

Now, take which of these suppositions you please, it is impossible to make personal identity to consist in anything but consciousness; or reach any further than that does....

John Locke. *An Essay Concerning Human Understanding*. Oxford: Clarendon Press, 1894.

MR. LOCKE'S ACCOUNT OF OUR PERSONAL IDENTITY

THOMAS REID (1710-1796)

It was evident even in his own time that Locke's memory theory of personal identity raised numerous difficulties. One of these challenges came from the Scottish philosopher, Thomas Reid, who was the founder of what has come to be known as the "common sense" school of philosophy. In the following selection from Essays on the Intellectual Powers of Man, *Reid argues that Locke's position on personal identity violates the principle of transitivity of identity, because—as his brave officer analogy shows—the failure to retain certain memories from the past would be that one is not, in fact, the very same person over time. Reid's own view was that the self was so indefinable that it is impossible to give a meaningful account of it.*

In a long chapter upon Identity and Diversity, Mr. Locke has made many ingenious and just observations, and some which I think cannot be defended. I shall only take notice of the account he gives of our own personal identity. His doctrine upon this subject has been censured by Bishop Butler, in a short essay subjoined to his *Analogy*, with whose sentiments I perfectly agree.

Identity, as was observed, supposes the continued existence of the being of which it is affirmed, and therefore can be applied only to things which have a continued existence. While any being continues to exist, it is the same being; but two beings which have a different beginning or a different ending of their existence cannot possibly by the same. To this, I think, Mr. Locke agrees.

He observes, very justly, that, to know what is meant by the same person, we must consider what the word *person* stands for; and he defines a person to be an intelligent being, endowed with reason and with consciousness, which last he thinks inseparable from thought.

From this definition of a person, it must necessarily follow, that, while the intelligent being continues to exist and to be intelligent, it must be the same person. To say that the intelligent being is the person, and yet that the person ceases to exist while the intelligent being continues, or that the person continues while the intelligent being ceases to exist, is to my apprehension a manifest contradiction.

One would think that the definition of a person should perfectly ascertain the nature of personal identity, or wherein it consists, though it might still be a question how we come to know and be assured of our personal identity.

Mr. Locke tells us, however, "that personal identity, that is, the sameness of a rational being, consists in consciousness alone, and, as far as this consciousness can be extended backwards to any past action or thought, so far reaches the identity of that person. So that whatever has the consciousness of present and past actions is the same person to whom they belong."

This doctrine has some strange consequences, which the author was aware of. Such as, that if the same consciousness can be transferred from one intelligent being to another, which he thinks we cannot show to be impossible, *then two or twenty intelligent beings may be the same person.* And if the intelligent being may lose the consciousness of the actions done by him, which surely is possible, then he is not the person that did those actions; so that *one intelligent being may be two or twenty different persons,* if he shall so often lose the consciousness of this former actions.

There is another consequence of this doctrine, which follows no less necessarily, though Mr. Locke probably did not see it. It is, *that a man may be, and at the same time not be, the person that did a particular action.*

Suppose a brave officer to have been flogged when a boy at school for robbing an orchard, to have taken a standard from the enemy in his first campaign, and to have been made a general in advanced life; suppose, also, which must be admitted to be possible, that, when he took the standard, he was conscious of his having been flogged at school, and that, when made a general, he was conscious of his taking the standard, but had absolutely lost the consciousness of his flogging.

These things being supposed, it follows, from Mr. Locke's doctrine, that he who was flogged at school is the same person who took the standard, and that he who took the standard is the same person who was made a general. Whence it follows, if there be any truth in logic, that the general is the same person with him who was flogged at school. But the general's consciousness does not reach so far back as his flogging; therefore, according to Mr. Locke's doctrine, he is not the person who was flogged. Therefore the general is, and at the same time is not, the same person with him who was flogged at school.

Leaving the consequences of this doctrine to those who have leisure to trace them, we may observe, with regard to the doctrine itself,

First, that Mr. Locke attributes to consciousness the conviction we have of our past actions, as if a man may now be conscious of what he did twenty years ago. It is impossible to understand the meaning of this, unless by consciousness he meant memory, the only faculty by which we have an immediate knowledge of our past actions.

Sometimes, in popular discourse, a man says he is conscious that he did such a thing, meaning that he distinctly remembers that he did it. It is unnecessary, in common discourse, to fix accurately the limits between consciousness and memory. This was formerly shown to be the case with regard to sense and memory: and therefore distinct remembrance is sometimes called sense, sometimes consciousness, without any inconvenience.

But this ought to be avoided in philosophy, otherwise we confound the different powers of the mind, and ascribe to one what really belongs to another. If a man can be conscious of what he did twenty years or twenty minutes ago, there is no use for memory, nor ought we to allow that there is any such faculty. The faculties of consciousness and memory are chiefly distinguished by this, that the first is an immediate knowledge of the present, the second an immediate knowledge of the past.

When, therefore, Mr. Locke's notion of personal identity is properly expressed, it is, that personal identity consists in distinct remembrance: for, even in the popular sense, to say that I am conscious of a part action means nothing else than that I distinctly remember that I did it.

Secondly, it may be observed, that, in this doctrine, not only is consciousness confounded with memory, but, which is still more strange, personal identity is confounded with the evidence which we have or our personal identity.

It is very true, that my remembrance that I did such a thing is the evidence I have that I am the identical person who did it. And this, I am apt to think, Mr. Locke meant. But to say that my remembrance that I did such a thing, or my consciousness, makes me the person who did it, is, in my apprehension, an absurdity too gross to be entertained by any man who attends to the meaning of it; for it is to attribute to memory or consciousness a strange magical power of producing its object, though that object must have existed before the memory or consciousness which produced it.

Consciousness is the testimony of one faculty; memory is the testimony of another faculty; and to say that the testimony is the cause of the thing testified, this surely is absurd, if any thing be, and could not have been said by Mr. Locke, if he had not confounded the testimony with the thing testified.

When a horse that was stolen is found and claimed by the owner, the only evidence he can have, or that a judge or witnesses can have, that this is the very identical horse which was his property, is similitude. But would it not be ridiculous from this to infer that the identity of a horse consists in similitude only? The only evidence I have that I am the identical person who did such actions is, that I remember distinctly I did them; or, as Mr. Locke expresses it, I am conscious I did them. To infer from this, that personal identity consists in consciousness, is an argument which, if it had any force, would prove the identity of a stolen horse to consist solely in similitude.

Thirdly, is it not strange that the sameness or identity of a person should consist in a thing which is continually changing, and is not any two minutes the same?

Our consciousness, our memory, and every operation of the mind, are still flowing like the water of a river, or like time itself. The consciousness I have this moment can no more be the same consciousness I had last moment, than this moment can be the last moment. Identity can only be affirmed of things which have a continued existence. Consciousness, and every kind of thought, are transient and momentary, and have no continued existence; and, therefore, if personal identity consisted in consciousness, it would certainly follow, that no man is the same person any two moments of his life; and as the right and justice of reward and punishment are founded on personal identity, no man could be responsible for his actions.

But though I take this to be the unavoidable consequence of Mr. Locke's doctrine concerning personal identity, and though some persons may have liked the doctrine the better on this account, I am far from imputing any thing of this kind to Mr. Locke. He was too good a man not to have rejected with abhorrence a doctrine which he believed to draw this consequence after it.

Fourthly, there are many expressions used by Mr. Locke, in speaking of personal identity, which to me are altogether unintelligible, unless we suppose that he confounded that sameness or identity which we ascribed to an individual with the identity which, in common discourse, is often ascribed to many individuals of the same species.

When we say that pain and pleasure, consciousness and memory, are the same in all men, this sameness can only mean similarity, or sameness of kind. That the pain of one man can be the same individual pain with that of another man is no less impossible, than that one man should be another man: the pain felt by me yesterday can no more be the pain I feel to-day, than yesterday can be this day; and the same thing may be said of every passion and of every operation of the mind. The same kind or species of operation may be in different men, or in the same man at different times; but it is impossible that the same individual operation should be in different men, or in the same man at different times.

When Mr. Locke, therefore, speaks of "the same consciousness being continued through a succession of different substances;" when he speaks of "repeating the idea of a past action, with the same consciousness we had of it at the first," and of "the same consciousness extending to actions past and to come"; these expressions are to me unintelligible, unless he means not the same individual consciousness, but a consciousness that is similar, or of the same kind.

If our personal identity consists in consciousness, as this consciousness cannot be the same individually any two moments, but only of the same kind, it would follow, that we are not for any two moments the same individual persons, but the same kind of persons.

As our consciousness sometimes ceases to exist, as in sound sleep, our personal identity must cease with it. Mr. Locke allows, that the same thing cannot have two beginnings of existence, so that our identity would be irrecoverably gone every time we ceased to think, if it was but for a moment.

Thomas Reid. *Essays on the Intellectual Powers of Man.* Essay Three: Of Memory (1785).

THE SELF AS AN ILLUSION

DAVID HUME (1711-1776)

In this highly provocative selection from A Treatise of Human Nature, *David Hume challenges the very notion of the self. Hume argued that all knowledge comes from sensory impression. What we call the self is simply a bundle of perceptions that succeed one another with great rapidity. Because these perceptions flow together in what seems to be a smooth and interrupted fashion, we have the illusion of personal identity, when in reality no such identity exists. The self, as he puts it, is simply a fiction.*

There are some philosophers who imagine we are every moment intimately conscious of what we call our self; that we feel its existence and its continuance in existence; and are certain, beyond the evidence of a demonstration, both of its perfect identity and simplicity....

Unluckily all these positive assertions are contrary to that very experience which is pleaded for them; nor have we any idea of self, after the manner it is here explained. For, from what impression could this idea be derived? This question it is impossible to answer without a manifest contradiction and absurdity; and yet it is a question which must necessarily be answered, if we would have the idea of self pass for clear and intelligible. It must be someone impression that gives rise to every real idea. But self or person is not any one impression, but that to which our several impressions and ideas are supposed to have a reference. If any impression gives rise to the idea of self, that impression must continue invariably the same, through the whole course of our lives; since self is supposed to exist after that manner. But there is no impression constant and invariable. Pain and pleasure, grief and joy, passions and sensations succeed each other, and never all exist at the same time. It cannot therefore be from any of these impressions, or from any other, that the idea of self is derived; and consequently there is no such idea.

But further, what must become of all our particular perceptions upon this hypothesis? All these are different, and distinguishable, and separable from each other, and may be separately considered, and may exist separately, and have no need of anything to support their existence. After what manner therefore do they belong to self, and how are they connected with it? For my part, when I enter most intimately into what I call myself, I always stumble on some particular perception or other, of heat or cold, light or shade, love or hatred, pain or pleasure. I never can catch myself at any time without a perception, and never can observe anything but the perception. When my perceptions are removed for any time, as by sound sleep, so long am I insensible of myself, and may truly be said not to exist. And were all my perceptions removed by death, and could I neither think, nor feel, nor see, nor love, nor hate, after the dissolution of my body, I should be entirely annihilated, nor do I conceive what is further requisite to make me a perfect nonentity. If anyone, upon serious and unprejudiced reflection, thinks he has a different notion of himself, I must confess I can reason no longer with him. All I can allow him is, that he may be in the right as well as I, and that we are essentially different in this particular. He may, perhaps, perceive something simple and continued, which he calls himself; though I am certain there is no such principle in me.

But setting aside some metaphysicians of this kind, I may venture to affirm of the rest of mankind, that they are nothing but a bundle or collection of different perceptions, which succeed each other with an inconceivable rapidity, and are in a perpetual flux and movement. Our eyes cannot turn in their sockets without varying our perceptions. Our thought is still more variable than our sight; and all our other senses and faculties contribute to this change: nor is there any single power of the soul, which remains unalterably the same, perhaps for one moment. The mind is a kind of theatre, where several perceptions successively make their appearance; pass, repass, glide away, and mingle in an infinite variety of postures and situations. There is properly no simplicity in it at one time, nor identity in different, whatever natural propension we may have to imagine that simplicity and identity. The comparison of the theatre must not mislead us. They are the successive perceptions only, that constitute the mind; nor have we the most distant notion of the place where these scenes are represented, or of the materials of which it is composed.

What then gives us so great a propension to ascribe an identity to these successive perceptions, and to suppose ourselves possessed of an invariable and uninterrupted existence through the whole course of our lives?...

We have a distinct idea of an object, that remains invariable and uninterrupted thorough a supposed variation of time; and this idea we call that of identity or sameness. We have also a distinct idea of several different objects existing in succession, and connected together by a close relation; and this to an accurate view affords as perfect a notion of *diversity*, as if there was no manner of relation among the objects. But though these two ideas of identity, and a succession of related objects be in themselves perfectly distinct, and even contrary, yet it is certain, that in our common way of thinking they are generally confounded with each other. That action of the imagination, by which we consider the uninterrupted and invariable object, and that by which we reflect on the succession of related objects, are almost the same to the feeling, nor is there much more effort of thought required in the latter case than in the former. The relation facilitates the transition of the mind from one object to another, and renders its passage as smooth as if it contemplated one continued object. This resemblance is the cause of the confusion and mistake, and makes us substitute the notion of identity, instead of that of related objects.

Thus we feign the continued existence of the perceptions of our senses, to remove the interruption: and run into the notion of a soul, and *self,* and substance, to disguise the variation. But we may farther observe, that where we do not give rise to such a fiction, our propension to confound identity with relation is so great, that we are apt to imagine I something unknown and mysterious, connecting the parts, beside their relation; and this I take to be the case with regard to the identity we ascribe to plants and vegetables. And even when this does not take place, we still feel a propensity to confound these ideas, though we are not able fully to satisfy ourselves in that particular, nor find anything invariable and uninterrupted to justify our notion of identity.

Thus the controversy concerning identity is not merely a dispute of words. For when we attribute identity, in an improper sense, to variable or interrupted objects, our mistake is not confined to the expression, but is commonly attended with a fiction, either of something invariable and uninterrupted, or of something mysterious and inexplicable, or at least with a propensity to such fictions. What will suffice to prove this hypothesis to the satisfaction of every fair enquirer, is to show from daily experience and observation, that the objects, which are variable or interrupted, and yet are supposed to continue the same, are such only as consist of a succession of parts, connected together by resemblance, contiguity, or causation. For as such a succession answers evidently to our notion of diversity, it can only be by mistake we ascribe to it an identity; and as the relation of parts, which leads us into this mistake, is really nothing but a quality, which produces an association of ideas, and an easy transition of the imagination from one to another, it can only be from the resemblance, which this act of the mind bears to that, by which we contemplate one continued object, that the error arises. Our chief business, then, must be to prove, that all objects, to which we ascribe identity, without observing their invariableness and uninterruptedness, are such as consist of a succession of related objects.

In order to this, suppose any mass of matter, of which the parts are contiguous and connected, to be placed before us; it is plain we must attribute a perfect identity to this mass, provided all the parts continue uninterruptedly and invariably the same, whatever motion or change of place we may observe either in the whole or in any of the parts. But supposing some very small or inconsiderable part to be added to the mass, or subtracted from it; though this absolutely destroys the identity of the whole, strictly speaking; yet as we seldom think so accurately, we scruple not to pronounce a mass of matter the same, where we find so trivial an alteration. The passage of the thought from the object before the change to the object after it, is so smooth and easy, that we scarce perceive the transition, and are apt to imagine, that 'tis nothing but a continued survey of the same object.

There is a very remarkable circumstance, that attends this experiment; which is, that though the change of any considerable part in a mass of matter destroys the identity of the whole, let we must measure the greatness of the part, not absolutely, but by its proportion to the whole. The addition or diminution of a mountain would not be sufficient to produce a diversity in a planet: though the change of a very few inches would be able to destroy the identity of some bodies. It will be impossible to account for this, but by reflecting that objects operate upon the mind, and break or interrupt the continuity of its actions not according to their real greatness, but according to their proportion to each other: And therefore, since this interruption makes an object cease to appear the same, it must be the uninterrupted progress o the thought, which constitutes the imperfect identity.

This may be confirmed by another phenomenon. A change in any considerable part of a body destroys its identity; but 'tis remarkable, that where the change is produced gradually and insensibly we are less apt to ascribe to it the same effect. The reason can plainly be no other, than that the mind, in following the successive changes of the body, feels an easy passage from the surveying its condition in one moment to the viewing of it in another, and at no particular time perceives any interruption in its actions. From which continued perception, it ascribes a continued existence and identity to the object.

But whatever precaution we may use in introducing the changes gradually, and making them proportionable to the whole, it is certain, that where the changes are at last observed to become considerable, we make a scruple of ascribing identity to such different objects. There is, however, another artifice by which we may induce the imagination to advance a step farther; and that is, by producing a reference of the parts to each other, and a combination to some common end or purpose. A ship, of which a considerable part has been changed by frequent reparations, is still considered as the same; nor does the difference of the materials hinder us from ascribing an identity to it. The common end, in which the parts conspire, is the same under all their variations, and affords an easy transition of the imagination from one situation of the body to another.

But this is still more remarkable, when we add a *sympathy* of parts to their common end, and suppose that they bear to each other, the reciprocal relation of cause and effect in all their actions and operations. This is the case with all animals and vegetables; where not only the several parts have a reference to some general purpose, but also a mutual dependence on, and connection with each other. The effect of so strong a relation is, that tho' every one must allow, that in a very few years both vegetables and animals endure a total change, yet we still attribute identity to them, while their form, size, and substance are entirely alter'd. An oak, that grows from a small plant to a large tree, is still the same oak; tho' there be not one particle of matter, or figure of its parts the same. An infant becomes a man-, and is sometimes fat, sometimes lean, without any change in his identity.

We may also consider the two following phenomena, which are remarkable in their kind. The first is, that though we commonly be able to distinguish pretty exactly betwixt numerical and specific identity, yet it sometimes happens, that we confound them, and in our thinking and reasoning employ the one for the other. Thus a man, who bears a noise, that is frequently interrupted and renewed, says, it is still the same noise; though tis evident the sounds have only a specific identity or resemblance, and there is nothing numerically the same, but the cause, which produced them. In like manner it may be said without breach of the propriety of language, that such a church, which was formerly of brick, fell to ruin, and that the parish rebuilt the same church of free-stone, and according to modern architecture. Here neither the form nor materials are the same, nor is there anything common to the two objects, but their relation to the inhabitants of the parish; and yet this alone is sufficient to make us denominate them the same. But we must observe, that in these cases the first object is in a manner annihilated before the second comes into existence; by which means, we are never presented in any one point of time with the idea of difference and multiplicity: and for that reason are less scrupulous in calling them the same.

Secondly, We may remark, that though in a succession of related objects, it be in a manner requisite, that the change of parts be not sudden nor entire, in order to preserve the identity, yet where the objects are in their nature changeable and inconstant, we admit of a, more sudden transition, than would otherwise be consistent with that relation. Thus as the nature of a river consists in the motion and change of parts; though in less than four and twenty hours these be totally altered; this hinders not the river from continuing the same during several ages. What is natural and essential to any thing is, in a manner, expected; and what is expected makes less impression, and appears of less moment, than what is unusual and extraordinary. A considerable change of the former kind seems really less to the imagination, than the most trivial alteration of the latter; and by breaking less the continuity of the thought, has less influence in destroying the identity.

We now proceed to explain the nature of *personal identity*, which has become so great a question ill philosophy, especially of late years in *England*, where all the more abstruse sciences are studied with a peculiar ardour and application. And here 'tis evident, the same method of reasoning must be continued. which has so successfully explained the identity of plants, and animals, and ships, and houses, and of all the compounded and changeable productions either of art or nature. The identity, which we ascribe to the mind of man, is only a fictitious one, and of a like kind with that which we ascribe to vegetables and animal bodies.' It cannot, therefore, have a different origin, but must proceed from a like operation of the imagination upon like objects.

But lest this argument should not convince the reader; though in my opinion perfectly decisive; let him weigh the following reasoning, which is still closer and more immediate. It is evident, that the identity, which we attribute to the human mind, however perfect we may imagine it to be, is not able to run the several different perceptions into one, and make them lose their characters of distinction and difference, which are essential to them. It is still true, that every distinct perception, which enters into the composition of the mind, is a distinct existence, and is different, and distinguishable, and separable from every other perception, either contemporary or successive. But, as, notwithstanding this distinction and separability, we suppose the whole train of perceptions to be united by identity, a question naturally arises concerning this relation of identity; whether it be something that really binds our several perceptions together, or only associates their ideas in the imagination. That is, in other words, whether in pronouncing concerning the identity of a person, we observe some real bond among his perceptions, or only feel one among the ideas we form of them. This question we might easily decide, if we would recollect what has been already proud at large, that the understanding never observes any real connection among objects, and that even the union of cause and effect, when strictly examined, resolves itself into a customary association of ideas. For from thence it evidently follows, that identity is nothing really belonging to these different perceptions, and uniting them together; but is merely a quality, which we attribute to them, because of the union of their ideas in the imagination, when we reflect u n them. Now the only qualities, which can give ideas a union in the imagination, am these three relations above-mentioned. There are the uniting principles in the ideal world, and without them every distinct object is separable by the mind, and may be separately considered, and appears not to have any more connection with any other object, than if disjoined by the greatest difference and remoteness. It is, therefore, on some of these three relations of resemblance, contiguity and causation, that identity depends; and as the very essence of these relations consists in their producing an easy transition of ideas; it follows, that our notions of personal identity, proceed entirely from the smooth and uninterrupted progress of the thought along a train of connected ideas, according to the principles above-explained.

The only question, therefore, which remains, is by what relations this uninterrupted progress of our thought is produced, when we consider the successive existence of a mind or thinking person. And here it is evident we must confine ourselves to resemblance and causation, and must drop contiguity, which has little or no influence in the present case.

To begin with resemblance; suppose we could see clearly into the breast of another, and observe that succession of perceptions, which constitutes his mind or thinking principle, and suppose that he always preserves the memory of a considerable part of past perceptions; it is evident that nothing could more contribute to the bestowing a relation on this succession amidst all its variations. For what is the memory but a faculty, by which we raise up the images of past perceptions? And as an image necessarily resembles its object, must not the frequent placing of these resembling perceptions in the chain of thought, convey the imagination more easily from one link to another, and make the whole seem like the continuance of one object? In this particular, then, the memory not only discovers the identity, but also contributes to its production, by producing the relation of resemblance among the perceptions. The case is the same whether we consider ourselves or others.

As to *causation*, we may observe, that the true idea of the human mind, is to consider it as a system of different perceptions or different existences, which are linked together by the relation of cause and effect, and mutually produce, destroy, influence, and modify each other.' Our impressions give rise to their correspondent ideas; said these ideas in their turn produce other impressions. One thought chases another, and draws after it a third, by which it is expelled in its turn. In this respect, I cannot compare the soul more properly to anything than to a republic or commonwealth, in which the several members are united by the reciprocal ties of government and subordination, and give rise to other persons, who propagate the same republic in the incessant changes of its parts. And as the same individual republic may not only change its members, but also its laws and constitutions; in like manner the same person may vary his character and disposition, as well as his impressions and ideas, without losing his identity. Whatever changes he endures, his several parts are still connected by the relation of causation. And in this view our identity with regard to the passions serves to corroborate that with regard to the imagination, by the making our distant perceptions influence each other, and by giving us a present concern for our past or future pains or pleasures.

As a memory alone acquaints us with the continuance and extent of this succession of perceptions, 'tis to be considered, u on that account chiefly, as the source of personal identity. Had we no memory, we never should have any notion of causation, nor consequently of that chain of causes and effects, which constitute our self or person. But having once acquired this notion of causation from the memory, we can extend the same chain of causes, and consequently the identity of car persons beyond our memory, and can comprehend times, and circumstances, and actions, which we have entirely forgot, but suppose in general to have existed. For how few of our past actions are there, of which we have any memory? Who can tell me, for instance, what were his thoughts and actions on the 1st of January 1715, the 11th of March 1719, and the 3rd of August 1733? Or will he affirm, because he has entirely forgot the incidents of these days, that the present self is not the same person with the self of that time; and by that means overturn all the most established notions of personal identity? In this view, therefore, memory does not so much produce as *discover* personal identity, by showing us the relation of cause and effect among our different perceptions. 'Twill be incumbent on those, who affirm that memory produces entirely our personal identity, to give a reason why we cm thus extend our identity beyond our memory.

The whole of this doctrine leads us to a

conclusion, which is of great importance in the present affair, viz. that all the nice and subtle questions concerning personal identity can never possibly be decided, and are to be regarded rather as gramatical than as philosophical difficulties. Identity depends on the relations of ideas; and these relations produce identity, by means of that easy transition they occasion. But as the relations, and the easiness of the transition may diminish by insensible degrees, we have no just standard, by which we can decide any dispute concerning the time, when they acquire or lose a title to the name of identity. All the disputes concerning the identity of connected objects are merely verbal, except so far as the relation of parts gives rise to some fiction or imaginary principle of union, as we have already observed....

David Hume. *A Treatise of Human Nature*. Ed. *L.A. Selby-Bigge.* Oxford: Clarendon Press, 1896.

8

ETHICS: WHAT IS RIGHT?

The word ethics comes from the Greek word *ethos*, meaning custom. The Latin equivalent of this term is *mores* (customs), from which we derive our words moral and morality. Although for our purposes we can use the terms ethics and morality interchangeably, there are those philosophers who argue that the two terms have slightly different meanings. In general, morality usually refers to specific moral codes that different communities or societies impose upon their members to prevent harm to others or to promote group cohesion. The Amish, for example, have their own very unique moral code and this code would be dramatically different from that of, let's say, conservative Jews or Western European liberals. The moral codes of different groups or cultures typically develop over long periods of time, and rarely are subject to intellectual scrutiny or critical examination.

Ethics, on the other hand, begins with an attitude of skepticism. It examines all moral views, including those that are perceived as sacrosanct, with a critical eye. This critical reflection on the truth or validity of moral positions is the hallmark of all legitimate ethical inquiry.

The scope of ethics is vast, indeed. As it is commonly understood, ethics addresses questions about how we ought to live our lives, what the nature of the good life is, and what is the proper way to interact with our fellow human beings (and perhaps with non-humans as well). Needless to say, there is very little in the realm of human activity that is not included somehow in the scope of ethics.

Since it is important to define fields of study as precisely as possible at the onset of any intellectual journal, our definition of will have to be broad enough to encompass the vast scope of ethical inquiry, while at the same time maintaining the focus on skepticism as the hallmark of this endeavor. For our purposes, then, we can define ethics simply as *the critical and rational examination of questions of right and wrong in human action.*

Getting Our Terms Straight

When the average person makes moral statements or judgments, they usually use certain terms interchangeably. For most people the terms *moral, right,* and *good* all refer to behavior that is judged to be acceptable or correct from their perspective, while *immoral, wrong* or *bad* refers to behavior that is judged to be unacceptable or incorrect. Although these terms carry more nuances than the person on the street may be aware of, for our purposes we can also use them interchangeably.

Quite often moral terms are used not only to describe behavior or action, but also to describe a person's character. Thus when we refer to someone as being a *moral person* we are making a judgment that his character is good or virtuous; conversely, when we refer to someone as being an *immoral person* we are claiming that his character is bad, wicked or evil.

There are two other terms that are often used in ethical discourse that should be kept in mind.

The term *amoral* means having no sense of right or wrong. Babies, small children, severely mentally handicapped individuals and sociopaths can be said to be amoral and, as such, are usually not deemed to be morally responsible for their actions. The word *non-moral* means outside the realm of morality. Fields of study, such as genetics and physics, or inanimate objects, such as guns or nuclear weapons are essentially non-moral. The old cliché, "Guns don't kill people, people do," therefore, is correct because guns themselves are neither moral nor immoral.

Searching for Objective Criteria

There's more to ethics than simple making claims about what is right and wrong.   In philosophical ethics one must also provide an objective basis for determining which actions are right or wrong in different circumstances. The reason for thois should be obvious: If we don't have any objective criteria for moral decision-making, then there really is no legtimate reason for choosing cone course of action over another. Our choices in life then simply become a matter of preference, rather like to choice whether to have pizza or hamburgers for dinner.

Take the example of drug use, for instance. It is not enough to say that drug use is wrong simply because one may find the practice personally repugnant or that it is morally acceptable simply because one enjoys recreational drug use. There has to be some kind of objective criteria that we can point to about the act that makes it right or wrong.

A moral theory will be objective if it is characterized by five essential criteria:

1. Rationality. Ethics is more than a matter of feeling, belief, or preference. If an ethical theory is to have any weight at all, it must be grounded in reasons that most sensible people would be willing to accept. Of course, it helps to have other rational people with whom to discuss and debate moral issues; otherwise ethical discourse becomes extremely difficult.

What does it mean to engage in rational moral discourse? In general, there are three essential steps involved in developing a rational argument: (1) Start from reasonable principles; (2) Argue logically from those principles; (3) Strive to be factually accurate.

In case you've forgotten, these ideas were developed in the chapter on Logic earlier in this text. The same logical principles that all philosopher follow when making arguments will apply with equal force in the field of ethics.

2. Openness. If the ethical theory that you espouse is truly rational, then you should be able to enter into moral arguments even with those who espouse views different from your own. You should also be open to the possibility that individuals with whom you are arguing may very well be able to persuade you of the merits of their theory and force you to abandon your own. Remember, our basic assumption is that other people are just as rational as you are. If we accept this assumption as true then we must acknowledge that we may be able to learn something about the moral life from our opponents. Even in those cases where someone else's moral theory may come into conflict with our own, at the very least, we must be open to the idea that his or her perspective can at least influence ours.

Unfortunately, most people enter into moral debates assuming that their own theory is perfect and that they will be the ones to persuade others to change their moral perspectives. How many times have you had an argument with someone only to realize that he was simply not listening to what you were saying because his mind had already been made up on the issue being discussed? This kind of rigid and dogmatic attitude makes doing ethics extremely difficult, if not impossible. It also prevents individuals from attaining moral maturity by preventing their own ethical perspective from evolving.

3. Universality. Most ethicists would also maintain that a viable ethical theory should also be universal in scope. Ethical theories are almost always articulated in the form of general rules of behavior. These rules are usually expressed in the form of a statement like, "Everyone ought to do x." There is, of course, some legitimate debate about what the term "everyone" here means. Does the everyone referred to mean every human being who has ever lived, everyone currently living, everyone in a particular society, or just everyone in our social group? In order to prevent one's moral theory from becoming too provincial, however, it is usually best to try to interpret the "everyone" in question in the broadest possible way.

4. Impartiality. If a moral theory is truly universal, then it must apply impartially to everyone. The principle of impartiality forbids us from treating one person differently from another when there is no legitimate reason for doing so.

This principle has been stated by Henry Sidgwick in the following way: "It cannot be right for A to treat B in a manner in which it would be wrong for B to treat A, merely on the grounds that they are different individuals, and without there being any difference between the natures and circumstances of the two that can be stated as a reasonable ground for the difference" (380). Therefore, the same moral rules that we demand others follow should apply equally to ourselves and to those close to us. If it is wrong to lie, for example, then it is as wrong to lie in our business dealings as it would be to lie to our family members. This is not to say that our attempts at applying moral rules impartially will be easy or that we will always be successful. It simply means that the goal of treating all those we have dealings with impartially should guide our moral decision-making.

5. Practicality. A theory that is so rigid and extreme that it cannot be practically implemented by human beings is no good to anyone. This does not mean that our moral theories and principles can't be idealistic, challenging, and lofty; it only means that our moral idealism must always be balanced by a practical consideration: can real human beings actually live according to such principles?

When choosing which moral principles to follow then, it is extremely important to ask a crucial question: can a person with the highest moral standards live according to this principle? If it would be difficult even for an ethical giant to follow the principles you espouse, then it is reasonable to assume that you will have difficulty living according to them.

The Big Theories

Although there are many different ethical theories that have been influential in Western thought, four are usually considered the "biggies" in the field of ethics—ethical egoism, utilitarianism, deontology, and virtue ethics. Most people's moral perspectives have been shaped by at least one of these theories, whether they recognize it or not.

Ethical Egoism. (*"An act is morally right if, and only if, it produces the greatest happiness—or the best possible outcome—for oneself."*) Ethical egoism is a theory that focuses exclusively what best serves the interest of the individual committing the act—namely you. When deciding whether or not to perform a particular act, the ethical egoist never considers the effect of the act on others, because the good of others is fundamentally morally irrelevant. Instead, he only considers whether the act will benefit him in the long-run. If it does, the act is morally right; if it doesn't, the act is morally wrong.

Utilitarianism. (*"An act is morally right if, and only if, it produces the greatest happiness—or the best possible outcome for all those who are affected by the act."*) Unlike the ethical egoist, the utilitarian is concerned not just with his own good, but the good of all those who are potentially affected by his actions. Using a hedonist calculus, the utilitarian weighs the positive and negative outcomes of his action. If the act produces greater net happiness for those who are affected by it, the act is morally right; if it produces greater net unhappiness, the act is wrong.

Deontology. (*"An act is morally right if, and only if, it accords with a universal rule that all can follow."*) Whereas the utilitarian looks exclusively to the consequences of his acts, the deontologist isn't interested in consequences at all. In fact, he considers the consequences of a given act to be morally irrelevant. Instead, he looks to intentions to determine if an act is right or wrong. If an act being considered can be universalized—that is, if it can be turned into a general rule that all can follow—then the act is right; if not, the act is wrong. According to this theory, acts like lying, cheating, stealing, or killing innocents can never be justified, because such actions can never be universalized.

Virtue Ethics. (*"An act is morally right, if, and only if, it is performed by a person of virtuous moral character."*) Virtue ethics is unique among the big theories we are discussing in that the proponent of this theory is not particularly interested in acts themselves, but rather the character of the person who is performing the act. According to this theory, a person who embodies virtues, such courage, justice, self-control, honesty, and the like, doesn't have to worry about his particular actions, because he so well-trained in the life of virtue that he almost can't help but do the right things habitually.

In general, we can fit all these theories into two main categories: consequentialist theories and non-consequentialist theories. Consequentialist theories, such as ethical egoism and ultilitarianism look, not surprisingly, to the consequences of an act to determine if that act is right or wrong. Non-consequentialist theories, such as deontology and virtue ethics, maintain that the rightness or wrongness of an act have nothing to do with the consequences of the act, but rather have to do with something intrinsic to the act itself (i.e., whether it can be turned into a universal law or whether it accords with some kind of recognized virtue).

Evaluating the Big Theories

So which of these big theories is the optimal one to follow? The answer is not quite so simple. In general, all of these theories have stood the test of time precisely because they provide clear and objective guidelines for moral actions. When you are involved in a situation where moral deliberation is required—for example, when you are trying to decide whether it would be morally justifiable to take office supplies from your place of employment for personal use—you can refer to any one of the moral theories that we've discussed for guidance. In doing so, you'll be far better off than the person, let's say, who based all of his moral decisions on gut-feeling, emotions, or blind obedience to some authority figure.

Of course, you won't get exactly the same sort of answers from these theories about what is the moral way to act in a given circumstance, precisely because they are all grounded in very different rational principles. To use the example of whether you should take supplies from your office, an ethical egoist might tell you that it's fine to take the supplies, if it's in your interest to do so, provided there's no chance of getting caught; a utilitarian, focused on the greatest happiness for the greatest number, would probably tell you that it's wrong to steal because you are hurting the company's bottom line and, therefore, placing all your fellow employee's jobs in jeopardy; a deontologist, of course, would tell you that it's wrong to steal under any circumstances, because the rule for stealing can't be universalized; finally, the virtue ethicist would remind you that honesty is a virtue in almost all cultures, and, therefore, a honest person would never even think of taking something that doesn't belong to him or her without the prior permission of the item's owner. Notice that, even when the proponents of different theories are in relative agreement about the right way to act in specific situation, they often base their justification or rationale on completely different, and sometimes contradictory, principles.

So which is the best theory to follow? I'm afraid we'll have to leave that to you to decide. As you work your way through some of the selections in this section of the text, you may find that one theory strikes you as being more persuasive than some of the others. Or you may find yourself wanting to combine the best aspects of two or more theories—for instance, the ethical egoist's healthy regard for self-interest with the virtue ethicist's concern for character. Or you may just find that none of the great theories are morally persuasive to you at all, and then you'll be forced to come up with your own approach to ethics.

The thing to remember about moral theories is that they are not just theories: they are meant to be practiced and lived out in your everyday life. So try one theory on for size, and then try on another. See which one fits best on you, and then commit yourself to living according to the principle that you've selected as much as possible.

EUTHYPHRO

PLATO (427-347 BCE)

Plato's dialogue, Euthyphro, *is one of the earliest examples of a virtue ethics approach to moral theory that we have in existence and a fine illustration of the Socratic approach to philosophy. All of Plato's Socratic dialogues center around a theme or question that becomes the focus of discussion for the participants in the dialogue. In* Euthyphro, *the question that Socrates raises is, "What is piety?" While this may seem like a fairly strange question, it actually is an important one, even in our own times. Just think about how many acts of atrocity are committed because the perpetrators felt they were doing the will of god—in other words, behaving piously. A proper understanding of the virtue of piety, Socrates believes, lays the foundation for true moral behavior, but first he has has to clear up some obvious misconceptions that young Euthyprho has concerning this virtue, a task that takes up the entire dialogue.*

1. Opening of the Dialogue

EUTHYPHRO: Why have you left the Lyceum, Socrates? and what are you doing in the Porch of the King Archon? Surely you cannot be concerned in a suit before the King, like myself?

SOCRATES: Not in a suit, Euthyphro; impeachment is the word which the Athenians use.

EUTH: What! I suppose that some one has been prosecuting you, for I cannot believe that you are the prosecutor of another.

SOC: Certainly not.

EUTH: Then some one else has been prosecuting you?

SOC: Yes.

EUTH: And who is he?

SOC: A young man who is little known, Euthyphro; and I hardly know him: his name is Meletus, and he is of the deme of Pitthis. Perhaps you may remember his appearance; he has a beak, and long straight hair, and a beard which is ill grown.

EUTH: No, I do not remember him, Socrates. But what is the charge which he brings against you?

SOC: What is the charge? Well, a very serious charge, which shows a good deal of character in the young man, and for which he is certainly not to be despised. He says he knows how the youth are corrupted and who are their corruptors. I fancy that he

must be a wise man, and seeing that I am the reverse of a wise man, he has found me out, and is going to accuse me of corrupting his young friends. And of this our mother the state is to be the judge. Of all our political men he is the only one who seems to me to begin in the right way, with the cultivation of virtue in youth; like a good husbandman, he makes the young shoots his first care, and clears away us who are the destroyers of them. This is only the first step; he will afterwards attend to the elder branches; and if he goes on as he has begun, he will be a very great public benefactor.

EUTH: I hope that he may; but I rather fear, Socrates, that the opposite will turn out to be the truth. My opinion is that in attacking you he is simply aiming a blow at the foundation of the state. But in what way does he say that you corrupt the young?

SOC: He brings a wonderful accusation against me, which at first hearing excites surprise: he says that I am a poet or maker of gods, and that I invent new gods and deny the existence of old ones; this is the ground of his indictment.

EUTH: I understand, Socrates; he means to attack you about the familiar sign which occasionally, as you say, comes to you. He thinks that you are a neologian, and he is going to have you up before the court for this. He knows that such a charge is readily received by the world, as I myself know too well; for when I speak in the assembly about divine things, and foretell the future to them, they laugh at me and think me a madman. Yet every word that I say is true. But they are jealous of us all; and we must be brave and go at them.

SOC: Their laughter, friend Euthyphro, is not a matter of much consequence. For a man may be thought wise; but the Athenians, I suspect, do not much trouble themselves about him until he begins to impart his wisdom to others, and then for some reason or other, perhaps, as you say, from jealousy, they are angry.

EUTH: I am never likely to try their temper in this way.

SOC: I dare say not, for you are reserved in your behaviour, and seldom impart your wisdom. But I have a benevolent habit of pouring out myself to everybody, and would even pay for a listener, and I am afraid that the Athenians may think me too talkative. Now if, as I was saying, they would only laugh at me, as you say that they laugh at you, the time might pass gaily enough in the court; but perhaps they may be in earnest, and then what the end will be you soothsayers only can predict.

EUTH: I dare say that the affair will end in nothing, Socrates, and that you will win your cause; and I think that I shall win my own.

2. The Nature of Euthyphro's Case

SOC: And what is your suit, Euthyphro? are you the pursuer or the defendant?

EUTH: I am the pursuer.

SOC: Of whom?

EUTH: You will think me mad when I tell you.

SOC: Why, has the fugitive wings?

EUTH: Nay, he is not very volatile at his time of life.

SOC: Who is he?

EUTH: My father.

SOC: Your father! my good man?

EUTH: Yes.

SOC: And of what is he accused?

EUTH: Of murder, Socrates.

SOC: By the powers, Euthyphro! how little does the common herd know of the nature of right and truth. A man must be an extraordinary man, and

have made great strides in wisdom, before he could have seen his way to bring such an action.

EUTH: Indeed, Socrates, he must.

SOC: I suppose that the man whom your father murdered was one of your relatives—clearly he was; for if he had been a stranger you would never have thought of prosecuting him.

EUTH: I am amused, Socrates, at your making a distinction between one who is a relation and one who is not a relation; for surely the pollution is the same in either case, if you knowingly associate with the murderer when you ought to clear yourself and him by proceeding against him. The real question is whether the murdered man has been justly slain. If justly, then your duty is to let the matter alone; but if unjustly, then even if the murderer lives under the same roof with you and eats at the same table, proceed against him. Now the man who is dead was a poor dependant of mine who worked for us as a field labourer on our farm in Naxos, and one day in a fit of drunken passion he got into a quarrel with one of our domestic servants and slew him. My father bound him hand and foot and threw him into a ditch, and then sent to Athens to ask of a diviner what he should do with him. Meanwhile he never attended to him and took no care about him, for he regarded him as a murderer; and thought that no great harm would be done even if he did die. Now this was just what happened. For such was the effect of cold and hunger and chains upon him, that before the messenger returned from the diviner, he was dead. And my father and family are angry with me for taking the part of the murderer and prosecuting my father. They say that he did not kill him, and that if he did, the dead man was but a murderer, and I ought not to take any notice, for that a son is impious who prosecutes a father. Which shows, Socrates, how little they know what the gods think about piety and impiety.

3. Drawing Euthyphro into Debate

SOC: Good heavens, Euthyphro! and is your knowledge of religion and of things pious and impious so very exact, that, supposing the circumstances to be as you state them, you are not afraid lest you too may be doing an impious thing in bringing an action against your father?

EUTH: The best of Euthyphro, and that which distinguishes him, Socrates, from other men, is his exact knowledge of all such matters. What should I be good for without it?

SOC: Rare friend! I think that I cannot do better than be your disciple. Then before the trial with Meletus comes on I shall challenge him, and say that I have always had a great interest in religious questions, and now, as he charges me with rash imaginations and innovations in religion, I have become your disciple. You, Meletus, as I shall say to him, acknowledge Euthyphro to be a great theologian, and sound in his opinions; and if you approve of him you ought to approve of me, and not have me into court; but if you disapprove, you should begin by indicting him who is my teacher, and who will be the ruin, not of the young, but of the old; that is to say, of myself whom he instructs, and of his old father whom he admonishes and chastises. And if Meletus refuses to listen to me, but will go on, and will not shift the indictment from me to you, I cannot do better than repeat this challenge in the court.

EUTH: Yes, indeed, Socrates; and if he attempts to indict me I am mistaken if I do not find a flaw in him; the court shall have a great deal more to say to him than to me.

4. First Attempt: Doing What I am Doing

SOC: And I, my dear friend, knowing this, am desirous of becoming your disciple. For I observe that no one appears to notice you—not even this Meletus; but his sharp eyes have found me out at once, and he has indicted me for impiety. And therefore, I adjure you to tell me the nature of piety and impiety, which you said that you knew so well, and of murder, and of other offences against the gods. What are they? Is not piety in every action always the same? and impiety, again—is it not always the opposite of piety, and also the same with itself, having, as impiety, one notion which includes whatever is impious?

EUTH: To be sure, Socrates.

SOC: And what is piety, and what is impiety?

EUTH Piety is doing as I am doing; that is to say, prosecuting any one who is guilty of murder, sacrilege, or of any similar crime—whether he be your father or mother, or whoever he may be—that

makes no difference; and not to prosecute them is impiety. And please to consider, Socrates, what a notable proof I will give you of the truth of my words, a proof which I have already given to others:—of the principle, I mean, that the impious, whoever he may be, ought not to go unpunished. For do not men regard Zeus as the best and most righteous of the gods?—and yet they admit that he bound his father (Cronos) because he wickedly devoured his sons, and that he too had punished his own father (Uranus) for a similar reason, in a nameless manner. And yet when I proceed against my father, they are angry with me. So inconsistent are they in their way of talking when the gods are concerned, and when I am concerned.

SOC: May not this be the reason, Euthyphro, why I am charged with impiety—that I cannot [accept] these stories about the gods? and therefore I suppose that people think me wrong. But, as you who are well informed about them approve of them, I cannot do better than assent to your superior wisdom. What else can I say, confessing as I do, that I know nothing about them? Tell me, for the love of Zeus, whether you really believe that they are true.

EUTH: Yes, Socrates; and things more wonderful still, of which the world is in ignorance.

SOC: And do you really believe that the gods fought with one another, and had dire quarrels, battles, and the like, as the poets say, and as you may see represented in the works of great artists? The temples are full of them; and notably the robe of Athene, which is carried up to the Acropolis at the great Panathenaea, is embroidered with them. Are all these tales of the gods true, Euthyphro?

EUTH: Yes, Socrates; and, as I was saying, I can tell you, if you would like to hear them, many other things about the gods which would quite amaze you.

SOC: I dare say; and you shall tell me them at some other time when I have leisure. But just at present I would rather hear from you a more precise answer, which you have not as yet given, my friend, to the question, What is 'piety'? When asked, you only replied, Doing as you do, charging your father with murder.

EUTH: And what I said was true, Socrates.

SOC: No doubt, Euthyphro; but you would admit that there are many other pious acts?

EUTH: There are.

SOC: Remember that I did not ask you to give me two or three examples of piety, but to explain the general idea which makes all pious things to be pious. Do you not recollect that there was one idea which made the impious impious, and the pious pious?

EUTH: I remember.

SOC: Tell me what is the nature of this idea, and then I shall have a standard to which I may look, and by which I may measure actions, whether yours or those of any one else, and then I shall be able to say that such and such an action is pious, such another impious.

EUTH: I will tell you, if you like.

SOC: I should very much like.

5. Second Attempt: That Which is Dear to the Gods

EUTH: Piety, then, is that which is dear to the gods, and impiety is that which is not dear to them.

SOC: Very good, Euthyphro; you have now given me the sort of answer which I wanted. But whether what you say is true or not I cannot as yet tell, although I make no doubt that you will prove the truth of your words.

EUTH: Of course.

SOC: Come, then, and let us examine what we are saying. That thing or person which is dear to the gods is pious, and that thing or person which is hateful to the gods is impious, these two being the extreme opposites of one another. Was not that said?

EUTH: It was.

SOC: And well said?

EUTH: Yes, Socrates, I thought so; it was certainly said.

SOC: And further, Euthyphro, the gods were admitted to have enmities and hatreds and differences?

EUTH: Yes, that was also said.

SOC: And what sort of difference creates enmity and anger? Suppose for example that you and I, my good friend, differ about a number; do differences of this sort make us enemies and set us at variance with one another? Do we not go at once to arithmetic, and put an end to them by a sum?

EUTH: True.

SOC: Or suppose that we differ about magni-

tudes, do we not quickly end the differences by measuring?

EUTH: Very true.

SOC: And we end a controversy about heavy and light by resorting to a weighing machine?

EUTH: To be sure.

SOC: But what differences are there which cannot be thus decided, and which therefore make us angry and set us at enmity with one another? I dare say the answer does not occur to you at the moment, and therefore I will suggest that these enmities arise when the matters of difference are the just and unjust, good and evil, honourable and dishonourable. Are not these the points about which men differ, and about which when we are unable satisfactorily to decide our differences, you and I and all of us quarrel, when we do quarrel?

EUTH: Yes, Socrates, the nature of the differences about which we quarrel is such as you describe.

SOC: And the quarrels of the gods, noble Euthyphro, when they occur, are of a like nature?

EUTH: Certainly they are.

SOC: They have differences of opinion, as you say, about good and evil, just and unjust, honourable and dishonourable: there would have been no quarrels among them, if there had been no such differences—would there now?

EUTH: You are quite right.

SOC: Does not every man love that which he deems noble and just and good, and hate the opposite of them?

EUTH: Very true.

SOC: But, as you say, people regard the same things, some as just and others as unjust,—about these they dispute; and so there arise wars and fightings among them.

EUTH: Very true.

SOC: Then the same things are hated by the gods and loved by the gods, and are both hateful and dear to them?

EUTH: True.

SOC: And upon this view the same things, Euthyphro, will be pious and also impious?

EUTH: So I should suppose.

SOC: Then, my friend, I remark with surprise that you have not answered the question which I asked. For I certainly did not ask you to tell me what action is both pious and impious: but now it would seem that what is loved by the gods is also hated by them. And therefore, Euthyphro, in thus chastising your father you may very likely be doing what is agreeable to Zeus but disagreeable to Cronos or Uranus, and what is acceptable to Hephaestus but unacceptable to Hera, and there may be other gods who have similar differences of opinion.

EUTH: But I believe, Socrates, that all the gods would be agreed as to the propriety of punishing a murderer: there would be no difference of opinion about that.

SOC: Well, but speaking of men, Euthyphro, did you ever hear any one arguing that a murderer or any sort of evil-doer ought to be let off?

EUTH: I should rather say that these are the questions which they are always arguing, especially in courts of law: they commit all sorts of crimes, and there is nothing which they will not do or say in their own defence.

SOC: But do they admit their guilt, Euthyphro, and yet say that they ought not to be punished?

EUTH: No; they do not.

SOC: Then there are some things which they do not venture to say and do: for they do not venture to argue that the guilty are to be unpunished, but they deny their guilt, do they not?

EUTH: Yes.

SOC: Then they do not argue that the evil-doer should not be punished, but they argue about the fact of who the evil-doer is, and what he did and when?

EUTH: True.

SOC: And the gods are in the same case, if as you assert they quarrel about just and unjust, and some of them say while others deny that injustice is done among them. For surely neither God nor man will ever venture to say that the doer of injustice is not to be punished?

EUTH: That is true, Socrates, in the main.

SOC: But they join issue about the particulars—gods and men alike; and, if they dispute at all, they dispute about some act which is called in question, and which by some is affirmed to be just, by others to be unjust. Is not that true?

EUTH: Quite true.

SOC: Well then, my dear friend Euthyphro, do tell me, for my better instruction and information, what proof have you that in the opinion of all the gods a servant who is guilty of murder, and is put in chains by the master of the dead man, and dies because he is put in chains before he who bound him can learn from the interpreters of the gods what he ought to do with him, dies unjustly; and that on behalf of such an one a son ought to proceed against his father and accuse him of murder. How would you show that all the gods absolutely agree in approving of his act? Prove to me that they do, and I will applaud your wisdom as long as I live.

EUTH: It will be a difficult task; but I could make the matter very clear indeed to you.

SOC: I understand; you mean to say that I am not so quick of apprehension as the judges: for to them you will be sure to prove that the act is unjust, and hateful to the gods.

EUTH: Yes indeed, Socrates; at least if they will listen to me.

6. The Third Attempt: That Which is Loved by *All* the Gods

SOC: But they will be sure to listen if they find that you are a good speaker. There was a notion that came into my mind while you were speaking; I said to myself: 'Well, and what if Euthyphro does prove to me that all the gods regarded the death of the serf as unjust, how do I know anything more of the nature of piety and impiety? for granting that this action may be hateful to the gods, still piety and impiety are not adequately defined by these distinctions, for that which is hateful to the gods has been shown to be also pleasing and dear to them.' And therefore, Euthyphro, I do not ask you to prove this; I will suppose, if you like, that all the gods condemn and abominate such an action. But I will amend the definition so far as to say that what all the gods hate is impious, and what they love pious or holy; and what some of them love and others hate is both or neither. Shall this be our definition of piety and impiety?

EUTH: Why not, Socrates?

SOC: Why not! certainly, as far as I am concerned, Euthyphro, there is no reason why not. But whether this admission will greatly assist you in the task of instructing me as you promised, is a matter for you to consider.

EUTH: Yes, I should say that what all the gods

love is pious and holy, and the opposite which they all hate, impious.

SOC: Ought we to enquire into the truth of this, Euthyphro, or simply to accept the mere statement on our own authority and that of others? What do you say?

EUTH: We should enquire; and I believe that the statement will stand the test of enquiry.

7. Socrates' Objection

SOC: We shall know better, my good friend, in a little while. The point which I should first wish to understand is whether the pious or holy is beloved by the gods because it is holy, or holy because it is beloved of the gods.

EUTH: I do not understand your meaning, Socrates.

SOC: I will endeavour to explain: we, speak of carrying and we speak of being carried, of leading and being led, seeing and being seen. You know that in all such cases there is a difference, and you know also in what the difference lies?

EUTH: I think that I understand.

SOC: And is not that which is beloved distinct from that which loves?

EUTH: Certainly.

SOC: Well; and now tell me, is that which is carried in this state of carrying because it is carried, or for some other reason?

EUTH: No; that is the reason.

SOC: And the same is true of what is led and of what is seen?

EUTH: True.

SOC: And a thing is not seen because it is visible, but conversely, visible because it is seen; nor is a thing led because it is in the state of being led, or carried because it is in the state of being carried, but the converse of this. And now I think, Euthyphro, that my meaning will be intelligible; and my meaning is, that any state of action or passion implies previous action or passion. It does not become because it is becoming, but it is in a state of becoming because it becomes; neither does it suffer because it is in a state of suffering, but it is in a state of suffering because it suffers. Do you not agree?

EUTH: Yes.

SOC: Is not that which is loved in some state either of becoming or suffering?

EUTH: Yes.

SOC: And the same holds as in the previous instances; the state of being loved follows the act of being loved, and not the act the state.

EUTH: Certainly.

SOC: And what do you say of piety, Euthyphro: is not piety, according to your definition, loved by all the gods?

EUTH: Yes.

SOC: Because it is pious or holy, or for some other reason?

EUTH: No, that is the reason.

SOC: It is loved because it is holy, not holy because it is loved?

EUTH: Yes.

SOC: And that which is dear to the gods is loved by them, and is in a state to be loved of them because it is loved of them?

EUTH: Certainly.

SOC: Then that which is dear to the gods, Euthyphro, is not holy, nor is that which is holy loved of God, as you affirm; but they are two different things.

EUTH: How do you mean, Socrates?

SOC: I mean to say that the holy has been acknowledged by us to be loved of God because it is holy, not to be holy because it is loved.

EUTH: Yes.

SOC: But that which is dear to the gods is dear to them because it is loved by them, not loved by them because it is dear to them.

EUTH: True.

SOC: But, friend Euthyphro, if that which is holy is the same with that which is dear to God, and is loved because it is holy, then that which is dear to God would have been loved as being dear to God; but if that which is dear to God is dear to him because loved by him, then that which is holy would have been holy because loved by him. But now you see that the reverse is the case, and that they are quite different from one another. For one is of a kind to be loved cause it is loved, and the other is loved because it is of a kind to be loved. Thus you appear to me, Euthyphro, when I ask you what is the essence of holiness, to offer an attribute only, and not the essence—the attribute of being loved by all the gods. But you still refuse to explain to me the nature of holiness. And therefore, if you please, I will ask you not to hide your treasure, but to tell me once more what holiness or piety really is, whether dear to the gods or not (for that is a matter about which we will not quarrel); and what is impiety?

EUTH: I really do not know, Socrates, how to express what I mean. For somehow or other our arguments, on whatever ground we rest them, seem to turn round and walk away from us....

8. An Inconclusive Ending

SOC: Then we must begin again and ask, What is piety? That is an enquiry which I shall never be weary of pursuing as far as in me lies; and I entreat you not to scorn me, but to apply your mind to the utmost, and tell me the truth. For, if any man knows, you are he; and therefore I must detain you, like Proteus, until you tell. If you had not certainly known the nature of piety and impiety, I am confident that you would never, on behalf of a serf, have charged your aged father with murder. You would not have run such a risk of doing wrong in the sight of the gods, and you would have had too much respect for the opinions of men. I am sure, therefore, that you know the nature of piety and impiety. Speak out then, my dear Euthyphro, and do not hide your knowledge.

EUTH: Another time, Socrates; for I am in a hurry, and must go now.

SOC: Alas! my companion, and will you leave me in despair? I was hoping that you would instruct me in the nature of piety and impiety; and then I might have cleared myself of Meletus and his indictment. I would have told him that I had been enlightened by Euthyphro, and had given up rash innovations and speculations, in which I indulged only through ignorance, and that now I am about to lead a better life.

Plato. "Euthyphro." *The Dialogues of Plato*. Vol. 2. Trans. by Benjamin Jowett. Oxford: Oxford University Press, 1892

REPUBLIC I-II

PLATO (427-347 BCE)

The question at the heart of Plato's masterwork, the Republic, is "what is justice?" Plato sets the dialogue in Piraeus, not far from Athens. Socrates and Glaucon, Plato's brother, are attending the festival of the goddess Bendis. Invited back to the home of Cephalus for supper, the discussion about justice quickly heats up with Cephalus, his son, Polemarchus, and the sophist, Thrasymachus all taking turns trying, with greater and lesser success, to define precisely what justice is. In Book II, Thrasymachus' position is taken over by Socrates' young friend, Glaucon, who challenges the very worth of justice as a virtue.

The importance of these opening arguments of the Republic *cannot be emphasized enough. What we have in this text is one of the greatest debates ever put on paper, about one of the most important virtues in Western ethics. In the arguments of Thrasymachus and Glaucon, Plato also presents us with one of the earliest known explications of the theory of Ethical Egoism, which in more recent times has been popularized in the writings of Ayn Rand and the political movement of libertarianism.*

BOOK I

I WENT down yesterday to the Piraeus with Glaucon, the son of Ariston, that I might offer up my prayers to the goddess; and also because I wanted to see in what manner they would celebrate the festival, which was a new thing. I was delighted with the procession of the inhabitants; but that of the Thracians was equally, if not more, beautiful. When we had finished our prayers and viewed the spectacle, we turned in the direction of the city; and at that instant Polemarchus, the son of Cephalus, chanced to catch sight of us from a distance as we were starting on our way home, and told his servant to run and bid us wait for him. The servant took hold of me by the cloak behind, and said, Polemarchus desires you to wait.

I turned round, and asked him where his master was.

There he is, said the youth, coming after you, if you will only wait.

Certainly we will, said Glaucon; and in a few minutes Polemarchus appeared, and with him Adeimantus, Glaucon's brother, Niceratus, the son of Nicias, and several others who had been at the procession.

Polemarchus said to me, I perceive, Socrates, that you and your companion are already on your way to the city.

You are not far wrong, I said.

But do you see, he rejoined, how many we are?

Of course.

And are you stronger than all these? for if not, you will have to remain where you are.

May there not be the alternative, I said, that we may persuade you to let us go?

But can you persuade us, if we refuse to listen to you? he said.

Certainly not, replied Glaucon.

Then we are not going to listen; of that you may be assured.

Adeimantus added: Has no one told you of the torch-race on horseback in honor of the goddess which will take place in the evening?

With horses! I replied. That is a novelty. Will horsemen carry torches and pass them one to another during the race?

Yes, said Polemarchus; and not only so, but a festival will be celebrated at night, which you certainly ought to see. Let us rise soon after supper and see this festival; there will be a gathering of young men, and we will have a good talk. Stay then, and do not be perverse.

Glaucon said: I suppose, since you insist, that we must.

Very good, I replied.

1. Cephalus

Accordingly we went with Polemarchus to his house; and there we found his brothers Lysias and Euthydemus, and with them Thrasymachus the Chalcedonian, Charmantides the Paeanian, and Cleitophon, the son of Aristonymus. There too was Cephalus, the father of Polemarchus, whom I had not seen for a long time, and I thought him very much aged. He was seated on a cushioned chair, and had a garland on his head, for he had been sacrificing in the court; and there were some other chairs in the room arranged in a semicircle, upon which we sat down by him. He saluted me eagerly, and then he said:

You don't come to see me, Socrates, as often as you ought: If I were still able to go and see you I would not ask you to come to me. But at my age I can hardly get to the city, and therefore you should come oftener to the Piraeus. For, let me tell you that the more the pleasures of the body fade away, the greater to me are the pleasure and charm of conversation. Do not, then, deny my request, but make our house your resort and keep company with these young men; we are old friends, and you will be quite at home with us.

I replied: There is nothing which for my part I like better, Cephalus, than conversing with aged men; for I regard them as travelers who have gone a journey which I too may have to go, and of whom I ought to inquire whether the way is smooth and easy or rugged and difficult. And this is a question which I should like to ask of you, who have arrived at that time which the poets call the "threshold of old age": Is life harder toward the end, or what report do you give of it?

I will tell you, Socrates, he said, what my own feeling is. Men of my age flock together; we are birds of a feather, as the old proverb says; and at our meetings the tale of my acquaintance commonly is: I cannot eat, I cannot drink; the pleasures of youth and love are fled away; there was a good time once, but now that is gone, and life is no longer life. Some complain of the slights which are put upon them by relations, and they will tell you sadly of how many evils their old age is the cause. But to me, Socrates, these complainers seem to blame that which is not really in fault. For if old age were the cause, I too, being old, and every other old man would have felt as they do. But this is not my own experience, nor that of others whom I have known. How well I remember the aged poet Sophocles, when in answer to the question, How does love suit with age, Sophocles—are you still the man you were? Peace, he replied; most gladly have I escaped the thing of which you speak; I feel as if I had escaped from a mad and furious master. His words have often occurred to my mind since, and they seem as good to me now as at the time when he uttered them. For certainly old age has a great sense of calm and freedom; when the passions relax their hold, then, as Sophocles says, we are freed from the grasp not of one mad master only, but of many. The truth is, Socrates, that these regrets, and also the complaints about relations, are to be attributed to the same cause, which is not old age, but men's characters and tempers; for he who is of a calm and happy nature will hardly feel the pressure of age, but to him who is of an opposite disposition youth and age are equally a burden.

I listened in admiration, and wanting to draw him out, that he might go on—Yes, Cephalus, I said; but I rather suspect that people in general are not convinced by you when you speak thus; they think that old age sits lightly upon you, not because of your happy disposition, but because you are rich, and wealth is well known to be a great comforter.

You are right, he replied; they are not convinced: and there is something in what they say; not, however, so much as they imagine. I might answer them as Themistocles answered the Seriphian who was abusing him and saying that he was famous, not for his own merits but because he was an Athenian: "If you had been a native of my country or I of yours, neither of us would have been famous." And to those who are not rich and are impatient of old age, the same reply may be made; for to the good poor man old age cannot be a light burden, nor can a bad rich man ever have peace with himself.

May I ask, Cephalus, whether your fortune was for the most part inherited or acquired by you?

Acquired! Socrates; do you want to know how much I acquired? In the art of making money I have been midway between my father and grandfather: for my grandfather, whose name I bear, doubled and trebled the value of his patrimony, that which he inherited being much what I possess now; but my father, Lysanias, reduced the property below what it is at present; and I shall be satisfied if I leave to these my sons not less, but a little more, than I received.

That was why I asked you the question, I replied, because I see that you are indifferent about money, which is a characteristic rather of those who have inherited their fortunes than of those who have acquired them; the makers of fortunes have a second love of money as a creation of their own, resembling the affection of authors for their own poems, or of parents for their children, besides that natural love of it for the sake of use and profit which is common to them and all men. And hence they are very bad company, for they can talk about nothing but the praises of wealth. That is true, he said.

Yes, that is very true, but may I ask another question? What do you consider to be the greatest blessing which you have reaped from your wealth?

One, he said, of which I could not expect easily to convince others. For let me tell you, Socrates, that when a man thinks himself to be near death, fears and cares enter into his mind which he never had before; the tales of a world below and the punishment which is exacted there of deeds done here were once a laughing matter to him, but now he is tormented with the thought that they may be true: either from the weakness of age, or because he is now drawing nearer to that other place, he has a clearer view of these things; suspicions and alarms crowd thickly upon him, and he begins to reflect and consider what wrongs he has done to others. And when he finds that the sum of his transgressions is great he will many a time like a child start up in his sleep for fear, and he is filled with dark forebodings. But to him who is conscious of no sin, sweet hope, as Pindar charmingly says, is the kind nurse of his age:

"Hope," he says, "cherishes the soul of him who lives in justice and holiness, and is the nurse of his age and the companion of his journey—hope which is mightiest to sway the restless soul of man."

How admirable are his words! And the great blessing of riches, I do not say to every man, but to a good man, is, that he has had no occasion to deceive or to defraud others, either intentionally or unintentionally; and when he departs to the world below he is not in any apprehension about offerings due to the gods or debts which he owes to men. Now to this peace of mind the possession of wealth greatly contributes; and therefore I say, that, setting one thing against another, of the many advantages which wealth has to give, to a man of sense this is in my opinion the greatest.

Well said, Cephalus, I replied; but as concerning justice, what is it?—to speak the truth and to pay your debts—no more than this? And even to this are there not exceptions? Suppose that a friend when in his right mind has deposited arms with me and he asks for them when he is not in his right mind, ought I to give them back to him? No one would say that I ought or that I should be right in doing so, any more than they would say that I ought always to speak the truth to one who is in his condition.

You are quite right, he replied.

But then, I said, speaking the truth and paying your debts is not a correct definition of justice.

Quite correct, Socrates, if Simonides is to be believed, said Polemarchus, interposing.

I fear, said Cephalus, that I must go now, for I have to look after the sacrifices, and I hand over the argument to Polemarchus and the company.

Is not Polemarchus your heir? I said.

To be sure, he answered, and went away laughing to the sacrifices.

2. Polemarchus

Tell me then, O thou heir of the argument, what did Simonides say, and according to you, truly say, about justice?

He said that the repayment of a debt is just, and in saying so he appears to me to be right.

I shall be sorry to doubt the word of such a wise and inspired man, but his meaning, though probably clear to you, is the reverse of clear to me. For he certainly does not mean, as we were just now saying, that I ought to return a deposit of arms or of anything else to one who asks for it when he is not in his right senses; and yet a deposit cannot be denied to be a debt.

True.

Then when the person who asks me is not in his right mind I am by no means to make the return?

Certainly not.

When Simonides said that the repayment of a debt was justice, he did not mean to include that case?

Certainly not; for he thinks that a friend ought always to do good to a friend, and never evil.

You mean that the return of a deposit of gold which is to the injury of the receiver, if the two parties are friends, is not the repayment of a debt—that is what you would imagine him to say?

Yes.

And are enemies also to receive what we owe to them?

To be sure, he said, they are to receive what we owe them; and an enemy, as I take it, owes to an enemy that which is due or proper to him—that is to say, evil.

Simonides, then, after the manner of poets, would seem to have spoken darkly of the nature of justice; for he really meant to say that justice is the giving to each man what is proper to him, and this he termed a debt.

That must have been his meaning, he said....

2a. The First Objection: The Possibility of Mistake

Well, there is another question: By friends and enemies do we mean those who are so really, or only in seeming?

Surely, he said, a man may be expected to love those whom he thinks good, and to hate those whom he thinks evil.

Yes, but do not persons often err about good and evil: many who are not good seem to be so, and conversely?

That is true.

Then to them the good will be enemies and the evil will be their friends? True.

And in that case they will be right in doing good to the evil and evil to the good?

Clearly.

But the good are just and would not do an injustice?

True.

Then according to your argument it is just to injure those who do no wrong?

Nay, Socrates; the doctrine is immoral.

Then I suppose that we ought to do good to the just and harm to the unjust?

I like that better.

But see the consequence: Many a man who is ignorant of human nature has friends who are bad friends, and in that case he ought to do harm to them; and he has good enemies whom he ought to benefit; but, if so, we shall be saying the very opposite of that which we affirmed to be the meaning of Simonides.

Very true, he said; and I think that we had better correct an error into which we seem to have fallen in the use of the words "friend" and "enemy."

What was the error, Polemarchus? I asked.

We assumed that he is a friend who seems to be or who is thought good.

And how is the error to be corrected?

We should rather say that he is a friend who is, as well as seems, good; and that he who seems only and is not good, only seems to be and is not a friend; and of an enemy the same may be said.

You would argue that the good are our friends and the bad our enemies?

Yes.

And instead of saying simply as we did at first, that it is just to do good to our friends and harm to our enemies, we should further say: It is just to do good to our friends when they are good, and harm to our enemies when they are evil?

Yes, that appears to me to be the truth.

2b. The Second Objection: The Prohibition Against Causing Harm

But ought the just to injure anyone at all?

Undoubtedly he ought to injure those who are both wicked and his enemies.

When horses are injured, are they improved or deteriorated?

The latter.

Deteriorated, that is to say, in the good qualities of horses, not of dogs?

Yes, of horses.

And dogs are deteriorated in the good qualities of dogs, and not of horses?

Of course.

And will not men who are injured be deteriorated in that which is the proper virtue of man?

Certainly.

And that human virtue is justice?

To be sure.

Then men who are injured are of necessity made unjust?

That is the result.

But can the musician by his art make men unmusical?

Certainly not.

Or the horseman by his art make them bad horsemen?

Impossible.

And can the just by justice make men unjust, or speaking generally, can the good by virtue make them bad?

Assuredly not.

Any more than heat can produce cold?

It cannot.

Or drought moisture?

Clearly not.

Nor can the good harm anyone?

Impossible.

And the just is the good?

Certainly.

Then to injure a friend or anyone else is not the act of a just man, but of the opposite, who is the unjust?

I think that what you say is quite true, Socrates.

Then if a man says that justice consists in the repayment of debts, and that good is the debt which a just man owes to his friends, and evil the debt which he owes to his enemies—to say this is not wise; for it is not true, if, as has been clearly shown, the injuring of another can be in no case just.

I agree with you, said Polemarchus.

Then you and I are prepared to take up arms against anyone who attributes such a saying to Simonides or Bias or Pittacus, or any other wise man or seer?

I am quite ready to do battle at your side, he said.

Shall I tell you whose I believe the saying to be?

Whose?

I believe that Periander or Perdiccas or Xerxes or Ismenias the Theban, or some other rich and mighty man, who had a great opinion of his own power, was the first to say that justice is "doing good to your friends and harm to your enemies."

Most true, he said.

Yes, I said; but if this definition of justice also breaks down, what other can be offered?

3. Thrasymachus: The Immoralist Position

Several times in the course of the discussion Thrasymachus had made an attempt to get the argument into his own hands, and had been put down by the rest of the company, who wanted to hear the end. But when Polemarchus and I had done speaking and there was a pause, he could no longer hold his peace; and, gathering himself up, he came at us like a wild beast, seeking to devour us. We were quite panic-stricken at the sight of him.

3a. Justice as the Advantage of the Stronger

He roared out to the whole company: What folly, Socrates, has taken possession of you all? And why, [do you act like idiots by giving] way to one another? I say that if you want really to know what justice is, you should not only ask but answer, and you should not seek honor to yourself from the refutation of an opponent, but have your own answer; for there is many a one who can ask and cannot answer. And now I will not have you say that justice is duty or advantage or profit or gain or interest, for this sort of nonsense will not do for me; I must have clearness and accuracy.

I was panic-stricken at his words, and could not look at him without trembling. Indeed I believe that if I had not fixed my eye upon him, I should have been struck dumb: but when I saw his fury rising, I looked at him first, and was therefore able to reply to him.

Thrasymachus, I said, with a quiver, don't be hard upon us. Polemarchus and I may have been guilty of a little mistake in the argument, but I can assure you that the error was not intentional. If we were seeking for a piece of gold, you would not imagine that we were "knocking under to one another," and so losing our chance of finding it. And why, when we are seeking for justice, a thing more precious than many pieces of gold, do you say that we are weakly yielding to one another and not doing our utmost to get at the truth? Nay, my good friend, we are most willing and anxious to do so, but the fact is that we cannot. And if so, you people who know all things should pity us and not be angry with us.

How characteristic of Socrates! he replied, with a bitter laugh; that's your ironical style! Did I not foresee—have I not already told you, that whatever he was asked he would refuse to answer, and try irony or any other shuffle, in order that he might avoid answering?

You are a philosopher, Thrasymachus, I replied, and well know that if you ask a person what numbers make up twelve, taking care to prohibit him whom you ask from answering twice six, or three times four, or six times two, or four times three, "for this sort of nonsense will not do for me"—then obviously, if that is your way of putting the question, no one can answer you. But suppose that he were to retort: "Thrasymachus, what do you mean? If one of these numbers which you interdict be the true answer to the question, am I falsely to say some other number which is not the right one?—is that your meaning?"—How would you answer him?

Just as if the two cases were at all alike! he said.

Why should they not be? I replied; and even if they are not, but only appear to be so to the person who is asked, ought he not to say what he thinks, whether you and I forbid him or not?

I presume then that you are going to make one of the interdicted answers?

I dare say that I may, notwithstanding the danger, if upon reflection I approve of any of them.

But what if I give you an answer about justice other and better, he said, than any of these? What do you deserve to have done to you?

Done to me!—as becomes the ignorant, I must learn from the wise— that is what I deserve to have done to me.

What, and no payment! A pleasant notion!

I will pay when I have the money, I replied.

But you have, Socrates, said Glaucon: and you, Thrasymachus, need be under no anxiety about money, for we will all make a contribution for Socrates.

Yes, he replied, and then Socrates will do as he always does— refuse to answer himself, but take and pull to pieces the answer of someone else.

Why, my good friend, I said, how can anyone answer who knows, and says that he knows, just nothing; and who, even if he has some faint notions of his own, is told by a man of authority not to utter them? The natural thing is, that the speaker should be someone like yourself who professes to know and can tell what he knows. Will you then kindly answer, for the edification of the company and of myself?

Glaucon and the rest of the company joined in my request, and Thrasymachus, as anyone might see, was in reality eager to speak; for he thought that he had an excellent answer, and would distinguish himself. But at first he affected to insist on my answering; at length he consented to begin. Behold, he said, the wisdom of Socrates; he refuses to teach himself, and goes about learning of others, to whom he never even says, Thank you.

That I learn of others, I replied, is quite true; but that I am ungrateful I wholly deny. Money I have none, and therefore I pay in praise, which is all I have; and how ready I am to praise anyone who appears to me to speak well you will very soon find out when you answer; for I expect that you will answer well.

Listen, then, he said; I proclaim that justice is nothing else than the interest of the stronger. And now why do you not praise me? But of course you won't.

Let me first understand you, I replied. Justice, as you say, is the interest of the stronger. What, Thrasymachus, is the meaning of this? You cannot mean to say that because Polydamas, the pancratiast, is stronger than we are, and finds the eating of beef conducive to his bodily strength, that to eat beef is therefore equally for our good who are weaker than he is, and right and just for us?

That's abominable of you, Socrates; you take the words in the sense which is most damaging to the argument.

Not at all, my good sir, I said; I am trying to understand them; and I wish that you would be a little clearer.

Well, he said, have you never heard that forms of government differ— there are tyrannies, and there are democracies, and there are aristocracies?

Yes, I know.

And the government is the ruling power in each State?

Certainly.

And the different forms of government make laws democratical, aristocratical, tyrannical, with a view to their several interests; and these laws, which are made by them for their own interests, are the justice which they deliver to their subjects, and him who transgresses them they punish as a breaker of the law, and unjust. And that is what I mean when I say that in all States there is the same principle of justice, which is the interest of the government; and as the government must be supposed to have power, the only reasonable conclusion is that everywhere there is one principle of justice, which is the interest of the stronger.

3b. Socrates' First Objection: Rulers' Errors

Now I understand you, I said; and whether you are right or not I will try to discover. But let me remark that in defining justice you have yourself used the word "interest," which you forbade me to use. It is true, however, that in your definition the words "of the stronger" are added.

A small addition, you must allow, he said.

Great or small, never mind about that: we must first inquire whether what you are saying is the truth. Now we are both agreed that justice is interest of some sort, but you go on to say "of the stronger"; about this addition I am not so sure, and must therefore consider further.

Proceed.

I will; and first tell me, Do you admit that it is just for subjects to obey their rulers?

I do.

But are the rulers of States absolutely infallible, or are they sometimes liable to err?

To be sure, he replied, they are liable to err.

Then in making their laws they may sometimes make them rightly, and sometimes not?

True.

When they make them rightly, they make them agreeably to their interest; when they are mistaken, contrary to their interest; you admit that?

Yes.

And the laws which they make must be obeyed by their subjects—and that is what you call justice?

Doubtless.

Then justice, according to your argument, is not only obedience to the interest of the stronger, but the reverse?

What is that you are saying? he asked.

I am only repeating what you are saying, I believe. But let us consider: Have we not admitted that the rulers may be mistaken about their own interest in what they command, and also that to obey them is justice? Has not that been admitted?

Yes.

Then you must also have acknowledged justice not to be for the interest of the stronger, when the rulers unintentionally command things to be done which are to their own injury. For if, as you say, justice is the obedience which the subject renders to their commands, in that case, O wisest of men, is there any escape from the conclusion that the weaker are commanded to do, not what is for the interest, but what is for the injury of the stronger?

Nothing can be clearer, Socrates, said Polemarchus.

Yes, said Cleitophon, interposing, if you are allowed to be his witness.

But there is no need of any witness, said Polemarchus, for Thrasymachus himself acknowledges that rulers may sometime command what is not for their own interest, and that for subjects to obey them is justice.

Yes, Polemarchus—Thrasymachus said that for subjects to do what was commanded by their rulers is just.

Yes, Cleitophon, but he also said that justice is the interest of the stronger, and, while admitting both these propositions, he further acknowledged that the stronger may command the weaker who are his subjects to do what is not for his own interest; whence follows that justice is the injury quite as much as the interest of the stronger.

But, said Cleitophon, he meant by the interest of the stronger what the stronger thought to be his interest—this was what the weaker had to do; and this was affirmed by him to be justice.

Those were not his words, rejoined Polemarchus.

Never mind, I replied, if he now says that they are, let us accept his statement. Tell me, Thrasymachus, I said, did you mean by justice what the stronger thought to be his interest, whether really so or not?

Certainly not, he said. Do you suppose that I call him who is mistaken the stronger at the time when he is mistaken?

Yes, I said, my impression was that you did so, when you admitted that the ruler was not infallible, but might be sometimes mistaken.

You argue like an informer, Socrates. Do you mean, for example, that he who is mistaken about the sick is a physician in that he is mistaken? Or that he who errs in arithmetic or grammar is an arithmetician or grammarian at the time when he is making the mistake, in respect of the mistake? True, we say that the physician or arithmetician or grammarian has made a mistake, but this is only a way of speaking; for the fact is that neither the grammarian nor any other person of skill ever makes a mistake in so far as he is what his name implies; they none of them err unless their skill fails them, and then they cease to be skilled artists. No artist or sage or ruler errs at the time when he is what his name implies; though he is commonly said to err, and I adopted the common mode of speaking. But to be perfectly accurate, since you are such a lover of accuracy, we should say that the ruler, in so far as he is a ruler, is unerring, and, being unerring, always commands that which is for his own interest; and the subject is required to execute his commands; and therefore, as I said at first and now repeat, justice is the interest of the stronger.

3c. Socrates' Second Objection: The Object of Rule

Indeed, Thrasymachus, and do I really appear to you to argue like an informer?

Certainly, he replied.

And do you suppose that I ask these questions with any design of injuring you in the argument?

Nay, he replied, "suppose" is not the word—I know it; but you will be found out, and by sheer force of argument you will never prevail.

I shall not make the attempt, my dear man; but to avoid any misunderstanding occurring between us in future, let me ask, in what sense do you speak of a ruler or stronger whose interest, as you were saying, he being the superior, it is just that the inferior should execute—is he a ruler in the popular or in the strict sense of the term?

In the strictest of all senses, he said. And now cheat and play the informer if you can; I ask no quar-

ter at your hands. But you never will be able, never.

And do you imagine, I said, that I am such a madman as to try and cheat Thrasymachus? I might as well shave a lion.

Why, he said, you made the attempt a minute ago, and you failed.

Enough, I said, of these civilities. It will be better that I should ask you a question: Is the physician, taken in that strict sense of which you are speaking, a healer of the sick or a maker of money? And remember that I am now speaking of the true physician.

A healer of the sick, he replied.

And the pilot—that is to say, the true pilot—is he a captain of sailors or a mere sailor?

A captain of sailors.

The circumstance that he sails in the ship is not to be taken into account; neither is he to be called a sailor; the name pilot by which he is distinguished has nothing to do with sailing, but is significant of his skill and of his authority over the sailors.

Very true, he said.

Now, I said, every art has an interest?

Certainly.

For which the art has to consider and provide?

Yes, that is the aim of art.

And the interest of any art is the perfection of it—this and nothing else?

What do you mean?

I mean what I may illustrate negatively by the example of the body. Suppose you were to ask me whether the body is self-sufficing or has wants, I should reply: Certainly the body has wants; for the body may be ill and require to be cured, and has therefore interests to which the art of medicine ministers; and this is the origin and intention of medicine, as you will acknowledge. Am I not right?

Quite right, he replied.

But is the art of medicine or any other art faulty or deficient in any quality in the same way that the eye may be deficient in sight or the ear fail of hearing, and therefore requires another art to provide for the interests of seeing and hearing—has art in itself, I say, any similar liability to fault or defect, and does every art require another supplementary art to provide for its interests, and that another and another without end? Or have the arts to look only after their own interests? Or have they no need either of themselves or of another?—having no faults or defects, they have no need to correct them, either by the exercise of their own art or of any other; they have only to consider the interest of their subjectmatter. For every art remains pure and faultless while remaining true—that is to say, while perfect and unimpaired. Take the words in your precise sense, and tell me whether I am not right.

Yes, clearly.

Then medicine does not consider the interest of medicine, but the interest of the body?

True, he said.

Nor does the art of horsemanship consider the interests of the art of horsemanship, but the interests of the horse; neither do any other arts care for themselves, for they have no needs; they care only for that which is the subject of their art?

True, he said.

But surely, Thrasymachus, the arts are the superiors and rulers of their own subjects?

To this he assented with a good deal of reluctance.

Then, I said, no science or art considers or enjoins the interest of the stronger or superior, but only the interest of the subject and weaker?

He made an attempt to contest this proposition also, but finally acquiesced.

Then, I continued, no physician, in so far as he is a physician, considers his own good in what he prescribes, but the good of his patient; for the true physician is also a ruler having the human body as a subject, and is not a mere moneymaker; that has been admitted?

Yes.

And the pilot likewise, in the strict sense of the term, is a ruler of sailors, and not a mere sailor?

That has been admitted.

And such a pilot and ruler will provide and prescribe for the interest of the sailor who is under him, and not for his own or the ruler's interest?

He gave a reluctant "Yes."

Then, I said, Thrasymachus, there is no one in any rule who, in so far as he is a ruler, considers or enjoins what is for his own interest, but always what is for the interest of his subject or suitable to his art; to that he looks, and that alone he considers in everything which he says and does.

3d. Thrasymachus' Second Position: Justice as Another's Good

When we had got to this point in the argument, and everyone saw that the definition of justice had been completely upset, Thrasymachus, instead of replying to me, said, Tell me, Socrates, have you got a nurse?

Why do you ask such a question, I said, when you ought rather to be answering?

Because she leaves you to snivel, and never wipes your nose: she has not even taught you to know the shepherd from the sheep.

What makes you say that? I replied.

Because you fancy that the shepherd or neatherd fattens or tends the sheep or oxen with a view to their own good and not to the good of himself or his master; and you further imagine that the rulers of States, if they are true rulers, never think of their subjects as sheep, and that they are not studying their own advantage day and night. Oh, no; and so entirely astray are you in your ideas about the just and unjust as not even to know that justice and the just are in reality another's good; that is to say, the interest of the ruler and stronger, and the loss of the subject and servant; and injustice the opposite; for the unjust is lord over the truly simple and just: he is the stronger, and his subjects do what is for his interest, and minister to his happiness, which is very far from being their own. Consider further, most foolish Socrates, that the just is always a loser in comparison with the unjust. First of all, in private contracts: wherever the unjust is the partner of the just you will find that, when the partnership is dissolved, the unjust man has always more and the just less. Secondly, in their dealings with the State: when there is an income tax, the just man will pay more and the unjust less on the same amount of income; and when there is anything to be received the one gains nothing and the other much. Observe also what happens when they take an office; there is the just man neglecting his affairs and perhaps suffering other losses, and getting nothing out of the public, because he is just; moreover he is hated by his friends and acquaintance for refusing to serve them in unlawful ways. But all this is reversed in the case of the unjust man. I am speaking, as before, of injustice on a large scale in which the advantage of the unjust is most apparent; and my meaning will be most clearly seen if we turn to that highest form of injustice in which the criminal is the happiest of men, and the sufferers or those who refuse to do injustice are the most miserable—that is to say tyranny, which by fraud and force takes away the property of others, not little by little but wholesale; comprehending in one, things sacred as well as profane, private and public; for which acts of wrong, if he were detected perpetrating any one of them singly, he would be punished and incur great disgrace—they who do such wrong in particular cases are called robbers of temples, and manstealers and burglars and swindlers and thieves. But when a man besides taking away the money of the citizens has made slaves of them, then, instead of these names of reproach, he is termed happy and blessed, not only by the citizens but by all who hear of his having achieved the consummation of injustice. For mankind censure injustice, fearing that they may be the victims of it and not because they shrink from committing it. And thus, as I have shown, Socrates, injustice, when on a sufficient scale, has more strength and freedom and mastery than justice; and, as I said at first, justice is the interest of the stronger, whereas injustice is a man's own profit and interest.

Thrasymachus, when he had thus spoken, having, like a bathman, deluged our ears with his words, had a mind to go away. But the company would not let him; they insisted that he should remain and defend his position; and I myself added my own humble request that he would not leave us. Thrasymachus, I said to him, excellent man, how suggestive are your remarks! And are you going to run away before you have fairly taught or learned whether they are true or not? Is the attempt to determine the way of man's life so small a matter in your eyes—to determine how life may be passed by each one of us to the greatest advantage?

And do I differ from you, he said, as to the importance of the inquiry?

You appear rather, I replied, to have no care or thought about us, Thrasymachus—whether we live better or worse from not knowing what you say you know, is to you a matter of indifference. Prithee, friend, do not keep your knowledge to yourself; we are a large party; and any benefit which you confer upon us will be amply rewarded. For my own part I

openly declare that I am not convinced, and that I do not believe injustice to be more gainful than justice, even if uncontrolled and allowed to have free play. For, granting that there may be an unjust man who is able to commit injustice either by fraud or force, still this does not convince me of the superior advantage of injustice, and there may be others who are in the same predicament with myself. Perhaps we may be wrong; if so, you in your wisdom should convince us that we are mistaken in preferring justice to injustice.

And how am I to convince you, he said, if you are not already convinced by what I have just said; what more can I do for you? Would you have me put the proof bodily into your souls?

Heaven forbid! I said; I would only ask you to be consistent; or, if you change, change openly and let there be no deception....

[Although Socrates presents four objections to Thrasymachus' position, in the interests of brevity we will limit ouselves to the last two, which are actually the most interesting]

3e. Socrates' Third Objection: Justice as Co-operation

...Well, I said, Thrasymachus, that matter is now settled; but were we not also saying that injustice had strength—do you remember?

Yes, I remember, he said, but do not suppose that I approve of what you are saying or have no answer; if, however, I were to answer, you would be quite certain to accuse me of haranguing; therefore either permit me to have my say out, or if you would rather ask, do so, and I will answer "Very good," as they say to storytelling old women, and will nod "Yes" and "No."

Certainly not, I said, if contrary to your real opinion.

Yes, he said, I will, to please you, since you will not let me speak. What else would you have?

Nothing in the world, I said; and if you are so disposed I will ask and you shall answer.

Proceed.

Then I will repeat the question which I asked before, in order that our examination of the relative nature of justice and injustice may be carried on regularly. A statement was made that injustice is stronger and more powerful than justice, but now justice, having been identified with wisdom and virtue, is easily shown to be stronger than injustice, if injustice is ignorance; this can no longer be questioned by anyone. But I want to view the matter, Thrasymachus, in a different way: You would not deny that a State may be unjust and may be unjustly attempting to enslave other States, or may have already enslaved them, and may be holding many of them in subjection?

True, he replied; and I will add that the best and most perfectly unjust State will be most likely to do so.

I know, I said, that such was your position; but what I would further consider is, whether this power which is possessed by the superior State can exist or be exercised without justice or only with justice.

If you are right in your view, and justice is wisdom, then only with justice; but if I am right, then without justice.

I am delighted, Thrasymachus, to see you not only nodding assent and dissent, but making answers which are quite excellent.

That is out of civility to you, he replied.

You are very kind, I said; and would you have the goodness also to inform me, whether you think that a State, or an army, or a band of robbers and thieves, or any other gang of evildoers could act at all if they injured one another? No, indeed, he said, they could not.

But if they abstained from injuring one another, then they might act together better?

Yes.

And this is because injustice creates divisions and hatreds and fighting, and justice imparts harmony and friendship; is not that true, Thrasymachus?

I agree, he said, because I do not wish to quarrel with you.

How good of you, I said; but I should like to know also whether injustice, having this tendency to arouse hatred, wherever existing, among slaves or among freemen, will not make them hate one another and set them at variance and render them incapable of common action?

Certainly.

And even if injustice be found in two only, will they not quarrel and fight, and become enemies to one another and to the just?

They will.

And suppose injustice abiding in a single person, would your wisdom say that she loses or that she retains her natural power?

Let us assume that she retains her power.

Yet is not the power which injustice exercises of such a nature that wherever she takes up her abode, whether in a city, in an army, in a family, or in any other body, that body is, to begin with, rendered incapable of united action by reason of sedition and distraction? and does it not become its own enemy and at variance with all that opposes it, and with the just? Is not this the case?

Yes, certainly.

And is not injustice equally fatal when existing in a single person—in the first place rendering him incapable of action because he is not at unity with himself, and in the second place making him an enemy to himself and the just? Is not that true, Thrasymachus?

Yes. And, O my friend, I said, surely the gods are just?

Granted that they are. But, if so, the unjust will be the enemy of the gods, and the just will be their friends?

Feast away in triumph, and take your fill of the argument; I will not oppose you, lest I should displease the company.

3f. Socrates' Fourth Objection: Justice as Happiness

Well, then, proceed with your answers, and let me have the remainder of my repast. For we have already shown that the just are clearly wiser and better and abler than the unjust, and that the unjust are incapable of common action; nay, more, that to speak as we did of men who are evil acting at any time vigorously together, is not strictly true, for, if they had been perfectly evil, they would have laid hands upon one another; but it is evident that there must have been some remnant of justice in them, which enabled them to combine; if there had not been they would have injured one another as well as their victims; they were but halfvillains in their enterprises; for had they been whole villains, and utterly unjust, they would have been utterly incapable of action. That, as I believe, is the truth of the matter, and not what you said at first. But whether the just have a better and happier life than the unjust is a further question which we also proposed to consider. I think that they have, and for the reasons which I have given; but still I should like to examine further, for no light matter is at stake, nothing less than the rule of human life.

Proceed.

I will proceed by asking a question: Would you not say that a horse has some end?

I should.

And the end or use of a horse or of anything would be that which could not be accomplished, or not so well accomplished, by any other thing?

I do not understand, he said.

Let me explain: Can you see, except with the eye?

Certainly not.

Or hear, except with the ear?

No. These, then, may be truly said to be the ends of these organs?

They may.

But you can cut off a vinebranch with a dagger or with a chisel, and in many other ways?

Of course.

And yet not so well as with a pruninghook made for the purpose?

True.

May we not say that this is the end of a pruninghook?

We may.

Then now I think you will have no difficulty in understanding my meaning when I asked the question whether the end of anything would be that which could not be accomplished, or not so well accomplished, by any other thing?

I understand your meaning, he said, and assent.

And that to which an end is appointed has also an excellence? Need I ask again whether the eye has an end?

It has.

And has not the eye an excellence?

Yes.

And the ear has an end and an excellence also?

True.

And the same is true of all other things; they have each of them an end and a special excellence?

That is so.

Well, and can the eyes fulfil their end if they are wanting in their own proper excellence and have a defect instead?

How can they, he said, if they are blind and cannot see?

You mean to say, if they have lost their proper excellence, which is sight; but I have not arrived at that point yet. I would rather ask the question more generally, and only inquire whether the things which fulfil their ends fulfil them by their own proper excellence, and fail of fulfilling them by their own defect?

Certainly, he replied.

I might say the same of the ears; when deprived of their own proper excellence they cannot fulfil their end?

True.

And the same observation will apply to all other things?

I agree.

Well; and has not the soul an end which nothing else can fulfil? for example, to superintend and command and deliberate and the like. Are not these functions proper to the soul, and can they rightly be assigned to any other?

To no other.

And is not life to be reckoned among the ends of the soul?

Assuredly, he said.

And has not the soul an excellence also?

Yes.

And can she or can she not fulfil her own ends when deprived of that excellence?

She cannot.

Then an evil soul must necessarily be an evil ruler and superintendent, and the good soul a good ruler?

Yes, necessarily.

And we have admitted that justice is the excellence of the soul, and injustice the defect of the soul?

That has been admitted.

Then the just soul and the just man will live well, and the unjust man will live ill?

That is what your argument proves.

And he who lives well is blessed and happy, and he who lives ill the reverse of happy?

Certainly.

Then the just is happy, and the unjust miserable?

So be it.

But happiness, and not misery, is profitable?

Of course.

Then, my blessed Thrasymachus, injustice can never be more profitable than justice.

Let this, Socrates, he said, be your entertainment at the Bendidea.

For which I am indebted to you, I said, now that you have grown gentle toward me and have left off scolding. Nevertheless, I have not been well entertained; but that was my own fault and not yours. As an epicure snatches a taste of every dish which is successively brought to table, he not having allowed himself time to enjoy the one before, so have I gone from one subject to another without having discovered what I sought at first, the nature of justice. I left that inquiry and turned away to consider whether justice is virtue and wisdom, or evil and folly; and when there arose a further question about the comparative advantages of justice and injustice, I could not refrain from passing on to that. And the result of the whole discussion has been that I know nothing at all. For I know not what justice is, and therefore I am not likely to know whether it is or is not a virtue, nor can I say whether the just man is happy or unhappy.

BOOK II

With these words I was thinking that I had made an end of the discussion; but the end, in truth, proved to be only a beginning. For Glaucon, who is always the most pugnacious of men, was dissatisfied at Thrasymachus's retirement; he wanted to have the battle out. So he said to me: Socrates, do you wish really to persuade us, or only to seem to have persuaded us, that to be just is always better than to be unjust?

I should wish really to persuade you, I replied, if I could....

4. Glaucon: The Ring of Gyges

[Glaucon raises his objection to Socrates' position]

They say that to do injustice is, by nature, good; to

suffer injustice, evil; but that the evil is greater than the good. And so when men have both done and suffered injustice and have had experience of both, not being able to avoid the one and obtain the other, they think that they had better agree among themselves to have neither; hence there arise laws and mutual covenants; and that which is ordained by law is termed by them lawful and just. This they affirm to be the origin and nature of justice; it is a mean or compromise, between the best of all, which is to do injustice and not be punished, and the worst of all, which is to suffer injustice without the power of retaliation; and justice, being at a middle point between the two, is tolerated not as a good, but as the lesser evil, and honored by reason of the inability of men to do injustice. For no man who is worthy to be called a man would ever submit to such an agreement if he were able to resist; he would be mad if he did. Such is the received account, Socrates, of the nature and origin of justice.

Now that those who practise justice do so involuntarily and because they have not the power to be unjust will best appear if we imagine something of this kind: having given both to the just and the unjust power to do what they will, let us watch and see whither desire will lead them; then we shall discover in the very act the just and unjust man to be proceeding along the same road, following their interest, which all natures deem to be their good, and are only diverted into the path of justice by the force of law. The liberty which we are supposing may be most completely given to them in the form of such a power as is said to have been possessed by Gyges, the ancestor of Croesus the Lydian. According to the tradition, Gyges was a shepherd in the service of the King of Lydia; there was a great storm, and an earthquake made an opening in the earth at the place where he was feeding his flock. Amazed at the sight, he descended into the opening, where, among other marvels, he beheld a hollow brazen horse, having doors, at which he, stooping and looking in, saw a dead body of stature, as appeared to him, more than human and having nothing on but a gold ring; this he took from the finger of the dead and reascended. Now the shepherds met together, according to custom, that they might send their monthly report about the flocks to the King; into their assembly he came having the ring on his finger, and as he was sitting among them he chanced to turn the collet of the ring inside his hand, when instantly he became invisible to the rest of the company and they began to speak of him as if he were no longer present. He was astonished at this, and again touching the ring he turned the collet outward and reappeared; he made several trials of the ring, and always with the same result—when he turned the collet inward he became invisible, when outward he reappeared. Whereupon he contrived to be chosen one of the messengers who were sent to the court; where as soon as he arrived he seduced the Queen, and with her help conspired against the King and slew him and took the kingdom.

Suppose now that there were two such magic rings, and the just put on one of them and the unjust the other; no man can be imagined to be of such an iron nature that he would stand fast in justice. No man would keep his hands off what was not his own when he could safely take what he liked out of the market, or go into houses and lie with anyone at his pleasure, or kill or release from prison whom he would, and in all respects be like a god among men. Then the actions of the just would be as the actions of the unjust; they would both come at last to the same point. And this we may truly affirm to be a great proof that a man is just, not willingly or because he thinks that justice is any good to him individually, but of necessity, for wherever anyone thinks that he can safely be unjust, there he is unjust. For all men believe in their hearts that injustice is far more profitable to the individual than justice, and he who argues as I have been supposing, will say that they are right. If you could imagine anyone obtaining this power of becoming invisible, and never doing any wrong or touching what was another's, he would be thought by the lookers-on to be a most wretched idiot, although they would praise him to one another's faces, and keep up appearances with one another from a fear that they too might suffer injustice. Enough of this.

Now, if we are to form a real judgment of the life of the just and unjust, we must isolate them; there is no other way; and how is the isolation to be effected? I answer: Let the unjust man be entirely unjust, and the just man entirely just; nothing is to be taken away from either of them, and both are to be perfectly furnished for the work of their respective lives. First, let the unjust be like other distinguished masters of craft; like the skilful pilot or physician, who knows intuitively his own powers and keeps within their limits, and who, if he fails at any point, is able to recover himself. So let the unjust make his unjust attempts in the right way, and lie hidden if he means to be great in his injustice (he who is found out is nobody): for the highest reach of injustice is, to be deemed just when you are not. Therefore I say that in the perfectly unjust man we must assume the most perfect injustice; there is to be no deduction, but we must allow him, while doing the most unjust acts, to have acquired the greatest reputation for justice. If he have taken a false step he must be able to recover himself; he must be one who can speak with effect, if any of his deeds come to light, and who can force his way where force is required by his courage and strength, and command of money and friends. And at his side let us place the just man in his nobleness and simplicity, wishing, as Aeschylus says, to be and not to seem good. There must be no seeming, for if he seem to be just he will be honored and rewarded, and then we shall not know whether he is just for the sake of justice or for the sake of honor and rewards; therefore, let him be clothed in justice only, and have no other covering; and he must be imagined in a state of life the opposite of the former. Let him be the best of men, and let him be thought the worst; then he will have been put to the proof; and we shall see whether he will be affected by the fear of infamy and its consequences. And let him continue thus to the hour of death; being just and seeming to be unjust. When both have reached the uttermost extreme, the one of justice and the other of injustice, let judgment be given which of them is the happier of the two.

Heavens! my dear Glaucon, I said, how energetically you polish them up for the decision, first one and then the other, as if they were two statues.

I do my best, he said. And now that we know what they are like there is no difficulty in tracing out the sort of life which awaits either of them. This I will proceed to describe; but as you may think the description a little too coarse, I ask you to suppose, Socrates, that the words which follow are not mine. Let me put them into the mouths of the eulogists of injustice: They will tell you that the just man who is thought unjust will be scourged, racked, bound—

will have his eyes burnt out; and, at last, after suffering every kind of evil, he will be impaled. Then he will understand that he ought to seem only, and not to be, just; the words of Aeschylus may be more truly spoken of the unjust than of the just. For the unjust is pursuing a reality; he does not live with a view to appearances—he wants to be really unjust and not to seem only—"His mind has a soil deep and fertile, Out of which spring his prudent counsels."

In the first place, he is thought just, and therefore bears rule in the city; he can marry whom he will, and give in marriage to whom he will; also he can trade and deal where he likes, and always to his own advantage, because he has no misgivings about injustice; and at every contest, whether in public or private, he gets the better of his antagonists, and gains at their expense, and is rich, and out of his gains he can benefit his friends, and harm his enemies; moreover, he can offer sacrifices, and dedicate gifts to the gods abundantly and magnificently, and can honor the gods or any man whom he wants to honor in a far better style than the just, and therefore he is likely to be dearer than they are to the gods. And thus, Socrates, gods and men are said to unite in making the life of the unjust better than the life of the just.

Plato. "Republic." *The Dialogues of Plato.* Vol. 3. Translated by Benjamin Jowett. Oxford: Oxford University Press, 1892.

NICOMACHEAN ETHICS

ARISTOTLE (384-322 BCE)

It has been reported that the Greek philosopher Aristotle wrote at least three works on ethics. The most famous of these is known as the Nicomachean Ethics, *named after his son, Nicomachus. The text presents one of the most lucid accounts of virtue theory that has ever been written. Indeed, the theory that Aristotle lays out in his* Ethics *was highly influential in antiquity as well as in the Middle ages. His treatment of the virtues provided the foundation for Thomas Aquinas' moral theory, and therefore is crucial for understanding Christian moral philosophy. In more recent times, thinkers such as Phillipa Foot and Alasdair MacIntyre have argued for a return to precisely the sort of virtue ethics that Aristotle presents in order to correct some of the imbalances in more modern approaches to moral philosophy.*

The selection presented in this text comes mainly from the first three books of the Ethics *in which Aristotle discusses (1) happiness as the end of all human action, (2) virtue as the key to happiness, (3) the important role that habit plays in the teaching of virtue, and (4) specific virtues such as courage, temperance and generosity.*

BOOK ONE

1. The Good as the End of All Action

Every art and every inquiry, and similarly every action and pursuit, is thought to aim at some good; and for this reason the good has rightly been declared to be that at which all things aim. But a certain difference is found among ends; some are activities, others are products apart from the activities that produce them. Where there are ends apart from the actions, it is the nature of the products to be better than the activities.

Now, as there are many actions, arts, and sciences, their ends also are many; the end of the medical art is health, that of shipbuilding a vessel, that of strategy victory, that of economics wealth. But where such arts fall under a single capacity—as bridle-making and the other arts concerned with the equipment of horses fall under the art of riding, and this and every military action under strategy, in the same way other arts fall under yet others—in all of these the ends of the master arts are to be preferred to all the subordinate ends; for it is for the sake of

the former that the latter are pursued. It makes no difference whether the activities themselves are the ends of the actions, or something else apart from the activities, as in the case of the sciences just mentioned.

2. The Search for a Supreme Good

If, then, there is some end of the things we do, which we desire for its own sake (everything else being desired for the sake of this), and if we do not choose everything for the sake of something else (for at that rate the process would go on to infinity, so that our desire would be empty and vain), clearly this must be the good and the chief good. Will not the knowledge of it, then, have a great influence on life? Shall we not, like archers who have a mark to aim at, be more likely to hit upon what is right? If so, we must try, in outline at least, to determine what it is, and of which of the sciences or capacities it is the object....

4. Happiness as the Supreme Good

Let us resume our inquiry and state, in view of the

fact that all knowledge and every pursuit aims at some good, what it is that we say political science aims at and what is the highest of all goods achievable by action. Verbally there is very general agreement; for both the general run of men and people of superior refinement say that it is happiness (*eudaimonia*), and identify living well and doing well with being happy; but with regard to what happiness is they differ, and the many do not give the same account as the wise. For the former think it is some plain and obvious thing, like pleasure, wealth, or honour; they differ, however, from one another—and often even the same man identifies it with different things, with health when he is ill, with wealth when he is poor; but, conscious of their ignorance, they admire those who proclaim some great ideal that is above their comprehension. Now some thought that apart from these many goods there is another which is self-subsistent and causes the goodness of all these as well. To examine all the opinions that have been held were perhaps somewhat fruitless; enough to examine those that are most prevalent or that seem to be arguable.

5. Mistaken Views Concerning the Supreme Good

...Now the mass of mankind are evidently quite slavish in their tastes, preferring a life suitable to beasts, but they get some ground for their view from the fact that many of those in high places share the tastes of Sardanapallus. A consideration of the prominent types of life shows that people of superior refinement and of active disposition identify happiness with honor; for this is, roughly speaking, the end of the political life. But it seems too superficial to be what we are looking for, since it is thought to depend on those who bestow honor rather than on him who receives it, but the good we divine to be something proper to a man and not easily taken from him.

Further, men seem to pursue honor in order that they may be assured of their goodness; at least it is by men of practical wisdom that they seek to be honored, and among those who know them, and on the ground of their virtue; clearly, then, according to them, at any rate, virtue is better. And perhaps one might even suppose this to be, rather than honor, the

end of the political life. But even this appears somewhat incomplete; for possession of virtue seems actually compatible with being asleep, or with lifelong inactivity, and, further, with the greatest sufferings and misfortunes; but a man who was living so no one would call happy, unless he were maintaining a thesis at all costs. But enough of this; for the subject has been sufficiently treated even in the current discussions. Third comes the contemplative life, which we shall consider later.

The life of money-making is one undertaken under compulsion, and wealth is evidently not the good we are seeking; for it is merely useful and for the sake of something else. And so one might rather take the aforenamed objects to be ends; for they are loved for themselves. But it is evident that not even these are ends; yet many arguments have been thrown away in support of them. Let us leave this subject, then....

7. Happiness and the "Function" of Human Beings

...Presumably, however, to say that happiness is the chief good seems a platitude, and a clearer account of what it is still desired. This might perhaps be given, if we could first ascertain the function of man. For just as for a flute-player, a sculptor, or an artist, and, in general, for all things that have a function or activity, the good and the 'well' is thought to reside in the function, so would it seem to be for man, if he has a function. Have the carpenter, then, and the tanner certain functions or activities, and has man none? Is he born without a function? Or as eye, hand, foot, and in general each of the parts evidently has a function, may one lay it down that man similarly has a function apart from all these? What then can this be? Life seems to be common even to plants, but we are seeking what is peculiar to man. Let us exclude, therefore, the life of nutrition and growth. Next there would be a life of perception, but it also seems to be common even to the horse, the ox, and every animal.

There remains, then, an active life of the element that has a rational principle; of this, one part has such a principle in the sense of being obedient to one, the other in the sense of possessing one and exercising thought. And, as 'life of the rational element' also has two meanings, we must state that life in the sense of activity is what we mean; for this seems to be the more proper sense of the term. Now if the function of man is an activity of soul which follows or implies a rational principle, and if we say 'so-and-so-and 'a good so-and-so' have a function which is the same in kind, e.g. a lyre, and a good lyre-player, and so without qualification in all cases, eminence in respect of goodness being added to the name of the function (for the function of a lyre-player is to play the lyre, and that of a good lyre-player is to do so well): if this is the case, and we state the function of man to be a certain kind of life, and this to be an activity or actions of the soul implying a rational principle, and the function of a good man to be the good and noble performance of these, and if any action is well performed when it is performed in accordance with the appropriate excellence: if this is the case, human good turns out to be activity of soul in accordance with virtue (*arete*), and if there are more than one virtue, in accordance with the best and most complete.

But we must add 'in a complete life.' For one swallow does not make a summer, nor does one day; and so too one day, or a short time, does not make a man blessed and happy....

8. External Goods Also Necessary for Happiness

...Yet evidently, as we said, [human happiness] needs the external goods as well; for it is impossible, or not easy, to do noble acts without the proper equipment. In many actions we use friends and riches and political power as instruments; and there are some things the lack of which takes the lustre from happiness, as good birth, goodly children, beauty; for the man who is very ugly in appearance or ill-born or solitary and childless is not very likely to be happy, and perhaps a man would be still less likely if he had thoroughly bad children or friends or had lost good children or friends by death. As we said, then, happiness seems to need this sort of prosperity in addition; for which reason some identify happiness with good fortune, though others identify it with virtue.

10a. Happiness and the Course of a Lifetime

Must no one at all, then, be called happy while he lives; must we, as Solon says, see the end? Even if we are to lay down this doctrine, is it also the case that a man is happy when he is dead? Or is not this quite absurd, especially for us who say that happiness is an activity? But if we do not call the dead man happy, and if Solon does not mean this, but that one can then safely call a man blessed as being at last beyond evils and misfortunes, this also affords matter for discussion; for both evil and good are thought to exist for a dead man, as much as for one who is alive but not aware of them; e.g. honors and dishonors and the good or bad fortunes of children and in general of descendants. And this also presents a problem; for though a man has lived happily up to old age and has had a death worthy of his life, many reverses may befall his descendants—some of them may be good and attain the life they deserve, while with others the opposite may be the case; and clearly too the degrees of relationship between them and their ancestors may vary indefinitely. It would be odd, then, if the dead man were to share in these changes and become at one time happy, at another wretched; while it would also be odd if the fortunes of the descendants did not for some time have some effect on the happiness of their ancestors.

10b. Further Thoughts on External Goods

But we must return to our first difficulty; for perhaps by a consideration of it our present problem might be solved. Now if we must see the end and only then call a man happy, not as being happy but as having been so before, surely this is a paradox, that when he is happy the attribute that belongs to him is not to be truly predicated of him because we do not wish to call living men happy, on account of the changes that may befall them, and because we have assumed happiness to be something permanent and by no means easily changed, while a single man may suffer many turns of fortune's wheel. For clearly if we were to keep pace with his fortunes, we should often call the same man happy and again wretched, making the happy man out to be chameleon and insecurely based. Or is this keeping pace with his fortunes quite wrong? Success or failure in life does not depend on these, but human life, as we said, needs these as mere additions, while virtuous activities or their opposites are what constitute happiness or the reverse.

The question we have now discussed confirms our definition. For no function of man has so much permanence as virtuous activities (these are thought to be more durable even than knowledge of the sciences), and of these themselves the most valuable are more durable because those who are happy spend their life most readily and most continuously in these; for this seems to be the reason why we do not forget them. The attribute in question, then, will belong to the happy man, and he will be happy throughout his life; for always, or by preference to everything else, he will be engaged in virtuous action and contemplation, and he will bear the chances of life most nobly and altogether decorously, if he is 'truly good' and 'foursquare beyond reproach'.

Now many events happen by chance, and events differing in importance; small pieces of good fortune or of its opposite clearly do not weigh down the scales of life one way or the other, but a multitude of great events if they turn out well will make life happier (for not only are they themselves such as to add beauty to life, but the way a man deals with them may be noble and good), while if they turn out ill they crush and maim happiness; for they both bring pain with them and hinder many activities. Yet even in these nobility shines through, when a man bears with resignation many great misfortunes, not through insensibility to pain but through nobility and greatness of soul.

If activities are, as we said, what gives life its character, no happy man can become miserable; for he will never do the acts that are hateful and mean. For the man who is truly good and wise, we think, bears all the chances life with nobility and always makes the best of circumstances, as a good general makes the best military use of the army at his command and a good shoemaker makes the best shoes out of the hides that are given him; and so with all other craftsmen. And if this is the case, the happy man can never become miserable; though he will not reach blessedness, if he meet with fortunes like those of Priam.

Nor, again, is he many-colored and changeable; for neither will he be moved from his happy state easily or by any ordinary misadventures, but only by many great ones, nor, if he has had many great misadventures, will he recover his happiness in a short time, but, if at all, only in a long and complete one in which he has attained many splendid successes.

When then should we not say that he is happy who is active in accordance with complete virtue and is sufficiently equipped with external goods, not for some chance period but throughout a complete life? Or must we add 'and who is destined to live thus and die as befits his life'? Certainly the future is obscure to us, while happiness, we claim, is an end and something in every way final. If so, we shall call happy those among living men in whom these conditions are, and are to be, fulfilled, but happy men. So much for these questions.

BOOK TWO

1. Moral Virtue and Habit

Virtue, then, being of two kinds, intellectual and moral, intellectual virtue in the main owes both its birth and its growth to teaching (for which reason it requires experience and time), while moral virtue comes about as a result of habit, whence also its name (*ethike*) is one that is formed by a slight variation from the word ethos (habit). From this it is also plain that none of the moral virtues arises in us by nature; for nothing that exists by nature can form a habit contrary to its nature. For instance the stone which by nature moves downwards cannot be habituated to move upwards, not even if one tries to train it by throwing it up ten thousand times; nor can fire be habituated to move downwards, nor can anything else that by nature behaves in one way be trained to behave in another. Neither by nature, then, nor contrary to nature do the virtues arise in us; rather we are adapted by nature to receive them, and are made perfect by habit.

Again, of all the things that come to us by nature we first acquire the potentiality and later exhibit the activity (this is plain in the case of the senses; for it was not by often seeing or often hearing that we got these senses, but, on the contrary, we had them before we used them, and did not come to have them by using them); but the virtues we get by first exercising them, as also happens in the case of the arts as well. For the things we have to learn before we can do them, we learn by doing them, e.g. men become builders by building and lyreplayers by playing the lyre; so too we become just by doing just acts, temperate by doing temperate acts, brave by doing brave acts.

This is confirmed by what happens in states; for legislators make the citizens good by forming habits in them, and this is the wish of every legislator, and those who do not effect it miss their mark, and it is in this that a good constitution differs from a bad one.

Again, it is from the same causes and by the same means that every virtue is both produced and destroyed, and similarly every art; for it is from playing the lyre that both good and bad lyre-players are produced. And the corresponding statement is true of builders and of all the rest; men will be good or bad builders as a result of building well or badly. For if this were not so, there would have been no need of a teacher, but all men would have been born good or bad at their craft. This, then, is the case with the virtues also; by doing the acts that we do in our transactions with other men we become just or unjust, and by doing the acts that we do in the presence of danger, and being habituated to feel fear or confidence, we become brave or cowardly. The same is true of appetites and feelings of anger; some men become temperate and good-tempered, others self-indulgent and irascible, by behaving in one way or the other in the appropriate circumstances. Thus, in one word, states of character arise out of like activities. This is why the activities we exhibit must be of a certain kind; it is because the states of character correspond to the differences between these. It makes no small difference, then, whether we form habits of one kind or of another from our very youth; it makes a very great difference, or rather all the difference....

3. Pleasure and Pain as the Test of Virtue

We must take as a sign of states of character the pleasure or pain that ensues on acts; for the man who abstains from bodily pleasures and delights in this very fact is temperate, while the man who is annoyed at it is self-indulgent, and he who stands his ground against things that are terrible and delights in this or at least is not pained is brave, while the man who is pained is a coward. For moral excellence is concerned with pleasures and pains; it is on account of the pleasure that we do bad things, and on account of the pain that we abstain from noble ones. Hence we ought to have been brought up in a particular way from our very youth, as Plato says, so as both to delight in and to be pained by the things that we ought; for this is the right education.

Again, if the virtues are concerned with actions and passions, and every passion and every action is accompanied by pleasure and pain, for this reason also virtue will be concerned with pleasures and pains. This is indicated also by the fact that punishment is inflicted by these means; for it is a kind of cure, and it is the nature of cures to be effected by contraries.

Again, as we said but lately, every state of soul has a nature relative to and concerned with the kind of things by which it tends to be made worse or better; but it is by reason of pleasures and pains that men become bad, by pursuing and avoiding these—either the pleasures and pains they ought not or when they ought not or as they ought not, or by going wrong in one of the other similar ways that may be distinguished. Hence men even define the virtues as certain states of impassivity and rest; not well, however, because they speak absolutely, and do not say 'as one ought' and 'as one ought not' and 'when one ought or ought not', and the other things that may be added. We assume, then, that this kind of excellence tends to do what is best with regard to pleasures and pains, and vice does the contrary.

The following facts also may show us that virtue and vice are concerned with these same things. There being three objects of choice and three of avoidance, the noble, the advantageous, the pleasant, and their contraries, the base, the injurious, the painful, about all of these the good man tends to go right and the bad man to go wrong, and especially about pleasure; for this is common to the animals, and also it accompanies all objects of choice; for even the noble and the advantageous appear pleasant.

Again, it has grown up with us all from our infancy; this is why it is difficult to rub off this passion, engrained as it is in our life. And we measure even our actions, some of us more and others less, by the rule of pleasure and pain. For this reason, then, our whole inquiry must be about these; for to feel delight and pain rightly or wrongly has no small effect on our actions.

Again, it is harder to fight with pleasure than with anger, to use Heraclitus' phrase, but both art and virtue are always concerned with what is harder; for even the good is better when it is harder. Therefore, for this reason also the whole concern both of virtue and of political science is with pleasures and pains; for the man who uses these well will be good, he who uses them badly will be bad.

That virtue, then, is concerned with pleasures and pains, and that by the acts from which it arises it is both increased and, if they are done differently, destroyed, and that the acts from which it arose are those in which it actualizes itself—let this be taken as said.

4. Becoming Virtuous

The question might be asked, what we mean by saying that we must become just by doing just acts, and temperate by doing temperate acts; for if men do just and temperate acts, they are already just and temperate, exactly as, if they do what is in accordance with the laws of grammar and of music, they are grammarians and musicians.

Or is this not true even of the arts? It is possible to do something that is in accordance with the laws of grammar, either by chance or at the suggestion of another. A man will be a grammarian, then, only when he has both done something grammatical and done it grammatically; and this means doing it in accordance with the grammatical knowledge in himself.

Again, the case of the arts and that of the virtues are not similar; for the products of the arts have their goodness in themselves, so that it is enough that they should have a certain character, but if the acts that are in accordance with the virtues have themselves a certain character it does not follow that they are done justly or temperately. The agent also must be in a certain condition when he does them; in the first place he must have knowledge, secondly he must choose the acts, and choose them for their own sakes, and thirdly his action must proceed from a firm and unchangeable character. These are not reckoned as conditions of the possession of the arts, except the bare knowledge; but as a condition of the possession of the virtues knowledge has little or no weight, while the other conditions count not for a little but for everything, i.e. the very conditions which result from often doing just and temperate acts.

Actions, then, are called just and temperate when they are such as the just or the temperate man would do; but it is not the man who does these that is just and temperate, but the man who also does them as just and temperate men do them. It is well said, then, that it is by doing just acts that the just man is produced, and by doing temperate acts the temperate man; without doing these no one would have even a prospect of becoming good.

But most people do not do these, but take refuge in theory and think they are being philosophers and will become good in this way, behaving somewhat like patients who listen attentively to their doctors, but do none of the things they are ordered to do. As the latter will not be made well in body by such a course of treatment, the former will not be made well in soul by such a course of philosophy.

6a. Defining Virtue

We must, however, not only describe virtue as a state of character, but also say what sort of state it is. We may remark, then, that every virtue or excellence both brings into good condition the thing of which it is the excellence and makes the work of that thing be done well; e.g. the excellence of the eye makes both the eye and its work good; for it is by the excellence of the eye that we see well. Similarly the excellence of the horse makes a horse both good in itself and good at running and at carrying its rider and at awaiting the attack of the enemy. Therefore, if this is true in every case, the virtue of man also will be the state of character which makes a man good and which makes him do his own work well.

How this is to happen we have stated already, but it will be made plain also by the following consideration of the specific nature of virtue. In everything that is continuous and divisible it is possible to take more, less, or an equal amount, and that either in terms of the thing itself or relatively to us; and the equal is an intermediate between excess and defect. By the intermediate in the object I mean that which is equidistant from each of the extremes, which is one and the same for all men; by the intermediate relatively to us that which is neither too much nor too little—and this is not one, nor the same for all. For instance, if ten is many and two is few, six is the intermediate, taken in terms of the object; for it exceeds and is exceeded by an equal amount; this is intermediate according to arithmetical proportion. But the intermediate relatively to us is not to be taken so; if ten pounds are too much for a particular person to eat and two too little, it does not follow that the trainer will order six pounds; for this also is perhaps too much for the person who is to take it, or too little—too little for Milo, too much for the beginner in athletic exercises. The same is true of running and wrestling. Thus a master of any art avoids excess and defect, but seeks the intermediate and chooses this—the intermediate not in the object but relatively to us.

If it is thus, then, that every art does its work well—by looking to the intermediate and judging its works by this standard (so that we often say of good works of art that it is not possible either to take away or to add anything, implying that excess and defect destroy the goodness of works of art, while the mean preserves it; and good artists, as we say, look to this in their work), and if, further, virtue is more exact and better than any art, as nature also is, then virtue must have the quality of aiming at the intermediate. I mean moral virtue; for it is this that is concerned with passions and actions, and in these there is excess, defect, and the intermediate. For instance, both fear and confidence and appetite and anger and pity and in general pleasure and pain may be felt both too much and too little, and in both cases not well; but to feel them at the right times, with reference to the right objects, towards the right people, with the right motive, and in the right way, is what is both intermediate and best, and this is characteristic of virtue. Similarly with regard to actions also there is excess, defect, and the intermediate. Now virtue is concerned with passions and actions, in which excess is a form of failure, and so is defect, while the

intermediate is praised and is a form of success; and being praised and being successful are both characteristics of virtue. Therefore virtue is a kind of mean, since, as we have seen, it aims at what is intermediate.

Again, it is possible to fail in many ways ..., while to succeed is possible only in one way (for which reason also one is easy and the other difficult-to miss the mark easy, to hit it difficult); for these reasons also, then, excess and defect are characteristic of vice, and the mean of virtue; For men are good in but one way, but bad in many.

6b. The Golden Mean

Virtue, then, is a state of character concerned with choice, lying in a mean, i.e. the mean relative to us, this being determined by a rational principle, and by that principle by which the man of practical wisdom would determine it. Now it is a mean between two vices, that which depends on excess and that which depends on defect; and again it is a mean because the vices respectively fall short of or exceed what is right in both passions and actions, while virtue both finds and chooses that which is intermediate. Hence in respect of its substance and the definition which states its essence virtue is a mean, with regard to what is best and right an extreme.

But not every action nor every passion admits of a mean; for some have names that already imply badness, e.g. spite, shamelessness, envy, and in the case of actions adultery, theft, murder; for all of these and suchlike things imply by their names that they are themselves bad, and not the excesses or deficiencies of them. It is not possible, then, ever to be right with regard to them; one must always be wrong. Nor does goodness or badness with regard to such things depend on committing adultery with the right woman, at the right time, and in the right way, but simply to do any of them is to go wrong. It would be equally absurd, then, to expect that in unjust, cowardly, and voluptuous action there should be a mean, an excess, and a deficiency; for at that rate there would be a mean of excess and of deficiency, an excess of excess, and a deficiency of deficiency. But as there is no excess and deficiency of temperance and courage because what is intermediate is in a sense an extreme, so too of the actions we have mentioned there is no mean nor any excess and deficiency, but however they are done they are wrong; for in general there is neither a mean of excess and deficiency, nor excess and deficiency of a mean.

7. Illustrating the Mean

We must, however, not only make this general statement, but also apply it to the individual facts. For among statements about conduct those which are general apply more widely, but those which are particular are more genuine, since conduct has to do with individual cases, and our statements must harmonize with the facts in these cases. We may take these cases from our table. With regard to feelings of fear and confidence courage is the mean..., while the man who exceeds in confidence is foolhardy, and he who exceeds in fear and falls short in confidence is a coward.

With regard to pleasures and pains—not all of them, and not so much with regard to the pains—the mean is temperance, the excess self-indulgence. Persons deficient with regard to the pleasures are not often found; hence such persons also have received no name. But let us call them 'insensible'.

With regard to giving and taking of money the mean is generosity, the excess and the defect extravagance and stinginess. In these actions people exceed and fall short in contrary ways; the prodigal exceeds in spending and falls short in taking, while the mean man exceeds in taking and falls short in spending. (At present we are giving a mere outline or summary, and are satisfied with this; later these states will be more exactly determined.)....

With regard to honour and dishonour the mean is proper pride, the excess is known as a sort of 'empty vanity', and the deficiency is undue humility....

With regard to anger also there is an excess, a deficiency, and a mean. Although they can scarcely be said to have names, yet since we call the intermediate person good-tempered let us call the mean good temper; of the persons at the extremes let the one who exceeds be called irascible, and his vice irascibility, and the man who falls short [can be called] an apathetic sort of person....

With regard to pleasantness in the giving of amusement the intermediate person is witty and the disposition wittiness, the excess is buffoonery and the person characterized by it a buffoon, while the man who falls short is a sort of boor and his state is boorishness....

9. Three Rules for Guidance

That moral virtue is a mean, then, and in what sense it is so, and that it is a mean between two vices, the one involving excess, the other deficiency, and that it is such because its character is to aim at what is intermediate in passions and in actions, has been sufficiently stated. Hence also it is no easy task to be good. For in everything it is no easy task to find the middle, e.g. to find the middle of a circle is not for every one but for him who knows; so, too, anyone can get angry—that is easy—or give or spend money; but to do this to the right person, to the right extent, at the right time, with the right motive, and in the right way, that is not for every one, nor is it easy; it is for this reason that goodness is both rare and laudable and noble.

(1) Hence he who aims at the intermediate must first depart from what is the more contrary to it, as Calypso advises: "Hold the ship out beyond that surf and spray." For of the extremes one is more erroneous, one less so; therefore, since to hit the mean is hard in the extreme, we must as a second best, as people say, take the least of the evils; and this will be done best in the way we describe. But we must consider the things towards which we ourselves also are easily carried away; for some of us tend to one thing, some to another; and this will be recognizable from the pleasure and the pain we feel. We must drag ourselves away to the contrary extreme; for we shall get into the intermediate state by drawing well away from error, as people do in straightening sticks that are bent.

(2) Now in everything the pleasant or pleasure is most to be guarded against; for we do not judge it impartially. We ought, then, to feel towards pleasure as the elders of the people felt towards Helen, and in all circumstances repeat their saying; for if we dismiss pleasure thus we are less likely to go astray. It is by doing this, then, (to sum the matter up) that we

shall best be able to hit the mean.

(3) But this is no doubt difficult, and especially in individual cases; for it is not easy to determine both how and with whom and on what provocation and how long one should be angry; for we too sometimes praise those who fall short and call them good-tempered, but sometimes we praise those who get angry and call them manly. The man, however, who deviates little from goodness is not blamed, whether he do so in the direction of the more or of the less, but only the man who deviates more widely; for he does not fail to be noticed. But up to what point and to what extent a man must deviate before he becomes blameworthy it is not easy to determine by reasoning, any more than anything else that is perceived by the senses; such things depend on particular facts, and the decision rests with perception. So much, then, is plain, that the intermediate state is in all things to be praised, but that we must incline sometimes towards the excess, sometimes towards the deficiency; for so shall we most easily hit the mean and what is right....

Aristotle. *Nicomachean Ethics*. Trans. W.D. Ross. Oxford: Clarendon Press, 1908. The text has been updated by the editor.

SELFLESS LOVE

JESUS OF NAZARETH (4 BCE-30 AD)

At the heart of the New Testament is the radical ethic of Jesus of Nazareth and his early followers that advocates the virtues of selfless love, compassion for the most vulnerable members of the society, and a life of radical poverty. The New Testament is so much a part of our culture in the West that we often forget just how unsettling the moral exhortations of Jesus are if they are taken seriously. Although it may be impossible to eliminate the centuries of dogmatic baggage that have influenced our reading of Scripture, if we take the time to read selections like those included below with a fresh eye—as though we had never encountered them before—what we are left with is basically a eudaimonistic ethic that proposes the most radical sort of altruistic behavior as the key to human happiness.

The Sermon on the Mount
Matthew 5:1-48

When Jesus saw the crowds, He went up on the mountain; and after He sat down, His disciples came to Him. He opened His mouth and began to teach them, saying,

"Blessed are the poor in spirit, for theirs is the kingdom of heaven.
Blessed are those who mourn, for they shall be comforted.
Blessed are the gentle, for they shall inherit the earth.
Blessed are those who hunger and thirst for righteousness, for they shall be satisfied.
Blessed are the merciful, for they shall receive mercy.
Blessed are the pure in heart, for they shall see God.
Blessed are the peacemakers, for they shall be called sons of God.
Blessed are those who have been persecuted for the sake of righteousness, for theirs is the kingdom of heaven.

Blessed are you when people insult you and persecute you, and falsely say all kinds of evil against you because of Me. Rejoice and be glad, for your reward in heaven is great; for in the same way they persecuted the prophets who were before you.

"You are the salt of the earth; but if the salt has become tasteless, how can it be made salty again? It is no longer good for anything, except to be thrown out and trampled under foot by men.

"You are the light of the world. A city set on a hill cannot be hidden; nor does anyone light a lamp and put it under a basket, but on the lampstand, and it gives light to all who are in the house. Let your light shine before men in such a way that they may see your good works, and glorify your Father who is in heaven.

"Do not think that I came to abolish the Law or the Prophets; I did not come to abolish but to fulfill. For truly I say to you, until heaven and earth pass away, not the smallest letter or stroke shall pass from the Law until all is accomplished. Whoever then annuls one of the least of these commandments, and teaches others to do the same, shall be called least in the kingdom of heaven; but whoever keeps and teaches them, he shall be called great in the kingdom of heaven.

"For I say to you that unless your righteousness surpasses that of the scribes and Pharisees, you will not enter the kingdom of heaven."

"You have heard that the ancients were told, 'You shall not commit murder' and 'Whoever commits murder shall be liable to the court.' But I say to you that everyone who is angry with his brother shall be guilty before the court; and whoever says to his brother, 'You good-for-nothing,' shall be guilty before the supreme court; and whoever says, 'You fool,' shall be guilty enough to go into the fiery hell. Therefore if you are presenting your offering at the altar, and there remember that your brother has something against you, leave your offering there before the altar and go; first be reconciled to your brother, and then come and present your offering. Make friends quickly with your opponent at law while you are with him on the way, so that your opponent may not hand you over to the judge, and the judge to the officer, and you be thrown into prison. Truly I say to you, you will not come out of there until you have paid up the last cent.

"You have heard that it was said, 'You shall not commit adultery'; but I say to you that everyone who looks at a woman with lust for her has already committed adultery with her in his heart. If your right eye makes you stumble, tear it out and throw it from you; for it is better for you to lose one of the parts of your body, than for your whole body to be thrown into hell. If your right hand makes you stumble, cut it off and throw it from you; for it is better for you to lose one of the parts of your body, than for your whole body to go into hell.

"It was said, 'Whoever sends his wife away, let him give her a certificate of divorce.'; but I say to you that everyone who divorces his wife, except for the reason of unchastity, makes her commit adultery; and whoever marries a divorced woman commits adultery.

Again, you have heard that the ancients were told, 'You shall not make false vows, but shall fulfill your vows to the Lord.' But I say to you, make no oath at all, either by heaven, for it is the throne of God, or by the earth, for it is the footstool of His feet, or by Jerusalem, for it is the City of the Great King. Nor shall you make an oath by your head, for you cannot make one hair white or black. But let your statement be, 'Yes, yes' or 'No, no'; anything beyond these is of evil.

You have heard that it was said, 'an eye for an eye, and a tooth for a tooth.' But I say to you, do not resist an evil person; but whoever slaps you on your right cheek, turn the other to him also. If anyone wants to sue you and take your shirt, let him have your coat also. Whoever forces you to go one mile, go with him two. Give to him who asks of you, and do not turn away from him who wants to borrow from you.

You have heard that it was said, 'You shall love your neighbor and hate your enemy.' But I say to you, love your enemies and pray for those who persecute you, so that you may be sons of your Father who is in heaven; for He causes His sun to rise on the evil and the good, and sends rain on the righteous and the unrighteous. For if you love those who love you, what reward do you have? Do not even the tax collectors do the same? If you greet only your brothers, what more are you doing than others? Do not even the Gentiles do the same? Therefore you are to be perfect, as your heavenly Father is perfect.

Who is the Greatest?
Mark 9:33-37

They came to Capernaum; and when He was in the house, He began to question them, "What were you discussing on the way?" But they kept silent, for on the way they had discussed with one another which of them was the greatest. Sitting down, He called the twelve and said to them, "If anyone wants to be first, he shall be last of all and servant of all." Taking a child, He set him before them, and taking him in His arms, He said to them, "Whoever receives one child like this in My name receives Me; and whoever receives Me does not receive Me, but Him who sent Me."

The Danger of Riches
Mark 10:17-31

As He was setting out on a journey, a man ran up to Him and knelt before Him, and asked Him, "Good Teacher, what shall I do to inherit eternal life?" And Jesus said to him, "Why do you call Me good? No one is good except God alone. You know the commandments, 'Do not murder, do not commit adultery, do not steal, do not bear false witness, do not defraud, honor your father and mother.'" And he said to Him, "Teacher, I have kept all these things from my youth up." Looking at him, Jesus felt a love for him and said to him, "One thing you lack: go and sell all you possess and give to the poor, and you will have treasure in heaven; and come, follow Me." But at these words he was saddened, and he went away grieving, for he was one who owned much property.

And Jesus, looking around, said to His disciples, "How hard it will be for those who are wealthy to enter the kingdom of God!" The disciples were amazed at His words. But Jesus answered again and said to them, "Children, how hard it is to enter the kingdom of God! It is easier for a camel to go through the eye of a needle than for a rich man to enter the kingdom of God." They were even more astonished and said to Him, "Then who can be saved?" Looking at them, Jesus said, "With people it is impossible, but not with God; for all things are possible with God."

Peter began to say to Him, "Behold, we have left everything and followed You. Jesus said, "Truly I say to you, there is no one who has left house or brothers or sisters or mother or father or children or farms, for My sake and for the gospel's sake, but that he will receive a hundred times as much now in the present age, houses and brothers and sisters and mothers and children and farms, along with persecutions; and in the age to come, eternal life. But many who are first will be last, and the last, first."

Servants of All
Mark 10:15-45

James and John, the two sons of Zebedee, came up to Jesus, saying, "Teacher, we want You to do for us whatever we ask of You." And He said to them, "What do you want Me to do for you?" They said to Him, "Grant that we may sit, one on Your right and one on Your left, in Your glory." But Jesus said to them, "You do not know what you are asking. Are you able to drink the cup that I drink, or to be baptized with the baptism with which I am baptized?"

They said to Him, "We are able." And Jesus said to them, "The cup that I drink you shall drink; and you shall be baptized with the baptism with which I am baptized. But to sit on My right or on My left, this is not Mine to give; but it is for those for whom it has been prepared."

Hearing this, the ten began to feel indignant with James and John. Calling them to Himself, Jesus said to them, "You know that those who are recognized as rulers of the Gentiles lord it over them; and their great men exercise authority over them. But it is not this way among you, but whoever wishes to become great among you shall be your servant; and whoever wishes to be first among you shall be slave of all. For even the Son of Man did not come to be served, but to serve, and to give His life a ransom for many."

The Greatest Commandment
Mark 12:28-34

One of the scribes came and heard them arguing, and recognizing that He had answered them well, asked Him, "What commandment is the foremost of all?" Jesus answered, "The foremost is, 'Hear, O Israel! The Lord our God is one Lord; and you shall love the Lord your God with all your heart, and with all your soul, and with all your strength.' "The second is this, 'You shall love your neighbor as yourself.' There is no other commandment greater than these." The scribe said to Him, "Right, Teacher; You have truly stated that He is one, and there is no one else besides him; and to love him with all the hear and with all the understanding and with all the strength, and to love one's neighbor as himself, is much more than all burnt offerings and sacrifices." When Jesus saw that he had answered intelligently, He said to him, "You are not far from the kingdom of God." After that, no one would venture to ask Him any more questions.

The Good Samaritan
Luke 10:30-37

Jesus replied and said, "A man was going down from Jerusalem to Jericho, and fell among robbers, and they stripped him and beat him, and went away leaving him half dead. And by chance a priest was going down on that road, and when he saw him, he passed by on the other side. Likewise a Levite also, when he came to the place and saw him, passed by on the other side. But a Samaritan, who was on a journey, came upon him; and when he saw him, he felt compassion, and came to him and bandaged up his wounds, pouring oil and wine on them; and he put him on his own beast, and brought him to an inn and took care of him. On the next day he took out two denarii and gave them to the innkeeper and said, 'Take care of him; and whatever more you spend, when I return I will repay you.' "Which of these three do you think proved to be a neighbor to the man who fell into the robbers' hands?" And he said, "The one who showed mercy toward him." Then Jesus said to him, "Go and do the same."

Where is Your Treasure?
Luke 12: 33-34

"Sell your possessions and give to charity; make yourselves money belts which do not wear out, an unfailing treasure in heaven, where no thief comes near nor moth destroys. For where your treasure is, there your heart will be also."

The Humble and the Exalted
Luke 14: 7-15

And He began speaking a parable to the invited guests when He noticed how they had been picking out the places of honor at the table, saying to them, "When you are invited by someone to a wedding feast, do not take the place of honor, for someone more distinguished than you may have been invited by him, and he who invited you both will come and say to you, 'Give your place to this man,' and then in disgrace you proceed to occupy the last place. But when you are invited, go and recline at the last place, so that when the one who has invited you comes, he may say to you, 'Friend, move up higher'; then you will have honor in the sight of all who are at the table with you. For everyone who exalts himself will be humbled, and he who humbles himself will be exalted." And He also went on to say to the one who had invited Him, "When you give a luncheon or

a dinner, do not invite your friends or your brothers or your relatives or rich neighbors, otherwise they may also invite you in return and that will be your repayment. But when you give a reception, invite the poor, the crippled, the lame, the blind, and you will be blessed, since they do not have the means to repay you; for you will be repaid at the resurrection of the righteous." When one of those who were reclining at the table with Him heard this, he said to Him, "Blessed is everyone who will eat bread in the kingdom of God!"

Discipleship Tested
Luke 14:25-35

Now large crowds were going along with Him; and He turned and said to them, "If anyone comes to Me, and does not hate his own father and mother and wife and children and brothers and sisters, yes, and even his own life, he cannot be My disciple. Whoever does not carry his own cross and come after Me cannot be My disciple. For which one of you, when he wants to build a tower, does not first sit down and calculate the cost to see if he has enough to complete it? Otherwise, when he has laid a foundation and is not able to finish, all who observe it begin to ridicule him, saying, 'This man began to build and was not able to finish.' Or what king, when he sets out to meet another king in battle, will not first sit down and consider whether he is strong enough with ten thousand men to encounter the one coming against him with twenty thousand? Or else, while the other is still far away, he sends a delegation and asks for terms of peace. So then, none of you can be My disciple who does not give up all his own possessions. Therefore, salt is good; but if even salt has become tasteless, with what will it be seasoned? It is useless either for the soil or for the manure pile; it is thrown out. He who has ears to hear, let him hear."

The Right Use of Money
Luke 16:9-13

"And I say to you, make friends for yourselves by means of the wealth of unrighteousness, so that when it fails, they will receive you into the eternal dwellings. He who is faithful in a very little thing is faithful also in much; and he who is unrighteous in a very little thing is unrighteous also in much. Therefore if you have not been faithful in the use of unrighteous wealth, who will entrust the true riches to you? And if you have not been faithful in the use of that which is another's, who will give you that which is your own? No servant can serve two masters; for either he will hate the one and love the other, or else he will be devoted to one and despise the other You cannot serve God and wealth."

FOUNDATIONS OF THE METAPHYSICS OF MORALS

IMMANUEL KANT (1724-1804)

Rejecting the idea that the consequences of an act should have any bearing on the morality of that act, the 18th century German philosopher Kant argues that motive alone determines the rightness and wrongness of an act. To act with a proper motive, he argues, means doing one's duty for its own sake, and that in turn means following what he calls his "supreme principle of morality"—the categorical imperative. The following selection comes from Foundations of the Metaphysics of Morals, *and lays out Kant's deontological ethical system.*

1. The Good Will

Nothing can possibly be conceived in the world, or even out of it, which can be called good without qualification, except a Good Will. Intelligence, wit, judgment, and the other *talents* of the mind, however they may be named, or courage, resolution, perseverance, as qualities of temperament, are undoubtedly good and desirable in many respects; but these gifts of nature may also become extremely bad and mischievous if the will which is to make use of them, and which, therefore, constitutes what is called *character,* is not good. It is the same with the *gifts of fortune.* Power, riches, honour, even health, and the general well-being and contentment with one's condition which is called *happiness,* inspire pride, and often presumption, if there is not a good will to correct the influence of these on the mind, and with this also to rectify the whole principle of acting, and adapt it to its end. The sight of a being who is not adorned with a single feature of a pure and good will, enjoying unbroken prosperity, can never give pleasure to an impartial rational spectator. Thus a good will appears to constitute the indispensable condition even of being worthy of happiness.

There are even some qualities which are of service to this good will itself, and may facilitate its action, yet which have no intrinsic unconditional value, but always presuppose a good will, and this qualifies the esteem that we justly have for them, and does not permit us to regard them as absolutely good. Moderation in the affections and passions, self-control and calm deliberation are not only good in many respects, but even seem to constitute part of the intrinsic worth of the person; but they are far from deserving to be called good without qualification, although they have been so unconditionally praised by the ancients. For without the principles of a good will, they may become extremely bad, and the coolness of a villain not only makes him far more dangerous, but also directly makes him more abominable in our eyes than he would have been without it.

A good will is good not because of what it performs or effects, not by its aptness for the attainment of some proposed end, but simply by virtue of the volition, that is, it is good in itself, and considered by itself is to be esteemed much higher than all that can be brought about by it in favour of any inclination, nay, even of the sum total of all inclinations. Even if it should happen that, owing to special disfavour of fortune, or the niggardly provision of a step-motherly nature, this will should wholly lack power to accomplish its purpose, if with its greatest efforts it should yet achieve nothing, and there should remain only the good will (not, to be sure, a mere wish, but the summoning of all means in our power), then, like a jewel, it would still shine by its own light, as a thing which has its whole value in itself....

2. Duty vs. Inclination

We have then to develop the notion of a will which deserves to be highly esteemed for itself, and is good without a view to anything further, a notion which exists already in the sound natural understanding, requiring rather to be cleared up than to be taught, and which in estimating the value of our actions always takes the first place, and constitutes the condition of all the rest. In order to do this we will take the notion of duty, which includes that of a good will, although implying certain subjective restrictions and hindrances. These, however, far from concealing it, or rendering it unrecognisable, rather bring it out by contrast, and make it shine forth so much the brighter.

I omit here all actions which are already recognised as inconsistent with duty, although they may be useful for this or that purpose, for with these the question whether they are done *from duty* cannot arise at all, since they even conflict with it. I also set aside those actions which really conform to duty, but to which men have *no* direct *inclination,* performing them because they are impelled thereto by some other inclination. For in this case we can readily distinguish whether the action which agrees with duty is done *from duty,* or from a selfish view. It is much harder to make this distinction when the action accords with duty, and the subject has besides a *direct* inclination to it. For example, it is always a matter of duty that a dealer should not overcharge an inexperienced purchaser, and wherever there is much commerce the prudent tradesman does not overcharge, but keeps a fixed price for everyone, so that a child buys of him as well as any other. Men are thus *honestly* served; but this is not enough to make us believe that the tradesman has so acted from duty and from principles of honesty: his own advantage required it; it is out of the question in this case to suppose that he might besides have a direct inclination in favour of the buyers, so that, as it were, from love he should give no advantage to one over another. Accordingly the action was done neither from duty nor from direct inclination, but merely with a selfish view.

On the other hand, it is a duty to maintain one's life; and, in addition, every one has also a direct inclination to do so. But on this account the often anxious care which most men take for it has no intrinsic worth, and their maxim has no moral import. They preserve their life *as duty requires,* no doubt, but not *because duty requires.* On the other hand, if adversity and hopeless sorrow have completely taken away the relish for life; if the unfortunate one, strong in mind, indignant at his fate rather than desponding or dejected, wishes for death, and yet preserves his life without loving it—not from inclination or fear, but from duty—then his maxim has a moral worth.

To be beneficent when we can is a duty; and besides this, there are many minds so sympathetically constituted that, without any other motive of vanity or self-interest, they find a pleasure in spreading joy around them, and can take delight in the satisfaction of others so far as it is their own work. But I maintain that in such a case an action of this kind, however proper, however amiable it may be, has nevertheless no true moral worth, but is on a level with other inclinations, *e. g.* the inclination to honour, which, if it is happily directed to that which is in fact of public utility and accordant with duty, and consequently honourable, deserves praise and encouragement, but not esteem. For the maxim lacks the moral import, namely, that such actions be done *from duty,* not from inclination. Put the case that the mind of that philanthropist were clouded by sorrow of his own, extinguishing all sympathy with the lot of others, and that while he still has the power to benefit others in distress, he is not touched by their trouble because he is absorbed with his own; and now suppose that he tears himself out of this dead insensibility, and performs the action without any inclination to it, but simply from duty, then first has his action its genuine moral worth. Further still; if nature has put little sympathy in the heart of this or that man; if he, supposed to be an upright man, is by temperament cold and indifferent to the sufferings of others, perhaps because in respect of his own he is provided with the special gift of patience and fortitude, and supposes, or even requires, that others should have the same—and such a man would certainly not be the meanest product of nature—but if nature had not specially framed him for a philanthropist, would he not still find in himself a source from whence to give himself a far higher worth than that of a good-natured temperament could be? Unquestionably. It is just in this that the moral worth of the character is brought out which is incomparably the highest of all, namely, that he is beneficent, not from inclination, but from duty.

To secure one's own happiness is a duty, at least indirectly; for discontent with one's condition, under a pressure of many anxieties and amidst unsatisfied wants, might easily become a great *temptation to transgression of duty*. But here again, without looking to duty, all men have already the strongest and most intimate inclination to happiness, because it is just in this idea that all inclinations are combined in one total. But the precept of happiness is often of such a sort that it greatly interferes with some inclinations, and yet a man cannot form any definite and certain conception of the sum of satisfaction of all of them which is called happiness. It is not then to be wondered at that a single inclination, definite both as to what it promises and as to the time within which it can be gratified, is often able to overcome such a fluctuating idea, and that a gouty patient, for instance, can choose to enjoy what he likes, and to suffer what he may, since, according to his calculation, on this occasion at least, he has [only] not sacrificed the enjoyment of the present moment to a possibly mistaken expectation of a happiness which is supposed to be found in health. But even in this case, if the general desire for happiness did not influence his will, and supposing that in his particular case health was not a necessary element in this calculation, there yet remains in this, as in all other cases, this law, namely, that he should promote his happiness not from inclination but from duty, and by this would his conduct first acquire true moral worth.

It is in this manner, undoubtedly, that we are to understand those passages of Scripture also in which we are commanded to love our neighbour, even our enemy. For love, as an affection, cannot be commanded, but beneficence for duty's sake may; even though we are not impelled to it by any inclination—nay, are even repelled by a natural and unconquerable aversion. This is *practical* love, and not *pathological*—a love which is seated in the will, and not in the propensions of sense—in principles of action and not of tender sympathy; and it is this love alone which can be commanded.

The second proposition is: That an action done from duty derives its moral worth, *not from the purpose* which is to be attained by it, but from the maxim by which it is determined, and therefore does not depend on the realization of the object of the action, but merely on the *principle of volition* by which the action has taken place, without regard to any object of desire. It is clear from what precedes that the purposes which we may have in view in our actions, or their effects regarded as ends and springs of the will, cannot give to actions any unconditional or moral worth. In what, then, can their worth lie, if it is not to consist in the will and in reference to its expected effect? It cannot lie anywhere but in the *principle of the will* without regard to the ends which can be attained by the action. For the will stands between its *à priori* principle, which is formal, and its *à posteriori* spring, which is material, as between two roads, and as it must be determined by something, it follows that it must be determined by the formal principle of volition when an action is done from duty, in which case every material principle has been withdrawn from it.

The third proposition, which is a consequence of the two preceding, I would express thus: *Duty is the necessity of acting from respect for the law.* I may have *inclination* for an object as the effect of my proposed action, but I cannot have *respect* for it, just for this reason, that it is an effect and not an energy of will. Similarly, I cannot have respect for inclination, whether my own or another's; I can at most, if my own, approve it; if another's, sometimes even love it; *i. e.* look on it as favourable to my own interest. It is only what is connected with my will as a principle, by no means as an effect—what does not subserve my inclination, but overpowers it, or at least in case of choice excludes it from its calculation—in other words, simply the law of itself, which can be an object of respect, and hence a command. Now an action done from duty must wholly exclude the influence of inclination, and with it every object of the will, so that nothing remains which can determine the will except objectively the *law,* and subjectively *pure respect* for this practical law, and consequently the maxim that I should follow this law even to the thwarting of all my inclinations.

Thus the moral worth of an action does not lie in the effect expected from it, nor in any principle of action which requires to borrow its motive from this expected effect. For all these effects—agreeableness of one's condition, and even the promotion of the happiness of others—could have been also brought about by other causes, so that for this there would have been no need of the will of a rational being;

whereas it is in this alone that the supreme and un-conditional good can be found. The pre-eminent good which we call moral can therefore consist in nothing else than *the conception of law* in itself, *which certainly is only possible in a rational being,* in so far as this conception, and not the expected effect, determines the will. This is a good which is already present in the person who acts accordingly, and we have not to wait for it to appear first in the result.

But what sort of law can that be, the conception of which must determine the will, even without paying any regard to the effect expected from it, in order that this will may be called good absolutely and without qualification? As I have deprived the will of every impulse which could arise to it from obedience to any law, there remains nothing but the universal conformity of its actions to law in general, which alone is to serve the will as a principle, *i. e.* I am never to act otherwise than so *that I could also will that my maxim should become a universal law.* Here now, it is the simple conformity to law in general, without assuming any particular law applicable to certain actions, that serves the will as its principle, and must so serve it, if duty is not to be a vain delusion and a chimerical notion. The common reason of men in its practical judgments perfectly coincides with this, and always has in view the principle here suggested. Let the question be, for example: May I when in distress make a promise with the intention not to keep it? I readily distinguish here between the two significations which the question may have: Whether it is prudent, or whether it is right, to make a false promise. The former may undoubtedly often be the case. I see clearly indeed that it is not enough to extricate myself from a present difficulty by means of this subterfuge, but it must be well considered whether there may not hereafter spring from this lie much greater inconvenience than that from which I now free myself, and as, with all my supposed *cunning,* the consequences cannot be so easily foreseen but that credit once lost may be much more injurious to me than any mischief which I seek to avoid at present, it should be considered whether it would not be more *prudent* to act herein according to a universal maxim, and to make it a habit to promise nothing except with the intention of keeping it. But it is soon clear to me that such a maxim will still only be based on the fear of consequences. Now it is a wholly different thing to be truthful from duty, and to be so from apprehension of injurious consequences. In the first case, the very notion of the action already implies a law for me; in the second case, I must first look about elsewhere to see what results may be combined with it which would affect myself. For to deviate from the principle of duty is beyond all doubt wicked; but to be unfaithful to my maxim of prudence may often be very advantageous to me, although to abide by it is certainly safer. The shortest way, however, and an unerring one, to discover the answer to this question whether a lying promise is consistent with duty, is to ask myself, Should I be content that my maxim (to extricate myself from difficulty by a false promise) should hold good as a universal law, for myself as well as for others? and should I be able to say to myself, "Every one may make a deceitful promise when he finds himself in a difficulty from which he cannot otherwise extricate himself"? Then I presently become aware that while I can will the lie, I can by no means will that lying should be a universal law. For with such a law there would be no promises at all, since it would be in vain to allege my intention in regard to my future actions to those who would not believe this allegation, or if they over-hastily did so would pay me back in my own coin. Hence my maxim, as soon as it should be made a universal law, would necessarily destory itself.

I do not, therefore, need any far-reaching penetration to discern what I have to do in order that my will may be morally good. Inexperienced in the course of the world, incapable of being prepared for all its contingencies, I only ask myself: Canst thou also will that thy maxim should be a universal law? If not, then it must be rejected, and that not because of a disadvantage accruing from it to myself or even to others, but because it cannot enter as a principle into a possible universal legislation, and reason extorts from me immediate respect for such legislation. I do not indeed as yet *discern* on what this respect is based (this the philosopher may inquire), but at least I understand this, that it is an estimation of the worth which far outweighs all worth of what is recommended by inclination, and that the necessity of acting from *pure* respect for the practical law is what constitutes duty, to which every other motive must give place, because it is the condition of a will being good *in itself,* and the worth of such a will is above everything....

3. Hypothetical and Categorical Imperatives

...But in order that in this study we may not merely advance by the natural steps from the common moral judgment (in this case very worthy of respect) to the philosophical, as has been already done, but also from a popular philosophy, which goes no further than it can reach by groping with the help of examples, to metaphysic (which does not allow itself to be checked by anything empirical (36), and as it must measure the whole extent of this kind of rational knowledge, goes as far as ideal conceptions, where even examples fail us), we must follow and clearly describe the practical faculty of reason, from the general rules of its determination to the point where the notion of duty springs from it.

Everything in nature works according to laws. Rational beings alone have the faculty of acting according *to the conception* of laws, that is according to principles, *i. e.* have a *will.* Since the deduction of actions from principles requires *reason,* the will is nothing but practical reason. If reason infallibly determines the will, then the actions of such a being which are recognised as objectively necessary are subjectively necessary also, *i. e.* the will is a faculty to choose *that only* which reason independent on inclination recognises as practically necessary, *i. e.* as good. But if reason of itself does not sufficiently determine the will, if the latter is subject also to subjective conditions (particular impulses) which do not always coincide with the objective conditions; in a word, if the will does not *in itself* completely accord with reason (which is actually the case with men), then the actions which objectively are recognised as necessary are subjectively contingent, and the determination of such a will according to objective laws is *obligation,* that is to say, the relation of the objective laws to a will that is not thoroughly good is conceived as the determination of the will of a rational being by principles of reason, but which the will from its nature does not of necessity follow.

The conception of an objective principle, in so far as it is obligatory for a will, is called a command (of reason), and the formula of the command is called an Imperative.

All imperatives are expressed by the word *ought* [or *shall*], and thereby indicate the relation of an objective law of reason to a will, which from its subjective constitution is not necessarily determined by it (an obligation). They say that something would be good to do or to forbear, but they say it to a will which does not always do a thing because it is conceived to be good to do it. That is practically *good,* however, which determines the will by means of the conceptions of reason, and consequently not from subjective causes, but objectively, that is on principles which are valid for every rational being as such. It is distinguished from the *pleasant,* as that which influences the will only by means of sensation from merely subjective causes, valid only for the sense of this or that one, and not as a principle of reason, which holds for every one.

A perfectly good will would therefore be equally subject to objective laws (viz. laws of good), but could not be conceived as *obliged* thereby to act lawfully, because of itself from its subjective constitution it can only be determined by the conception of good (38). Therefore no imperatives hold for the Divine will, or in general for a *holy* will; *ought* is here out of place, because the volition is already of itself necessarily in unison with the law. Therefore imperatives are only formulæ to express the relation of objective laws of all volition to the subjective imperfection of the will of this or that rational being, *e.g.* the human will.

Now all *imperatives* command either *hypothetically* or *categorically.* The former represent the practical necessity of a possible action as means to something else that is willed (or at least which one might possibly will). The categorical imperative would be that which represented an action as necessary of itself without reference to another end, *i.e.* as objectively necessary.

Since every practical law represents a possible action as good, and on this account, for a subject who is practically determinable by reason, necessary, all imperatives are formulæ determining an action which is necessary according to the principle of a will good in some respects. If now the action is good only as a means *to something else,* then the imperative is *hypothetical;* if it is conceived as good *in itself* and consequently as being necessarily the principle of a will which of itself conforms to reason, then it is *categorical.*

Thus the imperative declares what action possible by me would be good, and presents the practical rule in relation to a will which does not forthwith perform an action simply because it is good, whether because the subject does not always know that it is good, or because, even if it know this, yet its maxims might be opposed to the objective principles of practical reason.

Accordingly the hypothetical imperative only says that the action is good for some purpose, *possible* or *actual*. In the first case it is a Problematical, in the second an Assertorial practical principle. The categorical imperative which declares an action to be objectively necessary in itself without reference to any purpose, *i.e.* without any other end, is valid as an Apodictic (practical) principle.

Whatever is possible only by the power of some rational being may also be conceived as a possible purpose of some will; and therefore the principles of action as regards the means necessary to attain some possible purpose are in fact infinitely numerous. All sciences have a practical part, consisting of problems expressing that some end is possible for us, and of imperatives directing how it may be attained. These may, therefore, be called in general imperatives of Skill. Here there is no question whether the end is rational and good, but only what one must do in order to attain it. The precepts for the physician to make his patient thoroughly healthy, and for a poisoner to ensure certain death, are of equal value in this respect, that each serves to effect its purpose perfectly. Since in early youth it cannot be known what ends are likely to occur to us in the course of life, parents seek to have their children taught a *great many things,* and provide for their *skill* in the use of means for all sorts of arbitrary ends, of none of which can they determine whether it may not perhaps hereafter be an object to their pupil, but which it is at all events *possible* that he might aim at; and this anxiety is so great that they commonly neglect to form and correct their judgment on the value of the things which may be chosen as ends (40).

There is *one* end, however, which may be assumed to be actually such to all rational beings (so far as imperatives apply to them, viz. as dependent beings), and therefore, one purpose which they not merely *may* have, but which we may with certainty assume that they all actually *have* by a natural necessity, and this is *happiness.* The hypothetical imperative which expresses the practical necessity of an action as means to the advancement of happiness is Assertorial. We are not to present it as necessary for an uncertain and merely possible purpose, but for a purpose which we may presuppose with certainty and *à priori* in every man, because it belongs

to his being. Now skill in the choice of means to his own greatest well-being may be called *prudence,* in the narrowest sense. And thus the imperative which refers to the choice of means to one's own happiness, *i. e.* the precept of prudence, is still always *hypothetical;* the action is not commanded absolutely, but only as means to another purpose.

Finally, there is an imperative which commands a certain conduct immediately, without having as its condition any other purpose to be attained by it. This imperative is Categorical. It concerns not the matter of the action, or its intended result, but its form and the principle of which it is itself a result; and what is essentially good in it consists in the mental disposition, let the consequence be what it may. This imperative may be called that of Morality.

There is a marked distinction also between the volitions on these three sorts of principles in the *dissimilarity* of the obligation of the will. In order to mark this difference more clearly, I think they would be most suitably named in their order if we said they are either *rules* of skill, or *counsels* of prudence, or *commands* (*laws*) of morality. For it is *law* only that involves the conception of an *unconditional* and objective necessity, which is consequently universally valid; and commands are laws which must be obeyed, that is, must be followed, even in opposition to inclination. *Counsels,* indeed, involve necessity, but one which can only hold under a contingent subjective condition, viz. they depend on whether this or that man reckons this or that as part of his happiness; the categorical imperative, on the contrary, is not limited by any condition, and as being absolutely, although practically, necessary, may be quite properly called a command. We might also call the first kind of imperatives *technical* (belonging to art), the second *pragmatic* (to welfare), the third *moral* (belonging to free conduct generally, that is, to morals).

Now arises the question, how are all these imperatives possible? This question does not seek to know how we can conceive the accomplishment of the action which the imperative ordains, but merely how we can conceive the obligation of the will which the imperative expresses. No special explanation is needed to show how an imperative of skill is possible. Whoever wills the end, wills also (so far as reason decides his conduct) the means in his power which are indispensably necessary thereto. This proposition is, as regards the volition, analytical;

for, in willing an object as my effect, there is already thought the causality of myself as an acting cause, that is to say, the use of the means; and the imperative educes from the conception of volition of an end the conception of actions necessary to this end. Synthetical propositions must no doubt be employed in defining the means to a proposed end; but they do not concern the principle, the act of the will, but the object and its realization. *Ex. gr.,* that in order to bisect a line on an unerring principle I must draw from its extremities two interesecting ares; this no doubt is taught by mathematics only in synthetical propositions; but if I know that it is only by this process that the intended operation can be performed, then to say that if I fully will the operation, I also will the action required for it, is an analytical proposition; for it is one and the same thing to conceive something as an effect which I can produce in a certain way, and to conceive myself as acting in this way.

If it were only equally easy to give a definite conception of happiness, the imperatives of prudence would correspond exactly with those of skill, and would likewise be analytical. For in this case as in that, it could be said, whoever wills the end, wills also (according to the dictate of reason necessarily) the indispensable means thereto which are in his power. But, unfortunately, the notion of happiness is so indefinite that although every man wishes to attain it, yet he never can say definitely and consistently what it is that he really wishes and wills. The reason of this is that all the elements which belong to the notion of happiness are altogether empirical, *i.e.* they must be borrowed from experience, and nevertheless the idea of happiness requires an absolute whole, a maximum of welfare in my present and all future circumstances. Now it is impossible that the most clear-sighted, and at the same time most powerful being (supposed finite) should frame to himself a definite conception of what he really wills in this. Does he will riches, how much anxiety, envy, and snares might he not thereby draw upon his shoulders? Does he will knowledge and discernment, perhaps it might prove to be only an eye so much the sharper to show him so much the more fearfully the evils that are now concealed from him, and that cannot be avoided, or to impose more wants on his desires, which already give him concern enough. Would he have long life, who guarantees to him that it would not be a long misery? would he at least have health? how often has uneasiness of the body

restrained from excesses into which perfect health would have allowed one to fall? and so on. In short he is unable, on any principle, to determine with certainty what would make him truly happy; because to do so he would need to be omniscient. We cannot therefore act on any definite principles to secure happiness, but only on empirical counsels, *ex. gr.* of regimen, frugality, courtesy, reserve, &c., which experience teaches do, on the average, most promote well-being. Hence it follows that the imperatives of prudence do not, strictly speaking, command at all, that is, they cannot present actions objectively as practically *necessary;* that they are rather to be regarded as counsels (*consilia*) than precepts (*præcepta*) of reason, that the problem to determine certainly and universally what action would promote the happiness of a rational being is completely insoluble, and consequently no imperative respecting it is possible which should, in the strict sense, command to do what makes happy; because happiness is not an ideal of reason but of imagination, resting solely on empirical grounds, and it is vain to expect that these should define an action by which one could attain the totality of a series of consequences which is really endless. This imperative of prudence would however be an analytical proposition if we assume that the means to happiness could be certainly assigned; for it is distinguished from the imperative of skill only by this, that in the latter the end is merely possible, in the former it is given; as however both only ordain the means to that which we suppose to be willed as an end, it follows that the imperative which ordains the willing of the means to him who wills the end is in both cases analytical. Thus there is no difficulty in regard to the possibility of an imperative of this kind either.

On the other hand the question, how the imperative of *morality* is possible, is undoubtedly one, the only one, demanding a solution, as this is not at all hypothetical, and the objective necessity which it presents cannot rest on any hypothesis, as is the case with the hypothetical imperatives. Only here we must never leave out of consideration that we *cannot* make out *by any example,* in other words empirically, whether there is such an imperative at all; but it is rather to be feared that all those which seem to be categorical may yet be at bottom hypothetical. For instance, when the precept is: Thou shalt not promise deceitfully; and it is assumed that the necessity of this is not a mere counsel to avoid some other evil, so that it should mean: thou shalt not make a lying promise, lest if it become known thou shouldst destroy thy credit, but that an action of this kind must be regarded as evil in itself, so that the imperative of the prohibition is categorical; then we cannot show with certainty in any example that the will was determined merely by the law, without any other spring of action, although it may appear to be so. For it is always possible that fear of disgrace, perhaps also obscure dread of other dangers, may have a secret influence on the will. Who can prove by experience the non-existence of a cause when all that experience tells us is that we do not perceive it? But in such a case the so-called moral imperative, which as such appears to be categorical and unconditional, would in reality be only a pragmatic precept, drawing our attention to our own interests, and merely teaching us to take these into consideration.

We shall therefore have to investigate *à priori* the possibility of a categorical imperative, as we have not in this case the advantage of its reality being given in experience, so that [the elucidation of] its possibility should be requisite only for its explanation, not for its establishment. In the meantime it may be discerned beforehand that the categorical imperative alone has the purport of a practical law: all the rest may indeed be called *principles* of the will but not laws, since whatever is only necessary for the attainment of some arbitrary purpose may be considered as in itself contingent, and we can at any time be free from the precept if we give up the purpose: on the contrary, the unconditional command leaves the will no liberty to choose the opposite; consequently it alone carries with it that necessity which we require in a law.

Secondly, in the case of this categorical imperative or law of morality, the difficulty (of discerning its possibility) is a very profound one. It is an *à priori* synthetical practical proposition; and as there is so much difficulty in discerning the possibility of speculative propositions of this kind, it may readily be supposed that the difficulty will be no less with the practical.

In this problem we will first inquire whether the mere conception of a categorical imperative may not perhaps supply us also with the formula of it, containing the proposition which alone can be a categorical imperative; for even if we know the tenor of such an absolute command, yet how it is possible will require further special and laborious study,

which we postpone to the last section.

When I conceive a hypothetical imperative in general I do not know beforehand what it will contain until I am given the condition. But when I conceive a categorical imperative I know at once what it contains. For as the imperative contains besides the law only the necessity that the maxims shall conform to this law, while the law contains no conditions restricting it, there remains nothing but the general statement that the maxim of the action should conform to a universal law (47), and it is this conformity alone that the imperative properly represents as necessary.

4. First Formulation of the Categorical Imperative

There is therefore but one categorical imperative, namely this: *Act only on that maxim whereby thou canst at the same time will that it should become a universal law.*

Now if all imperatives of duty can be deduced from this one imperative as from their principle, then, although it should remain undecided whether what is called duty is not merely a vain notion, yet at least we shall be able to show what we understand by it and what this notion means.

Since the universality of the law according to which effects are produced constitutes what is properly called *nature* in the most general sense (as to form), that is the existence of things so far as it is determined by general laws, the imperative of duty may be expressed thus: *Act as if the maxim of thy action were to become by thy will a Universal Law of Nature.*

We will now enumerate a few duties, adopting the usual division of them into duties to ourselves and to others, and into perfect and imperfect duties.

1. A man reduced to despair by a series of misfortunes feels wearied of life, but is still so far in possession of his reason that he can ask himself whether it would not be contrary to his duty to himself to take his own life. Now he inquires whether the maxim of his action could become a universal law of nature. His maxim is: From self-love I adopt it as a principle to shorten my life when its longer duration is likely to bring more evil than satisfaction. It is asked then simply whether this principle founded on self-love can become a universal law of nature. Now we see at once that a system of nature

of which it should be a law to destroy life by means of the very feeling whose special nature it is to impel to the improvement of life would contradict itself, and therefore could not exist as a system of nature; hence that maxim cannot possibly exist as a universal law of nature, and consequently would be wholly inconsistent with the supreme principle of all duty.

2. Another finds himself forced by necessity to borrow money. He knows that he will not be able to repay it, but sees also that nothing will be lent to him, unless he promises stoutly to repay it in a definite time. He desires to make this promise, but he has still so much conscience as to ask himself: Is it not unlawful and inconsistent with duty to get out of a difficulty in this way? Suppose however that he resolves to do so, then the maxim of his action would be expressed thus: When I think myself in want of money, I will borrow money and promise to repay it, although I know that I never can do so. Now this principle of self-love or of one's own advantage may perhaps be consistent with my whole future welfare; but the question now is, Is it right? I change then the suggestion of self-love into a universal law, and state the question thus: How would it be if my maxim were a universal law? Then I see at once that it could never hold as a universal law of nature, but would necessarily contradict itself. For supposing it to be a universal law that everyone when he thinks himself in a difficulty should be able to promise whatever he pleases, with the purpose of not keeping his promise, the promise itself would become impossible, as well as the end that one might have in view in it, since no one would consider that anything was promised to him, but would ridicule all such statements as vain pretences.

3. A third finds in himself a talent which with the help of some culture might make him a useful man in many respects. But he finds himself in comfortable circumstances, and prefers to indulge in pleasure rather than to take pains in enlarging and improving his happy natural capacities. He asks, however, whether his maxim of neglect of his natural gifts, besides agreeing with his inclination to indulgence, agrees also with what is called duty. He sees then that a system of nature could indeed subsist with such a universal law although men (like the South Sea islanders) should let their talents rust, and resolve to devote their lives merely to idleness, amusement, and propagation of their species—in a word, to enjoyment; but he cannot possibly *will* that

this should be a universal law of nature, or be implanted in us as such by a natural instinct. For, as a rational being, he necessarily wills that his faculties be developed, since they serve him, and have been given him, for all sorts of possible purposes.

4. A fourth, who is in prosperity, while he sees that others have to contend with great wretchedness and that he could help them, thinks: What concern is it of mine? Let everyone be as happy as heaven pleases, or as he can make himself; I will take nothing from him nor even envy him, only I do not wish to contribute anything to his welfare or to his assistance in distress! Now no doubt if such a mode of thinking were a universal law, the human race might very well subsist, and doubtless even better than in a state in which everyone talks of sympathy and goodwill, or even takes care occasionally to put it into practice, but on the other side, also cheats when he can, betrays the rights of men, or otherwise violates them. But although it is possible that a universal law of nature might exist in accordance with that maxim, it is impossible to *will* that such a principle should have the universal validity of a law of nature. For a will which resolved this would contradict itself, inasmuch as many cases might occur in which one would have need of the love and sympathy of others, and in which, by such a law of nature, sprung from his own will, he would deprive himself of all hope of the aid he desires.

These are a few of the many actual duties, or at least what we regard as such, which obviously fall into two classes on the one principle that we have laid down. We must be *able to will* that a maxim of our action should be a universal law. This is the canon of the moral appreciation of the action generally. Some actions are of such a character that their maxim cannot without contradiction be even *conceived* as a universal law of nature, far from it being possible that we should *will* that it *should* be so. In others this intrinsic impossibility is not found, but still it is impossible to *will* that their maxim should be raised to the universality of a law of nature, since such a will would contradict itself. It is easily seen that the former violate strict or rigorous (inflexible) duty; the latter only laxer (meritorious) duty. Thus it has been completely shown by these examples how all duties depend as regards the nature of the obligation (not the object of the action) on the same principle....

5. Second Formulation of the Categorical Imperative

The will is conceived as a faculty of determining oneself to action *in accordance with the conception of certain laws*. And such a faculty can be found only in rational beings. Now that which serves the will as the objective ground of its self-determination is the *end*, and if this is assigned by reason alone, it must hold for all rational beings. On the other hand, that which merely contains the ground of possibility of the action of which the effect is the end, this is called the *means*....The ends which a rational being proposes to himself at pleasure as *effects* of his actions (material ends) are all only relative, for it is only their relation to the particular desires of the subject that gives them their worth, which therefore cannot furnish principles universal and necessary for all rational beings and for every volition, that is to say practical laws. Hence all these relative ends can give rise only to hypothetical imperatives.

Supposing, however, that there were something *whose existence* has *in itself* an absolute worth, something which, being *an end in itself*, could be a source of definite laws, then in this and this alone would lie the source of a possible categorical imperative, *i.e.* a practical law.

Now I say: man and generally any rational being *exists* as an end in himself, *not merely as a means* to be arbitrarily used by this or that will, but in all his actions, whether they concern himself or other rational beings, must be always regarded at the same time as an end. All objects of the inclinations have only a conditional worth, for if the inclinations and the wants founded on them did not exist, then their object would be without value. But the inclinations themselves being sources of want, are so far from having an absolute worth for which they should be desired, that on the contrary it must be the universal wish of every rational being to be wholly free from them. Thus the worth of any object which is *to be acquired* by our action is always conditional. Beings whose existence depends not on our will but on nature's, have nevertheless, if they are irrational beings, only a relative value as means, and are therefore called *things*; rational beings, on the contrary, are called *persons*, because their very nature points them out as ends in themselves, that is as something which must not be used merely as means, and so far therefore restricts freedom of action (and is an ob-ject of respect). These, therefore, are not merely subjective ends whose existence has a worth *for us* as an effect of our action, but *objective ends,* that is things whose existence is an end in itself: an end moreover for which no other can be substituted, which they should subserve *merely* as means, for otherwise nothing whatever would possess *absolute worth;* but if all worth were conditioned and therefore contingent, then there would be no supreme practical principle of reason whatever.

If then there is a supreme practical principle or, in respect of the human will, a categorical imperative, it must be one which (57), being drawn from the conception of that which is necessarily an end for every one because it is *an end in itself,* constitutes an *objective* principle of will, and can therefore serve as a universal practical law. The foundation of this principle is: *rational nature exists as an end in itself.* Man necessarily conceives his own existence as being so: so far then this is a *subjective* principle of human actions. But every other rational being regards its existence similarly, just on the same rational principle that holds for me: so that it is at the same time an objective principle, from which as a supreme practical law all laws of the will must be capable of being deduced. Accordingly the practical imperative will be as follows: *So act as to treat humanity, whether in thine own person or in that of any other, in every case as an end withal, never as means only.* We will now inquire whether this can be practically carried out.

To abide by the previous examples:

Firstly, under the head of necessary duty to oneself: He who contemplates suicide should ask himself whether his action can be consistent with the idea of humanity *as an end in itself.* If he destroys himself in order to escape from painful circumstances, he uses a person merely as *a mean* to maintain a tolerable condition up to the end of life. But a man is not a thing, that is to say, something which can be used merely as means, but must in all his actions be always considered as an end in himself. I cannot, therefore, dispose in any way of a man in my own person so as to mutilate him, to damage or kill him (58). (It belongs to ethics proper to define this principle more precisely so as to avoid all misunderstanding, *e.g.* as to the amputation of the limbs in order to preserve myself; as to exposing my life to danger with a view to preserve it, &c. This question is therefore omitted here.)

Secondly, as regards necessary duties, or those of strict obligation, towards others; he who is thinking of making a lying promise to others will see at once that he would be using another man *merely as a mean,* without the latter containing at the same time the end in himself. For he whom I propose by such a promise to use for my own purposes cannot possibly assent to my mode of acting towards him, and therefore cannot himself contain the end of this action. This violation of the principle of humanity in other men is more obvious if we take in examples of attacks on the freedom and property of others. For then it is clear that he who transgresses the rights of men, intends to use the person of others merely as means, without considering that as rational beings they ought always to be esteemed also as ends, that is, as beings who must be capable of containing in themselves the end of the very same action.

Thirdly, as regards contingent (meritorious) duties to oneself; is not enough that the action does not violate humanity in our own person as an end in itself, it must also *harmonise with* it. Now there are in humanity capacities of greater perfection, which belong to the end that nature has in view in regard to humanity in ourselves as the subject: to neglect these might perhaps be consistent with the *maintenance* of humanity as an end in itself, but not with the *advancement* of this end.

Fourthly, as regards meritorious duties towards others: the natural end which all men have is their own happiness. Now humanity might indeed subsist, although no one should contribute anything to the happiness of others, provided he did not intentionally withdraw anything from it; but after all this would only harmonise negatively not positively with *humanity as an end in itself,* if every one does not also endeavour, as far as in him lies, to forward the ends of others. For the ends of any subject which is an end in himself, ought as far as possible to be *my* ends also, if that conception is to have its *full* effect with me….

Kant's Critique of Practical Reason and Other Works on the Theory of Ethics. Trans. Thomas Kingsmill Abbott. 4th ed. London: Longman, Green, and Co., 1889.

UTILITARIANISM

JOHN STUART MILL (1806-1873)

Unlike Immanuel Kant, the 19th century English philosopher John Stuart Mill had absolutely no problems look-ing to the consequences of actions to determine if they were right or wrong. In the following selection from his work, Utilitarianism, *Mill claims that the morality of an act is determined by the degree to which it promotes "utility," which he defines as "the greatest happiness for the greatest number." This "greatest number" in-cludes all those who are affected by one's actions—human and nonhuman alike.*

CHAPTER 2
What Utilitarianism Is

The creed which accepts as the foundation of mor-als, Utility, or the Greatest Happiness Principle, holds that actions are right in proportion as they tend to promote happiness, wrong as they tend to produce the reverse of happiness. By happiness is intended pleasure, and the absence of pain; by un-happiness, pain, and the privation of pleasure. To give a clear view of the moral standard set up by the theory, much more requires to be said; in particular, what things it includes in the ideas of pain and plea-sure; and to what extent this is left an open question. But these supplementary explanations do not affect the theory of life on which this theory of morality is grounded—namely, that pleasure, and freedom from pain, are the only things desirable as ends; and that all desirable things (which are as numerous in the utilitarian as in any other scheme) are desirable either for the pleasure inherent in themselves, or as means to the promotion of pleasure and the preven-tion of pain.

Now, such a theory of life excites in many minds, and among them in some of the most estimable in feeling and purpose, inveterate dislike. To suppose that life has (as they express it) no higher end than pleasure—no better and nobler object of desire and pursuit—they designate as utterly mean and grovel-ling; as a doctrine worthy only of swine....

1. Higher and Lower Pleasures

It is quite compatible with the principle of utility to recognise the fact, that some kinds of pleasure are more desirable and more valuable than others. It would be absurd that while, in estimating all other things, quality is considered as well as quantity, the estimation of pleasures should be supposed to de-pend on quantity alone.

If I am asked, what I mean by difference of qual-ity in pleasures, or what makes one pleasure more valuable than another, merely as a pleasure, except its being greater in amount, there is but one possible answer. Of two pleasures, if there be one to which all or almost all who have experience of both give a de-cided preference, irrespective of any feeling of mor-al obligation to prefer it, that is the more desirable pleasure. If one of the two is, by those who are com-petently acquainted with both, placed so far above the other that they prefer it, even though knowing it to be attended with a greater amount of discon-tent, and would not resign it for any quantity of the other pleasure which their nature is capable of, we are justified in ascribing to the preferred enjoyment a superiority in quality, so far outweighing quantity as to render it, in comparison, of small account.

Now it is an unquestionable fact that those who are equally acquainted with, and equally capable of appreciating and enjoying, both, do give a most marked preference to the manner of existence which employs their higher faculties. Few human creatures would consent to be changed into any of the lower animals, for a promise of the fullest allowance of a beast's pleasures; no intelligent human being would consent to be a fool, no instructed person would be an ignoramus, no person of feeling and conscience would be selfish and base, even though they should be persuaded that the fool, the dunce, or the rascal is better satisfied with his lot than they are with theirs. They would not resign what they possess more than he for the most complete satisfaction of all the desires which they have in common with him. If they ever fancy they would, it is only in cases of unhappiness so extreme, that to escape from it they would exchange their lot for almost any other, however undesirable in their own eyes. A being of higher faculties requires more to make him happy, is capable probably of more acute suffering, and certainly accessible to it at more points, than one of an inferior type; but in spite of these liabilities, he can never really wish to sink into what he feels to be a lower grade of existence. We may give what explanation we please of this unwillingness; we may attribute it to pride, a name which is given indiscriminately to some of the most and to some of the least estimable feelings of which mankind are capable: we may refer it to the love of liberty and personal independence, an appeal to which was with the Stoics one of the most effective means for the inculcation of it; to the love of power, or to the love of excitement, both of which do really enter into and contribute to it: but its most appropriate appellation is a sense of dignity, which all human beings possess in one form or other, and in some, though by no means in exact, proportion to their higher faculties, and which is so essential a part of the happiness of those in whom it is strong, that nothing which conflicts with it could be, otherwise than momentarily, an object of desire to them.

Whoever supposes that this preference takes place at a sacrifice of happiness—that the superior being, in anything like equal circumstances, is not happier than the inferior— confounds the two very different ideas, of *happiness*, and *content*. It is indisputable that the being whose capacities of enjoyment are low, has the greatest chance of having them fully satisfied; and a highly endowed being will always feel that any happiness which he can look for, as the world is constituted, is imperfect. But he can learn to bear its imperfections, if they are at all bearable; and they will not make him envy the being who is indeed unconscious of the imperfections, but only because he feels not at all the good which those imperfections qualify. It is better to be a human being dissatisfied than a pig satisfied; better to be Socrates dissatisfied than a fool satisfied. And if the fool, or the pig, are a different opinion, it is because they only know their own side of the question. The other party to the comparison knows both sides....

2. Further Considerations on Happiness

According to the Greatest Happiness Principle...the ultimate end, with reference to and for the sake of which all other things are desirable (whether we are considering our own good or that of other people), is an existence exempt as far as possible from pain, and as rich as possible in enjoyments, both in point of quantity and quality; the test of quality, and the rule for measuring it against quantity, being the preference felt by those who in their opportunities of experience, to which must be added their habits of self-consciousness and self-observation, are best furnished with the means of comparison. This, being, according to the utilitarian opinion, the end of human action, is necessarily also the standard of morality; which may accordingly be defined, the rules and precepts for human conduct, by the observance of which an existence such as has been described might be, to the greatest extent possible, secured to all mankind; and not to them only, but, so far as the nature of things admits, to the whole sentient creation....

...If by happiness be meant a continuity of highly pleasurable excitement, it is evident enough that this is impossible. A state of exalted pleasure lasts only moments, or in some cases, and with some intermissions, hours or days, and is the occasional brilliant flash of enjoyment, not its permanent and steady flame. Of this the philosophers who have taught that happiness is the end of life were as fully aware as those who taunt them. The happiness which they meant was not a life of rapture; but moments of such, in an existence made up of few and transitory pains, many and various pleasures, with a decided predominance of the active over the passive, and having as the foundation of the whole, not to expect more from life than it is capable of bestowing. A life thus composed, to those who have been fortunate enough to obtain it, has always appeared worthy of the name of happiness. And such an existence is even now the lot of many, during some considerable portion of their lives. The present wretched education, and wretched social arrangements, are the only real hindrance to its being attainable by almost all.

The objectors perhaps may doubt whether human beings, if taught to consider happiness as the end of life, would be satisfied with such a moderate share of it. But great numbers of mankind have been satisfied with much less. The main constituents of a satisfied life appear to be two, either of which by itself is often found sufficient for the purpose: tranquillity, and excitement. With much tranquillity, many find that they can be content with very little pleasure: with much excitement, many can reconcile themselves to a considerable quantity of pain. There is assuredly no inherent impossibility in enabling even the mass of mankind to unite both; since the two are so far from being incompatible that they are in natural alliance, the prolongation of either being a preparation for, and exciting a wish for, the other. It is only those in whom indolence amounts to a vice, that do not desire excitement after an interval of repose: it is only those in whom the need of excitement is a disease, that feel the tranquillity which follows excitement dull and insipid, instead of pleasurable in direct proportion to the excitement which preceded it. When people who are tolerably fortunate in their outward lot do not find in life sufficient enjoyment to make it valuable to them, the cause generally is, caring for nobody but themselves. To those who have neither public nor private affections, the excitements of life are much curtailed, and in any case dwindle in value as the time approaches when all selfish interests must be terminated by death: while those who leave after them objects of personal affection, and especially those who have also cultivated a fellow-feeling with the collective interests of mankind, retain as lively an interest in life on the eve of death as in the vigour of youth and health. Next to selfishness, the principal cause which makes life unsatisfactory is want of mental cultivation. A cultivated mind - I do not mean that of a philosopher, but

any mind to which the fountains of knowledge have been opened, and which has been taught, in any tolerable degree, to exercise its faculties- finds sources of inexhaustible interest in all that surrounds it; in the objects of nature, the achievements of art, the imaginations of poetry, the incidents of history, the ways of mankind, past and present, and their prospects in the future. It is possible, indeed, to become indifferent to all this, and that too without having exhausted a thousandth part of it; but only when one has had from the beginning no moral or human interest in these things, and has sought in them only the gratification of curiosity.

Now there is absolutely no reason in the nature of things why an amount of mental culture sufficient to give an intelligent interest in these objects of contemplation, should not be the inheritance of every one born in a civilised country. As little is there an inherent necessity that any human being should be a selfish egotist, devoid of every feeling or care but those which centre in his own miserable individuality. Something far superior to this is sufficiently common even now, to give ample earnest of what the human species may be made. Genuine private affections and a sincere interest in the public good, are possible, though in unequal degrees, to every rightly brought up human being. In a world in which there is so much to interest, so much to enjoy, and so much also to correct and improve, every one who has this moderate amount of moral and intellectual requisites is capable of an existence which may be called enviable; and unless such a person, through bad laws, or subjection to the will of others, is denied the liberty to use the sources of happiness within his reach, he will not fail to find this enviable existence, if he escape the positive evils of life, the great sources of physical and mental suffering- such as indigence, disease, and the unkindness, worthlessness, or premature loss of objects of affection. The main stress of the problem lies, therefore, in the contest with these calamities, from which it is a rare good fortune entirely to escape; which, as things now are, cannot be obviated, and often cannot be in any material degree mitigated. Yet no one whose opinion deserves a moment's consideration can doubt that most of the great positive evils of the world are in themselves removable, and will, if human affairs continue to improve, be in the end reduced within narrow limits. Poverty, in any sense implying suffering, may be completely extinguished by the wisdom of society, combined with the good sense and providence of individuals. Even that most intractable of enemies, disease, may be indefinitely reduced in dimensions by good physical and moral education, and proper control of noxious influences; while the progress of science holds out a promise for the future of still more direct conquests over this detestable foe. And every advance in that direction relieves us from some, not only of the chances which cut short our own lives, but, what concerns us still more, which deprive us of those in whom our happiness is wrapt up. As for vicissitudes of fortune, and other disappointments connected with worldly circumstances, these are principally the effect either of gross imprudence, of ill-regulated desires, or of bad or imperfect social institutions.

All the grand sources, in short, of human suffering are in a great degree, many of them almost entirely, conquerable by human care and effort; and though their removal is grievously slow—though a long succession of generations will perish in the breach before the conquest is completed, and this world becomes all that, if will and knowledge were not wanting, it might easily be made—yet every mind sufficiently intelligent and generous to bear a part, however small and unconspicuous, in the endeavour, will draw a noble enjoyment from the contest itself, which he would not for any bribe in the form of selfish indulgence consent to be without.

And this leads to the true estimation of what is said by the objectors concerning the possibility, and the obligation, of learning to do without happiness. Unquestionably it is possible to do without happiness; it is done involuntarily by nineteen-twentieths of mankind, even in those parts of our present world which are least deep in barbarism; and it often has to be done voluntarily by the hero or the martyr, for the sake of something which he prizes more than his individual happiness. But this something, what is it, unless the happiness of others or some of the requisites of happiness? It is noble to be capable of resigning entirely one's own portion of happiness, or chances of it: but, after all, this self-sacrifice must be for some end; it is not its own end; and if we are told that its end is not happiness, but virtue, which is better than happiness, I ask, would the sacrifice

be made if the hero or martyr did not believe that it would earn for others immunity from similar sacrifices? Would it be made if he thought that his renunciation of happiness for himself would produce no fruit for any of his fellow creatures, but to make their lot like his, and place them also in the condition of persons who have renounced happiness? All honour to those who can abnegate for themselves the personal enjoyment of life, when by such renunciation they contribute worthily to increase the amount of happiness in the world; but he who does it, or professes to do it, for any other purpose, is no more deserving of admiration than the ascetic mounted on his pillar. He may be an inspiriting proof of what men can do, but assuredly not an example of what they *should*.

Though it is only in a very imperfect state of the world's arrangements that any one can best serve the happiness of others by the absolute sacrifice of his own, yet so long as the world is in that imperfect state, I fully acknowledge that the readiness to make such a sacrifice is the highest virtue which can be found in man. I will add, that in this condition the world, paradoxical as the assertion may be, the conscious ability to do without happiness gives the best prospect of realising, such happiness as is attainable. For nothing except that consciousness can raise a person above the chances of life, by making him feel that, let fate and fortune do their worst, they have not power to subdue him: which, once felt, frees him from excess of anxiety concerning the evils of life, and enables him, like many a Stoic in the worst times of the Roman Empire, to cultivate in tranquillity the sources of satisfaction accessible to him, without concerning himself about the uncertainty of their duration, any more than about their inevitable end.

Meanwhile, let utilitarians never cease to claim the morality of self devotion as a possession which belongs by as good a right to them, as either to the Stoic or to the Transcendentalist. The utilitarian morality does recognise in human beings the power of sacrificing their own greatest good for the good of others. It only refuses to admit that the sacrifice is itself a good. A sacrifice which does not increase, or tend to increase, the sum total of happiness, it considers as wasted. The only self-renunciation which it applauds, is devotion to the happiness, or to some of the means of happiness, of others; either of mankind collectively, or of individuals within the limits imposed by the collective interests of mankind.

3. Defending Utilitarianism

I must again repeat, what the assailants of utilitarianism seldom have the justice to acknowledge, that the happiness which forms the utilitarian standard of what is right in conduct, is not the agent's own happiness, but that of all concerned. As between his own happiness and that of others, utilitarianism requires him to be as strictly impartial as a disinterested and benevolent spectator. In the golden rule of Jesus of Nazareth, we read the complete spirit of the ethics of utility. To do as you would be done by, and to love your neighbour as yourself, constitute the ideal perfection of utilitarian morality. As the means of making the nearest approach to this ideal, utility would enjoin, first, that laws and social arrangements should place the happiness, or (as speaking practically it may be called) the interest, of every individual, as nearly as possible in harmony with the interest of the whole; and secondly, that education and opinion, which have so vast a power over human character, should so use that power as to establish in the mind of every individual an indissoluble association between his own happiness and the good of the whole; especially between his own happiness and the practice of such modes of conduct, negative and positive, as regard for the universal happiness prescribes; so that not only he may be unable to conceive the possibility of happiness to himself, consistently with conduct opposed to the general good, but also that a direct impulse to promote the general good may be in every individual one of the habitual motives of action, and the sentiments connected therewith may fill a large and prominent place in every human being's sentient existence. If the, impugners of the utilitarian morality represented it to their own minds in this its, true character, I know not what recommendation possessed by any other morality they could possibly affirm to be wanting to it; what more beautiful or more exalted developments of human nature any other ethical system can be supposed to foster, or what springs of action, not accessible to the utilitarian, such systems rely on for giving effect to their mandates.

The objectors to utilitarianism cannot always be charged with representing it in a discreditable light. On the contrary, those among them who entertain anything like a just idea of its disinterested character, sometimes find fault with its standard as being too high for humanity. They say it is exacting too much to require that people shall always act from the inducement of promoting the general interests of society. But this is to mistake the very meaning of a standard of morals, and confound the rule of action with the motive of it. It is the business of ethics to tell us what are our duties, or by what test we may know them; but no system of ethics requires that the sole motive of all we do shall be a feeling of duty; on the contrary, ninety-nine hundredths of all our actions are done from other motives, and rightly so done, if the rule of duty does not condemn them. It is the more unjust to utilitarianism that this particular misapprehension should be made a ground of objection to it, inasmuch as utilitarian moralists have gone beyond almost all others in affirming that the motive has nothing to do with the morality of the action, though much with the worth of the agent. He who saves a fellow creature from drowning does what is morally right, whether his motive be duty, or the hope of being paid for his trouble; he who betrays the friend that trusts him, is guilty of a crime, even if his object be to serve another friend to whom he is under greater obligations.

But to speak only of actions done from the motive of duty, and in direct obedience to principle: it is a misapprehension of the utilitarian mode of thought, to conceive it as implying that people should fix their minds upon so wide a generality as the world, or society at large. The great majority of good actions are intended not for the benefit of the world, but for that of individuals, of which the good of the world is made up; and the thoughts of the most virtuous man need not on these occasions travel beyond the particular persons concerned, except so far as is necessary to assure himself that in benefiting them he is not violating the rights, that is, the legitimate and authorised expectations, of any one else. The multiplication of happiness is, according to the utilitarian ethics, the object of virtue: the occasions on which any person (except one in a thousand) has it in his power to do this on an extended scale, in other words to be a public benefactor, are but exceptional; and on these occasions alone is he called on to consider public utility; in every other case, private utility, the interest or happiness of some few persons, is all he has to attend to. Those alone the influence of whose actions extends to society in general, need concern themselves habitually about large an object. In the case of abstinences indeed—of things which people forbear to do from moral considerations, though the consequences in the particular case might be beneficial—it would be unworthy of an intelligent agent not to be consciously aware that the action is of a class which, if practised generally, would be generally injurious, and that this is the ground of the obligation to abstain from it. The amount of regard for the public interest implied in this recognition, is no greater than is demanded by every system of morals, for they all enjoin to abstain from whatever is manifestly pernicious to society....

Again, Utility is often summarily stigmatised as an immoral doctrine by giving it the name of Expediency, and taking advantage of the popular use of that term to contrast it with Principle. But the Expedient, in the sense in which it is opposed to the Right, generally means that which is expedient for the particular interest of the agent himself; as when a minister sacrifices the interests of his country to keep himself in place. When it means anything better than this, it means that which is expedient for some immediate object, some temporary purpose, but which violates a rule whose observance is expedient in a much higher degree. The Expedient, in this sense, instead of being the same thing with the useful, is a branch of the hurtful.

Thus, it would often be expedient, for the purpose of getting over some momentary embarrassment, or attaining some object immediately useful to ourselves or others, to tell a lie. But inasmuch as the cultivation in ourselves of a sensitive feeling on the subject of veracity, is one of the most useful, and the enfeeblement of that feeling one of the most hurtful, things to which our conduct can be instrumental; and inasmuch as any, even unintentional, deviation from truth, does that much towards weakening the trustworthiness of human assertion, which is not only the principal support of all present social well-being, but the insufficiency of which does more than any one thing that can be named to keep back civilisation, virtue, everything on which human happiness on the largest scale depends; we feel that the violation, for a present advantage, of a rule of such transcendant expediency, is not expedient, and that he who, for the sake of a convenience to himself or to some other individual, does what depends on him to deprive mankind of the good, and inflict upon them the evil, involved in the greater or less reliance which they can place in each other's word, acts the part of one of their worst enemies.

Yet that even this rule, sacred as it is, admits of possible exceptions, is acknowledged by all moralists; the chief of which is when the withholding of some fact (as of information from a malefactor, or of bad news from a person dangerously ill) would save an individual (especially an individual other than oneself) from great and unmerited evil, and when the withholding can only be effected by denial. But in order that the exception may not extend itself beyond the need, and may have the least possible effect in weakening reliance on veracity, it ought to be recognised, and, if possible, its limits defined; and if the principle of utility is good for anything, it must be good for weighing these conflicting utilities against one another, and marking out the region within which one or the other preponderates.

Again, defenders of utility often find themselves called upon to reply to such objections as this—that there is not time, previous to action, for calculating and weighing the effects of any line of conduct on the general happiness. This is exactly as if any one were to say that it is impossible to guide our conduct by Christianity, because there is not time, on every occasion on which anything has to be done, to read through the Old and New Testaments. The answer to the objection is, that there has been ample time, namely, the whole past duration of the human species. During all that time, mankind have been learning by experience the tendencies of actions; on which experience all the prudence, as well as all the morality of life, are dependent. People talk as if the commencement of this course of experience had hitherto been put off, and as if, at the moment when some man feels tempted to meddle with the property or life of another, he had to begin considering for the first time whether murder and theft are injurious to human happiness. Even then I do not think that he would find the question very puzzling; but, at all events, the matter is now done to his hand.

It is truly a whimsical supposition that, if mankind were agreed in considering utility to be the test of morality, they would remain without any agreement as to what is useful, and would take no measures for having their notions on the subject taught to the young, and enforced by law and opinion. There is no difficulty in proving any ethical standard whatever to work ill, if we suppose universal idiocy to be conjoined with it; but on any hypothesis short of that, mankind must by this time have acquired positive beliefs as to the effects of some actions on their happiness; and the beliefs which have thus come down are the rules of morality for the multitude, and for the philosopher until he has succeeded in finding better.

That philosophers might easily do this, even now, on many subjects; that the received code of ethics is by no means of divine right; and that mankind have still much to learn as to the effects of actions on the general happiness, I admit, or rather, earnestly maintain. The corollaries from the principle of utility, like the precepts of every practical art, admit of indefinite improvement, and, in a progressive state of the human mind, their improvement is perpetually going on.

But to consider the rules of morality as improvable, is one thing; to pass over the intermediate generalisations entirely, and endeavour to test each individual action directly by the first principle, is another. It is a strange notion that the acknowledgment of a first principle is inconsistent with the admission of secondary ones. To inform a traveller respecting the place of his. ultimate destination, is not to forbid the use of landmarks and direction-posts on the way. The proposition that happiness is the end and aim of morality, does not mean that no road ought to be laid down to that goal, or that persons going thither should not be advised to take one direction rather than another. Men really ought to leave off talking a kind of nonsense on this subject, which they would neither talk nor listen to on other matters of practical concernment. Nobody argues that the art of navigation is not founded on astronomy, because sailors cannot wait to calculate the Nautical Almanack. Being rational creatures, they go to sea with it ready calculated; and all rational creatures go out upon the sea of life with their minds made up on the common questions of right and wrong, as well as on many of the far more difficult questions of wise and foolish. And this, as long as foresight is a human quality, it is to be presumed they will continue to do. Whatever we adopt as the fundamental principle of morality, we require subordinate principles to apply it by; the impossibility of doing without them, being common to all systems, can afford no argument against any one in particular; but gravely to argue as if no such secondary principles could be had, and as if mankind had remained till now, and always must remain, without drawing any general conclusions from the experience of human life, is as high a pitch, I think, as absurdity has ever reached in philosophical controversy.

The remainder of the stock arguments against utilitarianism mostly consist in laying to its charge the common infirmities of human nature, and the general difficulties which embarrass conscientious persons in shaping their course through life. We are told that a utilitarian will be apt to make his own particular case an exception to moral rules, and, when under temptation, will see a utility in the breach of a rule, greater than he will see in its observance. But is utility the only creed which is able to furnish us with excuses for evil doing, and means of cheating our own conscience? They are afforded in abundance by all doctrines which recognise as a fact in morals the existence of conflicting considerations; which all doctrines do, that have been believed by sane persons. It is not the fault of any creed, but of the complicated nature of human affairs, that rules of conduct cannot be so framed as to require no exceptions, and that hardly any kind of action can safely be laid down as either always obligatory or always condemnable. There is no ethical creed which does not temper the rigidity of its laws, by giving a certain latitude, under the moral responsibility of the agent, for accommodation to peculiarities of circumstances; and under every creed, at the opening thus made, self-deception and dishonest casuistry get in. There exists no moral system under which there do not arise unequivocal cases of conflicting obligation. These are the real difficulties, the knotty points both in the theory of ethics, and in the conscientious guidance of personal conduct. They are overcome practically, with greater or with less success, according to the intellect and virtue of the individual; but it can hardly be pretended that any one will be the less qualified for dealing with them, from possessing an ultimate standard to which conflicting rights and duties can be referred. If utility is the ultimate source of moral obligations, utility may be invoked to decide between them when their demands are incompatible. Though the application of the standard may be difficult, it is better than none at all: while in other systems, the moral laws all claiming independent authority, there is no common umpire entitled to interfere between them; their claims to precedence one over another rest on little better than sophistry, and unless determined, as they generally are, by the unacknowledged influence of considerations of utility, afford a free scope for the action of personal desires and partialities. We must remember that only in these cases of conflict between secondary principles is it requisite that first principles should be appealed to. There is no case of moral obligation in which some secondary principle is not involved; and if only one, there can seldom be any real doubt which one it is, in the mind of any person by whom the principle itself is recognised.

John Stuart Mill. *Utilitarianism*. London: Longmans, Green, Reader and Dyer, 1871.

9

POLITICAL PHILOSOPHY: WHAT IS JUST?

DAVID E. MCCLEAN

Non nobis solum nati sumus ortusque nostril partem patria vindicate, partem amici. (We are not born, do not live for ourselves alone; our country, our friends have a share in us.)   – Cicero, *De Officiis*

Every philosophy is under the illusion that it has no illusions because it has discovered the illusions of its predecessors.   – Reinhold Niebuhr

As philosophy is concerned with the application of critical intelligence, and often requires that one bring a skeptical mind to many types of inquiry, it might not be bad advice to suggest to a new student of political philosophy that he or she might do well to approach it *as* a philosopher would – bringing critical intelligence to the works of the various thinkers studied. The student might begin his or her inquiry with this heuristic:

All political philosophers were and are mistaken about a good many things, even where they proved or prove insightful about other things.

So, as one wades into the waters of political philosophy—as one wades into the waters of *any type of philosophical inquiry*—one could do worse than bring a large grain of salt along. One may be convinced, after all is said and done, that Plato (429 - 347 BCE), Aristotle (384-322 BCE) or Lenin (1870-1924) is right, more or less; but for the moment it might be best to avoid jumping to conclusions. Political philosophy—all philosophy—is full of interesting arguments, opinions and insights. Many philosophical conclusions ring true, even enduring the stresses of criticism over many years, but ultimately reveal themselves as only half-baked. Lurking behind what often seems to be a plausible set of assumptions about how a community or nation-state should be organized and governed, are collections of more basic assumptions, some of which are or were untested. One of the most basic assumptions concerns what we may call "the nature of Man." Other basic assumptions include: (i) women are not naturally equipped to govern; (ii) one's only real political loyalty can be to the city/city-state/nation of which one is a citizen or subject; (iii) some human beings are *naturally* subservient to other human beings; (iv) God ordains that a political community be organized in a certain way; and so forth. Like other people, a philosopher carries unexamined biases, even though it may appear as though he or she has purged all biases and is operating in a purely logical manner. That philosophers are "logic machines," operating with or from pure, unbiased perspectives when engaging in philosophical inquiry, is one of the great myths concerning philosophy and philosophers. The naïve acceptance of the myth of the detached and objective philosopher can mislead. It can also lead to real decisions, policies and consequences in the real world.

Two Foils: John Rawls and Carl Schmitt

In 1971 the American philosopher John Rawls (1921-2002) gave to the world an amazing work of systematic reasoning on matters political, *A Theory of Justice*—the first of its kind in many, many years. Systematic reasoning about politics had gone out of fashion prior to the appearance of this book (indeed, philosophy has its own cycles of fashion). Systematic reasoning in *political* philosophy—and in other areas of philosophical inquiry—was undermined by such movements as positivism, linguistic analysis, hermeneutics, pragmatism, and, more generally, postmodernism). In *A Theory of Justice*, Rawls attempted to establish the theoretical framework for what may be considered a just society. Rawls drew on the insights of another philosopher, IMMANUEL KANT (1724-1804), especially Kant's ethical philosophy, which was itself rooted in the larger project that was Kant's Critical Philosophy. In order to set the stage for the proper ordering of a society that would be just, Rawls told us, we have to start from what he called "the original position" and step behind what he called the "veil of ignorance." The ideas of the original position and the veil of ignorance were part of a thought experiment, one that was similar to other types of thought experiment that tried to get at the genesis of the rise of political communities ("How did political communities come about, anyway?"). Behind the veil of ignorance (according to this thought experiment) we would be deprived of any knowledge regarding how our personal attributes would situate us in the society we were about to (hypothetically) construct. The idea was that if we had no idea what would ultimately give us an advantage or what would impose a disadvantage, we would have a powerful incentive to construct a society in which, were we to be losers because of our status, we would not lose too much, and in which if we were winners, we would not win too much at the expense of the losers.

Rawls built upon Kant's claim that determining what is right to do in any given situation required the use of reason, for we are *essentially* rational creatures (not essentially white, or black, or bird watchers, or religious believers, or adventurers, or ballroom dancers). Reason, for both Kant and Rawls, is that faculty that allows us to formulate plans to attain our objectives. From this, Rawls goes one step further, and notes, with reference to Kant, that not only are we rational creatures, we are also *reasonable* creatures, and essentially so. Our reasonableness is what will allow us to construct a political community in which the members do not seek out their own interests, but will consider also the interests of others, for the sake of the community. It is also what will lead us to the conclusion that what is *just* must also be what is *fair*. A just society is one in which, with reference to the balance of human needs and wants in the aggregate, a condition exists that permits wealth but not at the expense of extreme poverty, for a society that distributes its resources (social welfare) in ways that produce large inequalities is one that distributes such resources in a matter that is unfair – one that no one in the original position would rationally sanction were there a real possibility that he or she would be the loser in such an arrangement.

Rawls wrote out of what is called The Social Contract Tradition in political philosophy, which includes Kant but also other philosophers. In the Social Contact Tradition, there tends to be thought experiments such as Rawls's—sustained reflections on the primordial or mythic point in time at which human beings determined it best to form political communities. It postulates or posits that human beings came together and constructed an agreement, a contract, by and through which rights would be preserved, and duties and constraints imposed on all contractors. Jean-Jacques Rousseau (1712-1778), John Locke (1632-1704), and Thomas Hobbes (1588-1679) were also part of this tradition, and each put forth ideas about that primordial point, the rationale for political community, the nature and basis of "equality" (etc.). However, as social contractarians (as these thinkers are called) begin not with historical facts but rather with *a priori* assumptions and traditions of thought, they tend to build upon assumptions that, in the eyes of many, seem shaky. For example, some critics of Rawls have argued that Rawls, in *A Theory of Justice*, merely built the foundation under a house that was already built, so to speak. That is, Rawls simply wrote an elaborate *apology* for a form of political life that he already valued, one based upon Western liberal principles of egalitarianism, democracy, and Liberalism. A tradition that was based upon ideas of natural law and natural rights, as articulated by his predecessors going back to Thomas Aquinas (1225-1274), John Locke, Hugo Grotius (1583-1645), Samuel Pufendorf (1632-1694) and others, contributed to a wholesale reconceptualization of the human being as infused with an inviolable set of entitlements that should be assumed so valuable as to override (at least most of the time) even the needs and desires of the community, or of the many. This was the rich intellectual loam from which *A Theory of Justice* emerged.

We in the Liberal West take these traditions of thought for granted; we swim in the waters of Liberalism as fish swim through actual water. We tend to think that our idea of "freedom," for example, is based upon some universal truth, some bedrock foundation ("We hold these truths to be self-evident, that all men are created equal, that they are endowed by their Creator with certain unalienable rights. . ."), and that there is a set way that any "reasonable" person would reckon in the original position. But is it the case that the most important thing about people is that they are rational, reasonable, and the bearers of rights? Are we not, also, filled with passions – love for our own particular cultures, commitment to our personal life goals and plans of life – and are we not also deeply conditioned by and embedded in a community that has given us, in many important ways, the very thoughts we think from day to day? As for our "reasonableness," are we as Rawls assumed we are? Philosopher Will Kymlicka (b. 1962) wonders:

> Consider Rawls's claim that impartial contractors would agree to distribute resources equally, unless the inequality is to the benefit of the least well-off. This principle [known as "The Difference Principle"] is chosen because impartial contractors are (according to Rawls) unwilling to risk being one of the undeserving losers in an inegalitarian society, even if that risk is small compared to the likelihood of being one of the winners. But, as Rawls admits, other assumptions about the dispositions of contractors are possible, in which case other principles would be chosen. If contractors are disposed to gamble, they might choose utilitarian principles which maximize the utility each contractor is likely to have in society, but which create the risk that they may end up being one of the people who is sacrificed for the great good of others (Singer, 193).

Kymlicka musses-up Rawl's neat assumptions (although Rawls would have his rejoinders to his critics in due course), and wonders whether human beings should be assumed to be so timid as to not assume the risk of a bet that they might actually wind up in a position to emerge "on top," rather than fall through the cracks, so to speak, into social oblivion or marginalization. Rawls assumes that "reasonable" people will behave in a predictable way when faced with the potential of serious loss. But it seems demonstrably false that this is so, unless of course one defines "reasonable" narrowly. People operate from a range of sensibilities, from a range of preferences, from sets of notions about what is relevant to their lives and what is irrelevant, about what makes life worth living and what makes life merely bearable. Some want to play it safe, while others prefer to take considerable risks, even if they might lose everything and have to start over again. Often, we even admire the risk-takers—write books and produce films about them.

Indeed, one of the criticisms of the thinking that pervades Liberalism is that it tends to boil down human beings to calculators, to a collection of bloodless rational actors who all share the same set of basic assumptions. Such thinking has been challenged by communitarians, who think, as did the Romantics that came to challenge the rationalism of the Enlightenment Project, that Liberalism's attempt to boil human beings down to no more than rational actors strips us of the things that make us most interesting (to us and to others) – our passions, our stories, our needs, our deepest hopes, our aspirations—the things that Rawls thought should not be permitted behind the veil. For these and other critics, the self is not merely a rational and predictable calculator, whether operating from behind some fancy called the veil of ignorance, or otherwise. The philosopher Daniel Dennett once called the human self a "center of narrative gravity." The notion that our stories, our narratives, are what most of us find the most important thing about ourselves is supported by other philosophers, including Alasdaire McIntyre (b. 1929) and Charles Taylor (b. 1931). While Liberalism has done great work to tame individual passions and cultural arrogance, demanding that one group's collective narrative should not be permitted to crowd out the collective narratives of others in a pluralistic democracy (Christianity over Islam, white over black, etc.), these thinkers have wondered if "coexistence" and pluralism has sometimes come at the price of erasing or blotting out the features of a life that make it worth living. Human beings are "rational animals," as Aristotle, Kant and Rawls would have it, but we are—arguably—much more than that. In addition, the communitarians would argue, no one can stand behind the veil of ignorance stripped of all that they are. A thought experiment is one, thing; fancy is another.

Yet Rawls's work is useful and instructive. The give and take with his critics led to a better and more tenable notion of Liberalism, which provided a set of arguments and a vocabulary with which liberal and pluralistic democracies can both understand themselves and defend themselves against "illiberal" ideas. Thanks to Rawls, we in the West no longer need to limit ourselves to John Locke, Benjamin Franklin (1706-1790), Thomas Paine (1737-1809) and Thomas Jefferson (1743-1846) for the intellectual underpinnings for the types of political communities constructed in the West. We can turn to a contemporary thinker, one who provided a rich and rigorous set of defenses for the type of political community we enjoy in the West. Rawls's political philosophy invites criticism, but the flaws in his theory of justice did not lead to catastrophic consequences (although some have argued that Rawls version of Liberalism, generally speaking, has led to an expansion of rights and a bloated welfare state that has become hard to maintain). We cannot be so sanguine about the errors of other political philosophers' works.

Carl Schmitt (1888-1985) was a German legal and political theorist, and an enthusiastic member of the Nazi Party, whose writings are now, once again – and, as far as some scholars are concerned, *oddly*—back in fashion (for a variety of reasons that we cannot explore here). He is known for, among other works, *Political Theology* and *The Idea of the Political*. Karl Schmitt is, arguably, the polar opposite of John Rawls. Not only did Schmitt not defend Liberalism, he disdained and rebuked it, and found it full of internal inconsistencies and false assumptions.

Indeed, not only did he find Liberalism problematic, but he found any notion of pluralism and cosmopolitanism to be the acme of absurdity. The idea of constructing a political community around Liberal and pluralistic ideas seemed, to Schmitt, to misunderstand the nature of Man (there's that phrase again). For Schmitt, Man is essentially dark, prone to evil, and the political community (i.e., the state) must keep this darkness in check. (This view about the darkness of human beings' essential nature is also held by many political conservatives in the West, although few would espouse Schmitt's conclusions concerning what is to be done about it.) As a Nazi, Schmitt was also aligned with notions of racial essentialism that were rampant in the Germany of his day, especially among those who were members of the Nazi party.

So strongly did Schmitt believe this philosophical anthropology about Man's essential darkness that he held that in order to save the political community from disintegration (which he witnessed in the case of Germany after World War I), the citizen-subject must accept certain hard facts about the limitations of his rights and freedoms. In Schmitt's political realism, which was more than mildly reminiscent of that of Hobbes and Machiavelli (1469-1527), politics and the state itself existed to preserve not rights or entitlements, but the *Volk*. As historian Mark Lilla (b. 1956) put it:

> Like a number of other German intellectuals, including Martin Heidegger, Ernst Jünger, and Gottfried Benn, Schmitt publicly supported the Nazis in the early days of the Third Reich. But . . . he went further than they did, becoming a committed, official advocate of the Nazi regime. Under the patronage of Hermann Göring, he was appointed to the Prussian State Council, received a professorship in Berlin, and edited an important legal journal. The Nazis obviously hoped that Schmitt would supply juridical respectability to Hitler's actions, and they were not disappointed. Soon after joining the party he wrote pamphlets defending the Führer principle, the priority of the Nazi Party, and racism, on the grounds that "all right [law] is the right of a particular *Volk*."

In support of his *Blut und Boden* political realism, in which "all right is the right of a particular *Volk*" (that is, a particular ethnic-racial group with attachment to a particular place), Schmitt held that all politics is, essentially, a game of "us" *versus* "them"—a game of determining who the "other" is as opposed to "us," and of determining the manner in which that "other" is to be engaged – or *dealt with*. More to the point, Schmitt wanted his German readers to understand that the matter wasn't merely about "us" and "them," but about "friends" and "enemies." Of course, the game of determining who the "enemy" is meant more and more sharply defining the nature of "us." The Nazi's notions of cultural and racial purity flowed, in part, from this type of thinking.

In his rejection of Liberalism Schmitt sketched, in both theoretical and legal terms, the role of the extreme unitary leader in the preservation of the *Volk*. Under cases of crisis or emergency, when the *Volk* (or, as it turned out in Nazi Germany, the purity of the *Volk*) is deemed to be threatened, the unitary leader is sanctioned to act in whatever ways he deems necessary, which may include the suspension of the common functions of government, even to the point that the law itself is suspended. This was Schmitt's Führer principle—the unitary leader is *self*-legitimating because, it is assumed, he embodies the essence of the *Volk*. Because of his theorizing, and in view of the position that Germany found itself in after the end of the World War I (Germany suffered a number of humiliations and its economy was a shambles), Schmitt was eagerly sought out by the Nazi Party because his ideas provided intellectual legitimacy to their nativist, racist, and statist worldviews and objectives. Indeed, among other things, Schmitt became known as "the crown jurist" of the Third Reich.

The belief that in times of crisis all the normal workings and legitimating mechanisms of government can be stripped away – notably its legislative and judicial functions – and centered in the person of one powerful unitary leader is what helped to build the bridge that allowed Adolf Hitler to step into power as Germany's supreme leader. Hitler, who would become "*The Führer*," would be the one to decide what was good or bad, right or wrong, moral or immoral for the German people. Schmitt declared that, ultimately, the sovereign is not the one who carries on the normal function of government and the wielding of state power, but the sovereign, ultimately, "is he who decides on the exception." The "exception" that Schmitt had in mind had to do with the power to actually suspend the law of the land in conditions of crisis or grave threat, such as was supposedly posed by the communists in Germany in the early 1930s (the Nazi's had held that the communists were seeking to foment revolution).

After the infamous Reichstag Fire of February 27, 1933 (the Reichstag was the seat of the German Parliament), Adolph Hitler, now German Chancellor and head of the coalition government, used Schmitt's theories to argue for the seizure of power, as Hitler and his supporters were able to convince enough now-primed government officials (including German President Paul von Hindenburg) that the fire was the work of Communist arsonists (although many historians have come to believe that the fire was actually set by the Nazis themselves as part of a plot to seize power, the fire being but a subterfuge):

> On the day following the fire, February 28, he [Hitler] prevailed on President Hindenburg to sign a decree "for the Protection of the People and the State" suspending the seven sections of the constitution which guaranteed individual and civil liberties. Described as a "defensive measure against Communist acts of violence endangering the state," the decree laid down that: "Restrictions on personal liberty, on the right of free expression of opinion, including freedom of the press; on the rights of assembly and association; and violations of the privacy of postal, telegraphic and telephonic communications; and warrants for house searches, orders for confiscations as well as restrictions on property, are also permissible beyond the legal limits otherwise prescribed" (Shire, 194).

From the notion that we are essentially rational and reasonable creatures to the notion that we are essentially defined by *Blut und Boden* commitments, political theorizing is fraught with dangers. The selection of Rawls and Schmitt for cursory discussion was intended only to highlight this point (and certainly not to draw any equivalence between these two thinkers). Whether it is correct to call Schmitt a "philosopher" or not is not pertinent to this cautionary introduction. Serious and sustained reflection and theorizing on the ways that political communities are to be ordered counts as doing political philosophy. Both Rawls and Schmitt were, by this definition, political philosophers. This is true of many dozens of other thinkers who have emerged over the centuries: Seneca the Younger (c. 1 BCE– CE 65), Cicero (106 – 46 BCE), Marcus Aurelius (120-180), Confucius (551–479 BCE), Mencius (372-289 BCE), Karl Marx (1818-1883), John Dewey (1859-1952), and many others.

As one commences reading what these thinkers had to say, one can ask oneself, with profit, these seven questions:

1. To what philosophical anthropology is this thinker committed?
2. What do we know now about the nature of human beings and even the world itself that this thinker did not know?

3. What circumstances or events likely influenced this thinker, and conditioned his or her views?
4. Is the thinker providing us with an unbiased argument, an argument that is value-laden, or an argument that begs the question?
5. What would it be like to live in the world in which this thinker would have us live?
6. What fallacies are afoot?
7. What assumptions and biases do I bring to my reading of the text?

Sources

Mark Lilla, "*The Enemy of Liberalism.*" *The New York Review of Books* (May 15, 1997).

Peter Singer, ed. *A Companion to Ethics.* Massachusetts: Blackwell Publishers, 1993.

William L. Shirer. *The Rise and Fall of the Third Reich: A History of Nazi Germany.* New York: Simon & Schuster, 1960.

CRITO

PLATO (424-348 BCE)

As you may recall from reading the Apology, at the end of Socrates' trial he has been found guilty of the charges leveled against him and the jury has decreed that his penalty be death. Socrates' accusers probably never expected to have to put him to death. It was assumed that he would escape from prison and the city of Athens would finally be rid of their resident nuisance. Unfortunately, Socrates' accusers failed to take into account the old gadfly's commitment to his philosophical convictions.

The Crito *opens as Socrates is awaiting his execution. During his trial, the state ship of Athens was on a sacred mission to Delos, and when it returned it was degreed that Socrates would finally be put to death. Crito, a good friend of Socrates, stops into his prison to try to convince him to flee before this happens. Besides providing a wonderful illustration of the Socratic method in action, the dialogue also offers a glimpse of Socrates' views on the relationship of citizens to the state. Socrates' rather controversial position is that, even when the state in which one lives is unjust, one is always obligated to obey the laws of that state.*

1. The Opening of the Dialogue

SOCRATES: Why have you come at this hour, Crito? it must be quite early?

CRITO: Yes, certainly.

SOC: What is the exact time?

CR: The dawn is breaking.

SOC: I wonder that the keeper of the prison would let you in.

CR: He knows me, because I often come, Socrates; moreover, I have done him a kindness.

SOC: And are you only just arrived?

CR: No, I came some time ago.

SOC: Then why did you sit and say nothing, instead of at once awakening me?

CR: I should not have liked myself, Socrates, to be in such great trouble and unrest as you are—indeed I should not: I have been watching with amazement your peaceful slumbers; and for that reason I did not awake you, because I wished to minimize the pain. I have always thought you to be of a happy disposition; but never did I see anything like the easy, tranquil manner in which you bear this calamity.

SOC: Why, Crito, when a man has reached my age he ought not to be repining at the approach of death.

CR: And yet other old men find themselves in similar misfortunes, and age does not prevent them from repining.

SOC: That is true. But you have not told me why you come at this early hour.

CR: I come to bring you a message which is sad and painful; not, as I believe, to yourself, but to all of us who are your friends, and saddest of all to me.

SOC: What? Has the ship come from Delos, on the arrival of which I am to die?

CR: No, the ship has not actually arrived, but she will probably be here to-day, as persons who have come from Sunium tell me that they have left her there; and therefore to-morrow, Socrates, will be the last day of your life.

SOC: Very well, Crito; if such is the will of God, I am willing; but my belief is that there will be a delay of a day.

CR: Why do you think so?

SOC: I will tell you. I am to die on the day after the arrival of the ship?

CR: Yes; that is what the authorities say.

SOC: But I do not think that the ship will be here until to-morrow; this I infer from a vision which I had last night, or rather only just now, when you fortunately allowed me to sleep.

CR: And what was the nature of the vision?

SOC: There appeared to me the likeness of a woman, fair and comely, clothed in bright raiment, who called to me and said: O Socrates, 'The third day hence to fertile Phthia shalt thou go.'

CR: What a singular dream, Socrates!

SOC: There can be no doubt about the meaning, Crito, I think.

CR: Yes; the meaning is only too clear.

2. Crito's "Reasons" for Socrates' Escape

Cr: But, oh! my beloved Socrates, let me entreat you once more to take my advice and escape. For if you die I shall not only lose a friend who can never be replaced, but there is another evil: people who do not know you and me will believe that I might have saved you if I had been willing to give money, but that I did not care. Now, can there be a worse disgrace than this—that I should be thought to value money more than the life of a friend? For the many will not be persuaded that I wanted you to escape, and that you refused.

SOC: But why, my dear Crito, should we care about the opinion of the many? Good men, and they are the only persons who are worth considering, will think of these things truly as they occurred.

CR: But you see, Socrates, that the opinion of the many must be regarded, for what is now happening shows that they can do the greatest evil to anyone who has lost their good opinion.

SOC: I only wish it were so, Crito; and that the many could do the greatest evil; for then they would also be able to do the greatest good—and what a fine thing this would be! But in reality they can do neither; for they cannot make a man either wise or foolish; and whatever they do is the result of chance.

CR: Well, I will not dispute with you; but please to tell me, Socrates, whether you are not acting out of regard to me and your other friends: are you not afraid that if you escape from prison we may get into trouble with the informers for having stolen you away, and lose either the whole or a great part of our property; or that even a worse evil may happen to us? Now, if you fear on our account, be at ease; for in order to save you, we ought surely to run this, or even a greater risk; be persuaded, then, and do

as I say.

SOC: Yes, Crito, that is one fear which you mention, but by no means the only one.

CR: Fear not—there are persons who are willing to get you out of prison at no great cost; and as for the informers, they are far from being exorbitant in their demands—a little money will satisfy them. My means, which are certainly ample, are at your service, and if you have a scruple about spending all mine, here are strangers who will give you the use of theirs; and one of them, Simmias the Theban, has brought a large sum of money for this very purpose; and Cebes and many others are prepared to spend their money in helping you to escape. I say, therefore, do not hesitate on our account, and do not say, as you did in the court that you will have a difficulty in knowing what to do with yourself anywhere else. For men will love you in other places to which you may go, and not in Athens only; there are friends of mine in Thessaly, if you like to go to them, who will value and protect you, and no Thessalian will give you any trouble. Nor can I think that you are at all justified, Socrates, in betraying your own life when you might be saved; in acting thus you are playing into the hands of your enemies, who are hurrying on your destruction. And further I should say that you are deserting your own children; for you might bring them up and educate them; instead of which you go away and leave them, and they will have to take their chance; and if they do not meet with the usual fate of orphans, there will be small thanks to you. No man should bring children into the world who is unwilling to persevere to the end in their nurture and education. But you appear to be choosing the easier part, not the better and manlier, which would have been more becoming in one who professes to care for virtue in all his actions, like yourself. And indeed, I am ashamed not only of you, but of us who are your friends, when I reflect that the whole business will be attributed entirely to our want of courage. The trial need never have come on, or might have been managed differently; and this last act, or crowning folly, will seem to have occurred through our negligence and cowardice, who might have saved you, if we had been good for anything; and you might have saved yourself, for there was no difficulty at all. See now, Socrates, how sad and discreditable are the consequences, both to us and you. Make up your mind then, or rather have your mind already made up, for the time of deliberation is over, and there is only one thing to be done, which must be done this very night, and, if we delay at all, will be no longer practicable or possible; I beseech you therefore, Socrates, be persuaded by me, and do as I say.

3. Socrates' Philosophical Principles:

3a. Always Follow the Path of Reason

SOC: Dear Crito, your zeal is invaluable, if a right one; but if wrong, the greater the zeal the greater the danger; and therefore we ought to consider whether I shall or shall not do as you say. For I am and always have been one of those natures who must be guided by reason, whatever the reason may be which upon reflection appears to me to be the best; and now that this chance has befallen me, I cannot repudiate my own words: the principles which I have hitherto honoured and revered I still honour, and unless we can at once find other and better principles, I am certain not to agree with you; no, not even if the power of the multitude could inflict many more imprisonments, confiscations, deaths, frightening us like children with hobgoblin terrors. What will be the fairest way of considering the question? Shall I return to your old argument about the opinions of men?—we were saying that some of them are to be regarded, and others not. Now were we right in maintaining this before I was condemned? And has the argument which was once good now proved to be talk for the sake of talking—mere childish nonsense? That is what I want to consider with your help, Crito:—whether, under my present circumstances, the argument appears to be in any way different or not; and is to be allowed by me or disallowed. That argument, which, as I believe, is maintained by many persons of authority, was to the effect, as I was saying, that the opinions of some men are to be regarded, and of other men not to be regarded. Now you, Crito, are not going to die to-morrow—at least, there is no human probability of this—and therefore you are disinterested and not liable to be deceived by the circumstances in which you are placed. Tell me then, whether I am right in saying that some opinions, and the opinions of some men only, are to be valued, and that other opinions, and the opinions of other men,

are not to be valued. I ask you whether I was right in maintaining this?

CR: Certainly.

SOC: The good are to be regarded, and not the bad?

CR: Yes.

SOC: And the opinions of the wise are good, and the opinions of the unwise are evil?

CR: Certainly.

SOC: And what was said about another matter? Is the pupil who devotes himself to the practice of gymnastics supposed to attend to the praise and blame and opinion of every man, or of one man only—his physician or trainer, whoever he may be?

CR: Of one man only.

SOC: And he ought to fear the censure and welcome the praise of that one only, and not of the many?

CR: Clearly so.

SOC: And he ought to act and train, and eat and drink in the way which seems good to his single master who has understanding, rather than according to the opinion of all other men put together?

CR: True.

SOC: And if he disobeys and disregards the opinion and approval of the one, and regards the opinion of the many who have no understanding, will he not suffer evil?

CR: Certainly he will.

SOC: And what will the evil be, whither tending and what affecting, in the disobedient person?

CR: Clearly, affecting the body; that is what is destroyed by the evil.

SOC: Very good; and is not this true, Crito, of other things which we need not separately enumerate? In questions of just and unjust, fair and foul, good and evil, which are the subjects of our present consultation, ought we to follow the opinion of the many and to fear them; or the opinion of the one man who has understanding? ought we not to fear and reverence him more than all the rest of the world: and if we desert him shall we not destroy and injure that principle in us which may be assumed to be improved by justice and deteriorated by injustice—there is such a principle?

CR: Certainly there is, Socrates.

SOC: Take a parallel instance:—if, acting under the advice of those who have no understanding, we destroy that which is improved by health and is deteriorated by disease, would life be worth having? And that which has been destroyed is—the body?

CR: Yes.

SOC: Could we live, having an evil and corrupted body?

CR: Certainly not.

SOC: And will life be worth having, if that higher part of man be destroyed, which is improved by justice and depraved by injustice? Do we suppose that principle, whatever it may be in man, which has to do with justice and injustice, to be inferior to the body?

CR: Certainly not.

SOC: More honourable than the body?

CR: Far more.

SOC: Then, my friend, we must not regard what the many say of us; but what he, the one man who has understanding of just and unjust, will say, and what the truth will say. And therefore you begin in error when you advise that we should regard the opinion of the many about just and unjust, good and evil, honourable and dishonourable.—'Well,' someone will say, 'but the many can kill us.'

CR: Yes, Socrates; that will clearly be the answer.

SOC: And it is true; but still I find with surprise that the old argument is unshaken as ever. And I should like to know whether I may say the same of another proposition—that not life, but a good life, is to be chiefly valued?

CR: Yes, that also remains unshaken.

SOC: And a good life is equivalent to a just and honourable one—that holds also?

CR: Yes, it does.

SOC: From these premises I proceed to argue the question whether I ought or ought not to try and escape without the consent of the Athenians: and if I am clearly right in escaping, then I will make the attempt; but if not, I will abstain. The other considerations which you mention, of money and loss of character and the duty of educating one's children, are, I fear, only the doctrines of the multitude, who would be as ready to restore people to life, if they were able, as they are to put them to death—and with as little reason. But now, since the argument has thus far prevailed, the only question which remains to be considered is whether we shall do rightly either in escaping or in suffering others to aid in our escape and paying them in money and thanks, or whether in reality we shall not do rightly; and if the latter, then death or any other calamity which may ensue on my remaining here must not be allowed to enter into the calculation.

CR: I think that you are right, Socrates; how then shall we proceed?

SOC: Let us consider the matter together, and do you either refute me if you can, and I will be convinced; or else cease, my dear friend, from repeating to me that I ought to escape against the wishes of the Athenians: for I highly value your attempts to persuade me to do so, but I may not be persuaded against my own better judgment. And now please to consider my first position, and try how you can best answer me.

CR: I will.

3b. Always Avoid Doing Wrong

SOC: Are we to say that we are never intentionally to do wrong, or that in one way we ought and in another way we ought not to do wrong, or is doing wrong always evil and dishonourable, as I was just now saying, and as has been already acknowledged by us? Are all our former admissions which were made within a few days to be thrown away? And have we, at our age, been earnestly discoursing with one another all our life long only to discover that we are no better than children? Or, in spite of the opinion of the many, and in spite of consequences whether better or worse, shall we insist on the truth of what was then said, that injustice is always an evil and dishonour to him who acts unjustly? Shall we say so or not?

CR: Yes.

SOC: Then we must do no wrong?

CR: Certainly not.

SOC: Nor, when injured, injure in return, as the many imagine; for we must injure no one at all?

CR: Clearly not.

SOC: Again, Crito, may we do evil?

CR: Surely not, Socrates.

SOC: And what of doing evil in return for evil, which is the morality of the many—is that just or not?

CR: Not just.

SOC: For doing evil to another is the same as injuring him?

CR: Very true.

SOC: Then we ought not to retaliate or render evil for evil to anyone, whatever evil we may have suffered from him. But I would have you consider, Crito, whether you really mean what you are saying. For this opinion has never been held, and never will be held, by any considerable number of persons; and those who are agreed and those who are not agreed upon this point have no common ground, and can only despise one another when they see how widely they differ. Tell me, then, whether you agree with and assent to my first principle, that neither injury nor retaliation nor warding off evil by evil is ever right. And shall that be the premise of our argument? Or do you decline and dissent from this? For so I have ever thought, and continue to think; but, if you are of another opinion, let me hear what you have to say. If, however, you remain of the same mind as formerly, I will proceed to the next step.

CR: You may proceed, for I have not changed my mind.

SOC: Then I will go on to the next point, which may be put in the form of a question:—Ought a man to do what he admits to be right, or ought he to betray the right?

CR: He ought to do what he thinks right.

SOC: But if this is true, what is the application? In leaving the prison against the will of the Athenians, do I wrong any? or rather do I not wrong those whom I ought least to wrong? Do I not desert the principles which were acknowledged by us to be just—what do you say?

CR: I cannot tell, Socrates; for I do not know.

4. Socrates' Arguments

4a. Obeying the Law

SOC: Then consider the matter in this way: Imagine that I am about to play truant (you may call the proceeding by any name which you like), and the laws and the government come and interrogate me: 'Tell us, Socrates,' they say; 'what are you about? are you not going by an act of yours to overturn us—the laws, and the whole state, as far as in you lies? Do you imagine that a state can subsist and not be overthrown, in which the decisions of law have no power, but are set aside and trampled upon by individuals?' What will be our answer, Crito, to these and the like words? Anyone, and especially a rhetorician, will have a good deal to say on behalf of the law which requires a sentence to be carried out. He will argue that this law should not be set aside; and shall we reply, 'Yes; but the state has injured us and given an unjust sentence.' Suppose I say that?

CR: Very good, Socrates.

SOC: 'And was that our agreement with you?' the law would answer; 'or were you to abide by the sentence of the state?' And if I were to express my astonishment at their words, the law would probably add: 'Answer, Socrates, instead of opening your eyes—you are in the habit of asking and answering questions. Tell us,—What complaint have you to make against us which justifies you in attempting to destroy us and the state?

4b. The State as Our Parent

SOC: In the first place did we not bring you into existence? Your father married your mother by our aid and begat you. Say whether you have any objection to urge against those of us who regulate marriage?' None, I should reply. 'Or against those of us who after birth regulate the nurture and education of children, in which you also were trained? Were not the laws, which have the charge of education, right in commanding your father to train you in music and gymnastic?' Right, I should reply. 'Well then, since you were brought into the world and nurtured and educated by us, can you deny in the first place that you are our child and slave, as your fathers were before you? And if this is true you are not on equal terms with us; nor can you think that you have a right to do to us what we are doing to you. Would you have any right to strike or revile or do any other evil to your father or your master, if you had one, because you have been struck or reviled by him, or received some other evil at his hands? You would not say this. And because we think right to destroy you, do you think that you have any right to destroy us in return, and your country as far as in you lies? Will you, O professor of true virtue, pretend that you are justified in this? Has a philosopher like you failed to discover that our country is more to be valued and higher and holier far than mother or father or any ancestor, and more to be regarded in the eyes of the gods and of men of understanding? also to be soothed, and gently and reverently entreated when angry, even more than a father, and either to be persuaded, or if not persuaded, to be obeyed? And when we are punished by her, whether with imprisonment or stripes, the punishment is to be endured in silence; and if she lead us to wounds or death in battle, thither we follow as is right; neither may anyone yield or retreat or leave his rank, but whether in battle or in a court of law, or in any other place, he must do what his city and his country order him; or he must change their view of what is just: and if he may do no violence to his father or mother, much less may he do violence to his country.' What answer shall we make to this, Crito? Do the laws speak truly, or do they not?

CR: I think that they do.

SOC: Then the laws will say: 'Consider, Socrates, if we are speaking truly that in your present attempt you are going to do us an injury. For, having brought you into the world, and nurtured and educated you, and given you and every other citizen a share in every good which we had to give, we further proclaim to any Athenian by the liberty which we allow him, that if he does not like us when he has become of age and has seen the ways of the city, and made our acquaintance, he may go where he pleases and take his goods with him. None of us laws will forbid him or interfere with him. Anyone who does not like us and the city, and who wants to emigrate to a colony or to any other city, may go where he likes, retaining his property. But he who has experience of the manner in which we order justice and administer the state, and still remains, has entered into an implied contract that he will do as we command him. And he who disobeys us is, as we maintain, thrice wrong; first, because in disobeying us he is disobeying his parents; secondly, because we are the authors of his education; thirdly, because he has made an agreement with us that he will duly obey our commands; and he neither obeys them nor convinces us that our commands are unjust; and we do not rudely impose them, but give him the alternative of obeying or convincing us;—that is what we offer, and he does neither. These are the sort of accusations to which, as we were saying, you, Socrates, will be exposed if you accomplish your intentions;

you, above all other Athenians.'

4c. Breaking the Laws as Promise Breaking

SOC: Suppose now I ask, why I rather than anybody else? they will justly retort upon me that I above all other men have acknowledged the agreement. 'There is clear proof,' they will say, 'Socrates, that we and the city were not displeasing to you. Of all Athenians you have been the most constant resident in the city, which, as you never leave, you may be supposed to love. For you never went out of the city either to see the games, except once when you went to the Isthmus, or to any other place unless when you were on military service; nor did you travel as other men do. Nor had you any curiosity to know other states or their laws: your affections did not go beyond us and our state; we were your especial favourites, and you acquiesced in our government of you; and here in this city you begat your children, which is a proof of your satisfaction. Moreover, you might in the course of the trial, if you had liked, have fixed the penalty at banishment; the state which refuses to let you go now would have let you go then. But you pretended that you preferred death to exile, and that you were not unwilling to die. And now you have forgotten these fine sentiments, and pay no respect to us the laws, of whom you are the destroyer; and are doing what only a miserable slave would do, running away and turning your back upon the compacts and agreements which you made as a citizen. And first of all answer this very question: Are we right in saying that you agreed to be governed according to us in deed, and not in word only? Is that true or not?' How shall we answer, Crito? Must we not assent?

CR: We cannot help it, Socrates.

SOC: Then will they not say: 'You, Socrates, are breaking the covenants and agreements which you made with us at your leisure, not in any haste or under any compulsion or deception, but after you have had seventy years to think of them, during which time you were at liberty to leave the city, if we were not to your mind, or if our covenants appeared to you to be unfair. You had your choice, and might have gone either to Lacedaemon or Crete, both which states are often praised by you for their good government, or to some other Hellenic or foreign state. Whereas you, above all other Athenians, seemed to be so fond of the state, or, in other words, of us, her laws (and who would care about a state which has no laws?), that you never stirred out of her; the halt, the blind, the maimed were not more stationary in her than you were. And now you run away and forsake your agreements. Not so, Socrates, if you will take our advice; do not make yourself ridiculous by escaping out of the city.

5. Socrates' Conclusions

SOC: 'For just consider, if you transgress and err in this sort of way, what good will you do either to yourself or to your friends? That your friends will be driven into exile and deprived of citizenship, or will lose their property, is tolerably certain; and you yourself, if you fly to one of the neighbouring cities, as, for example, Thebes or Megara, both of which are well governed, will come to them as an enemy, Socrates, and their government will be against you, and all patriotic citizens will cast an evil eye upon you as a subverter of the laws, and you will confirm in the minds of the judges the justice of their own condemnation of you. For he who is a corrupter of the laws is more than likely to be a corrupter of the young and foolish portion of mankind. Will you then flee from well-ordered cities and virtuous men? and is existence worth having on these terms? Or will you go to them without shame, and talk to them, Socrates? And what will you say to them? What you say here about virtue and justice and institutions and laws being the best things among men? Would that be decent of you? Surely not. But if you go away from well-governed states to Crito's friends in Thessaly, where there is great disorder and licence, they will be charmed to hear the tale of your escape from prison, set off with ludicrous particulars of the manner in which you were wrapped in a goatskin or some other disguise, and metamorphosed as the manner is of runaways; but will there be no one to remind you that in your old age you were not ashamed to violate the most sacred laws from a miserable desire of a little more life? Perhaps not, if you keep them in a good temper; but if they are out of temper you will hear many degrading things; you will live, but how?—as the flatterer of all men, and the servant of all men; and doing what?—eating and drinking in Thessaly, having gone abroad in order that you may get a dinner. And where will be your fine sentiments about justice and virtue? Say that you wish to live for the sake of your children—you want to bring them up and educate them—will you take them into Thessaly and deprive them of Athenian citizenship? Is this the benefit which you will confer upon them? Or are you under the impression that they will be better cared for and educated here if you are still alive, although absent from them; for your friends will take care of them? Do you fancy that if you are an inhabitant of Thessaly they will take care of them, and if you are an inhabitant of the other world that they will not take care of them? Nay; but if they who call themselves friends are good for anything, they will—to be sure they will.

'Listen, then, Socrates, to us who have brought you up. Think not of life and children first, and of justice afterwards, but of justice first, that you may be justified before the princes of the world below. For neither will you nor any that belong to you be happier or holier or juster in this life, or happier in another, if you do as Crito bids. Now you depart in innocence, a sufferer and not a doer of evil; a victim, not of the laws, but of men. But if you go forth, returning evil for evil, and injury for injury, breaking the covenants and agreements which you have made with us, and wronging those whom you ought least of all to wrong, that is to say, yourself, your friends, your country, and us, we shall be angry with you while you live, and our brethren, the laws in the world below, will receive you as an enemy; for they will know that you have done your best to destroy us. Listen, then, to us and not to Crito.'

This, dear Crito, is the voice which I seem to hear murmuring in my ears, like the sound of the flute in the ears of the mystic; that voice, I say, is humming in my ears, and prevents me from hearing any other. And I know that anything more which you may say will be vain. Yet speak, if you have anything to say.

CR: I have nothing to say, Socrates.

SOC: Leave me then, Crito, to fulfil the will of God, and to follow whither he leads.

Plato. "Crito." *The Dialogues of Plato.* Vol. 2. Trans. by Benjamin Jowett. Oxford: Oxford University Press, 1892.

THE TWO CITIES

AUGUSTINE (354-430)

The Catholic Church in the Middle Ages was in something of a bind when it came to the political realm. On the one hand, the Church was the dominant institution in Europe from the time of Constantine in the fourth century A.D., and therefore had to take political life seriously; on the other hand, however, the Christian's ultimate goal was directed towards eternal life with God in heaven. This tension between the Christian's earthly and heavenly kingdoms is nowhere better illustrated than in Augustine's monumental work, De Civitate Dei *(The City of God). In the end, true peace and ultimate fulfillment for the Christian can only be found in the next life, according to Augustine.*

Book XIV

Chapter 28

Of the nature of the two cities, the earthly and the heavenly.

Accordingly, two cities have been formed by two loves: the earthly by the love of self, even to the contempt of God; the heavenly by the love of God, even to the contempt of self. The former, in a word, glories in itself, the latter in the Lord. For the one seeks glory from men; but the greatest glory of the other is God, the witness of conscience. The one lifts up its head in its own glory; the other says to its God, "Thou are my glory, and the lifter up of my head." In the one, the princes and the nations it subdues are ruled by the love of ruling; in the other, the princes and the subjects serve one another in love, the latter obeying, while the former take thought for all. The one delights in its own strength, represented in the persons of its rulers; the other says to its God, "I will love you, O Lord, my strength." And therefore the wise men of the one city, living according to man, have sought for profit to their own bodies or souls, or both, and those who have known God "glorified Him not as God, neither were thankful, but became vain in their imaginations, and their foolish heart was darkened; professing themselves to be wise,"—

that is, glorying in their own wisdom, and being possessed by pride,—"they became fools, and changed the glory of the incorruptible God into an image made like to corruptible man, and to birds, and four-footed beasts, and creeping things." For they were either leaders or followers of the people in adoring images, "and worshipped and served the creature more than the Creator, who is blessed for ever." But in the other city there is no human wisdom, but only godliness, which offers due worship to the true God, and looks for its reward in the society of the saints, of holy angels as well as holy men, "that God may be all in all."

Book XV

Chapter 4

Of the Conflict And Peace Of The Earthly City.

But the earthly city, which shall not be everlasting (for it will no longer be a city when it has been committed to the extreme penalty), has its good in this world, and rejoices in it with such joy as such things can afford. But as this is not a good which can discharge its devotees of all distresses, this city is often divided against itself by litigations, wars, quarrels, and such victories as are either life-destroying or short-lived. For each part of it that arms against another part of it seeks to triumph over the nations through itself in bondage to vice. If, when it has conquered, it is inflated with pride, its victory is life-destroying; but if it turns its thoughts upon the common casualties of our mortal condition, and is rather anxious concerning the disasters that may befall it than elated with the successes already achieved, this victory, though of a higher kind, is still only shot-lived; for it cannot abidingly rule over those whom it has victoriously subjugated. But the things which this city desires cannot justly be said to be evil, for it is itself, in its own kind, better than all other human good. For it desires earthly peace for the sake of enjoying earthly goods, and it makes war in order to attain to this peace; since, if it has conquered, and there remains no one to resist it, it enjoys a peace which it had not while there were opposing parties who contested for the enjoyment of those things which were too small to satisfy both. This peace is purchased by toilsome wars; it is obtained by what they style a glorious victory. Now, when victory remains with the party which had the juster cause, who hesitates to congratulate the victor, and style it a desirable peace? These things, then, are good things, and without doubt the gifts of God. But if they neglect the better things of the heavenly city, which are secured by eternal victory and peace never-ending, and so inordinately covet these present good things that they believe them to be the only desirable things, or love them better than those things which are believed to be better,—if this be so, then it is necessary that misery follow and ever increase.

Book XIX

Chapter 13

Of the universal peace which the law of nature preserves through all disturbances, and by which everyone reaches his desert in a way regulated by the just judge.

The peace of the body then consists in the duly proportioned arrangement of its parts. The petite of the irrational soul is the harmonious repose of the appetites, and that of the rational soul the harmony of knowledge and action. The peace of body and soul is the well-ordered and harmonious life and health of the living creature. Peace between man and God is the well-ordered obedience of faith to eternal law. Peace between man and man is well-ordered concord. Domestic peace is the well-ordered concord between those of the family who rule and those who obey. Civil peace is a similar concord among the citizens. The peace of the celestial city is the perfectly ordered and harmonious enjoyment of God, and of one another in God. The peace of all things is the tranquillity of order. Order is the distribution which allots things equal and unequal, each to its own place. And hence, though the miserable, in so far as they are such, do certainly not enjoy peace, but are severed from that tranquillity of order in which there is no disturbance, nevertheless, inasmuch as they are deservedly and justly, miserable, they are by their very misery connected with order....

Chapter 14

Of the order and law which obtain in heaven and earth, whereby it comes to pass that human society is served by those who rule it.

The whole use, then, of things temporal has a reference to this result of earthly peace in the earthly community, while in the city of God it is connected with eternal peace. And therefore, if we were irrational animals, we should desire nothing beyond the proper arrangement of the parts of the body and the satisfaction of the appetites,—nothing, therefore, but bodily comfort and abundance of pleasures, that the peace of the body might contribute to the peace of the soul. For if bodily peace be awanting, a bar is put to the peace even of the irrational soul, since it cannot obtain the gratification of its appetites. And these two together help out the mutual peace of soul and body, the peace of harmonious life and health. For as animals, by shunning pain, show that they love bodily peace, and, by pursuing pleasure to gratify their appetites, show that they love peace of soul, so their shrinking from death is a sufficient indication of their intense love of that peace which binds soul and body in close alliance. But, as man has a rational soul, he subordinates all this which he has in common with the beasts to the peace of his rational soul, that his intellect may have free play and may regulate his actions, and that he may thus enjoy the well-ordered harmony of knowledge and action which constitutes, as we have said, the peace of the rational soul. And for this purpose he must desire to be neither molested by pain, nor disturbed by desire, nor extinguished by death, that he may arrive at some useful knowledge by which he may regulate his life and manners. But, owing to the liability of the human mind to fall into mistakes, this very pursuit of knowledge may be a snare to him unless he has a divine Master, whom he may obey without misgiving, and who may at the same time give him such help as to preserve his own freedom. And because, so long as he is in this mortal body, he is a stranger to God, he walks by faith, not by sight; and he therefore refers all peace, bodily or spiritual or both, to that peace which mortal man has with the immortal God, so that he exhibits the well-ordered obedience of faith to eternal law.

But as this divine Master inculcates two precepts—the love of God and the love of our neighbor—and as in these precepts a man finds three things he has to love—God, himself, and his neighbor—and that he who loves God loves himself thereby, it follows that he must endeavor to get his neighbor to love God, since he is ordered to love his neighbor as himself. He ought to make this endeavor in behalf of his wife, his children, his household, all within his reach, even as he would wish his neighbor to do the same for him if he needed it; and consequently he will be at peace, or in well-ordered concord, with all men, as far as in him lies. And this is the order of this concord, that a man, in the first place, injure no one, and, in the second, do good to every one he can reach. Primarily, therefore, his own household are his care, for the law of nature and of society gives him readier access to them and greater opportunity of serving them. And hence the apostle says, "Now, if any provide not for his own, and specially for those of his own house, he hath denied the faith, and is worse than an infidel." This is the origin of domestic peace, or the well-ordered concord of those in the family who rule and those who obey. For they who care for the rest rule—the husband the wife, the parents the children, the masters the servants; and they who are cared for obey—the women their husbands, the children their parents, the servants their masters. But in the family of the just man who lives

by faith and is as yet a pilgrim journeying on to the celestial city, even those who rule serve those whom they seem to command; for they rule not from a love of power, but from a sense of the duty they owe to others—not because they are proud of authority, but because they love mercy.

Chapter 17

What produces peace, and what discord, between the heavenly and earthly cities.

But the families which do not live by faith seek their peace in the earthly advantages of this life; while the families which live by faith look for those eternal blessings which are promised, and use as pilgrims such advantages of time and of earth as do not fascinate and divert them from God, but rather aid them to endure with greater ease, and to keep down the number of those burdens of the corruptible body which weigh upon the soul. Thus the things necessary for this mortal life are used by both kinds of men and families alike, but each has its own peculiar and widely different aim in using them. The earthly city, which does not live by faith, seeks an earthly peace, and the end it proposes, in the well-ordered concord of civic obedience and rule, is the combination of men's wills to attain the things which are helpful to this life. The heavenly city, or rather the part of it which sojourns on earth and lives by faith, makes use of this peace only because it must, until this mortal condition which necessitates it shall pass away. Consequently, so long as it lives like a captive and a stranger in the earthly city, though it has already received the promise of redemption, and the gift of the Spirit as the earnest of it, it makes no scruple to obey the laws of the earthly city, whereby the things necessary for the maintenance of this mortal life are administered; and thus, as this life is common to both cities, so there is a harmony between them in regard to what belongs to it.

But, as the earthly city has had some philosophers whose doctrine is condemned by the divine teaching, and who, being deceived either by their own conjectures or by demons, supposed that many gods must be invited to take an interest in human affairs, and assigned to each a separate function and a separate department,—to one the body, to another the soul; and in the body itself, to one the head, to another the neck, and each of the other members to one of the gods; and in like manner, in the soul, to one god the natural capacity was assigned, to another education, to another anger, to another lust; and so the various affairs of life were assigned,—cattle to one, corn to another, wine to another, oil to another, the woods to another, money to another, navigation to another, wars and victories to another, marriages to another, births and fecundity to another, and other things to other gods: and as the celestial city, on the other hand, knew that one God only was to be worshipped, and that to Him alone was due that service which the Greeks call latreia, and which can be given only to a god, it has come to pass that the two cities could not have common laws of religion, and that the heavenly city has been compelled in this matter to dissent, and to become obnoxious to those who think differently, and to stand the brunt of their anger and hatred and persecutions, except in so far as the minds of their enemies have been alarmed by the multitude of the Christians and quelled by the manifest protection of God accorded to them.

This heavenly city, then, while it sojourns on earth, calls citizens out of all nations, and gathers together a society of pilgrims of all languages, not scrupling about diversities in the manners, laws, and institutions whereby earthly peace is secured and maintained, but recognizing that, however various these are, they all tend to one and the same end of earthly peace. It therefore is so far from rescinding and abolishing these diversities, that it even preserves and adopts them, so long only as no hindrance to the worship of the one supreme and true God is thus introduced. Even the heavenly city, therefore, while in its state of pilgrimage, avails itself of the peace of earth, and, so far as it can without injuring faith and godliness, desires and maintains a common agreement among men regarding the acquisition of the necessaries of life, and makes this earthly peace bear upon the peace of heaven; for this alone can be truly called and esteemed the peace of the reasonable creatures, consisting as it does in the perfectly ordered and harmonious enjoyment of God and of one another in God. When we shall have reached that peace, this mortal life shall give place to one that is eternal, and our body shall be no more this animal body which by its corruption weighs down the

soul, but a spiritual body feeling no want, and in all its members subjected to the will. In its pilgrim state the heavenly city possesses this peace by faith; and by this faith it lives righteously when it refers to the attainment of that peace every good action towards God and man; for the life of the city is a social life.

Chapter 26

Of the peace which is enjoyed by the people that are alienated from God, and the use made of it by the people of God in the time of its pilgrimage.

Wherefore, as the life of the flesh is the soul, so the blessed life of man is God, of whom the sacred writings of the Hebrews say, "Blessed is the people whose God is the Lord." Miserable, therefore, is the people which is alienated from God. Yet even this people has a peace of its own which is not to be lightly esteemed, though, indeed, it shall not in the end enjoy it, because it makes no good use of it before the end. But it is our interest that it enjoy this peace meanwhile in this life; for as long as the two cities are commingled, we also enjoy the peace of Babylon. For from Babylon the people of God is so freed that it meanwhile sojourns in its company. And therefore the apostle also admonished the Church to pray for kings and those in authority, assigning as the reason, "that we may live a quiet and tranquil life in all godliness and love." And the prophet Jeremiah, when predicting the captivity that was to befall the ancient people of God, and giving them the divine command to go obediently to Babylonia, and thus serve their God, counselled them also to pray for Babylonia, saying, "In the peace thereof shall you have peace,"—the temporal peace which the good and the wicked together enjoy.

Chapter 27

That the peace of those who serve God cannot in this mortal life be apprehended in its perfection.

But the peace which is peculiar to ourselves we enjoy now with God by faith, and shall hereafter enjoy eternally with Him by sight. But the peace which we enjoy in this life, whether common to all or peculiar to ourselves, is rather the solace of our misery than the positive enjoyment of felicity. Our very righteousness, too, though true in so far as it has respect to the true good, is yet in this life of such a kind that it consists rather in the remission of sins than in the perfecting of virtues. Witness the prayer of the whole city of God in its pilgrim state, for it cries to God by the mouth of all its members, "Forgive us our debts as we forgive our debtors." And this prayer is efficacious not for those whose faith is "without works and dead," but for those whose faith "work by love." For as reason, though subjected to God, is yet "pressed down by the corruptible body,""so long as it is in this mortal condition, it has not perfect authority over vice, and therefore this prayer is needed by the righteous. For though it exercises authority, the vices do not submit without a struggle. For however well one maintains the conflict, and however thoroughly he has subdued these enemies, there steals in some evil thing, which, if it do not find ready expression in act, slips out by the lips, or insinuates itself into the thought; and therefore his peace is not full so long as he is at war with his vices. For it is a doubtful conflict he wages with those that resist, and his victory over those that are defeated is not secure, but full of anxiety and effort.

Amidst these temptations, therefore, of all which

it has been summarily said in the divine oracles, "Is not human life upon earth a temptation?" who but a proud man can presume that he so lives that he has no need to say to God, "Forgive us our debts?""And such a man is not great, but swollen and puffed up with vanity, and is justly resisted by Him who abundantly gives grace to the humble. Whence it is said, "God resists the proud, but giveth grace to the humble." In this, then, consists the righteousness of a man, that he submit himself to God, his body to his soul, and his vices, even when they rebel, to his reason, which either defeats or at least resists them; and also that he beg from God grace to do his duty, and the pardon of his sins, and that he render to God thanks for all the blessings he receives. But, in that final peace to which all our righteousness has reference, and for the sake of which it is maintained, as our nature shall enjoy a sound immortality and incorruption, and shall have no more vices, and as we shall experience no resistance either from ourselves or from others, it will not be necessary that reason should rule vices which no longer exist, but God shall rule the man, and the soul shall rule the body, with a sweetness and facility suitable to the felicity of a life which is done with bondage. And this condition shall there be eternal, and we shall be assured of its eternity; and thus the peace of this

Augustine. City of God. *Nicene and Post-Nicene Fathers. Vol. 2.* Ed. Philip Schaff. Buffalo, NY: Christian Literature Publishing Co., 1887.

THE PRINCE

NICCOLÒ MACHIAVELLI (1429-1527)

The great Renaissance historian, diplomat and philosopher, Niccolo Machivelli, held the position of Secretary to the Second Chancellery of the Republic of Florence from 1492-1512. Machiavelli's approach to political philosophy is about as far removed from that of Augustine as one could get. Focused almost exclusively on the exercise of political power, Machiavelli urges the would-be prince to separate his private and public morality. In his most famous work, Il Principe (The Prince), he argues that successful rulers need to be willing to act immorally at times, and to practice the political arts of manipulation, coercion, and deceit as needed to secure their power. It is based upon the ideas in this work, that the term "Machiavellian" has come down through history to be synonymous with treachery and deceit.

Chapter 15

Concerning things for which men, and especially princes, are praised or blamed.

It remains now to see what ought to be the rules of conduct for a prince towards subject and friends. And as I know that many have written on this point, I expect I shall be considered presumptuous in mentioning it again, especially as in discussing it I shall depart from the methods of other people. But, it being my intention to write a thing which shall be useful to him who apprehends it, it appears to me more appropriate to follow up the real truth of the matter than the imagination of it; for many have pictured republics and principalities which in fact have never been known or seen, because how one lives is so far distant from how one ought to live, that he who neglects what is done for what ought to be done, sooner effects his ruin than his preservation; for a man who wishes to act entirely up to his professions of virtue soon meets with what destroys him among so much that is evil.

Hence it is necessary for a prince wishing to hold his own to know how to do wrong, and to make use of it or not according to necessity. Therefore, putting on one side imaginary things concerning a prince, and discussing those which are real, I say that all men when they are spoken of, and chiefly princes for being more highly placed, are remarkable for some of those qualities which bring them either blame or praise; and thus it is that one is reputed liberal, another miserly, using a Tuscan term (because an avaricious person in our language is still he who desires to possess by robbery, whilst we call one miserly who deprives himself too much of the use of his own); one is reputed generous, one rapacious; one cruel, one compassionate; one faithless, another faithful; one effeminate and cowardly, another bold and brave; one affable, another haughty; one lascivious, another chaste; one sincere, another cunning; one hard, another easy; one grave, another frivolous; one religious, another unbelieving, and the like. And I know that every one will confess that it would be most praiseworthy in a prince to exhibit all the above qualities that are considered good; but because they can neither be entirely possessed nor observed, for human conditions do not permit it, it is necessary for him to be sufficiently prudent that he may know how to avoid the reproach of those vices which would lose him his state; and also to keep himself, if it be possible, from those which would not lose him it; but this not being possible, he may with less hesitation abandon himself to them. And again, he need not make himself uneasy at incurring a reproach for those vices without which the state can only be saved with difficulty, for if everything is considered carefully, it will be found that something which looks like virtue, if followed, would be his ruin; whilst something else, which looks like vice, yet followed brings him security and prosperity.

Chapter 16

Concerning liberality and meanness.

Commencing then with the first of the above-named characteristics, I say that it would be well to be reputed liberal. Nevertheless, liberality exercised in a way that does not bring you the reputation for it, injures you; for if one exercises it honestly and as it should be exercised, it may not become known, and you will not avoid the reproach of its opposite. Therefore, any one wishing to maintain among men the name of liberal is obliged to avoid no attribute of magnificence; so that a prince thus inclined will consume in such acts all his property, and will be compelled in the end, if he wish to maintain the name of liberal, to unduly weigh down his people, and tax them, and do everything he can to get money. This will soon make him odious to his subjects, and becoming poor he will be little valued by any one; thus, with his liberality, having offended many and rewarded few, he is affected by the very first trouble and imperilled by whatever may be the first danger; recognizing this himself, and wishing to draw back from it, he runs at once into the reproach of being miserly.

Therefore, a prince, not being able to exercise this virtue of liberality in such a way that it is recognized, except to his cost, if he is wise he ought not to fear the reputation of being mean, for in time he will come to be more considered than if liberal, seeing that with his economy his revenues are enough, that he can defend himself against all attacks, and is able to engage in enterprises without burdening his people; thus it comes to pass that he exercises liberality towards all from whom he does not take, who are numberless, and meanness towards those to whom he does not give, who are few.

We have not seen great things done in our time except by those who have been considered mean; the rest have failed. Pope Julius the Second was assisted in reaching the papacy by a reputation for liberality, yet he did not strive afterwards to keep it up, when he made war on the King of France; and he made many wars without imposing any extraordinary tax on his subjects, for he supplied his additional expenses out of his long thriftiness. The present King of Spain would not have undertaken or conquered in so many enterprises if he had been reputed liberal. A prince, therefore, provided that he has not to rob his subjects, that he can defend himself, that he does not become poor and abject, that he is not forced to become rapacious, ought to hold of little account a reputation for being mean, for it is one of those vices which will enable him to govern.

And if any one should say: Caesar obtained empire by liberality, and many others have reached the highest positions by having been liberal, and by being considered so, I answer: Either you are a prince in fact, or in a way to become one. In the first case this liberality is dangerous, in the second it is very necessary to be considered liberal; and Caesar was one of those who wished to become pre-eminent in Rome; but if he had survived after becoming so, and had not moderated his expenses, he would have destroyed his government. And if any one should reply: Many have been princes, and have done great things with armies, who have been considered very liberal, I reply: Either a prince spends that which is his own or his subjects' or else that of others. In the first case he ought to be sparing, in the second he ought not to neglect any opportunity for liberality. And to the prince who goes forth with his army, supporting it by pillage, sack, and extortion, handling that which belongs to others, this liberality is necessary, otherwise he would not be followed by soldiers. And of that which is neither yours nor your subjects' you can be a ready giver, as were Cyrus, Caesar, and Alexander; because it does not take away your reputation if you squander that of others, but adds to it; it is only squandering your own that injures you.

And there is nothing wastes so rapidly as liberality, for even whilst you exercise it you lose the power to do so, and so become either poor or despised, or else, in avoiding poverty, rapacious and hated. And a prince should guard himself, above all things, against being despised and hated; and liberality leads you to both. Therefore it is wiser to have a reputation for meanness which brings reproach without hatred, than to be compelled through seeking a reputation for liberality to incur a name for rapacity which begets reproach with hatred.

Chapter 17

Concerning cruelty and clemency, and whether it is better to be loved than feared.

Coming now to the other qualities mentioned above, I say that every prince ought to desire to be considered clement and not cruel. Nevertheless he ought to take care not to misuse this clemency. Cesare Borgia was considered cruel; notwithstanding, his cruelty reconciled the Romagna, unified it, and restored it to peace and loyalty. And if this be rightly considered, he will be seen to have been much more merciful than the Florentine people, who, to avoid a reputation for cruelty, permitted Pistoia to be destroyed.[*] Therefore a prince, so long as he keeps his subjects united and loyal, ought not to mind the reproach of cruelty; because with a few examples he will be more merciful than those who, through too much mercy, allow disorders to arise, from which follow murders or robberies; for these are wont to injure the whole people, whilst those executions which originate with a prince offend the individual only.

And of all princes, it is impossible for the new prince to avoid the imputation of cruelty, owing to new states being full of dangers. Hence Virgil, through the mouth of Dido, excuses the inhumanity of her reign owing to its being new, saying:

"Res dura, et regni novitas me talia cogunt Moliri, et late fines custode tueri."

Nevertheless he ought to be slow to believe and to act, nor should he himself show fear, but proceed in a temperate manner with prudence and humanity, so that too much confidence may not make him incautious and too much distrust render him intolerable.

Upon this a question arises: whether it be better to be loved than feared or feared than loved? It may be answered that one should wish to be both, but, because it is difficult to unite them in one person, it is much safer to be feared than loved, when, of the two, either must be dispensed with. Because this is to be asserted in general of men, that they are ungrateful, fickle, false, cowardly, covetous, and as long as you succeed they are yours entirely; they will offer you their blood, property, life, and children, as is said above, when the need is far distant; but when it approaches they turn against you. And that prince who, relying entirely on their promises, has neglected other precautions, is ruined; because friendships that are obtained by payments, and not by greatness or nobility of mind, may indeed be earned, but they are not secured, and in time of need cannot be relied upon; and men have less scruple in offending one who is beloved than one who is feared, for love is preserved by the link of obligation which, owing to the baseness of men, is broken at every opportunity for their advantage; but fear preserves you by a dread of punishment which never fails.

Nevertheless a prince ought to inspire fear in such a way that, if he does not win love, he avoids hatred; because he can endure very well being feared whilst he is not hated, which will always be as long as he abstains from the property of his citizens and subjects and from their women. But when it is necessary for him to proceed against the life of someone, he must do it on proper justification and for manifest cause, but above all things he must keep his hands off the property of others, because men more quickly forget the death of their father than the loss of their patrimony. Besides, pretexts for taking away the property are never wanting; for he who has once begun to live by robbery will always find pretexts for seizing what belongs to others; but reasons for taking life, on the contrary, are more difficult to find and sooner lapse. But when a prince is with his army, and has under control a multitude of soldiers, then it is quite necessary for him to disregard the reputation of cruelty, for without it he would never hold his army united or disposed to its duties.

Among the wonderful deeds of Hannibal this one is enumerated: that having led an enormous army, composed of many various races of men, to fight in foreign lands, no dissensions arose either among them or against the prince, whether in his bad or in his good fortune. This arose from nothing else than his inhuman cruelty, which, with his boundless valour, made him revered and terrible in the sight of his soldiers, but without that cruelty, his other virtues were not sufficient to produce this effect. And short-sighted writers admire his deeds from one point of view and from another condemn the principal cause of them. That it is true his other virtues would not have been sufficient for him may be proved by the case of Scipio, that most excellent man, not only of his own times but within the memory of man, against whom, nevertheless, his army rebelled in Spain; this arose from nothing but his too great forbearance, which gave his soldiers more license than is consistent with military discipline. For this he was upbraided in the Senate by Fabius Maximus, and called the corrupter of the Roman soldiery. The Locrians were laid waste by a legate of Scipio, yet they were not avenged by him, nor was the insolence of the legate punished, owing entirely to his easy nature. Insomuch that someone in the Senate, wishing to excuse him, said there were many men who knew much better how not to err than to correct the errors of others. This disposition, if he had been continued in the command, would have destroyed in time the fame and glory of Scipio; but, he being under the control of the Senate, this injurious characteristic not only concealed itself, but contributed to his glory.

Returning to the question of being feared or loved, I come to the conclusion that, men loving according to their own will and fearing according to that of the prince, a wise prince should establish himself on that which is in his own control and not in that of others; he must endeavour only to avoid hatred, as is noted.

Chapter 18

Concerning the way in which princes should keep faith.

Every one admits how praiseworthy it is in a prince to keep faith, and to live with integrity and not with craft. Nevertheless our experience has been that those princes who have done great things have held good faith of little account, and have known how to circumvent the intellect of men by craft, and in the end have overcome those who have relied on their word. You must know there are two ways of contesting,[*] the one by the law, the other by force; the first method is proper to men, the second to beasts; but because the first is frequently not sufficient, it is necessary to have recourse to the second. Therefore it is necessary for a prince to understand how to avail himself of the beast and the man. This has been figuratively taught to princes by ancient writers, who describe how Achilles and many other princes of old were given to the Centaur Chiron to nurse, who brought them up in his discipline; which means solely that, as they had for a teacher one who was half beast and half man, so it is necessary for a prince to know how to make use of both natures, and that one without the other is not durable. A prince, therefore, being compelled knowingly to adopt the beast, ought to choose the fox and the lion; because the lion cannot defend himself against snares and the fox cannot defend himself against wolves. Therefore, it is necessary to be a fox to discover the snares and a lion to terrify the wolves. Those who rely simply on the lion do not understand what they are about. Therefore a wise lord cannot, nor ought he to, keep faith when such observance may be turned against him, and when the reasons that caused him to pledge it exist no longer. If men were entirely good this precept would not hold, but because they are bad, and will not keep faith with you, you too are not bound to observe it with them. Nor will there ever be wanting to a prince legitimate reasons to excuse this non-observance. Of this endless modern examples could be given, showing how many treaties and engagements have been made void and of no effect through the faithlessness of princes; and he who has known best how to employ the fox has succeeded best.

But it is necessary to know well how to disguise this characteristic, and to be a great pretender and dissembler; and men are so simple, and so subject to present necessities, that he who seeks to deceive will always find someone who will allow himself to be deceived. One recent example I cannot pass over in silence. Alexander the Sixth did nothing else but deceive men, nor ever thought of doing otherwise, and he always found victims; for there never was a man who had greater power in asserting, or who with greater oaths would affirm a thing, yet would observe it less; nevertheless his deceits always succeeded according to his wishes, because he well understood this side of mankind.

Therefore it is unnecessary for a prince to have

all the good qualities I have enumerated, but it is very necessary to appear to have them. And I shall dare to say this also, that to have them and always to observe them is injurious, and that to appear to have them is useful; to appear merciful, faithful, humane, religious, upright, and to be so, but with a mind so framed that should you require not to be so, you may be able and know how to change to the opposite.

And you have to understand this, that a prince, especially a new one, cannot observe all those things for which men are esteemed, being often forced, in order to maintain the state, to act contrary to fidelity,[*] friendship, humanity, and religion. Therefore it is necessary for him to have a mind ready to turn itself accordingly as the winds and variations of fortune force it, yet, as I have said above, not to diverge from the good if he can avoid doing so, but, if compelled, then to know how to set about it.

For this reason a prince ought to take care that he never lets anything slip from his lips that is not replete with the above-named five qualities, that he may appear to him who sees and hears him altogether merciful, faithful, humane, upright, and religious. There is nothing more necessary to appear to have than this last quality, inasmuch as men judge generally more by the eye than by the hand, because it belongs to everybody to see you, to few to come in touch with you. Every one sees what you appear to be, few really know what you are, and those few dare not oppose themselves to the opinion of the many, who have the majesty of the state to defend them; and in the actions of all men, and especially of princes, which it is not prudent to challenge, one judges by the result.

For that reason, let a prince have the credit of conquering and holding his state, the means will always be considered honest, and he will be praised by everybody; because the vulgar are always taken by what a thing seems to be and by what comes of it; and in the world there are only the vulgar, for the few find a place there only when the many have no ground to rest on.

One prince of the present time, whom it is not well to name, never preaches anything else but peace and good faith, and to both he is most hostile, and either, if he had kept it, would have deprived him of reputation and kingdom many a time.

Chapter 19

That one should avoid being despised and hated.
Now, concerning the characteristics of which mention is made above, I have spoken of the more important ones, the others I wish to discuss briefly under this generality, that the prince must consider, as has been in part said before, how to avoid those things which will make him hated or contemptible; and as often as he shall have succeeded he will have fulfilled his part, and he need not fear any danger in other reproaches.

It makes him hated above all things, as I have said, to be rapacious, and to be a violator of the property and women of his subjects, from both of which he must abstain. And when neither their property nor their honor is touched, the majority of men live content, and he has only to contend with the ambition of a few, whom he can curb with ease in many ways.

It makes him contemptible to be considered fickle, frivolous, effeminate, mean-spirited, irresolute, from all of which a prince should guard himself as from a rock; and he should endeavour to show in his actions greatness, courage, gravity, and fortitude; and in his private dealings with his subjects let him show that his judgments are irrevocable, and maintain himself in such reputation that no one can hope either to deceive him or to get round him.

That prince is highly esteemed who conveys this impression of himself, and he who is highly esteemed is not easily conspired against; for, provided it is well known that he is an excellent man and revered by his people, he can only be attacked with difficulty. For this reason a prince ought to have two fears, one from within, on account of his subjects, the other from without, on account of external powers. From the latter he is defended by being well armed and having good allies, and if he is well armed he will have good friends, and affairs will always remain quiet within when they are quiet without, unless they should have been already disturbed by conspiracy; and even should affairs outside be disturbed, if he has carried out his preparations and has lived as I have said, as long as he does not despair, he will resist every attack, as I said Nabis the Spartan did.

But concerning his subjects, when affairs outside are disturbed he has only to fear that they will conspire secretly, from which a prince can easily secure himself by avoiding being hated and despised, and by keeping the people satisfied with him, which it is most necessary for him to accomplish, as I said above at length. And one of the most efficacious remedies that a prince can have against conspiracies is not to be hated and despised by the people, for he who conspires against a prince always expects to please them by his removal; but when the conspirator can only look forward to offending them, he will not have the courage to take such a course, for the difficulties that confront a conspirator are infinite. And as experience shows, many have been the conspiracies, but few have been successful; because he who conspires cannot act alone, nor can he take a companion except from those whom he believes to be malcontents, and as soon as you have opened your mind to a malcontent you have given him the material with which to content himself, for by denouncing you he can look for every advantage; so that, seeing the gain from this course to be assured, and seeing the other to be doubtful and full of dangers, he must be a very rare friend, or a thoroughly obstinate enemy of the prince, to keep faith with you.

And, to reduce the matter into a small compass, I say that, on the side of the conspirator, there is nothing but fear, jealousy, prospect of punishment to terrify him; but on the side of the prince there is the majesty of the principality, the laws, the protection of friends and the state to defend him; so that, adding to all these things the popular goodwill, it is impossible that any one should be so rash as to conspire. For whereas in general the conspirator has to fear before the execution of his plot, in this case he has also to fear the sequel to the crime; because on account of it he has the people for an enemy, and thus cannot hope for any escape.

Niccolò Machiavelli. *The Prince*. Trans. W.K. Marriott. New York: J.M. Dent and Sons, 1909.

LEVIATHAN

THOMAS HOBBES (1588-1679)

In his Leviathan, *the English philosopher Thomas Hobbes offers one of the earliest and most influential versions of what has come to be known as "social contract theory." Having lived through the English Civil War of 1642-1649, which ended with the beheading of King Charles II, Hobbes was deeply concerned with laying the foundations for a political society grounded in stability and peace. Hobbes begins by imagining a situation in which human beings live in the absence of government—the state of nature. In order to extricate themselves from a situation in which there is war of "all against all" and where life is "solitary, poor, nasty, brutish, and short," Hobbes envisions human beings coming together to create a commonwealth in which all political power is put in the hands of a sovereign, whose power Hobbes envisions as fairly absolute.*

CHAPTER 13
Of the Natural Condition of Mankind

Nature has made men so equal in the faculties of body and mind as that, though there be found one man sometimes manifestly stronger in body or of quicker mind than another, yet when all is reckoned together the difference between man and man is not so considerable as that one man can thereupon claim to himself any benefit to which another may not pretend as well as he. For as to the strength of body, the weakest has strength enough to kill the strongest, either by secret machination or by confederacy with others that are in the same danger with himself.

And as to the faculties of the mind, setting aside the arts grounded upon words, and especially that skill of proceeding upon general and infallible rules, called science, which very few have and but in few things, as being not a native faculty born with us, nor attained, as prudence, while we look after somewhat else, I find yet a greater equality amongst men than that of strength. For prudence is but experience, which equal time equally bestows on all men in those things they equally apply themselves unto. That which may perhaps make such equality incredible is but a vain conceit of one's own wisdom, which almost all men think they have in a greater degree than the vulgar; that is, than all men but themselves, and

a few others, whom by fame, or for concurring with themselves, they approve. For such is the nature of men that howsoever they may acknowledge many others to be more witty, or more eloquent or more learned, yet they will hardly believe there be many so wise as themselves; for they see their own wit at hand, and other men's at a distance. But this proveth rather that men are in that point equal, than unequal. For there is not ordinarily a greater sign of the equal distribution of anything than that every man is contented with his share.

From this equality of ability arises equality of hope in the attaining of our ends. And therefore if any two men desire the same thing, which nevertheless they cannot both enjoy, they become enemies; and in the way to their end (which is principally their own conservation, and sometimes their delectation only) endeavour to destroy or subdue one another. And from hence it comes to pass that where an invader hath no more to fear than another man's single power, if one plant, sow, build, or possess a convenient seat, others may probably be expected to come prepared with forces united to dispossess and deprive him, not only of the fruit of his labour, but also of his life or liberty. And the invader again is in the like danger of another.

And from this diffidence of one another, there is no way for any man to secure himself so reasonable as anticipation; that is, by force, or wiles, to master the persons of all men he can so long till he see no other power great enough to endanger him: and this is no more than his own conservation requireth, and is generally allowed. Also, because there be some that, taking pleasure in contemplating their own power in the acts of conquest, which they pursue farther than their security requires, if others, that otherwise would be glad to be at ease within modest bounds, should not by invasion increase their power, they would not be able, long time, by standing only on their defence, to subsist. And by consequence, such augmentation of dominion over men being necessary to a man's conservation, it ought to be allowed him.

Again, men have no pleasure (but on the contrary a great deal of grief) in keeping company where there is no power able to overawe them all. For every man looketh that his companion should value him at the same rate he sets upon himself, and upon all signs of contempt or undervaluing naturally endeavours, as far as he dares (which amongst them that have no common power to keep them in quiet is far enough to make them destroy each other), to extort a greater value from his contemners, by damage; and from others, by the example.

So that in the nature of man, we find three principal causes of quarrel. First, competition; secondly, diffidence; thirdly, glory.

The first maketh men invade for gain; the second, for safety; and the third, for reputation. The first use violence, to make themselves masters of other men's persons, wives, children, and cattle; the second, to defend them; the third, for trifles, as a word, a smile, a different opinion, and any other sign of undervalue, either direct in their persons or by reflection in their kindred, their friends, their nation, their profession, or their name.

Hereby it is manifest that during the time men live without a common power to keep them all in awe, they are in that condition which is called war; and such a war as is of every man against every man. For war consisteth not in battle only, or the act of fighting, but in a tract of time, wherein the will to contend by battle is sufficiently known: and therefore the notion of time is to be considered in the nature of war, as it is in the nature of weather. For as the nature of foul weather lieth not in a shower or two of rain, but in an inclination thereto of many days together: so the nature of war consisteth not in actual fighting, but in the known disposition thereto during all the time there is no assurance to the contrary. All other time is peace.

Whatsoever therefore is consequent to a time of war, where every man is enemy to every man, the same consequent to the time wherein men live without other security than what their own strength and their own invention shall furnish them withal. In such condition there is no place for industry, because the fruit thereof is uncertain: and consequently no culture of the earth; no navigation, nor use of the commodities that may be imported by sea; no commodious building; no instruments of moving and removing such things as require much force; no knowledge of the face of the earth; no account of time; no arts; no letters; no society; and which is worst of all, continual fear, and danger of violent death; and the life of man, solitary, poor, nasty, brutish, and short....

To this war of every man against every man, this also is consequent; that nothing can be unjust. The notions of right and wrong, justice and injustice, have there no place. Where there is no common power, there is no law; where no law, no injustice. Force and fraud are in war the two cardinal virtues. Justice and injustice are none of the faculties neither of the body nor mind. If they were, they might be in a man that were alone in the world, as well as his senses and passions. They are qualities that relate to men in society, not in solitude. It is consequent also to the same condition that there be no propriety, no dominion, no mine and thine distinct; but only that to be every man's that he can get, and for so long as he can keep it. And thus much for the ill condition which man by mere nature is actually placed in; though with a possibility to come out of it, consisting partly in the passions, partly in his reason.

The passions that incline men to peace are: fear of death; desire of such things as are necessary to commodious living; and a hope by their industry to obtain them. And reason suggesteth convenient articles of peace upon which men may be drawn to agreement. These articles are they which otherwise are called the laws of nature, whereof I shall speak more particularly in the two following chapters.

CHAPTER 14
Of the First and Second Natural Laws and of Contracts

THE right of nature, which writers commonly call jus naturale, is the liberty each man hath to use his own power as he will himself for the preservation of his own nature; that is to say, of his own life; and consequently, of doing anything which, in his own judgement and reason, he shall conceive to be the aptest means thereunto....

By liberty is understood, according to the proper signification of the word, the absence of external impediments; which impediments may oft take away part of a man's power to do what he would, but cannot hinder him from using the power left him according as his judgement and reason shall dictate to him.

A law of nature, lex naturalis, is a precept, or general rule, found out by reason, by which a man is forbidden to do that which is destructive of his life, or taketh away the means of preserving the same, and to omit that by which he thinketh it may be best preserved. For though they that speak of this subject use to confound jus and lex, right and law, yet they ought to be distinguished, because right consisteth in liberty to do, or to forbear; whereas law determineth and bindeth to one of them: so that law and right differ as much as obligation and liberty, which in one and the same matter are inconsistent.

And because the condition of man (as hath been declared in the precedent chapter) is a condition of war of every one against every one, in which case every one is governed by his own reason, and there is nothing he can make use of that may not be a help unto him in preserving his life against his enemies; it followeth that in such a condition every man has a right to every thing, even to one another's body. And therefore, as long as this natural right of every man to every thing endureth, there can be no security to any man, how strong or wise soever he be, of living out the time which nature ordinarily alloweth men to live. And consequently it is a precept, or general rule of reason: that every man ought to endeavour peace, as far as he has hope of obtaining it; and

when he cannot obtain it, that he may seek and use all helps and advantages of war. The first branch of which rule containeth the first and fundamental law of nature, which is: to seek peace and follow it. The second, the sum of the right of nature, which is: by all means we can to defend ourselves.

From this fundamental law of nature, by which men are commanded to endeavour peace, is derived this second law: that a man be willing, when others are so too, as far forth as for peace and defence of himself he shall think it necessary, to lay down this right to all things; and be contented with so much liberty against other men as he would allow other men against himself. For as long as every man holdeth this right, of doing anything he liketh; so long are all men in the condition of war. But if other men will not lay down their right, as well as he, then there is no reason for anyone to divest himself of his: for that were to expose himself to prey, which no man is bound to, rather than to dispose himself to peace....

To lay down a man's right to anything is to divest himself of the liberty of hindering another of the benefit of his own right to the same. For he that renounceth or passeth away his right giveth not to any other man a right which he had not before, because there is nothing to which every man had not right by nature, but only standeth out of his way that he may enjoy his own original right without hindrance from him, not without hindrance from another. So that the effect which redoundeth to one man by another man's defect of right is but so much diminution of impediments to the use of his own right original.

Right is laid aside, either by simply renouncing it, or by transferring it to another. By simply renouncing, when he cares not to whom the benefit thereof redoundeth. By transferring, when he intendeth the benefit thereof to some certain person or persons. And when a man hath in either manner abandoned or granted away his right, then is he said to be obliged, or bound, not to hinder those to whom such right is granted, or abandoned, from the benefit of it: and that he ought, and it is duty, not to make void that voluntary act of his own: and that such hindrance is injustice, and injury, as being sine jure; the right being before renounced or transferred. So that injury or injustice, in the controversies of the world, is somewhat like to that which in the disputations of scholars is called absurdity. For as it is there called an absurdity to contradict what one maintained in the beginning; so in the world it is called injustice, and injury voluntarily to undo that which from the beginning he had voluntarily done. The way by which a man either simply renounceth or transferreth his right is a declaration, or signification, by some voluntary and sufficient sign, or signs, that he doth so renounce or transfer, or hath so renounced or transferred the same, to him that accepteth it. And these signs are either words only, or actions only; or, as it happeneth most often, both words and actions. And the same are the bonds, by which men are bound and obliged: bonds that have their strength, not from their own nature (for nothing is more easily broken than a man's word), but from fear of some evil consequence upon the rupture.

Whensoever a man transferreth his right, or renounceth it, it is either in consideration of some right reciprocally transferred to himself, or for some other good he hopeth for thereby. For it is a voluntary act: and of the voluntary acts of every man, the object is some good to himself. And therefore there be some rights which no man can be understood by any words, or other signs, to have abandoned or transferred. As first a man cannot lay down the right of resisting them that assault him by force to take away his life, because he cannot be understood to aim thereby at any good to himself. The same may be said of wounds, and chains, and imprisonment, both because there is no benefit consequent to such patience, as there is to the patience of suffering another to be wounded or imprisoned, as also because a man cannot tell when he seeth men proceed against him by violence whether they intend his death or not. And lastly the motive and end for which this renouncing and transferring of right is introduced is nothing else but the security of a man's person, in his life, and in the means of so preserving life as not to be weary of it. And therefore if a man by words, or other signs, seem to despoil himself of the end for which those signs were intended, he is not to be understood as if he meant it, or that it was his will, but that he was ignorant of how such words and actions were to be interpreted.

The mutual transferring of right is that which men call contract.

There is difference between transferring of right to the thing, the thing, and transferring or tradition, that is, delivery of the thing itself. For the thing may be delivered together with the translation of the right, as in buying and selling with ready money, or exchange of goods or lands, and it may be delivered some time after.

Again, one of the contractors may deliver the thing contracted for on his part, and leave the other to perform his part at some determinate time after, and in the meantime be trusted; and then the contract on his part is called pact, or covenant: or both parts may contract now to perform hereafter, in which cases he that is to perform in time to come, being trusted, his performance is called keeping of promise, or faith, and the failing of performance, if it be voluntary, violation of faith....

If a covenant be made wherein neither of the parties perform presently, but trust one another, in the condition of mere nature (which is a condition of war of every man against every man) upon any reasonable suspicion, it is void: but if there be a common power set over them both, with right and force sufficient to compel performance, it is not void. For he that performeth first has no assurance the other will perform after, because the bonds of words are too weak to bridle men's ambition, avarice, anger, and other passions, without the fear of some coercive power; which in the condition of mere nature, where all men are equal, and judges of the justness of their own fears, cannot possibly be supposed. And therefore he which performeth first does but betray himself to his enemy, contrary to the right he can never abandon of defending his life and means of living.

But in a civil estate, where there a power set up to constrain those that would otherwise violate their faith, that fear is no more reasonable; and for that cause, he which by the covenant is to perform first is obliged so to do.

The cause of fear, which maketh such a covenant invalid, must be always something arising after the covenant made, as some new fact or other sign of the will not to perform, else it cannot make the covenant void. For that which could not hinder a man from promising ought not to be admitted as a hindrance of performing.

CHAPTER 15
Of Other Laws of Nature

FROM that law of nature by which we are obliged to transfer to another such rights as, being retained, hinder the peace of mankind, there followeth a third; which is this: that men perform their covenants made; without which covenants are in vain, and but empty words; and the right of all men to all things remaining, we are still in the condition of war.

And in this law of nature consisteth the fountain and original of justice. For where no covenant hath preceded, there hath no right been transferred, and every man has right to everything and consequently, no action can be unjust. But when a covenant is made, then to break it is unjust and the definition of injustice is no other than the not performance of covenant. And whatsoever is not unjust is just.

But because covenants of mutual trust, where there is a fear of not performance on either part (as hath been said in the former chapter), are invalid, though the original of justice be the making of covenants, yet injustice actually there can be none till the cause of such fear be taken away; which, while men are in the natural condition of war, cannot be done. Therefore before the names of just and unjust can have place, there must be some coercive power to compel men equally to the performance of their covenants, by the terror of some punishment greater than the benefit they expect by the breach of their covenant, and to make good that propriety which by mutual contract men acquire in recompense of the universal right they abandon: and such power there is none before the erection of a Commonwealth. And this is also to be gathered out of the ordinary definition of justice in the Schools, for they say that justice is the constant will of giving to every man his own. And therefore where there is no own, that is, no propriety, there is no injustice; and where there is no coercive power erected, that is, where there is no Commonwealth, there is no propriety, all men having right to all things: therefore where there is no Commonwealth, there nothing is unjust. So that the nature of justice consisteth in keeping of valid covenants, but the validity of covenants begins not but with the constitution of a civil power sufficient to compel men to keep them: and then it is also that propriety begins....

CHAPTER 17
Causes, Generation, and Definition of a Commonwealth

THE final cause, end, or design of men (who naturally love liberty, and dominion over others) in the introduction of that restraint upon themselves, in which we see them live in Commonwealths, is the foresight of their own preservation, and of a more contented life thereby; that is to say, of getting themselves out from that miserable condition of war which is necessarily consequent, as hath been shown, to the natural passions of men when there is no visible power to keep them in awe, and tie them by fear of punishment to the performance of their covenants, and observation of those laws of nature set down in the fourteenth and fifteenth chapters.

For the laws of nature, as justice, equity, modesty, mercy, and, in sum, doing to others as we would be done to, of themselves, without the terror of some power to cause them to be observed, are contrary to our natural passions, that carry us to partiality, pride, revenge, and the like. And covenants, without the sword, are but words and of no strength to secure a man at all. Therefore, notwithstanding the laws of nature (which every one hath then kept, when he has the will to keep them, when he can do it safely), if there be no power erected, or not great enough for our security, every man will and may lawfully rely on his own strength and art for caution against all other men. And in all places, where men have lived by small families, to rob and spoil one another has been a trade, and so far from being reputed against the law of nature that the greater spoils they gained, the greater was their honour; and men observed no other laws therein but the laws of honour; that is, to abstain from cruelty, leaving to men their lives and instruments of husbandry. And as small families did then; so now do cities and kingdoms, which are but greater families (for their own security), enlarge their dominions upon all pretences of danger, and fear of invasion, or assistance that may be given to invaders; endeavour as much as they can to subdue or weaken their neighbours by open force, and secret arts, for want of other caution, justly; and are remembered for it in after ages with honour.

Nor is it the joining together of a small number

of men that gives them this security; because in small numbers, small additions on the one side or the other make the advantage of strength so great as is sufficient to carry the victory, and therefore gives encouragement to an invasion. The multitude sufficient to confide in for our security is not determined by any certain number, but by comparison with the enemy we fear; and is then sufficient when the odds of the enemy is not of so visible and conspicuous moment to determine the event of war, as to move him to attempt.

And be there never so great a multitude; yet if their actions be directed according to their particular judgements, and particular appetites, they can expect thereby no defence, nor protection, neither against a common enemy, nor against the injuries of one another. For being distracted in opinions concerning the best use and application of their strength, they do not help, but hinder one another, and reduce their strength by mutual opposition to nothing: whereby they are easily, not only subdued by a very few that agree together, but also, when there is no common enemy, they make war upon each other for their particular interests. For if we could suppose a great multitude of men to consent in the observation of justice, and other laws of nature, without a common power to keep them all in awe, we might as well suppose all mankind to do the same; and then there neither would be, nor need to be, any civil government or Commonwealth at all, because there would be peace without subjection.

Nor is it enough for the security, which men desire should last all the time of their life, that they be governed and directed by one judgement for a limited time; as in one battle, or one war. For though they obtain a victory by their unanimous endeavour against a foreign enemy, yet afterwards, when either they have no common enemy, or he that by one part is held for an enemy is by another part held for a friend, they must needs by the difference of their interests dissolve, and fall again into a war amongst themselves.

It is true that certain living creatures, as bees and ants, live sociably one with another (which are therefore by Aristotle numbered amongst political creatures), and yet have no other direction than their particular judgements and appetites; nor speech, whereby one of them can signify to another what he thinks expedient for the common benefit: and therefore some man may perhaps desire to know why mankind cannot do the same. To which I answer,

First, that men are continually in competition for honour and dignity, which these creatures are not; and consequently amongst men there ariseth on that ground, envy, and hatred, and finally war; but amongst these not so.

Secondly, that amongst these creatures the common good differeth not from the private; and being by nature inclined to their private, they procure thereby the common benefit. But man, whose joy consisteth in comparing himself with other men, can relish nothing but what is eminent.

Thirdly, that these creatures, having not, as man, the use of reason, do not see, nor think they see, any fault in the administration of their common business: whereas amongst men there are very many that think themselves wiser and abler to govern the public better than the rest, and these strive to reform and innovate, one this way, another that way; and thereby bring it into distraction and civil war.

Fourthly, that these creatures, though they have some use of voice in making known to one another their desires and other affections, yet they want that art of words by which some men can represent to others that which is good in the likeness of evil; and evil, in the likeness of good; and augment or diminish the apparent greatness of good and evil, discontenting men and troubling their peace at their pleasure.

Fifthly, irrational creatures cannot distinguish between injury and damage; and therefore as long as they be at ease, they are not offended with their fellows: whereas man is then most troublesome when he is most at ease; for then it is that he loves to show his wisdom, and control the actions of them that govern the Commonwealth.

Lastly, the agreement of these creatures is natural; that of men is by covenant only, which is artificial: and therefore it is no wonder if there be somewhat else required, besides covenant, to make their agreement constant and lasting; which is a common power to keep them in awe and to direct their actions to the common benefit.

The only way to erect such a common power,

as may be able to defend them from the invasion of foreigners, and the injuries of one another, and thereby to secure them in such sort as that by their own industry and by the fruits of the earth they may nourish themselves and live contentedly, is to confer all their power and strength upon one man, or upon one assembly of men, that may reduce all their wills, by plurality of voices, unto one will: which is as much as to say, to appoint one man, or assembly of men, to bear their person; and every one to own and acknowledge himself to be author of whatsoever he that so beareth their person shall act, or cause to be acted, in those things which concern the common peace and safety; and therein to submit their wills, every one to his will, and their judgements to his judgement. This is more than consent, or concord; it is a real unity of them all in one and the same person, made by covenant of every man with every man, in such manner as if every man should say to every man: I authorise and give up my right of governing myself to this man, or to this assembly of men, on this condition; that thou give up, thy right to him, and authorise all his actions in like manner. This done, the multitude so united in one person is called a COMMONWEALTH; in Latin, CIVITAS. This is the generation of that great LEVIATHAN, or rather, to speak more reverently, of that mortal god to which we owe, under the immortal God, our peace and defence. For by this authority, given him by every particular man in the Commonwealth, he hath the use of so much power and strength conferred on him that, by terror thereof, he is enabled to form the wills of them all, to peace at home, and mutual aid against their enemies abroad. And in him consisteth the essence of the Commonwealth; which, to define it, is: one person, of whose acts a great multitude, by mutual covenants one with another, have made themselves every one the author, to the end he may use the strength and means of them all as he shall think expedient for their peace and common defence.

And he that carryeth this person is called sovereign, and said to have sovereign power; and every one besides, his subject.

The attaining to this sovereign power is by two ways. One, by natural force: as when a man maketh his children to submit themselves, and their children, to his government, as being able to destroy them if they refuse; or by war subdueth his enemies to his will, giving them their lives on that condition. The other, is when men agree amongst themselves to submit to some man, or assembly of men, voluntarily, on confidence to be protected by him against all others. This latter may be called a political Commonwealth, or Commonwealth by Institution; and the former, a Commonwealth by acquisition. And first, I shall speak of a Commonwealth by institution....

Thomas Hobbes. *Leviathan* (1651).

SECOND TREATISE OF GOVERNMENT

JOHN LOCKE (1632-1704)

Beginning from the same starting point as Thomas Hobbes—the idea of the state of nature—the English philosopher, John Locke, draws very different political conclusions. In his highly influential Second Treatise of Government, *Locke imagines the state of nature in which people live in relative peace because they recognize, even in this primitive state, a moral law of nature established by God. Although Locke's state of nature is not as nasty or brutish as Hobbes', it is nonetheless inconvenient, because the moral law in the state of nature is not always enforced consistently or fairly. As a result, human beings come together to form a political community and establish a government that is powerful enough to enforce the law. Unlike Hobbes, however, Locke places only limited powers in the hands of the government—powers that can be revoked by the people themselves if it violates their rights. Locke's ideas would prove highly influential in the modern era and would provide the inspiration for the ideas contained in the American Declaration of Independence.*

Chapter 2
Of the State of Nature

4. To understand political power right, and derive it from its original, we must consider, what state all men are naturally in, and that is, a state of perfect freedom to order their actions, and dispose of their possessions and persons, as they think fit, within the bounds of the law of nature, without asking leave, or depending upon the will of any other man.

A state also of equality wherin all the power and jurisdiction is reciprocal, no one having more than another; there being nothing more evident, than that the creatures of the same species and rank, promiscuously born to all the same advantages of nature, and the use of the same faculties, should also be equal one amongst another without subordination or subjection, unless the lord and master of them all should, by any manifest declaration of his will, set one above another, and confer on him, by an evident and clear appointment, an undoubted right to dominion and sovereignty....

6. But though this be a state of liberty, yet it is not a state of licence: though man in that state have an uncontrollable liberty to dispose of his person or possessions, yet he has not liberty to destroy himself, or so much as any creature in his possession, but where some nobler use than its bare preservation calls for it. The state of nature has a law of nature to govern it, which obliges every one: and reason, which is that law, teaches all mankind, who will but consult it, that being all equal and independent, no one ought to harm another in his life, health, liberty, or possessions: for men being all the workmanship of one omnipotent, and infinitely wise maker; all the servants of one sovereign master, sent into the world by his order, and about his business; they are his property, whose workmanship they are, made to last during his, not one another's pleasure: and being furnished with like faculties, sharing all in one community of nature, there cannot be supposed any such subordination among us, that may authorize us to destroy one another, as if we were made for one another's uses, as the inferior ranks of creatures are for our's. Every one, as he is bound to preserve himself, and not to quit his station willfully, so by the like reason, when his own preservation comes not

in competition, ought he, as much as he can, to preserve the rest of mankind, and may not, unless it be to do justice on an offender, take away, or impair the life, or what tends to the preservation of the life, the liberty, health, limb, or goods of another.

7. And that all men may be restrained from invading others rights, and from doing hurt to one another, and the law of nature be observed, which wills the peace and preservation of all mankind, the execution of the law of nature is, in that state, put into every man's hands, whereby everyone has a right to punish the transgressors of that law to such a degree, as may hinder its violation: for the law of nature would, as all other laws that concern men in this world 'be in vain, if there were no body that in the state of nature had a power to execute that law, and thereby preserve the innocent and restrain offenders. And if anyone in the state of nature may punish another for any evil he has done, every one may do so: for in that state of perfect equality, where naturally there is no superiority or jurisdiction of one over another, what any may do in prosecution of that law, everyone must needs have a right to do.

8. And thus, in the state of nature, one man comes by a power over another; but yet no absolute or arbitrary power, to use a criminal, when he has got him in his hands, according to the passionate heats, or boundless extravagancy of his own will; but only to retribute to him, so far as calm reason and conscience dictate, what is proportionate to his transgression, which is so much as may serve for reparation and restraint: for these two are the only reasons, why one man may lawfully do harm to another, which is that we call punishment. In transgressing the law of nature, the offender declares himself to live by another rule than that of reason and common equity, which is that measure God has set to the actions of men, for their mutual security; and so he becomes dangerous to mankind, the tie, which is to secure them from injury and violence, being slighted and broken by him. Which being a trespass against the whole species, and the peace and safety of it, provided for by the law of nature, every man upon this score, by the right he hath to preserve mankind in general, may restrain, or where it is necessary, destroy things noxious to them, and so may bring such evil on any one, who hath transgressed that law, as may make him repent

the doing of it, and thereby deter him, and by his example others, from doing the like mischief. And in the case, and upon this ground, every man hath a right to punish the offender, and be executioner of the law of nature....

10. Besides the crime which consists in violating the law, and varying from the right rule of reason, whereby a man so far becomes degenerate, and declares himself to quit the principles of human nature, and to be a noxious creature, there is commonly injury done to some person or other, and some other man receives damage by his transgression: in which case he who hath received any damage, has, besides the right of punishment common to him with other men, a particular right to seek reparation from him that has done it: and any other person, who finds it just, may also join with him that is injured, and assist him in recovering from the offender so much as may make satisfaction for the harm he has suffered.

11. From these two distinct rights, the one of punishing the crime for restraint, and preventing the like offence, which right of punishing is in everybody; the other of taking reparation, which belongs only to the injured party, comes it to pass that the magistrate, who by being magistrate hath the common right of punishing put into his hands, can often, where the public good demands not the execution of the law, remit the punishment of criminal offences by his own authority, but yet cannot remit the satisfaction due to any private man for the damage he has received. That, he who has suffered the damage has a right to demand in his own name, and he alone can remit: the damnified person has this power of appropriating to himself the goods or service of the offender, by right of self-preservation, as every man has a power to punish the crime, to prevent its being committed again, by the right he has of preserving all mankind, and doing all reasonable things he can in order to that end: and thus it is, that every man, in the state of nature, has a power to kill a murderer, both to deter others from doing the like injury, which no reparation can compensate, by the example of the punishment that attends it from everybody, and also to secure men from the attempts of a criminal, who having renounced reason, the common rule and measure God hath given to mankind, hath, by the unjust violence and slaughter he hath committed upon one,

declared war against all mankind, and therefore may be destroyed as a lion or a tiger, one of those wild savage beasts, with whom men can have no society nor security: and upon this is grounded that great law of nature, Whoso sheds man's blood, by man shall his blood be shed. And Cain was so fully convinced, that every one had a right to destroy such a criminal, that after the murder of his brother, he cries out, Everyone that finds me, shall slay me; so plain was it writ in the hearts of all mankind.

12. By the same reason may a man in the state of nature punish the lesser breaches of that law. It will perhaps be demanded, with death? I answer, each transgression may be punished to that degree, and with so much severity, as will suffice to make it an ill bargain to the offender, give him cause to repent, and terrify others from doing the like. Every offence, that can be committed in the state of nature, may in the state of nature be also punished equally, and as far forth as it may, in a commonwealth: for though it would be besides my present purpose, to enter here into the particulars of the law of nature, or its measures of punishment; yet, it is certain there is such a law, and that too, as intelligible and plain to a rational creature, and a studier of that law, as the positive laws of commonwealths; nay, possibly plainer; as much as reason is easier to be understood, than the fancies and intricate contrivances of men, following contrary and hidden interests put into words; for so truly are a great part of the municipal laws of countries, which are only so far right, as they are founded on the law of nature, by which they are to be regulated and interpreted.

13. To this strange doctrine, viz. That in the state of nature everyone has the executive power of the law of nature, I doubt not but it will be objected, that it is unreasonable for men to be judges in their own cases, that self-love will make men partial to themselves and their friends: and on the other side, that ill nature, passion and revenge will carry them too far in punishing others; and hence nothing but confusion and disorder will follow, and that therefore God hath certainly appointed government to restrain the partiality and violence of men. I easily grant, that civil government is the proper remedy for the inconveniencies of the state of nature, which must certainly be great, where men may be judges in their own

case, since it is easy to be imagined, that he who was so unjust as to do his brother an injury, will scarce be so just as to condemn himself for it: but I shall desire those who make this objection, to remember, that absolute monarchs are but men; and if government is to be the remedy of those evils, which necessarily follow from men's being judges in their own cases, and the state of nature is therefore not to how much better it is than the state of nature, where one man, commanding a multitude, has the liberty to be judge in his own case, and may do to all his subjects whatever he pleases, without the least liberty to anyone to question or control those who execute his pleasure? And in whatsoever he doth, whether led by reason, mistake or passion, must be submitted to? much better it is in the state of nature, wherein men are not bound to submit to the unjust will of another: and if he that judges, judges amiss in his own, or any other case, he is answerable for it to the rest of mankind.

14. It is often asked as a mighty objection, where are, or ever were there any men in such a state of nature? To which it may suffice as an answer at present, that since all princes and rulers of independent governments all through the world, are in a state of nature, it is plain the world never was, nor ever will be, without numbers of men in that state. I have named all governors of independent communities, whether they are, or are not, in league with others: for it is not every compact that puts an end to the state of nature between men, but only this one of agreeing together mutually to enter into one community, and make one body politic; other promises, and compacts, men may make one with another, and yet still be in the state of nature. The promises and bargains for truck, &c.; between the two men in the desert island, mentioned by Garcilasso de la Vega, in his history of Peru; or between a Swiss and an Indian, in the woods of America, are binding to them, though they are perfectly in a state of nature, in reference to one another: for truth and keeping of faith belongs to men, as men, and not as members of society.

15. To those that say, there were never any men in the state of nature...I...affirm, that all men are naturally in that state, and remain so, till by their own consents they make themselves members of some politic society; and I doubt not in the sequel of this discourse, to make it very clear....

Chapter 3
Of the State of War

16. THE state of war is a state of enmity and destruction: and therefore declaring by word or action, not a passionate and hasty, but a sedate settled design upon another man's life, puts him in a state of war with him against whom he has declared such an intention, and so has exposed his life to the other's power to be taken away by him, or any one that joins with him in his defense, and espouses his quarrel; it being reasonable and just, I should have a right to destroy that which threatens me with destruction: for, by the fundamental law of nature, man being to be preserved as much as possible, when all cannot be preserved, the safety of the innocent is to be preferred: and one may destroy a man who makes war upon him, or has discovered an enmity to his being, for the same reason that he may kill a wolf or a lion; because such men are not under the ties of the common law of reason, have no other rule, but that of force and violence, and so may be treated as beasts of prey, those dangerous and noxious creatures, that will be sure to destroy him whenever he falls into their power.

17. And hence it is, that he who attempts to get another man into his absolute power, does thereby put himself into a state of war with him; it being to be understood as a declaration of a design upon his life: for I have reason to conclude, that he who would get me into his power without my consent, would use me as he pleased when he had got me there, and destroy me too when he had a fancy to it; for nobody can desire to have me in his absolute power, unless it be to compel me by force to that which is against the right of my freedom, i.e. make me a slave. To be free from such force is the only security of my preservation; and reason bids me look on him, as an enemy to my preservation, who would take away that freedom which is the fence to it; so that he who makes an attempt to enslave me, thereby puts himself into a state of war with me. He that, in the state of nature, would take away the freedom that belongs to any one in that state, must necessarily be supposed to have a design to take away everything else, that freedom being the foundation of all the rest; as he that, in the state of society, would take away the freedom belonging to those of that society or commonwealth, must be supposed to design to take away from them everything else, and so be looked on as in a state of war.

18. This makes it lawful for a man to kill a thief, who has not in the least hurt him, nor declared any design upon his life, any farther than, by the use of force, so to get him in his power, as to take away his money, or what he pleases, from him; because using force, where he has no right, to get me into his power, let his pretence be what it will, I have no reason to suppose, that he, who would take away my liberty, would not, when he had me in his power, take away every thing else. And therefore it is lawful for me to treat him as one who has put himself into a state of war with me, i.e. kill him if I can; for to that hazard does he justly expose himself, whoever introduces a state of war, and is aggressor in it.

19. And here we have the plain difference between the state of nature and the state of war, which however some men have confounded, are as far distant, as a state of peace, good will, mutual assistance and preservation, and a state of enmity, malice, violence and mutual destruction, are one from another. Men living together according to reason, without a common superior on earth, with authority to judge between them, is properly the state of nature. But force, or a declared design of force, upon the person of another, where there is no common superior on earth to appeal to for relief, is the state of war: and it is the want of such an appeal gives a man the right of war even against an aggressor, though he be in society and a fellow subject. Thus a thief, whom I cannot harm, but by appeal to the law, for having stolen all that I am worth, I may kill, when he sets on me to rob me but of my horse or coat; because the law, which was made for my preservation, where it cannot interpose to secure my life from present force, which, if lost, is capable of no reparation, permits me my own defense, and the right of war, a liberty to kill the aggressor, because the aggressor allows not time to appeal to our common judge, nor the decision of the law, for remedy in a case where the mischief may be irreparable. Want of a common judge with authority, puts all men in a state of nature: force without right, upon a man's person, makes a state of war, both where there is, and is not, a common judge.

20. But when the actual force is over, the state of war ceases between those that are in society, and are equally on both sides subjected to the fair determination of the law; because then there lies open the remedy of appeal for the past injury, and to prevent future harm: but where no such appeal is, as in the state of nature, for want of positive laws, and judges with authority to appeal to, the state of war once begun, continues, with a right to the innocent party to destroy the other whenever he can, until the aggressor offers peace, and desires reconciliation on such terms as may repair any wrongs he has already done, and secure the innocent for the future; nay, where an appeal to the law, and constituted judges, lies open, but the remedy is denied by a manifest perverting of justice, and a barefaced wresting of the laws to protect or indemnify the violence or injuries of some men, or party of men, there it is hard to imagine anything but a state of war: for wherever violence is used, and injury done, though by hands appointed to administer justice, it is still violence and injury, however coloured with the name, pretences, or forms of law, the end whereof being to protect and redress the innocent, by an unbiassed application of it, to all who are under it; wherever that is not bona fide done, war is made upon the sufferers, who having no appeal on earth to right them, they are left to the only remedy in such cases, an appeal to heaven.

21. To avoid this state of war (wherein there is no appeal but to heaven, and wherein every the least difference is apt to end, where there is no authority to decide between the contenders) is one great reason of men's putting themselves into society, and quitting the state of nature: for where there is an authority, a power on earth, from which relief can be had by appeal, there the continuance of the state of war is excluded, and the controversy is decided by that power....

Chapter 5
Of Property

25. Whether we consider natural reason, which tells us, that men, being once born, have a right to their preservation, and consequently to meat and drink, and such other things as nature affords for their subsistence: or revelation, which gives us an account of those grants God made of the world to Adam, and to Noah, and his sons, it is very clear, that God, as king David says, has given the earth to the children of men; given it to mankind in common....

26. God, who hath given the world to men in common, hath also given them reason to make use of it to the best advantage of life, and convenience. The earth, and all that is therein, is given to men for the support and comfort of their being. And though all the fruits it naturally produces, and beasts it feeds, belong to mankind in common, as they are produced by the spontaneous hand of nature; and no body has originally a private dominion, exclusive of the rest of mankind, in any of them, as they are thus in their natural state: yet being given for the use of men, there must of necessity be a means to appropriate them some way or other, before they can be of any use, or at all beneficial to any particular man. The fruit, or venison, which nourishes the wild Indian, who knows no enclosure, and is still a tenant in common, must be his, and so his, i.e. a part of him, that another can no longer have any right to it, before it can do him any good for the support of his life.

Though the earth, and all inferior creatures, be common to all men, yet every man has a property in his own person: this nobody has any right to but himself. The labour of his body, and the work of his hands, we may say, are properly his. Whatsoever then he removes out of the state that nature hath provided, and left it in, he hath mixed his labour with, and joined to it something that is his own, and thereby makes it his property. It being by him removed from the common state nature hath placed it in, it hath by this labour something annexed to it, that excludes the common right of other men: for this labour being the unquestionable property of the labourer, no man but he can have a right to what that is once joined to, at least where there is enough, and as good, left in common for others.

He that is nourished by the acorns he picked up under an oak, or the apples he gathered from the trees in the wood, has certainly appropriated them to himself. Nobody can deny but the nourishment is his. I ask then, when did they begin to be his? When he digested? Or when he eat? Or when he boiled? Or when he brought them home? or when he picked them up? And it is plain, if the first gathering made them not his, nothing else could. That labour put a distinction between them and common: that added something to them more than nature, the common mother of all, had done; and so they became his private right. And will anyone say, he had no right to those acorns or apples, he thus appropriated, because he had not the consent of all mankind to make them his? Was it a robbery thus to assume to himself what belonged to all in common? If such a consent as that was necessary, man had starved, notwithstanding the plenty God had given him. We see in commons, which remain so by compact, that it is the taking any part of what is common, and removing it out of the state nature leaves it in, which begins the property; without which the common is of no use. And the taking of this or that part, does not depend on the express consent of all the commoners. Thus the grass my horse has bit; the turfs my servant has cut; and the ore I have digged in any place, where I have a right to them in common with others, become my property, without the assignation or consent of any body. The labour that was mine, removing them out of that common state they were in, hath fixed my property in them....

Chapter 7
Of Political or Civil Society

...87. Man being born, as has been proved, with a title to perfect freedom, and an uncontrolled enjoyment of all the rights and privileges of the law of nature, equally with any other man, or number of men in the world, hath by nature a power, not only to preserve his property, that is, his life, liberty and estate, against the injuries and attempts of other men; but to judge of, and punish the breaches of that law in others, as he is persuaded the offence deserves, even with death itself, in crimes where the heinousness of the fact, in his opinion, requires it. But because no political society can be, nor subsist, without having in itself the power to preserve the property, and in order thereunto, punish the offences of all those of that society; there, and there only is political society, where every one of the members hath quitted this natural power, resigned it up into the hands of the community in all cases that exclude him not from appealing for protection to the law established by

it. And thus all private judgment of every particular member being excluded, the community comes to be umpire, by settled standing rules, indifferent, and the same to all parties; and by men having authority from the community, for the execution of those rules, decides all the differences that may happen between any members of that society concerning any matter of right; and punishes those offences which any member hath committed against the society, with such penalties as the law has established: whereby it is easy to discern, who are, and who are not, in political society together. Those who are united into one body, and have a common established law and judicature to appeal to, with authority to decide controversies between them, and punish offenders, are in civil society one with another: but those who have no such common appeal, I mean on earth, are still in the state of nature, each being, where there is no other, judge for himself, and executioner; which is, as I have before showed it, the perfect state of nature.

88. And thus the commonwealth comes by a power to set down what punishment shall belong to the several transgressions which they think worthy of it, committed amongst the members of that society, (which is the power of making laws) as well as it has the power to punish any injury done unto any of its members, by any one that is not of it, (which is the power of war and peace;) and all this for the preservation of the property of all the members of that society, as far as is possible. But though every man who has entered into civil society, and is become a member of any commonwealth, has thereby quitted his power to punish offences, against the law of nature, in prosecution of his own private judgment, yet with the judgment of offences, which he has given up to the legislative in all cases, where he can appeal to the magistrate, he has given a right to the common-wealth to employ his force, for the execution of the judgments of the common-wealth, whenever he shall be called to it; which indeed are his own judgments, they being made by himself, or his representative. And herein we have the original of the legislative and executive power of civil society, which is to judge by standing laws, how far offences are to be punished, when committed within the common-wealth; and also to determine, by occasional judgments founded on the present circum-

stances of the fact, how far injuries from without are to be vindicated; and in both these to employ all the force of all the members, when there shall be need.

89. Whereever therefore any number of men are so united into one society, as to quit everyone his executive power of the law of nature, and to resign it to the public, there and there only is a political, or civil society. And this is done, where-ever any number of men, in the state of nature, enter into society to make one people, one body politic, under one supreme government; or else when any one joins himself to, and incorporates with any government already made: for hereby he authorizes the society, or which is all one, the legislative thereof, to make laws for him, as the public good of the society shall require; to the execution whereof, his own assistance (as to his own decrees) is due. And this puts men out of a state of nature into that of a commonwealth, by setting up a judge on earth, with authority to determine all the controversies, and redress the injuries that may happen to any member of the commonwealth; which judge is the legislative, or magistrates appointed by it. And where-ever there are any number of men, however associated, that have no such decisive power to appeal to, there they are still in the state of nature.

90. Hence it is evident, that absolute monarchy, which by some men is counted the only government in the world, is indeed inconsistent with civil society, and so can be no form of civil government at all: for the end of civil society, being to avoid, and remedy those inconveniencies of the state of nature, which necessarily follow from every man's being judge in his own case, by setting up a known authority, to which every one of that society may appeal upon any injury received, or controversy that may arise, and which every one of the* society ought to obey; where-ever any persons are, who have not such an authority to appeal to, for the decision of any difference between them, there those persons are still in the state of nature; and so is every absolute prince, in respect of those who are under his dominion.

91. For he being supposed to have all, both legislative and executive power in himself alone, there is no judge to be found, no appeal lies open to anyone, who may fairly, and indifferently, and with authority decide, and from whose decision relief and redress may be expected of any injury or inconvenience, that may be suffered from the prince, or by his order: so that such a man, however entitled, Czar, or Grand Seignior, or how you please, is as much in the state of nature, with all under his dominion, as he is with the rest of mankind: for where-ever any two men are, who have no standing rule, and common judge to appeal to on earth, for the determination of controversies of right betwixt them, there they are still in the state of nature, and under all the inconveniencies of it, with only this woful difference to the subject, or rather slave of an absolute prince: that whereas, in the ordinary state of nature, he has a liberty to judge of his right, and according to the best of his power, to maintain it; now, whenever his property is invaded by the will and order of his monarch, he has not only no appeal, as those in society ought to have, but as if he were degraded from the common state of rational creatures, is denied a liberty to judge of, or to defend his right; and so is exposed to all the misery and inconveniencies, that a man can fear from one, who being in the unrestrained state of nature, is yet corrupted with flattery, and armed with power....

Chapter 8
Of the Beginning of Political Societies

95. MEN being, as has been said, by nature, all free, equal, and independent, no one can be put out of this estate, and subjected to the political power of another, without his own consent. The only way whereby any one divests himself of his natural liberty, and puts on the bonds of civil society, is by agreeing with other men to join and unite into a community for their comfortable, safe, and peaceable living one amongst another, in a secure enjoyment of their properties, and a greater security against any, that are not of it. This any number of men may do, because it injures not the freedom of the rest; they are left as they were in the liberty of the state of nature. When any number of men have so consented to make one community or government, they are thereby presently incorporated, and make one body politic, wherein the majority have a right to act and conclude the rest.

96. For when any number of men have, by the

consent of every individual, made a community, they have thereby made that community one body, with a power to act as one body, which is only by the will and determination of the majority: for that which acts any community, being only the consent of the individuals of it, and it being necessary to that which is one body to move one way; it is necessary the body should move that way whither the greater force carries it, which is the consent of the majority: or else it is impossible it should act or continue one body, one community, which the consent of every individual that united into it, agreed that it should; and so everyone is bound by that consent to be concluded by the majority. And therefore we see, that in assemblies, empowered to act by positive laws, where no number is set by that positive law which impowers them, the act of the majority passes for the act of the whole, and of course determines, as having, by the law of nature and reason, the power of the whole.

97. And thus every man, by consenting with others to make one body politic under one government, puts himself under an obligation, to every one of that society, to submit to the determination of the majority, and to be concluded by it; or else this original compact, whereby he with others incorporates into one society, would signify nothing, and be no compact, if he be left free, and under no other ties than he was in before in the state of nature. For what appearance would there be of any compact? what new engagement if he were no farther tied by any decrees of the society, than he himself thought fit, and did actually consent to? This would be still as great a liberty, as he himself had before his compact, or any one else in the state of nature hath, who may submit himself, and consent to any acts of it if he thinks fit.

98. For if the consent of the majority shall not, in reason, be received as the act of the whole, and conclude every individual; nothing but the consent of every individual can make anything to be the act of the whole: but such a consent is next to impossible ever to be had, if we consider the infirmities of health, and avocations of business, which in a number, though much less than that of a common-wealth, will necessarily keep many away from the public assembly. To which if we add the variety of opinions, and contrariety of interests, which unavoidably happen in all collections of men, the coming into society upon such terms would be only like Cato's coming into the theatre, only to go out again. Such a constitution as this would make the mighty Leviathan of a shorter duration, than the feeblest creatures, and not let it outlast the day it was born in: which cannot be supposed, till we can think, that rational creatures should desire and constitute societies only to be dissolved: for where the majority cannot conclude the rest, there they cannot act as one body, and consequently will be immediately dissolved again....

Chapter 9
Of the Ends of Political Society and Government

123. If man in the state of nature be so free, as has been said; if he be absolute lord of his own person and possessions, equal to the greatest, and subject to no body, why will he part with his freedom? why will he give up this empire, and subject himself to the dominion and control of any other power? To which it is obvious to answer, that though in the state of nature he hath such a right, yet the enjoyment of it is very uncertain, and constantly exposed to the invasion of others: for all being kings as much as he, every man his equal, and the greater part no strict observers of equity and justice, the enjoyment of the property he has in this state is very unsafe, very unsecure. This makes him willing to quit a condition, which, however free, is full of fears and continual dangers: and it is not without reason, that he seeks out, and is willing to join in society with others, who are already united, or have a mind to unite, for the mutual preservation of their lives, liberties and estates, which I call by the general name, property.

124. The great and chief end, therefore, of men's uniting into commonwealths, and putting themselves under government, is the preservation of their property. To which in the state of nature there are many things wanting.

First, There wants an established, settled, known law, received and allowed by common consent to be the standard of right and wrong, and the common measure to decide all controversies between them: for though the law of nature be plain and intelligible to all rational creatures; yet men being biased by their interest, as well as ignorant for want of study of it, are not apt to allow of it as a law binding to them in the application of it to their particular cases.

125. Secondly, In the state of nature there wants a known and indifferent judge, with authority to determine all differences according to the established law: for everyone in that state being both judge and executioner of the law of nature, men being partial to themselves, passion and revenge is very apt to carry them too far, and with too much heat, in their own cases; as well as negligence, and unconcernedness, to make them too remiss in other men's.

126. Thirdly, In the state of nature there often wants power to back and support the sentence when right, and to give it due execution. They who by any injustice offended, will seldom fail, where they are able, by force to make good their injustice; such resistance many times makes the punishment dangerous, and frequently destructive, to those who attempt it.

127. Thus mankind, notwithstanding all the privileges of the state of nature, being but in an ill condition, while they remain in it, are quickly driven into society. Hence it comes to pass, that we seldom find any number of men live any time together in this state. The inconveniencies that they are therein exposed to, by the irregular and uncertain exercise of the power every man has of punishing the transgressions of others, make them take sanctuary under the established laws of government, and therein seek the preservation of their property. It is this makes them so willingly give up every one his single power of punishing, to be exercised by such alone, as shall be appointed to it amongst them; and by such rules as the community, or those authorized by them to that purpose, shall agree on. And in this we have the original right and rise of both the legislative and executive power, as well as of the governments and societies themselves.

128. For in the state of nature, to omit the liberty he has of innocent delights, a man has two powers.

The first is to do whatsoever he thinks fit for the preservation of himself, and others within the permission of the law of nature: by which law, common to them all, he and all the rest of mankind are one community, make up one society, distinct from all other creatures. And were it not for the corruption and vitiousness of degenerate men, there would be no need of any other; no necessity that men should separate from this great and natural community, and by positive agreements combine into smaller and divided associations.

The other power a man has in the state of nature, is the power to punish the crimes committed against that law. Both these he gives up, when he joins in a private, if I may so call it, or particular politic society, and incorporates int o any common-wealth, separate from the rest of mankind.

129. The first power, viz. of doing whatsoever he thought for the preservation of himself, and the rest of mankind, he gives up to be regulated by laws made by the society, so far forth as the preservation of himself, and the rest of that society shall require; which laws of the society in many things confine the liberty he had by the law of nature.

130. Secondly, The power of punishing he wholly gives up, and engages his natural force, (which he might before employ in the execution of the law of nature, by his own single authority, as he thought fit) to assist the executive power of the society, as the law thereof shall require: for being now in a new state, wherein he is to enjoy many conveniencies, from the labour, assistance, and society of others in the same community, as well as protection from its whole strength; he is to part also with as much of his natural liberty, in providing for himself, as the good, prosperity, and safety of the society shall require; which is not only necessary, but just, since the other members of the society do the like.

131. But though men, when they enter into society, give up the equality, liberty, and executive power they had in the state of nature, into the hands of the society, to be so far disposed of by the legislative, as the good of the society shall require; yet it being only with an intention in every one the better to preserve himself, his liberty and property; (for no rational creature can be supposed to change his condition with an intention to be worse) the power of the society, or legislative constituted by them, can never be supposed to extend farther, than the common good; but is obliged to secure every one's property, by providing against those three defects above mentioned, that made the state of nature so unsafe and uneasy. And so whoever has the legislative or

supreme power of any common-wealth, is bound to govern by established standing laws, promulgated and known to the people, and not by extemporary decrees; by indifferent and upright judges, who are to decide controversies by those laws; and to employ the force of the community at home, only in the execution of such laws, or abroad to prevent or redress foreign injuries, and secure the community from inroads and invasion. And all this to be directed to no other end, but the peace, safety, and public good of the people.

Chapter 11
Of the Extent of the Legislative Power.

....Sect. 142. These are the bounds which the trust, that is put in them by the society, and the law of God and nature, have set to the legislative power of every common-wealth, in all forms of government.

First, They are to govern by promulgated established laws, not to be varied in particular cases, but to have one rule for rich and poor, for the favourite at court, and the country man at plough.

Secondly, these laws also ought to be designed for no other end ultimately, but the good of the people.

Thirdly, they must not raise taxes on the property of the people, without the consent of the people, given by themselves, or their deputies. And this properly concerns only such governments where the legislative is always in being, or at least where the people have not reserved any part of the legislative to deputies, to be from time to time chosen by themselves.

Fourthly, the legislative neither must nor can transfer the power of making laws to anybody else, or place it anywhere, but where the people have.

Chapter 19
Of the Dissolution of Government

211. He that will with any clearness speak of the dissolution of government, ought in the first place to distinguish between the dissolution of the society and the dissolution of the government. That which makes the community, and brings men out of the loose state of nature, into one politic society, is the

agreement which every one has with the rest to incorporate, and act as one body, and so be one distinct common-wealth. The usual, and almost only way whereby this union is dissolved, is the inroad of foreign force making a conquest upon them: for in that case, (not being able to maintain and support themselves, as one intire and independent body) the union belonging to that body which consisted therein, must necessarily cease, and so every one return to the state he was in before, with a liberty to shift for himself, and provide for his own safety, as he thinks fit, in some other society. Whenever the society is dissolved, it is certain the government of that society cannot remain. Thus conquerors swords often cut up governments by the roots, and mangle societies to pieces, separating the subdued or scattered multitude from the protection of, and dependence on, that society which ought to have preserved them from violence. The world is too well instructed in, and too forward to allow of, this way of dissolving of governments, to need any more to be said of it; and there wants not much argument to prove, that where the society is dissolved, the government cannot remain; that being as impossible, as for the frame of an house to subsist when the materials of it are scattered and dissipated by a whirl-wind, or jumbled into a confused heap by an earthquake.

Sect. 212. Besides this over-turning from without, governments are dissolved from within,

First, when the legislative is altered. Civil society being a state of peace, amongst those who are of it, from whom the state of war is excluded by the umpirage, which they have provided in their legislative, for the ending all differences that may arise amongst any of them, it is in their legislative, that the members of a commonwealth are united, and combined together into one coherent living body. This is the soul that gives form, life, and unity, to the common-wealth: from hence the several members have their mutual influence, sympathy, and connection: and therefore, when the legislative is broken, or dissolved, dissolution and death follows: for the essence and union of the society consisting in having one will, the legislative, when once established by the majority, has the declaring, and as it were keeping of that will. The constitution of the legislative is the first and fundamental act of society, whereby provision is made for the continuation of their union, under the direction of persons, and bonds of laws, made by persons authorized thereunto, by the consent and appointment of the people, without which no one man, or number of men, amongst them, can have authority of making laws that shall be binding to the rest. When any one, or more, shall take upon them to make laws, whom the people have not appointed so to do, they make laws without authority, which the people are not therefore bound to obey; by which means they come again to be out of subjection, and may constitute to themselves a new legislative, as they think best, being in full liberty to resist the force of those, who without authority would impose any thing upon them. Everyone is at the disposure of his own will, when those who had, by the delegation of the society, the declaring of the public will, are excluded from it, and others usurp the place, who have no such authority or delegation.

221. There is therefore, secondly, another way whereby governments are dissolved, and that is, when the legislative, or the prince, either of them, act contrary to their trust.

First, The legislative acts against the trust reposed in them, when they endeavour to invade the property of the subject, and to make themselves, or any part of the community, masters, or arbitrary disposers of the lives, liberties, or fortunes of the people.

222. The reason why men enter into society, is the preservation of their property; and the end why they choose and authorize a legislative, is, that there may be laws made, and rules set, as guards and fences to the properties of all the members of the society, to limit the power, and moderate the dominion, of every part and member of the society: for since it can never be supposed to be the will of the society, that the legislative should have a power to destroy that which every one designs to secure, by entering into society, and for which the people submitted themselves to legislators of their own making; whenever the legislators endeavour to take away, and destroy the property of the people, or to reduce them to slavery under arbitrary power, they put themselves into a state of war with the people, who are thereupon absolved from any farther obedience, and are left to the common refuge, which God hath provided for all men, against force and violence. Whensoever there-

fore the legislative shall transgress this fundamental rule of society; and either by ambition, fear, folly or corruption, endeavour to grasp themselves, or put into the hands of any other, an absolute power over the lives, liberties, and estates of the people; by this breach of trust they forfeit the power the people had put into their hands for quite contrary ends, and it devolves to the people, who. have a right to resume their original liberty, and, by the establishment of a new legislative, (such as they shall think fit) provide for their own safety and security, which is the end for which they are in society. What I have said here, concerning the legislative in general, holds true also concerning the supreme executor, who having a double trust put in him, both to have a part in the legislative, and the supreme execution of the law, acts against both, when he goes about to set up his own arbitrary will as the law of the society. He acts also contrary to his trust, when he either employs the force, treasure, and offices of the society, to corrupt the representatives, and gain them to his purposes; or openly preengages the electors, and prescribes to their choice, such, whom he has, by sollicitations, threats, promises, or otherwise, won to his designs; and employs them to bring in such, who have promised before-hand what to vote, and what to enact. Thus to regulate candidates and electors, and new-model the ways of election, what is it but to cut up the government by the roots, and poison the very fountain of public security? for the people having reserved to themselves the choice of their representatives, as the fence to their properties, could do it for no other end, but that they might always be freely chosen, and so chosen, freely act, and advise, as the necessity of the common-wealth, and the public good should, upon examination, and mature debate, be judged to require. This, those who give their votes before they hear the debate, and have weighed the reasons on all sides, are not capable of doing. To prepare such an assembly as this, and endeavour to set up the declared abettors of his own will, for the true representatives of the people, and the lawmakers of the society, is certainly as great a breach of trust, and as perfect a declaration of a design to subvert the government, as is possible to be met with. To which, if one shall add rewards and punishments visibly employed to the same end, and all the arts of perverted law made use of, to take off and destroy all that stand in the way of such a design, and will not comply and consent to betray the liberties of their country, it will be past doubt what is doing. What power they ought to have in the society, who thus employ it contrary to the trust went along with it in its first institution, is easy to determine; and one cannot but see, that he, who has once attempted any such thing as this, cannot any longer be trusted.

223. To this perhaps it will be said, that the people being ignorant, and always discontented, to lay the foundation of government in the unsteady opinion and uncertain humour of the people, is to expose it to certain ruin; and no government will be able long to subsist, if the people may set up a new legislative, whenever they take offence at the old one. To this I answer, Quite the contrary. People are not so easily got out of their old forms, as some are apt to suggest. They are hardly to be prevailed with to amend the acknowledged faults in the frame they have been accustomed to. And if there be any original defects, or adventitious ones introduced by time, or corruption; it is not an easy thing to get them changed, even when all the world sees there is an opportunity for it. This slowness and aversion in the people to quit their old constitutions, has, in the many revolutions which have been seen in this kingdom, in this and former ages, still kept us to, or, after some interval of fruitless attempts, still brought us back again to our old legislative of king, lords and commons: and whatever provocations have made the crown be taken from some of our princes heads, they never carried the people so far as to place it in another line.

224. But it will be said, this hypothesis lays a ferment for frequent rebellion. To which I answer,

First, no more than any other hypothesis: for when the people are made miserable, and find themselves exposed to the ill usage of arbitrary power, cry up their governors, as much as you will, for sons of Jupiter; let them be sacred and divine, descended, or authorized from heaven; give them out for whom or what you please, the same will happen. The people generally ill treated, and contrary to right, will be ready upon any occasion to ease themselves of a burden that sits heavy upon them. They will wish, and seek for the opportunity, which in the change, weakness and accidents of human affairs, seldom

delays long to offer itself. He must have lived but a little while in the world, who has not seen examples of this in his time; and he must have read very little, who cannot produce examples of it in all sorts of governments in the world.

225. Secondly, I answer, such revolutions happen not upon every little mismanagement in public affairs. Great mistakes in the ruling part, many wrong and inconvenient laws, and all the slips of human frailty, will be born by the people without mutiny or murmur. But if a long train of abuses, prevarications and artifices, all tending the same way, make the design visible to the people, and they cannot but feel what they lie under, and see whither they are going; it is not to be wondered, that they should then rouse themselves, and endeavour to put the rule into such hands which may secure to them the ends for which government was at first erected; and without which, ancient names, and specious forms, are so far from being better, that they are much worse, than the state of nature, or pure anarchy; the inconveniencies being all as great and as near, but the remedy farther off and more difficult.

226. Thirdly, I answer, that this doctrine of a power in the people of providing for their safety a-new, by a new legislative, when their legislators have acted contrary to their trust, by invading their property, is the best fence against rebellion, and the probablest means to hinder it: for rebellion being an opposition, not to persons, but authority, which is founded only in the constitutions and laws of the government; those, whoever they be, who by force break through, and by force justify their violation of them, are truly and properly rebels: for when men, by entering into society and civil-government, have excluded force, and introduced laws for the preservation of property, peace, and unity amongst themselves, those who set up force again in opposition to the laws, do rebellare, that is, bring back again the state of war, and are properly rebels: which they who are in power, (by the pretence they have to authority, the temptation of force they have in their hands, and the flattery of those about them) being likeliest to do; the properest way to prevent the evil, is to shew them the danger and injustice of it, who are under the greatest temptation to run into it.

227. In both the fore-mentioned cases, when ei-

ther the legislative is changed, or the legislators act contrary to the end for which they were constituted; those who are guilty are guilty of rebellion: for if any one by force takes away the established legislative of any society, and the laws by them made, pursuant to their trust, he thereby takes away the umpirage, which everyone had consented to, for a peaceable decision of all their controversies, and a bar to the state of war amongst them. They, who remove, or change the legislative, take away this decisive power, which nobody can have, but by the appointment and consent of the people; and so destroying the authority which the people did, and nobody else can set up, and introducing a power which the people hath not authorized, they actually introduce a state of war, which is that of force without authority: and thus, by removing the legislative established by the society, (in whose decisions the people acquiesced and united, as to that of their own will) they untie the knot, and expose the people a-new to the state of war. And if those, who by force take away the legislative, are rebels, the legislators themselves, as has been shown, can be no less esteemed so; when they, who were set up for the protection, and preservation of the people, their liberties and properties, shall by force invade and endeavour to take them away; and so they putting themselves into a state of war with those who made them the protectors and guardians of their peace, are properly, and with the greatest aggravation, *rebellantes*, rebels.

John Locke. *Second Treatise of Government.* London: R. Butler, 1821.

10

AESTHETICS: WHAT IS ART?

STEPHAN T. MAYO

Aesthetics is one of two main branches of value theory in philosophy. Ethics is a study of values in human conduct. Aesthetics is a study of value in art. The word traces its origin to a Greek word that means sense appearance. However that could too narrowly define the field when we consider that art include prose and poetic literature. We could quibble that literature always has an auditory component. When we read literature the sounds and inflections of words accompany our thoughts. We could solve the problem by saying that aesthetics is a study of value in the plastic, visual, conceptual, auditory and performance arts.

The difficulty of answering the question: "What is art?" is a major one in aesthetics. The term has to cover a vast variety of media, from the plastic arts of painting and sculpture, to music, literature and the performing arts of dance, opera, and theater. It can even be expanded to certain performance sports like ice-skating, water ballet, diving and gymnastics. Seeking a common definition that covers the wide number of art productions from the earliest cave drawings to the latest experimental film is difficult. The definition would have to identify both Marcel Duchamp's *The Fountain* (which is a urinal set in a glass cube) and Michelangelo's *Pieta* as equally works of art. The most uncontroversial and agreed upon definition is that art is anything that is artificial, that is anything that humans make which is not simply something that exists in nature. Even that might be tested by, say Picasso's found object sculptures, many of which consist of natural objects. However Picasso juxtaposes these natural objects into unique forms. If, however, I place a twig in a frame and hang it on a museum wall that might qualify as art since I have taken it out of its natural context and intend it to be seen as though it were a production of an artist. We will see that Arthur Danto will claim that it is the referential nature of art that distinguishes it from natural objects (a twig on a tree doesn't refer to anything.) More provocatively Marshall McLuhan (*The Medium is the Message*) claimed that "art is anything we can get away with."

It should be obvious by the above that there is nothing uncontroversial about aesthetics including the very definition of art. Still the rumination and analyses of philosophers who think about these issues have consistently enhanced the enjoyment of those who love the arts because they highlight multiple features of the aesthetic experience. In this short introduction I want to briefly discuss how aesthetics interrelates with the other main branches of philosophy: metaphysics, epistemology, ethics and political philosophy.

Metaphysics

Metaphysics is a branch of philosophy that inquires about the being or reality of things. Aesthetics interrelates with metaphysics when one inquires about the ontological status of the work of art. What kind of being is it? Back in the 5th Century BC, the Greeks of ancient Athens interpreted aesthetics as a search for what made an object beautiful. Plato saw that there were many beautiful things such as paintings, mosaics, sculptures, lyric poetry, epic poetry, all beautiful but not Beauty Itself. When an artist makes a beautiful thing she mysteriously attunes herself with a secret reality that lies beneath and behind the concrete work of art, something that is not itself visible or tangible, i.e. to the Ideal universal and eternal Form (*eidos*) of Beauty Itself. In the Middle Ages, theologian/philosophers like St. Thomas Aquinas made beauty one of the transcendental properties of God. Thus God being infinitely beautiful created the world in which His beauty would be manifested both in the natural world and in the human artistic creations that imitated the natural world. Consequently the artist attempted to imitate the natural world in order to reveal the supernatural world beyond it.

Plato was suspicious of the artist as one who not only could reveal the natural world but could distort it as well. Since the natural world was only an imitation of the really real of the Ideal Forms, art was an imitation of an imitation. Better to forget about art and contemplate the pure Forms directly. In the nineteenth century, following the aesthetic writings of Immanuel Kant, the quest for beauty was augmented by the search for the sublime. Beauty is experienced when a perceived object most perfectly embodies our pre-formed idea of its nature. This felt sense of the aptness of the representation to the nature of what it represents is beauty. However, there are times when confronted with the immense forces of nature or by works of art which defy our ability to fully take them in and rationally interpret them. Subsequently we have emotional responses to the overwhelming visual and auditory array giving rise to the sense of the sublime—an experience which transcends reason.

The Achilles' heal of the representational view of art (judging a work on how well it could imitate, realistically depict, capture the true universal essence of a thing, or reveal the Divine origin of things) has always been music. What does music, especially non-vocal music, depict? Despite the best efforts of Romanticist artists and critics, not every piece of music tells a story or depicts a natural phenomenon. About the time of the invention of photography, artists, critics and public alike began to realize that the work of art had never been a mere imitation or copy of nature. Viewing a framed painting was not really like looking through a window, and Botticelli's women are worlds apart from a woman photographed or directly observed. Aestheticians focused on the art *object* itself, and not on any alleged *subject*, as art became less and less representational and more and more divorced from both natural and supernatural beings. If what we perceive in the work of art is the work of art, what is that, since certainly we do not merely perceive the raw materials from which the work is crafted? It is not oil paint blotches that we see in a Cezanne landscape, nor is it Montaigne Saint-Victoire as a real mountain. We enter the visual world of Cezanne and perceive the art object that conveys simultaneously a sense of depth and of flatness of the picture surface as well. We do not perceive isolated blobs of color, but shapes and forms in a style in a composition (the visual Cezannesque "world") unique to the artist. Susanne Langer will call this peculiar world the "virtual space" of the painting as distinguished from the actual dimensions of the canvas. Get too close to the work and it disappears. Not only does the form and unity disappear, but the medium (the materials and the psychological and emotional associations we have when we see the materials) disappear and only the bare materials remain (stretched canvas and oil paint smears.) Later abstract expressionist artists will present shape and color divorced (abstracted) entirely from a discernible subject matter. Artists such as Ad Reinhardt title their painting as *Number 43*, which depicts nothing at all discernible in nature.

The shift from the artist's subject to the artistic object by aestheticians brings us to the interrelationship between aesthetics and epistemology.

Epistemology

The mysteriousness of the reality of the artistic object gets clarified when we stop looking for the supernatural or natural origins of the work and concentrate on the intentional object of the work. Problems such as how a work of art such as a play, opera, dance or orchestral piece might exist in multiple manifestations or performances and yet remain a single work of art are also alleviated when we consider that the notation of the work allows the presentation of the artistic object to a variety of audiences or viewers. The work of art exists between the materials used by the artist or the performers and the consciousnesses of the audience or viewers. Without the pattern recognition aptitudes of our minds there would be no work of art. Aestheticians like Norman Goodman in *Art and Illusion* bring this relationship out in high definition. It should have been obvious to us that the glint of the sun emerging over the hills at dusk is not a light beaming from the back of the painting but a smear of titanium white oil paint, that a line can be perceived as a surface and a three-dimensional cube produced by grey tints juxtaposed against broad flat areas on a two-dimensional canvas. If an audience member jumps up onto the stage to save the damsel in distress, he has obviously mistaken the art object for natural reality. This brings us to an interesting set of questions. If the artwork is the phenomenal object and not the natural materials from which it is comprised, what is the relationship between art and truth? Verisimilitude may be one of the qualities that we appreciate in art as when a visitor waved at the painted sons of Charles Wilson Peale in his *The Staircase Group* or when Meryl Streep is praised for capturing the look, voice and mannerisms of Margaret Thatcher in the *Iron Lady*. However, the copy view of art hardly applies to the prostitutes in Picasso's cubist *Demoiselles d'Avignon* or to the form of a Mozart sonata. That having been said, we would still like the proposition "Sherlock Holmes smokes a pipe." to be true, whereas "Sherlock Holmes was a vampire" is understood as false.

There are several contenders for the criterion of truth in art. Some aestheticians claim that the deliberate intention of the artist is the basis of the true interpretation of the work of art. The art purists or formalists reject the intention-of-the-artist theory. The later say that appreciation of artistic form independent of any reference to a subject or the emotions or intentions of the creator of the art work is the aesthetic experience. We might appreciate the information we receive from the art work about history for example, or enjoy the patriotic emotions engendered in us about the heroes of the last war that art brings out. But these are not aesthetic qualities according to the purists. Only our appreciation of artistic form should constitute our aesthetic appreciation and the truth of the piece. Clive Bell and Roger Fry are proponents of the purist position. The intentions of the artist cannot be, according to them, what is truest about the work because the artist may not be conscious of what she is intending in the work, the work may not in fact successfully reflect the intentions of the artist and it doesn't make any difference anyway because the meaning the art work has must be derived from the form of the work itself. The audience may in fact give the work entirely different meaning than what the artist intended. And again, for the purist any extra-aesthetic meaning the work may have is irrelevant to the worth of the work aesthetically.

Another contender for the truth of a work of art comes from the Expressionists. For them the aesthetic experience is primarily the emotions that the work of art evokes in its audience, readers or viewers. That art works evoke a wide spectrum of emotions in us from terror, horror, sadness, nostalgia, anxiety, to awe, wonder, compassion, empathy, love, and reverence can hardly be denied. It is also uncontroversial that artists often attempt to convey in their productions emotions that they themselves feel in response to their own life's experience. The purists would however claim that the artist's own emotional history is irrelevant to the appreciation of the art object since whatever emotive elements are present in the object are the one's that are accessible and not the dark recesses of the artist's mind. If we cry when Mimi dies in the last scene of *La Bohème* because it reminds us of a recent loss of a close relative we are missing the appreciation of the artistic form. The expressionists however would say the tears are a proper response to the emotional expressiveness that is present in the swelling soberness in the minor key that Puccini has penned for the orchestra to play and the protagonists to sing. Suzanne Langer, who is a prominent proponent of the expressionist theory of art, states that music is the language of the emotions (Cf. *Feeling and Form*). It is not the actual emotions of the composer but the musical composition that exhibits a family resemblance with our emotional lives. For example, emotions and music are both temporal phenomena, they are both expressible in dynamic terms like *accelerando* and *decelerando*, *sostenuto* and *allegro*. This is why, she contends, that even absolute music, music that is totally abstracted from a natural reference, can elicit emotions because of the structural similarity with our own emotions. A similar analysis could be made for the connotation of words used by poets or the use of symmetry and asymmetry in architecture. The human psychological make-up formed within a historically based culture has already assigned emotional associations with the various elements in artistic media. The artist draws upon these emotively latent media elements in the composition of his works. Suffice it to say that the purists like Clive Bell and Roger Fry would find that any emotion evoked by the artwork (other than the, at times intense, satisfaction that comes from recognizing the form of the art object) to be distraught nonsense and outside the aesthetic realm.

Ethics and Political Philosophy

The relationship between Aesthetics and Ethics is intriguing because the artist/composer has always had an ambiguous relationship with society. On the one hand, she is dismissed as a craftsman or decorator, on the other a cultural hero (e.g. within the city-states of Renaissance Italy) or as national icon (e.g. the composers and authors of Tsarist Russia). On the one hand she is called upon to promote the revered ethical values of a society and on the other feared as a bohemian incendiary threatening the moral core of a culture.

Again the purists would say that expecting art works to either reinforce ethical or cultural values or to denigrate the same is a major category mistake. Aesthetic values have nothing to do with moral values. Since however art cannot be extracted fully from the historical contexts of not only the societies within which the artists work but also from classical aesthetic theories that associated art with beauty and alleged obligations of the human community to pursue beauty in the world and in the character of persons, the philosophy of art has attempted to show the relationship between art and moral and political values. Plato for one recognized the value of art as a medium for conveying moral and political values. In fact the pedagogy of ancient Athens consisted mainly in the singing of Homeric epic poetry in unison by the youth of the city-state. As the principal means of educating the sensibilities, psychic harmonies and civic responsibilities of the great-souled individual, Plato was in favor of severely censoring

Homeric depictions of both heroes and gods as vengeful, licentious, duplicitous or unjust. This one illustration of a classical art criticism shows that art has been historically both lionized as a central means of propagandizing moral, religious, cultural or political values and castigated as potentially dangerous to those values calling for censorship, prosecution, or banning by Church or State or both.

The Freudian and the Marxist aesthetics feature ethically relevant components. Freudian interpreters of art expression see art works as the result of a titanic struggle between the artist's asocial, uncultured, rapacious libidinous ego and the lawful, ethical, cultivated and sophisticated super-ego. Nietzsche anticipated the Freudian analysis in the nineteenth century. Marxists art critics find that artworks always represent the values of the dominant and exploitative class in a society. Thus they see contemporary artists who seek an unprecedented individualistic style (a style which not only invents a new work but an entirely new genre of work) to be the result of a bourgeois capitalistic celebration of the individual rights, justifying the liberty of corporations to exploit the laboring classes. Suffice it to say that any artist who seeks the public' recognition of her work will find the work judged not only on its aesthetic values but also for its negative or positive effect on the public sensibilities. The battle between the censors and the freedom of expression advocates goes on and on.

This brings us to one final consideration that many would have considered to be the most prominent concern of aestheticians. What makes a work of art a good work of art? There's no deficit of art critics out there trying to guide our weekend plans at the gallery, theater or recital hall. Aestheticians have conflicted over the very possibility of a single universal aesthetic standard for judging the myriad works and genres of art over the millennia as either good or bad art. Pluralists who reject a single all-encompassing standard contend that the criterion a great dance performance is distinct from the criterion for great literature, and so on. Aestheticians have tried to distinguish between subjective tastes (relative to a group or an individual) and aesthetic appreciation of the aesthetic qualities of the phenomenal objective. Sometimes called the subjective universal, these qualities rely as much upon the subjective projections of the audience or reader as the objective structure of the artwork to achieve the experience; and yet allegedly there is some quality of the object that evokes a universal human response to those sufficiently prepared to receive it. The assumption of all art critics is that their own evaluation of an artwork is generalizable to the aesthetically sophisticated audience.

One contemporary aesthetician is bold enough to offer a criterion for great art that transcends time, culture and the varying genres of art. Monroe Beardsley's provocative notion of compendiousness as a criterion of art bears noting (*The Aesthetic Point of View*). When a work of art is compendious it exhibits three sub-criteria: unity, complexity, and intensity. Works of art are good when they convey a depth of meaning, diversity or intensity with an economy of means or when a diversity of elements pull together in an overall unity of form. When a Chinese artist renders an old man trudging through the snow with a single stroke of a brush, the fullness of meaning with the economy of means is impressive. Minimalism is an example of this but Warhol's silk screens of the *Campbells Soup Can* might also qualify because he conveys the vast banality of commercial culture with a sparse use of materials. Needless to say that even the correct application of the Beardsleyan criterion to the myriads of art works will be contentious for aestheticians for the indefinite future.

REPUBLIC

PLATO (424-348 BCE)

Ever since the Cave drawings, until fairly recently in human history, many artists have attempted to imitate or copy nature as "realistically" as possible. At least much of the viewing public assumed that's what they were about. Since Plato believed that the reality (Beauty Itself) that the poets and artists were trying to imitate could not be perceived through the senses and only could be grasped through reason alone, he severely criticized and censored the arts. They were bound to distort, corrupt and falsify the truth. The misrepresentations of the comic playwright Aristophanes, whose play The Clouds depicted Plato's beloved teacher Socrates as an atheist, a charlatan and a moral reprobate, was case one for Plato's call for art censorship by the magistrates of the state.

BOOK X

[Socrates]: Of the many excellences which I perceive in the order of our State, there is none which upon reflection pleases me better than the rule about poetry.

[Glaucon]: To what do you refer?

To the rejection of imitative poetry, which certainly ought not to be received; as I see far more clearly now that the parts of the soul have been distinguished.

What do you mean?

Speaking in confidence, for I should not like to have my words repeated to the tragedians and the rest of the imitative tribe—but I do not mind saying to you, that all poetical imitations are ruinous to the understanding of the hearers, and that the knowledge of their true nature is the only antidote to them.

Explain the purport of your remark.

Well, I will tell you, although I have always from my earliest youth had an awe and love of Homer, which even now makes the words falter on my lips, for he is the great captain and teacher of the whole of that charming tragic company; but a man is not to be reverenced more than the truth, and therefore I will speak out.

Very good, he said.

Listen to me then, or rather, answer me.

Put your question.

Can you tell me what imitation is? for I really do not know.

A likely thing, then, that I should know.

Why not? for the duller eye may often see a thing sooner than the keener.

Very true, he said; but in your presence, even if I had any faint notion, I could not muster courage to utter it. Will you enquire yourself?

Well then, shall we begin the enquiry in our usual manner: Whenever a number of individuals have a common name, we assume them to have also a corresponding idea or form. Do you understand me?

I do.

Let us take any common instance; there are beds and tables in the world—plenty of them, are there not?

Yes.

But there are only two ideas or forms of them—one the idea of a bed, the other of a table.

True.

And the maker of either of them makes a bed or he makes a table for our use, in accordance with the idea—that is our way of speaking in this and similar instances—but no artificer makes the ideas themselves: how could he?

Impossible.

And there is another artist—I should like to know what you would say of him.

Who is he?

One who is the maker of all the works of all other workmen.

What an extraordinary man!

Wait a little, and there will be more reason for your saying so. For this is he who is able to make not only vessels of every kind, but plants and animals, himself and all other things --the earth and heaven, and the things which are in heaven or under the earth; he makes the gods also.

He must be a wizard and no mistake.

Oh! you are incredulous, are you? Do you mean that there is no such maker or creator, or that in one sense there might be a maker of all these things but in another not? Do you see that there is a way in which you could make them all yourself?

What way?

An easy way enough; or rather, there are many ways in which the feat might be quickly and easily accomplished, none quicker than that of turning a mirror round and round—you would soon enough make the sun and the heavens, and the earth and yourself, and other animals and plants, and all the, other things of which we were just now speaking, in the mirror.

Yes, he said; but they would be appearances only.

Very good, I said, you are coming to the point now. And the painter too is, as I conceive, just such another—a creator of appearances, is he not?

Of course.

But then I suppose you will say that what he creates is untrue. And yet there is a sense in which the painter also creates a bed?

Yes, he said, but not a real bed.

And what of the maker of the bed? Were you not saying that he too makes, not the idea which, according to our view, is the essence of the bed, but only a particular bed?

Yes, I did.

Then if he does not make that which exists he cannot make true existence, but only some semblance of existence; and if any one were to say that the work of the maker of the bed, or of any other workman, has real existence, he could hardly be supposed to be speaking the truth.

At any rate, he replied, philosophers would say that he was not speaking the truth.

No wonder, then, that his work too is an indis-

tinct expression of truth.

No wonder.

Suppose now that by the light of the examples just offered we enquire who this imitator is?

If you please.

Well then, here are three beds: one existing in nature, which is made by God, as I think that we may say—for no one else can be the maker?

No.

There is another which is the work of the carpenter?

Yes.

And the work of the painter is a third?

Yes.

Beds, then, are of three kinds, and there are three artists who superintend them: God, the maker of the bed, and the painter?

Yes, there are three of them.

God, whether from choice or from necessity, made one bed in nature and one only; two or more such ideal beds neither ever have been nor ever will be made by God.

Why is that?

Because even if He had made but two, a third would still appear behind them which both of them would have for their idea, and that would be the ideal bed and the two others.

Very true, he said.

God knew this, and He desired to be the real maker of a real bed, not a particular maker of a particular bed, and therefore He created a bed which is essentially and by nature one only.

So we believe.

Shall we, then, speak of Him as the natural author or maker of the bed?

Yes, he replied; inasmuch as by the natural process of creation He is the author of this and of all other things.

And what shall we say of the carpenter—is not he also the maker of the bed?

Yes.

But would you call the painter a creator and maker?

Certainly not.

Yet if he is not the maker, what is he in relation to the bed?

I think, he said, that we may fairly designate him as the imitator of that which the others make.

Good, I said; then you call him who is third in the descent from nature an imitator?

Certainly, he said.

And the tragic poet is an imitator, and therefore, like all other imitators, he is thrice removed from the king and from the truth?

That appears to be so.

Then about the imitator we are agreed. And what about the painter?—I would like to know whether he may be thought to imitate that which originally exists in nature, or only the creations of artists?

The latter.

As they are or as they appear? You have still to determine this.

What do you mean?

I mean, that you may look at a bed from different points of view, obliquely or directly or from any other point of view, and the bed will appear different, but there is no difference in reality. And the same of all things.

Yes, he said, the difference is only apparent.

Now let me ask you another question: Which is the art of painting designed to be—an imitation of things as they are, or as they appear—of appearance or of reality?

Of appearance.

Then the imitator, I said, is a long way off the truth, and can do all things because he lightly touches on a small part of them, and that part an image. For example: A painter will paint a cobbler, carpenter, or any other artist, though he knows nothing of their arts; and, if he is a good artist, he may deceive children or simple persons, when he shows them his picture of a carpenter from a distance, and they will fancy that they are looking at a real carpenter.

Certainly.

And whenever any one informs us that he has found a man knows all the arts, and all things else that anybody knows, and every single thing with a higher degree of accuracy than any other man—whoever tells us this, I think that we can only imagine to be a simple creature who is likely to have been deceived by some wizard or actor whom he met, and whom he thought all-knowing, because he himself was unable to analyse the nature of knowledge and ignorance and imitation.

Most true.

And so, when we hear persons saying that the tragedians, and Homer, who is at their head, know all the arts and all things human, virtue as well as vice, and divine things too, for that the good poet cannot compose well unless he knows his subject, and that he who has not this knowledge can never be a poet, we ought to consider whether here also there may not be a similar illusion. Perhaps they may have come across imitators and been deceived by them; they may not have remembered when they saw their works that these were but imitations thrice removed from the truth, and could easily be made without any knowledge of the truth, because they are appearances only and not realities? Or, after all, they may be in the right, and poets do really know the things about which they seem to the many to speak so well?

The question, he said, should by all means be considered.

Now do you suppose that if a person were able to make the original as well as the image, he would seriously devote himself to the image-making branch? Would he allow imitation to be the ruling principle of his life, as if he had nothing higher in him?

I should say not.

The real artist, who knew what he was imitating, would be interested in realities and not in imitations; and would desire to leave as memorials of himself works many and fair; and, instead of being the author of encomiums, he would prefer to be the theme of them.

Yes, he said, that would be to him a source of much greater honour and profit.

Then, I said, we must put a question to Homer; not about medicine, or any of the arts to which his poems only incidentally refer: we are not going to ask him, or any other poet, whether he has cured patients like Asclepius, or left behind him a school of medicine such as the Asclepiads were, or whether he only talks about medicine and other arts at second hand; but we have a right to know respecting military tactics, politics, education, which are the chiefest and noblest subjects of his poems, and we may fairly ask him about them. 'Friend Homer,' then we say to him, 'if you are only in the second remove from truth in what you say of virtue, and not in the third—not an image maker or imitator—and if you are able to discern what pursuits make men better or worse in private or public life, tell us what State was ever better governed by your help? The good order of Lacedaemon is due to Lycurgus, and many other cities great and small have been similarly benefited by others; but who says that you have been a good legislator to them and have done them any good? Italy and Sicily boast of Charondas, and there is Solon who is renowned among us; but what city has anything to say about you?' Is there any city which he might name?

I think not, said Glaucon; not even the Homerids themselves pretend that he was a legislator.

Well, but is there any war on record which was carried on successfully by him, or aided by his counsels, when he was alive?

There is not.

Or is there any invention of his, applicable to the arts or to human life, such as Thales the Milesian or Anacharsis the Scythian, and other ingenious men have conceived, which is attributed to him?

There is absolutely nothing of the kind....

Plato. "Republic." *The Dialogues of Plato*. Vol. 3. Trans. by Benjamin Jowett. Oxford: Oxford University Press, 1892.

OF THE STANDARDS OF TASTE

DAVID HUME (1711-1776)

The great 18th century Empiricist and Skeptic David Hume tackles the issue of aesthetic taste. Artistic appreciation is not, for Hume, a matter of rational judgment but rather a sentiment of delight produced in the art spectator. Now "taste" may be construed as subjective and individualistic. My taste for lima beans cannot be foisted upon you. I cannot say that you ought *to enjoy lima beans. However, I might be presumptuous to say that you ought to like Handel's music. In support for this presumption, Hume invokes the existence of Classic Works---works that have withstood the test of time. Consequently he proffers a notion of a subjective universal as a sentiment shared by those with the sufficient "delicacy" to experience it.*

1. The great variety of Taste, as well as of opinion, which prevails in the world, is too obvious not to have fallen under every one's observation. Men of the most confined knowledge are able to remark a difference of taste in the narrow circle of their acquaintance, even where the persons have been educated under the same government, and have early imbibed the same prejudices. But those, who can enlarge their view to contemplate distant nations and remote ages, are still more surprised at the great inconsistence and contrariety. We are apt to call barbarous whatever departs widely from our own taste and apprehension: But soon find the epithet of reproach retorted on us. And the highest arrogance and self-conceit is at last startled, on observing an equal assurance on all sides, and scruples, amidst such a contest of sentiment, to pronounce positively in its own favour.

2. As this variety of taste is obvious to the most careless enquirer; so will it be found, on examination, to be still greater in reality than in appearance. The sentiments of men often differ with regard to beauty and deformity of all kinds, even while their general discourse is the same. There are certain terms in every language, which import blame, and others praise; and all men, who use the same tongue, must agree in their application of them. Every voice is united in applauding elegance, propriety, simplicity, spirit in writing; and in blaming fustian, affectation, coldness and a false brilliancy: But when critics come to particulars, this seeming unanimity vanishes; and it is found, that they had affixed a very different meaning to their expressions. In all matters of opinion and science, the case it opposite: The difference among men is there oftener found to lie in generals than in particulars; and to be less in reality than in appearance. An explanation of the terms commonly ends the controversy; and the disputants are surprised to find, that they had been quarreling, while at bottom they agreed in their judgment.

3. Those who found morality on sentiment, more than on reason, are inclined to comprehend ethics under the former observation, and to maintain, that, in all questions, which regard conduct and manners, the difference among men is really greater than at first sight it appears. It is indeed obvious, that writers of all nations and all ages concur in applauding justice, humanity, magnanimity, prudence, veracity; and in blaming the opposite qualities. Even poets and other authors, whose compositions are chiefly calculated to please the imagination, are yet found, from HOMER down to FENELON, to inculcate the same moral precepts, and to bestow their applause and blame on the same virtues and vices. This great

unanimity is usually ascribed to the influence of plain reason; which, in all these cases, maintains similar sentiments in all men, and prevents those controversies, to which the abstract sciences are so much exposed. So far as the unanimity is real, this account may be admitted as satisfactory: But we must also allow that some part of the seeming harmony in morals may be accounted for from the very nature of language. The word *virtue*, with its equivalent in every tongue, implies praise; as that of *vice* does blame: And no one, without the most obvious and grossest impropriety, could affix reproach to a term, which in general acceptation is understood in a good sense; or bestow applause, where the idiom requires disapprobation. HOMER's general precepts, where he delivers any such will never be controverted; but it is obvious, that, when he draws particular pictures of manners, and represents heroism in ACHILLES and prudence in ULYSSES, he intermixes a much greater degree of ferocity in the former, and of cunning and fraud in the latter, than FENELON would admit of . The sage ULYSSES in the GREEK poet seems to delight in lies and fictions; and often employs them without any necessity or even advantage: But his more scrupulous son, in the FRENCH epic writer, exposes himself to the most imminent perils, rather than depart from the most exact line of truth and veracity.

4. The admirers and follows of the ALCORAN insist on the excellent moral precepts interspersed throughout that wild and absurd performance. But it is to be supposed, that the ARABIC words, which correspond to the ENGLISH, equity, justice, temperance, meekness, charity, were such as, from the constant use of that tongue, must always be taken in a good sense; and it would have argued the greatest ignorance, not of morals, but of language, to have mentioned them with any epithets, besides those of applause and approbation. But would we know, whether the pretended prophet had really attained a just sentiment of morals? Let us attend to his narration; and we shall soon find, that he bestows praise on such instances of treachery, inhumanity, cruelty, revenge, bigotry, as are utterly incompatible with civilized society. No steady rule of right seems there to be attended to; and every action is blamed or praised, so far only as it is beneficial or hurtful to the true believers.

5. The merit of delivering true general precepts in ethics is indeed very small. Whoever recommends any moral virtues, really does no more than is implied in the terms themselves. That people, who invented the word *charity*, and use it in a good sense, inculcated more clearly and much more efficaciously, the precept, *be charitable*, than any pretended legislator or prophet, who should insert such a *maxim* in his writings. Of all expressions, those, which, together with their other meaning, imply a degree either of blame or approbation, are the least liable to be perverted or mistaken.

6. It is natural for us to seek a Standard of Taste; a rule, by which the various sentiments of men may be reconciled; at least, a decision, afforded, confirming one sentiment, and condemning another.

7. There is a species of philosophy, which cuts off all hopes of success in such an attempt, and represents the impossibility of ever attaining any standard of taste. The difference, it is said, is very wide between judgment and sentiment. All sentiment is right; because sentiment has a reference to nothing beyond itself, and is always real, wherever a man is conscious of it. But all determinations of the understanding are not right; because they have a reference to something beyond themselves, to wit, real matter of fact; and are not always conformable to that standard. Among a thousand different opinions which different men may entertain of the same subject, there is one, and but one, that is just and true; and the only difficulty is to fix and ascertain it. On the contrary, a thousand different sentiments, excited by the same object, are all right: Because no sentiment represents what is really in the object. It only marks a certain conformity or relation between the object and the organs or faculties of the mind; and if that conformity did not really exist, the sentiment could never possibly have being. Beauty is no quality in things themselves: It exists merely in the mind which contemplates them; and each mind perceives a different beauty. One person may even perceive deformity, where another is sensible of beauty; and every individual ought to acquiesce in his own sentiment, without pretending to regulate those of others. To seek in the real beauty, or real deformity, is as fruitless an enquiry, as to pretend to

ascertain the real sweet or real bitter. According to the disposition of the organs, the same object may be both sweet and bitter; and the proverb has justly determined it to be fruitless to dispute concerning tastes. It is very natural, and even quite necessary to extend this axiom to mental, as well as bodily taste; and thus common sense, which is so often at variance with philosophy, especially with the skeptical kind, is found, in one instance at least, to agree in pronouncing the same decision.

8 But though this axiom, by passing into a proverb, seems to have attained the sanction of common sense; there is certainly a species of common sense which opposes it, at least serves to modify and restrain it. Whoever would assert an equality of genius and elegance between OGILBY and MILTON, or BUNYAN and ADDISON, would be thought to defend no less an extravagance, than if he had maintained a mole-hill to be as high as TENERIFFE, or a pond as extensive as the ocean. Though there may be found persons, who give the preference to the former authors; no one pays attention to such a taste; and we pronounce without scruple the sentiment of these pretended critics to be absurd and ridiculous. The principle of the natural equality of tastes is then totally forgot, and while we admit it on some occasions, where the objects seem near an equality, it appears an extravagant paradox, or rather a palpable absurdity, where objects so disproportioned are compared together.

9. It is evident that none of the rules of composition are fixed by reasonings *a priori*, or can be esteemed abstract conclusions of the understanding, from comparing those habitudes and relations of ideas, which are eternal and immutable. Their foundation is the same with that of all the practical sciences, experience; nor are they any thing but general observations, concerning what has been universally found to please in all countries and in all ages. Many of the beauties of poetry and even of eloquence are founded on falsehood and fiction, on hyperboles, metaphors, and an abuse or perversion of terms from their natural meaning. To check the sallies of the imagination, and to reduce every expression to geometrical truth and exactness, would be the most contrary to the laws of criticism; because it would produce a work, which, by universal experience, has been found the most insipid and disagreeable. But though poetry can never submit to exact truth, it must be confined by rules of art, discovered to the author either by genius or observation. If some negligent or irregular writers have pleased, they have not pleased by their transgressions of rule or order, but in spite of these transgressions: They have possessed other beauties, which were conformable to just criticism; and the force of these beauties has been able to overpower censure, and give the mind a satisfaction superior to the disgust arising from the blemishes. ARIOSTO pleases; but not by his monstrous and improbable fictions, by his bizarre mixture of the serious and comic styles, by the want of coherence in his stories, or by the continual interruptions of his narration. He charms by the force and clearness of his expression, by the readiness and variety of his inventions, and by his natural pictures of the passions, especially those of the gay and amorous kind: And however his faults may diminish our satisfaction, they are not able entirely to destroy it. Did our pleasure really arise from those parts of his poem, which we denominate faults, this would be no objection to criticism in general: It would only be an objection to those particular rules of criticism, which would establish such circumstances to be faults, and would represent them as universally blameable. If they are found to please, they cannot be faults; let the pleasure, which they produce, be ever so unexpected and unaccountable.

10. But though all the general rules of art are founded only on experience and on the observation of the common sentiments of human nature, we must not imagine, that, on every occasion the feelings of men will be conformable to these rules. Those finer emotions of the mind are of a very tender and delicate nature, and require the concurrence of many favourable circumstances to make them play with facility and exactness, according to their general and established principles. The least exterior hindrance to such small springs, or the least internal disorder, disturbs their motion, and confounds the operation of the whole machine. When we would make an experiment of this nature, and would try the force of any beauty or deformity, we must choose with care a proper time and place, and bring the fancy to a suitable situation and disposition. A perfect serenity of

mind, a recollection of thought, a due attention to the object; if any of these circumstances be wanting, our experiment will be fallacious, and we shall be unable to judge of the catholic and universal beauty. The relation, which nature has placed between the form and the sentiment will at least be more obscure; and it will require greater accuracy to trace and discern it. We shall be able to ascertain its influence not so much from the operation of each particular beauty, as from the durable admiration, which attends those works, that have survived all the caprices of mode and fashion, all the mistakes of ignorance and envy.

11. The same HOMER, who pleased at ATHENS and ROME two thousand years ago, is still admired at PARIS and at LONDON. All the changes of climate, government, religion, and language, have not been able to obscure his glory. Authority or prejudice may give a temporary vogue to a bad poet or orator, but his reputation will never be durable or general. When his compositions are examined by posterity or by foreigners, the enchantment is dissipated, and his faults appear in their true colours. On the contrary, a real genius, the longer his works endure, and the more wide they are spread, the more sincere is the admiration which he meets with. Envy and jealousy have too much place in a narrow circle; and even familiar acquaintance with his person may diminish the applause due to his performances. But when these obstructions are removed, the beauties, which are naturally fitted to excite agreeable sentiments, immediately display their energy and while the world endures, they maintain their authority over the minds of men.

12. It appears then, that, amidst all the variety and caprice of taste, there are certain general principles of approbation or blame, whose influence a careful eye may trace in all operations of the mind. Some particular forms or qualities, from the original structure of the internal fabric, are calculated to please, and others to displease; and if they fail of their effect in any particular instance, it is from some apparent defect or imperfection in the organ. A man in a fever would not insist on his palate as able to decide concerning flavours; nor would one, affected with the jaundice, pretend to give a verdict with regard to colours. In each creature, there is a sound and a defective state; and the former alone can be supposed to afford us a true standard of a taste and sentiment. If, in the sound state of theorgan, there be an entire or considerable uniformity of sentiment among men, we may thence derive an idea of the perfect beauty; in like manner as the appearance of objects in daylight, to the eye of a man in health, is denominated their true and real colour, even while colour is allowed to be merely a phantasm of the senses.

13. Many and frequent are the defects in the internal organs, which prevent or weaken the influence of those general principles, on which depends our sentiment of beauty or deformity. Though some objects, by the structure of the mind, be naturally calculated to give pleasure, it is not to be expected, that in every individual the pleasure will be equally felt. Particular incidents and situations occur, which either throw a false light on the objects, or hinder the true from conveying to the imagination the proper sentiment and perception.

14. One obvious cause, why many feel not the proper sentiment of beauty, is the want of that *delicacy* of imagination, which is requisite to convey a sensibility of those finer emotions. This delicacy every one pretends to: Every one talks of it; and would reduce every kind of taste or sentiment to its standard. But as our intention in this essay is to mingle some light of the understanding with the feelings of sentiment, it will be proper to give a more accurate definition of delicacy, than has hitherto been attempted. And not to draw our philosophy from too profound a source, we shall have recourse to a noted story in DON QUIXOTE.

15. It is with good reason, says SANCHO to the squire with the great nose, that I pretend to have a judgment in wine: this is a quality hereditary in our family. Two of my kinsmen were once called to give their opinion of a hogshead, which was supposed to be excellent, being old and of a good vintage. One of them tastes it; considers it; and after mature reflection pronounces the wine to be good, were it not for a small taste of leather, which he perceived in it. The other, after using the same precautions, gives also his verdict in favour of the wine; but with the reserve of a taste of iron, which he could easily distinguish. You cannot imagine how much they were both ridiculed for their judgment. But who laughed

in the end? On emptying the hogshead, there was found at the bottom, an old key with a leathern thong tied to it.

16. The great resemblance between mental and bodily taste will easily teach us to apply this story. Though it be certain, that beauty and deformity, more than sweet and bitter, are not qualities in objects, but belong entirely to the sentiment, internal or external; it must be allowed, that there are certain qualities in objects, which are fitted by nature to produce those particular feelings. Now as these qualities may be found in a smaller degree, or may be mixed and confounded with each other, it often happens, that the taste is not affected with such minute qualities, or is not able to distinguish all the particular flavours, amidst the disorder, in which they are presented. Where the organs are so fine, as to allow nothing to escape them; and at the same time so exact as to perceive every ingredient in the composition: This we call delicacy of taste, whether we employ these terms in the literal or metaphorical sense. Here then the general rules of beauty are of use; being drawn from established models, and from the observation of what pleases or displeases, when presented singly and in a high degree: And if the same qualities, in a continued composition and in a small degree, affect not the organs with a sensible delight or uneasiness, we exclude the person from all pretensions to this delicacy. To produce these general rules or avowed patterns of composition is like finding the key with the leathern thong; which justified the verdict of SANCHO's kinsmen, and confounded those pretended judges who had condemned them. Though the hogshead had never been emptied, the taste of the one was still equally delicate, and that of the other equally dull and languid: But it would have been more difficult to have proved the superiority of the former, to the conviction of every by-stander. In like manner, though the beauties of writing had never been methodized, or reduced to general principles; though no excellent models had ever been acknowledged; the different degrees of taste would still have subsisted, and the judgment of one man had been preferable to that of another; but it would not have been so easy to silence the bad critic, who might always insist upon his particular sentiment, and refuse to submit to his antagonist. But when

we show him an avowed principle of art; when we illustrate this principle by examples, whose operation, from his own particular taste, he acknowledges to be conformable to the principle; when we prove, that the same principle may be applied to the present case, where he did not perceive or feel its influence: He must conclude, upon the whole, that the fault lies in himself, and that he wants the delicacy, which is requisite to make him sensible of every beauty and every blemish, in any composition or discourse.

17. It is acknowledged to be the perfection of every sense or faculty, to perceive with exactness its most minute objects, and allow nothing to escape its notice and observation. The smaller the objects are, which become sensible to the eye, the finer is that organ, and the more elaborate its make and composition. A good palate is not tried by strong flavours; but by a mixture of small ingredients, where we are still sensible of each part, notwithstanding its minuteness and its confusion with the rest. In like manner, a quick and acute perception of beauty and deformity must be the perfection of our mental taste; nor can a man be satisfied with himself while he suspects, that any excellence or blemish in a discourse has passed him unobserved. In this case, the perfection of the man, and the perfection of the sense or feeling, are found to be united. A very delicate palate, on many occasions, may be a great inconvenience both to a man himself and to his friends: But a delicate taste of wit or beauty must always be a desirable quality; because it is the source of all the finest and most innocent enjoyments, of which human nature is susceptible. In this decision the sentiments of all mankind are agreed. Wherever you can ascertain a delicacy of taste, it is sure to meet with approbation; and the best way of ascertaining it is to appeal to those models and principles, which have been established by the uniform consent and experience of nations and ages.

18. But though there be naturally a wide difference in point of delicacy between one person and another, nothing tends further to encrease and improve this talent, than practice in a particular art, and the frequent survey or contemplation of a particular species of beauty. When objects of any kind are first presented to the eye or imagination, the sentiment, which attends them, is obscure and confused; and

the mind is, in a great measure, incapable of pronouncing concerning their merits or defects. The taste cannot perceive the several excellences of the performance; much less distinguish the particular character of each excellency, and ascertain its quality and degree. If it pronounce the whole in general to be beautiful or deformed, it is the utmost that can be expected; and even this judgment, a person, so unpracticed, will be apt to deliver with great hesitation and reserve. But allow him to acquire experience in those objects, his feeling becomes more exact and nice: He not only perceives the beauties and defects of each part, but marks the distinguishing species of each quality, and assigns it suitable praise or blame. A clear and distinct sentiment attends him through the whole survey of the objects; and he discerns that very degree and kind of approbation or displeasure, which each part is naturally fitted to produce. The mist dissipates, which seemed formerly to hang over the object: the organ acquires greater perfection in its operations; and can pronounce, without danger of mistake, concerning the merits of every performance. In a word, the same address and dexterity, which practice gives to the execution of any work, is also acquired by the same means in the judging of it.

19. So advantageous is practice to the discernment of beauty, that, before we can give judgment of any work of importance, it will even be requisite, that that very individual performance be more than once perused by us, and be surveyed in different lights with attention and deliberation. There is a flutter or hurry of thought which attends the first perusal of any piece, and which confounds the genuine sentiment of beauty. The relation of the parts is not discerned: The true characters of style are little distinguished: The several perfections and defects seem wrapped up in a species of confusion, and present themselves indistinctly to the imagination. Not to mention, that there is a species of beauty, which, as it is florid and superficial, pleases at first; but being found incompatible with a just expression either of reason or passion, soon palls upon the taste, and is then rejected with disdain, at least rated at a much lower value.

20. It is impossible to continue in the practice of contemplating any order of beauty, without be-

ing frequently obliged to form *comparisons* between the several species and degrees of excellence, and estimating their proportion to each other. A man, who has had no opportunity of comparing the different kinds of beauty, is indeed totally unqualified to pronounce an opinion with regard to any object presented to him. By comparison alone we fix the epithets of praise or blame, and learn how to assign the due degree of each. The coarsest daubing contains a certain lustre of colours and exactness of imitation, which are so far beauties, and would affect the mind of a peasant or Indian with the highest admiration. The most vulgar ballads are not entirely destitute of harmony or nature; and none but a person, familiarized to superior beauties, would pronounce their numbers harsh, or narration uninteresting. A great inferiority of beauty gives pain to a person conversant in the highest excellence of the kind, and is for that reason pronounced a deformity: As the most finished object, with which we are acquainted, is naturally supposed to have reached the pinnacle of perfection, and to be entitled to the highest applause. One accustomed to see, and examine, and weigh the several performances, admired in different ages and nations, can only rate the merits of a work exhibited to his view, and assign its proper rank among the productions of genius.

21. But to enable a critic the more fully to execute this undertaking, he must preserve his mind free from all prejudice, and allow nothing to enter into his consideration, but the very object which is submitted to his examination. We may observe, that every work of art, in order to produce its due effect on the mind, must be surveyed in a certain point of view, and not be fully relished by persons, whose situation, real or imaginary, is not conformable to that which is required by the performance. An orator addresses himself to a particular audience, and must have a regard to their particular genius, interests, opinions, passions, and prejudices; otherwise he hopes in vain to govern their resolutions, and inflame their affections. Should they even have entertained some prepossessions against him, however unreasonable, he must not overlook this disadvantage; but, before he enters upon the subject, must endeavour to conciliate their affection, and acquire their good graces. A critic of a different age or no-

tion, who should peruse this discourse, must have all these circumstances in his eye, and must place himself in the same situation as the audience, in order to form a true judgment of the oration. In like manner, when any work is addressed to the public, though I should have a friendship or enmity with the author, I must depart from this situation; and considering myself as a man in general, forget, if possible, my individual being and my peculiar circumstances. A person influenced by prejudice, complies not with this condition; but obstinately maintains his natural position, without placing himself in that point of view, which the performance supposes. If the work be addressed to persons of a different age or nation, he makes no allowance for their peculiar views and prejudices; but, full of the manners of his own age and country, rashly condemns what seemed admirable in the eyes of those for whom alone the discourse was calculated. If the work be executed for the public, he never sufficiently enlarges his comprehension, or forgets his interest as a friend or enemy, as a rival or commentator. By this means, his sentiments are perverted; nor have the same beauties and blemishes the same influence upon him, as if he had imposed a proper violence on his imagination, and had forgotten himself for a moment. So far his taste evidently departs from the true standard; and of consequence loses all credit and authority.

22. It is well known, that in all questions, submitted to the understanding, prejudice is destructive of sound judgment, and perverts all operations of the intellectual faculties: It is no less contrary to good taste; nor has it less influence to corrupt our sentiment of beauty. It belongs to *good sense* to check its influence in both cases; and in this respect, as well as in many others, reason, if not an essential part of taste, is at least requisite to the operations of this latter faculty. In all the nobler productions of genius, there is a mutual relation and correspondence of parts; nor can either the beauties or blemishes be perceived by him, whose thought is not capacious enough to comprehend all those parts, and compare then with each other, in order to perceive the consistence and uniformity of the whole. Every work of art has also a certain end or purpose, for which it is calculated; and is to be deemed more or less perfect, as it is more or less fitted to attain this end. The object

of eloquence is to persuade, of history to instruct, of poetry to please by means of the passions and the imagination. These ends we must carry constantly in our view, when we peruse any performance; and we must be able to judge how far the means employed are adapted to their respective purposes. Besides, every kind of composition, even the most poetical, is nothing but a chain of propositions and reasonings; not always, indeed, the justest and most exact, but still plausible and specious, however disguised by the colouring of the imagination. The persons introduced in tragedy and epic poetry, must be represented as reasoning, and thinking, and concluding, and acting, suitably to their character and circumstances; and without judgment, as well as taste and invention, a poet can never hope to succeed in so delicate an undertaking. Not to mention, that the same excellence of faculties which contributes to the improvement of reason, the same clearness of conception, the same exactness of distinction, the same vivacity of apprehension, are essential to the operations of true taste, and are its infallible concomitants. It seldom, or never happens, that a man of sense, who has experience in any art, cannot judge of its beauty; and it is no less rare to meet with a man who has a just taste without a sound understanding.

23. Thus, though the principles of taste be universal, and, nearly, if not entirely the same in all men; yet few are qualified to give judgment on any work of art, or establish their own sentiment as the standard of beauty. The organs of internal sensation are seldom so perfect as to allow the general principles their full play, and produce a feeling correspondent to those principles. They either labour under some defect, or are vitiated by some disorder; and by that means, excite a sentiment, which may be pronounced erroneous. When the critic has no delicacy, he judges without any distinction, and is only affected by the grosser and more palpable qualities of the object: The finer touches pass unnoticed and disregarded. Where he is not aided by practice, his verdict is attended with confusion and hesitation. Where no comparison has been employed, the most frivolous beauties, such as rather merit the name of defects., are the object of his admiration. Where he lies under the influence of prejudice, all his natural sentiments are perverted. Where good sense is

wanting, he is not qualified to discern the beauties of design and reasoning, which are the highest and most excellent. Under some or other of these imperfections, the generality of men labour; and hence a true judge in the finer arts is observed, even during the most polished ages, to be so rare a character; Strong sense, united to delicate sentiment, improved by practice, perfected by comparison, and cleared of all prejudice, can alone entitle critics to this valuable character; and the joint verdict of such, wherever they are to be found, is the true standard of taste and beauty.

24. But where are such critics to be found? By what marks are they to be known? How distinguish them from pretenders? These questions are embarrassing; and seem to throw us back into the same uncertainty, from which, during the course of this essay, we have endeavoured to extricate ourselves.

25. But if we consider the matter aright, these are questions of fact, not of sentiment. Whether any particular person be endowed with good sense and a delicate imagination, free from prejudice, may often be the subject of dispute, and be liable to great discussion and enquiry: but that such a character is valuable and estimable will be agreed in by all mankind. Where these doubts occur, men can do no more than in other disputable questions, which are submitted to the understanding: They must produce the best arguments, that their invention suggests to them; they must acknowledge a true and decisive standard to exist somewhere, to wit, real existence and matter of fact; and they must have indulgence to such as differ from them in their appeals to this standard. It is sufficient for our present purpose, if we have proved, that the taste of all individuals is not upon an equal footing, and that some men in general, however difficult to be particularly pitched upon, will be acknowledged by universal sentiment to have a preference above others.

26. But in reality the difficulty of finding, even in particulars, the standard of taste, is not so great as it is represented. Though in speculation, we may readily avow a certain criterion in science and deny it in sentiment, the matter is found in practice to be much more hard to ascertain in the former case than in the latter. Theories of abstract philosophy, systems of profound theology, have prevailed during one age: In a successive period, these have been universally exploded: Their absurdity has been detected: Other theories and systems have supplied their place, which again gave place to their successors: And nothing has been experienced more liable to the revolutions of chance and fashion than these pretended decisions of science. The case is not the same with the beauties of eloquence and poetry. Just expressions of passion and nature are sure, after a little time, to gain public applause, which they maintain for ever. ARISTOTLE, and PLATO, and EPICURUS, and DESCARTES, may successively yield to each other: But TERENCE and VIRGIL maintain an universal, undisputed empire over the minds of men. The abstract philosophy of CICERO has lost its credit: The vehemence of his oratory is still the object of our admiration.

27. Though men of delicate taste be rare, they are easily to be distinguished in society, by the soundness of their understanding and the superiority of their faculties above the rest of mankind. The ascendant, which they acquire, gives a prevalence to that lively approbation, with which they receive any productions of genius, and renders it generally predominant. Many men, when left to themselves, have but a faint and dubious perception of beauty, who yet are capable of relishing any fine stroke, which is pointed out to them. Every convert to the admiration of the real poet or orator is the cause of some new conversion. And though prejudices may prevail for a time, they never unite in celebrating any rival to the true genius, but yield at last to the force of nature and just sentiment. Thus, though a civilized nation may easily be mistaken in the choice of their admired philosopher, they never have been found long to err, in their affection for a favorite epic or tragic author.

28. But notwithstanding all our endeavours to fix a standard of taste, and reconcile the discordant apprehensions of men, there still remain two sources of variation, which are not sufficient indeed to confound all the boundaries of beauty and deformity, but will often serve to produce a difference in the degrees of our approbation or blame. The one is the different humours of particular men; the other, the particular manners and opinions of our age and country. The general principles of taste are uniform in human

nature: where men vary in their judgments, some defect or perversion in the faculties may commonly be remarked; proceeding either from prejudice, from want of practice, or want of delicacy; and there is just reason for approving one taste, and condemning another. But where there is such a diversity in the internal frame or external situation as is entirely blameless on both sides, and leaves no room to give one the preference above the other; in that case a certain degree of diversity in judgment is unavoidable, and we seek in vain for a standard, by which we can reconcile the contrary sentiments.

29. A young man, whose passions are warm, will be more sensibly touched with amorous and tender images, than a man more advanced in years, who take pleasure in wise, philosophical reflections concerning the conduct of life and moderation of the passions. At twenty, OVID may be the favourite author; HORACE at forty; and perhaps TACITUS at fifty. Vainly would we, in such cases, endeavour to enter into the sentiments of others, and divest ourselves of those propensities, which are natural to us. We choose our favourite author as we do our friend, from a conformity of humour and disposition. Mirth or passion, sentiment or reflection; whichever of these most predominates in our temper, it gives us a peculiar sympathy with the writer who resembles us.

30. One person is more pleased with the sublime; another with the tender; a third with raillery. One has a strong sensibility to blemishes, and is extremely studious of correctness: Another has a more lively feeling of beauties, and pardons twenty absurdities and defects for one elevated or pathetic stroke. The ear of this man is entirely turned towards conciseness and energy; that man is delighted with a copious, rich, and harmonious expression. Simplicity is affected by one; ornament by another. Comedy, tragedy, satire, odes, have each its partisans, who prefer that particular species of writing to all others. It is plainly an error in a critic, to confine his approbation to one species or style of writing, and condemn all the rest. But it is almost impossible not to feel a predilection for that which suits our particular turn and disposition. Such preferences are innocent and unavoidable, and can never reasonably be the object of dispute, because there is no standard, by which they can be decided.

31. For a like reason, we are more pleased, in the course of our reading, with pictures and characters, that resemble objects which are found in our own age or country, than with those which describe a different set of customs. It is not without some effort, that we reconcile ourselves to the simplicity of ancient manners, and behold princesses carrying water from the spring, and kings and heroes dressing their own victuals. We may allow in general, that the representation of such manners is no fault in the author, nor deformity in the piece; but we are not so sensibly touched with them. For this reason, comedy is not easily transferred from one age or nation to another. A FRENCHMAN or ENGLISHMAN is not pleased with the ANDRIA of TERENCE, or CLITIA of MACHIAVEL; where the fine lady, upon whom all the play turns, never once appears to the spectators, but is always kept behind the scenes, suitably to the reserved humour of the ancient GREEKS and modern ITALIANS. A man of learning and reflection can make allowance for these peculiarities of manners; but a common audience can never divest themselves so far of their usual ideas and sentiments, as to relish pictures which in no wise resemble them.

32. But here there occurs a reflection, which may, perhaps, be useful in examining the celebrated controversy concerning ancient and modern learning; where we often find the one side excusing any seeming absurdity in the ancients from the manners of the age, and the other refusing to admit this excuse, or at least, admitting it only as an apology for the author, not for the performance. In my opinion, the proper boundaries in this subject have seldom been fixed between the contending parties. Where any innocent peculiarities of manners are represented, such as those above mentioned, they ought certainly to be admitted; and a man, who is shocked with them, gives an evident proof of false delicacy and refinement. The poet's *monument more durable than brass*, must fall to the ground like common brick or clay, were men to make no allowance for the continual revolutions of manners and customs, and would admit of nothing but what was suitable to the prevailing fashion. Must we throw aside the pictures of our ancestors, because of their ruffs and fardingales? But where the ideas of morality and de-

cency alter from one age to another, and where vicious manners are described, without being marked with the proper characters of blame and disapprobation; this must be allowed to disfigure the poem, and to be a real deformity. I cannot, nor is it proper I should, enter into such sentiments; and however I may excuse the poet, on account of the manners in his age, I never can relish the composition. The want of humanity and of decency, so conspicuous in the characters drawn by several of the ancient poets, even sometimes by HOMER and the GREEK tragedians, diminishes considerably the merit of their noble performances, and gives modern authors an advantage over them. We are not interested in the fortunes and sentiments of such rough heroes: We are displeased to find the limits of vice and virtue so much confounded: And whatever indulgence we may give to the writer on account of his prejudices, we cannot prevail on ourself to enter into his sentiments, or bear an affection to characters, which we plainly discover to be blameable.

33. The case is not the same with moral principles, as with speculative opinions of any kind. These are in continual flux and revolution. The son embraces a different system from the father. Nay, there scarcely is any man, who can boast of great constancy and uniformity in this particular. Whatever speculative errors may be found in the polite writings of any age or country, they detract but little from the value of those compositions. There needs but a certain turn of thought or imagination to make us enter into all the opinions, which then prevailed, and relish the sentiments or conclusions derived from them. But a very violent effort is requisite to change our judgment of manners, and excite sentiments of approbation or blame, love or hatred, different from those to which the mind from long custom has been familiarized. And where a man is confident of the rectitude of that moral standard, by which he judges, he is justly jealous of it, and will not pervert the sentiments of his heart for a moment, in complaisance to any writer whatsoever.

34. Of all speculative errors, those, which regard religion, are the most excusable in compositions of genius; nor is it ever permitted to judge of the civility or wisdom of any people, or even of single persons, by the grossness or refinement of their theological principles. The same good sense, that directs men in the ordinary occurrences of life, is not harkened to in religious matters, which are supposed to be placed altogether above the cognizance of human reason. On this account, all the absurdities of the pagan system of theology must be overlooked by every critic, who would pretend to form a just notion of ancient poetry; and our posterity, in their turn, must have the same indulgence to their forefathers. No religious principles can ever be imputed as a fault to any poet, while they remain merely principles, and take not such strong possession of his heart, as to lay him under the imputation of bigotry or superstition. Where that happens, they confound the sentiments of morality, and alter the natural boundaries of vice and virtue. They are therefore eternal blemishes, according to the principle above mentioned; nor are the prejudices and false opinions of the age sufficient to justify them.

35. It is essential to the ROMAN catholic religion to inspire a violent hatred of every other worship, and to represent all pagans, mahometans, and heretics as the objects of divine wrath and vengeance. Such sentiments, though they are in reality very blameable, are considered as virtues by the zealots of that communion, and are represented in their tragedies and epic poems as a kind of divine heroism. This bigotry has disfigured two very fine tragedies of the FRENCH theatre, POLIEUCTE and ATHALIA; where an intemperate zeal for particular modes of worship is set off with all the pomp imaginable, and forms the predominant character of the heroes. 'What is this,' says the sublime JOAD to JOSABET, finding her in discourse with MATHAN, the priest of BAAL, 'Does the daughter of DAVID speak to this traitor? Are you not afraid, lest the earth should open and pour forth flames to devour you both? Or lest these holy walls should fall and crush you together? What is his purpose? Why comes that enemy of God hither to poison the air, which we breath, with his horrid presence?' Such sentiments are received with great applause on the theatre of PARIS; but at LONDON the spectators would be full as much pleased to hear ACHILLES tell AGAMEMNON, that he was a dog in his forehead, and a deer in his heart, or JUPITER threaten JUNO with a sound drubbing, if she will not be quiet.

36. RELIGIOUS principles are also a blemish in any polite composition, when they rise up to superstition, and intrude themselves into every sentiment, however remote from any connection with religion. It is no excuse for the poet, that the customs of his country had burthened life with so many religious ceremonies and observances, that no part of it was exempt from that yoke. It must for ever be ridiculous in PETRARCH to compare his mistress LAURA, to JESUS CHRIST. Nor is it less ridiculous in that agreeable libertine, BOCCACE, very seriously to give thanks to GOD ALMIGHTY and the ladies, for their assistance in defending him against his enemies.

David Hume. "Of the Standards of Taste." *The Harvard Classics*. Vol. 27. New York: P.F. Collier & Son, 1909–14.

THE BIRTH OF TRAGEDY

FRIEDRICH NIETZSCHE (1844-1900)

Friedrich Nietzsche reversed the roles of theology and art. Rather than art being an expression of theology, theology is an expression of artistic creativity. Since "God is Dead" for Nietzsche, the whole of Jewish and Christian theology expressed in the Old and New Testament *but also in* The Divine Comedy *by Dante Alighierri, had to have been the products of the fertile imaginations of the biblical authors and enhanced by the Florentine. Digging back further into the pagan artistry of Ancient Greece, Nietzsche uncovers two opposing divine inspirations of all subsequent artistic creators: the Apollonian and the Dionysian. Anticipating the psychology of Sigmund Freud, Nietzsche contrast the beautiful, rational, geometric, temperate and glorified aspect of psyche represented by the god Apollo, as opposed to the wild, frenetic, cruel, rapacious and passionate psyche represented by the god Dionysius. Though the Greeks depicted them as separate divinities, they form the energy of our own conflicted egos. Art is one with these unconscious natural forces—forces that hurl us towards death. Only the gods are immortal; but the creations of resolute artists are glorious in their tragic finality and vitality.*

1

We will have achieved much for scientific study of aesthetics when we come, not merely to a logical understanding, but also to the certain and immediate apprehension of the fact that the further development of art is bound up with the duality of the *Apollonian* and the *Dionysian*, just as reproduction similarly depends upon the duality of the sexes, their continuing strife and only periodically occurring reconciliation. We take these names from the Greeks, who gave a clear voice to the profound secret teachings of their contemplative art, not in ideas, but in the powerfully clear forms of their divine world. With those two gods of art, Apollo and Dionysus, we establish our recognition that in the Greek world there exists a huge contrast, in origin and purposes, between the visual arts, the Apollonian, and the non-visual art of music, the Dionysian.* These two very different drives go hand in hand, for the most part in open conflict with each other and simultaneously provoking each other all the time to new and more powerful offspring, in order to perpetuate in them the contest of that opposition, which the common word "Art" only seems to bridge, until at last, through a marvellous metaphysical act of the Greek "will," they appear paired up with each other and, as this pair, finally produce Attic tragedy, as much a Dionysian as an Apollonian work of art.

In order to bring those two drives closer to us, let us think of them first as the separate artistic worlds of *dream* and of *intoxication*, physiological phenomena between which we can observe an opposition corresponding to the one between the Apollonian and the Dionysian. According to the idea of Lucretius, the marvellous divine shapes first stepped out before the mind of man in a dream.* It was in a dream that the great artist saw the delightful anatomy of superhuman existence, and the Greek poet, questioned about the secrets of poetic creativity, would have also recalled his dreams and given an explanation similar to the one Hans Sachs provides in *Die Meistersinger*.

My friend, that is precisely the poet's work—

To figure out his dreams, mark them down.
Believe me, the truest illusion of mankind
Is revealed to him in dreams:
All poetic art and poeticizing
Is nothing but interpreting true dreams.

The beautiful appearance of the world of dreams, in whose creation each man is a complete artist, is the precondition of all plastic art, and also, in fact, as we shall see, an important part of poetry. We enjoy the form with an immediate understanding; every shape speaks to us; nothing is indifferent and unnecessary. For all the most intense life of this dream reality, we nevertheless have the shimmering sense of their *illusory quality*: That, at least, is my experience. For the frequency, indeed normality, of this response, I could point to many witnesses and the utterances of poets. Even the philosophical man has the presentiment that under this reality in which we live and have our being lies hidden a second, totally different reality and that thus the former is an illusion. And Schopenhauer specifically designates as the trademark of philosophical talent the ability to recognize at certain times that human beings and all things are mere phantoms or dream pictures. Now, just as the philosopher behaves in relation to the reality of existence, so the artistically excitable man behaves in relation to the reality of dreams: he looks at them precisely and with pleasure, for from these pictures he fashions his interpretation of life; from these events he rehearses his life for himself. This is not merely a case of the agreeable and friendly images which he experiences in himself with a complete understanding; they also include what is serious, cloudy, sad, dark, sudden scruples, teasing accidents, nervous expectations, in short, the entire "divine comedy" of life, including the Inferno—all this moves past him, not just like a shadow play—for he lives and suffers in the midst of these scenes—and yet also not without that fleeting sense of illusion. And perhaps several people remember, like me, amid the dangers and terrors of a dream, successfully cheering themselves up by shouting: "It is a dream! I want to dream it some more!" I have also heard accounts of some people who had the ability to set out the causality of one and the same dream over three or more consecutive nights. These facts

are clear evidence showing that our innermost beings, the secret underground in all of us, experiences its dreams with deep enjoyment and a sense of delightful necessity.

In the same manner the Greeks expressed this joyful necessity of the dream experience in their Apollo. Apollo, as the god of all the plastic arts, is at the same time the god of prophecy. In accordance with the root meaning of his association with "brightness," he is the god of light; he also rules over the beautiful appearance of the inner fantasy world. The higher truth, the perfection of this condition in contrast to the sketchy understanding of our daily reality, as well as the deep consciousness of a healing and helping nature in sleep and dreaming, is at the same time the symbolic analogy to the capacity to prophesy the truth, as well as to art in general, through which life is made possible and worth living. But also that delicate line which the dream image may not cross so that it does not work its effect pathologically— otherwise the illusion would deceive us as crude reality—that line must not be absent from the image of Apollo, that boundary of moderation, that freedom from more ecstatic excitement, that fully wise calm of the god of images. His eye must be "sun-like," in keeping with his origin; even when he is angry and gazes with displeasure, the consecration of the beautiful illusion rests on him. And so concerning Apollo one could endorse, in an eccentric way, what Schopenhauer says of the man trapped in the veil of Maja: "As on the stormy sea which extends without limit on all sides, howling mountainous waves rise up and sink and a sailor sits in a row boat, trusting the weak craft, so, in the midst of a world of torments, the solitary man sits peacefully, supported by and trusting in the *principium individuationis [principle of individuation]*" (*World as Will and Idea*, I.1.3). In fact, we could say of Apollo that the imperturbable trust in that principle and the calm sitting still of the man caught up in it attained its loftiest expression in him, and we may even designate Apollo himself as the marvellous divine image of the *principium individuationis*, from whose gestures and gaze all the joy and wisdom of "illusion," together with its beauty, speak to us.

In the same place Schopenhauer also described for us the tremendous *awe* which seizes a man when he suddenly doubts his ways of comprehending illusion, when the principle of reason, in any one of its forms, appears to suffer from an exception. If we add to this awe the ecstatic rapture, which rises up out of the same collapse of the *principium individuationis* from the innermost depths of a human being, indeed, from the innermost depths of nature, then we have a glimpse into the essence of the *Dionysian*, which is presented to us most closely through the analogy to *intoxication*. Either through the influence of narcotic drink, of which all primitive men and peoples speak in their hymns, or through the powerful coming on of spring, which drives joyfully through all of nature, that Dionysian excitement arises; as it intensifies, the subjective fades into complete forgetfulness of self. Even in the German Middle Ages, under the same power of Dionysus, constantly growing hordes thronged from place to place, singing and dancing; in these St. John's and St. Vitus's dances we recognize the Bacchic chorus of the Greeks once again, with its precursors in Asia Minor, right back to Babylon and the orgiastic *Sacaea [riotous Babylonian festival]*. There are people who, from a lack of experience or out of apathy, turn mockingly or pityingly away from such phenomena as from a "sickness of the people," with a sense of their own health. These poor people naturally do not have any sense of how deathly and ghost-like this very "health" of theirs sounds, when the glowing life of the Dionysian throng roars past them.

Under the magic of the Dionysian, not only does the bond between man and man lock itself in place once more, but also nature itself, no matter how alienated, hostile, or subjugated, rejoices again in her festival of reconciliation with her prodigal son, man. The earth freely offers up her gifts, and the beasts of prey from the rocks and the desert approach in peace. The wagon of Dionysus is covered with flowers and wreaths; under his yolk stride panthers and tigers. If someone were to transform Beethoven's *Ode to Joy* into a painting and not restrain his imagination when millions of people sink dramatically into the dust, then we could come close to the Dionysian. Now the slave a free man; now all the stiff, hostile barriers break apart, those things which necessity and arbitrary power or "saucy fashion" have established between men. Now, with the gospel of world harmony, every man feels himself not only united with his neighbour, reconciled and fused together, but also as one with him, as if the veil of Maja had been ripped apart, with only scraps fluttering around in the face of the mysterious primordial unity. Singing and dancing, man expresses himself as a member of a higher community: he has forgotten how to walk and talk and is on the verge of flying up into the air as he dances. The enchantment speaks out in his gestures. Just as the animals now speak and the earth gives milk and honey, so something supernatural also echoes out of him: he feels himself a god; he himself now moves in as lofty and ecstatic a way as he saw the gods move in his dream. The man is no longer an artist; he has become a work of art: the artistic power of all of nature, to the highest rhapsodic satisfaction of the primordial unity, reveals itself here in the transports of intoxication. The finest clay, the most expensive marble—man—is here worked and hewn, and the cry of the Eleusinian mysteries rings out to the chisel blows of the Dionysian world artist: "Do you fall down, you millions? World, do you have a sense of your creator?"

2

Up to this point, we have considered the Apollonian and its opposite, the Dionysian, as artistic forces which break forth out of nature itself, *without the mediation of the human artist*, and in which the human artistic drives are for the time being satisfied directly—on the one hand, as a world of dream images, whose perfection has no connection with an individual's high level of intellect or artistic education, on the other hand, as the intoxicating reality, which once again does not respect the individual, but even seeks to abolish the individual and to redeem him through a mystical feeling of collective unity. In comparison to these unmediated artistic states of nature, every artist is an "imitator," and, in fact, is an artist either of Apollonian dream or Dionysian intoxication or, finally—as in Greek tragedy, for example— simultaneously an artist of intoxication and of dreams. As the last, it is possible for us to imagine how he sinks down in Dionysian drunkenness and mystical obliteration of the self, alone and apart from the rapturous choruses, and how, through the Apollonian effects of dream, his own state now reveals itself to him, that is, his unity with the innermost basis of the world, *in a metaphorical dream picture*.

Having set out these general assumptions and comparisons, let us now approach the *Greeks*, in order to recognize to what degree and to what heights those *artistic drives of nature* were developed in them: in that way we will be in a position to understand more deeply and to assess the relationship of the Greek artist to his primordial images or, to use Aristotle's expression, his "imitation of nature." In spite of all their literature on dreams and numerous dream anecdotes, we can speak of the *dreams* of the Greeks only hypothetically, although with a fair degree of certainty. Given the incredibly clear and accurate plastic capability of their eyes, along with their intelligent and open love of colour, one cannot go wrong in assuming that, to the shame all those born later, their dreams also had a logical causality of lines and circumferences, colours, and groupings, a sequence of scenes rather like their best bas reliefs, whose perfection would certainly entitle us, if such a comparison were possible, to describe the dreaming Greek man as Homer and Homer as a dreaming Greek man, in a deeper sense than when modern man, with respect to his dreams, has the temerity to compare himself with Shakespeare.

On the other hand, we do not need to speak merely hypothetically when we are to expose the immense gap which separates the *Dionysian Greeks* from the Dionysian barbarians. In all quarters of the ancient world—setting aside here the newer worlds—from Rome to Babylon, we can confirm the existence of Dionysian celebrations, of a type, at best, related to the Greek type in much the same way as the bearded satyr, whose name and attributes are taken from the goat, is related to Dionysus himself. Almost everywhere, the central point of these celebrations consisted of an exuberant sexual promiscuity, whose waves flooded over all established family practices and its traditional laws. The very wildest bestiality of nature was here unleashed, creating that abominable mixture of lust and cruelty, which has always seemed to me the real "witches' cauldron." From the feverish excitement of those festivals, knowledge of which reached the Greeks from all directions by

land and sea, they were, it seems, for a long time completely secure and protected through the figure of Apollo, drawn up here in all his pride. Apollo could counter by holding up the head of Medusa, for no power was more dangerous than this massive and grotesque Dionysian force. Doric art has immortalized that majestic bearing of Apollo as he stands in opposition. This resistance became more questionable and even impossible as similar impulses finally broke out from the deepest roots of Hellenic culture itself: now the effect of the Delphic god, in a timely final process of reconciliation, limited itself to taking the destructive weapon out of the hand of the powerful opponent. This reconciliation is the most important moment in the history of Greek culture. Wherever we look, the revolutionary effects of this event manifest themselves. It was the reconciliation of two opponents, who from now on observed their differences with a sharp demarcation of the border line to be kept between them and with occasional gifts sent to honour each other, but basically the gap was not bridged over. However, if we see how, under the pressure of that peace agreement, the Dionysian power revealed itself, then we now understand the meaning of the festivals of world redemption and days of transfiguration in the Dionysian orgies of the Greeks, in comparison with that Babylonian Sacaea, which turned human beings back into tigers and apes.

In these Greek festivals, for the first time nature achieves its artistic jubilee. In them, for the first time, the tearing apart of the *principii individuationis [the principle of individuation]* becomes an artistic phenomenon. Here that dreadful witches' cauldron of lust and cruelty was without power. The strange mixture and ambiguity in the emotions of the Dionysian celebrant only remind him—as healing potions remind one of deadly poison—of that phenomenon that pain awakens joy, that the jubilation in his chest rips out cries of agony. From the most sublime joy echoes the cry of horror or the longingly plaintive lament over an irreparable loss. In those Greek festivals it was as if a sentimental feature of nature is breaking out, as if nature has to sigh over her dismemberment into separate individuals. The song and the language of gestures of such a doubly defined celebrant was for the Homeric

Greek world something new and unheard of, and in it Dionysian *music*, in particular, awoke fear and terror. If music was apparently already known as an Apollonian art, this music, strictly speaking, was a rhythmic pattern like the sound of waves, whose artistic power had been developed for presenting Apollonian states. The music of Apollo was Doric architecture expressed in sound, but only in intimate tones characteristic of the cithara. It kept at a careful distance, as something un-Apollonian, the particular element which constitutes the character of Dionysian music and, along with that, of music generally, the emotionally disturbing tonal power, the unified stream of melody, and the totally incomparable world of harmony. In the Dionysian dithyramb man is aroused to the highest intensity of all his symbolic capabilities; something never felt forces itself into expression, the destruction of the veil of Maja, the sense of oneness as the presiding genius of form, in fact, of nature itself. Now the essence of nature is to express itself symbolically; a new world of symbols is necessary, the entire symbolism of the body, not just the symbolism of the mouth, of the face, and of the words, but the full gestures of the dance, all the limbs moving to the rhythm. And then the other symbolic powers grow, those of the music, in rhythm, dynamics, and harmony—with sudden violence. To grasp this total unleashing of all symbolic powers, man must already have attained that high level of freedom from the self which desires to express itself symbolically in those forces. Because of this, the dithyrambic servant of Dionysus will be understood only by someone like himself! With what astonishment must the Apollonian Greek have gazed at him! With an amazement which was all the greater as he sensed with horror that all this might not be really so foreign to him, that, in fact, his Apollonian consciousness was, like a veil, merely covering the Dionysian world in front of him.

3

In order to grasp this point, we must dismantle that artistic structure of *Apollonian culture*, as it were, stone by stone, until we see the foundations on which it is built. Here we now become aware for the first time of the marvellous *Olympian* divine forms, which stand on the pediments of this building and whose actions decorate its friezes all around in illuminating bas relief. If Apollo also stands among them as a single god next to others and without any claim to a pre-eminent position, we should not on that account let ourselves be deceived. The same drive which made itself sensuously perceptible in Apollo gave birth to that entire Olympian world in general, and, in this sense, we are entitled to value Apollo as the father of that world. What was the immense need out of which such an illuminating society of Olympian beings arose?

Anyone who steps up to these Olympians with another religion in his heart and now seeks from them ethical loftiness, even sanctity, non-physical spirituality, loving gazes filled with pity, will soon have to turn his back despondently in disappointment with them. Here there is no reminder of asceticism, spirituality, and duty: here speaks to us only a full, indeed a triumphant, existence, in which everything present is worshipped, no matter whether it is good or evil. And thus the onlooker may well stand in real consternation in front of this fantastic excess of life, to ask himself with what magical drink in their bodies these high-spirited men could have enjoyed life, so that wherever they look, Helen laughs back at them, that ideal image of their own existence, "hovering in sweet sensuousness." However, we must call out to this onlooker who has already turned his back: "Don't leave them. First listen to what Greek folk wisdom expresses about this very life which spreads itself out here before you with such inexplicable serenity. There is an old legend that king Midas for a long time hunted the wise *Silenus*, the companion of Dionysus, in the forests, without catching him. When Silenus finally fell into the king's hands, the king asked what was the best thing of all for men, the very finest. The daemon remained silent, motionless and inflexible, until, compelled by the king, he finally broke out into shrill laughter and said these words, "Suffering creature, born for a day, child of accident and toil, why are you forcing me to say what would give you the greatest pleasure not to hear? The very best thing for you is totally unreachable: not to have been born, not to *exist*, to be *nothing*. The second best thing for you, however, is this—to die soon."

What is the relationship between the Olympian world of the gods and this popular wisdom? It is like the relationship of the entrancing vision of the tortured martyr to his torments.

Now, as it were, the Olympic magic mountain reveals itself and shows us its roots. The Greek knew and felt the terror and horrors of existence: in order to be able to live at all, he must have placed in front of him the gleaming dream birth of the Olympians. That immense distrust of the titanic forces of nature, that *Moira [Fate]* enthroned mercilessly above everything which could be known, that vulture of the great friend of man, Prometheus, that fatal lot of wise Oedipus, that family curse on the House of Atreus, which compelled Orestes to kill his mother, in short, that entire philosophy of the woodland god, together with its mythical illustrations, from which the melancholy Etruscans died off—that was overcome time after time by the Greeks, or at least hidden and removed from view, through the artistic *middle world [Mittelwelt]* of the Olympians. In order to be able to live, the Greeks must have created these gods out of the deepest necessity. We can readily imagine the sequential development of these gods: through that Apollonian drive for beauty there developed, by a slow transition out of the primordial titanic divine order of terror, the Olympian divine order of joy, just as roses break forth out of thorny bushes. How else could a people so emotionally sensitive, so spontaneously desiring, so singularly capable of *suffering*, have been able to endure their existence, unless the same qualities, with a loftier glory flowing round them, manifested themselves in their gods. The same impulse which summons art into life as the seductive replenishment for further living and the completion of existence also gave rise to the Olympian world, in which the Hellenic "Will" held before itself a transfiguring mirror. In this way, the gods justify the lives of men, because they themselves live it—that is the only satisfactory theodicy! Existence under the bright sunshine of such gods is experienced as worth striving for in itself, and the essential *pain* of the Homeric men refers to separation from that sunlight, above all to the fact that such separation is coming soon, so that people could now say of them, with a reversal of the wisdom of Silenus, "The very worst thing for them was to die

soon; the second worst was to die at all." When the laments resound now, they tell once more of short-lived Achilles, of the changes in the race of men, transformed like leaves, of the destruction of the heroic age. It is not unworthy of the greatest hero to long to live on, even as a day labourer. Thus, in the Apollonian stage, the "Will" spontaneously demands to keep on living, the Homeric man feels himself so at one with living, that even his lament becomes a song of praise.

Here we must now point out that this harmony, looked on with such longing by more recent men, in fact, that unity of man with nature, for which Schiller coined the artistic slogan "naive," is in no way such a simple, inevitable, and, as it were, unavoidable condition, like a human paradise, which we *necessarily* run into at the door of every culture: such a belief is possible only in an age which seeks to believe that Rousseau's Emile is also an artist and which imagines it has found in Homer an artist like Emile raised in the bosom of nature. Wherever we encounter the "naive" in art, we have to recognize the highest effect of Apollonian culture, which always first has to overthrow the kingdom of the Titans and to kill monsters and, through powerfully deluding images and joyful illusions, has to emerge victorious over the horrific depth of what we observe in the world and the most sensitive capacity for suffering. But how seldom does the naive, that sense of being completely swallowed up in the beauty of appearance, succeed! For that reason, how inexpressibly noble is *Homer*, who, as a single individual, was related to that Apollonian popular culture as the individual dream artist is to the people's capacity to dream and to nature in general. Homeric "naivete" is only to be understood as the complete victory of the Apollonian illusion. It is the sort of illusion which nature uses so frequently in order to attain her objectives. The true goal is concealed by a deluding image: we stretch our hands out toward this image, and nature reaches its goal through our deception. With the Greeks the "Will" wished to gaze upon itself through the transforming power of genius and the world of art; in order to glorify itself, its creatures had to sense that they themselves were worthy of being glorified; they had to see themselves again in a higher sphere, without this complete world of contemplation affecting them as an imperative or as a reproach. This is the sphere of beauty, in which they saw their mirror images, the Olympians. With this mirror of beauty, the Hellenic "Will" fought against the talent for suffering, which is bound up with artistic talent, and the wisdom of suffering, and, as a memorial of its victory, Homer stands before us, the naive artist.

Fredrich Neitzsche. *The Birth of Tragedy*. Trans. Ian Johnston, 2009. Used with permission.

WHAT IS ART?

LEO TOLSTOY (1828-1910)

Leo Tolstoy's What is Art? *presents a straightforward Expressive theory of art. Art is a means of expressing human emotions. He rejects theories like Plato's and Nietzsche's in which art seeks to reveal Beauty, the Divine or the Cosmic Will. Art communicates feelings and this is important socially in developing community. We can describe how someone else's sneeze can put us in contact with microbes that infect us; but Tolstoy doesn't explain how lines, form, color or motion can "infect" us with the emotions felt by the artist. In what sense does, say, a painting have feelings; and what is, say, a painting sad or blissful over or about? That analysis will await more contemporary aestheticians like Langer or Gombrich. In the excerpt's final section, Tolstoy describes something like an extrasensory perception of the viewer to the feelings of the artist with the work serving as a medium or soothsayer. This spiritual connection is, in fact, strengthened by the sincerity of the artist, which is even more remarkable considering that, here you are in the Metropolitan Museum of Art looking at a painting by an artist who is long since dead. Further Tolstoy believes that the more sincere the artist is the more successful she will be in expressing that emotion through her art. Thus peasant art is so much better than upper class art, besotted as the latter is with vanity and covetousness. Take that Salvador Dali!*

CHAPTER FIVE

In order correctly to define art, it is necessary, first of all, to cease to consider it as a means to pleasure and to consider it as one of the conditions of human life. Viewing it in this way we cannot fail to observe that art is one of the means of intercourse between man and man.

Every work of art causes the receiver to enter into a certain kind of relationship both with him who produced, or is producing, the art, and with all those who, simultaneously, previously, or subsequently, receive the same artistic impression.

Speech, transmitting the thoughts and experiences of men, serves as a means of union among them, and art acts in a similar manner. The peculiarity of this latter means of intercourse, distinguishing it from intercourse by means of words, consists in this, that whereas by words a man transmits his thoughts to another, by means of art he transmits his feelings.

The activity of art is based on the fact that a man, receiving through his sense of hearing or sight another man's expression of feeling, is capable of experiencing the emotion which moved the man who expressed it. To take the simplest example; one man laughs, and another who hears becomes merry; or a man weeps, and another who hears feels sorrow. A man is excited or irritated, and another man seeing him comes to a similar state of mind. By his movements or by the sounds of his voice, a man expresses courage and determination or sadness and calmness, and this state of mind passes on to others. A man suffers, expressing his sufferings by groans and spasms, and this suffering transmits itself to other people; a man expresses his feeling of admiration, devotion, fear, respect, or love to certain objects, persons, or phenomena, and others are infected by the same feelings of admiration, devotion, fear, respect, or love to the same objects, persons, and phenomena.

And it is upon this capacity of man to receive another man's expression of feeling and experience those feelings himself, that the activity of art is based.

If a man infects another or others directly, immediately, by his appearance or by the sounds he gives vent to at the very time he experiences the feeling; if he causes another man to yawn when he himself cannot help yawning, or to laugh or cry when he himself is obliged to laugh or cry, or to suffer when he himself is suffering—that does not amount to art.

Art begins when one person, with the object of joining another or others to himself in one and the same feeling, expresses that feeling by certain external indications. To take the simplest example: a boy, having experienced, let us say, fear on encountering a wolf, relates that encounter; and, in order to evoke in others the feeling he has experienced, describes himself, his condition before the encounter, the surroundings, the woods, his own lightheartedness, and then the wolf's appearance, its movements, the distance between himself and the wolf, etc. All this, if only the boy, when telling the story, again experiences the feelings he had lived through and infects the hearers and compels them to feel what the narrator had experienced is art. If even the boy had not seen a wolf but had frequently been afraid of one, and if, wishing to evoke in others the fear he had felt, he invented an encounter with a wolf and recounted it so as to make his hearers share the feelings he experienced when he feared the world, that also would be art. And just in the same way it is art if a man, having experienced either the fear of suffering or the attraction of enjoyment (whether in reality or in imagination) expresses these feelings on canvas or in marble so that others are infected by them. And it is also art if a man feels or imagines to himself feelings of delight, gladness, sorrow, despair, courage, or despondency and the transition from one to another of these feelings, and expresses these feelings by sounds so that the hearers are infected by them and experience them as they were experienced by the composer.

The feelings with which the artist infects others may be most various - very strong or very weak, very important or very insignificant, very bad or very good: feelings of love for one's own country, self-devotion and submission to fate or to God expressed in a drama, raptures of lovers described in a novel, feelings of voluptuousness expressed in a picture, courage expressed in a triumphal march, merriment evoked by a dance, humor evoked by a funny story, the feeling of quietness transmitted by an evening landscape or by a lullaby, or the feeling of admiration evoked by a beautiful arabesque - it is all art.

If only the spectators or auditors are infected by the feelings which the author has felt, it is art.

To evoke in oneself a feeling one has once experienced, and having evoked it in oneself, then, by means of movements, lines, colors, sounds, or forms expressed in words, so to transmit that feeling that others may experience the same feeling—this is the activity of art.

Art is a human activity consisting in this, that one man consciously, by means of certain external signs, hands on to others feelings he has lived through, and that other people are infected by these feelings and also experience them.

Art is not, as the metaphysicians say, the manifestation of some mysterious idea of beauty or God; it is not, as the aesthetical physiologists say, a game in which man lets off his excess of stored-up energy; it is not the expression of man's emotions by external signs; it is not the production of pleasing objects; and, above all, it is not pleasure; but it is a means of union among men, joining them together in the same feelings, and indispensable for the life and progress toward well-being of individuals and of humanity.

As, thanks to man's capacity to express thoughts by words, every man may know all that has been done for him in the realms of thought by all humanity before his day, and can in the present, thanks to this capacity to understand the thoughts of others, become a sharer in their activity and can himself hand on to his contemporaries and descendants the thoughts he has assimilated from others, as well as those which have arisen within himself; so, thanks to man's capacity to be infected with the feelings of others by means of art, all that is being lived through by his contemporaries is accessible to him, as well as the feelings experienced by men thousands of years ago, and he has also the possibility of transmitting his own feelings to others.

If people lacked this capacity to receive the thoughts conceived by the men who preceded them and to pass on to others their own thoughts, men would be like wild beasts, or like Kaspar Houser.

And if men lacked this other capacity of being infected by art, people might be almost more savage still, and, above all, more separated from, and more hostile to, one another.

And therefore the activity of art is a most important one, as important as the activity of speech itself and as generally diffused.

We are accustomed to understand art to be only what we hear and see in theaters, concerts, and exhibitions, together with buildings, statues, poems, novels. . . . But all this is but the smallest part of the art by which we communicate with each other in life. All human life is filled with works of art of every kind—from cradlesong, jest, mimicry, the ornamentation of houses, dress, and utensils, up to church services, buildings, monuments, and triumphal processions. It is all artistic activity. So that by art, in the limited sense of the word, we do not mean all human activity transmitting feelings, but only that part which we for some reason select from it and to which we attach special importance.

This special importance has always been given by all men to that part of this activity which transmits feelings flowing from their religious perception, and this small part of art they have specifically called art, attaching to it the full meaning of the word.

That was how man of old—Socrates, Plato, and Aristotle—looked on art. Thus did the Hebrew prophets and the ancient Christians regard art; thus it was, and still is, understood by the Mohammedans, and thus it still is understood by religious folk among our own peasantry.

Some teachers of mankind—as Plato in his *Republic* and people such as the primitive Christians, the strict Mohammedans, and the Buddhists—have gone so far as to repudiate all art.

People viewing art in this way (in contradiction to the prevalent view of today which regards any art as good if only it affords pleasure) considered, and consider, that art (as contrasted with speech, which need not be listened to) is so highly dangerous in its power to infect people against their wills that mankind will lose far less by banishing all art than by tolerating each and every art.

Evidently such people were wrong in repudiating all art, for they denied that which cannot be de-

nied - one of the indispensable means of communication, without which mankind could not exist. But not less wrong are the people of civilized European society of our class and day in favoring any art if it but serves beauty, i.e., gives people pleasure.

Formerly people feared lest among the works of art there might chance to be some causing corruption, and they prohibited art altogether. Now they only fear lest they should be deprived of any enjoyment art can afford, and patronize any art. And I think the last error is much grosser than the first and that its consequences are far more harmful.

CHAPTER FIFTEEN

...Art, in our society, has been so perverted that not only has bad art come to be considered good, but even the very perception of what art really is has been lost. In order to be able to speak about the art of our society, it is, therefore, first of all necessary to distinguish art from counterfeit art.

There is one indubitable indication distinguishing real art from its counterfeit, namely, the infectiousness of art. If a man, without exercising effort and without altering his standpoint on reading, hearing, or seeing another man's work, experiences a mental condition which unites him with that man and with other people who also partake of that work of art, then the object evoking that condition is a work of art. And however poetical, realistic, effectful, or interesting a work may be, it is not a work of art if it does not evoke that feeling (quite distinct from all other feelings) of joy and of spiritual union with another (the author) and with others (those who are also infected by it).

It is true that this indication is an internal one, and that there are people who have forgotten what the action of real art is, who expect something else form art (in our society the great majority are in this state), and that therefore such people may mistake for this aesthetic feeling the feeling of diversion and a certain excitement which they receive from counterfeits of art. But though it is impossible to undeceive these people, just as it is impossible to convince a man suffering from "Daltonism" [a type of color blindness] that green is not red, yet, for all that, this indication remains perfectly definite to those whose feeling for art is neither perverted nor atrophied, and it clearly distinguishes the feeling produced by art from all other feelings.

The chief peculiarity of this feeling is that the receiver of a true artistic impression is so united to the artist that he feels as if the work were his own and not someone else's - as if what it expresses were just what he had long been wishing to express. A real work of art destroys, in the consciousness of the receiver, the separation between himself and the artist—not that alone, but also between himself and all whose minds receive this work of art. In this freeing of our personality from its separation and isolation, in this uniting of it with others, lies the chief characteristic and the great attractive force of art.

If a man is infected by the author's condition of soul, if he feels this emotion and this union with others, then the object which has effected this is art; but if there be no such infection, if there be not this union with the author and with others who are moved by the same work - then it is not art. And not only is infection a sure sign of art, but the degree of infectiousness is also the sole measure of excellence in art.

The stronger the infection, the better is the art as art, speaking now apart from its subject matter, i.e., not considering the quality of the feelings it transmits.

And the degree of the infectiousness of art depends on three conditions:

1. On the greater or lesser individuality of the feeling transmitted;
2. on the greater or lesser clearness with which the feeling is transmitted;
3. on the sincerity of the artist, i.e., on the greater or lesser force with which the artist himself feels the emotion he transmits.

The more individual the feeling transmitted the more strongly does it act on the receiver; the more individual the state of soul into which he is transferred, the more pleasure does the receiver obtain, and therefore the more readily and strongly does he join in it.

The clearness of expression assists infection because the receiver, who mingles in consciousness with the author, is the better satisfied the more clearly the feeling is transmitted, which, as it seems to him, he has long known and felt, and for which he has only now found expression.

But most of all is the degree of infectiousness of art increased by the degree of sincerity in the artist. As soon as the spectator, hearer, or reader feels that the artist is infected by his own production, and writes, sings, or plays for himself, and not merely to act on others, this mental condition of the artist infects the receiver; and contrariwise, as soon as the spectator, reader, or hearer feels that the author is not writing, singing, or playing for his own satisfaction —does not himself feel what he wishes to express— but is doing it for him, the receiver, a resistance immediately springs up, and the most individual and the newest feelings and the cleverest technique not only fail to produce any infection but actually repel.

I have mentioned three conditions of contagiousness in art, but they may be all summed up into one, the last, sincerity, i.e., that the artist should be impelled by an inner need to express his feeling. That condition includes the first; for if the artist is sincere he will express the feeling as he experienced it. And as each man is different from everyone else, his feeling will be individual for everyone else; and the more individual it is—the more the artist has drawn it from the depths of his nature - the more sympathetic and sincere will it be. And this same sincerity will impel the artist to find a clear expression of the feeling which he wishes to transmit.

Therefore this third condition - sincerity - is the most important of the three. It is always complied with in peasant art, and this explains why such art always acts so powerfully; but it is a condition almost entirely absent from our upper-class art, which is continually produced by artists actuated by personal aims of covetousness or vanity.

Such are the three conditions which divide art from its counterfeits, and which also decide the quality of every work of art apart from its subject matter.

The absence of any one of these conditions excludes a work form the category of art and relegates it to that of art's counterfeits. If the work does not transmit the artist's peculiarity of feeling and is therefore not individual, if it is unintelligibly expressed, or if it has not proceeded from the author's inner need for expression—it is not a work of art. If all these conditions are present, even in the smallest degree, then the work, even if a weak one, is yet a work of art.

The presence in various degrees of these three conditions—individuality, clearness, and sincerity—decides the merit of a work of art as art, apart from subject matter. All works of art take rank of merit according to the degree in which they fulfill the first, the second, and the third of these conditions. In one the individuality of the feeling transmitted may predominate; in another, clearness of expression; in a third, sincerity; while a fourth may have sincerity and individuality but be deficient in clearness; a fifth, individuality and clearness but less sincerity; and so forth, in all possible degrees and combinations.

Thus is art divided from that which is not art, and thus is the quality of art as art decided, independently of its subject matter, i.e., apart from whether the feelings it transmits are good or bad.

But how are we to define good and bad art with reference to its subject matter?

Leo Tolstoy. *What is Art?* Trans. Alymer Maude, 1899.

THE AESTHETIC HYPOTHESIS

CLIVE BELL (1881-1964)

Clive Bell is a strong advocate of Formalism. He does not doubt that art is productive of subjective emotional responses in us. However true aesthetic experience is the evocation of a very refined emotion: the appreciation of significant form in a work of art. Anything outside of the line, color, form, and composition in the artwork is considered non-aesthetic for Bell. This would include the intentions of the artist or author, any information we might receive from the work about history or the real aspects of the model or subject matter. Also eliminated from aesthetic experience are any emotions that are triggered in us other than the delight we have in detecting the form present in the artwork. Thus if an artist uses his art to pander to popular feelings, like patriotism, bathos or sentimentality, she is on her way to producing bad art or non-art altogether.

It is improbable that more nonsense has been written about aesthetics than about anything else: the literature of the subject is not large enough for that. It is certain, however, that about no subject with which I am acquainted has so little been said that is at all to the purpose. The explanation is discoverable. He who would elaborate a plausible theory of aesthetics must possess two qualities—artistic sensibility and a turn for clear thinking. Without sensibility a man can have no aesthetic experience, and, obviously, theories not based on broad and deep aesthetic experience are worthless. Only those for whom art is a constant source of passionate emotion can possess the data from which profitable theories may be deduced; but to deduce profitable theories even from accurate data involves a certain amount of brain-work, and, unfortunately, robust intellects and delicate sensibilities are not inseparable. As often as not, the hardest thinkers have had no aesthetic experience whatever. I have a friend blessed with an intellect as keen as a drill, who, though he takes an interest in aesthetics, has never during a life of almost forty years been guilty of an aesthetic emotion. So, having no faculty for distinguishing a work of art from a handsaw, he is apt to rear up a pyramid of irrefragable argument on the hypothesis that a handsaw is

a work of art. This defect robs his perspicuous and subtle reasoning of much of its value; for it has ever been a maxim that faultless logic can win but little credit for conclusions that are based on premises notoriously false. Every cloud, however, has its silver lining, and this insensibility, though unlucky in that it makes my friend incapable of choosing a sound basis for his argument, mercifully blinds him to the absurdity of his conclusions while leaving him in full enjoyment of his masterly dialectic. People who set out from the hypothesis that Sir Edwin Landseer was the finest painter that ever lived will feel no uneasiness about an aesthetic which proves that Giotto was the worst. So, my friend, when he arrives very logically at the conclusion that a work of art should be small or round or smooth, or that to appreciate fully a picture you should pace smartly before it or set it spinning like a top, cannot guess why I ask him whether he has lately been to Cambridge, a place he sometimes visits.

On the other hand, people who respond immediately and surely to works of art, though, in my judgment, more enviable than men of massive intellect but slight sensibility, are often quite as incapable of talking sense about aesthetics. Their heads are not always very clear. They possess the data on which any system must be based; but, generally, they want the power that draws correct inferences from true data. Having received aesthetic emotions from works of art, they are in a position to seek out the quality common to all that have moved them, but, in fact, they do nothing of the sort. I do not blame them. Why should they bother to examine their feelings when for them to feel is enough? Why should they stop to think when they are not very good at thinking? Why should they hunt for a common quality in all objects that move them in a particular way when they can linger over the many delicious and peculiar charms of each as it comes? So, if they write criticism and call it esthetics, if they imagine that they are talking about Art when they are talking about particular works of art or even about the technique of painting, if, loving particular works they find tedious the consideration of art in general, perhaps they have chosen the better part. If they are not curious about the nature of their emotion, nor about the quality common to all objects that provoke it, they have my sympathy, and, as what they say if often charming and suggestive, my admiration too. Only let no one support that what they write and talk is aesthetics; it is criticism, or just "shop."

The starting-point for all systems of aesthetics must be the personal experience of a peculiar emotion. The objects that provoke this emotion we call works of art. All sensitive people agree that there is a peculiar emotion provoked by works of art. I do not mean, of course, that all works provoke the same emotion. On the contrary, every work produces a different emotion. But all these emotions are recognisably the same in kind; so far, at any rate, the best opinion is on my side. That there is a particular kind of emotion provoked by works of visual art, and that this emotion is provoked by every kind of visual art, by pictures, sculptures, buildings, pots, carvings, textiles, etc., etc., is not disputed, I think, by anyone capable of feeling it. This emotion is called the aesthetic emotion; and if we can discover some quality common and peculiar to all the objects that provoke it, we shall have solved what I take to be the central problem of aesthetics. We shall have discovered the essential quality in a work of art, the quality that distinguishes works of art from all other classes of objects.

For either all works of visual art have some common quality, or when we speak of "works of art" we gibber. Everyone speaks of "art," making a mental classification by which he distinguishes the class "works of art" from all other classes. What is the justification of this classification? What is the quality common and peculiar to all members of this class? Whatever it be, no doubt it is often found in company with other qualities; but they are adventitious—it is essential. There must be some one quality without which a work of art cannot exist; possessing which, in the least degree, no work is altogether worthless. What is this quality? What quality is shared by all objects that provoke our aesthetic emotions? What quality is common to Sta. Sophia and the windows at Chartres, Mexican sculpture, a Persian bowl, Chinese carpets, Giotto's frescoes at Padua, and the masterpieces of Poussin, Piero della Francesca, and Cezanne? Only one answer seems possible—significant form. In each, lines and colours combined in a particular way, certain forms and relations of forms, stir our aesthetic emotions. These relations and combinations of lines and colours, these aesthetically moving forms, I call "Significant Form"; and "Significant form" is the one quality common to all works of visual art.

At this point it may be objected that I am making aesthetics a purely subjective business, since my only data are personal experiences of a particular emotion. It will be said that the objects that provoke this emotion vary with each individual, and that therefore a system of aesthetics can have no objective validity. It must be replied that any system of aesthetics which pretends to be based on some objective truth is so palpably ridiculous as not to be worth discussing. We have no other means of recognising a work of art than our feeling for it. The objects that provoke aesthetic emotion vary with each individual. Aesthetic judgments are, as the saying goes, matters of taste; and about tastes, as everyone is proud to admit, there is no disputing. A good critic may be able to make me see in a picture that had left me cold things that I had overlooked, till at last, receiving the aesthetic emotion, I recognise it as a work of art. To be continually pointing out those parts, the sum, or rather the combination, of which unite to produce significant form, is the function of criticism. But it is useless for a critic to tell me that something is a work of art; he must make me feel it for myself. This he can do only by making me see; he must get at my emotions through my eyes. Unless he can make me see something that moves me, he cannot force my emotions. I have no right to consider anything a work of art to which I cannot react emotionally; and I have no right to look for the essential quality in anything that I have not *felt* to be a work of art. The critic can affect my aesthetic theories only by affecting my aesthetic experience. All systems of aesthetics must be based on personal experience—that is to say, they must be subjective.

Yet, though all aesthetic theories must be based on aesthetic judgments, and ultimately all aesthetic judgments must be matters of personal taste, it would be rash to assert that no theory of aesthetics can have general validity. For, though A, B, C, D are the works that move me, and A, D, E, F the works that move you, it may well be that x is the only quality believed by either of us to be common to all the works in his list. We may all agree about aesthetics, and yet differ about particular works of art. We may differ as to the presence or absence of the quality x. My immediate object will be to show that significant form is the only quality common and peculiar to all the works of visual art that move me; and I will ask those whose aesthetic experience does not tally with mine to see whether this quality is not also, in their judgment, common to all works that move them, and whether they can discover any other quality of which the same can be said.

Also at this point a query arises, irrelevant indeed, but hardly to be suppressed: "Why are we so profoundly moved by forms related in a particular way?" The question is extremely interesting, but irrelevant to aesthetics. In pure aesthetics we have only to consider our emotion and its object: for the purposes of aesthetics we have no right, neither is there any necessity, to pry behind the object into the state of mind of him who made it. Later, I shall attempt to answer the question; for by so doing I may be able to develop my theory of the relation of art to life. I shall not, however, be under the delusion that I am rounding off my theory of aesthetics. For a discussion of aesthetics, it need be agreed only that forms arranged and combined according to certain unknown and mysterious laws do move us in a particular way, and that it is the business of an artist so to combine and arrange them that they shall move

us. These moving combinations and arrangements I have called, for the sake of convenience and for a reason that will appear later, "Significant Form."

A third interpretation has to be met. "Are you forgetting about colour?" someone inquires. Certainly not; my term "significant form" included combinations of lines and of colours. The distinction between form and colour is an unreal one; you cannot conceive a colourless line or a colourless space; neither can you conceive a formless relation of colours. In a black and white drawing the spaces are all white and all are bounded by black lines; in most oil paintings the spaces are multi-coloured and so are the boundaries; you cannot imagine a boundary line without any content, or a content without a boundary lines. Therefore, when I speak of significant form, I mean a combination of lines and colours (counting white and black as colours) that moves me aesthetically.

Some people may be surprised at my not having called this "beauty." Of course, to those who define beauty as "combinations of lines and colours that provoke aesthetic emotion," I willingly conceded the right of substituting their word for mine. But most of us, however strict we may be, are apt to apply the epithet "beautiful" to objects that do not provoke that peculiar emotion produced by works of art. Everyone, I suspect, has called a butterfly or a flower beautiful. Does anyone feel the same kind of emotion for a butterfly or a flower that he feels for a cathedral or a picture/ surely, it is not what I call an aesthetic emotion that most of us feel, generally, for natural beauty. I shall suggest, later, that some people may, occasionally, see in nature what we see in art, and feel for her an aesthetic emotion; but I am satisfied that, as a rule, most people feel a very different kind of emotion for birds and flowers and the wings of butterflies from that which they feel for pictures, pots, temples and statues. Why these beautiful things do not move us as works of art move us is another, and not an aesthetic, question. For our immediate purpose we have to discover only what quality is common to objects that do move us as works of art. In the last part of this chapter, when I try to answer the question-"Why are we so profoundly moved by some combinations of lines and colours?" I shall hope to offer an acceptable explanation of why we are less profoundly moved by others.

Since we call a quality that does not raise the

characteristic aesthetic emotion "Beauty," it would be misleading to call by the same name the quality that does. To make "beauty" the object of the aesthetic emotion, we must give to the word an overstrict and unfamiliar definition. Everyone sometimes uses "beauty" in an unaesthetic sense; most people habitually do so. To everyone, except perhaps here and there an occasional aesthete, the commonest sense of the word is unaesthetic. Of its grosser abuse, patent in our chatter about "beautiful huntin'" and "beautiful shootin'," I need not take account; it would be open to the precious to reply that they never do so abuse it. Besides, here there is no danger of confusion between the aesthetic and the non-aesthetic use; but when we speak of a beautiful woman there is. When an ordinary man speaks of a beautiful woman he certainly does not mean only that she moves him aesthetically; but when an artist calls a withered old hag beautiful he may sometimes mean what he means when he calls a battered torso beautiful. The ordinary man, if he be also a man of taste, will call the battered torso beautiful, but he will not call a withered hag beautiful because, in the matter of women, it is not to the aesthetic quality that the hag may possess, but to some other quality that he assigns the epithet. Indeed, most of us never dream of going for aesthetic emotions to human beings, from whom we ask something very different. This "something," when we find it in a young woman, we are apt to call 'beauty.' We live in a nice age. With the man-in-the-street 'beautiful" is more often than not synonymous with "desirable": the word does not necessarily connote any aesthetic reaction whatever, and I am tempted to believe that in the minds of many the sexual flavour of the word is stronger than the aesthetic. I have noticed a consistency in those to whom the most beautiful thing in the world is a beautiful woman, and the next most beautiful thing a picture of one. The confusion between aesthetic and sensual beauty is not in their case so great as might be supposed. Perhaps there is none; for perhaps they have never had an aesthetic emotion to confuse with their other emotions. The art that they call "beautiful" is generally closely related to the women. A beautiful picture is a photograph of a pretty girl; beautiful music, the music that provokes emotions similar to those provoked by young ladies in musical farces; and beautiful poetry, the poetry that recalls the same emotions felt, twenty years earlier, for the rector's daughter. Clearly the word 'beauty" is used to connote the objects of quite distinguishable emotions, and that is a reason for not employing a term which would land me inevitably in confusions and misunderstandings with my readers.

On the other hand, with those who judge it more exact to call these combinations and arrangements of form that provoke our aesthetic emotions, not "significant form," but "significant relations of form," and then try to make the best of two worlds, the aesthetic and the metaphysical, by calling these relations "rhythm," I have no quarrel whatever. Having made it clear that by "significant form" I mean arrangements and combinations that move us in a particular way, I willingly join hands with those who prefer to give a different name to the same thing.

The hypothesis that significant form is the essential quality in a work of art has at least one merit denied to many more famous and more striking - it does help to explain things. We are all familiar with pictures that interest us and excite our admiration, but do not move us as works of art. To this class belongs what I call "Descriptive Painting" that is, painting in which forms are used not as objects of emotion, but as means of suggesting emotion or conveying information. Portraits of psychological and historical value, topographical works, pictures that tell stories and suggest situations, illustrations of all sorts, belong to this class. That we all recognise the distinction is clear, for who has not said that such and such a drawing was excellent as illustration, but as a work of art worthless? Of course many descriptive pictures possess, amongst other qualities, formal significance, and are therefore works of art; but many more do not. They interest us; they may move us too in a hundred different ways, but they do not move us aesthetically. According to my hypothesis they are not works of art. They leave untouched our aesthetic emotions because it is not their forms but the ideas or information suggested or conveyed by their forms that affect us.

Few pictures are better known or liked that Frith's "Paddington Station"; certainly I should be the last to grudge it its popularity. Many a weary forty minutes have I whiled away disentangling its fascinating incidents and forging for each an imaginary past and an improbable future. But certain though it is that

Frith's masterpiece, or engravings of it, have provided thousands with half-hours of curious and fanciful pleasure, it is not less certain that no one has experienced before it one half-second of aesthetic rapture—and this although the picture contains several pretty passages of colour, and is by no means badly painted. "Paddington Station" is not a work of art; it is an interesting and amusing document. In it line and colour are used to recount anecdotes, suggest ideas, and indicate the manners and customs of an age; they are not used to provoke aesthetic emotion. Forms and the relations of forms were for Froith not objects of emotion, but means of suggesting emotion and conveying ideas.

The ideas and information conveyed by "Paddington Station" are so amusing and so well presented that the picture has considerable value and is well, worth preserving. But, with the perfection of photographic processes and of the cinematograph, pictures of this sort are becoming otiose. Who doubts that one of those daily Mirror photographers in collaboration with a Daily mail reporter can tell us far more about "London day by day" than any royal Academician? For an account of manners and fashions we shall go, in future, to photographs, supported by a little bright journalism, rather than to descriptive painting. Had the imperial academicians of Nero, instead of manufacturing incredibly loathsome imitations of the antique, recorded in fresco and mosaic the manners and fashions of their day, their stuff, though artistic rubbish, would now be an historical gold-mine. If only they had been Friths instead of being Alma Tademas! But photography has made impossible any such transmutation of modern rubbish. Therefore it must be confessed that pictures in the Frith tradition are grown superfluous; they merely waste the hours of able men who might be more profitably employed in works of a wider beneficence. Still, they are not unpleasant, which is more than can be said for that kind of descriptive painting of which "The doctor" is the most flagrant example. Of course "The doctor" is not a work of art. In it form is not used as an object of emotion, but as a means of suggesting emotions. This alone suffices to make it nugatory; it is worse than nugatory because the emotion it suggests is false. What it suggests is not pity and admiration but a sense of complacency in our own pitifulness and generosity. It is sentimen-

tal. Art is above morals, or, rather, all art is moral because, as I hope to show presently, works of art are immediate means to good. Once we have judged a thing a work of art, we have judged it ethically of the first importance and put it beyond the reach of the moralist. But descriptive pictures which are not works of art, and, therefore, are not necessarily means to good states of mind, are proper objects of the ethical philosopher's attention. Not being a work of art, "The Doctor" has none of the immense ethical value possessed by all objects that provoke aesthetic ecstasy; and the state of mind to which it is a means, as illustration, appears to me undesirable.

The works of those enterprising young men, the Italian futurists, are notable examples of descriptive painting. Like the Royal Academicians, they use form, not to provoke aesthetic emotions, but to convey information and ideas. Indeed the published theories of the Futurists prove that their pictures ought to have nothing whatever to do with art. Their social and political theories are respectable, but I would suggest to young Italian painters that it is possible to become a Futurist in thought and action and yet remain an artist, if one has the luck to be born one. To associate art with politics is always a mistake. Futurist pictures are descriptive because they aim at presenting in line and colour the chaos of the mind at a particular moment; their forms are not intended to promote aesthetic emotion but to convey information. These forms, by the way, whatever may be the nature of the ideas they suggest, are themselves anything but revolutionary. In such futurist pictures as I have seen—perhaps I should except some by Severine—the drawing, whenever it becomes representative as it frequently does, is found to be in that soft and common convention brought into fashion by Besnard some thirty years ago, and much affected by Beaux-Art students ever since. As works of art, the Futurist pictures are negligible; but they are not to be judged as works of art. A good Futurist picture would succeed as a good piece of psychology succeeds; it would reveal, through line and colour, the complexities of an interesting state of mind. If futurist pictures seem to fail, we must seek an explanation, not in a lack of artistic qualities that they never were intended to possess, but rather in the minds the states of which they are intended to reveal.

Most people who care much about art find that

of the work that moves them most the greater part is what scholars call "Primitive." Of course there are bad primitives. For instance, I remember going, full of enthusiasm, to see one of the earliest Romanesque churches in Poitiers (Notre-Dame-la-Grande), and finding it as ill-proportioned, over-decorated, coarse, fat and heavy as any better class building by one of those highly civilised architects who flourished a thousand years earlier or eight hundred later. But such exceptions are rare. As a rule primitive art is good - and here again my hypothesis is helpful - for, as a rule, it is also free from descrip6tive qualities. In primitive art you will find no accurate representation; you will find only significant form. Yet no other art moves us so profoundly. Whether we consider Sumerian sculpture or pre-dynastic Egyptian art, or archaic Gree, or the Wei and T'ang masterpieces, or those early Japanese works of which I had the luck to see a few superb examples (especially two wooden Bodhisattvas) at the Shepherd's bush Exhibition in 1910, or whether, coming nearer home, we consider the primitive Byzantine art of the sixth century and its primitive developments amongst the western barbarians, or, turning far afield, we consider that mysterious and majestic art that flourished in Central and South America before the coming of the white men, in every case we observe three common characteristics—absence of representation, absence of technical swagger, sublimely impressive form. Nor is it hard to discover the connection between these three. Formal significance loses itself in preoccupation with exact representation and ostentatious cunning.

Naturally, it is said that if there is little representation and less saltimbancery in primitive art, that is because the primitives were unable to catch a likeness or cut intellectual capers. The contention is beside the point. There is truth in it, no doubt, though, were I a critic whose reputation depended on a power of impressing the public with a semblance of knowledge, I should be more cautious about urging it than such people generally are. For to support that the Byzantine masters wanted skill, or could not have created an illusion had they wished to do so, seems to imply ignorance of the amazingly dexterous realism of the notoriously bad works of that age. Very often, I fear, the misrepresentation of the primitives must be attributed to what the critics call, "wilful distortion." Be that as it may, the point is that, either from what of skill or want of will, primitives neither create illusions, nor make display of extravagant accomplishment, but concentrate their energies on the one thing needful - the creation of form. Thus have they created the finest works of art that we possess.

Let no one imagine that representation is bad in itself; a realistic form may be as significant, in its place as part of the design, as an abstract. But if a representative form has value, it is as form, not as representation. The representative element in a work of art may or may not be harmful; always it is irrelevant. For, to appreciate a work of art we need bring with us nothing from life, no knowledge of its ideas and affairs, no familiarity with its emotions. Art transports us from the world of man's activity to a world of aesthetic exaltation. For a moment we are shut off from human interests; our anticipations and memories are arrested; we are lifted above the stream of life. The pure mathematician rapt in his studies knows a state of mind which I take to be similar, if not identical. He feels an emotion for his speculations which arises from no perceived relation between them and the lives of men, but springs, inhuman or super-human, from the heart of an abstract science. I wonder, sometimes, whether the appreciators of art and of mathematical solutions are not even more closely allied. Before we feel an aesthetic emotion for a combination of forms, do we not perceive intellectually the rightness and necessity of the combination? If we do, it would explain the fact that passing rapidly through a room we recognise a picture to be good, although we cannot say that it has provoked much emotion. We seem to have recognised intellectually the rightness of its forms without staying to fix our attention, and collect, as it were, their emotional significance. If this were so, it would be permissible to inquire whether it was the forms themselves or our perception of their rightness and necessity that caused aesthetic emotion. But I do not think I need linger to discuss the matter here. I have been inquiring why certain combinations of forms move us; I should not have traveled by other roads had I enquired, instead, why certain combinations are perceived to be right and necessary, and why our perception of their rightness and necessity is moving. What I have to say is this: the rapt philosopher, and he who contemplates a work of art, inhabit a world with an intense and peculiar significance of its own; that significance is unrelated to the significance of life. In this world the emotions of life find no place. It is a world with emotions of its own.

To appreciate a work of art we need bring with us nothing but a sense of form and colour and a knowledge of three-dimensional space. That bit of knowledge, I admit, is essential to the appreciation of many great works, since many of the move moving forms ever created are in three dimensions. To see a cube or rhomboid as a flat pattern is to lower its significance, and a sense of three-dimensional space is essential to the full appreciation of most architectural forms. Pictures which would be insignificant if we saw them as flat patterns are profoundly moving because, in fact, we see them as related planes. If the representation of three-dimensional space is to be called "representation," then I agree that there is one kind of representation which is not irrelevant. Also, I agree that along with our feeling for line and colour we must bring with us our knowledge of space if we are to make the most of every kind of form. Nevertheless, there are magnificent designs to an appreciation of which this knowledge is not necessary: so, though it is not irrelevant to the appreciation of some works of art it is not essential to the appreciation of all. What we must say is that the representation of three-dimensional space is neither irrelevant nor essential to all art, and that every other sort of representation is irrelevant.

That there is an irrelevant representative or descriptive element in many great works of art is not in the least surprising. Why it is not surprising I shall try to show elsewhere. Representation is not of necessity baneful, and highly realistic forms may be extremely significant. Very often, however, representation is a sign of weakness in an artist. A painter too feeble to create forms that provoke more than a little aesthetic emotion will try to eke that little out by suggesting the emotions of life. To evoke the emotions of life he must use representation. Thus a man will paint an execution, and, fearing to miss with his first barrel of significant form, will try to hit with his second by raising an emotion of fear or pity. But if in the artist an inclination to play upon the emotions of life is often the sign of a flickering inspiration, in the spectator a tendency to seek, behind form, the emotions of life is a sign of defective sensibility always. It means that his aesthetic emotions are weak or, at any rate, imperfect. Before a work of art people who feel little or no emotion for pure form find themselves at a loss. They are deaf men at a concert. They know that they are in the presence of something great, but they lack the power of apprehending it. They know that they ought to feel for it a tremendous emotion, but it happens that the particular kind of emotion it can raise is one that they can feel hardly or not at all. And so they read into the forms of the work those facts and ideas for which they are capable of feeling emotion, and feel for them the emotions that they can feel—the ordinary emotions of life. When confronted by a picture, instinctively they refer back its forms to the world from which they came. They treat created form as though it were imitated form, a picture as though it were a photograph. Instead of going out on the stream of art into a new world of aesthetic experience, they turn a sharp corner and come straight home to the world of human interests. For them the significance of a work of art depends on what they bring to it; no new thing is added to their lives, only the old material is stirred. A good work of visual art carries a person who is capable of appreciating it out of life into ecstasy: to use art as a means to the emotions of life is to use a telescope of reading the news. You will notice that people who cannot feel pure aesthetic emotions remember pictures by their subjects; whereas people who can, as often as not, have no idea what the subject of a picture is. They have never noticed the representative element, and so when they discuss pictures they talk about the shapes of forms and the relations and quantities of colours. Often they can tell by the quality of a single line whether or not a man is a good artist. They are concerned only with lines and colours, their relations and quantities and qualities; but from these they win an emotion more profound and far more sublime than any that can be given by the description of facts and ideas.

This last sentence has a very confident ring —over-confident, some may think. Perhaps I shall be able to justify it, and make my meaning clearer too, if I give an account of my own feelings about music. I am not really musical. I do not understand music well. I find musical form exceedingly difficult to apprehend, and I am sure that the profounder subtleties of harmony and rhythm more often than not escape me. The form of a musical composition must be simple indeed if I am to grasp it honestly. My opinion about music is not worth having. Yet, sometimes, at a concern, though my appreciation of the music is limited and humble, it is pure. Sometimes, though I have poor understanding, I have a clean palate. Consequently, when I am feeling bright and clear and intent, at the beginning of a concert for instance, when something that I can grasp is being played, I get from music that pure aesthetic emotion that I get from visual art. It is less intense, and the rapture is evanescent; I understand music too ill for music to transport me far into the world of pure aesthetic ecstasy. But at moments I do appreciate music as pure musical form, as sounds combined acco4ding to the laws of a mysterious necessity, as pure art with a tremendous significance of its own and no relation whatever to the significance of life; and in those moments I lose myself in that infinitely sublime state of mind to which pure visual form transports me. How inferior is my normal state of mind at a concern. Tired or perplexed, I let slip my sense of form, my aesthetic emotion collapses, and I begin weaving into the harmonies, that I cannot grasp, the ideas of life. Incapable of feeling the austere emotions of art, I begin to read into the musical forms human emotions of terror and mystery, love and hate, and spend the minutes, pleasantly enough, in a world of turbid and inferior feeling. At such times, were the grossest pieces of onomatopoeic representation - the song of a bird, the galloping of horses, the cries of children, or the laughing of demons—to be introduced into the symphony, I should not be offended. Very likely I should be pleased; they would afford new points of departure for new trains of romantic feeling or heroic thought. I know very well what has happened. I have been using art as a means to the emotions of life and reading into it the ideas of life. I have been cutting blocks with a razor. I have tumbled from the superb peaks of aesthetic exaltation to the snug foothills of warm humanity. It is a jolly country. No one need to ashamed of enjoying himself there. Only no one who has ever been on the heights can help feeling a little crestfallen in the cosy valleys. And let no one imagine, because the has made merry in the warm tilth and quaint nooks of romance, that he can even guess at the austere and thrilling raptures of those who have climbed the cold, white peaks of art.

About music most people are as willing to be humble as I am. If they cannot grasp musical form and win from it a pure aesthetic emotion, they confess that they understand music imperfectly or not at all. They recognize quite clearly that there is a difference between the feeling of the musician for pure music and that of the cheerful concert-goer for what music suggests. The latter enjoys his own emotions, as he has every right to do, and recognises their inferiority. Unfortunately, people are apt to be less modest about their powers of appreciating visual art. Everyone is inclined to believe that out of pictures, at any rate, he can get all that there is to be got; everyone is ready to cry "humbug" and "imposter" at those who say that more can be had. The good faith of people who feel pure aesthetic emotions is called in question by those who have never felt anything of the sort. It is the prevalence of the representative element, I support. That makes the man in the street so sure that he knows a good picture when he sees one. For I have noticed that in matters of architecture, pottery, textiles, etc., ignorance and ineptitude are more willing to defer to the opinions of those who have been blest with peculiar sensibility. It is a pity that cultivated and intelligent men and women cannot be induced to believe that a great gift of aesthetic appreciation is at least as rare in visual as in musical art. A comparison of my own experience in both has enabled me to discriminate very clearly between pure and impure appreciation. Is it too much to ask that others should be as honest about their feelings for pictures as I have been about mine for music? For I am certain that most of those who visit galleries do feel very much what I feel at concerts. They have their moments of pure ecstasy; but the moments are short and unsure. Soon they fall back into the world of human interests and feel emotions, good no doubt, but inferior. I do not dream of saying that what they get from art is bad or nugatory; I say that they do not get the best that art can give. I do not say that they cannot understand art; rather I say that they cannot understand the state of mind of those who understand it best. I do not say that art means nothing or little to them; I say they miss its full significance. I do not suggest for one moment that their appreciation of art is a thing to be ashamed of; the majority of the charming and intelligent people with whom I am acquainted appreciate visual art impurely; and, by the way, the appreciation of almost all great writers has been impure. But provided that there be some fraction of pure aesthetic emotion, even a mixed and minor appreciation of art is, I am sure, one of the most valuable things in the world —so valuable, indeed, that in my giddier moments I have been tempted to believe that art might prove the world's salvation.

Yet, though the echoes and shadows of art enrich the life of the plains, her spirit dwells on the mountains. To him who woos, but woos impurely, she returns enriched what is brought. Like the sun, she warms the good seed in good soil and causes it to bring forth good fruit. But only to the perfect lover does she give a new strange gift—a gift beyond all price. Imperfect lovers bring to art and take away the ideas and emotions of their own age and civilisation. In twelfth-century Europe a man might have been greatly moved by a Romanesque church and found nothing in a T'ang picture. To a man of a later age, Greek sculpture meant much and Mexican nothing, for only to the former could he bring a crowd of associated ideas to be the objects of familiar emotions. But the perfect lover, he who can feel the profound significance of form, is raised above the accidents of time and place. To him the problems of archaeology, history, and hagiography are impertinent. If the forms of a work are significant its provenance is irrelevant. Before the grandeur of those Sumerian figures in the Louvre he is carried on the same flood of emotion to the same aesthetic ecstasy as, more than four thousand years ago, the Chaldean lover was carried. It is the mark of great art that its appeal is universal and eternal. Significant form stands charged with the power to provoke aesthetic emotion in anyone capable of feeling it. The ideas of men go buzz and die like gnats; men change their institutions and their customs as they change their coats; the intellectual triumphs of one age are the follies of another; only great art remains stable and unobscure. Great art remains stable and unobscure because the feelings that it awakens are independent of time and place, because its kingdom is not of this world. To those who have and hold a sense of the significance of form what does it matter whether the forms that move them were created in Paris the day before yesterday or in Babylon fifty centuries ago? The forms of art are inexhaustible; but all lead by the same road of aesthetic emotion to the same world of aesthetic ecstasy.

Clive Bell. *Art.* New York: Frederick A. Stokes, 1914.

ART, PHILOSOPHY, AND THE PHILOSOPHY OF ART

ARTHUR C. DANTO (1880-)

Arthur C. Danto returns us to our opening reflection on what defines a work of art. Meditating on Andy Warhol's pile of Brillo Boxes *and Duchamp's* The Fountain *(a urinal mounted in a glass square), Danto distinguishes use objects from art works by claiming that the latter are "representational," that is, they all stand for something. Here he is not reverting back to Plato's art as imitation or as realistic depictions. Rather Danto claim is that even the most abstract work of art has a reference, an intentional meaning. Trees are not trees as---whereas all paintings of trees are meant as something, whether as representative of trees, of the feelings that trees evoke in us, or they are meant as something simply to be looked at as a composition of colors and forms. Warhol's* Brillo Boxes *are not Brillo boxes that contain steel wool pads. They refer to the image of Brillo pads as typical of the images that proliferate in our contemporary consumerist society.*

One could ask why the image on the Brillo box is not just as representational as Warhol's Brillo Box since the former is meant to convey the notion that inside the box there is something that is desirable to bring home to use. In that case, commercial art is just as much art as the fine art in a museum. There are aestheticians who claim that what counts as art is its institutional settings and thus it is a societally constructed category. Art is what is stipulated to be art by the art institutional establishment, the gallery owners, critics, and museum directors. Danto might reply that it is not just the fact that art refers to an intended object that makes it art but that it refers to an object intended to be art and not some other meaning. In that case, we might ask what does it mean to intend something as art? What distinguishes some image intended as art from some image intended as advertisement? If I abstract from the object its commercial intention, what is left over that is art? And can something serve both as art and as something else, say, as an advertisement?

Not very many years ago, aesthetics— understood as the philosophy of art—was regarded as the dim, retarded offspring of two glamorous parents, its discipline and its subject. Philosophy in the twentieth century had become professionalized and technical, its methods formal, and its analytical aims the discovery of the most fundamental structures of thought, language, logic and science. Philosophical questions about art seemed peripheral and its answers cloudy—far too cloudy for those caught up in the reinvention of painting and music and literature to find much help in the dated, faded reflections of the aesthetician. And students with a primary interest in art who may have registered for courses in this condescendingly tolerated specialty found themselves confronting a perplexingly irrelevant literature. In 1954, the philosopher John Passmore published a paper with the accurate title "The Dreariness of Aesthetics," and it must have been just about then that the wit and painter Barnett Newman delivered one of his most quoted sayings: "Aesthetics is for art what ornithology is for the birds"—a sneer whose edge is blunted today by the fact that the vulgarism it echoes has faded from usage.

I have always had a passionate interest in art and a logical passion for philosophy, but nothing in my experience with either conflicted with the general dismal appraisal of aesthetics, and I am certain I should never have gotten involved with it had I not visited a singular exhibition at what was then the Stable Gallery on East 74th Street in New York in 1964. Andy Warhol had filled the space with piles of Brillo boxes, similar to if somewhat sturdier than those brashly stenciled cartons stacked in the storerooms of supermarkets wherever soap pads are sold. I was familiar of course with the exploitation of emblems of popular and commercial labels by the pop artists, and Warhol's portraits of Campbell's soup cans were legendary. But as someone who came to artistic age in the heroic period of Abstract Expressionism, when decisions for or against The Image were fraught with an almost religious agony, the crass and casual use of tacky images by the new artists seemed irreverent and juvenile. But the Warhol show raised a question which was intoxicating and immediately philosophical, namely why were his boxes works of art while the almost indistinguishable utilitarian cartons were merely containers for soap pads? Certainly the minor observable differences could not ground as grand a distinction as that between Art and Reality!

A philosophical question arises whenever we have two objects which seem in every relevant particular to be alike, but which belong to importantly different philosophical categories. Descartes for example supposed his experience while dreaming could be indistinguishable from his experience awake, so that no internal criterion could divide delusion from knowledge. Wittgenstein noted that there is nothing to distinguish someone's raising his arm from someone's arm going up, though the distinction between even the simplest action and a mere bodily movement seems fundamental to the way we think of our freedom. Kant sought a criterion for moral action in the fact that it is done from principles rather than simply in conformity with those principles, even though outward behavior might be indistinguishable between the two. In all these cases one must seek the differences outside the juxtaposed and puzzling examples, and this is no less the case when seeking to account for the differences between works of art and mere real things which happen exactly to resemble them.

This problem could have been raised at any time, and not just with the somewhat minimal sorts of works one might suspect the Brillo Boxes to be. It was always conceivable that exact counterparts to the most prized and revered works of art could have come about in ways inconsistent with their being works at all, though no observable differences could be found. I have imagined cases in which an artist dumps a lot of paint in a centrifuge she then spins, just "to see what happens"—and what happens is that it all splats against the wall in an array of splotches that cannot be told by the unaided eye from *The Legend of the True Cross*, by Piero della Francesca. Or an anarchist plants dynamite in the marble quarry, and the explosion results in a lot of lumps of marble which by a statistical miracle combine into a pile which *looks* like The Leaning Tower at Pisa. Or the forces of nature act through millennnia on a large piece of rock until something not to be told apart from the Apollo Belvedere results.

Nor are these imaginary possibilities restricted to painting, sculpture, and architecture. There are the famous chimpanzees who, typing at random, knocked out all the plays of Shakespeare. But Wordsworth sought to make poetry out of the most commonplace language, while Auden invented a style of reading poetry which was indistinguishable from ordinary talking—so for all anyone could tell, Moliere's M. Jourdain could have been speaking poetry rather than prose all his life. John Cage has made the division between music and noise problematic, leaving it possible that sets of sounds from the street could be music, while other sets which we would spontaneously suppose music happen not to be, just because of the circumstances of their production. And it takes little effort to imagine a dance in which the dancers do ordinary things in the ordinary ways; a dance could consist in someone sitting reading a book. I once saw Baryshnikov break into a football player's run on stage, and I thought it altogether wonderful. True, it may seem difficult to suppose art could have begun with these puzzling works - but it cannot be forgotten that when philosophy first noticed art it was in connection with the possibility of deception.

Now the "dreariness of aesthetics" was diagnosed as due to the effort of philosophers to find a definition of art, and a number of philosophical critics, much under the influence of Wittgenstein, contended that such a definition was neither possible nor necessary. It was not possible because the class of art works seemed radically open, so much so that no set of conditions could be imagined which would be necessary and sufficient for something to be a member. Luckily, there was no need for a definition, since we seem to have had no difficulty in picking out the works of art without benefit of one. And indeed something like this may very well have appeared true until the Warhol boxes came along. For if something is a work of art while something apparently exactly like it is not, it is extremely unlikely we could be certain we could pick the art work out even with a definition. Perhaps we really have no such skill at all. Still, to the degree that there is a difference, some theory is needed to account for it, and the problem of finding such a theory becomes central and urgent. Nor is this merely a matter of abstract concern to philosophers, for it is in response to a question which arose within the world of art itself. Philosophers of the tradition, to the degree that they had thought about art at all, thought chiefly about the art of their own time: Plato, about the illusionistic sculptures of his contemporaries; Kant, about the tasteful objects of the Enlightenment; Nietzsche, about Wagnerian opera; the Wittgensteinians, about the extraordinary proliferation of styles in the twentieth century, when a whole period of art history appeared to last about six months. But the Warhol boxes, though clearly of their time, raised the most general question about art that can be raised, as though the most radical possibilities had at last been realized. It was, in fact, as though art had brought the question of its own identity to consciousness at last.

However this identity is to be articulated, it is clear that it cannot be based upon anything works of art have in common with their counterparts. One prominent theorist, for example, regards paintings as very complex perceptual objects. So they are, but since objects can be imagined perfectly congruent with those which are not art works, these must have equivalent complexity at the level of perception. After all, the problem arose in the first place because

no perceptual difference could be imagined finally relevant. But neither can possession of so-called "aesthetic qualities' serve, since it would be strange if a work of art were beautiful but something exactly like it though not a work of art were not. In fact it has been a major effort of the philosophy of art to de-aestheticize the concept of art. It was Marcel Duchamp, a far deeper artist than Warhol, who presented as "readymades" objects chosen for their lack of aesthetic qualities—grooming combs, hat racks, and, notoriously, pieces of lavatory plumbing. "Aesthetic delectation is the danger to be avoided," Duchamp wrote of his most controversial work, *Fountain*, of 1917. It was precisely Duchamp's great effort to make it clear that art is an intellectual activity, a conceptual enterprise and not merely something to which the senses and the feelings come into play. And this must be true of all art, even that most bent upon gratifying the eye or ear, and not just for those works which are regarded as especially "philosophical," like Raphael's *School of Athens* or Mann's *The Magic Mountain*. Were someone to choreograph Plato's *Republic*, that would not, simply because of its exalted content, be more philosophical than *Coppelia* or *Petrouchka*. In fact these might be more philosophical, employing as they do real dancers imitating dancing dolls imitating real dancers!

Where are the components for a theory of art to be found? I think a first step may be made in recognizing that works of art are *representations*, not necessarily in the old sense of resembling their subjects, but in the more extended sense that it is always legitimate to ask what they are about. Warhol's boxes were clearly about something, had a content and a meaning, made a statement, even were metaphors of a sort. In a curious way they made some kind of statement about art, and incorporated into their identity the question of what that identity is—and it was Heidegger who proposed that it is a part of the essence of being a human that the question of what one is part of what one is. But nothing remotely like this could be true of a mere soap box. Dances, too, are representational, not simply in the way in which a pair of dancers may dance the dance the characters dance in the action they imitate, but in the same wide sense in which even the most resolutely abstract art has a pictorial dimension.

The Problem of Indiscernible Counterparts follows from the representationalistic character of works of art. Imagine a sentence written down, and then a set of marks which looks just like the written sentence, but is *simply* a set of marks. The first set has a whole lot of properties the second set lacks: it is in a language, has a syntax and grammar, says something. And its causes will be quite distinct in kind from those which explain mere marks. The structure then of works of art will have to be different from the structure of objects which merely resemble them.

Now of course not all representational things are works of art, so the definition has only begun. I shall not take the next steps here. All I have wished to show is the way that the philosophy of art has deep questions to consider, questions of representation and reality, of structure, truth, and meaning. In considering these things, it moves from the periphery to the center of philosophy, and in so doing it curiously incorporates the two things that give rise to it. For when art attains the level of self-consciousness it has come to attain in our era, the distinction between art and philosophy becomes as problematic as the distinction between reality and art. And the degree to which the appreciation of art becomes a matter of applied philosophy can hardly be overestimated.

Arthur C. Danto. "Art, Philosophy, and the Philosophy of Art." *Humanities*, Vol. 4, No. 1 (February 1983): 1-2. This text is in the public domain.

Made in the USA
Middletown, DE
05 January 2017